Creation and Blessing

Creation and Blessing

A Guide to the Study and Exposition of Genesis

Allen P. Ross

Baker Books

A Division of Baker Book House Co.
Grand Rapids, Michigan 49516

©1998, 1996 by Allen P. Ross

Published by Baker Books
a division of Baker Publishing Group
P.O. Box 6287, Grand Rapids, MI 49516-6287
www.bakerbooks.com

First hardcover edition published 1988
Third printing, May 1993

First paperback edition published 1996
Sixth printing, October 2005

Printed in the United States of America

Library of Congress Cataloging-in-Publication Data

Ross, Allen P.
    Creation and blessing
    Bibliography: p.
    Includes index.
    ISBN 0-8010-2107-3
       1. Bible. O.T. Genesis—Criticism, interpretation, etc. I. Title.
    BS1235.R73 1987
    222'11061   88-6173

Scripture quotations are from the author's own translation.

To my parents,
Victor and **Margaret Ross,**
who first opened to me the Holy Scriptures
and started me on my spiritual journey

Contents

Part 3. **The Patriarchal Narratives About Abraham**

Part 4. **The Patriarchal Narratives About the Descendants of Abraham**

Charts

12

Charts

Preface

The exposition of Old Testament narrative literature has often been a problem for Bible teachers and preachers. On the one hand, expositors may simply retell the stories (with or without dramatic embellishments) and then draw a few general lessons from them. The biblical narratives, however, are far more than illustrative stories. They are highly developed and complex narratives that form theological treatises. We do not do justice to them by oversimplifying them or overlooking their literary and theological motifs. On the other hand, expositors who have had more training in exegesis may make a detailed study of the passage in order to clarify the meaning of everything that happened or was said but may never come to the point of organizing the theological teaching of a passage in a way that is both clear and relevant to today's audience.

I have written this book for pastors, teachers, and all serious Bible students who wish to develop their understanding of the Book of Genesis (and narrative literature in general) and to increase their ability to expound it. I want to help the reader appreciate the major literary and theological motifs that form the theological ideas in the narratives and to demonstrate how these theological ideas can be developed into clear and accurate exposition. This book is not a commentary on Genesis, although it includes many interpretive comments. Rather, it is a guide to the study and exposition of the book.

The first four chapters include various introductory matters that will give the expositor a general idea of the nature and composition of Genesis as well as the various approaches to the study of the book that one will find represented in the commentaries and articles. I have suggested a step-by-step procedure that makes use of the best of modern scholarship but remains thoroughly orthodox. The rest of the book traces through the narratives in Genesis to show what such a procedure yields. The number and the variety of the passages in Genesis provide sufficient material to learn about the study and exposition of narrative literature.

For each of the narratives I have developed exegetical and expositional ideas, using the literary and theological motifs of the units. It is not my concern that the reader simply adopt these ideas and outlines. I would hope that the reader would develop the ideas more fully and improve the ways of saying things in the exposition. It is my concern that the reader catch something of a method that I believe is the simplest and most effective way of developing an expositional presentation out of a close analysis of the text, an expositional presentation that adequately treats the whole passage and is worded in a way that is true to the contextual meaning of the passage and relevant to the modern audience as well.

The material in this book is in no way intended to replace careful study of the text, which is absolutely essential for a clear and convincing exposition. I hope that this book inspires and aids the reader in such a study and thereby contributes to the exposition of the Scriptures. To that end I have included extensive bibliography for each narrative unit, as well as a general bibliography of the major commentaries and monographs on Genesis at the end of the book. References to outside sources have their full bibliographical data listed either at the end of the unit being discussed or, if they are general works, at the end of the book.

This book is largely the result of my teaching the exegetical exposition of the Pentateuch over the last eight years. I am indebted to my many students, who provided the forum for the discussions and who contributed to the development of the ideas by their participation. I am also grateful to Marie Janeway for carefully typing the manuscript and to David Aiken and Dorian Coover for their help in editing and proofreading the material.

Key to Transliteration

ʾ	א	ṭ	ט	p	ף פ פ
b	ב ב	y	י	ṣ	ץ צ
g	ג ג	k	ך כ כ	q	ק
d	ד ד	l	ל	r	ר
h	ה	m	ם מ	ś	שׂ
w	ו	n	ן נ	š	שׁ
z	ז	s	ס	t	ת ת
ḥ	ח	ʿ	ע		

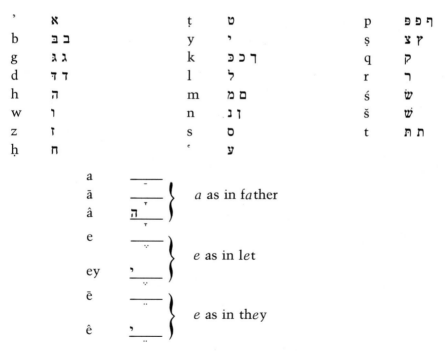

a ____ ̣

ā ____ ̣

â ה ____ ̣ } *a* as in father

e ____ ̤

ey י ____ ̤ } *e* as in let

ē ____ ̤

ê י ____ ̤ } *e* as in they

15

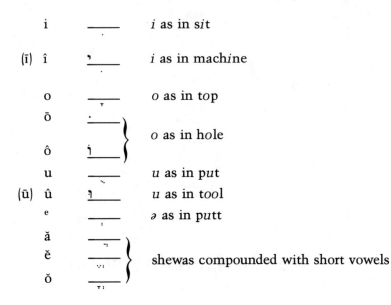

i		*i* as in s*i*t
(ī) î		*i* as in mach*i*ne
o		*o* as in t*o*p
ō		
ô		} *o* as in h*o*le
u		*u* as in p*u*t
(ū) û		*u* as in t*oo*l
e		*ə* as in p*u*tt
ă		
ĕ		} shewas compounded with short vowels
ŏ		

Abbreviations

ABR	*Australian Biblical Review*
ACQ	*American Church Quarterly*
AION	*Annali dell' istituto universitario orientale di Napoli*
AJBA	*Australian Journal of Biblical Archaeology*
AJSL	*American Journal of Semitic Languages and Literatures*
ANET	James B. Pritchard, ed. *Ancient Near Eastern Texts Relating to the Old Testament*
Ang	*Angelicum*
AOAT	*Alter Orient und Altes Testament*
ASAE	*Annales du service des antiquités de l'Égypte*
AThR	*Anglican Theological Review*
AUSS	*Andrews University Seminary Studies*
BA	*Biblical Archaeologist*
BAR	*Biblical Archaeology Review*
BASOR	*Bulletin of the American Schools of Oriental Research*
BCSBS	*Bulletin of the Canadian Society of Biblical Studies*
BDB	F. Brown, S. R. Driver, and C. A. Briggs, eds. *Hebrew and English Lexicon of the Old Testament*
BetM	*Bet(h) Mikra*
BETS	*Bulletin of the Evangelical Theological Society*

Bib	*Biblica*
BibRes	*Biblical Research*
BibSac	*Bibliotheca Sacra*
BiTr	*Bible Translator*
BJRL	*Bulletin of the John Rylands Library*
BSOAS	*Bulletin of the School of Oriental and African Studies*
BThB	*Biblical Theology Bulletin*
BTS	*Bible et terre sainte*
BZ	*Biblische Zeitschrift*
CanJTh	*Canadian Journal of Theology*
CBQ	*Catholic Biblical Quarterly*
CBQMS	Catholic Biblical Quarterly Monograph Series
ConQ	*Congregational Quarterly*
CT	*Christianity Today*
CTJ	*Calvin Theological Journal*
CTM	*Concordia Theological Monthly*
DBS	*Dictionnaire de la Bible, Supplément*
ErIs	*Eretz-Israel*
EvQ	*Evangelical Quarterly*
Exp	*Expositor*
Explor	*Exploration*
ExT	*Expository Times*
GKC	*Gesenius' Hebrew Grammar*, edited by E. Kautzsch, translated by A. E. Cowley
GTJ	*Grace Theological Journal*
HTR	*Harvard Theological Review*
HUCA	*Hebrew Union College Annual*
IDB	*Interpreter's Dictionary of the Bible*
IEJ	*Israel Exploration Journal*
IndThSt	*Indian Theological Studies*
Interp	*Interpretation*
ISBE	*International Standard Bible Encyclopedia*
JAAR	*Journal of the American Academy of Religion*
JANES	*Journal of the Ancient Near Eastern Society of Columbia University*
JAOS	*Journal of the American Oriental Society*
JASA	*Journal of the American Scientific Affiliation*
JBL	*Journal of Biblical Literature*
JBR	*Journal of Bible and Religion*
JCS	*Journal of Cuneiform Studies*
JEOL	*Jaarbericht van het Vooraziatisch-Egyptisch Genootschap "Ex Oriente Lux."*
JETS	*Journal of the Evangelical Theological Society*

JJS	*Journal of Jewish Studies*
JNES	*Journal of Near Eastern Studies*
JNWSL	*Journal of Northwest Semitic Languages*
JQR	*Jewish Quarterly Review*
JRE	*Journal of Religious Ethics*
JRelTh	*Journal of Religious Thought*
JSOR	*Journal of the Society of Oriental Research*
JSOT	*Journal for the Study of the Old Testament*
JSS	*Journal of Semitic Studies*
JThS	*Journal of Theological Studies*
KJV	King James Version
KS	*Kindred Spirit*
NIV	New International Version
Or	*Orientalia*
OTS	*Oudtestamentische Studiën*
OTWSA	*Ou Testamentiese Werkgemeenskap in Suid-Afrika*
PEFQSt	*Palestine Exploration Fund, Quarterly Statement*
PEQ	*Palestine Exploration Quarterly*
PN	M. Noth. *Die israelitischen Personennamen im Rahmen der gemeinsemitischen Namengebung*
RB	*Revue biblique*
RefRev	*Reformed Review*
RevQ	*Revue de Qumran*
RHR	*Revue de l'histoire des religions*
RSR	*Recherches de science religieuse*
RSV	Revised Standard Version
Sal	*Salesianum*
Scr	*Scripture*
StOr	*Studia Orientalia*
StPat	*Studia Patavina*
StTh	*Studia Theologica*
TAPhS	*Transactions of the American Philosophical Society*
Tar	*Tarbiz* [Hebrew]
TDOT	G. J. Botterweck, H. Ringgren, and H. J. Fabry, eds., *Theological Dictionary of the Old Testament*
ThS	*Theological Studies*
ThZ	*Theologische Zeitschrift*
TLZ	*Theologische Literaturzeitung*
TynB	*Tyndale Bulletin*
UF	*Ugarit-Forschungen*
UTQ	*University of Toronto Quarterly*
VigChr	*Vigiliae Christianae*
VT	*Vetus Testamentum*

VTS	*Vetus Testamentum Supplement*
WTJ	*Westminster Theological Journal*
ZAW	*Zeitschrift für die alttestamentliche Wissenschaft*
ZDMG	*Zeitschrift der deutschen morgenländischen Gesellschaft*

PART 1

The Study of Genesis

1

Approaches to Genesis

The starting point for this study is the presupposition that Scripture is revelation, a message from God to his people. Genesis thus has a dimension very different from the comparable literature of the ancient Near East.[1] As God's revelation, Genesis is authoritative. Consequently, in studying it, one must go beyond academic inquiry to discover its theologically applicable truths.

Such a study has many barriers. This literature was written ages ago for a particular people. It has highly developed levels of meaning for the religious community of Israel. And many of its genres are foreign to our way of thinking. It thus takes careful study with sound method to determine the timeless theological message of the text.

Not only must sound method be used in the study of the text, that method must be communicated along with the exposition. If the expositor has the goal of drawing people to the text in order for them to learn God's will, then the exposition must show that the interpretation was derived from the text. The expositor dare not give the impression that the meaning is mystical or derived arbitrarily. Once the expositor dem-

1. Biblical scholars commonly maintain that the Pentateuch should not automatically be treated differently than other literature; see John Skinner, *A Critical and Exegetical Commentary on Genesis,* 2d ed., International Critical Commentary (Edinburgh: T. & T. Clark, 1910), p. v.

onstrates that the message is from the text, then the exposition will carry the authority it must have to be effective.

Conservative scholarship has generally followed the traditional view that Moses wrote Genesis. Although the New Testament nowhere explicitly refers to Genesis as his work, references to the "law of Moses" have been interpreted to refer to the first five books. For centuries there was little disagreement over this conclusion.[2]

With the rise of philosophical rationalism, however, biblical scholars were no longer content to accept uncritically the traditions of the early rabbinical and Christian writings. Critical scholarship, as it has come to be called, took different approaches to the study of the Pentateuch, questioning the text, date, authorship, composition, and purpose of the literary units. Setting aside the ideas of revelation and inspiration, scholars worked solely with the text. In general, they attributed the Pentateuch to several sources in later periods.

We cannot embark here on a detailed analysis of their efforts. (See R. K. Harrison, *Introduction to the Old Testament* [Grand Rapids: Eerdmans, 1969]; and, from the critical side, Otto Eissfeldt, *The Old Testament: An Introduction* [New York: Harper & Row, 1965].) It is important to understand, though, how and why modern critical scholarship has drawn its conclusions about Genesis. Besides, such research has produced many insights that can add to the understanding of the text.

The Literary-Analytical Approach

The first systematic approach was the literary-analytical method. Although it purported to be a detailed analysis of the literary features of the text, the presuppositions of its proponents hindered it from being such.

The development of the approach was gradual, with each scholar building on and modifying the work of predecessors. At an early point

2. The view of Mosaic authorship found support in ancient tradition (biblical and extrabiblical), the ancient synagogue, the New Testament, the church fathers, and most commentators up to the time of modern criticism. See further Gleason Archer, *A Survey of Old Testament Introduction* (Chicago: Moody, 1964), pp. 100–101. Some have appealed to John 7:22 as supporting the Mosaic authorship of Genesis. The statement there ("Moses gave you circumcision") is called the law of Moses in verse 23. This could be a reference to Genesis 17:12, where circumcision was introduced, but there are other passages in the Pentateuch that legislate circumcision. Did Jesus have Genesis in mind when referring to circumcision? Perhaps, but it would be hard to prove. The division of the Hebrew canon into three parts—the Law (i.e., the Pentateuch, or "law of Moses"), the Prophets, and the Writings—is attested as early as the Prologue of Ecclesiasticus (Wisdom of Ben Sira) in approximately 190 B.C., and certainly in the New Testament (Luke 24:44).

Astruc (1753) attributed the different divine names and similar stories in Genesis to different literary sources: J (Yahweh) and E (Elohim). Eichhorn (1780) extended this analysis to the whole Pentateuch, concluding that the final editor was not Moses. De Wette (1805) said that Deuteronomy came from the time of Josiah and labeled it D. Ewald (1823) took E as the basic source, supplemented by additions from older sources. Delitzsch (1852) accepted as Mosaic the parts that were said to be from Moses but held that the other traditions were codified by later priests. Hupfeld (1853) divided the E source into E^1 (later known as P, for the priestly document) and E^2 (historical in nature). He noted that, except for the divine names used, E^2 was similar to J. He concluded that a final editor, or redactor (R), rearranged and mixed the traditions, leaving discrepancies and inconsistencies. Graf (1866) concluded that P came from the exile, although its historical sections were earlier. Kuenen (1869) argued for the unity of P. His arrangement was J (basic Torah), E (incorporated material), D (time of Josiah), and P (from the time of the exile). Wellhausen (1878) restated the approach forcefully and meticulously. It spread quickly in scholarly circles. (For a discussion of other influences on the formulation of the material, especially Wellhausen's work, see Umberto Cassuto, *The Documentary Hypothesis* [Jerusalem: Magnes, 1961], pp. 5–14.)

This general approach gave most of its attention to identifying the sources behind what had been considered the unified work of Moses. Although scholars differed over specific passages, there was general agreement concerning the sources. The J source was written in the southern kingdom by about 850 B.C. It was personal, biographical, and anthropomorphic, and it included prophetlike ethics and theological reflection. The E source was written in the northern kingdom about 750 B.C. It was more objective, less consciously tinged with ethical and theological reflection. An unknown redactor combined these two documents in the middle of the next century. Then, about 621 B.C., D was composed under Hilkiah for the reforms in Jerusalem. Finally, P was added sometime between 570 and 445 B.C. This source includes accounts of the origins and institutions of the theocracy, genealogies, and sacrificial ritual. (For this arrangement, see, among others, S. R. Driver, *An Introduction to the Literature of the Old Testament* [Edinburgh: T. & T. Clark, 1897], pp. 11–13.)

The method used to arrive at this reassignment of the authorship of the Pentateuch is fairly straightforward. First, to identify the literary sources involved the use of several criteria: changes in divine names (e.g., Elohim in Genesis 1:1–2:3 vs. Yahweh in Genesis 2:4–4:26); parallel narratives with contrasts and contradictions (e.g., the stories of the endangering of Sarah in Genesis 12 and 20); linguistic and stylistic differences in designations of persons, places, and objects (e.g., J uses "Canaanite," and E, "Amorite"); and the diversity of religious and moral ideas as well as the contemporary conditions and events they presuppose (e.g., in the Bethel narrative of J recorded in Genesis 28:13–16, 19, Yahweh stands upon the earth; but according to E in Genesis 28:10–12, 17–18, 20–22, a ladder bearing angels represents the bond between heaven and earth).

Second, to determine the date of the traditions the critical scholar followed an evolutionary approach. Anything that smacked of primitive ritual, magic, nature, or henotheism was early; and anything that was universal, ethical, free, or monotheistic was later. For example, Exodus 20:24–26 does not centralize worship and so is early (J), but Deuteronomy 12:1–26 calls for centralization (D), and Exodus 25 through Leviticus 9 assumes worship at one place and so is later (P). In short, highly developed ideas belong to later sources.

Scholarly reaction to this approach turned Pentateuchal studies into a debate. Conservatives, of course, were uneasy with the skepticism of critical scholars toward the text. They completely disagreed with the idea that the higher religious ideas had evolved through the creative genius of Israel. And they preferred to attempt to reconcile apparent discrepancies in the Bible rather than use them to support a theory of documentary sources.[3] Moreover, they found the entire approach futile, for segmenting the text into its sources and arranging it chronologically yielded very little constructive gain.

With the growth of archaeological evidence, scholarship began to see that the documentary hypothesis did not comport well with literary practices of the ancient Near East. For example, the criterion of the divine names was called into question when texts from the ancient Near East displayed a variety of names for deities engraved on the same monument. The criterion of doublets was also challenged on the basis of Semitic literary style. Subsequent studies demonstrated that repetition and parallelism were common. Rather than see them as evidence of different accounts that were pieced together, it made more sense to search for literary reasons for such repetitions. (J. P. Fokkelman [*Narrative Art in Genesis: Specimens of Stylistic and Structural Analysis.* Studia Semitica Neerlandica, 17 [Assen: Van Gorcum, 1975], pp. 1–8] appeals for a thorough synthetic study before resorting to diachronic studies.)

The criterion of stylistic differences also became suspect in the light

3. At times the documentary hypothesis exhibits circular reasoning. For a clever essay on the excesses in the approach, see Herman Wouk, *This Is My God* (Garden City, N.Y.: Doubleday, 1959), pp. 312–20. For an appraisal of the unity of Genesis 1–11, see Isaac M. Kikawada and Arthur Quinn, *Before Abraham Was: The Unity of Genesis 1–11* (Nashville: Abingdon, 1985).

of the discovery of new languages. Scholars have become more cautious in assigning lateness to a text on the basis of vocabulary or style.[4] Truly late words in a text could also be modernizations of ancient traditions. The use of religious ideas also had to be reevaluated in the light of modern studies. When law codes were discovered that were earlier than the Mosaic law, then it was no longer reasonable to relegate many of those ideas to a later time.

Critical scholarship began to see that the ancient development of stories and laws was different from what the literary-analytical approach suggested. Comparative studies suggested that a lengthy development in oral form lay behind the writing of the accounts, so that assigning a date for a document was not as important as tracing the ancient traditions. Form criticism thus became the predominant method.

The literary-analytical approach made scholars aware of literary phenomena such as variations in style, changes of names and terms, differing ideas, and repetition of (and in) narratives. But the assumption that these features prove multiple authorship and can be used to arrange a chronology of literary documents is unconvincing and unwarranted.

The Form-Critical Approach

Form criticism seeks to determine the genre, structure, setting, and intention of each literary unit in order to reconstruct the original tradition and to relate the texts to the people and institutions of ancient Israel. (See, for example, Edgar V. McKnight, *What Is Form Criticism?* [Philadelphia: Fortress, 1969], and Gene Tucker, *Form Criticism of the Old Testament* [Philadelphia: Fortress, 1971].)

Two factors shaped form criticism. First, archaeological discoveries indicated that Genesis 1–11 had a Sumerian-Akkadian background of the third and second millennia B.C. and that the patriarchal stories fit into the milieu of the second millennium and would be out of place against the Assyrian background of the first millennium. Second, the emphasis on oral tradition moved attention back to the formative stages

---

4. An analysis of the grammar, style, and vocabulary of the priestly material proves interesting. For recent studies on the date of the P material, see Robert Polzin, *Late Biblical Hebrew: Toward an Historical Typology of Biblical Hebrew Prose*, Harvard Semitic Monographs, 12 (Missoula, Mont.: Scholars, 1976), and especially the review article by Gary Rendsburg, "Late Biblical Hebrew and the Date of 'P,'" in *JAOS* 102 (1982): 65–80. Rendsburg concludes that the evidence points to a much earlier date for P than the previously proposed late date: "In fact, typologically the entire Pentateuch may be considered a unified work and may be dated to a time earlier than the composition of Joshua, Judges, and Samuel. This is not to say that writers of the Davidic period did not add such phrases as the boundaries given in Genesis 15:18, but as a whole the Pentateuch is ancient" (p. 78).

of the traditions. (See Christopher R. North, "The Place of Oral Tradition in the Growth of the Old Testament," *ExT* 61 [1949–50]: 292–96; H. Ringgren, "Oral and Written Transmission in the Old Testament," *StTh* 3 [1937]: 34–59.)

Hermann Gunkel, the pioneer of form criticism in biblical studies, realized that the newly discovered religious texts from Mesopotamia and Egypt exhibited striking similarities with the Old Testament literature and thereby provided opportunity for classifications. The method involves several steps. First, the critic must isolate the literary units by determining the logical bounds of each unit and by analyzing its self-sufficiency or relation to the context. Form critics may or may not rely on the literary classifications JEDP, but to them any unevenness in the text is due to multiple oral traditions behind it.

Second, the critic must identify the form or genre. In narrative the categories most frequently used are myths, folk tales, sagas, romances, novellas, legends, and historical narratives. Within the traditions there may be smaller units, such as blessings, oaths, hymns, or oracles. To verify the literary type, comparable samples must be found.

Form criticism assumes that poetic composition lies behind the stories in Genesis. Eissfeldt (*Old Testament*, pp. 33–56) distinguishes poetic narrative from historical narrative by listing the following features of poetic narrative: myth (a multiplicity of gods or angels), fairy tale (talking animals), saga (tribal etiology, folk etymology), and legend (patriarchal narratives where God is excessively prominent). Gunkel identifies six kinds of legends: etiological (e.g., explaining why human beings are sinful), ethnological (e.g., explaining why Canaan was enslaved), etymological (e.g., explaining the name Babel), ceremonial (e.g., explaining the Sabbath), geological (e.g., explaining salt near Sodom), and various unclassified types (*The Legends of Genesis*, trans. W. H. Carruth [Chicago: Open Court, 1901; reprint, New York: Schocken, 1964], pp. 24–35).

Third, the critic must establish the structure of the literary form. This task is fairly easy in hymnic and prophetic literature, but in narrative it involves tracing the motifs of similar stories (e.g., the wilderness stories have motifs of deprivation, murmuring, provision, and a lesson).

Fourth, the critic must identify the setting, or *Sitz im Leben*, for the unit. For example, hymnic literature was composed for the temple. Narrative literature is far more difficult. Gunkel said that the sagas of worship in Genesis may have originated in the places of which they treat and that the same may be said of other sagas that ascribe names to definite places (ibid., pp. 91–93).

Fifth, the critic must state the original intent of the story. This step often requires tracing its transmission and redaction history. For example, the tracing of the "sister sagas" in Genesis 12, 20, 26 has yielded these conclusions: the original core of the tradition belongs to the pre-conquest tribe of Isaac in Palestine, but in the later tribal unification the account was embellished and transferred to the more famous ancestor, Abram. In its development, the unit was embellished with speeches, the moral sensitivity became stronger, God's intervention became less tangible, and the story was transferred to more familiar peoples and powers (Gerar was not known, so Pharaoh was substituted). (See Klaus Koch, *The Growth of the Biblical Tradition, the Form Critical Method*, trans. S. M. Cupitt [New York: Scribner's Sons, 1969], pp. 111–31, esp. p. 128.)

An approach as involved as the form-critical method needs a detailed response; the following comments provide only a basic evaluation. At the outset we may note that form criticism is concerned with the final, fixed form as a part of the study rather than simply dividing the text into sources. The method is more interested in literary types than literary documents, recognizing that the traditions had earlier histories than the documentary hypothesis granted. On the other hand, form criticism embraces a naturalistic approach that accepts the idea that monotheism developed from polytheism, that miracles were unlikely, and that the records cannot be actual history.[5]

Form criticism assumes that (1) the sagas existed as oral units first, (2) these units were collected into cycles of stories, and (3) these collections were edited and embellished as they were developed into a book. While this schema may have been true to some extent, it probably was not entirely the case. For example, it would be plausible for parts of Genesis if Israel retained any knowledge of primeval history from their Mesopotamian background or if the patriarchal stories were passed down orally. However, this view does not preclude the stories' being written down at approximately the same time they were related orally. (See Kenneth A. Kitchen, *Ancient Orient and Old Testament* [Chicago: Inter-Varsity, 1966], pp. 135–38). We cannot simply assume a long oral tradition followed by a gradual embellishment of every account.

Form criticism frequently compares similar accounts in contemporaneous literature (e.g., the various flood stories). The emphasis on the comparison of ancient Near Eastern literature is often helpful. Whether they always represent common types of stories or not must be demonstrated case by case. In many cases the parallels are not convincing.

5. Form criticism concludes that the traditions of Genesis reached their form by the time of the monarchy but that they do not represent history (as appears, for example, in the succession narrative of Samuel). This view follows the general assumption that "uncivilized" races produce no history, only song and saga.

With regard to the various steps of form criticism, we may note both values and dangers. First, the separation of a text into originally independent units with different meanings may not be helpful for studying narrative literature in cases where the author is trying to develop a unified argument. Taking units in isolation without due regard for their part in the context does not contribute to the task of exegesis, which is to discover the intent of the final writer. Recognizing literary units within the present form of the text, however, is basic to exegesis.

Second, the identification of literary forms can be helpful, provided the forms are not labeled according to historical credibility.

Third, in developing the literary structure, there is the danger of forcing a narrative into a parallel structure or designating elements that do not fit as later embellishments. But if the literary unit exhibits the same structure and motifs that may be found in other passages and other literature, then we must determine the nature and function of that form and its use in the present context.

Fourth, the identification of the story's setting is very helpful if it can be legitimately reconstructed. Many reconstructions, however, are too subjective.

Fifth, regarding the intent of the author, we may agree that the exegete must attempt to articulate the purpose of the final writer in telling the story to Israel. However, the attempt to trace the development of the tradition through a long period of redactional history is not possible with any degree of certainty. Moreover, it is not necessary, because the final, written copy is the canonical text. Nevertheless, it is sometimes helpful to think of what the narrative meant to the original audience, what it meant to subsequent generations, and how it might be interpreted by different believing communities.

The Traditio-Historical Approach

This approach analyzes the compositional, historical, ideological, and psychological elements of the Hebrew text for the purpose of discovering the formation and transmission of Israelite traditions in the preliterary stage. The basic features of this method further developed the prevalent ideas in critical scholarship. Its proponents were critical of the old documentary hypothesis because of the emphasis on literary documents. They stressed that an understanding of ancient Hebrew psychology would provide the solution to the history of the traditions that lay behind the text and explain the difficulties in the text (e.g., the relationship between the one and the many, the personification of the individual to represent the tribe). They also contended that traditions were originally oral and not literary and that these traditions were then collected into complexes of traditions and suffered corruptions in transmission (e.g., the disciples of the prophets worked up the oracles and solidified them later in writing). In addition, the proponents of this approach placed a greater emphasis on comparative mythology and assumed that throughout the ancient world there was a diffusion of one pattern of sacral kingship and cultic activity, which could be reconstructed if close, compositional analysis were undertaken.[6]

Their first task is to trace the transmission of the story. The approach assumes that oral transmission was by memory, that the story was accompanied by an interpretation, and that it was reformulated by communities in various locations. For example, the story of Jacob at Bethel in Genesis 28:10–22 was first the account of a Canaanite etiology (vv. 18–19), then it dealt with a spiritual experience in the life of Jacob (vv. 15–16), and finally the *heilsgeschichte* motif was added during the period of the monarchy (vv. 13–14). Part of the development of the stories involved their being redacted into a literary unit. This redactor, however, was not a collector according to the old literary analytical view but a creative editor. For example, in combining the Jacob-Esau stories and the Jacob-Laban stories, he transformed them from old tales into their current cycles and added theophanies at critical points to link them (e.g., Bethel in 28:10–22; Mahanaim in 32:1–2; Peniel in vv. 22–32; and Shechem in 33:18–20). Finally, in the postexilic period they became normative for faith.

The traditio-historical critic also has the task of discovering the forces at work in the formation and reformulation of the stories. For example, priests shaped the traditions about Israel's origins, the sacrifices, and chronicles; the Levites transmitted Deuteronomic materials; wise men developed wisdom material; and prophets collected oracles. (See G. von Rad, *Studies in Deuteronomy*, Studies in Biblical Theology, 9 [London: SCM, 1953].) The locations also were important: southern locations (Jerusalem) would be concerned with kingship and the temple site; northern locations (Shechem and Gilgal), with covenant traditions. Furthermore, the setting gave the social, political, and religious dynamics to the traditions: elders in the gate shaped the legal material and Deuteronomic material was passed on in the covenant renewals.

6. See J. Pedersen, *Israel, Its Life and Culture*, trans. Aslaug Møller (Copenhagen: S. L. Møller, 1926); and Aubrey Johnson, *The One and the Many in the Israelite Conception of God* (Cardiff: University of Wales, 1942). Views on writing differ among the proponents of this approach. Eduard Nielsen, argues that writing was the work of a specialist and therefore played an insignificant role (*Oral Tradition* [London: SCM, 1954]). Also writing from the traditio-historical perspective, Sigmund Mowinckel contends that the psalms were interpreting ritual and therefore belonged to the annual autumnal festival known as the enthronement festival (*The Psalms in Israel's Worship*, trans. D. R. Ap-Thomas [Nashville: Abingdon, 1962]).

To avoid the pitfalls of earlier methods, these scholars posited two, long-developing, contemporaneous collections: the P group (Genesis through Numbers) and the D group (Deuteronomy through Kings). But to these critics the key to the meaning lies more in the development of the traditions than in the collections themselves.

It is difficult to evaluate this approach because of the diverse emphases of the scholars. On the whole, however, we may note that one type of source criticism has been substituted for another. More specifically, the traditio-historical approach often treats the material as parallel, contemporary, and more or less coterminal strata. While this emphasis may appear to be good, it allows one to select at random various elements from the Bible or ancient literature to weave the tradition. Seeing everything on a level rather than in a historical development may lead the exegete to ignore important distinctions in the traditions that are due to changing times and circumstances.[7]

The approach can also be criticized for its emphasis on oral tradition. Basically, there is a misrepresentation of the relationship between oral tradition and writing in the ancient Near East. Oral tradition was usually accompanied by written documents for the transmission of anything important. Literacy was fairly widespread from the earliest periods, as archaeological discoveries suggest.[8] Albright asserts, "The prolonged and intimate study of the many scores of thousands of pertinent documents from the ancient Near East proves that sacred and profane documents were copied with greater care than is true of scribal copying in Graeco-Roman times" (*From the Stone Age to Christianity* [Garden City, N.Y.: Doubleday, 1957], p. 79). The emphasis on oral tradition is thus probably overstated.

The correlation of biblical material with mythology may also be challenged. The assumption that a common mythological pattern was diffused throughout the ancient world may be valid, but it does not account for the distinct religious ideas of ancient Israel. With the critical disintegration of the Mosaic tradition, it is impossible to explain the historical origin of the faith in Yahweh. It is unsatisfactory and without parallel to ascribe the faith to chance coalescence of religious ideas springing up

7. The work of R. A. Carlson in Samuel illustrates this tendency: in his view, the moving of the ark to Jerusalem is the annual enthronement festival, and the adultery of David and Bathsheba is the sacred marriage part of the ritual (*David, the Chosen King: A Traditio-Historical Approach to the Second Book of Samuel* [Uppsala: Alqvist & Wiksells, 1964]).

8. Mustering evidence from "the hundreds of thousands of clay tablets from Mesopotamia and the acres of hieroglyphic texts and scenes from Egypt," Kitchen contends that to transmit anything important the ancient Near East employed writing (*Ancient Orient,* p. 136). Note that the Proto-Sinaitic inscriptions were written by slave-miners in approximately 1450 B.C. Note Judges 8:14, where the young man accidentally encountered at Succoth wrote down the names of the city's elders.

here and there in different situations. Moreover, the comparisons with ancient myth are often forced and unnatural. (See, for example, Carlson, *David*, on the events in David's story or Mowinckel's use of the Babylonian *akitu* festival.) Finally, the emphasis on the history of the traditions engages a method that is too subjective. Indeed, the lack of agreement over the reconstructions calls the method into question.

This approach, however, has several positive emphases. It employs archaeological evidence and compositional analysis; and its emphasis on oral tradition and Hebrew psychology, taken in moderation, can prove helpful.

The Rhetorical-Critical Approach

It comes as no surprise that such an emphasis on compositional analysis and literary parallels would lead to a greater emphasis among scholars on rhetoric. In recent years biblical scholars have been concerned less with the origin and transmission of the narratives than with the literary shape of the present form of the text. This area is the emphasis of so-called canonical criticism; see Brevard S. Childs, *Introduction to the Old Testament as Scripture* (Philadelphia: Fortress, 1979).

The phrase "rhetorical criticism" was first used in an address by James Muilenburg in 1968. He called for study of the nature of Hebrew literary composition as an extension of form criticism. ("Form Criticism and Beyond," *JBL* 88 [1969]: 1–18). This new synchronic emphasis would be primarily concerned with matters of structure and texture.[9]

In the recent examples of rhetorical criticism, certain features of the literature are employed in the analysis of the structure: scenes, parts of scenes, strophes, direct discourse, and acts. Narrative literature can thereby be broken down into its constituent levels.[10] The analysis of sounds, syllables, words, phrases, and sentences—texture, in rhetorical criticism—likewise follows certain patterns. These include the repeti-

9. For a discussion of the various works, see Vernon K. Robbins and John H. Patton, "Rhetoric and Biblical Criticism," *Quarterly Journal of Speech* 66 (1980): 327–37. For a sample of thorough synchronic analysis, see Fokkelman, *Narrative Art*, as well as his *Narrative Art and Poetry in the Books of Samuel: King David* (Assen: Van Gorcum, 1981).

10. There are different emphases in the works of those following this approach. Some stress genre studies and diachronic studies more than others; see Roy F. Melugin, "Muilenburg, Form Criticism, and Theological Exegesis," in *Encounter with the Text*, ed. Martin J. Buss (Philadelphia: Fortress, 1979); and Mary Savage, "Literary Criticism and Biblical Studies: A Rhetorical Analysis of the Joseph Narrative," in *Scripture in Context*, ed. Carl D. Evans, William H. Hallo, and John B. White (Pittsburgh: Pickwick, 1980), pp. 79–100. See also S. Bar-Efrat, "Some Observations on the Analysis of Structure in Biblical Narrative," *VT* 30 (1980): 154–73. For a good introduction to analysis of narrative, see Robert Alter, *The Art of Biblical Narrative* (New York: Basic, 1981).

tion of thoughts or key words, word plays or paronomasia, repetition of sounds such as assonance or alliteration, adumbration, inclusio (or inverted correspondence), and a host of other literary devices. (See Michael Fishbane, *Text and Texture: Close Readings of Selected Biblical Texts* [New York: Schocken, 1979].)

Rhetorical criticism has interested theologians as well as literary critics. It enables the theologian to understand the theological ideas of the text more fully, because the structure and the texture are not merely ornamental—they are the means for directing the reader's focus in the story. For samples of writings by literary scholars, see Kenneth R. R. Gros Louis, ed., *Literary Interpretations of Biblical Narratives* (Nashville: Abingdon, 1974).

The structure and texture focus attention persuasively by arousing an emotional response in addition to an intellectual reaction to the narrative. For example, repetition, the hallmark of Hebrew rhetoric, centers the thought and gives unity and continuity to the narrative (James Muilenburg, "A Study in Hebrew Rhetoric: Repetition and Style," *VTS* 1 [1953]: 97–111). But it frequently does so in a way that makes a lasting impression on the reader, for it carries forward the emotional and intellectual connotations of the previous use.

There are cautions in the use of rhetorical criticism, as there are in any approach. First, if the study ignores altogether the origin and transmission of the text, it may arbitrarily ascribe meanings that go beyond the intent of the passage. The basic meaning of a text must be tied to its historical setting and purpose. The biblical scholar thus cannot work simply on the level of synchronic studies. Second, rhetorical criticism must be coupled with the study of genre. In this area the correlation with form criticism is strongest. In studying structure and texture of a narrative, it is important to relate these findings to the literary form, for the form indicates the function in many cases.

Conclusion

With such an accumulation of ideas presented for the Pentateuch over the last few centuries, the modern scholar is faced with a formidable task. Since there are strengths and weaknesses in all the approaches, as well as many variations of each approach, most modern scholars are eclectic to some degree. The conservative scholar, for example, wants to be open to helpful advances but at the same time must discern what is compatible with the understanding of Scripture as God's revelation.

Modern scholars are comfortable with *rhetorical criticism* because it gives some freedom from the endless debate over higher criticism. The approach is not so much concerned with which verse was added later or which section came from an old Canaanite tradition. Rather, the study is concerned with the final fixed form of the text. One danger, however, is that the interpreter may assign a meaning to the unit that may be far removed from the original intent. This is a danger for those eager to see contemporary issues in the text.[11] Another is that the interpreter may engage in a thorough analysis of the narrative without carrying the study to the purpose of the genre or the theological point within the book.

Many of the emphases of *traditio-historical criticism* are helpful: oral tradition, Hebrew psychology, comparative literature, and compositional analysis—provided they are taken with caution.

It is important for the exegetical expositor to understand the different types of literature, and to this end, *form criticism* can be helpful. But here too there must be substantial evidence for the assignment of types—that is, convincing samples. Also, the interpreter must be able to demonstrate with some degree of plausibility the original setting.

While it is difficult to see much that was beneficial in the *literary-analytical approach*, we may acknowledge that it did alert scholars to the variations and tensions within the text. Although more recent studies have capitalized on the literary features as part of the narrator's art, it is possible that they also reflect sources used in the compilation of Genesis. On the broadest level, we may observe the difference in style between Genesis 1–11, 12–36, and 37–50, three very different sections. On a narrower level, we may observe differences in style between chapters themselves; the creation, for example, in Genesis 1:1–2:3 varies considerably from the style of Genesis 2:4–25. Sources were probably used in the writing of Genesis—sources that were brought by ancestors from Mesopotamia, sources and records of the ancestral families kept by the patriarchs, genealogical records, and the like. It is reasonable to suggest that Moses gathered ancient records and traditions, and it makes better sense for the message of the book in the Pentateuch.[12]

11. The work of Phyllis Trible, *Texts of Terror: Literary-Feminist Readings of Biblical Narratives* (Philadelphia: Fortress, 1984), may illustrate this danger. The book has excellent insights into the text of the selected passages but does not articulate the meaning of the units in context apart from their use for studying the terrorized women.

12. A case could be made for Moses as the author of the sections that critical scholarship has assigned to P. In this view, as Moses compiled the old traditions (the sections designated as JE), he freely added and explained items from his perspective. For example, the Table of Nations is divided between J ("these are the sons of" sections) and P (sections that are more full, often using *yālad*, "begot"). One could argue that Moses used the old skeleton list and added the material about Nimrod, the founding of the great empires, the Canaanite boundaries, and the cliché list of tribes. This hypothesis would explain the difference in style (at the heart of source criticism is the idea that no single author would have written the Pentateuch as it stands) but would not require a late date for the compilation.

We come naturally to the question of the creativity of such a writer-compiler. How free was he to reshape the traditions for his purposes? If his primary concern was a theological interpretation and not simply a report of ancient happenings, then some interpretive shaping would be expected. By the choice of words in the dialogue or the narrative, the arrangement of material in poetic style, interpretive additions, or the inclusion or deletion of material, the writer gave a definite shape and direction to the final form of the text.[13] Without altering the facts of the traditions, he formed a theological treatise based on the material gathered. This treatise, not the sources, has been identified as the inspired and authoritative message from God.

What, then, can be said of later additions and reshapings? It is likely that there were additions, modifications, and clarifications made in the text. One clear example is Genesis 14:14, which reports that Abram chased the armies to Dan. Not only was Dan not yet born, but also the migration of the tribe of Dan to the north came later than Moses. A wholesale reshaping of the traditions by successive generations, however, seems out of the question.

13. The writer has the freedom to choose the Hebrew vocabulary and constructions to record dialogue that would not have been spoken in classical Hebrew. For example, Exodus 2:10 has the daughter of Pharaoh naming Moses. It is unlikely that she would have made a wordplay on an Egyptian name (mōšeh, "Moses") with a Hebrew expression (mᵉšîtîhû, "I have drawn him out"). But the writer could form such a word play by his choice of words to translate her statement. Furthermore, dialogue and narrative alike can be set in poetic style. For example; the participants in the story of Job would not have spoken in poetry. Probably the material has been recast for mnemonic and rhetorical purposes. Genesis 26:5 illustrates the use of interpretive additions. Abraham "obeyed my voice, and kept my charge, my commandments, my statutes, and my laws." This statement could very well be a free interpretation of an original idea that Abraham was obedient, because the terms used in the present form are the technical legal terms from the later period of the giving of the law. In essence it would be saying: Abraham was obedient to whatever God said; it was as if he obeyed the law of Moses. Finally, the mere omission of material may be significant for interpretation. If the Chronicler omits the sin of David, for example, then we must conclude that a specific presentation of David is being developed. We are getting a true picture of David, but not the whole picture.

2

Method for Studying Genesis

I shall now outline a method for the exegetical exposition
of the Book of Genesis that is consonant with an orthodox, exegetical,
and critical approach. By *critical* I mean that it satisfies the demands of
literary-analytical investigation, with sound judgments on the nature,
purpose, and composition of the text. By *exegetical* I mean that the basic
investigation uses the Hebrew text and that the meaning is derived from
the text. And by *orthodox* I mean that the integrity of the text as the
inspired and authoritative Scripture is maintained.[1]

The discussion that follows stresses the literary and theological considerations, two areas that have been neglected frequently by commentaries and expositions. In the discussion of the chapters of Genesis, I
shall not devote as much time to the grammatical, syntactic, cultural,
or historical backgrounds and connections in the text. Such material is
usually described in detail in the better commentaries. My concern is

1. I do not say that critical questions should be ignored or that diachronic studies
have no value. Careful scholars must consider all the data and be able to offer plausible
solutions to the critical questions. They can do so within the framework of belief that
Scripture is a record of divine revelation. For a helpful summary of several paths to
follow in the analysis of Scripture, paths that deviate from critical methods in several
ways, see Alan R. Millard, "Approaching the Old Testament," *Themelios*, n.s., 2 (1977):
34–39.

that, along with that material, the expositor be able to determine the literary and theological aspects of the text. This determination will involve concentration on literary genre, narrative structure, rhetorical devices, the unified theological point of the narrative, and the correlation with the theology of the book and with the Bible as a whole.

Ultimately, the discussion of the literary and theological features will contribute to the development of the theological lesson and will, in turn make it easier to formulate the expositional ideas and outlines. In the discussion of the narratives of Genesis, I have included the formulation of my ideas and outlines to illustrate how each narrative could be developed for modern application, while remaining true to the meaning of the text in its historical and contextual setting. I have not intended to provide the complete exegesis for each narrative; however, my ideas and conclusions are certainly based on such exegetical studies.

This chapter presents a method for studying Genesis, following a certain order of steps. It must be recognized, however, that in practice the order of study varies considerably with different passages. Such an order, however, provides a convenient way to understand the aspects of a full analysis.

Determination of the Literary Unit

The foundational step in the procedure is identification of the literary unit, for this information will determine the contents of the exposition. Identifying the unit is not always simply a matter of deciding where a story begins and ends; rather, it is a matter of studying the structure and motifs of the possible unit, along with the surrounding contexts.

For example, Genesis 36 seems to be a unit. But if Genesis 37:1 belongs to this unit, with Genesis 37:2 beginning the next section, as I shall argue, then the unit contrasts Jacob with the advancement of Esau. This conclusion changes the point of the exposition.

Literary units may incorporate several different genres. A story could include a genealogy, an oracle, a cultic law, or a blessing. In that case the connection of the different genres must be carefully explained. Or the individual parts could be treated separately, provided the exegetical treatment is related to the context in the final form of the text. One must avoid the *isolated* study of such a part, whether it is treated as a later addition or as a part of the original composition.

Appraisal of the Narrative

A close reading of the narrative will isolate the things that must be studied. By a close reading I mean that the expositor will work through the text with whatever translations, commentaries, and dictionaries may be needed, for the purpose of identifying the points that must be studied.

Some of the items to note would be (1) critical problems; (2) difficult grammatical and textual expressions and constructions; (3) important theological words about the nature and works of God; (4) unusual expressions, figures of speech, word plays, repetition, and literary allusions; (5) literary patterns, structures, forms, and the use of direct quotations; (6) significant uses of tenses, moods, and cases; and (7) any patterns or motifs that build on prior narratives.

How detailed the study of these things will be is up to the expositor. Research into such matters obviously requires a certain amount of ability to find the information as well as time to think it through so that the exposition will clearly present the findings. Too often exposition of Old Testament narratives lacks precision and depth because these matters have not been adequately investigated.

Resolution of Critical Matters

Lower, or textual, criticism will not be a frequent task in Genesis, apart from the poetic passages. Nevertheless, because of the variety of English Bibles today, the expositor will have to determine the best reading whenever a textual difficulty arises. Sound method involves a knowledge of the relative strengths and weaknesses of the various manuscripts and versions, a knowledge of the tendencies of the scribes, and a knowledge of the rules of textual criticism for evaluating the evidence. For a general work on the subject, see Ralph W. Klein, *Textual Criticism of the Old Testament* (Philadelphia: Fortress, 1974).

Higher criticism concerns the authorship, date, occasion, and unity of the text. The expositor will probably have surveyed such issues before studying individual passages, but the specific questions raised about the stories, oracles, and laws in the book must be given more than a cursory consideration. Expositors too often ignore the genuine difficulties in the text.

Conservative scholarship rightly rejects the critical views that the stories were fabricated tales or idealized events told for some didactic purpose. The narratives themselves give the impression that the events happened, and the rest of the Bible confirms this view. Yet, the literary art of the writer brings some creativity and interpretation to bear on the traditions.

Philological Studies

No expositor has the time to study all the important words as completely as possible. But we must know exactly what the words mean in the context and be able to demonstrate their meanings with other uses or illustrate them with nontheological uses.

Several kinds of words require a more thorough investigation: (1) words that are central to the interpretation of the passage (e.g., "righteous" in Gen. 18:22–23), (2) basic theological terms (e.g., "grace" in 6:8), (3) words that are difficult (e.g., "strive" in 6:3), or (4) words that involve puns or popular etymologies (e.g., *ya'ăqōb*, "Jacob," and *'āqab*, "supplant, deceive," in 27:36).

The method for studying words involves both the etymology and the usage of the word. Great caution needs to be exercised in tracing the etymology—a matter that is often the work of the specialist. The expositor must guard against using an etymology, or a definition primarily derived from a cognate Semitic language listed in a dictionary or commentary, unless that meaning be validated by usage. Of course, if the word is a rare word, then etymology and evidence from the versions will have to be used cautiously.

Most words that will be studied are frequent enough that usage can be the prominent concern for the expositor. How a word is used in the literature determines its meaning, especially if it is used in the same context or by the same writer or in the same literary genre or in the same period of time by other writers. The process simply involves studying the passages where the word is used and then categorizing the different meanings of the word. The results enable the expositor to see the range of meanings in the word and then determine which precise meaning best fits the immediate context.

Naturally, more information will be gathered than can be used in the exposition. The expositor will have to select what is most helpful in developing the message of the passage. In some cases word studies will constitute the essence of the message (such as "evil," "repent," "blot out," "strive," and "grace" in Gen. 6:1–8).

Literary Analysis

The process of exegesis must include the analysis of the structure and texture of the literary unit. In determining the meaning of the passage, we must consider the deliberate design of the unit, the rhetorical devices the writer used in forming that unit, the setting of the account within the broader circle of narratives, the character sketches and descriptive clauses that color the narrative, the use of dialogue, and the unfolding of the plot in which the basic conflicts are resolved.

In this step the expositor is the literary critic in the true sense of the expression. The criticism must evaluate the overall effect of the biblical presentation, the impact of its arrangement, and the purpose for the poetic features. Some of the most common literary features of Genesis are anthropomorphic or metaphorical language describing God, the use of dialogue in the plot, and types and archetypes upon which later Scripture draws.[2] If possible, the study should attempt to specify the literary genre of the unit. If it can be described within Semitic and biblical types, then not only will there be a basis for comparison of texts and an understanding of the function of the unit, there will also be assistance in outlining the material.

G. Herbert Livingston offers examples of literary types developed through exegesis (*The Pentateuch in Its Cultural Environment* [Grand Rapids: Baker, 1974]). For example, Genesis 18:16–33 records an intercession: it has an orientation, or setting, involving a divine soliloquy and a divine word to Abraham (vv. 16–22), a sequence of dialogue (vv. 23–32), and a concluding observation (v. 33). Livingston then compares other intercession narratives in Exodus 5:19–6:1; 17:1–7; 31:18–32:16; 32:30–35; 33:7–23; Numbers 11:4–25; 12:10b–16. Such comparisons add insight into the purpose and meaning of a passage.

In addition, a literary study should ascertain the tone or mood of the passage—the attitude of the writer to the subject, and what responses (intellectual and emotional) might be expected from the audience. The alert expositor will catch the tone of the passage and communicate it in presenting the message.

Grammatical and Syntactic Analysis

From the outset, the study will require precise understanding of the grammar and syntax. In narrative literature the most difficult classifications will come in the dialogue and in the poetic sections—usually the most significant parts of the narratives.

2. When anthropomorphic language is used when God is speaking or acting, the interpreter must be careful not to take the text literally. Anthropomorphic language is a necessary means of communicating the divine will to humans; it is a form of condescension in revelation. Second, in narrative literature the dialogue often provides the significance of the story, especially if that dialogue includes a speech from the Lord. (In what better place may one find the center of theology than the words of the Lord?) Finally, Genesis contains much archetypal material. Cain, for example, is an archetype of a certain kind of person. John can thus say that everyone who hates a brother is like Cain (1 John 3:12)—there are many antitypes, or fulfillments. In the case of a type, there is only one antitype. Passover, for example, is a type of Christ; we do not look for another antitype. But an antitype can become an archetype. Jesus is the second Adam, so in some way Adam was a type of Christ (as well as an archetype of humankind). Jesus, then, by virtue of being the second Adam, becomes the archetype of those who conform to his image. In Genesis, the ancestors all represent the tribes that came from them, so that when one reads about Jacob, called Israel, that story represents more than an original event in the life of the patriarch.

It will soon become clear that, in certain passages, two or three interpretations of a particular form or construction make perfectly good sense
in the context. In such cases the other aspects of the exegetical process—
that is, the study of the words, the structure, the tone, and so forth—
may lead to the better choice.

There may not be a large number of insights from the grammar in a
given passage, but this step in the process will enable the expositor to
be sure that the interpretation fits the grammar and syntax. Frequently,
however, we will be able to make precise interpretations that may not
be reflected clearly in English translations. For example, the change from
the cohortatives to the obligatory imperfect in Genesis 12:1–3—as well
as the change in Hebrew vocabulary for the English word "curse"—is a
refinement that the English does not reflect ("but the one who treats
you lightly *I must curse*"). There are similar refinements in just about
every passage in Genesis; reliance on the English text by expositors will
miss them.

Exegetical Synthesis

The exegesis of a passage must demonstrate the unity and progression
of the narrative. The simplest way to capture the unity, and the most
helpful for the next two steps in the process, is to make a full exegetical
outline of the material and then write a summary of the passage in one
sentence.

An exegetical outline is developed from summaries of the individual
ideas or verses of the text. These individual sections are united by common themes or constructions to form the larger divisions of the passage,
for which a summary must then be written. When an outline is developed in this manner, it will include everything that is in the passage and
will express the relationships between the parts, enabling the interpreter
to see the narrative structure apart from all the descriptive and qualifying
sections.

An exegetical outline uses full sentences to express complete thoughts
about the contents of the section. Since this outline describes the contents, the sentences should be descriptive and historical.

Observe the following sample of an exegetical outline of Genesis
11:1–9:

     I. Prologue: The human race was united by one language (1).
    II. Human endeavor: Migrating to the land of Shinar, the people
        resolved to build a grandiose city and tower to preserve their
        identity and their unity (2–4).

     A. Event: The people migrated to, and settled in Shinar's fertile valley (2).

     B. Resolution: The people resolved to make bricks and build a city and a tower so that they might preserve their name and their unity (3–4).

       1. Ingenuity: They resolved to make bricks out of the materials available to them (3).

       2. Ambition: They resolved to develop a tower-city to make a name for themselves and to prevent scattering (4).

         a. Purpose: They wished to preserve their name (4a).

         b. Fear: They did not want to be scattered abroad (4b).

III. The Lord's intervention: Investigating the enterprise of the human race and knowing the dangerous potential of their unified pride, the Lord confounded their speech and scattered them abroad (5–8).

     A. Event: The Lord descended to investigate their building (5).

     B. Resolution: Knowing their potential was dangerously evil, the Lord resolved to scatter them across the face of the earth (6–8).

       1. Observation: The Lord concluded that nothing would be withheld from their designs (6).

       2. Resolution: The Lord resolved to destroy their unity (7).

       3. Solution: The Lord scattered them across the face of the earth so that their project ceased (8).

IV. Epilogue: The human race was disunited and scattered by the Lord's making a babble of their one language at Babel (9).

Several observations must be made here. First, every outline need not be as detailed as this one; for lengthy passages the points may be more comprehensive. Second, it is helpful to use topics to introduce the points, but this is not always possible. Third, using the past tense in the outline gives a better historical perspective. Fourth, the summaries should not simply restate what is in the subpoints but should condense the basic ideas. In short, the expositor tries to capture the argument of the passage without simply restating the verses.

Once all the parts of a narrative have been outlined, it is helpful to write a one-sentence summary of the entire passage, a synopsis of the unit. Limiting it to one sentence rather than a paragraph forces us to show the unity and the subordination of the parts. In short, it requires us to decide upon the central point of the unit and to determine how the other parts are related to it. We may write the summary by condensing the major points of the outline. The summary of Genesis 11:1–9 would be:

When the human race settled together to preserve their unity and to develop their fame by building a grandiose city-tower, the Lord interrupted their collective apostasy and scattered them across the face of the earth by confusing the language that united them.

Observe that the first half of the passage has been subordinated to the second half in the wording of this sentence. I interpreted the story to be primarily about the judgment of the Lord and not about the building of the tower—the building is foundational to the judgment. In the main clause I used a compound predicate: "The Lord interrupted . . . and scattered." In this way some of the reason for the scattering, which surfaces in the exegesis, comes through in the summary statement.

The formulation of an exegetical outline and summary statement is of great value in the entire process of exegetical exposition. If the expositor can develop this kind of exegetical synthesis, it will reflect a clear understanding of the passage. Moreover, it will be a safeguard that the exposition to follow will in fact reflect the point of the story and correlate all the parts correctly.

Development of the Theology

In the final analysis the narrative unit has something to say theologically. It may include many theological motifs and statements, but together they will express a unified theological idea. Accordingly, the exposition should develop the theology of the passage; failure to do so will inevitably leave the exposition on the level of storytelling, historical inquiry, or Bible trivia.

There is a great deal of debate over biblical theology—its method, its value, and even its possibility. One helpful approach is that of Walther Eichrodt, with its emphasis on the covenant (*Theology of the Old Testament*, 2 vols., trans. J. A. Baker [Philadelphia: Westminster, 1961–67]).[3] At the risk of oversimplification, I would say that a good starting point would be to try to discover what the passage says about the covenant God, about his creation, and about the relationship that exists or does not exist between them.

The exegetical summary of the passage will probably lead directly into the formulation of the theological point of the unit. It should be possible to formulate a statement about God and his will or his actions or about the actions of human beings in relationship to God's will. Once

3. The attempt to do biblical theology assumes that the text has unity and that all the texts in their final fixed form in the canon also have unity. Some do not see a unity; G. von Rad, for example, sees the text as a compilation of testimonies of Israel's faith.

again the statement should be a complete thought, and it should account for the entire unit. However, it should now be written as a theological statement rather than a historical description.

In narrative material it is important to watch for the narrator's statements of interpretation and for direct statements of the Lord in response to human actions or activities. If no such statements appear, then conclusions must be drawn by inference from the context. By concordance study, topical-index study, and even through word studies, the exegete can usually discover the theological ideas.

In identifying the theological ideas of the material the reader will discover that there are frequently two strands that must be correlated: those ideas with God as the subject, and those with humans. One could say that God is the subject of Genesis. Since the text is usually cast in the form of biography, however, the subject matter is more often about human choices and actions in the light of what is known about God.

In Genesis 11:1–9, for example, the story centers on the judgment of God in the affairs of humans. The theological statement we make must express truth that is applicable in other, similar situations: God opposes any enterprise that is characterized by pride and collective disobedience. Or from another side: Those who exalt themselves in disobedience to God may expect the judgment of God. Thus, the idea must be broadened from the particular instance in the narrative, which is one example of the outworking of the theological truth, to the general theological principle it conveys.

Naturally, our theological idea must be validated with the rest of God's revelation. This safeguard prevents the expositor from stating the point incorrectly. For example, one might say that God *always* does such and such, when in fact the most that can be said from a given passage may be that God *may* do such and such. Narrative literature describes what happened, and so we learn that it is possible; whether or not that happening is normative must be determined from the clear teachings of Scripture. We must be sure that the theological idea we develop is true. The correlation of other passages will provide the necessary qualifications.

Eventually the study will have to correlate New Testament uses of the material or comparable ideas expressed in the New Testament. This step must be reserved until the Old Testament material has been thoroughly studied, however, in order to avoid reading New Testament ideas into an Old Testament passage.

Development of the Exposition

The next step is the relevant and orderly presentation of the material in exposition, in either written or spoken form. There are many ways to present it in modern exposition—some more effective than others. The following method is an effective way to develop an exposition that is exegetically precise as well as relevant.

The expositor must first formulate the expository idea, the central idea of the message. This step may be one of the most difficult parts of the process. In a clear, positive sentence, drawn from the exegesis of the passage, state the applicable theological point the entire passage is making. It should not be limited to one of the sections of the narrative, and it certainly must not be something extraneous brought into the text, for the exegetical exposition will have to show how that idea was derived from the text.[4] The wording should not now be historical and descriptive, for that would remove the lesson from the present audience; neither should the wording be totally contemporary, for that would leave the meaning for the original audience out of the picture. The wording should express the *timeless* theological truth that the passage teaches, in a way that would be applicable to the original situation as well as to the contemporary corresponding situations. When this step is done the message will be relevant—and tied to the text.

One way to develop this expository idea is to rework the summary statement of the passage with the theological ideas in mind. In many cases the expository idea will be a restatement of the biblical theology. One that could be used for Genesis 11:1–9 is *God will subjugate the proud who rebel against his will.* This sentence is a straightforward, powerful assertion drawn from the passage. I used the general word "subjugate" because the specific idea of confusion of languages does not apply to other acts of pride. In choosing this verb, I was thinking of how God abases the proud and of how the judgment is talionic (here the confusion of the language strikes at the source of their strength, one language). If the passage were less specifically connected to a unique event in the ancient past, then the words in the statement would not have to be generalized so much. But once the message is put on the general level of God's subjugating proud rebellion, comparable biblical teachings can be correlated so that people can see that the lesson is a part of the broader teaching about God's response to the type of pride that leads to collective apostasy.

In a similar manner, the major points of the exegetical outline, and

---

4. Frequently today in the preaching of Old Testament narrative, the would-be expositor creatively embellishes the narrative in an attempt to make it interesting or relevant, filling in the details and circumstances that the biblical writer left out. Such an expositor frequently draws applications from the material just added to the text. The resulting sermon may be biblical or reflect a biblical philosophy of life, but it did not come from the text being used.

possibly the subpoints, may be recast to form theological statements. (If the passage is too difficult—such as the genealogy in Genesis 36—we may be unable to present the subpoints in any relevant theological form). If we develop the outline this way, it will enable the audience to see that the full exposition is derived from the passage.[5] We may find it necessary to combine points or redivide points in forming the exposition, which provides no problem as long as the contextual meaning is not destroyed. For Genesis 11:1–9, then, we could write the following expositional outline:

I. Immense pride (hubris) is rebellion against God (2–4).
   A. Pride leads to disobedience to God's Word (2).
   B. Ingenuity strengthens proud ambition (3).
   C. Ambition and fear motivate pride (4).
II. God will not permit proud, rebellious acts to succeed (5–8).
   A. God investigates the activities of arrogant mortals (5).
   B. God knows the danger of collective apostasy (6–7).
   C. God cuts off the expectations of such pride (8).

Verse 1 may be used as a prologue, and verse 9 as a concluding summary, especially with its wordplay on the name "Babel."

The substance of the exposition must be the exegetically derived material that led to these ideas. The exposition must explain from the text how the parts contribute to the central theological point that the passage is making. All the relevant studies must be brought to bear in the discussion. If the work has been done, the expositor need not worry about what to put in the exposition.

Application of the Lesson

It should be a relatively simple matter to move from the exegetically derived theological statement to the application, but application is frequently omitted. If the literature is didactic, if it is a message from God, then it must suggest a proper course of action or proper way of thinking. The expositor should, therefore, express this element in a specific, pos-

5. Too many so-called expositors simply make the one central idea the substance of their message. The narrative may be read or retold, but the sermon is essentially their central expository idea—it is explained, illustrated, and applied without further recourse to the text. This approach is not valid exegetical exposition. In exegetical exposition, the *substance* of the exposition must be clearly derived from the text so that the central idea unfolds in the analysis of the passage and so that all parts of the passage may be interpreted to show their contribution to the theological idea.

itive application. This step will be facilitated by correlating it with other Scriptures, but it should be drawn from the message of the passage itself.

Resources

There are many resources available for the study of the Book of Genesis; every individual working in the text will no doubt develop a personal preference for those books that are the most useful. In my discussions of the individual units, I include after each unit a selected bibliography of books and articles that may be helpful on each specific passage. At the end I provide a more thorough bibliography—but the list is by no means exhaustive. In this section I should like to list and describe the several basic commentaries that might offer the greatest help in developing exegetical expositions.

Every commentary has helpful information, but every commentary also demands critical use. The Jewish work by Umberto Cassuto (*A Commentary on the Book of Genesis,* 2 vols.) is excellent for the detailed study of Genesis 1–12. It is wordy and may take the reader into more minutia than desired, but the observations are worthwhile. *The First Book of the Bible: Genesis,* by Benno Jacob, is a translated and abridged edition of his original German work. The English copy is nowhere near as valuable as the original but will provide material that otherwise would not be available. Derek Kidner's brief commentary, *Genesis,* has many practical and theological comments on the text. *Genesis: A Commentary,* by Gerhard von Rad, has merit for theological insights, although most of these have to be used with great caution. Ephraim A. Speiser's commentary *Genesis,* in the Anchor Bible series, provides a good deal of help, especially for the literary and cultural background. The three-volume set on Genesis by Claus Westermann has many good things in it, but unless the expositor is able to sort through an amalgamation of critical views, the work may be more confusing than helpful.

Of the older works, George Bush, *Notes, Critical and Practical on the Book of Genesis* (1857), Franz Delitzsch, *A New Commentary on Genesis* (1888–89), and S. R. Driver, *The Book of Genesis* (1948), all have helpful comments on the text. Of course, when using these older works the exegete must check the ideas with modern scholarship.

In the recent works on the narratives of Genesis, three books are worthy of consideration (although others could be mentioned). The first is *Narrative Art in Genesis* by J. Fokkelman (1975), which covers Genesis 11:1–9 and the Jacob stories. This book will help the expositor understand the literary features of exegetical exposition. Another is Walter Brueggemann, *Genesis. Interpretation: A Bible Commentary for Teaching and Preaching* (1982). Brueggemann's concern is similar to mine, but he entertains many critical views. Nevertheless, the discussion will prompt the expositor to develop his or her thinking in the meaning of the text. The third book is George Coats's *Genesis, with an Introduction to Narrative Literature.* Coats has many good insights, but here also many critical views must be evaluated.

The Nature of Genesis

$\mathbf{T}$his chapter will determine the nature of Genesis by analyzing the literary types that may have been incorporated in the work: myth, etiology, history, and tradition.

Myth

It is common to find portions of Genesis described as myth or as mythic in origin. Wilhelm De Wette long ago noted that all ancient peoples had myth: "Symbols and myths are necessarily used, by a rude people, to clothe abstract truths" (*A Critical and Historical Introduction to the Canonical Scriptures of the Old Testament*, trans. Theodore Parker [Boston: Little & Brown, 1850], p. 23). Genesis, he claimed, used them as drapery for religious truth. More recently, Carmino De Catanzaro reiterated the position that much of Genesis 1–11 was mythology: "Its purpose is, in part, that of filling in a gap by relating the origins of things in symbolic form where the author lacked more precise, scientific knowledge" ("Man in Revolt: A Study in the Primeval History of the Book of Genesis," *CanJTh* 4 [1958]: 285).

Theodore Gaster also views much of Genesis as myth, the old mythical stories having been retold to provide illustration for truth (*Myth,*

Legend, and Custom in the Old Testament [New York: Harper & Row, 1969], pp. xxv–xxxvi). Gaster suggests, for example, that Paradise illustrates humankind's constant sacrifice of innocence for intellect. Such stories developed so much, however, that often the original myth survives only by a chance word. Gaster maintains that myth is the natural language of religion, transmuting the historical data into religious truth. Edmund Leach agrees: "All stories which occur in the Bible are myths for the devout Christian, whether they correspond to historical fact or not" (*Genesis as Myth* [London: J. Cape, 1969], p. 7).

The pioneer in the study of myth in Genesis is Hermann Gunkel. Kaiser says:

> It is with the name and results of Hermann Gunkel that any researcher in Genesis must reckon. As early as 1895 Gunkel began to draw the contrasts between history and the contents of Genesis 1–11. In 1901 he introduced his famous Genesis commentary with these words: "Are the narratives of Genesis history or legend? For the modern historian this is no longer an open question." ["The Literary Form of Genesis 1–11," in *New Perspectives on the Old Testament*, ed. J. Barton Payne (Waco, Tex.: Word, 1970), p. 50]

Genesis 1–11 cannot be considered history, according to Gunkel, because (1) these chapters originate in oral tradition, whereas history is found in written documents; (2) they deal with family stories, whereas history relies on outside evidence; (3) they narrate the impossible, whereas history tells the possible; (4) they are poetic and intended to delight and inspire, whereas history seeks to inform; and (5) they are different in form from the true Hebrew historiography as seen in 1 Samuel 9–20, where we find searching, uncomplimentary documents of David's court.[1] The influence of Gunkel spread in the study of Genesis. Skinner, for example, said, "We are not entitled to assume *a priori* that Israel is an exception to the general rule that a legendary age forms the ideal background of history: whether it be so or not must be determined on the evidence of its records" (*Commentary on Genesis*, p. v).

Toward a Definition

Certain limitations must be put on the concept in order to understand it. For some, myth is reality—in the terms of poetry, drama, and sym-

---

1. These major distinctions listed by Gunkel do not stand close scrutiny, as Kaiser has shown. Concerning the first, there is much more to be said for the strength of oral tradition and its complementary written records (K. A. Kitchen, *Ancient Orient and Old Testament* [Chicago: Inter-Varsity, 1966], pp. 135–37). Concerning the stories' nature as family stories, the beginnings of the race must begin with families and lead to great, public events. Concerning their being poetry, we have examples of the writer's poetry within the narratives, and for the most part the rest is prosaic.

bol—to evoke another dimension, that of being suspended between heaven and earth and yet partaking of both at the same time. (See Thorir K. Thordarson, "The Mythic Dimension," VT 24 [1974]: 220.)

Barr is not content to view myth as symbol. All language is symbolic in one sense, Barr reasons, but this fact does not make it myth. It cannot be just another way of speaking (Barr, "The Meaning of 'Mythology' in Relation to the Old Testament," VT 9 [1959]: 3–4).

For Childs, the essence of myth is human understanding of reality. By it people attempt to order the multiplicity of impressions about growth and decay, birth and death, or rising and setting, into a unified whole. To accomplish this ordering, Childs continues, myth projects the present reality back to a primeval age to show that what happened once continues to influence the world and destiny (Myth and Reality in the Old Testament [Naperville, Ill.: Allenson, 1960], pp. 17–20).

Mircea Eliade's comments provide a helpful summary. He writes:

> Myth narrates a sacred history; it relates an event that took place in primordial Time, the fabled time of the "beginnings." In other words, myth tells how, through the deeds of Supernatural Beings, a reality came into existence, be it the whole of reality, the Cosmos, or only a fragment of reality—an island, a species of plant, a particular kind of human behavior, an institution. . . . The actors in myths are Supernatural Beings. They are known primarily by what they did in the transcendent times of the "beginnings." . . . In short, myths describe the various and sometimes dramatic breakthroughs of the sacred (or the "supernatural") into the World. It is this sudden breakthrough of the sacred that really *establishes* the World and makes it what it is today. [Myth and Reality (New York: Harper & Row, 1963), pp. 5–6]

Eliade reiterates emphatically that the cosmogonic myth is "true," since the existence of the world is there to prove it.

Myth and the Old Testament

If myth is not merely symbolic language but rather an expression of the world view of reality by ancient men and women, then we have sufficient understanding to determine if it was used in Genesis. *Reality* in the Old Testament differs radically from the prevailing view of the ancient world. The Hebrews believed in an absolutely sovereign God who brought them into existence as a nation. Their concept of time was not cyclical but eschatological and full of hope, their ritual was not cosmic but redemptive, and their concept of space was not limited to the primeval but actualized in history. In a word, according to Childs (Myth and Reality, pp. 42, 70–71), the new reality was Israel within her concept of history. (Childs holds that the writers broke the myth and used what they could to serve their purposes.)

Concerning the concept of Israel's world view, we find another radical break with mythical ideas. Myth deals in correspondences (for example, vegetation dies when and because the god dies). Since myth represents a total world view in a relevant cultural group, it cannot be used to refer to a phrase here or a word there. Myth as a totality shaped and expressed the mind of ancient people (see Barr, "Meaning of 'Mythology,' " p. 3).[2]

With these concepts of myth in mind, we conclude that Genesis is not myth. (See also Frankfort's view that the Hebrews broke with the mode of speculation that had prevailed prior to their time, in H. Frankfort et al., *Before Philosophy* [New York: Penguin, 1946], p. 237.) The Hebrew faith departed radically from the mythological concepts of world reality and of harmony by correspondences between the human and divine. Barr says, "The main battle of the Hebrew faith is fought against the confusion of human and divine, of God and nature." Barr adds that, while vestiges of myth from the world around may survive, "they now have to be understood in their relation to a totality which is shaped largely by its repudiation of the characteristic mythological pattern of correspondence" ("Meaning of 'Mythology,' " p. 7). The Israelite concept of reality in their history enforced the differences, so that whatever survivals of myth as may exist in the language are controlled by the historical sense.

Thordarson concluded that, as far as positive forces of nature were concerned, mythology was done away in Yahwism. The negative forces such as Death and Chaos and the Underworld, he allowed, were preserved in their mythological meaning ("Mythic Dimension," p. 218).

Gerhard Hasel was not satisfied with even that allowance. Studying the alleged mythical allusions in the creation account of Genesis, Hasel concluded that the individual terms are actually used as polemics:

> This investigation of crucial terms and motifs in the creation account of Gen. 1 in conjunction with a comparison of respective ancient Near Eastern analogues has repeatedly pointed into one direction. The cosmology of Gen. 1 exhibits in a number of crucial instances a sharply antimythical polemic. With a great many safeguards Gen. 1 employs certain terms and motifs, partly taken from ideologically and theologically incompatible predecessors and partly chosen in deliberate contrast to comparable ancient Near Eastern concepts, and uses them with a meaning and empha-

2. C. Westermann points out that, methodologically, we must consider religiohistorical parallels in light of the total phenomenological conception of the works in which such parallels appear. Single terms must not be torn from their cultural moorings and treated in isolation from the total concept ("Sinn und Grenze religionsgeschichtlicher Parallelen," *TLZ* 90 [1965], col. 489–96).

sis not only consonant with but expressive of the purpose, worldview, and understanding of reality as expressed in this Hebrew account of creation. Due to our laying bare of main aspects of the polemic nature of Genesis cosmology with its consistent antimythical thread running through Gen. 1, one does not do justice to this particular emphasis in Gen. 1 when one speaks in the instances considered of a "demythologizing" [W. H. Schmidt] of mythical motifs, which are said to be "reshaped and assimilated" [Gunkel], "defused" [G. Fohrer], "broken" [Childs], "removed" [McKenzie], or whatever description one may use. It does also not do justice to the antimythical polemic of Gen. 1 to speak of the historicization of myth [Noth]. It appears that the Genesis cosmology represents not only a "complete break" [Sarna] with the ancient Near Eastern mythological cosmologies but represents a parting of the spiritual ways brought about by a conscious and deliberate antimythical polemic which meant an undermining of the prevailing mythological cosmologies. ["The Polemic Nature of the Genesis Cosmology," *EvQ* 46 (1974): 91]

Not only is mythology foreign to the Hebrews' concept of reality, but it raises questions about truth. The New Testament assures the reader that the Old Testament presents actual events. The fact remains, however, that we are dealing with exceptional literature. The truth we find in these narratives goes beyond the event and describes the reality of life in a typological or archetypical manner. The narratives are timeless, as well as being centered in time, but they are not myth. Isolated terms that are not part of a total world view must be viewed as poetic descriptions from a common cultural setting, or as antimythical polemics.

Etiology

The word "etiology" means a study of causes. It is usually a short explanatory comment at the end of a story. Sigmund Mowinckel explains:

The etiological saga is always built on a reality. However, this reality is not an event, much less a historical event, but a condition, something existing, a topographical, ethnologic, cultic, or customary phenomenon of a permanent sort. The action seeks to explain the origin and existence of this continually existing condition. [*Tetrateuch-Pentateuch-Hexateuch* (Berlin: A. Töpelmann, 1964), p. 81]

Childs points out that those who use etiology commonly assume that (1) the interest for which it was composed lay at the end of the narrative, (2) the effect is primary and the causation is secondary, (3) the effect evoked the cause, and (4) because etiology is involved, this connection is artificial and nonhistorical ("The Etiological Tale Re-examined," *VT* 24 [1974]: 396).

Problem of Etiology

Scholars have been perplexed about the relationship between the cause and the effect, that is, whether the etiology gave rise to the story or whether it embellished it. The problem is compounded in that the discussions are based on reconstructions in the text. The critical view has argued that, under the influence of tradition, there was a reshaping of the original idea of the story for an etiological use in the "historical" narrative.[3]

How, then, does etiology pertain to historicity? In his criticism of the Alt-Noth school, Bright argued that, if etiology is a literary form it cannot be used to establish or deny historicity. With this position Albright agrees, stating:

> Since all ancient literary composition had to conform to fixed patterns of oral delivery and formal styles of writing . . . the ultimate historicity of a given datum is never conclusively established nor disproved by the literary framework in which it is imbedded: there must always be external evidence. ["The Israelite Conquest of Canaan in the Light of Archaeology," *BASOR* 74 (1939): 12][4]

Bright also argued against the use of etiology as a creative force of tradition. According to Bright, "Nothing is more fundamentally wrong in the method of Alt and Noth than this. . . ." He continues:

> I should not wish to deny that the aetiological factor is present. . . . But I should like to submit that, *where historical tradition is concerned*, not only can it be proved that the aetiological factor is often secondary in the formation of these traditions, *it cannot be proved that it was ever primary*. [*Early Israel*, p. 91]

3. See Burke O. Long, *The Problem of Etiological Narrative in the Old Testament* (Berlin: A. Töpelmann, 1968). In the critical view, for example, the oldest form of Genesis 22 was a cult saga that legitimized the redemption of child sacrifice with the sacrifice of an animal but was used to explain why Israel offered lambs rather than children (von Rad, *Genesis*, pp. 238, 243).

4. Bright notes that ancient scribes had to conform to the forms of the time, and so forms themselves cannot be the final arbiter of historicity. Form criticism cannot pass final verdict on historicity. Novels today may be fiction or biography; newscasts may be models of objectivity or propaganda (John Bright, *Early Israel in Recent History Writing* [London: SCM, 1956], p. 90).

For many critics, an etiological element makes the tradition automatically suspect, for if an etiological factor created the story, it could
hardly be historical. Etiology does occur, because Genesis explains many
things to the nation of Israel. But in all probability these stories were
selected because they explained things; moreover, the etiological factors
are usually responsible for only a single detail or application from the
story.

Concluding Evaluation

Etiology can be a legitimate motif in the narratives, but an etiology
presumes the tradition and therefore cannot be the cause of the tradition.
Childs concludes, "Thus it is a methodological error to seek a form
critical warrant in the genre of the etiology as a means to by-pass the
historical question and to seek to deduce the cause from the effect"
("Etiological Tale Re-examined," p. 393).

History

If the world view of the Old Testament writers is governed by a historical sense rather than by mythology, then it is necessary to consider
what that sense involved. Most modern scholars have not been willing
to call Genesis "history," unless it is distinguished from modern philosophies of history. Norman Porteous explains insightfully,

> The emphasis on the various types of literature and the tracking down
> of traditions do not of necessity throw doubt on the historicity of the
> events which are recorded. In practice, however, the classifying of tradi-
> tions and their association with cultic situations has led to a certain
> sceptical attitude to their historicity. Moreover ... the fact that Israel's
> religious traditions make frequent reference to supernatural interven-
> tions is usually enough to make the historian look askance at them and
> assume that the actual course of events must have been very different.
> ["Old Testament and History," in *Annual of the Swedish Theological
> Institute*, vol. 8, ed. Hans Kosmala (Leiden: E. J. Brill, 1972), pp. 22–23]

Conflict with Modern History

Although there are problems with understanding history for any era,
many would contrast ancient history with modern, which, it is presumed, can normally be verified by outside sources. The difficulty is
that history, in contrast to the exact sciences, in which causation can
be empirically determined under repeated identical conditions, is a social science, in which conditions never repeat. Porteous comments that
we never get down to the bare facts of history except in the most su-

perficial sense, for the facts of history are *interpreted* facts, and the interpretation varies from one historian to another (ibid., p. 25).

In analyzing the earlier Old Testament, critical scholars diminish its value as history. One reason is the absence of outside sources that verify the contents. (See Millar Burrows, "Ancient Israel," in *The Idea of History in the Ancient Near East,* ed. Robert Claude Denton [New Haven: Yale University Press, 1955], p. 101.) Albrecht Alt addressed this problem, saying:

> Can we go on to describe this decisive process in historical detail? The condition and the nature of the tradition that has come down to us make it very difficult. For no foreign nation observed the growth of Israel or left an account of it; and as far as Isarel's own literature is concerned, not only are there absolutely no records, in the strict sense, of the very early period, but it also lies far beyond the time which was fresh in the memory of the first true historians, writing during the foundation of the monarchy. We are dependent on a collection of sagas which were transmitted orally for a long time before they were put into literary form. [*Essays on Old Testament History and Religion,* trans. R. A. Wilson (Garden City, N.Y.: Doubleday, Anchor Books, 1968), pp. 3–4]

Archaeological and historical materials may essentially substantiate the ideas of the accounts, but they do not offer the kind of verification that historians require.

A second reason that these works are not considered to be history is the intertwining of religious ideas with the events. The supernatural element has troubled historians. Nevertheless, if philosophies of history vary between historians, then our task is to extract the biblical philosophy of history and then to trace the connection of causes and effects and draw out the intended lessons of moral and political wisdom.

The Scriptures as History

Judged by its distinct ideas in the ancient world, the Bible must be considered a unique type of history. Speiser writes that "the Bible is both a primary and unique source on the subject of the idea of history, for the book as a unit is essentially a work of history" ("The Biblical Idea of History in Its Common Near Eastern Setting," *IEJ* 7 [1957]: 207). Within the ancient world the historical framework distinguished Israel from the pagans; as G. Ernest Wright asserts, Israel learned about God from historical acts (*God Who Acts* [London: SCM, 1952], p. 44). The exodus, for example, taught Israel that God had chosen her.

Cassuto concludes that "Israel has the distinction of being the first of the civilized peoples to create historiography in the full and precise meaning of the word" (*Biblical and Oriental Studies*, vol. 1, trans. Israel Abrahams [Jerusalem: Magnes, 1973], p. 8). This historiography, however, was a history of a particular kind. Scripture was never intended to be a mere chronicle of events or the biography of a nation. It is not oblivious to the historical process; however, the Pentateuch deals with primeval history, the times of the patriarchs, and the gradual incubation of national consciousness among a people unused to independence.[5] This special kind of history shows that the Old Testament's world view transcends the historian's plane; it is not history for history's sake but records of past events for the purpose of educating people spiritually. It presents a theological view of history, interpreting with a divine cause as well as a human one.

The Background of Israelite History

The two major centers of civilization preceding Israel were Mesopotamia and Egypt. Speiser concludes that "Egypt and Mesopotamia were as mutually incompatible as totalitarianism and democracy—and for precisely the same reasons ("Biblical Idea of History," p. 207).

According to Speiser Israel's world view of hope and freedom was closer to that of Mesopotamia than that of Egypt. In the land of Mesopotamia, the *ziqqurratu,* or temple tower, was an aspiration to forge a living bond between heaven and earth, joining the mortal and the immortal. The pyramids, on the other hand, were monumental tributes to dead kings. The former tells of hope; the latter, of resignation.

Israel, regarded as the cultural descendant of the Mesopotamian civilization because of the roots of the patriarchs and the cultural ties, retained Mesopotamian traditions and concepts. Consequently, scholars look to Mesopotamian literature to find the sources for Genesis or the concepts that inform it.

The Nature of Biblical History

With this background in mind we may attempt to describe the philosophy of history present in the biblical literature. M. H. Segal writes:

> The Pentateuch does not give us history. It tells us nothing of the events in the primeval ages beyond a few examples of the moral deterioration of mankind prior to the call of Abraham. Of Abraham it tells us nothing of his life before the call. It says nothing of the centuries-long story of

---

5. The only parts that do not address themselves to history in one way or another, Speiser says, are Psalms, Proverbs, Job, Ecclesiastes, and Song of Solomon, but the fact they are in the canon shows that it is a special kind of history ("Biblical Idea of History," p. 207).

Israel in Egypt before the oppression. [*The Pentateuch* (Jerusalem: Magnes, 1967) p. 23.]

The biblical account is actually a unique distillation of history. (See Speiser, "Biblical Idea of History," p. 202.) It is less interested in recording events for the sake of history than in using these events as vehicles for communicating the verities of biblical faith. The Bible presents an interpretation of significant events from the perspective of Yahwistic faith.

In the biblical idea of history, the conviction concerning the reality and authority of Yahweh is the point of departure for any evaluation. Robinson says, "The Bible takes it as axiomatic that God controls history, reveals himself in history, and directs it towards a final goal" ("Historical Summaries of Biblical History," *EvQ* 47 [1975]: 195; see also David Noel Freedman, "The Biblical Idea of History," *Interp* 21 [1967]: 38).

The Essence of Biblical History

At the center of Israel's interest in the interpretation of history is the covenant. God chose his people through Abraham and made a covenant with them through him. Genesis uses this theme as the central point of its interest in recording past events. The narratives were selected and interpreted theologically to teach the covenant faith. Israel's history looked back to what God had done (in the election) and looked forward to the promise fulfilled (in the liberation and ultimately in the eschaton); in between was the interpretation of events according to the faith.[6] Burrows states that these ideas were present from the earliest times:

The conception of Israel's history as grounded in a divine choice and a divine act of deliverance from bondage and as consisting in the fulfillment of promises made to the remote ancestors of the Israelites was already dominant in the religious traditions of the people before the works of history were written. ["Ancient Israel," p. 112]

Historicity

Can the texts, then, be described as historical? In contrast to modern views that stress the interpretations and minimize the events themselves, we may say that it is reasonable to suppose that interpretation is a response to *something* that demands interpretation. Or, as Speiser says of the patriarchal material:

6. Speiser notes that biblical history bridges the two cultures: Israel is to be liberated from the one, in accordance with freedom of the other. Such liberation marked the birth of the nation ("Biblical Idea of History," p. 211).

It cannot be set down as fancy. The author retells events in his own inimitable way: he does not invent them. What is thus committed to writing is tradition, in the reverent care of literary genius. Where that tradition can be independently checked, it proves to be authentic. ["Biblical Idea of History," p. 210; see also Porteous, "Old Testament and History," p. 29]

The writer simply recorded the ancient traditions that had already become important in the memory of Israel. The fact that he interpreted those events in accord with a specific belief need not negate their historicity.

Tradition

If ancient tradition were used in Genesis, then clarification of those traditions is in order. Genesis is filled with accounts of individuals and individual events in the remote past. This kind of record, with names, genealogies, and connections to subsequent events in the memory of Israel, has been variously designated as legend, tradition, or, most commonly, saga.

In evaluation of the work of Gunkel, Albright says,

Against Wellhausen, Gunkel saw that the narratives of Genesis were a prose form of early poetic traditions, often going back to a high antiquity.... Gunkel was well aware of the great antiquity of the sagas of Genesis. He failed, however, to recognize that much "saga" is orally transmitted history, just as much "history" is a more sophisticated form of saga. It is hard to distinguish between saga and dramatic historical presentation. Besides, we now know that the traditions of Genesis had been handed down with extraordinary fidelity for many centuries before they were put into prose, usually in abbreviated form, about the tenth century B.C. [Introduction to Gunkel, *Legends of Genesis*, p. viii][7]

Von Rad contends that saga is to be treated not as fantasy but as tradition:

Let us hold fast to this: by no means is saga merely the product of poetic fantasy; rather, it comprises the sum total of the living historical recol-

7. According to Albright, "In general it is a pity that Carruth chose the rendering 'legends' for the German *Sagen*, since German *Sage* in its usual modern sense was taken over from Norse *saga*, which refers to a prose or more rarely poetic narrative of historical origin and coloring. If we remember that Gunkel did not attempt to prejudge the historicity of a given narrative by calling it *Sage*—regardless of what 'legend' may seem to mean in the context—we shall not be misled" (Introduction, pp. xi–xii).

lection of peoples, in it is mirrored in fact and truth the history of a people. It is the form in which a people thinks of its own history. [*Genesis*, p. 31]

We may say that the memory of ancient events and persons in the heritage of Israel, preserved by oral tradition and by writing, provided the nation with her historical past as well as her common experience.

The Background of the Traditions

Much has been written during the past century about the Mesopotamian background of the early part of Genesis. It now seems clear that both the Hebrew and the Babylonian traditions are independent versions. The foundational points of contact are the creation, the frame of lists of seven or ten names, the story of the flood, Nimrod, and Babel.[8]

When Genesis 1–11 is compared with *Atraḫasis,* the structure and content show a Mesopotamian connection. *Atraḫasis* has the creation of humans, their multiplying on earth, and their attracting punishment from the gods—plague, famine (twice), and flood—but surviving by a family in a boat, ending with the reestablishment of man and society. There is an undeniable common framework.[9] The differences are that it is polytheistic, with a plurality of the gods and a divided counsel, humankind becomes a labor-saver for the gods, and there is no fall or sense of sin (Millard, "New Babylonian 'Genesis' Story," pp. 5–7).[10]

8. See A. R. Millard, "A New Babylonian 'Genesis' Story," *TynB* 18 (1967): 18; W. F. Albright, "The Babylonian Matter in the Pre-Deuteronomic Primeval History (JE) in Genesis 1–11," *JBL* 58 (1939): 91–103. Unger states that both sources give us forms of primitive traditions of the beginnings of the universe and of human beings. They are traditions common to all civilized nations of antiquity. Modifications occurred in time, and the polytheistic corruptions entered various recensions. Genesis, Unger concludes, presents the original form these traditions must have assumed (*Archaeology and the Old Testament* [Grand Rapids: Zondervan, 1954], p. 37). Von Rad also attests to the point that Israel found such traditions in Canaan when she moved in and in turn brought other ideas, likewise ancient, from her pre-Palestinian dwelling places (*Genesis,* p. 64).

9. See W. G. Lambert and A. R. Millard, *Atra-ḫasis, the Babylonian Story of the Flood* (Oxford: At the Clarendon Press, 1969); Kenneth A. Kitchen, "The Old Testament in Its Context"; part 1, "From the Origins to the Eve of the Exodus," *Theological Students' Fellowship Bulletin* 59 (1971): 4. Millard notes that the narrative of creation and the narrative of the flood are similarly continuous in both accounts ("New Babylonian 'Genesis' Story," pp. 14–15).

10. As far as the Hebrew *tᵉhom,* "sea," is concerned, it is not a personal name, nor is there a hint of God's doing battle with the sea, as there is with the Babylonian goddess Tiamtu ("sea"). The sea in Genesis is only an unruly element to be tamed. The pagan paradise story is also different. There human beings were made to do the grievous toil the Igigu would not do willingly, thus freeing the gods from toil. In the making of human beings, god and man mingled together in the clay, with spitting (= giving life?) parallel to God's inbreathing in Genesis. In the Babylonian account, the offense that led to the flood was the people's noise, not their sin.

The major consideration, though, is that the overall framework is present. According to Kitchen,

> We seem to have a situation of parallel traditions (not borrowings) within the inner diversity of peoples having a common heritage in Mesopotamia: in each case, creation, man's dissent from deity, flood and renewal as a total entity, but differently presented by Hebrews and Babylonians.
>
> Nor is the evidence of Atrakhasis accidental or entirely isolated. The same fundamental pattern is implicit in the Sumerian King List, with its kings (who must follow a creation) who reign before a flood, then the flood, then the re-establishment of kingship (the keynote of ancient society). And the Sumerian flood-story of c. 1600 B.C. would seem, when complete, to have included the creation of man, a punishment other than flood(?), then dissent between men and gods resulting in the flood, the saving of many by boat, and restoration. So, the over-all tradition is not an atypical feature in Mesopotamia. ["Old Testament in Its Context," p. 5]

In addition to the narrative framework, Kitchen points out that the combination of lists (or genealogies) and narrative—such as one finds in Genesis 1–11—is not unknown in the Mesopotamian world:

> The use of lists, statistics, etc., is commonplace in Ancient Near Eastern literature, and cannot be used to determine authorship; longstanding attempts in Old Testament studies to segregate such matter under such ciphers as "P" fly directly in the face of ancient modes of composition and must therefore be dismissed as meaningless and irrelevant. [ibid.]

These lists, it might be noted, show very consistent patterns, including the addition of notes about individuals whenever the author/compiler deemed it appropriate. The Sumerian king list also annotates certain names on the list. This stylistic pattern in no way destroys the unity of the literature.

In this brief sketch of the points of contact in the literature, we have observed the general framework, patterns of style and format, as well as general themes. We conclude, with others, that the two traditions must be parallel traditions, perhaps going back to one source.

The Transmission of Traditions

Besides the primeval traditions and genealogies brought from the East, the family traditions of the patriarchs would have been handed down from generation to generation. Joseph, and later Moses, would have had every facility for recording and preserving the traditions that the ancestors brought with them (ibid., p. 6).

This vast collection of records and traditions then had to be formed into a unified, cohesive work. Moses, under divine inspiration, selected the materials for this work, arranged them in the most effective way, and drew out their greater significance by the choice of terms and use of literary devices employed in his interpretive telling of the traditions.

It is apparent, though, that the revising did not obscure the distinctions in the material. The primeval narratives are very different from the patriarchal stories, and the Joseph stories are not like the patriarchal traditions.[11] Moreover, within the narrative stylistic differences reflect earlier units and patterns.

Conclusion

The classification of the genre of Genesis is not a simple matter. The work is part of the Pentateuch, the law in general, but it is not exactly legal literature. The work is cast in narrative style, but it is not a simple reporting of past events, and it is not a complete history of the ancestors. What it reports happened, but how it explains it is theological interpretation. Accordingly, myth must be ruled out as a possible genre for the narratives; and saga or legend connotes a negative classification that is not productive.

It may be necessary to classify the three sections of Genesis individually. The primeval events are ancient traditions cast in a poetic narrative form that lends itself readily to oral transmission. The patriarchal events are reports about the ancestors that were retained in the family records. And the Joseph material forms a short story with its arc of tension and its resolution. But within each section there are other genres such as linking genealogies, theophanies, oracles, blessings, and tribal sayings.

The debate over the compilation of these reports and traditions continues. The critical view may allow that the traditions reflect an early origin (either inside Israel or outside) but it maintains that they were not compiled until much later in the nation's experience. But there does not seem to be any compelling evidence for dating the composition relatively late. In the view of R. K. Harrison,

11. Thomas E. Ridenhour suggests that the Joseph section is the product not of nomadic people but of a settled and sophisticated people with literary ability. He follows von Rad in stating that it is not etiology but ancient wisdom literature ("The Old Testament and the Patriarchal Traditions" [Ph.D. diss., Duke University, 1972], p. 51). See also G. von Rad, "The Joseph Narrative and Ancient Wisdom," in *The Problem of the Hexateuch and Other Essays*, trans. E. W. Trueman Dicken (New York: McGraw-Hill, 1966), pp. 292–300; K. A. Kitchen, "Some Egyptian Background to the Old Testament," *Tyndale House Bulletin* 5 (1960): 4–18; Gerhard von Rad, "The Story of Joseph," in *God at Work in Israel*, trans. John H. Marks (Nashville: Abingdon, 1980), pp. 19–35.

Almost the entire body of Pentateuchal material could have been easily extant in practically its present form by the late Joshua period. No doubt the passing of time brought certain editorial activities to bear upon the Hebrew text in the form of explanatory glosses, insertions, and revisions of language and spelling, consistent with the practices of Babylonian, Egyptian, and other Near Eastern scribes. Even when cognizance has been taken of this situation, there appears to be no substantial ground for denying that the Pentateuch in virtually its extant form was in existence by the time of Samuel. [*Introduction to the Old Testament* (Grand Rapids: Eerdmans, 1969), p. 541]

This final, fixed form of the text retains all the types of literature passed down and collected by the ancestors. The final product is not simply a collection but *a theological shaping of the reports and traditions for the instruction of Israel under the Sinaitic covenant.* Genesis, then, in the broadest sense, belongs in the Torah, for it is a theological explanation of what led up to and transpired at Sinai. The book forms a prologue to the law.

Accordingly, the primary concern in the interpretation of this book is to relate each theological idea to the covenantal concerns of the law. More than being reports of Israel's ancestral history, the records and traditions are didactic, as they anticipate the clear development of the covenant stipulations and promises. If the text had as its purpose the writing of a simple history, it would have been more comprehensive and would have suppressed the didactic, theological interpretations. If the text had as its purpose the writing of laws, it would not have used the form of narrative reports. As it stands, Genesis is part of the Torah tradition in the form of theological interpretation of significant events in Israel's traditions. The task of the expositor, therefore, is to determine how the structure and texture of the final composition work together in the development of a theological treatise.

4

The Composition of Genesis

If indeed the Book of Genesis is the product of literary formation, and if it is also a theological treatise, then there must be a complementary development of the literary structure and theological motifs. This chapter will trace the structure of the book and the major theological themes.

A survey of Genesis reveals that, in its present, canonical form, the book is a unified work, for it exhibits a consistent structure, a common theme, and a progressive development of that theme within the structure. The book arranges the traditions from the past in a series of sections, entitled $tôl^edôt$ ("generations" or "account"), that develop the motif of divine blessing, in order to present the historical basis in tradition for the election and covenant of the seed of Abraham.

The Theme of Genesis

Even a casual reading of the Book of Genesis reveals the prominence of the theme of blessing. The entire book turns on this motif and its antithetical motif, cursing.[1] God's blessing gives the seed to the patriarchs

---

1. For a brief survey, see Claus Westermann, *Blessing in the Bible and the Life of the Church*, trans. Keith Crim (Philadelphia: Fortress, 1978). The motifs of blessing and

and the land to the seed; the cursing alienates, subjugates, and disinherits. Later, prophets and historians expanded the motifs and applied them to future events.

The word *bārak* means "to bless, enrich" (A. Murtonen, "The Use and Meaning of the Words *L^ebarek* and *B^erakah* in the Old Testament," *VT* 9 [1959]: 166–68). A study of its uses in Genesis shows that the giving of a blessing bestowed prosperity with respect to fertility of land and fertility of life. The gift of divine blessing included the empowerment to achieve what was promised. God was therefore always the ultimate source of the blessing, even when it was communicated by an individual.

The blessing in Genesis enriched that which was good. In Genesis 1:1–2:3, for example, God blessed animal life, human life, and the seventh day—all part of the creation that he had pronounced good. Everything in creation was good, but that which was blessed was enriched beyond its normal quality. God's blessing on the patriarchs granted unusual provision from above, so that the family could multiply and prosper phenomenally and enjoy a special status above the rest of the race. Since this blessing was from God, it came with the requirements of faith and obedience. Participation in the blessing of God was not for unbelievers who turned aside to evil.

The antithetical idea of cursing is normally expressed with the verb *ʾārar*, which means "to impose a ban or a barrier, a paralysis on movement or other capabilities" (Herbert Chanan Brichto, *The Problem of Curse in the Hebrew Bible* [Philadelphia: Society of Biblical Literature and Exegesis, 1963], p. 217; see also J. Scharbert, "*ʾārar,*" *TDOT*, vol. 1, pp. 405–18). Such power of cursing was not given to just anyone; it was given to authorities of society and state. Ultimately, the power to curse belonged to God or an agency endowed by God with special power to invoke a curse. Anyone could imprecate, but imprecation was effectual only when it invoked the supernatural power (Brichto, *Problem of Curse,* p. 115). The curse in Genesis involved separation or alienation from the place of blessing, or even from those who were blessed. For example, Cain was cursed and as a result had to flee from the fertile soil and the presence of the Lord.

Occasionally there were acts of judgment that did the work of the curse without actually pronouncing a curse. In such cases there was no need for the warning that a curse brings, for the removal from the place of blessing was by swift intervention. And on occasion there were cir-

cursing supply major themes in the Bible that are only beginning to be developed by exegetes. R. A. Carlson applies it in his work on Samuel, seeing the *berakah* ideology tied to the land with intense anti-Canaanite feeling (*David, the Chosen King* [Uppsala: Alqvist & Wiksells, 1964], p. 28).

cumstances and events (such as famine, death, and oppression) that indicated that a curse was present.

A curse was occasioned by some evil act that destroyed life or disrupted God's established order or institutions. In Genesis the curse is prominent in the first eleven chapters, for that part of the book traces the spread of sin once humans came to know "good and evil." The emphasis on the curse is replaced in the patriarchal narratives by the prominence of the blessing, except for the warning of a curse for those who oppose God's program and God's people (12:1–3).

In this way we may trace the message of the book through the motifs of God's blessing and cursing at the founding of the theocracy. When evil spoiled God's blessed creation and drew the divine curse, God set about to establish his program to restore blessing to the world through promises to his chosen seed, promises that looked beyond the narratives of Genesis to the establishment of the promised theocracy.

There is another side to this tension between blessing and cursing, a conflict that works out on the human level and corresponds to the blessing and cursing. The motifs of good and evil characterize the human activities and circumstances in this struggle. That which is good is harmonious with the divine will; that which is evil conflicts with the divine will. "Good" describes obedient activities and pleasing circumstances meant to benefit and enhance life; "evil" depicts sinful activities and unpleasant circumstances that interrupt and hinder life, causing pain and suffering. God blesses the good but curses the evil; God's blessing in turn brings about good things, but his cursing ultimately destroys life.

In the beginning all God's creation is called "good" (1:10, 12, 18, 21, 25, 31)—in fact, the creation of human life is "very good." But in the garden the humans were tempted with the tree of the knowledge of good and evil (2:9, 17; 3:5, 22), and thinking that they would gain divine power over life, to alter it for better or for worse, they fell into sin and succeeded only in bringing evil into the human experience. Here began the conflict between good and evil. And so in the very first setting God instructed Cain to do good (4:7), for if he did not, sin would overwhelm him. With the experience of evil, however, early men and women were prone to disobey God and stray from his blessing.

The motif of evil thus appears throughout the narratives of Genesis, reminding us of the sinful nature of the race and its unhappy circumstances. The basic use of this motif describes the evil acts of humans. Prior to the flood the human nature became very evil, so that evil multiplied (6:5). The judgment of the flood was the only recourse for such wickedness. But even after the judgment there was the recognition that the human heart is evil from childhood (8:21). During the early sojourn of Abram we encounter the spread of evil again in civilization (13:13), painfully reminding us of the need for God's blessing. But even in the chosen family evil surfaced (37:2) in the activities of Joseph's brothers. The bright spot was Joseph's refusal to do that which was evil before the Lord (39:9).

The words for evil also describe the painful deeds done to God's people. When Lot eventually took a stand for the Lord, the wicked sinners threatened to *deal worse* with him (19:9). Tensions of this sort were so common that treaties had to be made to keep people from doing *harm* to each other (26:29 and 31:52). But God ultimately protected his servant from evil: he did not allow Laban to say anything good or evil (24:50) or do good or evil (31:24, 29). Jacob was confident that God had not allowed Laban to harm him (v. 7), and so later praised the angel who delivered him from evil (48:16). "Evil" also describes the treachery of Joseph's brothers as they sold him into slavery (50:20) and blamed his disappearance on an evil beast (37:20, 33). In the process of time when Joseph tested his brothers, he accused them of repaying evil for good (44:4). Only at the end of the book do the brothers express how evil they had been, when they appealed to Joseph for forgiveness (50:17).

Evil actions bring evil results, and Genesis emphasizes this as well. The treachery of the brothers brought nothing but misery to Jacob (44:29, 34), so that before Pharaoh he had to admit that his days had been few and evil (47:9). But even before this, the evil in the race had brought great judgment from God, first at the flood, and then at the destruction of Sodom. But God used such calamities to advance his cause of blessing; for example, in the days of Joseph the bad cows (41:19–21, 27) signified the bad years of the famine—the occasion for the elevation of Joseph as deliverer of his people.

The text of Genesis also occasionally indicates the divine and human perception of evil. In addition to the passage that records how God saw that the race was evil (6:5), we read how the thing that Judah's sons did was evil in the eyes of the Lord (38:10), and so swift judgment followed. And on the human side we read how Esau's wives were evil to Isaac (28:8). In the final analysis the human and the divine perception of evil come together in the wisdom of Joseph, who explained that what his brothers did for him was intended for *evil* but that evil was actually part of God's plan for *good*. Here we see how God's persistent plan to bless can actually triumph over evil and turn it back into good, as it had at the beginning of creation.

Juxtaposed with the motif of evil throughout the book is the motif of good—from the beginning tension between good and evil to the final triumph of good over evil in God's plan to restore the blessing. Beginning with the creation we see that *good* describes God's blessed provision for the race. All creation was good (chap. 1), as was the food (2:9), the gold

(v. 12), and life itself, whether a newborn child (30:20) or a long life of peace with God (15:15; 25:8). The bounty of the earth was also good, as evidenced by the seven good years that God would send to Egypt (41:5, 22, 24, 26, 35) before the bad years—an interpretation that was good in the eyes of Pharaoh (41:37). At the heart of God's goodness to his people was the promise of the blessing, for when that promise was reiterated, good things were included (32:10, 12). Accordingly, other rulers gave to God's people good land (20:15; 45:18, 20; 47:6, 11) and good gifts (45:23 [26:29?]), all because God's plan was intended for *good* (50:20).

It is fitting, then, that people who wished to share in God's blessing should treat others well. Certainly Abram was concerned that things go well with him in Egypt (12:13)—and they did, in a way (v. 16), but not as he had planned. Later, Joseph too hoped that things would go well with him (40:14), and in time they did because he was faithful. God's advice to Cain, that if he did well he would find acceptance (4:7), fell on deaf ears not only in that story but in the subsequent accounts as well. In fact, many of the acts of evil were perverted perceptions of good. For example, the sons of God saw that the daughters of men were beautiful and took all they wanted (6:2). This good appearance of women (24:16; 26:7) made them vulnerable to such advances. Another example occurs in the story of Lot; when Lot tried to protect the angels from the evil men of the city, he willingly surrendered his daughters so that the men could do what seemed good in their eyes (19:8; see also 34:18). Here too Joseph's testing and instruction of his brothers brought the correct perception, for he accused them of repaying his good with their evil (44:4) and then explained that their evil was actually a part of God's good plan (50:20).

It will be clear in the exposition of Genesis that the motifs of blessing and cursing and good and evil appear repeatedly, tracing the theological message of the book. They vividly portray why and how God set about to establish his plan through the seed of Abraham. The conflict between good and evil rises up again and again in the narratives, sometimes with the motifs clearly expressed and sometimes implied. At each stage in the development of God's theocratic program, as evil threatened to jeopardize the blessing, the Lord either prevented it or overcame it. For those who persisted in opposing the Lord and his blessing, swift judgment was guaranteed; but for those who, by faith, submitted to him and obeyed his Word, then blessing was assured.

The Structure of Genesis

The structure of the book is marked by an initial section and then ten further sections with headings. The major structural word of the book is *tôlᵉdôt*, expressed in the clause "these are the generations of. . . ." The word is a feminine noun from *yālad*, "to give birth" (properly derived from the *hiphil* stem of the verb, meaning "to beget"). It is often translated as "generations," "histories," or simply "descendants."[2]

This word has been traditionally viewed as a heading of a section. Reconstructing the outline according to this view would yield the arrangement below. (See C. F. Keil and F. Delitzsch, *Biblical Commentary on the Old Testament: The Pentateuch*, trans. James Martin [Grand Rapids: Eerdmans, 1949 reprint], pp. 70–71; Bush, *Notes*, p. 57; Leupold, *Exposition of Genesis*, vol. 1, pp. 109–11.)

1. Creation (1:1–2:3)
2. Tôl^edôt of the heavens and the earth (2:4–4:26)
3. Tôl^edôt of Adam (5:1–6:8)
4. Tôl^edôt of Noah (6:9–9:29)
5. Tôl^edôt of Shem, Ham, and Japheth (10:1–11:9)
6. Tôl^edôt of Shem (11:10–26)
7. Tôl^edôt of Terah (11:27–25:11)
8. Tôl^edôt of Ishmael (25:12–18)
9. Tôl^edôt of Isaac (25:19–35:29)
10. Tôl^edôt of Esau, the father of Edom (twice) (36:1–8; 36:9–37:1)
11. Tôl^edôt of Jacob (37:2–50:26)

The critical views on this arrangement vary, but scholars generally assign the term to P. Speiser says,

> The term that is most typical of this source—one might call it *P*'s signature—is *tôl^edôt*, etymologically "begettings," and hence also genealogy, line, family tree (v 1, vi 9, x 1, etc.), and by extension also story, history; in the latter sense we find this term used in ii 4, and perhaps also in xxxvii 2. [*Genesis*, p. xxiv][3]

Speiser takes it as a heading in all places except for 2:4, 25:19, and 37:2. In these places he contends that it means "story" or "history" and refers to the preceding narrative.

2. BDB lists the meanings as "generations" or "account of men and their descendants" (p. 410). Ludwig Koehler and Walter Baumgartner (*Lexicon in Veteris Testamenti: Libros*, 2d ed [Leiden: E. J. Brill, 1958], p. 1021) define it as "descendants." P. J. Wiseman takes it as "family history in its origins" (*New Discoveries in Babylonia about Genesis*, 2d ed. [London: Marshall, Morgan & Scott, 1936], p. 50).

3. For a stylistic and grammatical study of the formula, based on the Jacob section of Genesis, see Peter Weimer, "Die Toledot-Formel in der priesterschriftlichen Geschichtsdarstellung," *BZ* 18 (1974): 65–93. The article traces the pattern based on the standard of the Jacob cycle and is primarily concerned with grammatical structure. See also M. H. Woudstra, "The *Tol^edot* of the Book of Genesis and Their Redemptive-Historical Significance," *CTJ* 5 (1970): 185. Woudstra does not accept the critical view; he is presenting Samuel B. Külling's discussion of B. Holwerda's views.

Skinner doubts that this word referred to what preceded; he explains that, as a redactional insertion, it served as a heading, originally followed by a word in the genitive (*Commentary on Genesis*, pp. 39–40). Driver says that the word's significance was "the particulars about a man and descendants" (*Book of Genesis* [1920 ed.], p. 19; Driver thought that the form in 2:4 should have been in 1:1).

In order to understand the significance of the word *tôlᵉdôt*, we must interpret its meaning in the present arrangement of the book. Since *tôlᵉdôt* is related to the word *yālad*, it refers to the product or the result of its subject, which is marked out by the subjective genitive. This subject marks the starting point in the narrative; the section combines narrative and genealogy to move from this point to the end of the *tôlᵉdôt*. The heading thus summarizes the ensuing discussion, which traces the development of the subject from a starting point to an end.

Besides the traditional approach that sees *tôlᵉdôt* as a consistent heading throughout and the critical approach that takes it as belonging to P as a later insertion, there is the view that was presented by P. J. Wiseman and accepted by R. K. Harrison that these are similar to the colophons of clay tablets and therefore refer to the preceding material in the narrative (Wiseman, *New Discoveries*, p. 8; Harrison, *Introduction to the Old Testament* [Grand Rapids: Eerdmans, 1969], p. 548). They argue that the traditions were recorded on clay tablets and then collected into the present form of Genesis.

The colophon view cannot be accepted, however, because the evidence from cuneiform is unconvincing and the outworking of the arrangement in Scripture is impossible. When one studies the colophons on the tablets, it becomes clear that they are not like the *tôlᵉdôt* of Genesis.[4] In the cuneiform tablets, the titles are repetitions of the tablet's first line and not a description of the contents, the owner seems to be the present owner and not the original owner, and the Akkadian

---

4. In the passage in Genesis 2:4, the parallels to the colophon would be five: (1) the title for the narrative would be "these are the generations of the heaven and the earth," (2) the date would be found in the clause "when the LORD God made earth and heaven," (3) the serial number of the series would consist in the account being written on six days on six tablets, (4) the conclusion statement announcing the finish of the series would be seen in the 2:1–3 passage, and (5) the name of the owner or writer finds only the correspondence in the Lord God (P. J. Wiseman, *Creation Revealed in Six Days* [London: Marshall, Morgan & Scott, 1949], p. 46). Examples of cuneiform texts and colophon markers appear in Alexander Heidel, *The Babylonian Genesis* (Chicago: University of Chicago Press, 1951), pp. 25, 30. For a summary description of the forms, see A. Leo Oppenheim, *Ancient Mesopotamia* (Chicago: University of Chicago Press, 1964), pp. 240–41. For the consistent anonymity of the cuneiform texts (only two extant texts reveal their authors), see W. W. Hallo, "New Viewpoints on Cuneiform Literature," *IEJ* 12 (1962): 14; and W. G. Lambert, "A Catalogue of Texts and Authors," *JCS* 16 (1962): 59.

equivalent of *tôl^edôt* is not used in the formulas. When one attempts to trace the proposed arrangement within Genesis it becomes clear that the system is unworkable. If these are references to what has immediately preceded, then the word in 5:1 should have come at the end of the story of Adam (4:16) and not later. Another passage that would be improbable as a concluding form is 10:1, the *tôl^edôt* of the sons of Noah. It is unlikely that it looks back to the flood and the curse, especially in view of 10:32. Besides the problems of harmonization, there is also the difficulty of having the story of Abraham preserved by Ishmael (the *tôl^edôt* of Ishmael would be the colophon concluding that preceding history), having Isaac keep Ishmael's archives, Esau those of Jacob, and Jacob those of Esau.

Along with these difficulties is the fact that nowhere in the Bible does *tôl^edôt* refer *clearly* to what has preceded; in every place it can and often must refer to what follows. For example, the word begins a genealogy at the end of Ruth. In the expression "these are the generations of Perez" (Ruth 4:18), Perez is the point of departure and not the prominent person. Such a usage would be similar to the "generations of Terah" in Genesis 11:27. Likewise in Numbers 3:1, the *tôl^edôt* of Aaron and Moses cannot conclude the census of chapters 1 and 2. However, if the *tôl^edôt* in Genesis are taken in reference to the sections that follow, they fit perfectly. From 2:4 onward, every occurrence is followed by an account of what issued from the starting point just named.

Even in Genesis 2:4, the formula fits as a heading. Wiseman himself recognizes that 2:1–3 forms a natural conclusion for the creation account. Genesis 2:4a would then be the heading of the next section; 2:4b would be the beginning dependent clause (much like the *Enuma Elish* text "when above . . ."). The structure here is similar to Genesis 5:1:

> 2:4 These are the *tôl^edôt* of the heavens and the earth when they were created;
> When Yahweh God made earth and heaven. . . .
> 5:1 This is the book of the *tôl^edôt* of Adam;
> When God created man. . . .

It must also be pointed out that "Yahweh God" is used exclusively in 2:4–3:24. This fact would suggest connecting the contents of the passage with the title in 2:4.

The *tôl^edôt* heading announces the historical development from the ancestor (or beginning point) and could be translated paraphrastically "this is what became of _____," or "this is where it started from" (with reference to the following subject.)[5] Genesis 2:4, then, introduces the subject of what became of the heaven and the earth, and 2:4b–4:26 delineates what subsequently happened in and to the cosmos. What follows, of course, is the story of the fall, the murder of Abel, and the development of sin within expanding civilization. The story does not simply present another creation account; it traces the events from the point of the climax of creation to its corruption by sin.

When the passages are studied with this structure in mind, the composition makes sense. The term cannot be narrowed to mean "genealogy," because the contents are frequently broader.[6] It cannot depict biographies or histories, because, as Woudstra comments, "The Bible does not present histories of people; it contains no biographies; but it draws lines from a starting point to an end point. If it were otherwise, we should have had a *tôl⁽e⁾dôt* of Abraham and of Joseph, but we look in vain for such" ("*Tol⁽e⁾dot* of Genesis," p. 188).

Rather, each section is a narrative depicting what became of someone (normally) in details relevant to the purpose of Genesis. The *tôl⁽e⁾dôt* of Terah is not about Terah but is primarily concerned with what became of Terah, namely, Abraham and his kin. The *tôl⁽e⁾dôt* of Isaac has Jacob at its center, with other parts relating to Esau. The *tôl⁽e⁾dôt* of Jacob traces the family from him through the life of Joseph. The person named after *tôl⁽e⁾dôt* is usually not the central character in the narrative but the person of origin.

Assuming, therefore, that the word is the heading of a section and means basically "this is what became of _____," we may observe that the development in each section follows a narrowing process. The writer concerns himself with where the ways begin to part. After the new beginnings with Noah, the writer supplies the *tôl⁽e⁾dôt* of Shem, Ham, and Japheth. But immediately afterward, the *tôl⁽e⁾dôt* of Shem is selected. The next *tôl⁽e⁾dôt* is that of Terah, one out of Shem. This account is concerned with the life of Abraham. The line then narrows to the son of Abraham, Isaac, but the *tôl⁽e⁾dôt* of Ishmael is given first in a tidying up process of the line not chosen. The same development holds true of the next generation: before the *tôl⁽e⁾dôt* of Jacob is developed, Esau is dealt with.

We may also observe that the material within each *tôl⁽e⁾dôt* reflects the development of the book itself. Noting the motifs of blessing and

5. This view is stated in the words of Woudstra, who is presenting Holwerda's view (Woudstra, *Tol⁽e⁾dot* of Genesis," p. 187). Derek Kidner's position is similar (*Genesis,* p. 23).

6. K. A. Kitchen's suggestion of "succession" may be a good translation if it can be distinguished from "descendants" ("The Old Testament in Its Context"; part 1, "From the Origins to the Eve of the Exodus," *Theological Students' Fellowship Bulletin* 59 [1971]: 2).

cursing in the analysis of the sections, we discover within each $tôl^edôt$ a deterioration from blessing to cursing until Genesis 12:1–2, from which point the trend moves to the promise of blessing. From this point on there is a constant striving for the place of blessing, but still there is deterioration, for the later patriarchs do not measure up to Abraham. The family, as a consequence, at the end of the book is not in the land of blessing but in Egypt, waiting for a visitation from God. Kidner succinctly expresses this development by stating that "man had travelled far from Eden to *a coffin*, and the chosen family far from Canaan to *Egypt*" *(Genesis,* p. 224). When we survey the development of this grand structure of the book, it will become evident that, as Woudstra says, "the $tôl^edôt$ formulas have not been subsequently added to an already existing text, but are the very fabric around which the whole of Genesis has been constructed" (*"Tol^edot* of Genesis," pp. 188–89).

Within the sections of the book important theological themes form the developing message of Genesis. The following survey of each $tôl^edôt$ offers a glimpse of the direction that an exhaustive exegesis would explore.

Creation (1:1–2:3)

The first section of the book is not headed by a $tôl^edôt$, and logically so. The section forms the introduction to the book. The significance of this section is that the work of creation is wrapped in divine blessing. Animal life (1:22), human life (v. 28), and the seventh day (2:3) are all blessed specifically. Humankind, the image of God, enjoying sovereignty over the creatures of the earth and observing the rest of God, has a blessed beginning.

The account of creation (primarily 1:1–2:3, but further information gathered from 2:4–25) not only forms the theological starting point of the book but also provides a vivid portrayal of the work of God in transforming chaos into a creation that is complete, fully blessed, and at rest. The nature and work of God revealed in this section will be repeated throughout Genesis, and so a more detailed analysis is required at this point (see chart 1).

Analysis of the material in this chapter yields a framework that is foundational to the theology of the book. Essentially the work of creation is a correction of chaos. Emptiness, formlessness, darkness, and the deep are replaced or altered with a creation that is pronounced good and is blessed by God.

A paradigm thus emerges in the prologue of the book: God breaks through the darkness with his light (bringing good over evil), sets about making divisions from the darkness and the deep (the lasting symbol of chaos), provides fertile land that will be heavily vegetated, designates appointed times and seasons (ordering the cycles of life), blesses the

Chart 1. **Basic Elements in the Creation Account**

Title: God created the universe

Chaos: Waste and void, darkness on the deep

Creation: Spirit of God hovering over the face of the water
  Day 1: Light out of darkness, day and night separated
  Day 2: Waters above and below separated: heaven
  Day 3: Seas gathered and dry land appears: vegetation
  Day 4: Heavenly luminaries formed to rule and divide times
  Day 5: Marine life and birds created and blessed
  Day 6: Animal life created and blessed; human life created, blessed, and
    commissioned

Completion:
  Day 7: Creation marked with sanctified rest

Chart 2. **Theological Themes in the Creation Account**

Day	Activity	Theological Themes
1	Light created; light divided from darkness	Revelation of God's *goodness* and *separation* from evil
2	Heaven divided from waters below	*Separation* from evil abyss (deep)
3	Land appears for vegetation	Provision of *fertile land* for all types of vegetation
4	Luminaries designated to rule times and seasons	Designation of *appointed times* and seasons for ordering creation
5	Living creatures of the sea and air created and blessed	Provision and blessing of all kinds of *animal life*
6	Land animals created and blessed;	
	human life created and blessed and commissioned to have dominion	Provision of *human life* (seed) and blessing of *fertility* and *dominion* over creation
7	Completion of creation and designation of the seventh day	Provision of sanctifying, or *theocratic, rest*

earth with all kinds of living creatures, and creates human life in his image, with the blessing of fertility and the commission to rule. With creation in perfect order and fullness, the sanctifying theocratic rest can begin (see chart 2).

Genesis gives no explanation of the chaos, but we may gather from the words used and from parallel passages that it was a judgment on rebellion, that Satan was somehow involved, and that oppressive evil existed instead of the fullness of life. If creation is a remedy for this chaos, then God's work through the six days anticipates his work in bringing about blessing after the fall. God reveals himself to people (Abram, and thereby to Israel), separates them from the darkness of this evil and chaotic world, orders their life around the seasons and requires

seasonal homage, blesses them with fertile land and livestock, provides
fertility for the family, and enables them to have dominion in the earth.
The culmination of this creative development is that human beings and
their world may enjoy the theocratic rest of God.

The Tôl°dôt of the Heavens and the Earth (2:4–4:26)

The second section of the book explains what became of the creation:
through the beguiling temptation, evil invaded and enslaved the human
race. Everything in God's perfect order was devastatingly altered. Accordingly, we could entitle this section "The Second Chaos: The Fall
and Its Results."

The section begins with an anthropomorphic description of the creation of Adam and Eve and then traces the deterioration through the sin
and the curse to the expansion of sin in the descendants. As if in answer
to the three blessings of the creation account, this section supplies a
threefold cursing (of the serpent, in 3:14; of the ground, in v. 17; and of
Cain, in 4:11). Man no longer serves God but the ground; no longer does
he rule, but he survives. In the deteriorating life, however, there is a
token of grace and a ray of hope: God places a preserving mark on Cain,
and people begin to proclaim the name of the Lord.

This tôl°dôt section begins with a detailed account of the creation of
Adam and Eve to show how ominous the fall was. The stories in chapter 4
provide the aftermath, showing how evil advanced once it entered the
human family. But the central section is the most critical. It introduces
the theological themes listed in chart 3.

Here is the second chaos. The elements are generally parallel to the
first, with its symbols of evil, emptiness, disorder, and death. God must
now restore the good creation. Requiring human obedience and faith, he
will set about making good triumph over evil, bringing life out of death,
and setting boundaries to order life and dominion (see chart 4).

The reestablishment of the created order is difficult. Throughout
Genesis there is a perpetual struggle between good (that which promotes
and enhances life) and evil (that which destroys creation and brings
pain), the forces of life and the forces of death, the blessing and the
cursing. The work of re-creation moves from promise to fulfillment,
promising the seed, the land, the dominion, and the rest. It works with
promise because God chose to make faith in his Word the requirement
for receiving and enjoying the blessing.

The means of this renewal is the same as creation—the Word of the
Lord. The creation came into existence in response to the powerful creative Word; the fulfillment of the promise to bless will come about
through those who by faith obey his Word. Blessing cannot be achieved

Chart 3. **Theological Themes in Genesis 3**

Human Activity and Experience	Theological Themes
Sin	
Disobeyed God's commandment	Disobedience to God's Torah brings complete ruin
Were beguiled into believing a lie	Evil must use deception, whereas obedience must discern the truth (light out of darkness)
Desired to know "good and evil" rather than just the good	Experience of evil (pain) with the good (care) unravels the creation
Desired to be wise but ended up only hiding in fear	Wisdom begins with the fear of the Lord and obeys his law
Were carried away with the goodness and beauty of the fruit	People must be satisfied with what God provides and calls good
Judgment	
Perpetual enmity between forces of evil and the human race	Conflict between good and evil remains, but good will triumph
Painful labor in childbirth and in harvesting	Life will be difficult, necessitating blessing for fertility and rest
Tension over desire and dominion in the human family	Tensions necessitate a divine choice for ordering life
Prospect of death and decay, but the race will continue	Transitory and frail nature calls for hope in the promise of life
Grace	
Clothed with animal skins and kept from the garden	There is divine provision for the guilty

Chart 4. **Humankind's Need for God's Re-creative Work**

Creation	Chaos	Re-Creation
God's creation: very good (light)	Earth's devastation: evil (darkness) throughout	God's program: separation from evil; restoration of good
God's blessing: • fertility • dominion • earth's bounty	Sin's curse: • pain in birth • deception, hubris • painful, scarce subsistence	God's blessing: • promised seed (many) • sovereignty (kings) • promised land (rich)
Completion marked by Sabbath rest	Perpetual toil and conflict of good and evil	God's promise: theocratic rest set apart to God in peace
Summary: perfect life	Summary: death	Summary: hope of life in spite of death

through any other way—certainly not through disobedience that comes through deception and hubris.

Genesis 4–11 traces the spread of sin throughout the world, showing the great need for the divine plan of redemptive blessing. But this tracing works through the different sections with different emphases. In chapter 4 we have the initial development of the curse, or what is basically the spread-of-sin motif. (For a discussion of this motif and the others in Gen. 1–11, see David J. A. Clines, *The Theme of the Pentateuch*, JSOT Supp. 10 [Sheffield: Sheffield University Press, 1978], pp. 61–77.)

The story of Cain and Abel builds on the motifs of chapter 3. Here is the first outworking of the conflict between seeds, and sin triumphs. At the heart of the story is once again good and evil. God advised Cain to do good so that all would be well, but he chose evil by killing his brother (thus destroying creation) and then, out of deception and hubris, denied knowledge of and responsibility for it. The resultant curse on Cain and the land corresponds to the original envy he had for his brother's blessing.

The second half of the chapter develops the spread-of-sin motif even further. Here there is not simply male domination but the taking of two wives; here there is not simply a murder but an arrogant boasting of "undoing creation" and demanding protection for it. The subtle theme of creation comes through the formulation of culture—again part of the deception when hubris, pride, bigamy, and murder characterize this cultured race. A remnant appears, however, with its calling out in the name of the Lord, a reminder of God's and Adam's calling out at creation.

The Tôlᵉdôt of the Book of Adam (5:1–6:8)

This next *tôlᵉdôt* takes up another parallel theme, leaving the spread-of-sin theme understood. The prominent theme now is death—everyone died, except one who walked with God (a term that recalls the Lord's walking to and fro in the garden). The end-of-life motif is the essence of this section.

The literary design of the section highlights the downward movement. The unit begins with a reiteration of creation in bliss, using the verb *bārak* (5:1–2), but throughout the genealogy the blessing that began the race is enshrouded by the notice of the descendants' deaths. Then at the end of genealogy, the text records the birth of Noah as a comfort from the curse, using the word *'ārar*. The *tôlᵉdôt* concludes with a report of God's intense displeasure over human existence (6:1–8)—a report that stands in the strongest of contrasts with the beginning verses.

This concluding part (6:1–8) announces death as the plan of God— not just the regular deaths of people, but the end of all flesh. The cause was the great hubris on the part of the humans, taking all the women they wanted and living in moral abandonment. The evaluation of God reflects antithetically the creation: there God saw that everything was *good*, but here he saw that the intent of human plans was only *evil* continually. This development was a tremendous pain to the heart of God, recalling the pain of the curse. Now the Spirit would no longer shield the race, let alone hover over it. The observation of God, the withdrawal of the Spirit, and the evil of the race together introduce the theme of uncreation in the next section. The single bright spot in God's dealings with the human race is that the remnant finds grace.

The Tôlᵉdôt of Noah (6:9–9:29)

This passage contains both judgment (the curse of the flood) and blessing (God delivers the remnant and promises never again to curse the ground as he did). But the downward trend characterizes this section too, for the account begins with Noah's righteousness and ends with his lying drunk and naked in the tent and with Canaan's being cursed. The members of the new age brought evil with them.

The entire section may be described as an account of uncreation and re-creation. The worldwide flood returns the earth to the original chaos, in which the fertile land was covered by the deep (here the fountains of the deep open up to flood the earth), and all life outside the ark ended. Gradually the waters abated, the land appeared, and things began to grow, so that a new creation appeared. Here, the second Adam through his obedience preserved all life, worshiped the Lord with a sacrifice, and received the blessings and responsibilities that were first given in Eden. At this point the blessing motif emerges in a way that it had not since the garden; it becomes more and more prominent in overcoming the effect of the curse.

The new covenant made after the flood was a covenant of grace in which the Lord promised never again to judge the world with such a flood. In short, there would be no further return to the chaos of the primal deep. The death of all flesh by the flood would lead some to think that the taking of life (destroying creation) was permissible. Human beings were thus prohibited from shedding blood. Only God can alter life for good or evil. Sinful people must not tamper with creation. Rather, they must be fruitful and multiply—the original work of procreation given to Adam and Eve.

The human race, however, retains an experiential knowledge of evil, a fact painfully displayed in the scene of Noah's drunkenness. The theme of nakedness is repeated with this second Adam, but with an ironic twist. Here it does not represent integrity, but indecency and susceptibility to evil. The occasion brings out the worst in Ham, and so an oracle of cursing is pronounced on whole sections of the race that follow in that depravity. Those who live in defiance of God's order, giving full expression to the evil in their hearts, forfeit the blessing of bounty, dominion, and rest, and inherit enslavement instead. On the other hand, the blessing now focuses on Shem and his descendants. In a world where evil abounds, the blessing now belongs to those who act with integrity.

The Tôl°dôt of the Sons of Noah (10:1–11:9)

As the population expands from Noah's sons, the subject of the book turns to the nations. This section begins with the fruitful population from Shem, Ham, and Jepheth and ends with the dispersion at Babel. It is a stroke of genius to place such a story after the Table of Nations, especially when it precedes the table chronologically. In the literary presentation, it both explains the fruitful population and leaves the reader looking for some provision of divine blessing in the world.

The theme of this section is confusion and dispersion. It records the final stage in God's universal judgments on the sinful race, for this judgment holds the race in check. The sin here is once again hubris—people in pride refusing to obey the Lord and attempting to make a name for themselves by their enterprise. The divine Judge foresaw that nothing would be withheld from them, and so he scattered them across the face of the earth. In this incident we have another "uncreation" theme, for harmony, unity, and peace are not possible for a scattered, rebellious people.

The Table of Nations (chap. 10) naturally calls for the account of the dispersion (11:1–9). The table surveys the world of nations known to Israel, arranging them in the threefold division after the oracle of Noah. The Israelites would know these names through ancient wars and tribal federations. The list is a witness to disunity, destruction, and subjugation. It is not a reminder of unity, goodness, or blessing in life.

What, then, becomes of the Creator's plan for a race that would obey his commandments, receive his blessings, and enjoy his good creation in theocratic rest? (von Rad, *Genesis,* pp. 152–55). The realization of such a plan would not be found in these existing nations, even if united by language and geography. Rather, God would have to form a new nation from one man (creation theme), through whom he would make his covenant of blessing.

The Tôl°dôt of Shem (11:10–26)

Based upon the universal scope of the expanding race in the previous section, the present genealogy forms a transition, narrowing the focus from the line of Shem to Abram. Anyone familiar with Abram would catch the significance immediately, for the theme now shifts from dispersion and chaos to the beginning of God's program to restore blessing.

The Tôl°dôt of Terah (11:27–25:11)

While chapters 1–11 portrayed the race in rebellion to what God had intended, chapters 12–25 recount God's development of the promised blessing through Abram. This section tells what became of Terah; it traces the life of Abraham in the development of the promised blessing and thereby is the foundation for the rest of the Book of Genesis, the Pentateuch, and the Old Testament. We may title the subject matter of this *tôl^edôt* "The Promise of the Blessing to Abraham and His Seed."

On the divine side is movement toward fulfillment of the promised blessings, and on the human side is development toward obedience. God promises to build Abram's nation and bless her with fertility, the bounty of the earth, and dominion so that she may be the means of blessing to a world under the curse. But God's people must respond to God's Word in obedience (unlike the parents did in the garden), in humility (unlike the proud ancestors, who rebelled), and in faith. But along the way the tension of good and evil continues, the evil using the devices of earlier times to threaten to destroy God's creation of a nation for blessing and service.

The Abraham stories should be studied in relation to the promises of the land and the seed. The narratives are not pieced together at random but show repetition and parallelism to stress the promise and the obedience. The cycle of stories begins with the call of Abram in 12:1–9 (11:27–32 forms a brief prologue to the stories), concentrates on the promises in chapters 16–21, and concludes with the sacrifice of Isaac in 22:1–19. As outlined below, the accounts of the call of Abram and the sacrifice of Isaac form an inclusio for the section; and the developments of the land promises and seed promises have parallel motifs.

    I. Call of Abram (12:1–9)
       Overview of the Abram stories: Call to travel to a new land; promise of blessing (become a great nation); obedience of Abram; confirmation of the promised blessing (land); response of sacrifice and proclamation.
   II. Development of the promise: Focus on the *land* (12:10–15:21).
      A. Threat: Famine in the land; deception when away from the land; deliverance from Egypt by plagues (12:10–20).
      B. Separation: Controversy with Lot over the land; relinquishing the best of the land to Lot; division of the family (Lot among evil men); promise of land lavishly confirmed to Abram (13).
      C. Rescue of Lot: Abram's intercession in battle when land invaded; his rescue of Lot with the people of Sodom; blessing received from Melchizedek (14).
      D. Enactment of the covenant: Complaint of childlessness; promise sworn to by sacred oath; prophecy of sojourn in

bondage out of the land; prophecy of rest and return to the
land (15).

III. Development of the promise: Focus on the *seed* (16–21).

    A. Threat: Barrenness in the womb; Abram listening to his wife
about Hagar; Hagar delivered in the wilderness; Ishmael, the
false seed, receiving an antiblessing (16).

    B. Separation: Circumcision instructed for covenanters; prom-
ise of seed lavishly restated (kings and a multitude of nations); names changed; circumcision obediently performed
(17).

    C. Rescue of Lot: Visitation of angels to confirm the promise;
intercession of Abraham through prayer; rescue of Lot from
Sodom; destruction of wicked sinners from the land (chaos
in preparation of blessing); incest in cave; Moab and Ammon
(18–19).

    D. Repeated threat: Wife endangered by deception in the land;
deliverance in a warning dream; life for innocence, death for
guilt; barrenness removed by prayer; choice of land (20).

    E. Fulfillment of the covenant: Seed (Isaac) born amid great
rejoicing but then hostility and deliverance from Ishmael;
Hagar again delivered in the wilderness; treaty of Beersheba;
peaceful sojourn in the land (the promised seed now dwelling
in the Promised Land) (21).

IV. Test of Abraham (22:1–19).

Restatement of the Abraham theme; call to travel to a new land
(cf. 12:1); demand of the life of the promised seed; obedience of
Abraham with travel and sacrifice; response of sacrifice and
naming; confirmation of promised blessing and of seed with
dominion in the land.

V. Epilogue: The transfer of the promise to the seed (22:20–25:11).

    A. Transition (22:20–24).

    B. Land: Abraham purchases a portion of the land to ensure the
future possession (23).

    C. Seed: Abraham prepares for the marriage of Isaac for the
continuation of the promise (24).

    D. Dominion: Abraham sends away his sons so that the birth-
right is preserved for Isaac (25:1–11).

The Abrahamic stories include many theological plots and motifs.
The promise gradually develops with the obedient servant, but tension
from threats and disobedience because of deception jeopardize the program. Initial threats begin each section—the famine of the land (chap. 12)
parallels the barrenness of Sarai (chap. 16). The presence of the evil Ca-

naanites also poses a danger; Lot's lifting up his eyes and choosing the rich land on the basis of false appearances (similar to Eve's temptation, as the allusion to the garden in 13:10 suggests) twice interrupts Abraham's pursuit of the promise. And the danger to the promise of the seed through deception (chap. 20) carries foward the act in chapter 12—it is lingering on—just as the final hostility from Hagar and her son (chap. 21) is a reminder of the earlier tension (chap. 16).

Ultimately the promised blessing takes shape because of the obedience of Abraham, a fact that is clearly set forth in 12:4 and 22:12. His first obedience is explained in 15:6 as belief in the Lord for imputed righteousness; but his additional obedience adds the further explanation that he feared the Lord. At first Abraham believed the Lord and obeyed the Word; because he obeyed the Word, he received righteousness and God's solemn oath to bless. And then Abraham believed the covenant promises, and because he did, he kept the sign of the covenant, interceded for righteousness, and received the promised seed. But at the end, Abraham also feared the Lord, and because he did, he obeyed the Word, relinquished Isaac, and received the child back again. This progression in faith is the way of blessing.

The Tôlᵉdôt of Ishamel (25:12–18)

The next two sections trace the story to the major sons of Abraham; the first unit traces the line of Ishmael, which is not the chosen line, and the second section returns to the promised seed, Isaac. This section on Ishmael is important because God granted a blessing to Ishmael as the son of Abraham and Hagar. Other sons of Abraham received no such blessing.

The Tôlᵉdôt of Isaac (25:19–35:29)

To answer what became of Isaac, the narrative tells the story of Jacob, his son, the struggle within the family, and the emergence of the tribes of Israel. The section could thus be titled "The Development of the Promise Through the Seed of Abraham." The blessing given to Abram will now be transferred to Jacob through Isaac, his father.

The narratives about Isaac recede into the background of the Jacob cycle. After the account of the births of Jacob and Esau, the narrative turns to Isaac (chap. 26) to affirm that, as the promised seed, he had inherited the blessing from his father. The literary parallels between Isaac and Abraham affirm this continuity: Isaac's wife was also barren for many years, but he prayed for the seed; Isaac too was faced with a famine, but he did not go down to Egypt; Isaac deceived a ruler about his wife, and he too was spared; Isaac reopened the wells of his father, and when hostility began he continued to enjoy God's provision; and finally, Isaac also made a treaty with Abimelech. The repetition of the motifs shows that the promises were passed on from one generation to the next.

The continuation of the themes of blessing and deception may be attested in the life of Jacob as well as Isaac. The Jacob stories, however, intensify the two themes of deception and of blessing, even though the two are mutually incompatible. The blessing is central to the stories, as chart 5 below shows, but the deception and evil make the development of the blessing difficult.

As with the Abrahamic stories and later the Joseph stories, the Jacob narratives center on a journey. It is necessitated by deception (unlike Abram's but similar to Joseph's) and is out of the Promised Land (again unlike Abram's but comparable to Joseph's). The journey is to develop into a nation of tribes with great possessions (as with Joseph) but involves a return to the land (parallel with the journey of Abram but not of Joseph, who only has a promise of the return).

The Jacob stories can be arranged according to the Jacob-Esau cycle and the Jacob-Laban cycle, the former bracketing the latter. The former show how Jacob came to be the heir (on the human level but in harmony with the oracle to his mother), and the latter show how the promises began to be fulfilled. The transition from cycle to cycle is made with a night vision of the angelic presence (chaps. 28 and 32). And then another divine revelation occurs when Jacob contemplates the journey to Egypt (chap. 46). (See Claus Westermann, *The Promises to the Fathers*, trans. David E. Green [Philadelphia: Fortress, 1980].)

Throughout the Jacob stories the attention is on the efforts to attain the blessing (or an alternate blessing) or to divert the blessings. But God works through deception, animosity, favoritism, jealousy, and human schemes to elect the line, produce the tribes, enrich the family, and restore them to the land. The theological emphasis of this section, then, must be the further development of God's blessing. Faith, obedience, separation from evil, and worship are the responsibilities of the members of the covenant; unbelief, envy, hatred, jealousy, and integration with pagans all provide the foil for the program. The conflict of good and evil is very pronounced in this section.

The structure of the Jacob stories fits a general chiasm (see Michael Fishbane, *Text and Texture* [New York: Schocken, 1979], p. 42; see chart 5). This type of structure provides a balance to the development of the narrative, presaging and reflecting the parallel themes but centering on the fulfillment of the promises of the seed (the tribes) and its prosperity (flocks).

The journey out of the land thus enabled the promise to flourish. Fertility of human life and animal life was provided by God in Laban's

Chart 5. **Literary Development of the Jacob Narrative**

(Preceded by *tôlᵉdôt*)

A Oracle sought; Rebekah struggles in childbirth; *bekorah* birthright; birth; themes of strife, deception, fertility (25:19–34).

   B Interlude: strife; deception; *berakah* blessing; covenant with foreigner (26).

     C Deception; *berakah* stolen; fear of Esau; flight from land (27:1–28:9).

       D Encounter (< *pagaʿ*) with the divine at sacred site near border; *berakah* (28:10–22).

         E Internal cycle opens: arrival; Laban at border; deception; wages; Rachel barren; Leah fertile (29:1–30:21).

           F Rachel fertile; Jacob increases the herds (30:22–43).

         E' Internal cycle closes: departure; Laban at border; deception; wages (31).

       D' Encounters (< *pagaʿ*) with divine beings at sacred sites near border; *berakah* (32).

     C' Deception planned; fear of Esau; *berakah* gift returned; return to land (33).

   B' Interlude: strife; deception; covenant with foreigner (34).

A' Oracle fulfilled; Rachel struggles in childbirth; *berakah*; death resolutions (35:1–22).

(Succeeded by *tôlᵉdôt*)

land, but the question of dominion (especially concerning Esau) and exclusion from the Promised Land (brought about by deception) necessitated the return and the deliverance.

The Tôlᵉdôt *of Esau (36:1–8)*

Prior to the narratives tracing what became of Jacob, the promised seed, the attention focuses on Esau, the other son of Isaac, from whom Jacob wrested the birthright and the blessing. Earlier in Genesis the line of Ishmael was given before the *tôlᵉdôt* of Isaac, the chosen seed; now, after Isaac's *tôlᵉdôt* (the Jacob and Esau stories), the writer deals with what became of Esau before turning to the chosen seed, the descendants of Jacob. This stylistically highlighted parallelism prompts the reader to compare Esau with Ishmael and Jacob with Isaac (Weimar, "Toledot-Formel," pp. 68–69).

The Tôlᵉdôt *of Esau, the Father of Edom (36:9–37:1)*

A further accounting of the development of Esau's line is added because of the great significance of these Edomite, Amalekite, and Horite chieftains (36:9–43). The writer, in tracing the development of Esau's line a step further, evidently wishes to heighten the contrast between its expanse and the simple sojournings of Jacob (37:1, provided as a contrast and a transition). The notion that these kings ruled in the land before any king reigned over the Israelites (36:31) suggests that this list carries up to the monarchy.

The Tôl°dôt of Jacob (37:2–50:26)

This section of the book focuses on Joseph and his brothers, the founding fathers of the tribes. In essence, the narratives relate why the tribes were in Egypt and how they were each related to the promised blessings. The family had deteriorated to the point of merging with the Canaanites. To preserve the line of blessing, God amazingly moved through the exigency of the evil will of the brothers to bring about good through Joseph's administration.

The Joseph stories continue the major themes of the earlier narratives. Just as God protected and prospered the patriarch Jacob outside the land, so he would prosper and protect the tribes in Egypt. In addition, their journey out of the land was caused by deception and hubris—the age-old sins of the fathers that interfered with the Creator's development of blessing for the world. These stories, however, do not end with a return to the land.

The structure thus cannot follow a chiasm. Rather, it is built on repetition to stress the sovereign work of God in bringing good out of evil. We find two dreams of the teen-aged Joseph, two dreams later in prison, two dreams of Pharaoh, two imprisonments for Joseph, and two journeys of the brothers. The following outline summarizes the literary structure.

I. Cycle one: Testing of Joseph (37–41).
After God elects Joseph to administer his program in exile, two rounds of testing reveal that Joseph is faithful.
   A. Election and rejection: Through dreams God elects the faithful Joseph to be the ruler, but he is envied, hated, and sold into slavery by his brothers (37).
      1. Evil: Destruction of life through jealousy (cf. Cain), and deception of the father with the blood of the kid (cf. chap. 27).
      2. Good: Faithful servant of the father, faithful servant in Egypt.
   B. Interlude—rebuke of Judah: Through a series of unusual circumstances, evil is judged and righteousness triumphs, showing in Judah that the program of election cannot be set aside (38).
   C. Faithfulness and suffering: Through another period of testing Joseph shows himself to be faithful (39–40).
      1. Faithful servant of Potiphar, refusing temptation to evil.

      2. Once again falsely accused, with his cloak as evidence.
      3. Once again thrown into prison after faithful service.
      4. Faithful steward in prison, retaining faith in the promise of God (revealed in his dreams) by interpreting dreams in spite of the circumstances.
   D. Fulfillment of destiny: Having remained faithful in spite of envy, hatred, temptation, and enslavement, Joseph rises to power (cf. the end of chap. 38) (41).
      1. Means (as a test): Pharaoh's two dreams.
      2. Interpretation of the dreams: Good and evil years.
      3. Instruction: Live wisely according to what God's plans are.
II. Cycle two: Testing of the brothers (42–45).
   Whereas Joseph's tests were designed to demonstrate his faithfulness, the testing of the brothers was necessitated by past unfaithfulness. The point was that participation in God's program of blessing cannot permit evil (i.e., acts and attitudes that destroy life).
   A. First test (to set up the second): Will good overcome evil? (42).
      1. Joseph accuses them of spying (what they had done to him) and demands Benjamin as proof of their truthfulness.
      2. Joseph puts money in their sacks and imprisons one of them (as they had done to him) to raise their consciousness about evil.
   B. Second test (completion): Will they preserve life? (43).
      1. Joseph gives them all good things but shows favoritism to Benjamin, causing envy in the brothers.
      2. Joseph puts the cup in Benjamin's sack to give them the opportunity to abandon their brother, as they had abandoned him.
   C. Aftermath (44–45).
      1. Good triumphs over evil now, as Judah magnanimously stands for Benjamin (he had learned much in chap. 38).
      2. Joseph reveals himself to his brothers and explains the work of God in delivering his people.

The last several chapters of the book may be considered transitional chapters. The family moved to Egypt, the names of the family were entered in the record, the family settled in Goshen by Pharaoh's goodness, the nation enjoyed the protection of Joseph's wise administration, the blessings of the family were carefully recorded, as were, finally, the burial in Canaan and the promise of divine visitation. The book ends with a promise of future blessings.

The repetition of the theme of exile in the Joseph and Jacob cycles displays a tension theologically. If evil threatens to destroy the ongoing work of God to bless the world and if it meets with disciplinary acts and with sojournings away from the fertile land, how should the people of God conduct themselves? And is the promise of God really in jeopardy?

Naturally God protects and delivers his people. Laban twice could not do "good or evil" to the covenant people (24:50; 31:29). And when God predicted the Egyptian exile (15:13–14), he ensured Israel's safety. Ultimately, the covenant is safe because it is the Lord's covenant.

These narratives also teach the covenanters how to live in bondage when they know that the promise of God belongs to them, for participation in the blessings of the covenant requires obedience. They are to do what is good and shun what is evil, never losing sight of their destiny. They are to fear God, love the brethren, forgive one another, and make provision for the future. In short, the way of wisdom begins to surface in these stories, a wisdom that the parents in the garden mistakenly sought through disobedience. It cannot be developed by doing evil, for evil undermines and destroys God's good creation.

It takes such wisdom to endure this evil world while waiting for the fulfillment of the promises. God had promised the blessings of seed, land, and dominion. Fertility in the family and increase in their possessions began with the patriarchs. And now with Joseph there was a beginning in the expectation of dominion. But the servant who comes to such prominence must be a faithful steward of the covenant, one who resists evil and clings to that which is good.

The Purpose of Genesis

Given this literary and theological analysis, and being somewhat influenced by the setting of the book in the Pentateuch,[7] I now summarize the purpose of the Book of Genesis. The major concern is to describe the destiny of the covenant people. Related concerns include the nature of the covenant God who created his people, the nature of God's people within creation, and the beginning of the covenant code in the revealed acts of God.

7. The interpretation stands on the basis of the analysis of the text. However, an understanding of the author and setting of any given piece of literature helps to sharpen the focus of the interpretation. Naturally, if this work were cast in the exilic period, the significance of the interpretation would vary considerably.

The Destiny of the Covenant People

Genesis supplies the historical basis for God's covenant with Israel, the seed of Abraham, whom God called out of the scattered nations. This idea can be traced through the entire Pentateuch, for, as Segal states, *"the real Theme of the Pentateuch is the selection of Israel from the Nations and its Consecration to the Service of God and His Laws in a Divinely-appointed land."* He adds, "The central event in the development of this theme is the divine covenant with Abraham and its twofold promise to make his offspring into the people of God and to give them the land of Canaan as an everlasting inheritance" (*The Pentateuch* [Jerusalem: Magnes, 1967], p. 23).

Within the development of this theme, Genesis forms an indispensable prologue to the drama that unfolds in Exodus. As the literary and historical background to the summons to go forth from Egypt to a promised land, Genesis demonstrates that such a command fulfilled a covenant with the founding father of the tribes.

The outworking of this divine plan begins with creation and develops toward the selection of Abram through a series of universally catastrophic events. Genesis 1–11, according to Segal, explains "the reason for setting apart the worship of God in the world of a special people, Israel, in a special land, Canaan" (Segal, p. 29). He observes that there are two opposite progressions in this prologue. There is the orderly creation of God, with its climax in man's being blessed, and there is the totally disintegrating work of sin, with its two greatest curses being the flood and the dispersion. The first progression demonstrates God's intent to bring about perfect order from the beginning, in spite of what the reader may know of human experience.

The second progression demonstrates the great need of God's intervention in the human race to provide the solution for human corruption. Humankind begins to be corrupted at the fall, where sin incurred the curse and ruined the race. This race, its moral deterioration connected with the advance of civilization, was corrupted beyond repair and had to be destroyed by the flood. After this judgment, however, the new humanity again exhibited the old nature. Human insolence now had far-reaching effects. Obscenity, arrogance, and ambition brought universal decadence and dispersion.

The inspired writer has thus taken ancient traditions and constructed a "coherent theological picture of man's revolt against his maker and its terrible consequences" (Carmino J. De Catanzaro, "Man in Revolt: A Study in the Primaeval History of the Book of Genesis," *CanJTH* 4 [1958]: 291). These narratives precede Abraham in time and leave the reader looking for a solution, which comes through the election and program of blessing through Abraham (Gen. 12–50). Segal writes:

> It was the moral deterioration of general mankind dispersed over the lands of the earth (ch x) that led to the election of a particular people who would cultivate the divine law in a particular land, and serve as a model for the nations of the world and as a source of blessing for all humanity (as promised to the three patriarchs, Gen. xii, 3b; xxii, 18; xxvi, 4b; xxviii, 14b). [*Pentateuch*, p. 28]

The text displays this work of God by focusing all attention on one man and his seed. God's saving will in fact extends to the scattered nations through one who is loosened from his ties among the nations and made the founder of a new nation, the recipient of promises reaching even beyond Israel. Only with 12:1–3 does the significance of the universal preface to saving history become understandable (von Rad, *Genesis*, p. 150), and only in light of the prologue does the beginning of chapter 12 become fully clear.

Genesis is the basis for the Book of Exodus. The impetus of the exodus is God's remembering the covenant with Abraham: "God heard their moaning, and God remembered his covenant with Abraham and Isaac and Jacob. God looked upon the Israelites, and God took notice of them" (Exod. 2:24–25). In fact, the final events and the closing words of Genesis anticipate the exodus: "God will surely take notice of you and bring you up from this land which He promised on oath to Abraham, to Isaac, and to Jacob" (Gen. 50:24). This statement of Joseph is reiterated by Moses as he took the bones of the patriarch out of Egypt in the exodus (Exod. 13:19). (See Kitchen, "Old Testament in Its Context," p. 9. We find reference to the God of Abraham, Isaac, and Jacob in Exod. 3:16 and to the God of the fathers in 4:5).

Genesis thus provides Israel with the historical and theological basis for her existence as the chosen people. Israel could trace her ancestry to the patriarch Abraham, whom God had elected out of the dispersed nations and to whom God had made the great covenantal promises of posterity, land, and dominion.

Because of the importance of lineal offspring, the first promised blessing, much space is devoted to the family concerns of the patriarchs, such as their acquiring wives, sons and heirs, and birthrights and blessings. After the oracle of Jacob (Gen. 49), the Pentateuch spans four centuries as the tribes grow. Genesis thus stands forth as a statement of the birthright of the tribes of Israel as they labored in Egypt and were called to leave it.

Recognizing that they had indeed become the great nation promised in the blessing to Abraham, they would realize also that there was no

future in Egypt, in Sodom, or in Babylon; their future was in the land
that had been promised by divine oath, the land of Canaan. Even as the
patriarchs had struggled with deceit, famine, racial integration, and persecution, Israel's attainment of the Promised Land would also be through
much struggle. The inhabitants of the land, whose sins are catalogued
elsewhere, would have to be dispossessed.

Moreover, their destiny was not bondage but freedom. The promise
spoke of kings, dominion, and theocratic rest, not forced labor in the
service of others. The curse involved banishment, alienation, and sub-
servience; God promised blessing. Consequently, the message of Genesis
would inspire the people of God to seize their destiny.

The Nature of the Covenant God

A careful analysis of the revelation of God in Genesis yields a full
picture of the nature of the Lord. This understanding, quite naturally,
would be essential for instilling faith in the covenant promises. An outline of the categories of theology will provide an introductory survey of
this emphasis.

1. God is a living God.
    a. He is described as speaking, seeing, hearing, resting, breathing,
       and so forth (1, 2, 3, 17, 18).
    b. He existed before the creation of this universe (1).
    c. He created humankind according to his likeness and image (1,
       2, 5).
    d. He entered the world with human form and human acts such
       as eating, talking, wrestling, or showing himself (12, 18, 32).
    e. He revealed himself by appearances (12, 18), visions (15, 46),
       dreams (20, 28, 31, 37, 40–41), and oracles (25).
2. God is sovereign.
    a. He was known as the Most High God (14).
    b. He created everything and gave names to different items and to
       individuals (1–2, 17, 32).
    c. He issued commandments (2–3, 9, 26).
    d. He brought the flood and then caused it to end (6–8).
    e. He confused human language and dispersed the nations (11).
    f. He issued prophecy (15, 46).
    g. He promised the land of Canaan to his people (12, 17, etc.).
    h. He promised kings from the womb of Sarah (17); he set up
       people in political power (41).
    i. He controlled people's dreams (15, 28, 31, 37, 40–41).
    j. He destroyed Sodom with great devastation (19) but spared in-
       nocent people (18–20).

  k. He tested people (22); he disciplined with crippling (32).
  l. He ruled over nations' economies and over life itself (40–41).
  m. He elected people (12, 25, 37).
3. God is powerful.
  Many of the above points could be repeated here with an emphasis on divine ability. To them we may add:
  a. He prevented Enoch from dying (5).
  b. He brought plagues on Pharaoh (12).
  c. He protected Abram (15).
  d. He controlled the womb (20–21, 25, 30).
  e. He controlled the fertility of the flocks (30).
  f. He crippled with a touch (32).
4. God is righteous (and a righteous judge).
  a. He punished disobedience with death (2).
  b. He declared the curse oracle as just recompense for the sin (3–4).
  c. He destroyed the whole creation because humankind was very evil (6–8).
  d. He dispersed the nations because of their proud rebellion (11).
  e. He determined to bless and curse in accordance with how the nations dealt with his servant (12).
  f. He refused to destroy the innocent with the righteous, in order that the nation might learn that he is righteous (18).
  g. He dealt with innocent Abimelech in righteousness (20).
  h. He made things right for Leah and Rachel (29–30) and for Jacob in his work with Laban (31).
  i. He made things right for faithful Joseph but brought discipline to those who were guilty of evil.
5. God is holy.
  Although this theme is not predominant in Genesis, it overlaps with the discussion of righteousness in some passages, such as the flood narrative. The only clear statement, though, is in the sanctification of the Sabbath day (2:3).
6. God is good.
  a. He created everything good and affirmed afterward that it was very good (1).
  b. He corrected what was not good (2).
  c. He commanded Cain to do well (4).
  d. He opposed evil throughout Genesis (6, etc.).
  e. He provided reward for his faithful servant (15).
  f. He planned affairs for good, whereas human beings planned evil (50).
7. God is gracious.

a. He freely gave humankind permission to enjoy all of creation (2).
b. He provided skins for the sinners (3).
c. He protected Cain from avengers (4).
d. He gave grace to Noah (6).
e. He remembered Noah (8) and Abraham (19).
f. He provided water and protection in the wilderness (16, 21).
g. He preserved the righteous in the covenant (19).
h. He intervened even when humans failed (12, 20, 26).
i. He gave the promise to Jacob, the deceiver (28).
j. His angels preserved his servant (28, 32).
k. He delivered in answer to prayer (32).
l. He gave bounty to his servant (33).
m. His grace was desired (43).

The Nature of God's People Within Creation

In order to obtain a fuller picture of the will of God, it is important to survey the book's ideas about human nature, especially of the people of God within his creation. Here too an outline will provide an easy survey.

1. All creation.
   Everything was created in perfect order and harmony, but after the fall there was the cursed earth (3–4), famine (12, 26, 41), and death. The divine plan to restore blessing was indicated by wells of water (16, 20–21, 24, 26, 29) as well as by the fertility of flocks, crops, and people.
2. Humans before the fall.
   a. The body was created from the dust of the ground—it was perishable (2).
   b. The spirit was given from the Lord, imparting life (2).
   c. Human life (*nepeš*) is a combination of physical body and divine breath.
   d. Blood may have been the connecting link between the material and immaterial parts, in view of the importance placed on it (4, 9).
   e. Humankind, male and female, was created in the image of God. Human life was similar to God, but the rest of creation was after its own kind. The term "image" refers not to form but to function, with the communicable attributes that God imparted. This function included fellowship with God, service of God, obedience to God, administration for God, and imitation of God

(esp. in procreation, naming, prophesying, and influencing for righteousness).

   f. Male and female united became one flesh, living in their integrity. They were a complementary unity, spiritually and intellectually equal.

3. Humans after the fall.

   a. The immediate results of sin were guilt, fear, denial, pain, conflict, and death (3, 5, 23, etc.).

   b. The nature of fallen human beings was evil: evil plans and corrupt, violent acts (6); moral abandonment (9); perverse evil (13, 19), and other evil acts (38, 50).

   c. Individual evil acts included envy (4, 37), hatred (27, 37), murder (4, 34), polygamy (6), pride (11), and incest (19).

   d. Human beings could create cultural and practical implements (4).

   3. Men and women were still capable of integrity (12, 20, 26).

   f. Humankind was still in the image of God (9).

4. The covenant people.

   a. They had faith in the Lord (15:6) and were faithful (e.g., 37, 39, 48–49).

   b. They were characterized by righteousness: moral acts (9), righteous intercession (18), rescue of captives (14), championing rights in controversy (31), fighting for what is right (38), resisting sin (39).

   c. They were obedient: walking with the Lord (5–6, 17), obeying the Lord's commands (7), obeying God's Word (12, 17), offering to God (22), obeying all the statutes (26), and obeying even when tempted (39).

   d. They worshiped the Lord: making pleasing sacrifices (4, 8), building altars (12–13, 22, 26, 28, 35, 46), making proclamation of the faith (4, 12), praying, (18, 20, 25), tithing (14, 28), setting up pillars (28, 35), anointing with oil and vowing (28).

   e. They were gracious: forgiving (45, 50), generous (13), unselfish (44), and hospitable (18).

   f. They were capable of great wisdom (Joseph stories).

   g. They were essentially concerned about passing on and preserving the covenant (15, 25, 27, etc.).

   h. They were susceptible to evil:

      (1) deception (12, 20, 26–27, 29–30, 33–34, 37–39, 42ff.)

      (2) murder (34, 37)

      (3) strife (13, 29–30, 45)

      (4) immorality (9, 16, 35)

      (5) stealing (31)

i. They were dishonest as well as untrustworthy: they needed treaties for mutual protection (21, 26, 31, 34).

The Beginnings of the Covenant Relationship

Everything in Genesis moves toward establishment of the covenant blessings as a restoration of the creation blessing. A study of this aspect of the theology of the book would take into consideration the nature of the covenant, the promises of the covenant, exclusion from the covenant, the sign of the covenant, and the covenant stipulations.

The covenant stipulations ultimately were formulated into the legal code of Israel. One of the most important—but often overlooked—themes in Genesis, however, is the foundation of the law. The means by which God would bring blessing is through the obedience of his covenant people, and that obedience required certain standards for discerning good and evil. The following outline surveys some of the early legal precedents that became part of the law itself.

1. Law in general.
   a. God gave commandments to the parents in the garden (2:16–17) and judged them on the basis of their compliance (3:8–24).
   b. Abraham reversed the disobedience of the parents by obeying all the commandments and statutes from God (26:5).
   c. Throughout the book, individuals served God by obeying his commandments to them. The general designation for this obedience is "walked with God" (5:22; 6:9; 17:1).
   d. Disobedience to God's righteous will—that is, doing evil—brought the curse of death (2:17), the flood (6:3, 7; 7:22–23), plagues (12:17), judgment on the nations (15:14), judgment on sinners (19; 38:7–10), warning of death for adultery (20:7), and a reckoning for guilt (42:22).
2. Cultic law: The people of God find that approval from God in the sinful world requires cultic acts. Genesis shows many of these, which the law later incorporated.
   a. The Sabbath day was founded in creation (2:1–3).
   b. Seasons were ordered for service and worship (1:14).
   c. Sacrificial worship was at the center of the believer's gratitude: God clothed Adam and Eve with animal skins (3:21); Cain and Abel brought their offerings (4:3); Noah sacrificed a sweet savor offering (8:20–22); the people were never to eat the blood (9:4); the patriarchs built many altars to attest to God's presence and promise (e.g., 12:7–8; 13:4; 18; 26:25; 35:3–7); substitution with animal sacrifice was taught on what would become the temple mount (22:2, 12–13); the covenant was initiated by

sacrifice and oath (15:9–21); treaties and boundaries were established by sacrifice (31:54); and oil was poured out on the altar (28:18).

   d. Places of worship became important: Beer Lahai Roi (24), Bethel (28); false places (e.g., ziggurat) were ruined (11).

   e. A priestly blessing was an oracle from God (14:17, 19).

   f. Tithing was the natural response of the faithful (14:20; 28:22).

   g. Circumcision was a sacred rite (17:10–14; 21:4) and not to be profaned (34:14–31).

   h. Intercession (18:16–33) served to bring about conformity to righteousness.

   i. Solemn oaths were a part of the cultic life (14:22; 21:22–23; 24:2–3; 25:33; 26:28; 31:43–54; 47:29; 50:25).

   j. Prayer brought deliverance (20; 24:12–15; 25:21; 32:11).

   k. Proclamation at the altar began (4:26; 12:8; 13:4; 21:33; 26:25).

   l. Religious vows were to be kept (28:20; 35).

   m. Diet law: the sinew of the hip was not eaten (32:32), and there was a distinction between the clean and the unclean animals (7:2, 8). The sin of intoxication was also deplored (9:20–25).

   n. Uncleanness was to be shunned (see the laws in Leviticus 12–19): household idols were to be removed (35:2); homosexuality forbidden (19:7); incest rebuked (19:37–38); uncovering the nakedness of the father brought loss of inheritance (35:22 and 49:3–4); marriage with Canaanites prohibited (24; 28; 38); separation from pagan nations required (13:13; 19:37–38; 31:43–55; 34:23; 21:22–34); avoidance of pagan superstitions advised (30:14); idols buried (35:2); and the whore burned (38:24).

3. The Decalogue: The foundation of the Ten Commandments appears in the events of Genesis.

   a. God was recognized as sovereign over all things that the pagans worshiped (1), and so would tolerate no false idols (35:1–5).

   b. Humankind was made in the image of God, and so it would be futile to make images (1:26).

   c. The Sabbath day commemorated the creation (2:1–3) and therefore served as a sign of the new creation.

   d. People were to honor their fathers and mothers rather than live in moral abandonment (9:24–29; 35:22).

   e. Killing was evil (4:8, 11, 23; 9:6; 27:41; 34:25–30; 37:18), for it destroys creation.

   f. Committing adultery was prohibited (26:11; 39:7–9; 12:19 and 20:3–7—under the penalty of death).

   g. Stealing was wrong (14:1–12 [stealing at first meant kidnapping]; 31:19; 40:15).

    h. Bearing false witness or swearing falsely was prohibited (I combine here the ninth commandment and the taking of the name of God in vain) (21:22–23; 37:32; 39:14), for false accusation, or false testimony, was deceptive and destructive. Lying was wrong (12:13; 20:2; 26:7; and many other samples of troubling deceptions).

    i. Coveting was wrong (in 3:6–7, the words used are from the tenth commandment, showing that such strong desire prompted other sins).

4. The *Mishpatim:* The many situational laws in Exodus 21–23 and the rest of the Pentateuch find their basis in Genesis.

    a. Foundation for marriage (1:18–24); problem with two or more wives (4:19; 6:1–4 for harems; 29:28 for sisters); intermarriage and violation of marriage rights by rape (34).

    b. Levirate customs for carrying on the name of the deceased (38).

    c. Inheritance laws and possession of property: not taking another's goods (14:23); purchase of the cave (23); selection of the true heir and the dismissal of others (25:1–6); being cheated out of the proper inheritance (31:14); wages (31:7, 41); right of transfer (25:31).

    d. Necessity of love for others; hated brother (27:41; 37) sisters' tension (29–30); fear of retaliation (50:15); quarrels (13; 45:24).

    e. Treatment of servants and slaves: handmaid (16; 21); submission to masters (16:6, 9); treatment of strangers (18:1–8).

2

The Primeval Events

pre-Abraham

The record of the primeval events, Genesis 1:1–11:26, forms the prologue for the book. It demonstrates convincingly and graphically the need for God's blessing in the world; for ever since humankind acquired the knowledge of good and evil, evil became the dominant force, bringing corruption and chaos into God's creation and incurring the divine curse. This prologue explains why God called Abram and inaugurated a program of blessing through his covenant.

The early chapters of Genesis develop several major themes. The introduction to this section records how the Lord created the universe out of a primordial chaos. The beginning, then, saw a perfect and harmonious creation enjoying the blessing of God. But a second chaos was ushered in at the fall, and so the Lord made new decrees and provisions for men and women in the new order. Yet this new order witnessed the spread of sin more than the triumph of good. The Lord consequently destroyed the world and everything in it, except the recipients of grace. Out of this second watery chaos the Lord renewed the earth and commissioned the second Adam to begin anew; but before long, sin reared its ugly head and man fell again. As the human race multiplied, it united in proud rebellion against the Lord. Consequently, the Lord brought judgment into the world yet again, scattering and hopelessly dividing the human race. At the end of this record of the constant spread of evil and the corresponding intervention of the Lord, there is no renewal, no new beginning. The reader is thereby prepared for the call of Abram.

5

The Creation of the Universe by the Word of God
(Gen. 1:1–2:3)

If the creation around us displays the glory of God (Ps. 19), how much more the account of the origin of that creation in Genesis! From beginning to end the emphasis in the passage is on God's sovereign majesty. He is the subject; his actions, although expressed simply and briefly, are lofty and inspiring. Accordingly, exposition of this section must concentrate on the nature of God as it is displayed through the work of creation.

To understand the importance of this revelation about God to the theological message of the book requires a knowledge of its proper contexts. In its historical context the account contrasts radically with other stories of creation in the ancient Near East. This fact can be appreciated only by studying the ancient records with all their polytheistic and confusing elements. In fact, a knowledge of pagan religion in general will be helpful in measuring the impact of the creation narrative on its Israelite audience.

The literary context is, of course, the religious writings of ancient Israel. The account of creation forms the starting point of the prologue to Genesis, which in turn is the foundation of the whole Pentateuch. In other words, the account is essentially a theological treatise.

Theological Ideas

The task of the expositor is to discover the main point of the theological treatise. To do so, it is essential to ask why the new nation of Israel needed to have this material and to have it written as it is. At the outset we observe that the portrayal of God as the Creator and Sustainer of all life has great bearing on the fact that God was now creating Israel as a new nation among the nations (Deut. 32:6–9). The God who created Israel as his own people is the sovereign God who created the universe and all that is in it. The implications would be inescapable: since the theocracy is founded by the sovereign God of creation, the law, the customs, and the beliefs associated with it are all consonant with the plan of creation. Creation is thus the theological starting point, explaining what kind of God was establishing his theocracy and how powerful his Word was in doing so.

Several theological ideas inform this basic theme. First, the text reveals the sovereignty of the God of creation. Since everything that exists in the universe was made by him, it must therefore be under his control. The impact of this truth in the ancient world would have been staggering. It was a world plagued by the worship of false gods, who challenged the Lord for Israel's affections and allegiance. But those gods were identified with the sun, moon, stars, animals, rivers, and a host of other things. In short, everything that the pagans worshiped God had made. Consequently, their gods should pose no real threat to Israel, for the creation must be subject to the Creator. From their beginning the Israelites witnessed how their sovereign God destroyed the gods of Egypt (Exod. 18:11; Num. 33:4) and then the gods of Canaan (Josh. 10:12–13, if we assume that the sun and the moon also represented their gods).

Second, the account lays the foundation for the law, God's Word to his people. If indeed God was before all things and made everything—including the things pagans worshiped—how foolish it would be to have any gods besides him. If God made humans as his image to represent him on earth, how foolish it would be to make an image of God. If God himself set aside one day for rest and sanctified it, should not God's people who were seeking to please him observe one special day as well? In numerous ways the law finds its rationale in creation. This idea is strengthened by the fact that God created by his powerful and authoritative Word. Later, when Israel received "the Word of the Lord," they knew it was that creative word. Should they not obey this powerful word, as all creation had? Could they not trust it?

Third, the passage reveals the activity of God in redemption. At the beginning there was darkness over the deep, and there was waste and void; but at the end there was a marvelous creation at rest, blessed and sanctified by God. This creation narrative traces how God transformed the chaos into the cosmos, turned darkness into light, and altered that which was unprofitable to that which was good, holy, and worth blessing. This direction in the passage parallels the direction of the message in the Pentateuch as a whole, in which God redeems Israel from the darkness and chaos of Egypt and leads them on toward blessing and rest. The pattern of God's redemptive work thus first begins to unfold at creation. Genesis 1:1–2:3, then, confirms the teaching that God, the sovereign Creator, is in fact the Redeemer and Lawgiver and that he accomplishes his work through his powerful Word.

Structure and Synthesis

Structure

A brief survey of the passage reveals a definite structure in the pattern of six days of creation. The narrative for each day typically includes the divine speech ("God said"), the statement of the fulfillment of his decree ("and it was so" or "and there was"), the divine evaluation ("it was good"), and then the concluding sequence ("evening and morning came").

The seventh day (2:1–3) breaks with this pattern. Here, instead of creation and evaluation, there is finishing, ceasing, blessing, and sanctifying. The emphasis of the seventh day must then be the perfect completion of all creation. Indeed, the pattern of the words and clauses seems to underscore this emphasis. There are thirty-five words in the Hebrew text of these three verses, a multiple of seven. The three middle clauses (2:2a, 2:2b, and 2:3a) in the original have seven words each, and the adjective "seventh" is within each clause. The reader receives a strengthened impression that the seventh day is a celebration of completion.

The analysis of the beginning of the account, 1:1–2, has been debated over the years (see appendix 1). The problem concerns the relationship of the clauses in verse 2 to the statement in verse 1. In the Hebrew text the clause beginning verse 2, "now the earth was waste and void," clearly begins with a disjunctive ("now," or some other circumstantial translation) rather than a conjunctive ("and") or sequential ("and then") formation. This construction signifies that verse 2 is not the result of or a development from verse 1. Consequently, many scholars have posited a gap between the verses, allowing for the fall of Satan between the original creation and the chaos reported in verse 2. Others would rather take verse 1 as the title of the entire account of creation, verse 2 as a description of the chaos at the beginning of the creation, and then verse 3

Chart 6. **Corresponding Activity in the Days of Creation**

Formlessness (*tōhû*)		Emptiness (*bōhû*)	
Day	Item Created	Day	Item Created
1	Light with darkness	4	Lights for the day and night
2	Sea and sky	5	Creatures for the water and air
3	Fertile earth	6	Creatures for the fertile earth

as the beginning of the work of creation to form the universe as we know it. This view suggests that the creation of our universe was a re-creation following a chaos and that the account of an original creation and the explanation of the chaos are not provided in Genesis 1—although they are taught elsewhere in Scripture.

It is worth observing that "waste and void" in verse 2 gives a key to the six days of creation, the first three correcting the waste or formlessness, and the next three correcting the void or emptiness. This division is also attested by the parallelism between the days (see chart 8). The structure of this chapter thus includes the introduction (1:1–2), the six days of creation (1:3–31), and then the conclusion (2:1–3).

Summary Message

Out of the darkened chaos God sovereignly and majestically created the entire universe in six days, bringing about perfect order and abundant fullness for people to enjoy and to rule, and then blessed and sanctified the seventh day, which marked the completion of creation.

Exegetical Outline

    I. Introduction: God, through his Spirit, created the entire universe out of the dark chaos (1:1–2).
        A. Title: God created the universe (1).
        B. Circumstances: The earth was chaotic and enveloped in darkness, but the Spirit of God was ensuring creation (2).
    II. Development: In six days God, by his powerful Word, called into existence a perfect, harmonious, and fruitful creation to be enjoyed and ruled by human beings (1:3–31).
        A. In three days God brought about order and form through his sovereign creative acts (3–13).
            1. Day 1: God created light and sovereignly divided it from the darkness (3–5).
            2. Day 2: God created the sky and sovereignly separated the waters above and below it (6–8).

　　　3. Day 3: God created sea and dry land and sovereignly blessed the earth (9–13).

　　B. In three more days God brought about fullness and harmony within the created universe through his sovereign creative acts (14–31).

　　　1. Day 4: God created luminaries in the heavens to govern the temporal order (14–19).

　　　2. Day 5: God created animal life for sea and sky and sovereignly blessed them with fruitfulness (20–23).

　　　3. Day 6: God created animal life for the land and human life to rule over creation and sovereignly blessed them all with fruitfulness (24–31).

　III. Conclusion: God blessed and sanctified the seventh day because on it he ceased from all his creative work (2:1–3).

　　A. By the seventh day God had completely finished his creative work (1).

　　B. God blessed and sanctified the seventh day because on it he ceased his work (2–3).

Development of the Exposition

The exposition of the passage should be developed in accordance with the structure in order to present the exegetically derived theological ideas accurately. While it is important to stress the fact of the creation in time and space, it is also important to give attention to the timeless theological truths that creation reveals about the person and works of the Lord.

I. God transforms chaos into creation (1:1–2).

The wording of this first point reflects the interpretation that verse 1 is a summary statement and that verse 2 provides circumstantial clauses. If one argued for an original creation in verse 1, then the wording of this point would be quite different.

A. God is the sovereign Creator of all that exists (1).

The first verse declares the message of the chapter in summary fashion: God created everything. What is so striking about this great theological truth is that God ('ĕlōhîm) is introduced simply as the one who existed before anything in our universe. The plural form of the word, a specialized use of the plural to signify his majestic potentialities, adds to the emphasis on his sovereign power.

The verb used for create (bārāʾ) is used in Scripture exclusively for the activity of God (see appendix 2). Humans may make (*ʿāśâ*), form (*yāṣar*), or build (*bānâ*); to the Hebrew, however, God creates. The verb does not in and of itself mean creation out of nothing; it basically means to produce something new, fresh, and perfect. In this verse the verb refers to the activities of the six days to follow.

What God created is here called "the heavens and the earth," a poetic expression (merism) signifying the whole universe. Other examples of this poetic device are "day and night" (meaning all the time) and "man and beast" (meaning all created physical beings). "Heaven and earth" thus indicates not only the heaven and the earth but everything in them. Genesis 2:4 also uses this expression in a restatement of the work of creation throughout the six days.

All this activity is "in the beginning" (*bᵉrēʾšît*). "Beginning" refers to the first phase of a step, which must be the beginning of our universe as we know it. Accordingly, John 1:1 precedes Genesis 1:1 in our theological reckoning.

The point of the verse, then, is that God is absolutely sovereign over all matter. Such sovereignty demands allegiance, for to acknowledge the Creator naturally leads to submission to him.

B. The chaos necessitates the transformation into the creation (2a).

It is clear from the contents of verse 2 that something is drastically wrong at the outset. Two clauses set down the circumstances as chaotic; the first states that the earth was "waste and void" (*tōhû wābōhû*), or "formlessness and emptiness." "Void" (*bōhû*) is a relatively rare word, occurring only two other times in Scripture, in both cases joined with "waste" (*tōhû*) to describe a judgment of God (Jer. 4:23; Isa. 34:11). In fact, the Jeremiah passage constructs an antithesis to this creation account, tracing a dismantling of creation by the judgment of God. "Waste and void" cannot describe an intermediate stage in God's work of creation. Not only does the syntax (*wāw* disjunctive) argue against that sequence, but Isaiah 45:18 states that God did not make this world as a waste (*tōhû*). This key phrase in Genesis 1:2 indicates that the world must be shaped and peopled before it may be pronounced "good." The following narrative shows how God brought this world from its primitive condition of desolation and waste to its fullness and order.

Not only was the earth "waste and void," but, according to the second circumstantial clause, "darkness" (*ḥōšek*) was upon the face of the deep. Darkness throughout the Bible represents evil and death—it is not conducive to life. Some uses of the motif of darkness include the plague of darkness on Egypt (Exod. 10:15; Ps. 105:28), the wicked (1 Sam. 2:9), wicked enemies (Ps. 35:6), death (Job 3:4–5), the day of the Lord in judgment (Isa. 13:10), and a parallelism with calamity (ra'; Isa. 45:7). Neither is darkness a positive good in Genesis; rather, it is dispelled by the first act of creation.

This darkness covered the face of t^ehôm. This term refers to the salty deep, the ocean, and thereby figuratively to the abyss. Students of comparative mythology often associate the word with the Akkadian Ti'amat, a goddess identified with the salty sea. In that Eastern culture's mythology, Apsu, fresh water, is Ti'amat's male counterpart in the pantheon. In Genesis, however, the "deep" is not spoken of in mythological terms: it is simply the primeval ocean and not a goddess in rebellion.

In the first part of Genesis 1:2, there is thus an ominous, uncomfortable tone. The clauses describe not the results of divine creation but a chaos at the earliest stage of this world. It is not the purpose of Genesis to tell the reader how the chaos came about (any more than it is interested in identifying the serpent in chap. 3). The expositor must draw some conclusions from other passages with similar descriptions. If one can posit that the fall of Satan (Ezek. 28) brought about the chaos in God's original creation, then Genesis 1 describes a re-creation, or God's first act of redemption, salvaging his world and creating all things new. This picture is similar to how it will be at the end of the age when God judges the world and then makes all things new. But Genesis is more interested in God's work as Creator, and so the circumstantial clauses report the chaos only briefly.

C. The Spirit of God ensures the creation (2b).

In contrast to the first two clauses of verse 2, a third clause offers a positive thought—"the Spirit of God was hovering over the face of the waters [māyim]." The arena is now the life-giving water and not the chaotic, abysslike deep. The activity belongs to the Spirit of God, not an awesome wind sweeping across the waters, as some have translated it (the verb "hovering" argues against such a rendering). This verb (rāḥap) basically means "flutter, fly"; it is used in Deuteronomy 32:11 to describe an eagle stirring up the nest, fluttering over its young. In much the same way, the unformed, lifeless mass of the watery earth was under the care of the divine Spirit, who hovered over it, ensuring its future development.

II. God creates everything by his powerful Word (1:3–31).

A. God brings about form and order in creation (3–13).

The second section of the passage traces the creation of the universe through six days. The first three days remedy the formlessness.

1. God sovereignly creates light and divides it from darkness (3–5). At the beginning of the account the reader learns that the means of creation was the Word of God. The first verb, "and he said," sets the tone for this emphasis throughout the chapter and the rest of the biblical revelation (Ps. 33:9; John 1:1–3; 1 Cor. 8:6; Col. 1:16). What God said in his creative decree makes the point more striking: "Let there be ... and there was." The verbs used here ($y^e h\hat{\imath}$ ... $wayh\hat{\imath}$) are related to the holy name Yahweh, the great I Am. The use of these words suggests a significant word play: God, who in Exodus 3:14 is known as "I Am" (*'ehyeh* explains *Yahweh*), says, "Let there be" ($y^e h\hat{\imath}$), "and there was" (*wayhî*). It is not surprising, then, that John records that Jesus Christ is the Word of God, who created everything (John 1:3). In Genesis, Israel learned that the Word of the Lord is the powerful transforming word that was first manifested in creation.

That which God calls into existence at the outset is light (*'ôr*), immediately changing a world enveloped in darkness. It is natural light, physical light; but it is much more. The Bible shows again and again that light and darkness signify mutually exclusive realms, especially in spiritual matters of good and evil. Throughout Scripture light is the realm of God and the righteous; darkness is the domain of the Evil One and death. Light represents that which is holy, pure, true, life-giving, and gladdening. For example, when God brought the judgment of darkness on Egypt, Israel enjoyed light in their dwellings (Exod. 10:21–23). When Israel followed the Lord's light through the wilderness by night, they were assured of his presence. When they were instructed to keep the lamps burning in the Holy Place, they knew that there was something symbolic about that light. In the act of creating light in the darkened arena of the world, God thus also manifested his nature and will.

After the creation of light God announced his evaluation: it was good. The idea of the word "good" (*ṭôb*) is that the light is useful, fitting, and healthy. That which is good is conducive for and enhances life—so light is good, not the darkness.

Since darkness yet remained, God then divided it from this light. From the beginning God's people would thus learn that God makes divisions (*bādal*). In Israel's law the Lord would make divisions between the holy and the profane (Lev. 10:10; 11:47), between the Holy Place and the Most Holy Place (Exod. 26:33), and in fact between Israel and the nations (Lev. 20:24, 26). Even in the breastpouch of the priest, light and dark objects, the Urim and Thummim, were used for decisions. The division of light from darkness in creation thus displays the will of God as a foretaste of the law.

After the light and the darkness attained their separate spheres, God named them "day" (*yôm*) and "night" (*lāylâ*). The act of naming in the ancient Near East was an act of sovereign dominion, often associated with creation. In the Babylonian account of creation, *Enuma Elish* (tablet 1, lines 1–2, 7–8), when the writer wished to state that nothing existed, he said that nothing was named. In Genesis also, naming attests to the sovereignty of the Creator. Later God entrusted his dominion over the earth to Adam by letting him name all the living creatures.

The meaning of the term "day" (*yôm*) in this chapter has received varying interpretations. Although the word normally means a twenty-four-hour day, it can also mean a longer general period of time (Isa. 61:2) or an idiom "when" (as in Gen. 2:4). In this chapter, however, it must carry its normal meaning. Support for this view includes the following: (1) elsewhere, whenever *yôm* is used with a number, it means a twenty-four-hour period; (2) the Decalogue bases the teaching of the Sabbath day on the six days of creation and the seventh day of rest; (3) from the fourth day on, there are days, years, signs, and seasons, suggesting that the normal system is entirely operative; and (4) if *yôm* refers to an age, then the text would have to allow for a long period of "day" and then a long period of "night"—but few would argue for the night as an age. It seems inescapable that Genesis presents the creation in six days.

2. God sovereignly creates a division for the waters (6–8). On the second day God created an expanse in the atmosphere to separate the waters above from the waters below. This "firmament" (from Latin *firmamentum*, something made solid) is poetically described elsewhere as a tent curtain (Ps. 104:2), a veil (Isa. 40:22), clear pavement like sapphire (Exod. 24:10), and molten glass (Job 37:18). This atmospheric expanse was a necessary progression in the development of creation. Up to this point the atmosphere may have been like a dense fog; there may have been little visibility and very little light shining through. With the creation of the expanse God thus set a division between the cloud masses above and the waters below.

The text reports that it happened as decreed: "and it was so." The word "so" (*kēn*, from *kûn*) is much stronger than it may seem. It means that, like an established thing, the light and darkness found their fixed place in the order of creation. The expression was not used for the division between the light and darkness, because that separation was alternating; this separation was spatial and unchanging. Conversely, the creation of the expanse dividing the waters is not called "good," because the work of God with the water is not yet completed.

The sovereignty of God appears in this day's activity in his naming the expanse "heavens" (*šāmāyim*) and also in his control over this domain. Pagan mythology considered the heavens to be the dominion of the high gods. According to Genesis, however, God not only created this domain but also controlled it by making a division in it. The theological significance of this teaching involves Israel's confidence in the Lord as the supreme God of the heavens and Israel's compliance with all the divisions and distinctions he made in his creation.

3. God provides fertility for the earth (9–13). On the third day God caused the dry land to appear and the earth to flourish with growth. The emphasis now begins to shift from bringing order to bringing fullness.

God continued his work of bringing order to creation by decreeing that fertile land appear through the gathering of the waters into reservoirs he called "seas" (*yammîm*). In this report we learn that God set the boundaries for the seas, demonstrating his sovereign control over them. The fact that the Canaanites worshiped *Prince Yam*, a deification of the cosmic ocean, adds greater significance to this portrayal of God's sovereignty.

On the emerging dry land God caused all manner of vegetation to appear ("let the earth vegetate vegetation," or as Cassuto has it, "Let the earth be covered with a fresh green mantle of verdure" [*A Commentary on the Book of Genesis,* vol. 1, p. 40]). This vegetation (*deše'*) seems to be the general term, and herbage (*'ēśeb*) and trees (*'ēṣ*) seem to be subdivisions of it (an interpretation supported by vv. 29–30, which attest to only two kinds: plants and trees).

This decree for fertility stands in bold relief to the ancient mythologies. In Canaan, for example, the religious myth claimed that Baal could produce fertility. At the end of the year Baal died—an idea that explained why the crops died—and was said to be captured by a god "Death" (*Mot*) and carried away to the abyss, the domain of Prince Sea. But in the spring the goddess Anat, Baal's consort, rescued him in a bloody battle, defeating Prince Sea in the process. The reappearance of Baal thus ensured that the crops would grow in the new year and accounted for the change of seasons in the spring. Most of the ancient religions had such rituals, designed to induce the gods to produce crops and fruit (and life as well).

In contrast to corrupt accounts of fertility, the text of Genesis simply but powerfully reports that God gathered the seas together and decreed that the fertile earth produce vegetation. Fertility is a self-perpetuating process decreed by God, a created capacity from the true Lord of life. There is no god Sea, just the seas that God controls. Vegetation does not result from some pagan god's springtime ascendancy through depraved ritual. It results from the majestic Word of the sovereign Lord of creation.

B. God brings about fullness and harmony in creation and establishes dominion for humankind (14–31).

1. God appoints luminaries to regulate the divisions (14–19). The fourth day records how God created the luminaries—the sun, moon, and stars—to rule over the heavens. The language here describes the phenomena; the sun is not *in* the atmosphere—it is far beyond it—but *appears to be* in the heavens. Likewise, it is possible to interpret the passage with the meaning that the sun, moon, and stars now appeared for the first time, not that they were only now brought into existence.

Whatever the time and manner of their creation, these heavenly luminaries have as their function to dominate the day and the night, to serve as signs for the fixed seasons, and to rule over the heavens. The verse may be translated "signs for the fixed seasons [a hendiadys], that is, days and years" (an explicative *wāw*).

The sun, moon, and stars are thus all God's creation, attesting to his glory and ruling over time by his decree. Not so in the mythology of the pagans. Sun gods, moon gods, and the whole astrological arrangement form the pantheons of the pagans. They thought of these heavenly orbs as objects of worship, as forces of destiny that were serviceable for divining through alignments and eclipses. What folly it was to follow the astrological charts of the Babylonians or to look to the sun god of the Egyptians, thinking that the answers to destiny were there. Rather, Israel must trust in the personal God who created all these stars and planets by his Word and must give no credence or respect to the gods of the pagans.

Moreover, both earthly and heavenly bodies are all subject to the will of the Creator. They are witnesses to the glory of God (Ps. 19)—and no more. To look to the sun or the stars should direct the true believer's thoughts to the Creator. But humans most often rejected the Creator and worshiped the creation (Rom. 1).

2. God creates life in sea and sky (20–23). On the fifth day God created all the living creatures that inhabit the seas and that fly across the skies. This passage declares that life came into being by the direct command of God. Vegetation is not included here, for to the Hebrew mind that is not life (i.e., not *nepeš ḥayyâ*).

Although these verses are concerned with general categories of living things, the great sea creatures (*tannînim*) are singled out for special attention. The pagans worshiped the great sea creatures as dragons and monsters in rebellion that had to be subdued. In ancient Canaan Lotan (the equivalent of Hebrew's Leviathan) was the name of this great force. The Torah subdues this view rather simply by reporting that God created (*bārā'*) them. Canaan may fear and venerate them as gods, but Israel knew that they were just another part of God's perfect and harmonious creation. Only the Creator, Job would learn, can control Leviathan. Here too the blessing of fertility is granted by the sovereign decree. God, not some pagan ritual, is the source of life and fertility.

3. God creates life for the land, human life for his service (24–31). The sixth day reveals both the culmination and the goal of creation. After bringing order and fullness to the creation, God created human life to enjoy and rule the now habitable world.

First, God created animals for the earth after their kind. Here again God created in kinds, or species. So far the expression "kind" (*mîn*) has been used for vegetation, both plants and trees, water creatures, air creatures, and now land creatures (domesticated, creeping, and game animals). God continually makes boundaries and sets limits for the self-perpetuating creation, boundaries that the law will employ in teaching the principles of holiness and cleanness.

But the crowning point of creation is human life. Like the animals, humans were formed from the ground, given provision of food, and blessed with fruitfulness. But humans are far more than animals. The text shows that human life was set apart in relation to God by the divine plan ("let us make man"), by the divine pattern ("as our image"), and by the divine purpose ("let him have dominion").

The expression "let us make man" introduces the climax of God's creative activity. This plural verb has caused a fair amount of debate in theological circles. The form can be explained as either a plural of majesty or a potential plural, expressing the wealth of potentials in the divine being. This verb harmonizes with the plural "God" (*'ĕlōhîm*) used in verse 1 and following, which, although plural in form, takes a singular verb. These plurals do not explicitly refer to the triunity of the Godhead but do allow for that doctrine's development through the process of progressive revelation.

The divine pattern is that human life, male and female, be the "image" of God (the preposition "in" probably is a *bêt* of essence—"as," and not "in"). The term "image" (*ṣelem*) is used in the Old Testament for actual forms and shapes of idols (1 Sam. 6:5, 11) and reliefs (Ezek. 23:14). The term "likeness" (*dᵉmût*), which is more abstract, further explains the meaning of "image." It describes a similarity (e.g., "like a man," in Ezek. 1:10).

The term "image" has been variously explained as personality, nature (as body and spirit), or capacity for moral decision. It does not signify a physical representation of corporeality, for God is a spirit. The term must therefore figuratively describe human life as a reflection of God's spiritual nature; that is, human life has the communicated attributes that came with the inbreathing (Gen. 2:7). Consequently, humans have spiritual life, ethical and moral sensitivities, conscience, and the capacity to represent God. The significance of the word "image" should be connected to the divine purpose for human life. Von Rad has made the analogy that, just as kings set up statues of themselves throughout the border of their land to show their sovereign domain, so God established his representatives on earth (*Theology*, vol. 1, p. 146).

Human life, male and female, thus has great capacity and responsibility by virtue of being the image of God. First, humans may produce life—their own, spiritual-physical life. If humans are to imitate God, then creating life is a basic part of that task. A man and a woman can produce a living soul. This privilege is part of their blessing from God, a blessing that includes divine enablement. For believers, childbirth is an act of worship, a sharing in the work of God, the one who created life.

Second, humans are to have dominion over the world. The terms used suggest putting down opposition and were perhaps used in anticipation of the conflict with evil. As the Scriptures unfold, however, one realizes how humans have failed at this task. The New Testament states that "we do not yet see all things under his dominion," but Jesus Christ, the express image of the Father, will ultimately re-establish such dominion (Heb. 2:8–9).

In Israel, and later in the church, the redeemed of the Lord have been sensitive to the design of the Creator. Believers have attempted to fulfill God's purposes for them by using the spiritual capacities he imparted to them. Now believers are called on to be conformed to the image of Christ, who is the image of the Father. God's new creation must trample underfoot all evil forces, taking into captivity every wicked thought and deed. Whereas the original dominion was both physical and spiritual, the Christian's is primarily spiritual. In both cases, however, God provides spiritual and physical blessings, so that his "image" might effectively represent him on earth.

III. God culminates creation with the blessing of holiness (2:1–3).

The seventh day, which later became the sign of the Sinaitic covenant with Israel, reports the Sabbath of God as the blessed culmination of creation.

A. God completes his work of creation (1).

The repetition in this last section of the narrative stresses the culmination of and cessation from creation. The key word here is the well-known "rest" (*šābat*, "to rest"; *šabbāt*, "the Sabbath"). The word actually means "cease," more than "rest" as understood today. It is not a word that refers to remedying exhaustion after a tiring week of work.

Rather, it describes the enjoyment of accomplishment, the celebration of completion.

The New Testament uses the concept of Sabbath rest in a spiritual sense. Believers have ceased from their labors and have entered into that divine rest (Heb. 4). Yet there remains a rest in the world of peace to come. Salvation, to the writer of Hebrews, is the new beginning of the theocratic rest begun in the creation.

B. God distinguished his rest by sanctification (2–3).

On the seventh day God not only ceased from his work of creation, he sanctified the day in commemoration of it. The word "sanctify" (< qiddēš) must be studied thoroughly in conjunction with "rest." Israel was to set apart one day in seven to worship and serve the Lord—not simply to engage in common relaxation and entertainment. It was a reminder that they, the nation of Israel, were God's creation too—that they were God's holy nation. The day belonged to God. The point is that those who enjoy Sabbath rest must be set apart to him and must set their actitivies apart to him.

The entire narrative with all its details and motifs yields a clear, unified idea that accounts for all the parts: *God, by his powerful Word, transforms the chaos into a holy and blessed creation.* This truth is the fundamental, basic teaching of the account of creation.

The significance of this theological point figured prominently in the activities of the people of God from age to age. Israel, for example, in their religious experience from Egypt, realized that, out of that darkened and chaotic pagan world, God brought them into existence as his people, teaching them the truth, distinguishing that truth from error, providing abundance for them, commissioning them to be his representatives, and promising them theocratic rest. Dominion, fruitfulness, and rest would be theirs in the Land of Promise.

The world was plagued with pagan gods and false ideas, but Israel knew that they were created by the true God and that God would defeat the pagans' gods in the process of establishing theocratic rest. The report that his powerful Word was the agent of creation clearly shows that his creation did then, and must always, obey that Word.

This passage is significant also in the lives of Christians. Above and beyond asserting the fact of creation in much the same way it did for Israel, the passage provides an important theological lesson. The believer enters into a life of Sabbath rest from works and embarks on a life of holiness in that rest. We learn from the creation account (1) that God is a redeeming God who changes darkness to light, death to life, and chaos to blessing; (2) that God is absolutely sovereign over all life and all pagan ideas that would contend for our allegiance; and (3) that God works by his powerful Word—to create, to redeem, and to sanctify. Obedience to his powerful Word, either the written Word or the living Word, our Savior, will transform believers into his glorious image.

Bibliography

Anderson, Bernhard, W., ed. *Creation in the Old Testament*. Philadelphia: Fortress, 1984. (Essays by Gunkel, von Rad, Eichrodt, Westermann, and others.)

Armerding, Carl E. "An Old Testament View of Creation." *Crux* 12 (1974–75): 3–4.

Asselin, D. T. "The Notion of Dominion in Genesis 1–3." *CBQ* 16 (1954): 277–94.

Barker, Kenneth L. "The Value of Ugaritic for Old Testament Studies." *BibSac* 133 (1976): 119–29 (esp. p. 121).

Clifford, Richard J. "The Hebrew Scriptures and the Theology of Creation." *ThS* 46 (1985): 507–23.

Clines, D. J. A. "The Etymology of Hebrew Ṣelem." *JNWSL* 3 (1974): 19–25.

Hasel, Gerhard F. "The Meaning of 'Let Us' in Gen. 1:26." *AUSS* 13 (1975): 58–66.

————— . "The Polemic Nature of the Genesis Cosmology." *EvQ* 46 (1974): 81–102.

————— . "The Significance of the Cosmology in Genesis 1 in Relation to Ancient Near Eastern Parallels." *AUSS* 10 (1972): 1–20.

Heidel, Alexander. *The Babylonian Genesis*. 2d ed. Chicago: University of Chicago Press, 1951.

Hoffmeier, James K. "Some Thoughts on Genesis 1 and 2 and Egyptian Cosmology." *JANES* 15 (1983): 39–50.

Kaiser, Walter C. "The Literary Form of Genesis 1–11." In *New Perspectives in the Old Testament*, edited by J. B. Payne, pp. 48–65. Waco, Tex.: Word, 1970.

May, Herbert Gordon. "The Creation of Light in Genesis 1:3–5." *JBL* 58 (1939): 203–11.

Petersen, David L. "Yahweh and the Organization of the Cosmos." *JSOT* 13 (1979): 47–64.

Shea, William H. "The Unity of the Creation Account." *Origins* 5 (1978): 9–38.

Smith, Gary V. "Structure and Purpose in Genesis 1–11." *JETS* 20 (1977): 307–19.

Waltke, Bruce K. "The Creation Account in Genesis 1:1–3." Part 1, "Introduction to Biblical Cosmology"; part 2, "The Restitution Theory"; part 3, "The Initial Chaos Theory and the Precreation Chaos Theory"; part 4, "The Theology of Genesis 1"; part 5, "The Theology of Genesis 1," continued. *BibSac* 132 (1975): 25–36, 136–44, 216–28, 327–42; 133 (1976): 28–41.

6

The Creation of Man and Woman in the Garden
(Gen. 2:4–25)

T his passage is the first part of the *tôl^e dôt* of the heavens and earth, which runs through chapter 4. This first *tôl^e dôt* traces what became of the universe God had so marvelously created: it was cursed through disobedience, so that deterioration and decay spread rapidly throughout the human race. This point may be demonstrated by the presence of the motif of cursing. Whereas the word "bless" was used three times in the account of creation, the word for "curse" appears three times in this *tôl^e dôt*. Beginning with Genesis 2:4, then, we have one of the most important sections in the book—it makes painfully obvious the need for the restoration of the blessing.

The first unit in this *tôl^e dôt*, Genesis 2:4–25, provides the necessary introduction to the record of the fall and the resultant curse. The magnitude of that sin and destruction can be fully understood only when the nature and purpose of humankind is understood. To know what God had invested in human life and what he had expected of it is to know what was lost at the fall.

The record of the creation of man and woman in the garden is not another, divergent tradition of creation; it is a rehearsing of the creation of man and woman that establishes their nature and place in God's world. The narrator incorporates just what he needs to lay the foundation for chapter 3, in a way that is didactic in its own right. Anyone reading this section carefully can gain a fresh appreciation for the design of the Creator, and a similar reading of chapter 3 will reveal its allusions and references to this section. Clearly, the sections are inexorably bound together. Critical studies that are primarily concerned with original meanings of isolated sections overlook the unity of the final fixed form of the narrative and make the discovery of the main theme difficult. Here, by establishing the nature and place of humankind, the biblical writer prepares for the discussion to follow.

Theological Ideas

If the story of creation presented the foundation of the theocracy with the purpose of calling allegiance to the sovereign Creator, the story of the creation of the man and the woman explains that humans have the God-given capacity and responsibility to serve the Lord with integrity. The impartation of the breath of life, the provision of bounty in the place of service, the declaration of the first commandment, and the provision of help all work together to develop this central theological message.

But another theological theme has great relevance. Whereas the first chapter stressed the importance of the Word of the Lord as the powerful means of creation (everything obeyed God's decree), the second employs it as the test of obedience. The Word of the Lord in this unit comes in the form of a command to be obeyed, one that the man and the woman are able to obey in view of their created nature. The Word of the Lord is direct; it brings the announcement of provision along with the prohibition. The whole story, of course, would be most instructive for the nation receiving the Ten Commandments.

The theological motifs of the passage also bring great significance to God's design for the institution of marriage. That the man and the woman correspond and become one flesh must not be limited to the physical level. They help one another serve the Lord and keep his command so that they might continue their life as his representatives in the world.

Structure and Synthesis

Structure

The narrative has several distinct sections: the account of the creation of the man (2:4b–7), the planting of the garden (vv. 8–9), the digression to survey the rivers (vv. 10–14), the commandment (vv. 15–17), and the creation of the woman (vv. 18–25). To limit the exposition to any of these sections would destroy the development of the theological message leading up to chapter 3. It is far better to treat the entire unit as it develops with its separate parts: the creation of human life against the background of the chaos (2:4b–7); the commandment of God for obedient service amid the bountiful provision of the garden (vv. 8–17); and the completion of human life by the provision of a corresponding partner for the man (vv. 18–25).

The structure of the first few verses is worth noting, since it parallels the beginning of chapter 1. As with Genesis 1:1, there is a summary statement of the section (2:4a). This sentence is followed by a temporal clause (v. 4b) with several circumstantial clauses (vv. 5–6), laying the foundation for the main point in the narrative (v. 7). Parallel to 1:2, there are three circumstantial clauses: two negative ones ("before any sprig of the field was in the earth" and "before any grain of the field grew") and one positive one ("now a mist used to go up from the earth and water all the surface of the ground"). But in 2:5, each of the negative clauses also has a corresponding causal clause ("because the LORD God had not caused it to rain on the earth" and "there was no man to till the ground"). The writer uses the clauses basically to say that this $tôl^edôt$ begins in the primeval days. But the structure, designed to reflect Genesis 1:1–3, underscores that this section is tracing in detail what became of that creation (see chart 7).

The chapter also makes significant use of speaking. First, there is the Word of the Lord in the commandment, giving both permission and prohibition. Coming immediately after the creation of human life with spiritual capacity, this direct communication must be given prominence. But the Lord also spoke in his evaluation of Adam's being alone and his resolution to make the corresponding helper. This speech is not a direct communication to the man; nevertheless, it must be interpreted in the light of the command. Then, Adam also spoke. We learn that he named the animals, an act that reflected the Creator's design and purpose of his being the representative of God. This speaking was the means by which the man came to the same conclusion as God's second speech—he was alone. Finally, the man spoke in joy over the provision of the woman, a praise that reflected God's resolution to give him the corresponding helper.

Summary Message

With the world in its infancy, the Lord God created the first man with the capacity to serve God and the responsibility to keep God's com-

Chart 7. **Parallels Between Creation Accounts**

Element	Gen. 1:1–3	Gen. 2:4–7
Summary	In the beginning God created the heaven and the earth.	These are the *tôl^edôt* of the heaven and earth when they were created, when the Lord God made earth and heaven,
Circumstantial clauses—two negative and one positive	Now the earth was waste and void,	Before any sprig of the field was in the earth,
	and darkness was upon the face of the deep,	and before any grain of the field grew—because the Lord God had not caused it to rain on the earth, and there was no man to till the ground—
	and the Spirit of God was hovering over the face of the waters.	and a mist used to go up from the ground and water the surface of the soil.
Main clause	And God said, "Let there be light," and there was light.	And the Lord God formed the man from the dust of the ground, and breathed into his nostrils the breath of life, and the man became a living being.

mandments, placing him in a perfect environment with every provision and completing him with a corresponding partner in the service of God.

Exegetical Outline

Title: The record of what happened to God's creation (4).
  I. Before the earth was cultivated and flourishing, the Lord God formed the man with the capacity to serve him (5–7).
    A. Circumstances: The earth was uncultivated and unproductive for lack of any rain and any man, but the soil was being watered by a mist (5–6).
    B. Creation: The Lord God formed the man out of the dust from the ground and imparted his life-giving breath to him (7).
  II. Into a bountiful garden environment the Lord God placed the man as God's own spiritual servant and gave him a commandment that he might enjoy life (8–17).
    A. Provision: The Lord God prepared a garden in Eden with all that the heart could desire (8–14).
      1. In the garden that God planted was the tree of life as well as the tree of the knowledge of good and evil (8–9).
      2. The garden was the source of life to the rich and productive regions of the world (10–14).
    B. Prohibition: The Lord God placed man in the garden to serve him and to obey the commandment (15–17).

    1. God placed the man in this setting to serve him (15).

    2. God gave the man his first commandment that the man might enjoy life and not die (16–17).

III. Because there was no corresponding partner for the man in the service of God, the Lord God provided the woman, thereby perfecting creation (18–23).

    A. Circumstances: The man's condition of being alone, intensified by his observation of the animal world, was not good (18–20).

        1. The Lord God determined to make a corresponding helper to complete man (18).

        2. The Lord God made man aware of his loneliness when he began to exercise his dominion over the animals (19–20).

    B. Creation: The Lord God created a woman from the life of the man to be his corresponding partner in the service of God (21–23).

        1. Out of the sleeping man the Lord God formed Eve to correspond to him physically and spiritually (21–22a).

        2. To the delight of the man, the Lord God presented her as the man's new partner (22b–23).

IV. Epilogue: This act of creation is the foundation of marriage in society—one man and one woman united in one life without fear of exploitation (24–25).

Development of the Exposition

The passage begins with the title for the entire *tôlᵉdôt* section of 2:4–4:26. Enough has been said already in chapter 4 about this matter. It would be helpful, however, to use that material in arguing the nature of this account (i.e., the title of the section serves notice that what follows is a description of what became of the universe).

I. Humankind has the capacity to serve God (5–7).

A. Primeval beginning (5–6).

The first two verses of this section provide the setting for the creation of human life. The writer thinks of a time before there were any wild shrubs (Gen. 21:15; Job 30:4, 7) in the earth or cultivated grain in the fields, because there was no rain and no man to till the ground. The only hint of the beginning of fertility is that a mist used to go up from the "earth" (*ʾereṣ*) to water the surface of the "ground" (*ʾadāmâ*, the fertile soil). The point of these clauses is that, in a world that had yet to flourish with fertility, the Lord God was preparing for abundant growth. But more important, when joined with verse 7, this part of the passage plays a subordinate role: before the earth could flourish under God's blessing, God focused his attention on the crowning point of creation, human life.

The clauses foreshadow two ominous notes of Genesis: rain and tilling the ground. Certainly the narration comes from a perspective in which these were common aspects of life. But the mention of man's tilling the ground anticipates the expulsion from the garden under the curse (3:23), and the mention of rain anticipates the great flood (6:17; 7:4).

B. Human life (7).

Against such a background, the narrative carefully describes God's creation of human life. What strikes the reader immediately is the new designation of the Creator—the Lord God (*Yahweh 'ĕlōhîm*). (Speiser [*Genesis*, p. 16] suggests that, in accordance with Mesopotamian practice, the determinative "god" was written with the personal name.) In contrast to the use in chapter 1 of *'ĕlōhîm* alone, with its emphasis on the sovereignty and power of God, this *tôlᵉdôt* uses the name *Yahweh*, with its emphasis on the personal and covenantal nature of God. After all, the Lord breathes life into the man and directly declares his commandment to him.

The Lord God's creative act is here portrayed with the word *yāṣar*, "formed." The term signifies that this act of creation was by design, an idea demonstrated by the use of a related noun later in the book: "Every intent [*yēṣer*] of the thoughts of his heart was evil" (6:5). The idea of intent or design in forming the man can also be illustrated by the participial use of this verb, which means "potter" (*yôṣer*; e.g., Jer. 18:2–4).

Besides stressing that humankind is a work of art according to the design of the Creator, the passage also explains that humankind is earthly. The whole act is clarified by the notice that the Lord God used dust from the ground to form the man. The paronomasia in the line underscores this fact: "The Lord God formed the man [*hā'ādām*] from the dust of the ground [*hā'ădāmâ*]." "Man" (*'ādām*) in this section thus refers to the first human, but then also to humankind. Since the first man came from the ground, he and all human beings are inseparably bound to it (see Job 4:19; 10:9; Isa. 29:16). Moreover, the allusion to this passage after the fall retains the proper perspective: "dust you are" (Gen. 3:19).

To this body of dust was imparted the "breath [*nᵉšāmâ*] of life." This word for breath is used in the Bible for God and for the life imparted to man—never for animals (see Mitchell, "Old Testament Usage"). Here the very breath of God is being given in a moment of inspiration. This breath brings more than animation to the man of earth (2:7); it brings spiritual understanding (Job 32:8) and a functioning conscience (Prov. 20:27). In short, we may conclude that moral capacity is granted to human beings by virtue of this inbreathing. It truly is a breath of life; that is, it produces life. It probably is this inbreathing that constitutes humankind as the image of God.

Finally, according to Genesis 2:7, the combining of the physical body and the divine breath produces the "living being." This expression is often translated "living soul." The Hebrews, however, did not think in terms of a soul apart from the body. Rather, the word (nepeš, "soul," describes the whole person—the soul in the body, or a human being with all the appetites (nepeš may include the idea of "throat," in the sense of a breathing person). The expression "living being" is used for animals (e.g., 2:19), but "image" never is; nor, apparently, is "breath of life." Like the animals, man is a living, breathing being; unlike the animals, however, he arrived at that state in a way that assuredly distinguishes him from the animals.

By this verse, then, the nation of Israel would see that humankind was created with great care and planning, so that it would have the capacity to serve the Lord God. Without the details of God's providing men and women with these spiritual capacities, the rest of the chapter would not carry the same force.

II. Humankind has the responsibility to keep God's commandments in order to enjoy life (8–17).

A. Abundant provisions (8–14).

The record of the creation of human beings includes God's provision for them and their responsibility to him. This second section of the passage begins with a description of the bountiful provision God made for the man. Since the garden also provides the setting for the testing, the purpose of the lavish description must inevitably lead to the giving of the commandment—Adam can enjoy it all but must not eat the forbidden fruit.

The focus of this description quickly turns to the trees in the garden, for they will form a major motif in chapter 3. The grammatical constructions probably indicate that the tree of life produced life (that is, it is not a genitive of attribute meaning "a living tree"), and the tree of knowledge produced knowledge—or rather, the eating of it would. With the mention of this tree, we are introduced to "good and evil," a predominant theme of Genesis. To eat from this tree would bring the experience of "good and evil." An individual would bring evil alongside the existing good and would be able to elevate life or put it in danger.

The tree of life was apparently a means of preserving life in the blissful state.

The description of the garden is followed by a long parenthetical section that traces the rivers flowing out from the one source and the precious gems and gold that were in that region (2:10–14). The text, by its construction, is digressing to relate the richness of the lands of the known world to the origin of the garden. According to Westermann, "The purpose is to state that the rivers which bring fertility (= blessing) to the world have their origin in the river which brings fertility (= blessing) to the garden of God" (*Genesis*, vol. 1, p. 216). The mention of precious gems forms a motif in the primeval tradition (Ezek. 28:13) that will be predominant in the eschaton (Rev. 21:18–21), as if to say that paradise will be restored. In fact, the term "paradise" has become applicable to both the garden and heaven. (The word comes from the Greek translation of "garden"; see also Luke 23:43.)

B. Obedient service (15–17).

The vocabulary in verses 15–17 strikingly points to the spiritual nature of the man's responsibility. First, the word translated "placed" is actually from the word for "rest" (*nûaḥ*). It means "placed" in this passage, but the choice of a word with overtones of "rest" is important (cf. *śîm*, "put," in 2:8). The word is cognate to "rest" (*menûḥâ*), which is used in Psalm 95:11 to refer to rest in the Promised Land. Genesis 2:15 thus must have some connection with the biblical teaching of Sabbath rest in the Bible (see vv. 1–3 and Heb. 3:7–4:11).

The two infinitives (translated "to serve it" and "to keep it") are also significantly chosen. These two verbs are used throughout the Pentateuch for spiritual service. "Keep" (*šāmar*) is used for keeping the commandments and taking heed to obey God's Word; "serve" (*ʿabad*) describes the worship and service of the Lord, the highest privilege a person can have. Whatever activity the man was to engage in in the garden (and there is no reason to doubt that physical activity was involved), it was described in terms of spiritual service of the Lord.

Cassuto questions whether the idea of gardening should even be retained (*Commentary on Genesis*, vol. 1, pp. 122–23). He notes the meanings of these words but adds the observation that "to till the ground" was a result of the expulsion from the garden after the curse (3:23) and therefore could not be the original purpose. Also, at that expulsion, the task of keeping (*šāmar*) the way to the tree was given over to the angels. The use of the two verbs at the end of chapter 3 suggests that the original purpose of man's being put in the garden was more significant than previously thought. Cassuto also contends that variant readings in some manuscripts suggest that the verbs are not infinitives with suffixes but gerunds (meaning "for serving and keeping"). The evidence for the textual reading may not be overwhelmingly convincing, and the argument based on the contrast with the result of the curse may be explained as a change of object only, but the significant words selected do support a higher purpose than gardening, as it later came to be known.

Verse 16 continues the emphasis with the use of *ṣiwwâ*, "command," the major word for commandment in the law. Here is the first commandment given in the Bible, and it concerns life or death for good or evil. As with God's subsequent commands, there are positive blessings and negative prohibitions. In this passage, all earthly goods and pleasures are at the man's disposal (the infinitive stressing "you may eat to your heart's content"), except this one tree of the knowledge of good and evil (the infinitive strengthening the certainty of the death: "You shall surely die"). Westermann explains that this prohibition in no way means that the man will be deprived of anything. It actually enlarges his potential; for by hearing it and obeying it, the man stands in a new relationship with the one giving the command (*Genesis*, vol. 1, p. 224).

This concept of death needs thorough study because it is a major theme in Genesis, especially in the early part of the book concerning the spread of sin. The basic idea seems to be more of alienation or separation rather than cessation or annihilation. The death predicted here certainly includes physical death, as Genesis 5 attests, but it involves more than just physical death, in view of the struggle in the surrounding context between God's blessing and cursing.

The man, who was created with spiritual capacity and provided with God's bounty, must therefore live obediently in his service of God, for his life is at stake.

III. Humankind has the provision of complementary help in serving God and keeping his commandments (18–25).

The third section of the passage describes the creation of the woman as the man's complement. This section is also the foundation of the institution of marriage, so it has great bearing on the mainstay of Israel's society. Whatever interpretations are given to the comments about the woman and marriage, they must be developed in light of the context: God intended that the man and the woman be a spiritual, functional unity, walking in integrity, serving him, and keeping his commandments. If this pattern prevailed, the nation would live and prosper under God's good hand of blessing.

A. The man's incompleteness (18–20).

The narrative begins with the striking announcement by God that the man is not yet as God had planned to be. Adam is alone, and that state is not good—the only thing in creation that is not good in God's opinion. Since the idea of "good" describes that which is appropriate and fitting within the purpose of creation, the man's being alone was not good, because he could not do all that God had planned for humankind. As he began to function as God's representative, naming the animals that God brought to him, he became very aware of his solitude. Being alone is a negative concept, for the full life is found in community (see Eccl. 4:9–12; Jer. 16:1–9). The tension of the man's incompleteness continues to build until God fulfills his resolution of verse 18.

B. Humankind's completeness (21–25).

Certain expressions in this context require careful attention. One is the word "helper" (ʿēzer), a term seldom given the proper exposition. It may be difficult to improve on the English translation; however, it is important for the exposition to trace its usage. In that way it will soon become apparent that "helper" is not a demeaning term. God is usually the one described as the "helper" (Exod. 18:4; Deut. 33:7; 1 Sam. 7:12; Ps. 20:2; 46:1). The word essentially describes one who provides what is lacking in the man, who can do what the man alone cannot do. (The Septuagint translated the word with boēthos, which elsewhere describes a physician.) The man was thus created in such a way that he needs the help of a partner. Or we may say that human beings cannot fulfill their destiny except in mutual assistance (see Delitzsch, *New Commentary on Genesis*, vol. 1, p. 140).

A second expression that the expositor must explain is kᵉnegdô, "corresponding to him." This word means "according to his opposite" (neged meaning "opposite," "over against," or "counterpart"). It means that the woman would share the man's nature; that is, whatever the man received at creation, she too would have. In support of this view we may recall that Genesis 1:27 makes it clear that the image of God is "male and female." The man and the woman thus corresponded physically, socially, and spiritually. As Delitzsch describes her, the woman by relative difference but essential equality would be man's fitting complement. What he lacked ("not good") she supplied; and it would be safe to say that what she lacked, he supplied, for life in common requires mutual help.

The idea of "one flesh" expresses the complete personal community of one man and one woman as spiritual unity. The passage does not deal with any restrictions or instructions of the one over the other, because they form a spiritual and intellectual unity. They are living in their integrity, absolutely without sin, as the motif of nakedness suggests. Prior to the fall there was no need of hierarchy or submission, since the pair had not experienced evil in any way.

Genesis, then, unfolds the careful planning of God simply and profoundly. The man was made aware that he by himself was incomplete, so that, when God prepared the woman and presented her to him, he was overjoyed. At last he found the complementary partner, for the woman shared his nature. His joyful couplet stresses this relation with his "flesh of my flesh" and "bone of my bones," and it culminates in the paronomasia between "woman" and "man" (*'iššâ* and *'îš*, although from different roots, sound the same). The point of this jubilant cry is that the creation of humankind has reached its goal in the complementary partnership of man and woman. This emphasis on the meaning of woman is unique in ancient Near Eastern texts.

The epilogue to the passage explains that this account provides the foundation of marriage. (The "therefore" [*'al kēn*] formula is frequent in Genesis.) If God is the speaker then the verse must be in the future tense; but if the narrator (the view more consistent with usage), then it would be translated in the present tense: "This is why a man leaves." The divine plan for marriage, then, is one man and one woman becoming one flesh and living together in their integrity. For the sake of the wife the man leaves the strong bond of his parents and unites with her.

The final verse informs us that the two were naked and had no shame. They were at ease with one another, without fear of exploitation for evil. This integrity was shattered by the fall and regained only gradually and imperfectly in marriage as the two begin to feel at ease with each other. Their nakedness was literal, but it also signified something far more—as chapter 3 will show.

The main point of the whole unit, then, could be stated as follows: *God has prepared human beings, male and female, with the spiritual capacity and communal assistance to serve him and to keep his commands so that they might live and enjoy the bounty of his creation.* People have spiritual capacity, moral responsibility, and mutual assistance—albeit flawed by sin—because God so designed life. In writing such an expositional idea I used the present perfect to reflect the view that the narrative is about an act of creation in the remote past but that it still describes human nature and responsibility.

The primary application of this theological idea relates to the people of God under Moses, as the epilogue to the passage indicates. The passage tells how God prepared humans with a specific design and moral capacity; how he set them in a luxuriant land to be his servants, warning them that before them was life or death, depending on their obedience to his commandments; and how he gave them the community of marriage for their joy and help. These motifs reappear in the message of Deuteronomy 30:11–20, which sets out the instructions for the nation of Israel. Verses 15 through 20 read as follows:

See, I have set before you today life and good, death and evil, in that I
command you today to love the LORD your God, to walk in his ways, and
to keep his commandments, his statutes, and his judgments, that you
may live and multiply; and the LORD your God will bless you in the land
which you go to possess. But if your heart turns away so that you do not
hear, and are drawn away, and worship other gods and serve them, I announce to you today that you shall surely perish; you shall not prolong
your days in the land which you cross over Jordan to go in and possess.
I call heaven and earth as witnesses today against you, that I have set
before you life and death, blessing and cursing; therefore, choose life,
that both you and your descendants may live; that you may love the
LORD your God, that you may obey his voice, and that you may cling to
him, for he is your life and the length of your days; and that you may
dwell in the land which the LORD swore to your fathers, to Abraham,
Isaac, and Jacob, to give them.

The Christian likewise can relate this passage to the teachings of the
New Testament. Accordingly, when people are regenerated they become
new creations. They have a renewed spiritual capacity to serve God and
obey his commandments (see John 20:22 for the inbreathing of the Spirit).
And they too see that the communal assistance within marriage is a
vital part of meeting the design of the Creator.

Bibliography

Amiran, Ruth. "Myths of the Creation of Man and the Jericho Statues." *BA-
SOR* 167 (1962): 23–25.

Andreasen, Niels-Erik. "Adam and Adapa: Two Anthropological Characters."
AUSS 19 (1981): 179–94.

Buchanan, G. W. "The Old Testament Meaning of the Knowledge of Good and
Evil." *JBL* 75 (1956): 114–20.

Clark, William. "A Legal Background to the Yahwist's Use of 'Good and Evil'
in Genesis 2–3." *JBL* 88 (1969): 266–78.

Clines, D. J. A. "The Tree of Knowledge and the Law of Yahweh." *VT* 24 (1974):
8–14.

Engnell, I. " 'Knowledge' and 'Life' in the Creation Story.' *VTS* 3 (1955): 103–19.

Gordis, R. "The Knowledge of Good and Evil in the Old Testament and the
Qumran Scrolls." *JBL* 76 (1957): 123–38.

James, E. D. *The Tree of Life: An Archaeological Study.* Leiden: E. J. Brill, 1966.

McKenzie, John L. "The Literary Characteristics of Genesis 2–3." *ThS* 15 (1954):
541–72.

Marcus, R. "The Tree of Life in Proverbs." *JBL* 62 (1943): 117–20.

May, H. G. "The Sacred Tree on Palestine Painted Pottery." *JAOS* 59 (1939): 251–59.

Mitchell, T. C. "The Old Testament Usage of Nᵉšāmâ." *VT* 11 (1961): 177–87.

Nielson, E. "Creation and the Fall of Man." *HUCA* 43 (1972): 1–22.

Rosenzweig, Michael L. "A Helper Equal to Him." *Judaism* 139 (1986): 277–80.

Speiser, E. A. "The Rivers of Paradise." In *Oriental and Biblical Studies*, edited by J. J. Finkelstein and Moshe Greenberg, pp. 23–34. Philadelphia: University of Pennsylvania Press, 1967.

Walsh, Jerome T. "Genesis 2:4–3:24: A Synchronic Approach." *JBL* 96 (1977): 161–77.

Witfall, W. "The Breath of His Nostrils: Gen. 2:7." *CBQ* 36 (1974): 237–40.

7

The Temptation and the Fall
(Gen. 3:1–7)

The subject matter in these verses is the temptation that led to disobedience. The unit provides a perfect test case for the subject of temptation, for the disobedience cannot be blamed on the environment, and certainly not on heredity. The reader sees in this story the clear working of temptation.

The story is archetypical, as are so many of the stories in Genesis. On the literal level the account reports how sin entered into the human race. It explains that the human race came into its fallen state through the disobedience of the human parents in the garden, for God surely did not create humans in their present condition. The presence of evil in the race began in the garden.

On the archetypical level the story describes the process of temptation that occurs repeatedly in human experience. Here the story achieves its didactic element teaching us not to be ignorant of Satan's devices (2 Cor. 2:11). Accordingly, the people of God may learn to resist the Tempter.

Theological Ideas

Several theological ideas come to the fore in this brief section. One concerns the Word of the Lord once again. In chapter 1, the Word of the

130

Lord was the powerful means of creation—everything achieved its fixed place in the universe because it obeyed (cf. Ps. 33:9). In chapter 2, the Word of the Lord was formulated into a direct commandment for the humans to obey. But now in chapter 3, there is some question over the precise wording and meaning of the commandment of the Lord. It cannot be fortuitous that Eve lacks precision in the wording, whereas the serpent does not. This contrast in itself would be a sufficient lesson for the nation that received the Lord's commandments and decisions (i.e., the Torah).

Behind the discussion between Eve and the serpent about the precise wording of the commandment is the issue of the divine motive in giving the law. A second theological motif to develop would thus be the integrity of God. How can anyone eagerly obey the commandments of God unless it can be demonstrated that his laws are good for the people? An appreciation of God's goodness is essential to the keeping of the law.

In this context it may be helpful to compare the descriptions of the pagan deities in all their caprice as well as the symbols and representations of their power. One such symbol was the serpent. If the nations of the ancient Near East surrounding Israel venerated the serpent as the life-giving goddess of the earth, then the representation in this passage strikes a remarkably antithetical theme. The story takes on a polemic nature.

Finally, this passage contains early traces of wisdom motifs. The desire to be wise has remained with humankind throughout the ages, but the acquisition of biblical wisdom is quite different than the attempt made by Eve. According to later sages, the beginning of wisdom is the fear of the Lord, but in this account the desire for wisdom follows a course of disobedience. No one can achieve divine wisdom in this way. Consequently, this disobedience resulted in Adam and Eve's fearing the Lord, as the next unit will state (v. 8)—but this fear is very different from that which Proverbs 1:7 enjoins.

Structure and Synthesis

Structure

The account of the temptation is, of course, part of the larger context about sin and the curse. But it would be very difficult to include the entire chapter in one exegetical exposition if one is to do justice to the passage. The first seven verses form a unit on the temptation and the fall into sin, and the rest of the chapter records the results.

The passage develops with dialogue and description. The dialogue is between the serpent and the woman over the nature of the command. In 3:1b, the serpent used the commandment in the form of a question in order to engage the woman in conversation. The woman's attempt to paraphrase the commandment in response to the question reveals several telling changes (vv. 2–3); the serpent then boldly denied the Word of the Lord (v. 4). It is interesting that three times the Word of the Lord is quoted, but never appropriately: once it is questioned in a misleading way, once it is paraphrased with major changes, and once it is flatly denied.

The analysis of the descriptions in the story must incorporate the repetition of words as well as the use of circumstantial clauses. Probably Genesis 2:25 should be used as a general connecting verse between the two passages, for it lays the foundation for the motif of nakedness in chapter 3. If it is used to begin this narrative, then it forms an inclusio with verse 7, which records that the man and the woman knew that they were naked. In between these two notices of nakedness is the explanation of how Adam and Eve moved from innocent nakedness to shameful nakedness, or from integrity to guilt.

The mention of "naked" (ʿărûmmîm) in 2:25 also forms a significant word play on the word "subtle" (ʿārûm) in the description of the serpent (3:1). This play underscores the fact that the integrity of the human was the target of the serpent's attack—it was his area of expertise.

Another motif that ties the structure together is that of knowing. The serpent's explanation of the prohibition was that God "knows" (yōdēaʿ) that if they eat they will become like God, "knowing" (yōdeʿê) good and evil (v. 5). Then, when the woman concentrated on the tree (v. 6), she saw that it was good, pleasant, and desirable—the knowledge of evil was not in her thoughts. But after the man and the woman ate from the tree, "they knew [wayyēdeʿû] that they were naked" and tried to cover themselves (v. 7). Now the knowledge of evil was overwhelming. Westermann notes that "being ashamed is rather a reaction to being discovered unmasked" (Genesis, vol. 1, p. 236).

The structure of verse 6 is also significant. The circumstantial clauses of the first half of the verse may be subordinated to the second: "When she saw . . ., she took. . . ." The significant point, then, is the shift from Eve's thinking to the rapid succession of events in the verbs: "she took . . . and ate . . . and gave . . . and he ate also." The dialogue and the descriptions retard the progress of the account as if to hold it out for investigation; but once the temptation is finished, the story line follows rapidly with the account of the fall.

Summary Message

The serpent raised serious doubt about the Word of God and the goodness of God in giving the commandment, with the result that the appeal of the forbidden tree to the senses of the woman prompted her to eat from the tree and also to give to her husband.

Exegetical Outline

   I. Prologue: The humans were unashamedly naked (2:25), but the serpent was the craftiest of all God's creatures (3:1a).

  II. The serpent engaged the woman in a discussion about the prohibition of God's Word (1b–3).

    A. The serpent questioned the woman about God's commandment (1b).

    B. The woman explained what God had said, but in the process made several significant changes (2–3).

      1. She disparaged the privileges God had given (2–3a).

      2. She added to the prohibition (3b).

      3. She minimized the penalty for disobedience (3c).

 III. The serpent denied the penalty for sin, raising doubts about the integrity of God in giving the commandment (4–5).

    A. The serpent boldly denied the Word of the Lord (4).

    B. The serpent cast doubt on the integrity of God (5).

 IV. When the woman concentrated on the forbidden tree with all its appeal to her senses, she disobeyed the Lord and ate from the tree and gave to her husband to eat (6).

    A. The appeal of the forbidden fruit to the senses was sufficient to draw the woman into sin (6a).

      1. Practical: It was good for food.

      2. Aesthetic: It was pleasing to look at.

      3. Spiritual: It would make one wise.

    B. The woman ate and gave also to her husband to eat (6b).

  V. Aftermath: The man and the woman suffered the consequences of their disobedience, namely, the knowledge of sin (7).

Development of the Exposition

Although other developments of this passage are possible, I would concentrate on the theme of temptation that leads to the fall. The section on the dialogue serves to remove the barriers to sin, and the appeal to the senses then prompts the sin.

I. Temptation raises questions about the Word of God (1–3).

A. The Tempter (1a).

After God comes the serpent, whom the New Testament identifies as the devil (Rev. 12:9). In the former chapters what God said was very clear; now what God said becomes a matter of debate prompted by the serpent. The Word of the Lord in the preceding chapters brought life and order; the words of the serpent now bring chaos and death. God's Word is older than Satan's lies, but Satan's lies are so shrewdly expressed that they are most often effective.

The prologue to the story introduces the nature of the serpent as "shrewd," or "crafty." This line could be treated prior to the first point of the exposition, but it may be more effective to include it as part of the work of temptation. That the Tempter was a serpent indicates that temptation came in a disguise. It came from a subordinate creature, one over whom humans were to exercise dominion (cf. Matt. 16:21–23). The appeal from a subordinate apparently took Eve by surprise, for she was engaged in conversation before she had a chance to think.

The appearance of a crafty snake prompting Eve to sin is a mystery. The text is interested neither in the origin of evil in the snake nor in the nature of the snake. It primarily is concerned with what the snake said. The narrative leaves all the other questions enshrouded in mystery.

The description of the serpent as "shrewd" ('ārûm) is powerful, in view of the notice in the preceding verse that the two of them were naked ('ărûmmîm). The word "shrewd" (or "crafty") carries the idea of being wary, of knowing where the traps lay and the dangers lurked. That quality of shrewdness is not evil in itself, for according to Proverbs 1:4, the naive person and the simpleton need to cultivate it. But here the craftiness will be used for an evil purpose. This word play with "naked" supports the idea that the mention of their nakedness implies that they were oblivious to evil, not knowing where the dangers lay.

B. The Tempter's question (1b).

Not only did temptation come in disguise and craftiness, but it raised questions about the commandment of God. (Note that the serpent could speak only of "God"; the name "Yahweh," or the Lord, belonged to the context of the relation of humans to God.) The method was shrewd and calculated. It was not a direct denial of God's commandment—not yet, anyway. The question raised was not easy to answer, for it left several possible answers open. Its purpose, however, was to engage the woman in a discussion about the commandment. It gave the woman an oppor-tunity to justify herself and defend God.

C. The Tempter's discovery (2–3).

In the woman's response to the serpent's question, it became clear that the precision of the Word of the Lord had not been retained. There are three changes that she made. First, she minimized the provision of the Lord. The Lord had said, "You may freely eat" ('ākōl tō'kēl), but Eve simply said, "We may eat" (nō'kēl). Second, she added to the prohibition. The Lord had said nothing about touching the tree, but Eve said that God (she used the serpent's designation) said, "Neither shall you touch it" (wᵉlō' tiggᵉ'û). Von Rad says that it is as though she wanted to set a law for herself by means of this exaggeration (Genesis, p. 86). Third, she weakened the penalty for the sin. God had declared, "You shall surely die" (môt tāmût), but Eve said, "lest you die" (pen-tᵉmūtûn). Concentration on such a forbidden object very easily led her to these modifications—unless Adam had told her incorrectly.

The changes that were made between this verse and the giving of the commandment are within the legitimate range of interpretation. There is no violation in free paraphrasing of the words of the Lord. However, if the precise wording of the original commandment is weakened, the appeal to sin grows stronger. "Lest you die" carries the meaning of God's warning, but it does not clearly retain the certainty of the penalty of death. As Westermann commented, "A command that is questioned is no longer the original command" (Genesis, vol. 1, p. 239).

II. Temptation raises doubts about the integrity of God (4–5).

A. The Tempter's denial of God's Word (4).

When the serpent saw that the woman had not retained a precise knowledge of God's words, he denied the penalty of death. It is striking here that his words were much closer to the original decree; he said, "You shall not surely die [lō'-môt tᵉmūtûn]." The construction of the Hebrew stresses the boldness of this denial: "not—you shall surely die." In the normal construction the negative would precede the finite verb, but here it is simply placed in front of the entire construction. What was at first a question about the prohibition now became a denial of the consequence of disobedience.

Here is the lie that has allured the human race from the beginning (see John 8:44): there is no punishment for disobedience. But the Bible again and again makes it clear that no one can get away with sin. Disobedience brings death.

B. The Tempter's explanation of God's motive (5).

Not only did the serpent deny the Word of God, but he also raised doubts about the integrity of God in order to justify the disobedience. His explanation of God's motive in giving the law was that God was jealous and was holding them back from their destiny. According to the serpent, God knew that when they ate they would be like God, knowing good and evil. The Tempter thus held out the promise of divinity to them.

This knowledge of good and evil was and is intriguing. Adam and Eve lived in a setting that God himself had pronounced "good." Yet they were now led to believe that there was greater good held back from them, that somehow they could elevate life for the better. But with the knowledge of good there was also the knowledge of evil, that potential of putting life in danger or of destroying it altogether. This potential they underestimated.

In raising doubt about God's integrity, the serpent motivated them to sin with the promise of divinity. The idea of becoming like God has an appeal that is almost irresistible (note the thought in Isa. 14:14, which, although probably not a reference to Satan, does portray the magnitude of this temptation). Yet, being led by a subordinate is, as Kidner remarks, "a curious way to achieve divinity" (*Genesis*, p. 68).

III. Temptation succeeds with an appeal to the senses (6).

A. The appeal of sin (6a).

The work of the Tempter was finished. He had removed the barrier to their eating—Eve was no longer convinced that God would punish them for it. And he had brought them to the brink of sin with his rationalization—Eve thought that God was holding them back from divinity. Now the appeal of the forbidden fruit was sufficient to draw them into sin.

Practicality for food, aesthetic beauty, and the potential for wisdom—the physical, emotional, and spiritual senses—all worked together to draw Eve into sin. The new possibilities of life enticed Eve to eat. This threefold description of what Eve perceived seems to be reflected in John's "lust of the flesh, lust of the eyes, and the pride of life" (1 John 2:16). Natural desires for food, beauty, and knowledge are gifts from God but are to be used within his restrictions. The world ignores these restrictions.

The words used in Eve's reflection are significant. First, the words *ta'ăwâ* ("pleasant") and *neḥmād* ("desirable") are cognate to the Hebrew verbs translated "covet" in the Ten Commandments; both verbs are used in Deuteronomy 5:21, but only the second occurs in Exodus 20:17. Strong desire such as Eve's, or coveting as the commandment prohibits, is usually followed by an unlawful taking, as it was here. This story, then, would have been instructive for Israel about the folly of acting on desire. Second, Eve's reflection concentrates on the potential good of the fruit and ignores the evil that there is in disobedience. And third, the use of the word for wisdom (*lĕhaśkîl*, "to make one wise") introduces the strongest appeal to the woman. To be wise is to have mental and spiritual acumen. She clearly believed the serpent's lie but realized her mistake too late. Later Paul would say that the world by its wisdom did not know God and that the wisdom of the world is foolishness with God (1 Cor. 1:26–2:16; 3:18).

B. The act of sin (6b).

Finally, the sin of Eve is reported, but it is reported in rapid succession with a sequence of verbs: she took, she ate, she gave, and he ate also. It is typical of narrative art in Genesis that more time is given to the dialogue and the tension; afterward the resolution is quickly reported. It is a way of stressing that the didactic material comes in the dialogue and the description.

The comment that the man ate also is important. The text thereby shows that he needed no temptation with clever words—he simply went along with the crime. His way that led to transgression was willful conformity. The New Testament says that Eve was beguiled, but man sinned willfully (1 Tim. 2:14; Rom. 5:12, 17–19).

Kidner makes an interesting observation on the coincidence of words used in the Bible; he notes that the verbs "take" and "eat" describe a very simple act in the garden. That act, however, required a very costly remedy, for the Lord himself would have to taste death before these verbs became verbs of salvation (Genesis, p. 68).

IV. Aftermath: The knowledge of evil brings alienation (7).

The results, of course, were anticlimactic. Their eyes (i.e., their understanding) were opened, but the promise of divine enlightenment did not come about. What was right before was now very wrong. They knew more, but that additional knowledge was evil. They saw more, but what they now saw they spoiled by seeing. Mistrust and alienation replaced the security and intimacy they had enjoyed. They attempted futilely to cover themselves with leaves.

The message to Israel, and to all God's people, should now be clear: *A thorough knowledge of the Word of God and an unwavering trust in the goodness of God are absolutely essential for spiritual victory over the world, the flesh, and the devil.* The appeal by the Tempter to humankind's desire to know, under the guise of spiritual development, is thereby set aside. In practical terms, this lesson would mean for Israel that the subtle claims of the pagans to achieve divinity and superior knowledge through their corrupt practices were false. The people of God were to avoid the satanic appeal to an elevated life and superior knowledge if that appeal also required transgressing God's barriers.

It is no surprise, then, that the Old Testament is filled with instructions for the people to know the Word of God, to memorize it, and to use it to discern truth from error (e.g., Deut. 6:5–9, 13–25; Ps. 119:9–16). Accordingly, we find that Jesus resisted temptation by his superior knowledge of the Word of God—he quoted three times from Deuteronomy—when he was engaged by Satan's use of the Word (Matt. 4). The temptations offered to Jesus were also shrewd; they were temptations to physical and spiritual achievements by disobedience to the Father. Such temptations can be rejected only through the use of Scripture (Heb. 5:14).

God's people must therefore have a wholehearted trust in the goodness of God, a precise knowledge of the Word of God, and an obedient fear of God himself. They must remember that they are human and not divine and therefore must obey him. True wisdom may be attained through compliance with the commandments of the Lord.

Bibliography

Coats, G. W. "The God of Death: Power and Obedience in the Primeval History." *Interp* 29 (1975): 227–39.

Combs, E. "The Political Teaching of Genesis I–XI." In *Studia Biblica*, pp. 105–10. *JSOT* Supplement 11. Sheffield: Sheffield University Press, 1979.

Gordis, R. "The Significance of the Paradise Myth." *AJSL* 52 (1935–36): 84–86.

Habel, N. C. "Ezekiel 28 and the Fall of the First Man." *CTM* 38 (1967): 516–24.

Joines, K. R. "The Serpent in Gen. 3." *ZAW* 87 (1975): 1–11.

May, H. G. "The King in the Garden of Eden: A Study of Ezekiel 28:12–19." In *Israel's Prophetic Heritage: Essays in Honor of James Muilenberg*, edited by Bernhard W. Anderson and Walter Harrelson, pp. 166–76. New York: Harper and Brothers, 1962.

Reicke, Bo. "The Knowledge Hidden in the Tree of Paradise." *JSS* 1 (1956): 193–201.

Sayce, A. T. "The Serpent in Genesis." *ExT* 20 (1909): 562.

Stern, H. S. "The Knowledge of Good and Evil." *VT* 8 (1958): 405–18.

8

The Oracles of God at the Fall
(Gen. 3:8–24)

The second part of Genesis 3 reports the effects of sin in the human race. It is therefore a natural extension of the first seven verses of the chapter, which report the temptation and the disobedience. In fact, the present narrative continues the development begun at the beginning of the tôlᵉdôt. As George Coats says, "The structure of the unit leans on two pillars: an account of paradise gained (2:8–17) and an account of paradise lost (3:1–24)." He adds that they could not have been independent of each other but that they stand together as a unit, the one a reflex of the other (*Genesis*, p. 51). Whereas Adam and Eve had life, they now will have death; where they had pleasure, they now will have pain; where abundance, now a meager sustenance by toil; where perfect harmony with God and with each other, now alienation and conflict.

The passage falls into three sections: the confrontation by the Lord, in which the sinners, hearing him, fear and hide in the midst of the garden; the oracles of the Lord, in which the new order is declared for the serpent, the woman, and the man; and the provision of clothing from the Lord, in which the human instinct to cover guilt is superseded by the Lord.

139

Different kinds of genre are employed in this section. Most noticeably there are oracles from the Lord, written in poetic form. But we also find narrative report that includes dialogue (interrogation) in the first part and soliloquy in the last part. The general classification of the whole unit must be the same as in the other parts of the *tôl^edôt*, for the same variety exists. Von Rad rightly observes that the unit teaches doctrine, a particular world view (*Genesis*, p. 63). And yet, as we have observed, it is written in the form of history. It uses past events as the basis of, and pattern for, the teaching. Coats concludes that the genre of the section so far (2:4–3:24) could be classified as *report*, a genre that communicates events for the sake of the communication and its implications (*Genesis*, p. 47). But Coats then adds that such a classification does not mean that it is history writing, and accordingly he labels the section "Paradise Tale." This is an unwarranted interpretation.

Theological Ideas

The major theological theme of the narrative encompasses the Lord's response to the disobedience. At first the Lord interrogated the participants in order to obtain a confession. Then he declared the new conditions of life, in view of the presence of evil: conflict, pain, and death. But finally, he provided clothing for the humans and kept them away from the tree of life. The Lord once again is the sovereign and majestic subject of the narrative. Whereas his previous actions revealed him as the Creator and Benefactor, this narrative demonstrates him to be a compassionate Judge of sinners.

In conjunction with this dominant theme, the passage clarifies the task and the hope of human beings. What must sinners do? They must confess their sin and trust in God's goodness for provision of life. What can sinners hope for? They can look forward to release from the curse and anticipate the ultimate victory over evil. These themes would be illuminating for Israel, a nation of slaves toiling and perishing at the hand of the Egyptians, for in hearing the oracles they could understand why such evil existed, and they could hope for relief and victory.

Many subordinate theological motifs contribute to this overall picture. First, there is the divine provision for the confessing sinners. An animal's life was apparently taken and its skin used to cover their shame. Here began the pattern of substitution that the Israelites would experience every time an animal was sacrificed in their place and its skin given to the priests. In addition, the symbolism of clothing finds its beginning here. Adam and Eve first clothed themselves with leaves, which was the proper response to shame and guilt, but the only satisfactory clothing would have to come from God.

Second, angels (cherubim) guard the way to the tree of life. The way to life is available, but only in the way God would provide it. Later in the tabernacle the embroidered curtains held up the images of cherubim before the people, warning them that access to God and to life is prevented for sinners in a sinful state. Likewise, Leviticus 26 and Deuteronomy 11 make it clear that temporal and spiritual blessings in the Land of Promise were available to those who followed the way God established in the law.

Third, the effect of evil on human nature and human relations is vividly portrayed in the passage. We discover fear as a result of guilt, self-vindication before confession, perpetual conflict within the human experience, and the struggle for domination and manipulation among humans. But life continues with the birth of children, and hope exists with the anticipation of a victorious seed.

The Christian expositor thinks of Jesus Christ, the last Adam (1 Cor. 15:45), the Seed of the woman (Gal. 3:16–19; 4:4), in relation to this narrative. With the revelation of the New Testament we are able to see how the human race would ultimately gain victory—it would come through one who took upon himself the curse of the whole world. The motifs in this chapter—toil, sweat, thorns, the conflict, the tree, death, dust, and the seed—all will be reflected in the experience of the Christ, who became the curse, sweat great drops of blood in bitter agony, wore a crown of thorns, hung on a tree until he was dead, and was placed in the dust of death (cf. Ps. 22:15). This culmination of God's provision for the sinful race, however, does not come into focus in Genesis 3:8–24.

Structure and Synthesis

Structure

In addition to the overall development of the narrative in the three major sections mentioned above, there is also a deliberate arrangement in an inverted (chiastic) order. First, there is the Lord's interrogation of the man (3:9–12) and then the interrogation of the woman (v. 13). These are followed by the oracle for the serpent (vv. 14–15), the oracle for the woman (v. 16), and finally the oracle for the man (vv. 17–19). We thus have man—woman—serpent—woman—man. The focus on the serpent is central to the arrangement, which is where the perpetual struggle of good and evil is announced.

Certain motifs in this narrative serve to unite the passage with the whole *tôlᵉdôt* section. The references in the interrogation to the prohibited tree (3:11) and the confessions of having eaten from that tree (vv. 12–13) clearly show the dependence of this passage on the former. Or again, the words of the Lord in observing that the man and the woman had become like God continue the theme of knowing good and evil (2:17; 3:5; and here). Finally, the expulsion of man from the garden "to till the ground from which he was taken" (3:23) recalls and explains the circumstantial clause at the beginning (2:5). The verbs "till" (ʿābad) and "keep" (šāmar) now appear at the end of the story with a different force and use than they had earlier (2:15). Eating from one tree kept the humans from eating from the other; or if we say it in terms of the spiritual reality behind the story, when the human beings disobeyed God and experienced evil, they were prevented from living on perpetually in that state.

Summary Message

After the Lord God elicited a confession of sin from the self-vindicating sinners, he decreed just punishments for them (which were also promises of future relief), necessitating the divine provisions for covering their shame and preventing their living perpetually under the curse.

Exegetical Outline

   I. The Lord God called Adam and Eve to confess their disobedience, but they delayed their confession with attempts to vindicate themselves (8–13).

     A. Adam and Eve, ashamed of their nakedness and afraid of God, hid in the midst of the trees (8).

     B. In response to the Lord's interrogation, Adam eventually confessed that he ate, but only after blaming God for giving him the woman (9–12).

     C. In response to the Lord's interrogation, Eve also confessed, but only after shifting the blame to the serpent (13).

  II. The Lord God decreed righteous judgments—on the serpent, the woman, and the man—which also promised future relief and ultimate victory (14–19).

     A. In his curse on the serpent, God declared that there would be perpetual conflict between good and evil until the seed of the woman triumphed (14–15).

     B. In his oracle for the woman, God declared that there would be increased pain in childbirth and male domination in life (16).

     C. In his oracle for the man, God declared that there would be a curse on the earth, making human survival a painful experience that would end only through death (17–19).

 III. The Lord God provided skins to cover the nakedness of the man and his wife and prevented them from living forever in their sinful condition (20–24).

A. Adam demonstrated their faith in the Lord's words by naming his wife Eve (20).
B. God made provision for their sin and shame by providing
animal skins to clothe them (21).
C. God prevented their living on under the curse by driving
them out of the garden and hindering their return (22–24).

Development of the Exposition

A passage as complex as this one certainly lends itself to several expositions. It is most important, however, that one exposition cover the
entire narrative to show its unity and progression.

I. God calls sinners to confess their sin, not to attempt to excuse themselves (8–13).

A. Sinners, aware of their sin, avoid God through fear (8).

This verse could very easily be taken with the last section as another
result of the fall; or perhaps better, verse 7 could be joined with this
unit. Such a division would give the present narrative a nice inclusio—
their clothing themselves at the beginning and God's clothing them at
the end. Verses 7 and 8 could thus be incorporated in both the preceding
exposition and in this one.

At any rate, verse 8 indicates that the interrogation by God is of sinners hiding in fear and shame. It is not the report of sinners seeking
God, as popular expositions sometimes imply. The man and the woman
heard the sound of the Lord God moving about in the garden and they
hid themselves, a hiding that Adam explained was occasioned by fear.
(For a discussion of "cool of the day," see Cassuto, *Commentary on
Genesis*.)

There is no indication in the narratives of Genesis of long delays
between events. It appears that the temptation and fall occurred immediately after Adam and Eve's being created and placed in the garden,
possibly on the seventh day, and immediately after the sin there was the
presence of the One who knows how to ask questions. The pace makes
it hard to substantiate the popular idea that humankind enjoyed a long
period of unbroken fellowship with the Lord God in the garden. After
they sinned, then, they sensed the awesome presence of God, and they
hid themselves.

B. Sinners, confronted by God's penetrating Word, must confess their sin and not excuse themselves (9–13).

In this section the exegetical exposition must look very closely at the
Hebrew words and word order to catch the emphases in the dialogue.

1. *The man's confession (9–12)*. There are two sets of questions for the man. First, there is the rhetorical question, "Where are you?" (That God said it to the man and that the answer is not literal but explanatory indicate it is rhetorical.) Adam's answer centers on his fear because he was naked. The motif of nakedness, introduced before, obviously stands for more than a lack of covering, in view of the shame and fear that was generated over it. From this event on, all sinners will fear the Lord God when their guilt is uncovered.

Second, there is the question about Adam's disobedience. Here the word order in the Hebrew places prominence on the tree that was forbidden: "Did you, from the tree that I commanded you not to eat from, eat?" The question was whether or not he ate, but the relative clause reminded him that that eating was a direct violation of the commandment. The issue from God's point of view was clear-cut.

Adam's confession was delayed by attempts to transfer the blame to God and to the woman. The Hebrew construction (independent nominative absolute with a relative clause) indicates such an effort: "The woman, whom you gave to be with me, she gave me from the tree, and I ate." The words focus on the woman, but the relative clause blames God for providing the woman. Nevertheless, the truth finally came out: "I ate."

2. *The woman's confession (13)*. The Lord's question to the woman is worded very emphatically with a demonstrative pronoun: "What is this you have done?" It has the force of saying, "What in the world have you done?" or "Do you realize what you have done?"

Here too the woman transferred the responsibility, in this case to the serpent for beguiling her. This explanation, as well as the man's earlier one, is correct, but it does not excuse the disobedience. Ultimately her confession to God's original question came out: "I ate."

In the dialogue the Lord shows his majesty and potency by asking penetrating questions, and the humans appear fearful and defensive with evasive excuses. Eventually they did confess, and it was sufficient.

II. God declares the punishments for sin and the prospects for the sinners (14–19).

It is important at the outset for the exposition to establish the nature of these oracles. They are not commandments to be obeyed but declarations of how life now must be. For example, if a woman avoids pain in childbirth or a man, sweat in his labor, they have not violated a commandment. That they must find ways to avoid pain and prevent sweat proves that the oracles are in effect. Moreover, the oracles are not simply curses. The decrees include provisions for relief and victory as well as the punishments. In fact, the word "curse" (*'ārûr*) is used only of the serpent—from whom the Lord did not seek a confession.

A. The fall brought a perpetual struggle between good and evil (14–15).

With the curse on the serpent there is the first hint that something other than the reptile was present. Verse 14 appears to bring a curse on the animal as a perpetual reminder of the event, but verse 15 suggests that some force behind the serpent would perpetuate the struggle that took place in the garden. Accordingly, many interpreters over the years have concluded that the curse is on satanic forces as well as the reptile.

In the first part of the curse the focus seems to be on the animal used in the temptation. A comparison used in the construction shows that the serpent would be cursed more than the rest of the animals. All creation would now lie under a curse, but the serpent more so for his part in the crime. This use of the comparative degree recalls Genesis 3:1, where we were told that the serpent was more crafty than all the other animals. The punishment was thus talionic.

The idea of the curse must be clearly explained in these passages. The basic idea I presented in chapter 3 is that "curse" has the idea of banishment from the place of blessing. All of creation would now be barred from the fullness of fertility and harmony, but the serpent more than all the rest. The terms that explain his cursing speak of humility: crawling on his belly and eating dust (along with his food).

The second part of the serpent's curse pertains to a perpetual conflict that will end with the seed of the woman delivering the crushing blow after receiving the crippling blow. Much has been written about the seed of the woman, but it usually concentrates on the connection with the victory of Christ over Satan. But there is more to this passage. The immediate seed of the woman would be Cain, and then all of humanity, for she was the mother of all living. The seed of the serpent is not so easy, but by New Testament times it may have included all who rejected the Lord and opposed his kingdom (cf. "you are of your father the devil," in John 8:44). Along the way, we may say, anything that represented the forces of evil could be included in the seed of the serpent. In Genesis 4, there is an immediate outworking of the conflict between Cain, the seed of the woman, and sin that is couching at the door, whose desire was to have Cain. This struggle between good and evil would always be there in the human race, but ultimately the seed of the woman would bruise the head of the serpent's seed.

B. The fall brought the woman pain in childbirth and domination by the male (16).

In the oracle for the woman, one part deals with childbirth and the other with her relationship to the man. The first introduces great pain into the process of bearing and rearing children. The Hebrew construction must be interpreted carefully: "I will greatly multiply your pain *in* your conception." "Conception" precisely locates the pain. That this is the correct interpretation may be seen in the rest of the verse: "*in* pain you shall bring forth children."

The expositor must study the words used in this part very carefully. First, since there is no pain in conception, the word "conception" must be taken as a synecdoche representing the whole process that begins with conception. The parallel "bring forth" may give us further understanding on what is in mind. Second, the word for "pain" ($'i\d{s}\d{s}^eb\hat{o}n$) may not be limited to physical suffering in the process of childbirth. It basically means "painful toil" but can be applied to emotional as well as physical pain. The woman's susceptibility to the emotional and physical pain associated with the process of, and ability for, childbearing may have been what Peter had in mind in his description of "weaker vessels" (1 Peter 3:7).

The second part of the pronouncement on the woman also requires a close exegesis in the text. It has traditionally been translated with a supplied future tense: "Your desire *shall be* for your husband." In such a construction, however—a nominal sentence without a verb—the tense of the supplied verb must be drawn from the context. To determine what the context suggests requires a careful study of "desire."

The Hebrew word "desire" ($t^e\check{s}\hat{u}q\hat{a}$) has some of the same uses that the English word has. In this passage it is commonly explained to mean that the woman would be drawn to her husband, probably so explained on the basis of the usage in Song of Solomon. But the word also occurs in this context of Genesis with quite another meaning. According to its use in Genesis 4:7, "desire" probably should be interpreted to describe prompting to evil. The idea of the verse would then be that, because the woman prompted the man to sin in giving him something to eat, that is, taking the lead rather than maintaining a partnership, the man would have dominion over her. I would thus translate, "Your desire *was* to your husband, but he shall have the mastery over you." The punishment, then, would also be talionic for the woman. This view also finds support in verse 17 ("because you obeyed your wife").

Important to the understanding of this line is the meaning of "rule" ($m\bar{a}\check{s}al$). This word cannot be weakened to mean leadership alone, as many expositors wish to do. It is a term that describes dominion, mastery, lordship. It can have a rather harsh application. The significant point about this verse is that it is part of the punishment oracle for sin. To attempt to make it teach the submission of the woman to her husband and the loving leadership of the husband to his wife completely misses the point. Those are qualities taught in the New Testament as part of the work of the Holy Spirit; this verse is part of the oracle for sin.

How would this oracle then apply in successive generations? It may be argued that the male domination in the history of the human race is a perpetual reminder of the fall, just as is the serpent's crawling on the ground. But if Eve is an archetype, that is, if she represents every woman as Adam represents every man, then the story portrays a characteristic of human nature—the woman at her worst would be a nemesis to the man, and the man at his worst would dominate the woman.

The Christian exposition of this passage will necessarily carry the ideas to the New Testament teachings on the same theme. For believers in Jesus Christ, life in the Spirit removes the sting of the curse, so that a much more harmonious and loving relationship is envisioned than that which is declared to be a result of evil in the human race.

C. The fall brought the man the prospect of painful toil until death (17–19).

As mentioned above, the oracle for the man begins with an observation that he *obeyed* his wife and ate (note the Hebrew idiom for "obey"). There is an indication here of Adam's passiveness in the sin (note how his participation is almost an afterthought in v. 6). We may then observe that he was not beguiled; he sinned wilfully at his wife's prompting and brought sin into the human race by his act.

The judgment here is also talionic: he ate (as did she), and so he would experience painful toil in eating. The punishment would be a perpetual reminder of the sin. His work in scratching out a subsistence will be painful toil (the same word used for the pain of the woman) because the ground would be cursed, or hindered from enjoying fertility.

The man's difficult toil in life would continue until he died (a gracious provision in view of the suffering) and returned to dust to become the serpent's prey once again (see v. 14). His death, then, would not only underscore the fact that the serpent caused death to replace life but also be a reminder that human beings were earthbound, dust. So much for ambitions of divinity. Humankind may think of being like God, but God declared, "Dust you are, and unto the dust you shall return."

Shakespeare graphically portrays the irony of this in *Hamlet* (V, 1). Hamlet speaks to Horatio in the churchyard, just after finding the skull of Yorick:

To what base uses we may return, Horatio! Why may not imagination trace the noble dust of Alexander till 'a[he] find it stopping a bunghole? . . . Alexander died, Alexander was buried, Alexander returneth to dust;

the dust is earth, of earth we make loam, and why of that loam, whereto
he was converted, might they not stop a beer-barrel?

Imperious Caesar, dead and turn'd to clay,
Might stop a hole to keep the wind away.
O that that earth, which kept the world in awe,
Should patch a wall t' expel the winter's flaw!

The oracles thus all reflect talionic justice: they sinned by eating, and
so would suffer to eat; she led her husband to sin, and so would be
mastered by him; they brought pain into the world by their disobedience,
and so would have painful toil in their respective lives; and the serpent
ruined the human race, and so he would be destroyed. These declarations
list the inevitable consequences of disobedience. As long as sinful life
exists all of this evil consequence will continue, for all of it will be
repeated. The original sin of Adam and Eve brought into the race the
conflict between good and evil, with the consequent painful toil, hard-
ship, alienation, and death. Every act of disobedience perpetuates the
same effects. The only hope left from the oracles is that the human race
will not live forever in this state—death will be a release—and that there
will ultimately be victory over the seed of the serpent.

III. God makes gracious provisions for the believing sinners (20–24).

The final section of the passage stresses God's provision of protection
for the man and the woman. Now that the new order of life is fully
operative, God extends his grace to his people.

A. Faith overcomes the doom of the curse (20).

The expositor will have to look at this verse very carefully in order
to appreciate its significance in the context. At first it seems out of
place. But a closer analysis of the meaning of, and motivation for, the
name, especially in contrast with the prospect of death as a punishment
for sin, will show that it indicates Adam's faith. The whole incident
shows that they accepted their lot in a fallen world (now Adam named
his wife; in chap. 4 the woman named her children) but held on to the
positive side of it—life would continue. Their look is uplifted in faith
(contrast Cain's bitterness after his interrogation).

The name "Eve" (ḥawwâ, "living" or "life-giver"), interpreted by the
narrator as "the mother of all living [ḥay]," signifies that the woman
became a pledge in the continuation of the race, in spite of the curse.
The name celebrates the survival of the race and the victory over death.

By anticipating life it also commemorates the establishment of a new order.

B. Grace covers the sinners' shame (21).

The present verse does not mention grace or shame but strongly indicates by its contents that both were meant in the event. God's clothing of Adam and Eve with animal skins shows the divine improvement on their human effort to cover their nakedness. According to Marcus Dods,

> It is also to be remarked that the clothing which God provided was in itself different from what man had thought of. Adam took leaves from an inanimate, unfeeling tree; God deprived an animal of life, that the shame of His creature might be relieved. This was the last thing Adam would have thought of doing. To us life is cheap and death familiar, but Adam recognized death as the punishment of sin. Death was to early man a sign of God's anger. And he had to learn that sin could be covered not by a bunch of leaves snatched from a bush as he passed by and that would grow again next year, but only by pain and blood. Sin cannot be atoned for by any mechanical action nor without expenditure of feeling. Suffering must ever follow wrongdoing. From the first sin to the last, the track of the sinner is marked with blood. Once we have sinned we cannot regain permanent peace of conscience save through pain, and this not only pain of our own. The first hint of this was given as soon as conscience was aroused in man. It was made apparent that sin was a real and deep evil, and that by no easy and cheap process could the sinner be restored. The same lesson has been written on millions of consciences since. Men have found that their sin reaches beyond their own life and person, that it inflicts injury and involves disturbance and distress, that it changes utterly our relation to life and to God, and that we cannot rise above its consequences save by the intervention of God Himself, by an intervention which tells us of the sorrow He suffers on our account.
>
> For the chief point is that it is God who relieves man's shame. [*The Book of Genesis*, pp. 25–26]

C. God prevents the extension of life (22–24).

The story closes with the Lord's reasoned decision to prevent humankind from extending life in such a painful state. The reasoning in verse 22 may be literal, that humans actually had become like God in this respect, but it may also be irony, for in general they had become anything but divine. It is clear that whatever they had become was evil, for God acted to prevent them from continuing on perpetually in that condition. Consequently, he drove them out from the garden and stationed his angels and the flashing sword (possibly a reference to lightning) at the entrance of the garden.

The lesson from this narrative is timeless: *Sinful rebellion against God brings pain, conflict, and death; but confession to God ensures God's gracious provisions.* If the preceding narrative was a test case for temptation, then this narrative is one for the inevitable results of sin. Israel would be warned through it and instructed to confess their sin and receive God's gracious provisions in spite of the curse.

The point from the beginning to the end is the institution of the new order of existence for humankind, which will remain until the end of the age. Life as it was for Israel, or as it is today, is not the way God created it. There was a break in the continuity from creation to the present condition. This passage explains why men and women labor in toil and agony and conflict all their days, and why they die. Sin has wrought this dilemma, and nothing short of the removal of sin will end it.

By this report Israel would also learn that all the dealings of God with sinners can be traced back to the first disobedience. Their God was a saving God, however, to which the provision of clothes for Adam and Eve attested. In Israel sacrifices were made according to the prescribed manner of the law: the animals' lives were taken in exchange for the human seeking atonement, and the skins were given to the priests for their use. (No priest could read this passage without thinking of the connection.) The sinful worshiper thus lived because of God's gracious institution.

The human race of course lives on in the present evil world, and so the curse remains in effect. But for the believer, Israelite or New Testament Christian, there are better prospects. The sting of the curse has been removed in view of the glorious prospects that lie ahead. There is no going back to the garden; the only way now is on to glory to join the last Adam, who died as the curse for the human race and changed death into life through his resurrection from the dead.

Bibliography

Alonso-Schökel, L. "Sapiential and Covenant Themes in Genesis 2–3." *Theology Digest* 13 (1965): 3–10.

Cooke, G. A. *A Text Book of the North Semitic Inscriptions*, p. 135. Oxford: Clarendon, 1903.

Foh, Susan T. "What Is the Woman's Desire?" *WTJ* 37 (1975): 376–83.

Heller, Jan. "Der Name Eva." *Archiv Orientální* 26 (1958): 636–56.

Kapelrud, A. S. "The Gates of Hell and the Guardian Angels of Paradise." *JAOS* 70 (1950): 151–56.

Key, A. F. "The Giving of Proper Names in the OT." *JBL* 83 (1964): 55–59.

Lidsbarski, M. *Ephemeris für Semitische Epigraphik,* vol. 1, p. 30. Giessen: J. Richer'sche Verlagsbuchhandlung, 1902.

Martin, R. A. "The Earliest Messianic Interpretation of Genesis 3:15." *JBL* 84 (1965): 425–27.

Nielsen, E. "Creation and the Fall of Man: A Cross-Disciplinary Investigation." *HUCA* 43 (1972): 1–22.

Ross, Allen P. "Woman: After the Fall." *KS* 5, no. 1 (1981): 10–11, 23.

————. "Woman: Fulfilled in Christ." *KS* 5, no. 4 (1981): 14–16.

————. "Woman: In the Beginning." *KS* 4 (1980): 9–11.

Sagan, Carol. "In Pain Shalt Thou Bring Forth Children." *BAR* 5 (1979): 28.

Stitzinger, Michael F. "Genesis 1–3 and the Male/Female Role Relationship." *GTJ* 2 (1981): 23–44.

Vorster, W. S. "The Messianic Interpretation of Gen. 3:15: A Methodological Problem." *OTWSA* 15–16 (1972–73): 108–18.

Waterman, L. "The Curse in the 'Paradise Epic.'" *JAOS* 39 (1919): 322–28.

Williams, A. J. "The Relationship of Genesis 3:20 to the Serpent." *ZAW* 89 (1977): 357–74.

Witfall, Walter, "Genesis 3:15—a Protoevangelium?" *CBQ* 36 (1974): 361–65.

9

The Story of Cain and Abel
(Gen. 4:1–16)

The subject matter of Genesis 4 is the spread of sin from the family to the society. In the first part of the chapter, the story of Cain and Abel, the narrative relates how the destruction of the original creation involved not only husband and wife but brother and brother. Here was a man in rebellion against his brother and against God; he did not submit to God and care for his brother but destroyed his brother and denied responsibility for it. In every aspect, then, the rebellion described in this story was a decline from the paradise story.

Yet, God protected the life of the rebellious brother, so that he could live on in the world, albeit separated from the blessing. This theme is developed more fully in the second half of the chapter, studied in the next unit. There the story shows how individuals in primeval history became historical generations. Civilizations of godless people flourished under common grace—but the record makes it clear that their origins were in Cain.

The two units in Genesis 4 would have been very significant for the nation of Israel. They were moving into a world of cities and cultural interests. Music, art, and industry were on every hand. Societies in rebellion against God, however, would be antagonistic to Israel, rejecting her sacrifices and being eager to destroy her. On the one hand, the nation would be warned of bitter opposition; on the other hand, she would be instructed to continue to sacrifice to God in faith and in unity.

Theological Ideas

Basically the story is about Cain, even though the story line also concerns Abel and the Lord as principal characters. Cain and Abel provide us with archetypical repesentations of two kinds of people in a setting of worship. The plot of the story develops from the Lord's rejection of Cain and his offering. Cain thereupon became angry, rejected the Lord's advice, murdered his brother, denied the knowledge and responsibility for his crime, and protested the punishment for it. The "way of Cain" (Jude 11), then, is unbelief that may manifest itself in envy of God's dealing with the righteous, in murderous acts, in denial of responsibility for one's brother, and in refusal to accept the punishment.

Many motifs also pertain to the law. First, sacrifices were to be offered to God from a heart of faith. With such a motivation the sacrifice was bound to represent the first and the best of the worshiper's possessions. Second, Israelites did have responsibility for one another. They were one another's keepers in the covenant and dared not destroy the life of a brother. Third, homicidal blood would pollute the land and require purification. Shed blood would cry out for vengeance, accusing the murderer of the crime. Fourth, punishment for the guilty was at the foundation of society. Fifth, God made provision against blood revenge through the protective care of the guilty, here by decree, and later by the establishment of the cities of refuge. Sixth, life without God or his blessing was a dangerous life without protection. Godless society was reduced to seeking compensation wherever it could find it. And seventh, the elder brother was rejected in favor of the younger for inheritance. Cain showed himself unfaithful and rebellious and therefore was disqualified, for the line of blessing would now proceed through Abel's replacement.

Structure and Synthesis

Structure

The general structure of the story underscores its main point. For example, the contrast between the beginning and the ending is significant. At the beginning, Eve says at the birth of Cain, "I have created a man with the LORD." The conclusion of the story reports Cain's departure and his relation to the Lord: "Cain went away from the presence of the LORD" (v. 16). His land, Nod, is a place without the Lord, even though his beginning was considered to be from the Lord.

The development of the story works around two sections that contain the Lord's dialogue with Cain, verses 3–7 and 9–16. These two parts are separated by the report of the murder in verse 8. The central emphasis of the first section may be discovered in the Lord's interrogation and advice for the troubled Cain; the emphasis of the second part lies in the Lord's interrogation and condemnation of the guilty Cain.

That Cain's sin is against a brother is stressed by the antithetical arrangement of the lines in the first five verses. The clauses alternate between the two brothers, reporting on first one and then the other (see chart 8). Afterward the writer focuses on Cain, but always in reference to his relationship with Abel, his brother. The epithet "his brother" (or "your brother" or "my brother") appears seven times, as does the name Abel, thus stressing their relationship. In contrast, the name Cain occurs fourteen times in the first seventeen verses of the chapter. The narrative thus clearly contrasts the brothers.

It is also obvious that the design and the motifs of this story are parallel to the narrative of chapter 3. For example, the verb "know" occurs in 4:1 and 4:9, reflecting 2:17, 3:5, and 3:7; Cain had to hide himself after his condemnation (4:14), and Adam and Eve hid themselves in fear (3:8); Cain brought an offering from the fruit of the ground (4:3), and Eve ate from the fruit of the tree (3:6); God interrogated Cain before and after his sin (4:6, 10), and God interrogated the first sinners (3:9, 11, 13); God used the words of his oracle for the woman (3:16) in his warning for Cain (4:7); the voice of Abel's blood cried out against Cain (4:10), and the voice of the Lord God was heard in the garden (3:8); Cain denied being his brother's keeper (4:9), and God placed the man in the garden to keep it (2:15) but subsequently installed the angels to keep the way to the tree (3:24); finally, Cain was cursed (4:11), and the serpent and the ground were cursed (3:14, 17). The cumulative effect of these repeated words and themes serves to show that the present story is an extension of the preceding account.

Chart 8. **Literary Development of the Cain and Abel Story**

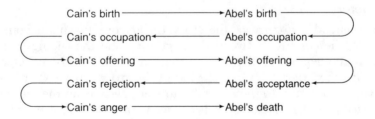

Summary Message

In spite of God's warning against sin, Cain, a tiller of the ground, murdered his brother, Abel, a shepherd of the sheep, because his brother's offering was accepted and his was not; he denied responsibility for the crime; and he protested the severity of the punishment, prompting God to provide protection for him.

Exegetical Outline

I. When Cain's offering was not accepted but Abel's was, Cain became very angry (1–5).

    A. The participants: Cain and Abel were born to Eve; the first-born—considered a provision from the Lord—became a tiller of the ground, and the second, a shepherd of the sheep (1–2).

        1. Eve gave birth to Cain and Abel, the birth of Cain being considered a provision of the Lord (1–2a).

        2. Abel became a shepherd of the sheep, but Cain a tiller of the ground (2b).

    B. The occasion: Cain and Abel brought sacrifices to the Lord, Abel's being accepted but Cain's rejected—a rejection that enraged Cain (3–5).

        1. Cain brought an offering, but Abel brought the best he had (3–4a).

        2. When Abel and his offering were preferred over Cain and his offering, Cain was enraged (4b–5).

II. In spite of the Lord's warning to master sin, Cain murdered his brother (6–8).

    A. The Lord interrogated Cain about his anger and advised him to do that which was right (6–7).

    B. Cain deliberately killed his brother in the field (8).

III. When the Lord questioned Cain about the murder of his brother, Cain denied any knowledge of it and any responsibility for his brother (9).

IV. When the Lord established the punishment for the crime, Cain protested the severity of it, drawing a gracious protection from the Lord (10–15).

    A. The Lord banished Cain from the fertile land (10–12).

    B. Cain protested the severity of the punishment, fearing blood revenge (13–14).

    C. The Lord graciously provided protection for the murderer (15).

V. Epilogue: Cain fled from the presence of the Lord (16).

Development of the Exposition

In such a narrative, with principal characters and dialogue, the organization of the exposition could be developed from one of two angles. The Lord could be the subject of the discussion, since he dominates in the interrogation and decree. However, I have chosen in the exegetical outline and the expositional development to concentrate on Cain, for the story line throughout focuses on him. In the exposition I would develop Cain as the archetype of antagonistic unbelief and focus the study on that description as it gradually unfolds throughout the story.

I. Unbelief becomes anger over God's approval of those more faithful (1–5).

The first section of the story sets out the occasion for the crime. One brother apparently pleased God and found acceptance; but the other brother, thinking himself to be just as acceptable, was filled with envy and rage. The issue is how one reacts to seeing oneself passed over and another blessed. If we are self-righteous, we will react as Cain did.

A. Auspicious beginning (1–2).

The narrative gradually unfolds the description of Cain as an unbeliever. In the first stage of the development, however, the account of the births of the two boys, there is no hint of the evil to come, only the brightest of prospects. The exegesis of verse 1 uncovers this idea. The child was named Cain (qayin), with the sentiment of the mother being, "I have created [qānîtî] a man with the LORD." The paronomasia relates the name to the verb by sounds (the two Hebrew words are unrelated etymologically) to suggest that this sentiment was the significance of the name. Eve's statement is full of hope and faith. She says, in effect, "God made man, and now with the help of the Lord, I have made the second man." Cain, by virtue of being the firstborn, was considered a work of God.

There is a slightly ominous note in the contrast of the boys' occupations. Cain is a "tiller of the ground," but Abel is a "keeper of the sheep." While there is nothing wrong with either occupation (both were important in the nation), there is a hint of the place of each man in the nature of things, for Cain lines up with an occupation that resulted from the fall (3:23), but Abel with men's and women's original purpose of having dominion over animals (1:28). The writer is perhaps suggesting— and only suggesting—that Cain was more naturally identified with the curse than was Abel.

Westermann notes that this narrative prologue pattern occurs again

Chart 9. **Parallels Between the Brothers Narratives**

Event	Cain and Abel	Jacob and Esau
Birth of two sons	4:1–2a	25:24–26
Naming of offspring	4:1b	25:25b, 26b
Occupation of both sons	4:2b	25:27

in Genesis 25:24–27 (see chart 9), which records the births of Jacob and Esau (*Genesis*, vol. 1, pp. 292–93). The parallel continues in that there is conflict between the two brothers, although in the later stories Esau only threatens to kill his brother.

B. Missed opportunity (3–5a).

The second part, the development of the occasion for the murder, provides a further unveiling of Cain's true nature in relationship to Abel's. At the time of worship (apparently the end of a season or a proclaimed time to sacrifice), both young men brought their offerings (both are called *minḥâ*, which in the Levitical code describes an acceptable offering). The Hebrew construction describing Abel's offering is elaborate, the writer stressing that Abel went out of his way to please God: he "brought of the firstlings of his flock and of their fat." This construction, a hendiadys, is better translated: "He brought the fattest of the firstlings of his flock." Later the law required that worshipers give the best that they had to God, which included the firstborn of the flock that was the fattest or healthiest (e.g., Exod. 13:2, 12; see also Lev. 22:17–25). In contrast to Abel's offering, Cain's is simply mentioned— he brought an offering of the fruit of the ground. Cassuto concludes that, whereas the one worshiper went out of his way to please God, the other simply discharged a duty (*Commentary on Genesis*, vol. 1, p. 205).

That there was something wrong with Cain's attitude or motivation may be seen immediately in the Lord's response: "And the LORD respected Abel and his offering, but he did not respect Cain and his offering." In each case the person is mentioned before the offering, which suggests that the kind of offering is not as important to the story as the attitude of the person making the offering. Here again we can see that Cain is not right.

The expositor will have to survey some of the suggestions offered for interpreting the verb *šāʿâ*, "had respect." How did they know one was accepted and the other was not? Some suggest that fire fell and consumed Abel's offering but not Cain's, or that Abel's flocks flourished but Cain's crops withered, or that the Lord simply spoke, or that they knew inwardly. This is an incidental question, for the text merely makes the point that God rejected Cain and his offering.

C. Angry response (5b).

A further indication of Cain's lack of faith was his response to God's displeasure with his offering. He was clearly jealous over his brother's acceptance by God, and so became very angry. This anger, which was not the response that would be expected from a humble believer, prompted a warning from the Lord himself.

II. Unbelief disregards the warnings against sin (6–8).

A. Divine warning (6–7).

Cain was so angry over the rejection of his offering that God warned him of the peril he was in. Whereas Eve had to be talked into her sin by the serpent, it appears that Cain would not be talked out of his intended sin, even by the Lord himself (Kidner, *Genesis*, p. 74).

The words of the Lord will take the most time in the exegesis of this section, not only because of their difficulty, but also because of their importance to the exposition as a whole. They begin with interrogation and then move to paternal advice. At the center of the speech is the concept of doing well: "If you do well, there is uplift; but if you do not do well, sin is couching at the door, and its desire is for you, but you can have the mastery over it." Here, then, is the predicted conflict (3:15) between good and evil arising immediately. The point of the statement, even though put in a conditional clause, is that Cain was to do well ("good").

In view of the preventive nature of this advice, the exposition's application would probably come back to reiterate the point—*do what is right and you will master sin.* Cain's anger was reflected in his facial expression; if he did well, however, even that would all change.

But if he did not do well, sin was about to overwhelm him, according to the Lord. Sin is personified as an animal couching at the door and ready to pounce on Cain, whose anger made him susceptible to this evil influence. Perhaps there is more in this passage, however, than a personification. The participle "couching" or "lies" (*rōbēṣ*) is cognate to an Akkadian term used of a type of demon. The first edition of the Jewish Publication Society's *Torah* offered the translation: "Sin is the demon at the door." If such a translation is legitimate, then there is a connection with the oracle about the seed of the serpent.

It is important that the expositor elaborate on how the Lord's words reflect the oracle about the woman: "Your desire [was] to your husband, but he shall have the mastery over you." A comparison of the Hebrew in 4:7 with 3:16 clearly shows that the Lord was warning Cain by reminding him of the fatal outcome of the earlier conflict.

B. Calloused disobedience (8).

But Cain does not want the mastery over sin. No sooner had the Lord's warning ended than Cain set upon his brother and murdered him. The Hebrew wording shows that it was premeditated ("Cain rose up against Abel his brother and slew him").

Here, too, there is a parallel construction with chapter 3. We have the speech (Satan's in 3:4–5, God's in 4:6–7), the circumstantial clause ("when she saw" in 3:6, "when they were" in 4:8), and then the sin ("she ate" in 3:6, and "he killed him" in 4:8).

III. Unbelief repudiates the responsibility for sin (9).

Just as he did in the previous narrative, the Lord came to the sinner with a question, a rhetorical question that sought a confession or some indication of guilt or shame. The Lord knew where Abel was, as verse 10 clarifies, but he sought a confession from Cain.

Cain's response reveals even more of his nature: he denies any knowledge of the murder and repudiates the responsibility for his brother. (The exposition will need to trace the repetition in these chapters of "know" [yādaʿ] and "keep" [šāmar]). The lie is one thing, but the repudiation of responsibility for a brother is very telling. In all probability the answer to Cain's question should be yes. If a nation or family is to survive, the people must be responsible for the well-being of one another. Of course, the answer that Cain expected was a decisive *no*.

IV. Unbelief protests the punishment for sin (10–14).

A. Divine judgment (10–12).

The Lord answered his own question (v. 9) and cut across Cain's defiant answer. The wording of the condemnation speech parallels that of chapter 3: "What is this you have done?" Cain may have denied the murder, but the blood testified against him by crying out to God. Westermann says,

> This is one of the monumental sentences in the Bible. It needs no explanation and retains its validity through the centuries for each generation. The most important word in the sentence is אלי, "to me." It is no empty sentence that the blood of the victim cries out; there is someone there to whom it cries out. Cain cannot hide his deed. [*Genesis*, vol. 1, p. 305]

The Lord's speech moves instantly from accusation to judgment, as if the insolent answer that Cain had given indicated there would be no confession forthcoming. The declaration "you are cursed from the fertile soil" may be a conscious reversal of the wording in 3:17, "Cursed is the fertile soil because of you." Accordingly, there is an advance on the curse—it now attaches to the son of Adam. Cain will be banished from the land. But the fertile soil was in some way in collusion with Cain by virtue of its receiving the blood. The abundant fertility will thus be hindered greatly, and Cain will have great difficulty scratching out his food.

Moreover, Cain will be a ceaseless wanderer (*nāʿ wānād* is a hendiadys, "a wanderer and a fugitive," meaning "a wandering fugitive"; the Latin and the Greek managed to capture the paronomasia here: *vagus et profugus, stenōn kai tremōn*). Perhaps the difficulty of getting a decent yield from the soil would contribute to Cain's endless wandering. At any rate, the murderer is banished from the fertile land and must flee into exile in the east.

B. Rebellious protest (13–14).

In Cain's response to the judgment of God, we discover the last clue to his character: "My punishment is too great to bear." The exegete will have to study this line carefully because of the different ways that commentators take it. "Punishment" is actually "iniquity" (*ʿāwōn*), leading some to suggest that Cain was crying out for forgiveness. However, Cain nowhere is portrayed with the slightest hint of remorse. The word should thus be taken in one of its developed senses, that of punishment for the iniquity (a metonymy).

Westermann observes that there is a familiar ring to the words of Cain; they sound like some of the laments in the psalms in that they have the three main parts—*you* drive me out, *I* must hide, and *they* may kill me (*Genesis*, vol. 1, pp. 309–10). This comparison does not suggest that the punishment would be softened, only that the lamentable state was worse than death. It is unbearable, for, as Cain explains, to be driven away meant that he had to sever all relationships with the family and, more important, with the Lord of blessing.

V. Unbelief continues under divine protection (15–16).

Common grace is manifested here. The Lord put some kind of protection on Cain so that he would survive (speculation on what the mark was will probably be futile; von Rad's suggestion of the first tattoo is surely wide of the mark). The action shows essentially what God thought of blood revenge. God became the protector of the murderer, promising vengeance on the avenger.

Cain's last act of defiance was his settling in the land of Nod and building a city (as the next section will show). There is an ironic word play on "Nod," for this was the word used for "fugitive." One might say he lived in the "land of wanderings."

The narrative art of this story effectively presents a picture of a man without faith, a man in rebellion against God. The expositor can approach this subject from two perspectives, that of the righteous who must tolerate such a person, or that of the wicked. If the latter is chosen, then the thrust of the message would be a warning about the penalty for rebellion and advice for averting it. Rather than concentrate on another whom God has favored and try to discredit or destroy him, the potentially rebellious person must concentrate on doing what is right to overcome evil.

The message to the righteous would be to continue to serve God in piety, knowing that such service will alienate them from the wicked individual who is only outwardly religious. The devout must expect that the wicked will oppose them in a host of subtle ways. Both types of people were in ancient Israel; both are in any assembly gathered for worship.

John concentrates on the theme of love for the brethren and uses Cain as an illustration: "For this is the message that you have heard from the beginning, that we should love one another, not as Cain, who was of the wicked one and murdered his brother. . . . Do not marvel my brethren if the world hates you" (1 John 3:11–13). This use of the story in the New Testament is certainly at the heart of the message, but it is only a part of it.

I would word the expository idea in this way: *Those who worship must have as their goal always to please God so that they will not allow sin (envy and hatred) to work its ruinous ways in their lives.* This formulation centers on the warning that God gave Cain but includes all the major facets of the story. Anytime a person is filled with envy and anger over God's blessing on others, there will be disaster if that anger is allowed to run its course. Cain has become the abiding example of this pattern.

In a sermon delivered in the holy season, Gerhard von Rad concentrated on one aspect of the story of Cain—the blood crying out. His correlation with the New Testament illustrates another of many emphases that can be developed:

At the beginning of Passiontide it is fitting to say a word about the extent of the damage done by man. Man approaching the cross is a brother-murderer from the very beginning. The interpreter may also properly sketch out the lines of cultural history—the division of humanity into various states of life, the existence of two altars. And Cain continues to travel the road he has taken—founding cities and the musical arts, developing the art of forging so that the sword comes to be regarded as an approved implement—and the song of Lamech madly celebrates the native force and the boundlessness of revenge (Gen. 4:17–24).

But the sermon should center on verse 10: as far as human understanding is concerned, inconceivable and inexpiable is the accusing cry of the blood of our brother Abel, a cry that ascends to God day and night. This should be the starting point for the dispelling of manifold and familiar misunderstandings: Abel's blood, even the best and dearest, never brings salvation in the presence of God; instead it increases the burden of the curse. But Christ's blood "speaks more graciously than the blood of Abel" (Heb. 12:24). Thus the Bible speaks of two kinds of blood and their voices before God: one of these is millionfold, and its message is accusation, while the other is the blood of the One, and it brings healing. [*Biblical Interpretations in Preaching*, p. 22]

Bibliography

Borger, R. "Genesis IV 1." *VT* 9 (1959): 85–86.

Castellino, G. R. "Genesis 4:7." *VT* 10 (1960): 442–45.

De Catanzaro, C. J. "The Early Chapters of Genesis—a History of Salvation." *ACQ* 4 (1964): 174–81.

————. "Man in Revolt: A Study in the Primaeval History of the Book of Genesis." *CanJTh* 4 (1958): 285–92.

Gevirtz, S. "West-Semitic Curses and the Problem of the Origins of Hebrew Law." *VT* 11 (1961): 137–58.

Gruber, Mayer I. "The Tragedy of Cain and Abel: A Case of Depression." *JQR* 69 (1978): 89–97.

————. "Was Cain Angry or Depressed? Background of a Biblical Murder." *BAR* 6 (1980): 34–36.

Hauser, Alan J. "Linguistic and Thematic Links Between Genesis 4:1–6 and Genesis 2–3." *JETS* 23 (1980): 297–306.

Kline, Meredith G. "Oracular Origin of the State." In *Biblical and Near Eastern Studies.* Edited by Gary A. Tuttle, pp. 132–40. Grand Rapids: Eerdmans, 1978.

Levin, Saul. "The More Savory Offering: A Key to the Problem of Gen. 4:3–5." *JBL* 98 (1979): 85.

Morris, L. "The Biblical Use of the Term 'Blood.' " *JThS*, n.s., 6 (1955–56): 77–82.

Rad, Gerhard von. *Biblical Interpretations in Preaching.* Translated by John E. Steely. Nashville: Abingdon, 1977.

Riemann, Paul A. "Am I My Brother's Keeper?" *Interp* 24 (1970): 482–91.

Snaith, N. H. "Sacrifices in the Old Testament." *VT* 7 (1957): 308–17.

Waltke, Bruce K. "Cain and His Offering." *WTJ* 48 (1986): 363–72.

Zimmerli, W. "Zur Exegese von Genesis 4:1–16." *Der evangelische Erzieher* 20 (1968): 200–203.

10

The Beginning of Civilization
(Gen. 4:17–26)

The narrative now traces the line of Cain through to its full development. What became of the person who rebelled against God and left the land of blessing in angry defiance of the laws and the sacrifices? He prospered. His line took the lead in producing cities, music, weapons, agricultural implements—in short, civilization. Such activity may have been their way to cope with life under the curse; it was their only recourse in a bitter life. Being separated from God, Cain's line enhanced their life with these refinements.

The righteous descendants of Adam do not figure in this discussion. No doubt they used culture, as the later Israelites did, to the glory of God; but the text stresses something else as the predominant theme of their life, for which they would be remembered. Seth, the replacement of Abel, fathered Enosh, and then people began to worship the Lord. As great as all the inventions of civilization were, this step was greater by far.

Theological Ideas

As with the preceding passage, some ideas in this account must be stated negatively, and some may be stated positively. On the negative

164

side, this narrative says a great deal about godless society's disregard for what God had done. The institution of marriage was changed to satisfy human desires, and so we find the first bigamist. In addition, the value of life was disdained as Lamech took the murder by Cain a step further. These negative examples were important for the teaching of the law. God's nation would have to preserve the institution of marriage and protect human life as God had intended it.

On the positive side, we may observe that the retention of the knowledge of the Lord was the most important aspect of life for the righteous. The righteous also built cities and made various implements, but they would also say as the psalmist later said, "Except the LORD build the house, they labor in vain who build it" (Ps. 127:1). But to use culture in the worship and service of the Lord would not be in vain.

Structure and Synthesis

Structure

There are distinct genres in this section of the chapter. One that is immediately noticeable is *genealogy*. Most commentators include Genesis 4:1 to form the complete genealogy of the line of Cain, bringing the number to seven names. Within the genealogy there are a few explanatory comments with regard to the contributions of individuals.

The *taunt song* of verses 23–24 forms another genre within the section. This ancient song of Lamech's indicates the evil side of expanding society.

The last two verses in the chapter form a fitting contrast with the preceding material. Here we find a *report* of the birth of Seth, with a reminder of the murder and a note on the antiquity of true worship. It is interesting to observe that the beginning of this section (v. 25) parallels verse 1 ("Adam knew his wife"), and the end of it (v. 26b) contrasts with the beginning of this passage in verse 17 ("called the name of the city after the name of his son").

The narrative thus contains three sections: Cain's family and the building of the city and the growth of culture (vv. 17–22), Lamech's taunt song and exploitation of vengeance (vv. 23–24), and Seth's family and the knowledge of the Lord (vv. 25–26). In the exposition it may be most effective to unite the first two parts to form a contrast with the last.

Summary Message

In contrast to Cain's descendants, who, while altering the institutions of God and disdaining the value of life, produced cities, music, and all kinds of implements for the good life, the descendants of Adam through Seth primarily promoted the worship of the Lord.

Exegetical Outline

    I. The family of Cain altered the institutions of God and disdained the value of life but at the same time produced cities, music, and all types of implements for the good life (17–24).
      A. Cain fathered Enoch, after whom he named a city and through whom the line developed to Lamech (17–18).
        1. Birth: Cain knew his wife and fathered Enoch (17a).
        2. Memorial: Cain built a city and named it after his son (17b).
        3. Descendants: Enoch continued the line of descendants toward Lamech (18).
      B. Lamech, who through two wives fathered those who produced all kinds of implements for the enjoyment and convenience of life, exulted over killing a youth (19–24).
        1. Altering God's institution of marriage, Lamech took two wives and fathered those who produced cultural things (19–22).
        2. Disdaining the value of life, Lamech exulted in his prowess of killing a youth and his expectation of greater vengeance than Cain (23–24).
    II. The family of Adam through Seth preserved the worship of the Lord God through birth and proclamation (25–26).
      A. Birth: Adam knew his wife and fathered a son (25a).
      B. Memorial: Seth was named to commemorate God's provision of the son (25b).
      C. Descendants: Seth continued the line to Enosh, at which time people began to proclaim the name of the Lord (26).

Development of the Exposition

I. The world prides itself on its cultural advancements (17–24).

A. The city becomes the lasting monument (17).

The society described here is a society away from God, as the preceding section of the chapter so vividly concluded. The story is about the family of the fugitive that attempts to evade the effects of the curse by ingenuity and enterprise. Their prosperity is great, but it is an empty prosperity apart from God.

The building of the city seems to be a defiant act by Cain, for he was condemned to be a ceaseless wanderer in the earth. The naming of the city was an attempt to retain the name of his son in the memory of the descendants (Enoch may mean "dedication"). The psalmist later spoke of the ungodly who give their name to their works and leave all that they have in the inheritance as they pass off the scene (Ps. 49:10–12). If they have nothing else in life, they are like the beasts of the field.

B. The advances of culture bring enjoyment and convenience (18–22).

The next section of the narrative is important for two reasons. First, in the line from Lamech there are a number of beginnings: tenting, music, weapons, and implements. This cultural growth brings delight to the families, as is seen by the names using *yûbāl* (note the possible etymological connection to Israel's delightful concept of Jubilee) and the mention of Naamah (*naʿămâ*), a name similar to Naomi. The exegete must be very careful in interpreting such names. We must not make too much out of the meanings of names if there is no convincing evidence. In this passage, however, there may be some etymological connection with words that indicate joy and happiness.

The second important feature of this section concerns the order of the genealogy. It is interesting to compare the lists of descendants through Cain with those through Seth in the next chapter (see chart 10). The line through Cain is a genealogy of seven names, the last-named entry having three sons (and one daughter); the line through Seth is a list of ten names, the last-named entry having three sons. It appears that the lists were arranged selectively to achieve this comparable structure.

Chart 10. **Descendants of Cain and Seth**

The Line of Cain	The Line of Seth
Adam	Adam
Cain	Seth
Enoch	Enosh
Irad	Kenan
Mehujael	Mahalalel
Methushael	Jared
Lamech	Enoch
Jabal	Methuselah
Jubal	Lamech
Tubal-Cain	Noah
(Naamah)	Shem
	Ham
	Japheth

Moreover, the seventh from Adam through Seth was Enoch, who walked with God and did not die (Gen. 5:24). The seventh from Adam through Cain (and perhaps contemporary with Enoch) was Lamech, who boasted of killing a young man. In the two lists, speeches are attributed to only two of the people listed—the two Lamechs. Lamech the descendant of Cain sang a taunt song of his prowess in killing the youthful warrior, but Lamech the descendant of Seth named Noah in the hope that he would bring people comfort from the pain of the curse (v. 29). Moses evidently juxtaposed the two genealogies to show the contrast between the way of Cain and the way of Seth.

C. The value of marriage and life are altered by human indulgence (23–24).

At the heart of this narrative about the advances in civilization is the additional information about advancing rebellion against God. First, there was bigamy, a problem that society would face for ages to come. Malachi, though, reminded the people of his age that God originally made man and woman as one, so that there might be a godly seed (2:15). The prophet's message based on Genesis was a warning for the people to put away their foreign wives.

Second, there was disdain for life. Here we have Lamech's taunt song; it seems to be "a demonstration of strength for the benefit of the women" (Coats, *Genesis*, p. 68; see also Gevirtz, *Patterns*). Lamech slew a youth (probably a youthful warrior) who had offended him. Killing, the first sin committed outside the garden, was thus here to stay. After taking vengeance on the lad, Lamech demanded greater leniency in the vengeance that might come his way than that afforded to Cain. Lamech's use of *hārag*, "killed," the same word used in the account of Cain's murder, provides the link between the two crimes. But Lamech exploited the divine provision by expecting to be avenged seventy times seven (or seventy-seven times). Perhaps Jesus alluded to this passage when he said that the way of the righteous would be to forgive seventy times seven (Matt. 18:22).

II. The priority of the righteous is to preserve the knowledge of the Lord (25–26).

The chapter ends with a contrast to Cain's family—there were godly people on earth. The text does not say that all the Sethites were righteous and all the Cainites were wicked, nor would such a position harmonize with the account of the flood, in which all but eight people perished. But it can be said that instances of faith were more likely to be found in the family that led to Abram.

A. *The faithful commemorate God's provision (25).*

In words reminiscent of Genesis 4:1, the birth of Seth is reported. Eve once again displayed her faith with the expression of the sentiment over her son, whom she named Seth (*šēt*): "For God has appointed [*šāt*] me another seed instead of Abel, whom Cain slew." The motivation for the name is at one time a poignant reminder of the murder and a hopeful anticipation of things to come. The name Seth may mean something like "new beginning" or "foundation." On this child their hopes were renewed. With this child they once again enjoyed God's provision.

B. *The faithful proclaim God's nature (26).*

Seth fathered Enosh, and a new beginning occurs: the faith of the mother is strong, for people (note the indefinite subject for the passive verb) began "to call on the name of the LORD." This expression will require a good deal of study in the exposition of Genesis. The verb *qārā'*, "call," can be used for naming (cf. 4:17, 25), reading, proclaiming, summoning, and praying. Usage of this expression in the Pentateuch supports the idea of proclamation more than praying (cf. Gen. 12:8; Exod. 34:6; Lev. 1:1). The meaning of *šēm*, "name," also requires interpretation, since the word is actually followed by the name itself. The word "name" often refers to characteristics or attributes (see Isa. 9:6). The idea of this line is that people began to make proclamation about the nature of the Lord ("began to make proclamation of the Lord by name").

Benno Jacob says that to "call upon the name of the Lord" is to make an exclamation containing the name "LORD." Jacob adds, "This is a preliminary announcement of the exclamation of the second Lamech at the birth of his son Noah in 5,29 where the word 'the LORD' reappears. Enosh is still alive at Noah's birth (5,29)" (*First Book of the Bible*, p. 39). This is the oldest reference to the worship of Yahweh. It shows that the name Yahweh was known by God's people from earliest times.

The narrative thus describes the first affluent society, self-indulgent and self-gratifying, building cities and developing civilization but doing so in defiance of God and his laws. Into the midst of this world God brought his nation Israel, and later the church, as his kingdom of priests (Exod. 19:6 and 1 Peter 2:5) to worship the Lord and proclaim his name.

This record informs the reader that some who traced their lineage to Seth, God's replacement for Abel, began to proclaim their faith. They, as well as Noah, Abram, and others, proclaimed the Lord by their worship and their words. Some people, albeit a remnant, thus were not caught up in the good life but were more concerned about spiritual

170

things. Israel could trace their heritage to Enosh in spiritual matters as well. The people of God have always been able to use the advances of culture for their task, but they have had to learn to keep things in proper perspective. The evidence of this perspective, and the safeguarding of it, lies in the message of the narrative: *In an affluent and self-indulgent society, the righteous must preserve the knowledge of the Lord.* How difficult it was to do so can be seen in the history of Israel and then of the church. As Westermann says,

> When J in the same context also associates the beginning of the worship of God with primeval time, he is pointing out that worship is as determinative for the whole history of humankind as is the work of civilization and that its universal aspect should not be lost sight of by way of the partial. [*Genesis*, vol. 1, p. 344]

Bibliography

Finkelstein, J. J. "The Antediluvian Kings: A University of California Tablet." *JCS* 17 (1963): 39–51.

Gevirtz, S. *Patterns in the Early Poetry of Israel,* pp. 25–34. Chicago: University of Chicago Press, 1963.

Gowen, H. H. "The Cainite and Sethite Genealogies of Gen. 4 and 5." *AThR* 2 (1924): 326–27.

Malamat, A. "King Lists of the Old Babylonian Period and Biblical Genealogies." *JAOS* 88 (1968): 163–73.

Manley, G. T. "The God of Abraham." *TynB* 14 (1964): 3–7.

Miller, J. M. "The Descendants of Cain: Notes on Gen. 4." *ZAW* 86 (1974): 164–74.

Miller, P. D. "Yeled in the Song of Lamech." *JBL* 85 (1966): 477–78.

North, R. "The Cain Music." *JBL* 83 (1964): 373–89.

Sandmel, Samuel. "Gen. 4:26b." *HUCA* 32 (1961): 19–29.

Wilson, R. R. *Genealogy and History in the Biblical World.* New Haven: Yale University Press, 1977.

11

The Outworking of the Curse in the Human Race
(Gen. 5)

A new *tôlᵉdôt* section begins here with the dual purpose of linking the record of Adam and his generation to the story of Noah, and of showing the result of sin in the human race. This passage also forms a balance with the preceding narrative: if in spite of sin there was such progress, what became of the curse? The answer, of course, is that, in spite of human achievements, death reigned from Adam's time on through the generations.

Theological Ideas

The predominant theme of the chapter is death—"and he died" occurs eight times on the list. That death is in contrast to the divine blessing and due to the presence of the curse is clearly indicated by the beginning and ending of the chapter. Genesis 5 seems to be displaying the reign of death in contrast to the desire of God. The exegete must thus explain the significance of this theme by relating it to the earlier chapters of the book.

Another significant theological idea in the passage is that of walking with God. Enoch (and later Noah) walked with God (see also Mic. 6:8; Mal. 2:6). The exposition will have to develop this concept very clearly, since the passage presents "walking with God" as an alternative to the living-and-dying cycle of the genealogy. The discussion by F. J. Helfmeyer in *TDOT* (vol. 3, pp. 392–95) will be helpful.

Structure and Synthesis

Structure

A genealogy is a little difficult to work with, but this one lends itself nicely to an exegetical exposition. The structure has ten panels of names in the list from Adam to Noah, with Noah's three sons at the end of the list. The pattern used in each part records that someone lived x years, fathered the one who would be the next entry on the list, and then lived y more years and fathered sons and daughters; it then concludes with the total number of years he lived and records that he died.

The writer digresses from this rigid pattern in three places—at the beginning with Adam, in the seventh panel with Enoch, and at the end with Noah. These three parts will be of the greatest interest to the expositor, for, with their additional information, they form a marked contrast to the routine of the genealogy.

The genealogy is a vertical list, showing descent from Adam through Seth and Enoch to Noah. The other vertical list in Genesis (11:10–31) continues the line to Abram (one of three sons of Terah listed at the end of that genealogy). Together these genealogies link Abram to Noah and to Adam in the line in which faith had on occasion surfaced. It suggests that the family and ancestry of Abram were closer to the truth than was the rest of the world.

Summary Message

After God created man and woman in his image and with his blessing, the human race, living under the curse, multiplied continually and died just as regularly—with the exception of Enoch who walked with God— all of which prompted a hope for relief from the curse.

Exegetical Outline

Title: This is what became of Adam (1a)
  I. After 130 years, Adam, who was created in God's image and blessed by God, fathered Seth in his image and then died at the age of 930 (1b–5).
     A. God made human beings as his image and blessed them (1b–2).

    B. Adam fathered Seth after his image and then died (3–5).

II. After 105 years, Seth fathered Enosh and then died at the age of 912 (6–8).

III. After 90 years, Enosh fathered Kenan and then died at the age of 905 (9–11).

IV. After 70 years, Kenan fathered Mehalalel and then died at the age of 910 (12–14).

V. After 65 years, Mahalalel fathered Jared and then died at the age of 895 (15–17).

VI. After 162 years, Jared fathered Enoch and then died at the age of 962 (18–20).

VII. After 65 years, Enoch fathered Methuselah and then walked with God for 300 years until God took him (21–24).

    A. Enoch fathered Methuselah at age 65 (21).

    B. After the birth of Methuselah, Enoch walked with God for 300 years (22–23).

    C. Because Enoch walked with God, God took him (24).

VIII. After 187 years, Methuselah fathered Lamech and then died at the age of 969 (25–27).

IX. After 182 years, Lamech fathered Noah, hoping for comfort from the curse, and then died at the age of 777 (28–31).

X. After 500 years, Noah fathered Shem, Ham, and Japheth (32).

Development of the Exposition

There are a number of ways that a section like this could be handled in exposition. One effective way would be to treat in an extended introduction the predominant theme of death, the pattern of names and formulas, and the purpose as a link from Adam to Noah and then to concentrate on the three sections with additional material as the exposition proper. The treatment of these three parts will display a contrast with the theme of death.

I. Humankind's purpose is to represent God and enjoy his blessing (1b–5).

The first section that has additional interpretive material is the introduction to the genealogy. By repeating themes from the creation account, the writer shows God's intention for the human race. The narrative begins with the creation and blessing of Adam as the image of God (note that "image" and "likeness" are reversed here from the earlier account). The expositor should not miss the emphasis on the blessing of the image at creation, nor the intended contrast with the theme of death that suddenly takes over the passage.

The idea here is also that whatever "image" involved was passed on to the son, for Seth was in the image of his father. The spiritual capacities that were imparted to Adam and Eve, that endowed them with the ability and responsibility to represent God on earth, were passed on by natural reproduction. Even in a cursed world human beings are in the image of God (as Gen. 9:6 reiterates) and may yet serve him and enjoy his blessing.

In spite of this marvelous reminder of what God had in mind for his creation, a sudden shift in the mood alerts the reader that something is terribly wrong. Adam died. If ever one doubted whether the warning "you shall surely die" (2:17) was ever fulfilled, one needs only to read on in this record. The New Testament also stresses the point that by one man sin entered into the world, and death by sin (Rom. 5:12).

The Christian expositor will have to correlate the New Testament's teachings on life under the curse of death. In the new creation in Christ Jesus, people have the responsibility of conforming to the image of Christ, who is the express image of the Father, in order to represent him on earth and enjoy his blessings.

II. Humankind's responsibility is to walk with God (21–24).

The second section that has additional interpretive material is the panel of Enoch, the seventh from Adam. This one exception to the reign of death provides a ray of hope for the human race, as if to say that death was not the final answer. One man "walked with God" and God "took him." The New Testament reports the tradition that Enoch preached about the coming judgment (Jude 14). Here was a man who lived in obedience and fellowship with God and served as God's spokesperson. For him God overruled death.

The expositor must clarify the expressions in this passage. First, the report that God "took him" needs attention. A concordance study will eventually lead to the story of Elijah's transport to glory. Accordingly— and in view of the fact that, instead of reporting that Enoch died, the writer says that God took him—we may conclude that Enoch was trans- lated out of this life without suffering death.

A clear explanation is also required for Enoch's walk with God, for this experience was undoubtedly held up as the model for others to follow in their earthly pilgrimage. In contrast to the other panels, the report about Enoch prefers the verb "he walked with God" (hithallēk). Enoch did not "live"—he walked with God. Enoch did not "die"—he walked with God, and God took him. Moreover, that "walk" lasted three hundred years. The expression became a common description of the life of fellowship and obedience with the Lord, as if to say that walking with the Lord was a step above mere living. To walk with the Lord was commanded of Israel (Lev. 26:3; see also v. 12); it remains the standard for the believer's life (Col. 2:6; Rev. 3:4).

The comments by Marcus Dods on this subject may be helpful in making specific connections to the life of faith:

> Only once is the monotony broken; but this in so striking a manner as to rescue us from the idea that the historian is mechanically copying a barren list of names. For in the seventh generation, contemporaneous with the culmination of Cain's line in the family of Lamech, we come upon the simple but anything but mechanical statement: "Enoch walked with God and he was not; for God took him." The phrase is full of meaning. Enoch walked with God because he was His friend and liked His company, because he was going in the same direction as God, and had no desire for anything but what lay in God's path. We walk with God when He is in all our thoughts; not because we consciously think of Him at all times, but because He is naturally suggested to us by all we think of; as when any person or plan or idea has become important to us, no matter what we think of, our thought is always found recurring to this favorite object, so with the godly man everything has a connection with God and must be ruled by that connection. When some change in his circumstances is thought of, he has first of all to determine how the proposed change will affect his connection with God—will his conscience be equally clear, will he be able to live on the same friendly terms with God and so forth. When he falls into sin he cannot rest till he has resumed his place at God's side and walks again with Him. This is the general nature of walking with God; it is a persistent endeavour to hold all our life open to God's inspection and in conformity to His will; a readiness to give up what we find does cause any misunderstanding between us and God; a feeling of loneliness if we have not some satisfaction in our efforts at holding fellowship with God, a cold and desolate feeling when we are conscious of doing something that displeases Him. This walking with God necessarily tells on the whole life and character. As you instinctively avoid subjects which you know will jar upon the feelings of your friend, as you naturally endeavour to suit yourself to your company, so when the consciousness of God's presence begins to have some weight with you, you are found instinctively endeavouring to please Him, repressing the thoughts you know He disapproves, and endeavouring to educate such dispositions as reflect His own nature.
>
> It is easy then to understand how we may practically walk with God— it is to open to Him all our purposes and hopes, to seek His judgment on our scheme of life and idea of happiness—it is to be on thoroughly friendly terms with God. . . . Things were not made easy to Enoch. In evil days, with much to mislead him, with everything to oppose him, he had by faith and diligent seeking, as the Epistle to the Hebrews says, to

cleave to the path on which God walked, often left in darkness, often
thrown off the track, often listening but unable to hear the footfall of
God or to hear his own name called upon, receiving no sign, but still
diligently seeking the God he knew would lead him only to good. [*Book
of Genesis*, pp. 51–53]

III. Humankind's hope is for relief from the curse (28–31).

The third significant departure from the pattern of the genealogy
comes at the end of the list with the birth of Noah. The text includes
the words of Lamech at the naming of Noah, words that express hope
for relief from the curse: "And he called his name Noah [*nōaḥ*], saying,
'This one shall comfort us [*yᵉnaḥămēnû*] concerning our work and toil
of our hands, because of the ground which the LORD has cursed.' " This
expression is based on a word play on the name of Noah (the sound of
nōaḥ is similar to the sound of the verb *nāḥam*); "Noah" does not mean
"comfort" but prompts the sentiment through the word play.

The name Noah is also the basis for the motif of resting, in the next
tôlᵉdôt section of the book. Life under the curse was very painful for
these early bearers of the curse, and so Lamech hoped for relief and
comfort through this man Noah. Human life under the curse was also
painful to God, and so God used Noah as part of his plan to relieve the
world of the pain, but not in the way Lamech thought.

Here, then, was the second bright prospect in an otherwise depressing
existence. First, Enoch walked with God and escaped the curse of death;
now, Noah's life brought the prospect for comfort under the curse.

The chapter surely stresses that death had invaded the human family.
But this motif provides the backdrop for the primary interest of the
narrative, that there is evidence of grace throughout—life, fertility (note
the stress on "sons and daughters"), Enoch's translation, and the prospect
of rest and comfort. No doubt, these aspects of life under the curse
carried over from God's creation of humankind as his image and with
his blessing and from men's and women's awareness of this original
intent.

Israel had to learn to cope with death and pain in their life, as indeed
all do. But they learned that *those who enjoy the blessing of the calling
of God may anticipate victory over the curse as they walk with the
Lord.* They could learn this lesson from this chapter in Genesis. God
had created Israel to be his people, to represent him on earth, and to
carry forth his blessing. Their enjoyment of many of these blessings,
however, demanded a walk with God.

In a similar way the church today is to exemplify the image of God in the world. Believers today also look for their translation to glory, for they also hope for relief from the curse, as indeed the whole world does, groaning for the day of redemption (Rom. 8:22). In the meantime, however, they must walk with the Lord.

Bibliography

Gil, M. "Enoch in the Land of Eternal Life." *Tar* 38 (1968–69): 322–37.

Hallo, W. W. "Beginning and End of the Sumerian King List in the Nippur Recension." *JCS* 17 (1963): 52–57.

Hartman, T. C. "Some Thoughts on the Sumerian King List and Genesis 5 and 11b." *JBL* 91 (1972): 25–32.

Hasel, Gerhard F. "The Genealogies of Gen. 5 and 11 and Their Alleged Babylonian Background." *AUSS* 16 (1978): 361–74.

——— . "Genesis 5 and 11: Chronogenealogies: The Biblical History of Beginnings." *Origins* 7 (1980): 23–37.

Kraeling, E. G. "The Interpretations of the Name Noah in Genesis 5:29." *JBL* 48 (1929): 138–43.

Malamat, A. "King Lists of the Old Babylonian Period and Biblical Genealogies." *JAOS* 83 (1968): 163–73.

Martin, F. "A Famine Element in the Flood Story." *JBL* 45 (1926): 129–33.

Miller, J. Maxwell. "In the 'Image' and 'Likeness' of God." *JBL* 91 (1972): 289–304.

Morgenstern, J. "A Note on Genesis 5:29." *JBL* 49 (1930): 306–9.

Parnham, F. S. "Walking with God." *EvQ* 46 (1974): 117–18.

Rowley, H. H. "The Future Life in the Old Testament." *ConQ* 33 (1955): 116–32.

Snaith, N. H. "The Meaning of 'The Paraclete.' " *ExT* 57 (1945–46): 48–49.

Stigers, Harold G. "Critique II of 'The Biblical Calendar of History.' " *JASA* 22 (1970): 102–5.

Whybray, R. N. "Proverbs VIII 22–31 and Its Supposed Prototypes." *VT* 15 (1965): 504–14.

Wilson, Robert R. "The Old Testament Genealogies in Recent Research." *JBL* 94 (1975): 169–89.

Yamauchi, Edwin M. "Critique of 'The Biblical Calendar of History.' " *JASA* 22 (1970): 99–101.

12

God's Grief over the Wickedness of Humankind
(Gen. 6:1–8)

The present section of Genesis has been the subject of debate for centuries, most scholars considering it to be one of the most difficult passages to interpret in the Pentateuch. At the center of the discussion is the identity of the "sons of God" and the "daughters of men." Most of the early church fathers interpreted the sons of God to be angels, probably because of certain manuscripts of the Septuagint. But this view was met with resistance from rabbinical circles, for their position was more commonly that the sons of God were human judges. In fact, there was a curse pronounced on anyone taking the angel view (*Genesis Rabba* 26.5). Later, in the medieval period and especially in the Roman church, there was a preference for the interpretation that the sons of God were Cainites, and the daughters of men, Sethites. Now, in the modern period, critical scholarship is more apt to interpret the sons of God as lesser gods in the heavenly pantheon, taking the passage as a remnant of a Canaanite myth.

Whatever view the expositor takes of some of these details in the passage, the passage as a whole is clearly portraying how wicked the human race had become and indicating that death would be the punishment. This judgment would be severe because the sin was great. It must be remembered that these eight verses are part of the *tôleḏôt* section that began with Genesis 5:1. The theme throughout these two narrative sections is that death is the judgment for the sinful race. In this second narrative, though, the theme is heightened to the urgency and severity of death because of gross evil in the spread of sin.

Theological Ideas

The central theme of this passage is the wickedness of the human race. This point, expressed so strongly in verse 5, demands more attention than the problem of the sons of God. Evil, one of the major themes of Genesis, is God's description of the race—a very great evil. All the related expressions used in this report of the Lord's observation of humankind also warrant detailed study.

Several other theological motifs in this passage stem from the wickedness of men and women. The idea that the Lord was grieved over human sin and "repented" over having made humankind certainly needs interpretation. These anthropomorphic expressions convey the divine response to sin that leads God to the decision to destroy what he had created. God's grief over sin thus forms an important part of the theology of divine judgment.

While judgment may be the predominant aspect of God's reaction to sin in this narrative, grace also surfaces very clearly (v. 8). A thorough study of "grace" (*ḥēn*) within its semantic field is in order. Many expositors ignore this verse and its location at the end of the *tôleḏôt* section, emphasizing rather the righteousness of Noah. But that theme must await the next *tôleḏôt* section. In the present section the writer is contrasting the fate of Noah with the fate of the rest of the race—he found grace.

Structure and Synthesis

Structure

The structure of the passage follows two parallel developments, both of which are filled with allusions to earlier sections of the book. The major structural indicators are "the sons of God saw" in verse 2 and "the LORD saw" in verse 5. The sons of God saw that the daughters were *good*, and they took all they wanted; the Lord saw that humankind was *evil*, and he was grieved and decided to blot out his creation.

The first part includes a report of the circumstances (v. 1), an exposition of the crisis (v. 2), and an oracle of judgment (v. 3). The report in verse 4 then shows the complications of the crisis, suggesting a cultural identity for the offspring of these marriages. The second part of the narrative includes a revelation of the Lord's evaluation of the human race (v. 5), his grief over having created human beings (v. 6), and his oracle of judgment (v. 7). Verse 8 then shows a way out of the devastating judgment.

Within this structure the literary allusions bring the pattern into sharper focus. The wording of verse 2 recalls the fall of Eve in the garden (3:6), for when she saw that the tree was *good,* she *took* and ate. In that passage the motivation was to be like God; in this passage the barriers between the "sons of God" and the human race also seem to be challenged.

The wording of verse 6 recalls the hopes of Lamech in 5:29, and both in turn reflect the curse oracle in 3:17: "grieve," "make," and "repent" reflect Lamech's "toil," "labor," and "comfort," as the exposition will show. Obviously the perspective was very different.

This little narrative forms a unit by itself. It features a point of tension that it develops from the perspective of the divine reaction as well as human complications, and it offers a resolution for the tension. It parallels the accounts of Pharaoh and Sarai in Genesis 12:10–20 and of David and Bathsheba in 2 Samuel 11–12. In all three stories the conflict begins when boundaries are overstepped in the matter of marriage; in all three stories the stages of seeing and taking are followed by the intervention of God (cf. Westermann, *Genesis,* vol. 1, p. 367).

The parallel structure within the narrative, the parallel motifs alluded to within the story, and parallel stories in other contexts all stress the direction the passage must go. Humans cannot seize divinity; they cannot overstep their bounds and blur God's distinctions. Such evil must be brought to a halt by divine intervention.

Summary Message

In response to the wickedness on the earth, in which superhuman beings overstepped their bounds and humankind's thoughts and deeds were completely evil, the Lord God determined to destroy all living creatures except the recipients of grace.

Exegetical Outline

I. When superhuman beings overstepped their bounds by taking as wives all the women they wanted, giving rise to the appearance of ancient heroes, the Lord warned that he would withdraw his protection (1–4).

A. Wickedness: Superhuman beings, seeing the beauty of human women, took them as wives (1–2).

      B. Oracle: The divine Lord placed a limit on his protection of human life (3).

      C. Qualification: The Nephilim, the ancient heroes, appeared on earth after the marriages (4).

  II. When the Lord saw how grievously wicked humankind was, he determined to destroy all living creatures from the earth except Noah, who found grace (5–8).

      A. Wickedness: All of men's and women's thoughts and actions were evil all the time (5).

      B. Oracle: Because the Lord was grieved over humankind, he determined to destroy all living creatures (6–7).

        1. Emotional: The Lord was grievously pained by humankind (6).

        2. Volitional: The Lord determined to destroy all living creatures from the earth (7).

      C. Qualification: Noah found grace in the eyes of the Lord (8).

Development of the Exposition

I. God places a limit on the extent of human wickedness (1–4).

A. Corrupt practices (1–2).

The first part of the narrative describes the severity of the evil that was emerging: the sons of God took all the daughters of men that they wished. Such unions occurred at a time when the race *began* to multiply (see other uses of the *hiphil* of *ḥālal* to indicate beginnings in 4:26; 9:20; 10:8; 11:6). In other words, while the human family was following the divine directive to multiply and fill the earth (1:28), evil also was abounding.

There are four predominant interpretations of the "sons of God": they are (1) the line of Seth, the godly line; (2) fallen angels; (3) lesser gods within the pantheon; or (4) despots, powerful rulers. The literature on the matter will provide the reasons for and the problems with each view. To me, the view that sees a godly line versus a wicked line of humans does justice neither to the terms used nor to the passage as a whole. The story shows hubris—a proudful overstepping of boundaries. The story describes these "sons of God" as a lusty, powerful lot, striving for fame and fertility. The view that takes them as lesser gods is, of course, built on the idea that pagan mythology lies behind the narrative. There are major problems with that idea, as have been discussed before.

I find most attractive a combination of the "angel" view and the "despot" view. Fallen angels left their habitation and indwelt human despots and warriors, the great ones of the earth. We know from Daniel 10:13, 20 that great kings and kingdoms of the earth had "princes" ruling behind them, powerful spirits with whom Michael had to fight; we also know from Ezekiel 28:11–19 that the king of Tyre may have been associated in the prophet's mind with Satan, the anointed cherub. It is no surprise that, in the literature of the ancient Near East, kings were described as divine, half-divine, or demigods. Pagans revered such great leaders as gods or as offspring of the gods. In Ugaritic the "sons of god[s]" (bn 'lm) refers to members of the pantheon as well as great kings of the earth. In the Ugaritic legend of the Dawn, the chief god of the pantheon, El, is in danger of becoming senile. In a sacred rite of the birds, he seduces two human women in one lewd section of the literature. This union of a god and human women produced "Dawn" and "Dusk" (šḥr and šlm), who seem to become goddesses representing Venus. Gods were thus thought to have their origin in copulation between a god and humans. Accordingly, any superhuman individual or giant would suggest to the ancient people some kind of unusual origin.

The view that interprets the "sons of God" solely as powerful rulers does not, in my opinion, make enough use of the literary connections with pagan literature. The expression "sons of god," when taken in context of these verses and when viewed against the background of the ancient Near East, suggests that more than powerful rulers are involved. Moreover, the expression in the Bible refers to angels (see, e.g., Job 1:6)

If this analysis is correct, then we have in the story an explanation of how corrupt the world got when this unparalleled violation took place. Furthermore, the story would also become a polemic against subsequent beliefs of the pagans that giants, powerful rulers, and men of renown were of divine origin and that immortality was achieved by hubris and immorality. The entire cult of the Canaanites was centered on fertility rites by sympathetic magic in which people engaged in sexual intercourse with hierodules at the temple. As Israel encountered such corruption she had the law of God which stressed the separation of such sexual activities from the sanctuary and denied that divinity could be achieved by defying God's barriers.

The polemic would then be saying that the "sons of God" that the pagans often spoke of were not lesser gods of the pantheon who entered the world of humans for their pleasure. Rather, the "sons of God" were basically human beings. There may have been demonic or spirit activity or power behind them, but they were just another low order of humans. Their taking any women they wished (the origin of harems?) was an attempt to satisfy their baser instincts. The offspring of these marriages may have been famous and powerful but, contrary to popular thinking, were not god-kings. They were flesh, as the text states; they would die, in due course, like all members of the human race. When God judged the world, as he subsequently did, no giant, no alleged deity, and no pagan ideology would have power against him. God simply allotted the days and announced the end.

Here, then, humankind had overstepped the boundaries again, trying to assume the role of divinity and hoping to achieve immortality. God, through Moses, set the record straight by confronting the mythological ideas directly: do not believe the gentile myths concerning the divine origin of the men of renown; in the end all must die, for all are flesh ("the end of all flesh"). The passage goes on to say that those who survive the judgment and become immortal do so by grace alone; moreover, those who are recipients of grace will walk with him in righteousness, not living according to the corrupt practices of the world.

B. Divine intervention (3–4).

The first oracle reported in the passage records the decision to limit the days of human beings on the earth (v. 3). This verse is also fraught with problems. First, the meaning of the first verb, translated "strive" (yādôn), is in question because it occurs only here in the Old Testament. There are several possibilities presented in the literature; Speiser's view that it means "protect" or "shield" (based on an Akkadian cognate) is rather compelling. Others prefer to follow the Septuagint translation "remain," which at least fits the context. The point seems to be that the Lord would not allow the race to continue on in such debauchery; rather, there would be a limit.

This time limit raises the second problem in the passage. The expositor will have to decide whether the number signifies the new age limit for people or whether it specifies the time left for the race before the flood. The second view is far easier to defend, in view of the continued longevity in people (at least past 120 years) after this time.

II. God plans to destroy the entire world because of the pervasive wickedness of the human race (5–7).

A. Corrupt hearts (5).

The fifth verse of the passage records the Lord's evaluation of the race. Whereas the preceding account (v. 2) described the practices without moral evaluation, this part provides the evaluation without restating the practices. We must assume, in view of the juxtaposition of the two parts and especially in view of the parallel structure, that the "wickedness" of verse 5 includes the corrupt practices of verses 1–2.

The description of the race is ominous: The "LORD saw that the wickedness of man was great in the earth, and that every intent of the thoughts of his heart was only evil continually." All the words here call for study, but the key word is "intent" (*yēṣer*). This noun is cognate to the verb used in Genesis 2:7 for the formation of the man—God had made human beings by design (*yāṣar*), but they had taken their God-given capacities and devised evil continually. There is hardly a stronger statement in the Bible about the evil of the human heart. The knowledge of good and evil has led to this low point.

B. Divine intervention (6–7).

The revelation of the Lord's response may be divided into two sections: his pain and his plan. Verse 6 reports how the wickedness of the race pained the Lord's heart (note the contrast between the heart of the wicked and the heart of the Lord). The text says that the Lord was sorry (*wayyinnāḥem*) that he had made (*ʿāśâ*) man in the earth, and it grieved him (*wayyitʿaṣṣēb*) in his heart. As has been mentioned above, these words reflect the words of Lamech in 5:29, which in turn reflect the wording of the curse. Painful toil had entered with the curse, and Lamech longed for comfort (*niḥam*) from the painful toil (*mēʿiṣṣᵉbôn*) in the earth that the Lord cursed. But now we read that God was sorry (*niḥam*) that he made (*ʿāśâ*) man because it grieved him (*ʿāṣab*). Here we learn why pain was brought into the world as a result of sin— God was pained by sin. But now, rather than "comfort" (the *piel*) the humans in their sinful plight, God was "sorry" (the *niphal*) that he made them. This anthropomorphic description of God's response to sin underscores the point of the passage: men and women are so desperately wicked that they grieve God's heart to the extent that, rather than comfort them, God will destroy them.

The second section reveals what God would do about the pain: "I will destroy mankind that I have created." The verb is literally "blot out" (*māḥâ*); its uses in the Bible provide an interesting study. One striking use is the word of the prophet: "And I will stretch over Jerusalem the line of Samaria and the plummet of the house of Ahab, and I *will wipe* Jerusalem as one *wipes* a dish, *wiping* it and turning it upside down" (2 Kings 21:13). The verb indicates a complete removal of one thing from another—in Genesis, of the human race from the earth (cf. also Ps. 51:1, which refers to blotting out transgressions). The judgment will include all living creatures on the face of the earth.

An interesting parallel occurs in Exodus 32. In his anger over the nation's idolatry, the Lord was determined to destroy the entire nation and begin again with Moses (v. 10). Through Moses' intercession the Lord relented (*niḥam*) from the harm that he would do to the people.

Afterward Moses prayed that the sin of the people might be forgiven, saying, "If not, blot me out [< *māḥâ*] from your book that you have written" (v. 32). The Lord responded by saying, "Whoever has sinned against me, I will blot him out of my book" (v. 33). The interpretation of these verses is, of course, another matter entirely. At this point it is simply worth noting the similar themes and terminology. God's pain over sin, especially idolatrous activities, prompts him to blot out the wicked.

III. God provides grace to escape the judgment (8).

The exposition could treat this verse as a subpoint under the previous section, as the exegetical outline listed it; however, it may be significant enough to warrant a separate point in the development of the message. The exposition, then, would first move from sin to the divine decree to limit life, and then again from evaluation of the sinfulness of the race to the divine decree to destroy life, but would culminate with the clear provision of grace. Even though swift judgment would fall on the human race, that judgment would be delayed (120 years) and some would escape (by grace).

A close study of the word for grace will support the idea that it signifies unmerited favor. If the word is given its proper meaning, it means that the recipients of grace actually deserved the judgment too. The discussion of Noah's righteousness comes in the next section. Here, Noah received sovereign grace and escaped the catastrophe. No one escapes divine judgment apart from grace.

The passage in its entirety is clear enough, in spite of the difficulty of some of the details. God's people are recipients of grace; they are spared from the divine wrath on the wicked. Noah and his family received the favor of God and so escaped the corruption and destruction of the wicked world. That doom was certain, in spite of pagan attempts to circumvent it, because it came from the sovereign decree of the Lord. Pagan corruption that confused the boundaries between the spirit world and the human world, that gratified the flesh, and that devised wickedness would not long be tolerated by the Spirit of God.

In the time of Moses, Israel also knew that they were chosen by God and recipients of his favor. They also knew that God would judge the corrupt pagan world for its idolatry and fornication. They too would fall under the judgment of God if they indulged in the sexual idolatry of the pagans (which, on occasion, they did). They, as God's people, would meet the Nephilim, the Anakim, and the Rephaim when they entered the land. But Israel would learn that these men were mere mortals and not demigods. Giants too would fall when the Lord fought for Israel (Num. 13:30–33; 14:6–9).

This passage also has meaning for the end of the age (which is why I worded the main points to fit the original setting as well as the present). The message of the New Testament that parallels Genesis 6–8 is that the corrupt world will be swept away by judgment before God's remnant will begin a new order. Jesus said,

> But as the days of Noah were, so also will the coming of the Son of Man be. For as in the days before the flood, they were eating and drinking, marrying and giving in marriage, until the day that Noah entered the ark, and did not know until the flood came and took them all away, so shall the coming of the Son of Man be. [Matt. 24:37–39]

God's plan to bring about his theocratic blessing involves the removal of the wicked. It is sometimes alarming to look around today and observe how satanic and corrupt the world has become. Many pagan ideas and symbols are reemerging in religious practices, reminding us that we wrestle not against flesh and blood but against principalities and powers (Eph. 6:12) that make subtle appeals to the senses. Only God's warning of imminent judgment provides the clarification: even those claiming the rights of divinity and power will die, for they are mere, sinful mortals. Adam and Eve were the first to learn it, and others did so after them—one does not become like God by rebelling against God, and one cannot rebel against God's order and survive. The point of the passage is that *the wickedness of pagan idolatry and fornication (in spite of their claims) brings pain to God and judgment to the world, a judgment that can be escaped only by God's grace.*

Bibliography

Bustanoby, A. "The Giants and the Sons of God." *Eternity* 15 (1964): 19–20.

Cassuto, U. "The Episode of the Sons of God and the Daughters of Man." In *Biblical and Oriental Studies*, vol. 1, *Bible*, pp. 17–28. Jerusalem: Magnes, 1973.

Clines, David J. A. "The Significance of the 'Sons of God' Episode (Genesis 6:1–4) in the Context of the 'Primeval History' (Genesis 1–11)." *JSOT* 13 (1979): 33–46.

Eslinger, Lyle. "A Contextual Identification of the $b^e n\hat{e}$ $h\bar{a}$'$\check{e}l\bar{o}h\hat{i}m$ and $b^e n\hat{e}$ $h\bar{a}$'$\bar{a}\underline{d}\bar{a}m$ in Genesis 6:1–4." *JSOT* 13 (1979): 65–73.

Kline, Meredith G. "Divine Kingship and Genesis 6:1–4." *WTJ* 24 (1961–62): 187–204.

Murphy, R. E. "Yēṣer in the Qumran Literature." *Bib* 39 (1958): 334–44.

Parunak, H. Van Dyke. "A Semantic Survey of NḤM." *Bib* 56 (1975): 512–32.

Speiser, E. A. "YDWN, Gen. 6:3." *JBL* 75 (1956): 126–29.

Tur-Sinai, N. H. "The Riddle of Genesis VI:1–4." *ExT* 71 (1959–60): 348–50.

VanGemeren, Willem A. "The Sons of God in Genesis 6:1–4 (An Example of Evangelical Demythologization?)." *WTJ* 43 (1981): 320–48.

Wickham, L. R. "The Sons of God and the Daughters of Men: Gen. 6:2 in Early Christian Exegesis." *OTS* 19 (1974): 135–47.

13

The Judgment of the Flood
(Gen. 6:9–8:22)

When studying the story of the flood, the expositor must remember the account is one of swift and terrible judgment on sinful rebellion. The narrative begins by contrasting Noah with his generation, the way of the righteous with the way of open rebellion against God. It continues by describing how God judged the wicked and started a new order with the righteous. It concludes with the sacrifice of a worshiping community that escaped the great judgment. In it all, Noah became the means of saving the race.

Most critical scholarship is convinced that two distinct accounts of the flood are present here (J and P). In the commentaries these two sources may be discussed separately without any attempt to treat the final form of the text as we now have it (Skinner, Gunkel, and von Rad treat them separately; Speiser notes the sources and then discusses the narrative as a whole). In other words, many critical scholars ignore the work of the "redactor," to whom they attribute the final stage in the development of the text. By way of contrast, Martin Kessler analyzes the passage rhetorically and evaluates the critical approach in the process. He concludes that the normal criteria of the documentary hypothesis fail in the examination of the narrative, stating that "there are no 'seams'

188

in Gen. 7; the garment is of one piece and if materials should be of different provenance, their joining has been executed with such artistry that they have been dissolved in the whole" ("Rhetorical Criticism," p. 17). Kessler does not reject the necessity of historical criticism but shows that it vastly underrated the literature. (Kessler's article is well worth reading in conjunction with the account of the flood.)

There is no problem in saying that a compiler, possibly Moses himself, may have used sources in constructing this theological treatise about the flood. To attempt to isolate the possible sources and interpret them separately, however, simply ignores the purpose of exegesis, which is to interpret the text of Scripture as it now stands. To attempt to reconstruct any sources that might be behind a piece of literature is quite a different type of investigation.

In the present structure of the Book of Genesis, this passage begins a tôlᵉdôt section that continues through chapter 9. The section traces what became of Noah: it tells of his righteousness in a corrupt world; his obedience to the Lord's commands in preparing the ark; his deliverance from the flood; his worship after the flood; his reception of the covenant promises, blessings, and commands; and his drunkenness and nakedness in the tent. The section ends on a note much lower than that with which it begins.

The parallels to the beginning of Genesis must not be missed in these next few units in the book. In this first unit the fountains of the deep and the windows of heaven brought a flood over the whole earth (chaos), but then the waters abated and dry land appeared as the seas were once again gathered into their places (creation). In the next unit, Noah was commissioned to be fruitful and multiply and replenish the earth, for he now was the new man of the earth. But then in the following unit Noah's failure was displayed in his lying naked, just as the knowledge of nakedness was evidence of the fall. In both cases curses resulted from the failures. There is thus a deliberate parallel between Adam and Noah and between Adam's world and Noah's world. With Noah there is a new beginning of God's creation, but there is also a new beginning of evil.

Theological Ideas

The obvious theme of this narrative unit is divine judgment on sinners. The account shows God to be the judge of the whole earth, judging the wicked and the world in which they did wickedness. In this judgment God made distinctions between the righteous and the wicked (cf. also Gen. 19) and also between the clean and the unclean (vividly portrayed in the animals chosen for the ark). The clean animals may have been for sacrificial purposes, showing that that which is clean belongs to God, just as the righteous belonged to God.

A related theme is the deliverance from judgment by divine grace. God preserved his remnant from the flood by prior announcement and special provision. One teaching would be that those who claim to be recipients of grace should walk with God in righteousness. Other Scriptures (e.g., Ps. 1) show that an untarnished, separated believer in this life can look forward to being separated from sinners in the judgment.

These two motifs of judgment on sinners and deliverance from the judgment had a special significance for Israel. On a smaller scale but in a similar way, the Lord judged the wicked Egyptians with water and brought Israel through the flood of the sea to worship him on the other side with sacrifices (Exod. 14–15). It is not surprising that many expressions used in Noah's account—the judgment on sinners, the deliverance of the righteous, the walking in righteousness, and the sacrifice of clean animals—are also used in the instruction of the nation in the law.

Why would God use a flood to bring judgment? Were there no other ways to do it? Several observations may be offered here. First, God is sovereign over all creation and frequently uses nature to judge humankind. The sea has always been a symbol of chaos—something that human beings cannot control (Job 38:8–11). But God has power over it and all nature (see Ps. 29, which alludes to the flood).

Second, the great flood would be a most effective way of purging the world—certainly the most graphic. It would wash the earth clean, so that not a trace of the wicked or their wickedness would be found. God thus purified the earth of all but the remnant. Later the law used the terminology of washing with water as a symbol for purging before worship (e.g., Lev. 8:6, 21). The New Testament also drew on these motifs (e.g., Titus 3:5).

Third, the flood was used by God to start a new creation. The first creation with Adam was paralleled here by the second with Noah. Just as the dry land appeared from the waters of the chaos in Genesis 1:9, so here the waters abated until the ark came to rest on Ararat. Once Noah and his family emerged from the ark into God's new creation, he was commissioned to be fruitful and have dominion as Adam had been. The use of a flood that enveloped the whole earth was thus God's way of beginning again. The narrative of the flood, then, includes the uncreation/re-creation theme.

Structure and Synthesis

Structure

The entire account of the flood was arranged according to a pattern of antithetical parallelism in which the second half of the story reflects the first half in reverse (i.e., in a chiasm; see chart 11). There are other ways to diagram this chapter, or the entire section dealing with the Noah narratives (see articles by Anderson, Wenham, or Shea listed in the bibliography). But chart 11 demonstrates the reversal that characterizes the uncreation/re-creation theme, the entire reversal centering on the divine remembrance of Noah. Here is the balance between the judgment on sinners and the deliverance of the recipients of grace. Other structural patterns in the narrative itself may be observed in the discussion of the text.

Summary Message

Because the race was corrupt and filled with violence, the Lord destroyed it and its world with a devastating flood but used Noah, his righteous servant, to save creation and establish a new order after the judgment of the flood.

Exegetical Outline

Title: This is what became of Noah (6:9a).
    I. God instructed Noah, his righteous servant, to prepare the ark, because a great flood would destroy the corrupt, violent race (6:9b–22).
        A. Noah was righteous in a world that was characterized by evil (9b–12).
            1. Noah was righteous and walked with God (9b–10).
            2. The entire human race was corrupt and filled with violence (11–12).

Chart 11. Structure of the Flood Narrative

Title: "These are the generations of Noah."
Introduction: Noah's righteousness and Noah's sons (6:9–10).
A God resolves to destroy the corrupt race (6:11–13).
  B Noah builds an ark according to God's instructions (6:14–22).
    C The Lord commands the remnant to enter the ark (7:1–9).
      D The flood begins (7:10–16).
        E The flood prevails 150 days, and the mountains are covered (17:17–24).
        F God remembers Noah (8:1a).
      E' The flood recedes 150 days, and the mountains are visible (8:1b–5).
      D' The earth dries (8:6–14).
    C' God commands the remnant to leave the ark (8:15–19).
  B' Noah builds an altar (8:20).
A' The Lord resolves not to destroy humankind (8:21–22).

  B. God instructed Noah to prepare an ark to save himself and his family and every creature because the entire world was to be destroyed by a flood (13–22).

   1. God forewarned Noah of the destruction to come (13).

   2. God instructed Noah to build the ark (14–21).

   3. Noah did as the Lord had commanded him (22).

 II. After Noah, his family, and the animals entered the ark, the Lord destroyed the entire earth and all its inhabitants by a great flood (7:1–24).

  A. In obedience to the Lord's instructions, Noah, his family, and the animals entered the ark (1–9).

  B. The Lord brought a great flood on the earth, and every living thing was destroyed (10–24).

   1. Those who entered the ark on the day the flood began were shut in safely by the Lord (10–16).

   2. The waters prevailed over the whole earth, so that every living thing died (17–24).

 III. When the flood receded and the earth was once again inhabitable, Noah obediently emptied the ark and faithfully offered a sacrifice that God accepted (8:1–22).

  A. God began to restore the world by ending the storm and eliminating its effect (1–5).

   1. God remembered Noah (1a).

   2. God began to restore the earth (1b–5).

  B. Noah waited until the earth was inhabitable before leaving the ark (6–19).

   1. He tested the new environment by releasing birds (6–12).

   2. He emptied the ark after he saw the condition of the earth (13–19).

  C. The Lord accepted Noah's sacrifice of the clean animals and withdrew his curse of the flood (20–22).

   1. Noah sacrificed a pleasing sacrifice to the Lord (20).

   2. The Lord resolved not to judge the evil race in this manner again (21–22).

Development of the Exposition

The three parts of the above exegetical outline form a helpful expository development—the commission to build the ark and preserve creation, the judgment of the wicked outside the ark, and the sacrificial worship of the remnant after the completion of the judgment. I doubt that any part of this narrative could be treated apart from the whole;

since it is so long, however, the exposition will have to synthesize portions of the whole and be selective in the details to be discussed.

I. God instructs the righteous to prepare to escape the judgment of the wicked (6:9–22).

A. The righteous walk with God, but the wicked corrupt the earth (9–12).

In this section the narrative contrasts Noah with the corrupt generation. The expositor must clarify the critical words "righteous," "blameless," "corrupt," and "violence."

Noah is described as "a just and blameless man" ('îš ṣaddîq tāmîm), or as Cassuto puts it, "a wholly righteous man" (taking the second adjective as an adverb). "Blameless" describes a perfect, flawless, or complete individual. In Leviticus it is used to describe the sacrificial animals as perfect, without blemish. The term is also used of Abraham (Gen. 17:1). But "righteous" is the main word in Noah's description. It describes both a covenantal relationship and proper conduct within the covenant. By this word we learn that Noah was conforming to the requirements of the relationship he had with God. However we define the word "righteous" in this passage, it is clear that the righteous person belongs to God (see also Gen. 18). This description is further qualified by the report that Noah walked with God (note the word order of v. 9b, placing "Noah" at the beginning and the end).

The corruption of the earth is reported in two stages: verse 11 states that the earth was corrupt and full of violence, and then verse 12 records that *God saw* the earth (recalling the wording of Gen. 1 and 6:5) that it was corrupt. And, if this report were not enough, a causal clause is added to explain that all flesh had corrupted itself. Three times in these two verses the term "corrupt" (wattiššāḥēt, nišḥātâ, hišḥît) is used. This word, as well as "violence" (ḥāmās), gives a graphic description of human nature at its worst. Psalm 14 also speaks of the race's corruption and then elaborates on it. The evil that God saw filled the earth, with the exception of Noah.

B. God resolves to make a distinction between the righteous and the wicked (13–22).

The second part of chapter 6 records how the Lord resolved to do something about the wickedness on the earth. The expositor must not miss the word play in verse 13, with "destroy" (mašḥîtam) reflecting "corrupted" (hišḥît) in the preceding verse. Here is talionic justice; the human race had *corrupted* its way on the earth, and so God would *destroy* them. The use of the word in both places shows its basic meaning to be that of ruining or devastating (see its reference to the destruction of Sodom in Gen. 13:10). Because of the violence, the great evil on the earth, God announced that the end of all flesh was at hand.

A contrast and comparison along the way with the flood stories of the ancient Near East proves helpful. In the Babylonian account there is no emphasis on sin as the reason for the flood; instead, the gods are bothered by the noise of humans.

The construction of the ark with all its details also makes an interesting comparative study with the accounts of the flood in the pagan literature. The biblical ark appears to be far more seaworthy than the monstrosities the other stories describe.

The rest of the chapter records the instructions for building and filling the ark (vv. 14–21) and then the refrain of Noah's obedience. While the details of the instruction need clarification in the exposition, the note that "Noah did according to all that God commanded him—so did he" is most important. Here the reader may catch a glimpse of what it means to walk with God, or to be righteous. The report of Noah's obedience to God's commands in such a perverse generation would have been instructive for Israel under the law. Brueggemann says,

> The narrator wants the listening community to turn to Noah, to consider that in this troubled exchange between creator and creation there is the prospect of fresh alternative. Something new is at work in creation. Noah is the new being (2 Cor. 5:17) for whom none of the other data applies. He is the fully responsive man who accepts creatureliness and lets God be God. So the presentation of faithful Noah is rather like a refrain:
>
> > He . . . did all that God commanded him (6:22). Noah did all that the Lord had commanded him (7:5) . . . as God had commanded Noah (7:9).
>
> Noah regards God's commands as promises of life (cf. John 12:50). [Genesis, pp. 79–80]

II. The Lord destroys the wicked and their world but saves a remnant through the obedience of one man (7:1–24).

A. The Lord ensures the deliverance of the righteous from judgment (1–9).

The chapter opens with the Lord's command for Noah to take his family and the animals into the ark. At the outset, the restatement that Noah was righteous is striking ("for you have I seen righteous before me in this generation"). This virtue must be contrasted with the corruption that God saw in the world, reported in chapter 6. The repetition strengthens the basic theological motif that links the chapters.

The term "blot out," translated "destroy" (māḥâ), occurs again in verse 4. This statement repeats the announcement of the destruction in Genesis 6:7. When the destruction is over, the wicked will be gone.

Once again the obedience motif is present, for after reporting the command to enter the ark, the text says that "Noah did according to all the LORD commanded him" (v. 5). It is further repeated in verse 9 after the elaboration of the entering into the ark ("as God had commanded Noah").

B. The Lord's judgment completely destroys the wicked and their world (10–24).

The record following is one of catastrophic judgment by God. It is expedient that this generation of sinners should die so that all others might be warned of the coming wrath of God. But the development of the narrative follows two sides: those who entered the ark were safely shut in by the Lord, but all those outside the ark died. Noah, then, sailed through the judgment to a new age; catastrophe does not interrupt God's desire to bless the world.

Martin Kessler compares the texts of the two entrance reports (7:8–9, 14–16), two sections that have often been explained as contradictory accounts from two different sources. Kessler observes how similar they are materially.

1. Each list has four categories of animals.
2. While the command in verse 2 has the compound adjective "from all" and the preposition "from," the first entrance report uses the preposition three times and the second report uses the simple adjective "all" six times, summing up the command twice with the repetition of "from all."
3. "Clean and unclean" is repeated from the command, and "male and female," a typical P-phrase, is used in both reports.
4. "Clean and unclean" suggests a reference to the command that calls for seven pairs of clean animals.
5. Both reports relate that animals "came to Noah, to the ark" and end with the obedience formula.
6. The second report is more fully developed, suggesting careful enumeration.
7. Both reports borrow liberally from what has been considered P-vocabulary in Genesis 1: "ground" (1:25), "beast" (v. 24), "male and female" (v. 27), "kind" (v. 12), and "creeping thing" (v. 24).
8. The style of both is enumerative.

Kessler concludes that convincing evidence is lacking that the two accounts are contradictory in any way. He takes the view that the writer created "variation by design"; that is, he wrote an alternate, duplicating, materially synonymous account, in the spirit of parallelismus membrorum ("Rhetorical Criticism," pp. 8–9). For an exhaustive analysis of the entire chapter, see Kessler's whole article.

The narrative of the flood testifies to God's power and freedom over his creation. It shows him to be a God who judges sin in deadly anger. Such a judgment protects every suceeding word of grace from any kind of innocuousness. God's gracious redemption is meaningful in light of judgment. It is clear that the narrative is more interested in the moral aspects of the flood than in all the physical details. The cause is stressed— the monstrous acts of sin performed in their habitual courses. There is no mixture of good, no relenting, just violence and corruption. Basically, the chapter answers the question What is the end of humanity? Can men and women pursue their lives immorally and enjoy the pleasures of this world with reckless abandon? Is this life final or preparatory? With the narrative the answer is clear—everything that had breath died.

But the expense seems so great. It is always harsh to see such judgments reported or predicted. There is no word concerning the terror of the lost and no note of hesitancy in the remnant. The verdict is incontestable: no part of the sinful world can remain.

The account of the judgment shows an eschatological event. This point cannot be missed. Jesus interpreted the passage in an analogy with the final judgment, in which all the wicked will be swept away and only the righteous will enter into the new age.

III. The righteous remnant that God delivers establishes a new order in the earth (8:1–22).

The culmination of the narrative would be most encouraging for believing Israel. Noah, the recipient of grace, the righteous man who walked with God, survived the judgment on the wicked and established a new order in the "life to come." God will again redeem his remnant from the judgments.

A. God restores his creation after the judgment is complete (1–19).

The first part of this chapter details the creation theme, telling how the waters abated, dry land appeared, foliage grew, and humankind again inhabited the earth. Throughout Israel's history this pattern would reappear: after any catastrophic judgment God would begin anew with the remnant.

The chapter begins with the communication that God remembered (wayyizkōr 'ĕlōhîm) Noah and all the living creatures in the ark. This expression says far more than that God suddenly recalled the plight of the remnant. A study of the word "remember" (*zākar*) will show, as Childs says, that "God's remembering always implies his movement toward the object. . . . The essence of God's remembering lies in his acting toward someone because of a previous commitment" (*Memory and Tradition*, p. 34). To say "God remembered Noah" is to say that God faithfully kept his promise to Noah by intervening to end the flood.

The theme of rest figures prominently in this section, picking up the ultimate significance of the name given by Lamech (5:29). When the text says that the ark came to rest (*wattānaḥ*, in 8:4), or that the bird did not previously find a resting place (*mānôaḥ*, in v. 9), there is probably more to the theme than a physical landing on dry ground. (Cassuto traces the theme on *nûaḥ/nōaḥ*.)

B. The restored remnant acknowledges their gratitude to the Lord in worship (20–22).

The sacrifice of Noah forms the major point in the final section of the narrative. Noah built an altar to the Lord and offered burnt offerings (*ʿōlōt*) on it of every clean beast. In response the Lord was pleased to accept the sacrifice: "And the LORD smelled a sweet savor [*rêaḥ hannîḥōaḥ (<nûaḥ)*]." The terminology in these verses reflects Leviticus 1, which legislates the whole burnt offering and describes it as a sweet aroma offering. The whole burnt offering represented the worshiper's total surrender and dedication to the Lord, and the expression of the Lord's smelling the sweet fragrance represented God's acceptance. The people of God were to be a worshiping people, offering to their God the praise of their lips and the best of their possessions.

After the flood, Noah could see that, in addition to the wrath of God on earth, there was also redemption and restoration. No human ever experienced this truth so strongly. How could Noah best express his gratitude to God? According to Maurice, he wanted to say, "We confess that Thou hast made us rulers; help us to govern; we know that the world can crush us; help us not to fear it, but Thee; we are sure that we have rebelled against Thee; we bless Thee that Thou upholdest us and unitest us to Thee" (*Doctrine of Sacrifice*, p. 25). The true worshiper, who by God's grace escaped the catastrophe, thus confessed his submission to and dependence on God through sacrificial worship. The foundation of this sacrifice is laid in God's fixed purpose to assert righteousness in the world, to bring men and women out of a wrong state and to establish them in a true state. In a word, God restored human dependence on him by making people aware of their impotence. By his sacrifice Noah expressed his submission to the gracious government of God in his life and in his world; by it he confessed the evil in himself and his fellows, which had brought ruin upon the world; and by it he acknowledged the wonder of the wisdom of God in redeeming and restoring life. God would say again and again that the human heart was only evil continually. But when people expressed their faith and submission through sacrifice, God would smell the sweet aroma and say again and again that he was well pleased and that he would dwell with them and be their God (see further ibid., pp. 18–32). Accordingly, the Lord promised that such a judgment would never again come on the human race, even though they were filled with evil. The order of creation with its seasons and times would continue.

The expository idea of the entire narrative could be worded as follows: *God will judge the wicked with severe and catastrophic judgment in order to start life over with a worshiping community.* I word this statement with a future tense because at any given moment in history the lesson of this narrative is a warning of imminent judgment on the corrupt race. It is the prerogative and the will of the holy God to purge the world of evil.

Another way to capture the idea is to say that, in the midst of the catastrophic judgment (of the flood) in which the sovereign Lord of creation destroys the wicked world, the servant of God—the recipient of grace—obediently prepares for the life to come and embarks on it in worship. In commenting on this extreme form of judgment, Dods says:

> This event then gives us some measure by which we can know how much God will do to maintain holiness upon earth. In this catastrophe every one who strives after godliness may find encouragement, seeing in it the Divine earnestness of God for good and against evil. There is only one other event in history that so conspicuously shows that holiness among men is the object for which God will sacrifice everything else. There is no need now of any further demonstration of God's purpose in this world and His zeal for carrying it out. . . . The Flood has not been forgotten by almost any people under heaven, but its moral result is *nil.* But he whose memory is haunted by a dying Redeemer, by the thought of One Whose love found its most appropriate and practical result in dying for him, *is* prevented from much sin, and finds in that love the spring of eternal hope. [*Book of Genesis*, pp. 66–67]

Bibliography

Anderson, Bernhard W. "From Analysis to Synthesis: The Interpretation of Genesis 1–11." *JBL* 97 (1978): 23–39.

Battenfield, James R. "Atra-Ḥasīs: A Survey." *GTJ* 12 (1971): 3–22.

Bright, John. "Has Archaeology Found Evidence of the Flood?" In *The Biblical Archaeologist* vol. 1, edited by G. Ernest Wright and David Noel Freedman, pp. 32–40. Garden City, N.Y.: Doubleday, 1961.

Brueggemann, Walter. "Kingship and Chaos (A Study in Tenth Century Theology)." *CBQ* 33 (1971): 317–22.

───── ."Weariness, Exile, and Chaos." *CBQ* 34 (1972): 19–38.

Childs, Brevard S. *Memory and Tradition in Israel.* Naperville, Ill.: Allenson, 1962.

Clark, W. M. "The Flood and the Structure of the Pre-patriarchal History." *ZAW* 83 (1971): 184–211.

───── ."The Righteousness of Noah." *VT* 21 (1971): 261–80.

Fensham, F. C. "The Destruction of Mankind in the Near East." *AION*, n.s., 15 (1966): 31–37.

───── ."The Obliteration of the Family as Motif in the Near Eastern Literature." *AION*, n.s., 19 (1969): 191–99.

Fisher, E. "*Gilgamesh* and Genesis: The Flood Story in Context." *CBQ* 32 (1970): 392–403.

Frymer-Kensky, Tikva. "What the Babylonian Flood Stories Can and Cannot Teach Us About the Genesis Flood." *BAR* 4:4 (November/December 1978): 32–41.

Gage, Warren Austin. *The Gospel of Genesis*, pp. 7–15. Winona Lake, Ind.: Carpenter, 1984.

Hämmerby-Dupuyr, D. "Some Observations on the Assyro-Babylonian and Sumerian Flood-Stories." *AUSS* 6 (1968): 1–18.

Hasel, Gerhard F. "The Biblical View of the Extent of the Flood." *Origins* 2 (1975): 77–95.

───── ."The Fountains of the Great Deep." *Origins* 1 (1974): 67–72.

───── ."Semantic Values of Derivatives of the Hebrew Root Š'R." *AUSS* 11 (1973): 152–69.

───── ."Some Issues Regarding the Nature and Universality of the Genesis Flood." *Origins* 5 (1978): 83–98.

Heidel, Alexander. *The Gilgamesh Epic and the Old Testament Parallels.* Chicago: University of Chicago Press, 1946.

Kaplan, C. "The Flood in the Book of Enoch and Rabbinics." *JSOR* 15 (1931): 22–24.

Kessler, Martin. "Rhetorical Criticism of Genesis 7." In *Rhetorical Criticism: Essays in Honor of James Muilenberg*, edited by Jared J. Jackson and Martin Kessler, pp. 1–17. Pittsburgh: Pickwick, 1974.

Kramer, Samuel Noah. "Reflections on the Mesopotamian Flood." *Expedition* 9 (1967): 12–18.

Lambert, W. G. "New Light on the Babylonian Flood." *JSS* 5 (1960): 113–23.

Lambert, W. G., and Millard, A. R. *Atra-Hasis: The Babylonian Story of the Flood. With the Sumerian Flood Story, by M. Civil.* Oxford: At the Clarendon Press, 1969.

Lapointe, R. "The Divine Monologue as a Channel of Revelation." *CBQ* 32 (1970): 161–81.

Lemche, Neils Peter. "The Chronology in the Story of the Flood." *JSOT* 18 (1980): 52–62.

Mallowan, M. E. L. "Noah's Flood Reconsidered." *Iraq* 26 (1964): 62–82.

Maurice, F. B. *The Doctrine of Sacrifice Deduced from the Scriptures.* 2d ed. London: Macmillan, 1893.

Millard, A. R. "A New Babylonian 'Genesis' Story." *TynB* 18 (1967): 3–18.

Mitchell, T. C. "The Old Testament Usage of Nešāmâ." *VT* 11 (1961): 177–87.

————— ."The Study of Genesis 1–11." *TynB* 3 (1957): 3–4.

Oesterley, W. O. E. "The Dove with the Olive-Leaf (Gen VIII 8–11)." *ExT* 18 (1906–7): 377–78.

Raikes, R. L. "The Physical Evidence of Noah's Flood." *Iraq* 28 (1966): 52–63.

Scott, R. B. Y. "The Hebrew Cubit." *JBL* 77 (1958): 205–14.

Shea, William H. "The Structure of the Genesis Flood Narrative and Its Implications." *Origins* 6 (1979): 8–29.

Toombs, L. E. "Clean and Unclean." *IDB*, vol. 1, p. 643.

Ullendorf, E. "The Construction of Noah's Ark." *VT* 4 (1954): 95–96.

Wenham, Gordon J. "The Coherence of the Flood Narrative." *VT* 28 (1978): 336–48.

Woolley, L. "Stories of the Creation and the Flood." *PEQ* 88 (1956): 14–21.

14

The Covenant of God Through Noah
(Gen. 9:1–17)

This passage is completely given over to God's initiative in making a covenant with all humankind. The repetition of the commission given to Adam demonstrates that with Noah there is a new beginning, but one that required a covenant. It was now necessary to have a covenant with obligations for men and women and promises from God because people might begin to wonder whether God held life cheap or whether the taking of life was a small matter. This covenant through Noah declared that God held life sacred and that humankind too must preserve life in the earth.

Theological Ideas

The major idea in this unit is the establishment of an unconditional, unilateral covenant. From this point on, the God of Israel would be known as a covenant-making and covenant-keeping God. Naturally, this motif has bearing on subsequent covenants that God made with his people. Just like this covenant, those later covenants had stipulations for the people and promises and signs from God. The exposition of this narrative must therefore develop the concept of covenant within the developing message of Genesis.

In addition to this concept, the passage unfolds the continuing re-creation theme with the comparison between Noah and Adam. Here the study must retrace the original design of the Creator for blessing and commissioning humankind in the image of God. This passage alludes to the former by the use of "be fruitful," "multiply," and "fill the earth." It also parallels the garden scene with the permission to eat any animal, but with a prohibition against eating blood.

Another theme that is important to the Levitical laws is the value of blood. The blood of an animal, according to Leviticus, belongs to God. Humans dare not eat it. Moreover, the blood of human beings is the life of the flesh. Humans dare not spill it, for human beings are in the image of God. For the crime of murder, then, society would have the right to take the murderer's life.

Structure and Synthesis

Structure

The narrative falls into two parts. As Westermann notes,

> The parts, 9:1–7 and 9:8–17, have each their own message, but belong together as the divine addresss that concludes the flood. . . . The two parts really contain only one message—the first renews the blessing over the living beings saved from the flood, the second promises that there shall never again be a flood. Everything else is subordinated to this. [*Genesis,* vol. 1, p. 461]

In his discussion Westermann shows that this passage is parallel to Genesis 8:21–22 (although he classifies 9:1–17 as P and 8:21–22 as J). The promise that there shall never again be a flood (9:8–17) corresponds to 8:21, and the decree that the rhythm of life will continue with order (9:1–7) corresponds to 8:22. We may say that chapter 9 confirms those previous promises by the establishing of a covenant.

The structure of each part of the narrative contains parallel opening and closing lines, forming inclusios. Verse 1 records the commission to be fruitful and multiply and fill the earth. Then, after detailing the provision of food and the prohibition regarding blood, the section closes with a restatement of this commission. The force of the inclusio is to strengthen the unity of the section and to maintain the prominent idea of producing life. Verse 9 reports God's decision to make a covenant with Noah and his descendants. Then, after detailing the recipients of the covenant and the sign and the promises of the covenant, the section closes with a restatement of the establishment of the covenant and the giving of the sign.

Several structural clues indicate that the two sections form a unit. First, the covenant surfaces in the two parts. For example, verse 7 gives the stipulations in the positive statement, "But you [w^e'*attem*], be fruitful." (This contrast is with the preceding negative stipulation not to shed the blood of human beings.) Then, in verse 9, God promises what he will do: "But as for me [*wa*'*ǎnî*], I am about to establish my covenant with you."

Another link between the two sections may be formed with the repetition of phrases describing the extent of the provisions and prohibitions: in verse 2, "every animal of the earth," "every fowl of the air," "everything that moves on the earth," and "every fish of the sea"; in verse 3, "every moving thing that lives" and "everything"; in verse 5, "every animal"; in verse 10, "every living creature," "every beast of the earth," and "every beast of the earth"; in verse 12, "every living creature"; in verse 15, "every living creature of all flesh" and "all flesh"; in verse 16, "every living creature of all flesh"; and in verse 17, "all flesh."

The constant repetition and variation of this emphasis, which is a continuation from the flood narrative, unites these two sections and points to the extent of the workings of the covenant. All living creatures are at humankind's disposal for food, as long as the blood is not included; but God will make a covenant to protect all living creatures on the earth. In a word, life is valuable, for God will protect it, and humankind must not abuse it.

Finally, the structure is united with the introductory formula of the address to Noah and his sons after the flood. Verse 1 reports, "And God blessed Noah and his sons and said. . . ." Verse 8 likewise begins, "And God said to Noah and his sons." And verse 17 concludes, "And God said to Noah."

The exposition thus incorporates all seventeen verses in the development of the theological message. Accordingly, the narrative unit provides a nice balance, delineating the responsibilities and laws for Noah and then the promises and the sign from God.

Summary Message

Demonstrating his high regard for life, God established a new order with the blessing of fruitfulness and the prohibition of taking another person's life and promised by covenant never to destroy every living creature again by such a flood—the rainbow being the reminder of this gracious covenant.

Exegetical Outline

    I. God established the new order by blessing Noah as he had Adam and by instructing humankind that, rather than destroy human life, they must populate the earth and preserve life (1–7).

        A. God began the new order by blessing Noah as he had Adam and by allowing people to eat meat without blood (1–4).

            1. Blessing: Human beings were to be fruitful and multiply (1).

            2. Provision: Human beings were allowed to eat of every living thing (2–3).

            3. Prohibition: Human beings were not to eat animals alive, that is, with the blood in them (4).

        B. God prohibited people from shedding human blood, for humans were in the image of God (5–6).

            1. Any violation of the law of shedding blood would be punished by God (5).

            2. Anyone who shed the blood of another person would be put to death, for humans were in the image of God (6).

        C. God reiterated his instructions for humankind to fill the earth (7).

    II. God promised with an unconditional, enduring covenant that he would never again destroy the world with such a flood and sealed his promise with the sign of the rainbow (8–17).

        A. God promised with a covenant that he would never again destroy the world with such a flood (8–11).

        B. God sealed his covenant with the sign of the rainbow, reminding himself and the race of the covenant promise (12–16).

        C. God reiterated the sign of the covenant of peace (17).

Development of the Exposition

The unity of the passage is based on the value of life: after the flood, people might think that life was worthless to God, but God's commandments to and covenant with Noah showed that the contrary was true. The exposition should retain this theme through its development.

I. People have the responsibility to produce and preserve life on the earth (1–7).

A. *God commissions humankind to produce life (1, 7).*

The text clearly shows that Noah was the second Adam; that is, he was blessed as God's image bearer and given the same commandments.

"Be fruitful, and multiply, and fill the earth [$p^e r\hat{u}$ $\hat{u}r^e b\hat{u}$ $\hat{u}mil'\hat{u}$ 'et-hā'āreṣ]" restates the earlier commission of Genesis 1:28. In both passages the commission is introduced by "and God blessed" (waybārek), thus bestowing the ability to be fruitful. In verse 7, the verb "swarm" (širṣû) is added, making another allusion to the beginning (1:20).

It would be worth noting in passing that these verbs are used in Exodus 1:7 to describe how the Israelites flourished in the land of Egypt. It is clear that in that passage Moses was portraying the people of Israel as obediently following the divine commission from God and enjoying God's blessing.

B. God instructs humankind to protect life (2–4).

The parallels with the beginning of Genesis continue. God provided Noah and his descendants with food (cf. 9:3 with 1:29) but now also opened the animal world to them for food. Humankind now lived with the reality of killing, and so the animal world would be afraid of humans. But within the lavish provision ("every moving thing") there is prohibition—"only flesh with its life, its blood, you shall not eat" (cf. 2:16–17). The point of the prohibition is that people may eat flesh as long as it no longer has life in it—and the blood represented the life. The text is prohibiting not simply the consumption of blood but rather the pulsating lifeblood.

C. God prohibits the violation of life (5–6).

There are two parts to this section: divine reprisal for any violation of the law of blood (v. 5) and punishment for the shedding of human blood (v. 6). That they belong together is evident from the mention of human life in both verses.

Repetition is used to unite and strengthen the ideas here. The particle 'ak, "only, surely," begins both verse 4 and verse 5, forming a continuation. In verse 4 it is translated "but" or "only," making the exception to the provision of flesh. In verse 5 it is translated "surely," introducing the penalty for any violation of the preceding prohibition.

Another word that is repeated is the verb "I will require" ('edrōš). The structure of verse 5 is governed by this verb: "Surely your own blood will I require; at the hand of every beast will I require it; and at the hand of man and every man's brother will I require." The whole emphasis is put on the verb by this threefold repetition. The command not to kill is thus reformulated to express God's absolute lordship over every life.

We thus learn that humankind does not have unlimited power over life just because God does. God's warnings in this section taught people to safeguard life, both in how they ate meat and in how they preserved human life on the earth. By these teachings humankind would learn that law was necessary for the stability of life in the new order, that wickedness could not go unchecked as it had before. It might again attain dimensions that nothing short of a flood could correct. Human government was instituted in these early provisions. Israel later had the laws against bloodshed and eating blood more fully formulated as part of the Sinaitic covenant.

II. God promises to preserve his creation (8–17).

The second half of the passage records the making of the unconditional covenant that ensures that there will not be another watery judgment like the flood. This covenant does not depend on human obedience to the laws given to Noah; rather, men's and women's compliance with the laws will allow them to live and enjoy this covenant.

A. God promises to preserve life (8–11).

In this section the nature and the extent of the covenant is explained. God instituted this covenant as a gracious provision of protection for all creation. The basic point of this covenant is that God gave assurance that what he agreed to do would be done.

B. God uses a sign as a reminder of the pledge (12–17).

The covenant is cosmic and universal, as seen from the great sign, the rainbow. As it arched over the horizon after the rains, it formed an all-embracing sign of God's faithfulness to his word of grace. Von Rad observes that the bow (qešet) is the same word for the regular battle bow, and so it makes a vivid description of what was going on: God hung up his "battle bow" to be a sign of peace (*Genesis*, p. 134). Dods again is helpful as he elaborates on this sign.

> They accepted it as a sign that God has no pleasure in destruction, that he does not give way to moods, that he does not always chide, that if weeping may endure for a night joy is sure to follow. If any one is under a cloud, leading a joyless, heartless life, if any one has much apparent reason to suppose that God has given him up to catastrophe, and lets things run as they may, there is some satisfaction in reading this natural emblem and recognising that without the cloud, nay, without the cloud breaking into heavy sweeping rains there cannot be the bow, and that no cloud of God's sending is permanent, but will one day give place to unclouded joy. [*Book of Genesis*, pp. 73–74]

The sign of the covenant was to all flesh. It was a token of God's pledge to humankind. Israel would be strengthened, as would all covenanters, to see in the skies again and again the pledge of God that he keeps his promise of grace to the human race. In addition, it was a reminder that judgment was completed for that age. The cycle once more came around in the end of the age, albeit in a different form, before there was complete peace and rest.

The main point of this section is that God's covenant turns judgment into grace. The emblem of the bow was the sign of the covenant, serving to remind the participants to keep the stipulations. Here God, who is omniscient, would perpetually "remind" himself never to flood the world again. The use of "I will remember" in verses 15 (we̱zākartî) and 16 (lizkōr) recalls the usage of the verb in 8:1, "and God remembered [wayyizkōr] Noah." As noted earlier, the verb "remember" is used frequently to describe God's faithfulness to his covenant promises.

Within the whole context of the flood narrative, the message at the conclusion is one of peace and preservation. The previous section has been one of judgment, not unlike war. Covenant treaties were often made after wars in order to ensure peace, a sequence that seems to be occurring here. God would definitely judge sin, but he would also make a covenant of peace with the survivors. His covenant of peace would reign over the new era, in which humankind had the responsibility to take life seriously. We may word it this way: *Humankind is responsible to preserve life (i.e., produce and protect life) because they are regularly reminded that life is precious to God.*

If the entire narrative of the flood is typical of the great judgment at the end of the age (Matt. 24:37), then this narrative anticipates the future time of peace when swords will be beaten into plowshares (Isa. 2:4)—the new age that will dawn after the great judgment on the world of sin. In the meantime, however, life continues in the present order. The divine will of forbearance is at work until the end of the age. This provision we call common grace. Believers understand this forbearance and wait patiently until all things will be made new. Believers attempt to live obediently to their covenant God, reminded every time they see a rainbow that divine wrath will give way to peace, for judgment is God's strange work (Isa. 28:21).

Bibliography

Albright, W. F. "The Hebrew Expression for 'Making a Covenant' in Pre-Israelite Documents." *BASOR* 121 (1951): 21–22.

Barr, J. "The Image of God in the Book of Genesis—a Study of Terminology." *BJRL* 51 (1968–1969): 11–26.

Dewar, C. L. "The Biblical Use of the Term 'Blood.' " *JThS*, n.s., 4 (1953): 204–8.

McCarthy, D. J. "The Symbolism of Blood and Sacrifice." *JBL* 88 (1969): 166–76.

Mawdsley, Ralph D. "Capital Punishment in Gen. 9:6." *Central Bible Quarterly* 18 (1975): 20–25.

Tur-Sinai, N. H. "Ohoth ('Signs') in the Bible and in the Lachish Letters." *Tar* 20 (1949): 49–57.

15

The Oracle of Noah–
the Curse of Canaan
(Gen. 9:18–29)

This bizarre little story about Noah's drunkenness and exposure, along with the resultant cursing of Canaan, has perplexed students of Genesis for a long time. Why does Noah, the spiritual giant of the preceding narratives, appear in such a bad light? What exactly did Ham do to Noah? Who is Canaan, and why should he be cursed for something he did not do? Although such problems preoccupy much of the study of the passage, their solutions are tied to the more basic question of the purpose of the narrative within the theological message of Genesis.

Theological Ideas

The most significant element of this passage is the blessing and cursing, the two motifs that occur repeatedly throughout the book. Another important stage in the development of these motifs is found in the oracle of Noah. Ham's impropriety toward the nakedness of his father prompted an oracle with far-reaching implications: Canaan was cursed, but Shem (the ancestor of Israel) and Japheth enjoyed the blessing. It seems almost incredible that a relatively minor event would have such major repercussions. But consistently in Genesis one finds that the fate of both people and nations is determined by occurrences with the ancestors that seem trivial and commonplace. The main characters of these stories acted on natural impulse in their own interests, but the narrator was concerned with the greater significance of their actions. Out of the virtues and vices of Noah's sons grew the virtues and vices of the families of the world.

The purpose of this section in Genesis is to portray the characteristics of the three branches of the human race in relation to blessing and cursing. In pronouncing the oracle, Noah discerned the traits of his sons and, in a moment of insight, determined that the attributes of their descendants were embodied in his sons' personalities. Because these sons were primogenitors of the families of the earth, the narrator is more interested in the greater meaning of the oracle with respect to tribes and nations in his day than with the children of Shem, Ham, and Japheth.

The oracle of Noah, far from being concerned solely with the fortunes of the immediate family, thus actually pertains to vast movements of ancient peoples. Portraying their tendencies as originating in individual ancestors, Genesis anticipates the expected destinies of these tribes and nations. On the basis of their actions, they would either share in the blessing or be cursed. Within the general oracle of Noah there seems to be an emphasis on the Canaanites, who are the antagonists in the Book of Genesis. What else would Israel think of when they read that Canaan had been cursed in antiquity?

Besides the prominent themes of blessing and cursing in the oracle, this passage makes several other theological contributions. In the first place, Ham's acting with moral abandonment seems to be the antithesis of honoring his father (which later became one of the Ten Commandments). In connection with this incident there is also the idea of talionic justice, a motif that has surfaced earlier in the book. Because Ham caused a breach in his family, his own descendants would be cursed. Related to this issue is the concept that the sins of the fathers would be visited on the children—a theme also found in the Decalogue. Finally, moral issues are also presented here as the occasion for other sins. Drunkenness, nakedness, and moral abandonment are all decried by this story. Accordingly, sobriety, modesty, and filial honor are all enjoined by Moses.

Structure and Synthesis

Structure

It is fairly easy to see that the passage essentially has the record of the event and the oracle, with the oracle being based on the event. There

is also a brief prologue that introduces the family members as the ancestors of the entire human population (vv. 18–19) and a conclusion
(vv. 28–29) that probably applies to the whole *tôleḏôt* section.

The two main sections—the event and the oracle—are parallel in
their organization. The event tells what Noah did, how Ham reacted to
it, and then how Shem and Japheth rectified the situation; the section
with the oracle begins with a note about Noah's waking from his stupor
and realizing what had transpired and then proceeds to the curse on
Canaan and the blessing on Shem and Japheth. In the event section,
Ham is twice identified as "the father of Canaan" (vv. 18, 22), an inserted
explanation that lays the foundation for the curse oracle.

That the oracle stresses Canaan can be seen from its repetition of the
name in all three lines. With the additional references to Canaan in the
report of the event, the point of the passage can hardly be ignored.
Before the blessing can be developed among those who are righteous,
those who act with moral abandonment must be removed. To Israel the
latter would primarily mean Canaanites.

Genesis 49 is a parallel passage; it records Jacob's oracle concerning
the future of the tribes. In both passages—here at the end of the primeval
events and there at the end of the patriarchal stories—the one giving the
oracle uses the nature and actions of his sons to anticipate their descendants' destinies. What makes a curse or a blessing from an old man
binding on his descendants? The expositor will have to take a careful
look at this phenomenon, for unless the oracles came from God, they
would not be prophetic.

Summary Message

Noah cursed Canaan, the descendant of Ham, with slavery but blessed
Shem and Japheth because, when he had become intoxicated and had
lain naked in his tent, Ham had responded with disrespect, whereas
Shem and Japheth had respectfully covered their father's nakedness.

Exegetical Outline

    I. Prologue: The entire earth was populated by those who de-
       scended from Shem, Ham, and Japheth—Ham being the father
       of Canaan (18–19).
   II. Event: In response to Noah's intoxication and nakedness, Ham
       acted with disrespect, but Shem and Japheth acted with rever-
       ence in covering their father (20–23).
      A. Noah's behavior: After planting a vineyard, Noah became
         drunk and lay naked in his tent (20–21).
      B. The sons' response: Ham acted with disrespect, but his
         brothers covered their father's nakedness (22–23).

III. Oracle: Upon learning what Ham had done, Noah pronounced
   an oracle, cursing Canaan with abject slavery and blessing Shem
   and Japheth (24–27).
   A. Noah's knowledge: Waking from the wine, Noah learned
      how his youngest son had acted (24).
   B. Noah's oracle:
      1. Canaan, the son of Ham, would be cursed with abject
         slavery (25).
      2. The Lord, the God of Shem, would be blessed, so that
         Shem would be served by Canaan (26).
      3. Japheth would be enlarged and settle in Shem's tents,
         causing Canaan to serve him (27).
IV. Epilogue: Noah lived 350 years after the flood and died at the
   age of 950 years (28–29).

Development of the Exposition

The prologue and epilogue form important links to the context and
provide background information for this narrative, although they need
not be included in the actual exposition of the unit. The event and the
oracle form the essence of this narrative.

I. God's people must respond to incidents of decadence with ethical purity rather than moral abandonment (20–23).

With this expository point we may summarize the event that led up
to the oracle. In writing this statement I am using Noah's behavior as
the tension and the reactions of the sons as the right and wrong ways
to respond.

A. Decadent behavior (20–21).

The behavior of Noah after the flood provided the occasion for the
violation by Ham. Noah acted so differently from before the flood that
some commentators have suggested that a diffferent person, or at least
a different source, is in view here. The text, however, simply presents
one man who had walked in righteousness with God but who planted
a vineyard, became drunk, and lay naked in his tent. Or as Francisco
says, "With the opportunity to start an ideal society, Noah was found
drunk in his tent" ("Curse on Canaan," p. 678).

Noah is described as a "man of the soil" in verse 20. This epithet is
probably designed to say more than that he was a farmer. In view of his
being the patriarch of the survivors of the flood, Noah would be considered as the master of the earth, or as Rashi understood it, the Lord of

the earth (Ben Isaiah and Sharfman, *The Pentateuch and Rashi's Commentary,* p. 84). This view harmonizes with the identification of Noah as the second Adam.

This man of the soil proceeded (*wayyāḥel*) to plant a vineyard. The primeval narratives present various beginnings, most of which are not very good. After the flood there are three—Noah's planting a vineyard, Nimrod's becoming a hunter (Gen. 10:8), and the building of the tower by the people of Shinar (11:6). The use of the same verb (*ḥālal*) in these three passages provides an ominous connection.

The exposition of this story will have to consider what Noah did wrong. Some commentators exonerate him completely, and others categorically condemn his activity. The man perhaps was simply overwhelmed by what he had produced. Planting a vineyard does not seem problematic; the vine in the Bible is considered noble. The psalmist described wine as God's provision, stating that it "gladdens the heart of man" (104:15). A parable in Judges has a vine saying, "Should I give up my wine, which cheers both God and men?" (9:13). Not only did the fruit of the vine alleviate the pain of the curse of the ground (cf. Gen. 5:29), but it also formed the symbol of the coming bliss in the messianic age. Zechariah 8:12 and Isaiah 25:6 describe the future age with this motif (cf. the point of the turning of the water to wine in John 2 as a sign).

Although wine alleviates to some degree the painful toil of this life, the Old Testament warned of the moral dangers attending this new step in human enterprise. Those who served the Lord in the temple (Lev. 10:9), those taking vows (Num. 6:2–4), and those making leadership decisions (Prov. 31:4–5) were warned of its use. The story of Noah shows two degrading effects of the abuse of wine—drunkenness and nakedness. While no blame is attached to his planting the vineyard, it is difficult to ignore the prophetic oracles that use nakedness and drunkenness in their descriptions of chaotic tragedies (see, e.g., Hab. 2:15; Lam. 4:21). The Old Testament may not have prohibited the use of wine for everyone, but it never excused drunkenness and nakedness.

Along with the primary intent of the narrative to set the stage for the oracle, the point here forms a polemic against pagan ideas and practices. The ancient Near East saw Armenia as the original home of wine, but Egyptian literature attributed its invention to the god Osiris, and Greek literature attributed it to Dionysius. The Genesis account, by contrast, reports that the beginning of wine and its effect on humans was anything but divine. It had all the trappings of depravity. Cursing and slavery, rather than festive joy, proceeded from its introduction into the world. The passage implies that any nation that indulges in the excessive use of wine and in nakedness is already in slavery.

B. Moral abandonment (22).

Noah's behavior prompted the violation by Ham. Ham, whom the text identifies as the father of Canaan, "saw his father's nakedness and told his two brothers outside" (v. 22). What Ham did has been the subject of a great deal of speculation. The expositor will discover that many writers believe that Ham did nothing at all. Many believe that two traditions have been spliced together here and that Canaan was the one who did the wrong. Rice asserts, "All the tensions of Gen. 9:18–27 are resolved when it is recognized that this passage contains two parallel but different traditions of Noah's family" ("Curse That Never Was," p. 7). But positing two traditions does not resolve the tension; instead, it raises another. If the parts of the story were from different traditions, why were they combined to form this narrative?

It seems clear enough that the story is contrasting Ham with his two brothers in the event of seeing the father's nakedness—and Ham is the father of Canaan. The oracle curses Ham's descendants but blesses the descendants of Shem and Japheth. If Canaan rather than Ham had been the guilty one, then why was Ham not included in the blessing? The story places the violation on Ham but the curse on Canaan.

Many interpretations have been given for this violation, some of which see more in the text than is actually there. The discussions usually take "he saw his nakedness" as a euphemism for some sin. Cassuto speculates that the pre-Torah account may have been uglier but was reduced to minimal proportions (*Commentary on Genesis*, vol. 2, pp. 150–52). The Talmud records the view that castration took place which suggests an original story similar to Greek and Semitic stories about family power struggles (*Sanh.* 70a). The only possible textual support for such a violent crime would come from Genesis 9:24, which says that Noah "found out what his youngest son *had done* to him." It is not clear, however, how the brothers' act of covering up their naked father would correct such a deed.

Bassett suggests, on the basis of the idiomatic "uncover the nakedness," that Ham engaged in sexual intercourse with Noah's wife and that Canaan was cursed because he was the offspring of that union. Bassett argues that to "see another's nakedness" is the same as sexual intercourse and that a later redactor who missed the idiomatic meaning added the words in 9:23 (a convenient way to dispose of a problem for the view!).

The evidence for this interpretation is minimal. The expression "to see the nakedness" is used in Scripture for shameful or defenseless exposure. But this wording is quite different from the idiom for sexual violation, "to uncover the nakedness" (see Lev. 18 and 20). This latter construction (*gillâ ʿerwâ*) is used in Leviticus 18 and 20 to describe the evil sexual conduct of the Canaanites. Leviticus 20:17 is the only place where "see" (rā'â) is used, but there it is in a parallel construction with "uncover" (gillâ). This one usage cannot be made the basis for an idiomatic meaning of sexual intercourse. Rather, the clear idiom influences the meaning of "see" in that context.

According to Genesis 9:21, Noah *uncovered himself* (the stem is reflexive). If there had been any occurrence of sexual violation, one would have expected to read, "Ham uncovered his father's nakedness." Moreover, as Rice observes, if Ham had committed incest with his mother, he would not likely have told his two brothers, nor would the Torah pass over such an inauspicious beginning for the detested Canaanites ("Curse That Never Was," pp. 12–13).

There is thus no clear evidence that Ham actually did anything other than see the nakedness of his father. To Noah, however, such an act was serious enough to prompt the oracle on Ham's descendants (who would be openly guilty in their customs of what many suspect Ham of doing). It is difficult for people living in the modern world to understand and appreciate the modesty and discretion of privacy called for in ancient morality. Nakedness in the Old Testament was from the beginning a thing of shame for fallen humankind. To Adam and Eve as sinners, the state of nakedness was both undignified and vulnerable. Their covering of their nakedness was a sound instinct, for it provided a boundary for fallen human relations. To be exposed meant to be unprotected; to see someone uncovered was to bring dishonor and to gain advantage for potential exploitation. A similar commentary on seeing nakedness as a gross violation of honor is related by Herodotus in the story of Gyges, who, when seeing the nakedness of Candaules' wife—which Herodotus said was a shame among the Lydians—either had to kill Candaules or had to be killed himself (*Herodotus* 1.8–13).

By mentioning that Ham entered and saw his father's nakedness, the text emphasizes that this seeing was the disgusting thing. Ham's errant looking, a moral flaw, represented the first step in the abandonment of a moral code. This violation of a boundary destroyed the honor of Noah. (For similar taboos against such "looking," cf. Gen. 19:26; Exod. 33:20; Judg. 13:22; 1 Sam. 6:19). Ham desecrated a natural and sacred barrier. His going out to tell his brothers about it without covering the old man aggravated the act. Because of this breach of domestic and filial propriety (the expositor must keep in mind that these are not little boys), Ham could expect nothing less than the oracle against his own family's honor.

C. Righteous conduct (23).

Shem and Japheth acted to preserve the honor of their father by covering him with *the* garment (v. 23). The definiteness of the noun gives the impression that Ham completed Noah's uncovering by bringing the garment out to his brothers. The text is very careful to state that the brothers did not see their father's nakedness. Their approach was cautious, their backs turned to Noah with the garment on their shoulders. In contrast to the brevity of the narrative as a whole, this verse draws out the story in great detail in order to dramatize the brothers' sensitivity and piety. The point cannot be missed—this attitude is the antithesis of the hubris of Ham.

II. God will bless the righteous but curse those who act with moral abandonment (25–27).

An act of hubris cannot end without repercussions. A humiliation in like manner will follow according to the principle of talionic justice. Ham made an irreparable breach in his father's family; a curse will thus be put on his family. The oracle that follows, although including blessing and cursing, is essentially a curse, for the blessing gains its meaning in contrast to the curse on Canaan.

A. The curse (25).

With the brief notice that Noah knew what his youngest son had done to him, the narrative bridges the event and the oracle. The verb could indicate that Noah found out, or that he intuitively knew.

In the ancient world the curse was only as powerful as the one making it. Anyone could imprecate, but imprecation was effectual only when God was invoked. The Torah had no magical ideas such as sorcery and divination (Exod. 22:18). The curse may have found its way into Israel as part of an oath to protect its institutions. One who committed serious transgressions against them was delivered up to misfortune, the activation of which belonged to the Lord (Deut. 28; Josh. 6:26; 1 Sam. 26:19). The curse was thus a means of seeing that the will of the Lord was executed in divine judgment on anyone profaning what was sacred. It was an expression of faith in the just rule of God, for one who cursed had no other resource. The words had no power in themselves, unless the Lord performed them. It was thus in every sense an oracle. God himself would bring about the curse if it was indeed his desire to do so. In this passage the honor of Noah and the sanctity of the family had been treated lightly. Noah therefore pronounced the oracle of cursing; the Lord would fulfill it.

The second half of the verse explains that slavery is the curse. This fate meant certain subjugation and loss of freedom. But Noah was not content to state that Canaan would be enslaved. By using the superlative genitive, "servant of servants" (ʿebed ʿăbādîm), he declared that it would be the most abject slavery. Canaan would serve his relatives, Shem and Japheth.

But who was Canaan? Was it right to curse someone for the actions of another? The Torah does incorporate judgment from one generation to another, the sins of the fathers being visited on the children (Exod. 20:5). But in such cases the one judged deserves to be punished (cf. "to those who hate me" in Exod. 20:5). A later generation may be judged for the sin of an ancestor if they are of like mind and deed. Otherwise they may simply bear the fruit of some ancestor's sin (e.g., see Josh. 9:27).

It is unlikely that Canaan was singled out for the curse because he was the youngest son of Ham (who was Noah's youngest son). On the contrary, the Torah, which shows that God deals justly with all people, suggests that Noah anticipated in him the evil traits that marked his father Ham. The text has prepared the reader for this conclusion by twice pointing out that Ham was the father of Canaan, a phrase that signifies more than lineage. Even though the oracle of cursing would weigh heavily on Ham as he saw his family marred, it was directed to his distant descendants, who retained the traits.

In this regard it must be clarified that the Canaanite people, not the man, are in view for the fulfillment of the oracle. The names Canaan, Shem, and Japheth all represent the people who were considered to be their descendants. By this extension the oracle predicts the curse on the Canaanites and is much wider than a son's being cursed for his father, although the oracle springs from the incident. The oracle was thus a prophetic announcement concerning the future nations (as Gen. 49 was for the future tribes). To the Hebrew mind, the Canaanites were the most natural embodiment of Ham. Everything the Canaanites did in their pagan existence was symbolized by the attitude of Ham. From the moment the patriarchs entered the land, these tribes were there with their corrupting influence (Gen. 13:13; 15:16; 18:20–21; chaps. 19 and 38).

The Torah warned the people of the exodus about the wickedness of the Canaanites in terms that call to mind the violation of Ham (Lev. 18:2–6). There follows a lengthy listing of such vile practices of the Canaanites (vv. 7–23) that the text must employ euphemisms to represent their deeds ("nakedness" is used twenty-four times). Because of these sins the Canaanites were defiled and were to be driven out before the Israelites.

The constant references to "nakedness" and "uncovering" in this passage in Leviticus, designating the people of Canaan as a people enslaved sexually, clearly reminds the reader of the action of Ham, the father of Canaan. No Israelite who knew the culture of the Canaanites could read the story of their ancestor without making the connection. But the descendants had advanced far beyond the sin of the ancestor. The attitude that led to the deed of Ham came to full fruition in the Canaanites. These descendants were not cursed because of what Ham did: they were cursed because they acted as their ancestor had. That moral abandonment was fully developed in the Canaanites, which it took an oracle of the Lord to reveal and announce.

B. The blessing (26–27).

The blessing is given to Shem, but the wording is unexpected—the God of Shem is blessed. The expositor should not miss the word play on the name; Delitzsch says, "[Yahweh] makes Himself a name in becoming the God of Shem, and thus entwines His name with that of Shem, which means the name" (*New Commentary on Genesis*, p. 296). By blessing the God of the man (and of the tribe), the man himself is blessed. The idea is that Shem would ascribe his good fortune to the Lord, for his advantage would be his relationship to the Lord.

Here too the point of the oracle looks forward to the descendants. It would be clear to Israel, who found themselves in such a personal, covenantal relationship with the Lord, that they were the heirs of the blessing. As they encountered the Canaanites, they would know that the blessing subjugated the Canaanites to them.

The announcement of Japheth's share in the blessing is strengthened by another word play: "May the LORD enlarge [*yapt*] Japheth [*yepet*]." There will be peaceful cohabitation between Japhethites and Shemites, or at least alliance in the subjugation of Canaan, for Japheth will "dwell in the tents of Shem."

The critical part of this narrative is most certainly the oracle of cursing and blessing, and the dominant feature of that oracle is the cursing of Canaan. The Canaanites would be doomed to perpetual slavery because they would follow in the moral abandon of their distant ancestor. Their subjugation would be contrasted to the blessing on the others: Shem would have spiritual blessings by virtue of knowing the Lord; Japheth would have temporal blessings with the prospect of participation with Shem. This curse narrative immediately precedes the listing of the families and the descendants in Genesis 10. If there was any question as to whom the narrator was referring, the lines could be traced immediately.

The point of the story in context, then, is God's preparation for the giving of the land to Abram, the heir of Shem's blessing. This point would then typify the preparation of the land for Israel's inheritance. For Israel to receive the blessing of the promise of the fathers, the curse on the Canaanites had to be exacted. The wicked activities of the Canaanites demonstrated clearly that they were indeed cursed. As a part of the theological justification for Israel's subjugation of the Canaanites, this passage had great significance. The point could be worded to reflect this principle: *God will bless the righteous but curse those who live in moral abandonment.* People living in dark debauchery without any familial respect but only aggressive hubris are enslaved already by their lusts and are doomed for divine destruction. Those who want to please the divine Father should cultivate piety and reverence for the divine institutions.

On the whole, this brief story expresses the recoiling of Israelite morality at the licentious habits engendered by a civilization that had deteriorated into an orgiastic people to whom nothing was sacred. Being enslaved by their vices, the Canaanites were to be enslaved by others.

It is not possible to take the oracle as an etiology, answering the questions concerning why the Canaanites had sunk so low or why they were enslaved by others. At no time in the history of Israel was there a complete subjugation of Canaan. Many cities were conquered, and at times Canaanites were enslaved, but Israel failed to accomplish her task fully. These Canaanites survived until the final colony at Carthage was destroyed in 146 B.C. by the Romans. There was thus really no time in the history of Israel to fit a retrospective view such as an etiology would demand.

Rather, the oracle states a futuristic view in broad, general terms. It is a sweeping oracle announcing in part and imprecating in part the fate of the families descending from these individuals. It is broad enough to include massive migrations of people in the second millennium as well as individual wars and later subjugations.

The intended realization, according to the design of the writer, would be the period of the conquest. Israel was called to conquer the Canaanites. At the same time as the Israelite wars against the Canaanites (down through the battle of Taanach), waves of Sea Peoples began to sweep through the land against the Hittites, Canaanites, and Egyptians. Neiman states, "The Greeks and the Israelites, willy-nilly, were allies against the Canaanites and the Hittites during that great world conflict which came down through the historical memory of many peoples by many different names" ("Date and Circumstances," p. 131).

In their invasions these people from the north sought to annex the coastland territory and make homes for themselves. Israel felt herself in the strongest moral contrast to the Canaanites (as Shem had felt to Ham). Any help from the Japhethites would be welcomed. Such a spirit of tolerance toward the Gentiles would not have been possible in the later period of Israel's history. The curse oracle thus originated at a time *before the conquest,* when the Canaanites were still formidable enemies.

In all probability the event and its oracle were recorded to remind the

Israelites of the nature and origin of the Canaanites, to warn them about such abominations, and to justify their subjugation and dispossession through holy warfare. Israel received the blessing, but Canaan received the curse.

Bibliography

Allen, D. C. *The Legend of Noah.* Urbana, Ill.: Illini, 1963.

Bassett, F. W. "Noah's Nakedness and the Curse on Canaan: A Case of Incest?" *VT* 21 (1971): 232–37.

Ben Isaiah, Abraham, and Benjamin Sharfmen. *The Pentateuch and Rashi's Commentary: Genesis.* New York: S. S. & R., 1949.

Brichto, Herbert Chanan. *The Problem of "Curse" in the Hebrew Bible.* Philadelphia: Society of Biblical Literature and Exegesis, 1963.

Brow, John P. "Peace Symbolism in Ancient Military Vocabulary." *VT* 21 (1971): 20–23.

Cohen, H. H. *The Drunkenness of Noah.* University: University of Alabama Press, 1974.

Dijk, H. J. van. "A Neglected Connotation of Three Hebrew Verbs." *VT* 18 (1968): 16–30.

Emerton, J. A. "A Consideration of Some Alleged Meanings of ידע in Hebrew." *JSS* 15 (1970): 145–80.

Figart, Thomas O. *A Biblical Perspective on the Race Problem,* esp. pp. 55–58. Grand Rapids: Baker, 1973.

Francisco, Clyde T. "The Curse on Canaan." *CT* 8 (1964): 678–80.

Hoftijzer, J. "Some Remarks to the Tale of Noah's Drunkenness." *OTS* 12 (1958): 22–28.

Neiman, David. "The Date and Circumstances of the Cursing of Canaan." In *Biblical Motifs,* edited by Alexander Altmann, pp. 113–34. Cambridge: Harvard University Press, 1966.

Rice, Gene. "The Curse That Never Was (Genesis 9:18–27)." *JRelTh* 29 (1972): 5–27.

Ross, Allen P. "The Curse of Canaan." *BibSac* 137 (1980): 223–40.

Scharbert, Josef. "ארר 'rr; מְאֵרָה *me'ērāh.*" *TDOT,* vol. 1, pp. 405–18.

Selms, A. van. "The Canaanites in the Book of Genesis." *OTS* 12 (1958): 182–213.

Shufelt, J. E. "Noah's Curse and Blessing, Gen. 9:18–27." *CTM* 17 (1946): 737–42.

Yamauchi, Edwin M. "Slaves of God." *BETS* 9 (1966): 6–9.

16

The Table of Nations
(Gen. 10)

T he tenth chapter of Genesis remains one of the least satisfactorily studied passages in the book. When compared to the volumes produced on other sections of Genesis, the efforts to understand the structure and meaning of this passage in its context have been sparse. Westermann laments this fact, noting that most writers merely address themselves to the location of the individual names or to the classification of the sections into sources (*Genesis*, vol. 1, p. 66).

At first glance it does not appear that the table is the stuff of which exciting exegetical expositions are made. Upon closer examination of the text, however, the exegete will find very important information. The Table of Nations gives us a survey of the most significant descendants of the sons of Noah. It all appears to be a witness to the fulfillment of the divine commission to fill the earth (9:1); but the present *tôlᵉdôt* section includes also the account of the dispersion at Babel. When we also consider that account, we learn the reason that the nations spread out and filled the earth, separating into different areas with different languages—it was divine judgment on a rebellious people.

This *tôlᵉdôt* section (10:1–11:9) thus also has the aspect of deterioration in the narrating of the material; only, in contrast to the previous sections, here there is no ray of hope. The reader is left with the people of the earth hopelessly scattered across the face of the earth, divided from one another and from God. This section, then, is the climax of the primeval events and the transition to the patriarchal narratives, for it leaves the reader wondering what will happen next.

Theological Ideas

The theological ideas communicated through this chapter must be formulated in conjunction with the surrounding context. The oracle of blessing and cursing in the last chapter tells us why it was important to identify the surrounding nations; the account of the dispersion at Babel tells us how the nations came to be scattered and divided. In addition to those two bits of information, this chapter demonstrates that all the nations came from one man, Noah. The implications of these ideas within the theological message of the book require a detailed investigation into the chapter.

Structure and Synthesis

Structure

Patterns   The first thing in Genesis 10 that strikes the reader is the arrangement of the table into three groups, headed by Shem, Ham, and Japheth. This division reflects a pattern in the early part of Genesis. The genealogy of Cain (Gen. 4) ends with three sons (Jabal, Jubal, and Tubal-Cain). The genealogy from Adam to Noah (chap. 5) includes ten names, and the last person on the list (Noah) has three sons (Shem, Ham, and Japheth). The genealogy from Noah to Terah (chap. 11) also includes ten names (counting Noah), and the last person on the list (Terah) has three sons as well (Abram, Nahor, and Haran). The patterns appear to reflect parallel uses of the genealogical records; the division into three lines offers a natural arrangement.

On investigation the reader is struck by a deliberate pattern in the selection of names for the table. For example, of the sons of Japheth, who number seven, two are selected for further listing. From those two sons come seven grandsons, completing a selective list of fourteen names under Japheth. With Ham's thirty descendants and Shem's twenty-six, the grand total is seventy (or seventy-one, depending on how some are explained). Cassuto believes that this total is an attempt to show that the placing of the nations around Israel (which is not listed) is by divine providence (*Commentary on Genesis*, vol. 2, pp. 177–80). He suggests that the seventy nations correspond to the number of the families of

Israel, for God arranged their boundaries according to the number of the Israelites (Deut. 32:8). At least the numerical symmetry of the table shows a unified and ordered arrangement.

Names While the table clearly lists families (10:32), there are also individuals in the chapter. Genesis 6–9 presents Noah, Shem, Ham, and Japheth as four individuals, recording their births, ages, and activities. That an event is said to have taken place in the days of Peleg (10:25) would suggest that he too was thought to be an individual. Moreover, all the names in the line of Shem (as recorded in chap. 11) are presented as actual individuals. Nimrod is depicted in the chapter as an individual (vv. 8–12). In fact, one of the reasons the Nimrod section is classified by the critics as J is that it describes an ancient hero and is not merely a genealogy.

In addition to the names of individuals, tribal names also appear in the table. Besides the declarative statement that families are among the entries (10:32), the names themselves also provide proof for this observation. The Kittim, Dodanim, Mizraim, Ludim, Ananim, Lehabim, Naphtuhim, Patrusim, Casluhim, and Caphtorim (vv. 4, 6, 13) are all plural nouns and must represent tribes rather than actual sons.

In addition, names with the gentilic ending î ("-ites")—the Jebusites, Amorites, Girgashites, Hivites, Arkites, Sinites, Arvadites, Zemarites, and Hamathites—are also found in the table (vv. 16–18). These include the names of cities, and the gentilic ending depicts tribes in those locations.

Some names on the list are clearly designated as places: Babylon, Erech, Akkad, Calneh, Shinar, Asshur, Nineveh, Rehoboth Ir, Calah, and Resen (vv. 10–12). Other place names are listed without being clearly designated as geographical locations although usage suggests they are such. Sidon (v. 15) normally represents the city in Phoenicia. Magog (v. 2) is elsewhere called the land of Gog. Tarshish, Elishah, Gomer, Meshech, Havilah, and Sheba (vv. 2, 4, 28–29) are known as locations in the Bible.

If this table simply assigns fabled ancestors to the various nations, then there are exegetical problems with the tradition of Genesis. The chapter includes famous people, well-known cities and places, tribes and nations, as well as a number of names that could be individuals but are known later as peoples. Since the word "eponymous" is used so widely for the mystical personages of pagan traditions, it seems inappropriate for Genesis, for these biblical traditions not only rejected mythical concepts but frequently included polemics against them. But if the word can be limited to its basic meaning of a founder or ancestor who gave his name to the people or place, then there is no problem, for that view does not call the tradition into question. In other words, as Wiseman says, "The tradition of these relationships, where they are listed in the genealogical manner ('begot'), goes back to an initial physical relationship" ("Genesis 10," p. 17).

The names thus include names of tribes, cities, inhabitants of those cities, and countries, along with various individuals. This view does not nullify the possibility that there actually were ancestors, or founders, who descended from the sons of Noah, the survivors of the flood.

Formulas   The table is constructed with a variation of style that has created a tension for scholars for some time. Part of it follows a $b^e n\hat{e}$ ("sons of") formula, and part of it follows a $y\bar{a}lad$ ("begot") formula.

The word $b^e n\hat{e}$, the construct plural of $b\bar{e}n$ ("son"), occurs fourteen times (twice seven) in the chapter. It presents the family and hereditary relationships coming from a father or ancestor. Of the nearly five thousand uses in the Bible, this word most often depicts a literal son or grandson (or children in general). But in the table the word is used with geographical terms. Elishah and Tarshish, for example, are among the "sons of" Javan (v. 4). This usage is comparable to 1 Chronicles 2:51, where Salma is called the father of Bethlehem. The ancient world frequently used terms of family relationships to denote political and civic relationships: a father was a more powerful nation, a son was a dependent tribe, brothers were allies, and daughters were suburbs.

This idea of dependency or subordination of the "son" to the ancestor or sovereign occurs fairly frequently among figurative uses of $b\bar{e}n$. One example is Ahaz's message to Tiglath-Pileser, "I am your servant and your son" (2 Kings 16:7). Moreover, membership in a group by virtue of identification with the nature of the "father" is also a frequent use. The phrase "sons of Belial" characterize people according to moral or ethical standing. Such uses, then, depict a connection, derivation, subordination, or dependency on the source word.

The looser sense of $b\bar{e}n$ thus describes a relationship in which the "son" derives a quality or essence from the ancestor, or one in which the "son" is subordinate to and dependent on the ancestor. It is not difficult, then, to see how the term could be applied to a city that had been founded by an ancestor or to a tribe started by an ancestor.

The term $y\bar{a}lad$, the other key word in the genealogical formula, means "to bear" or "to bring forth." A study of this term leads in the same direction as $b\bar{e}n$. It too may have a figurative sense in which cities and nations are said to be begotten. Genesis 10 indicates that Egypt, a country, begot the Ludim, a tribe (v. 13). Canaan, possibly a land, begot Sidon, a city (v. 15). The intent again would be to show that the "father" was actually the ancestor or founder of the tribe or city and that the "sons," produced by "begetting," are dependencies, nationally and politically.

It may be concluded that the Table of Nations offers a realistic picture of developing nations, portraying their movements and developments at the dawn of world history. In using the terms $b\bar{e}n$ and $y\bar{a}lad$, the writer may very well be tracing tribal relationships back to ancestral connections in the remote past, from whom the nations of the earth developed. Because of this understanding, the writer of the table maps the various families of the earth to show their common origin. Moreover, because Genesis is concerned with tracing the blessing of God on his people, one is not surprised to find at the turning point of the book a table emphasizing ancestral connections to the three who were blessed (9:1).

Variation of Style   As we have seen, the two expressions "sons of" and "begot" are somewhat similar in their meaning in the passage. But what explains their use here?

The heading of the chapter is "These are the particulars [$t\hat{o}l^ed\hat{o}t$] of the sons of [$b^en\hat{e}$] Noah, Shem, Ham, and Japheth; and sons were born [$wayyiww\bar{a}l^ed\hat{u}$] to them after the flood." Both terms occur in the heading.

In the line of Japheth only $b^en\hat{e}$ is used for the fourteen names. However, the record is not meant to be complete with this listing; from these names were spread the isles of the sea (v. 5), a continuing development.

The line of Ham uses both terms. The sons of ($b^en\hat{e}$) Ham are four: Cush, Mizraim, Put, and Canaan. The sons of ($b^en\hat{e}$) Cush are five; the sons of ($b^en\hat{e}$) Raamah are two. But Cush begot ($y\bar{a}lad$) Nimrod, who founded the empires in the east; Mizraim begot ($y\bar{a}lad$) various Egyptian tribes; and Canaan too begot ($y\bar{a}lad$) a number of peoples dwelling in the land.

In the line of Shem both terms are used as well. At the outset the account declares that sons were born ($y\bar{a}lad$) to Shem, the father of all the sons of ($b^en\hat{e}$) Eber, and the brother of Japheth.

The sons of ($b^en\hat{e}$) Shem are five, the sons of ($b^en\hat{e}$) Aram, four. Then the passage indicates that Arphaxad, a son of Shem, begot ($y\bar{a}lad$) Shelah, and Shelah begot ($y\bar{a}lad$) Eber. To Eber two sons were born ($yullad$): Peleg and Joktan. Joktan begot ($y\bar{a}lad$) thirteen tribes. The table describes these thirteen as the sons of ($b^en\hat{e}$) Joktan.

The title announced the passage to be the $t\hat{o}l^ed\hat{o}t$ of the $b^en\hat{e}$ Noah; the summary describes the results. The word $t\hat{o}l^ed\hat{o}t$, coming from $y\bar{a}lad$, supplies the key to the use of the terms. The table is not concerned with a simple list of the sons of the ancestors; rather, it is concerned with tracing "what became of" these sons. Within the structure of the $b^en\hat{e}$ Noah, the passage is focusing on the great development and movement of families that were of interest to Israel. The *bānîm* ("sons") provides the point of departure, and the *yālad* points out the development. It is the writer's concern to emphasize the development of certain people; *yālad* introduces those sections and reminds the readers that the table begins with *tôledôt*.

The term *yālad* was used to introduce readers to the development of the kingdoms in the east and the expansion of Egyptian tribes leading to the inclusion of the Philistines. It also identified the inhabitants of the land being given to Israel, the chosen line that descended through Arphaxad to Eber (the famous ancestor of the Hebrews), and the Arabian tribes bearing the closest ties with Israel. But where there are *yālad* sections, there are closing reminders that these are the sons of (*benê*) Ham and the sons of (*benê*) Shem. The term *yālad* is used to bring in the emphasis of the *tôledôt* and to blend with *benê* for continuity.

The use of these two terms is precise. The term *bēn* points to the ancestor; the term *yālad* (and related forms) points to the descendants. The former emphasizes the beginning; the latter, the continuing results. By using these terms correctly, the writer, in one table, bridged the past with the present, thus forming a major transition in the book.

Structure of the Table   The structure of the table, in its final form in Genesis 10, is as follows:

Table heading: "Now these are the generations [*tôledôt*] of Shem, Ham, and Japheth, the sons of [*benê*] Noah; and sons [*bānîm*] were born [*yiwwāledû*] to them after the flood" (1).

1. *Japheth (2–5)*
   Heading: "The sons of [*benê*] Japheth . . ." (2).
   Expansion: "And the sons of [*benê*] Gomer . . ." (3).
                   "And the sons of [*benê*] Javan . . ." (4).
   Colophon: "From these the coastlands of the nation were separated into their lands, every one according to his language, according to their families, into their nations" (5).
2. *Ham (6–20)*
   Heading: "And the sons of [*benê*] Ham . . ." (6).
   Expansion: "And the sons of [*benê*] Cush . . ." (7a).
                   "And the sons of [*benê*] Raamah . . ." (7b).
                   "Now Cush begot [*yālad*] . . ." (8–12).
                   "And Mizraim begot [*yālad*] . . ." (13–14).
                   "And Canaan begot [*yālad*] . . ." (15–19).

Colophon: "These are the sons of [$b^en\hat{e}$] Ham, according
                             to their families, according to their languages,
                             by their lands, by their nations" (20).

3. *Shem (21–31)*
   Heading: "And also to Shem, the father of all the children
                             of [$b^en\hat{e}$] Eber, and the older brother of Japheth,
                             children were born [$yullad$]. The sons of [$b^en\hat{e}$]
                             Shem . . ." (21–22).

   Expansion: "And the sons of [$b^en\hat{e}$] Aram . . ." (23).
                             "And Arphaxad begot [$y\bar{a}lad$] . . ." (24a).
                             "And Shelah begot [$y\bar{a}lad$] . . ." (24b).
                             "And two sons were born [$yullad$] to Eber
                             . . . " (25).
                             "And Joktan begot [$y\bar{a}lad$] . . . " (26–29a).

   Colophon: "All these were the sons of [$b^en\hat{e}$] Joktan" (29b–
                             30).

   Colophon: "These are the sons of [$b^en\hat{e}$] Shem, according
                             to their families, according to their languages,
                             by their lands, according to their nations" (31).

   Final colophon: "These are the families of the sons of [$b^en\hat{e}$]
                             Noah, according to their genealogies [$l^et\hat{o}l^ed\bar{o}$-
                             $t\bar{a}m$], by their nations; and out of these the na-
                             tions were separated on the earth after the flood"
                             (32).

Colophons Each section of this plan has its own heading and its
own colophon, which reiterates the specific emphasis of the section.
One element found in each of the endings is $l^emi\check{s}p^eh\bar{o}t\bar{a}m$ ("according
to their families"). This use of a standard form of classification most
commonly refers to physically related clans, normally a national subdivision. In this passage it is a subdivision of $g\hat{o}y$ ("nation"). This division, of course, is a major point in the table, according to 10:32.

A second element in the endings is $li l\check{s}\bar{o}n\bar{o}t\bar{a}m$ ("according to their
languages [tongues]"). Part of the criteria for the listings in the table is
the languages the families or tribes spoke.

A third element is $b^eg\hat{o}y\bar{e}hem$ ("in their nations"). Nations are usually
composed of persons closely associated by common descent, language,
or history and are usually organized as a political state (which is objective and impersonal, and usually coordinate with a kingdom). Here a
different preposition is used; b^e normally suggests location but could be
taken as a standard of measurement ("by").

The fourth element is $b^e\,ar\d{s}\bar{o}t\bar{a}m$ ("in their lands"). The division of
the families uses national boundaries for some of the distinctions.

The sons of Noah are thus divided by means of anthropological, linguistic, political, and geographical criteria. For this reason the table includes names of people, tribes, countries, and cities. The order of these elements is not always the same, and one can observe the differences (see chart 12).

Shem and Ham, both of which have *yālad* sections, are arranged in identical order. All three end with nations, showing perhaps that in the final analysis these names are units with national and political affiliations. Japheth, having lands at the beginning, is predominantly geographical and linguistic and has little tribal emphasis. Conversely, Ham and Shem, beginning with families, appear to emphasize tribal details. They are not restricted to areas (although area is important) but in fact overlap. The *yālad* additions, showing the development of tribes and clans, support this emphasis of the summary endings.

While one cannot oversimplify the arrangement of the table into geopolitical or ethnolinguistic arrangements, one can see that Moses had in mind a definite plan in tracing out the developing families. In doing so he used four criteria to categorize the names he selected for his grand purpose. He was thus able to compile a document portraying the early advances of the beginning nations.

Types of Genealogies   Scholars generally conclude that there are two major types of genealogical lists: those that trace lineage and those that chart alliances. They can be identified by form as well as nature. When a genealogy gives only one line of descent from an ancestor, then it is called a "linear genealogy." When a genealogy expresses more than one line of descent from an ancestor, then it exhibits segmentation or branching and is called a "segmented genealogy." The function is directly related to the form (see Wilson, "Old Testament Genealogies," p. 179).

The function of the linear type is to link the name with the ancestor. The function of the segmented type is more varied. It may be used for domestic purposes, mirroring the changes in society; for political or legal purposes, showing the tribal alliances; or for religious purposes, celebrating some festival (ibid., pp. 180–81).

Segmented genealogies emphasize that tribal affiliation was essential for treaties and alliances. The tribe was stronger than the individual, and tribal affiliations added to that strength. Charts that register blood

Chart 12.   **Order of Elements
in the Table of Nations**

Son	Elements
Japheth	lands, languages, families, nations
Ham	families, languages, lands, nations
Shem	families, languages, lands, nations

ties reflect the social and political relationships necessary for defending and maintaining their tribal groups. In the ancient world a kindred group was more than a family grown large.

Segmented genealogies have symmetrical patterns; but they also have a certain fluidity, so that they may undergo rapid adjustments to reflect real or desired changes in ties. Genealogies also have depth; linear lists in the ancient world may go back as far as nineteen names or more, and segmented lists usually express societal structure with ten, twelve, or fourteen names. Although they may be symmetrical, they are never stereotyped.

By relating the biblical material to these genealogical patterns of the ancient Near East, we can see that Genesis 5 and 11 fit the pattern of the linear lists, linking individuals from one era to another. Genesis 10, although unique, more closely illustrates the segmented pattern. This Table of Nations, then, traces affiliation of tribes to show relationships, on the basis of some original physical connections. Showing such kinship was necessary for confederations, intermarriage, habitations, possessions of lands, and holy war.

Conclusion   Genesis 10 is a structured arrangement of the important nations of the ancient world. The writer clearly is emphasizing the development of those nations that were of primary importance to Israel (yālad sections), within the overall structure of the table (the bᵉnê arrangement).

Summary Message

From Shem, Ham, and Japheth descended all the nations of the world in their lands and according to their languages, among whom were the Canaanite tribes, who occupied the land of Canaan, and the eastern powers, who derived from Nimrod of the Hamitic line.

Exegetical Outline

Title: This is what became of Shem, Ham, and Japheth after the flood (1).
  I. The descendants of Japheth settled in the north and west and became the founders of the Greek and Scythian tribes (2–5).
  II. The descendants of Ham settled in the area of Egypt and Canaan, and from these tribes came the founders of the great cities of the east (6–20).
    A. The descendants of Ham were Cush, Mizraim, Put, and Canaan (6).
    B. The descendants of Cush were the people of the Arabian peninsula (7).

    C. Expansion: Nimrod founded the great cities of the east (8–12).
    D. The descendants of Mizraim were the tribes of northern Africa (13–14).
    E. Expansion: Canaan produced the Canaanite tribes (cliché list) in the land promised to Israel (15–20).
  III. The descendants of Shem, the ancestor of Eber, settled in the eastern lands and in the region of the Persian Gulf (21–31).
    A. The descendants of Shem were Elam, Asshur, Arphaxad, Lud, and Aram (21–22).
    B. The descendants formed the major tribes of the eastern gulf regions (23–31).
Colophon: These were the divisions of the nations (32).

Development of the Exposition

There are not too many satisfying ways to treat this passage in an exposition. One would certainly not wish to go name by name through the table; such an exercise would be tedious and academic. It would probably be far better to arrange a topical exposition and to select the names and descriptions in support of the ideas. Perhaps the most important topics that could be drawn from a study of this passage would be (1) the human race is united by virtue of its beginnings from one family—it is really one family; (2) the human race is hopelessly divided by language, race, territory, and politics, all of which raise the question of the cause for such division; and (3) the divided nations all stand in some relation to the divine plan for blessing and cursing, as witnessed by the oracle of Noah and the deliberate emphases within the table. These ideas can be united in an expositional idea that could be used for the chapter in context: *The human race, although united by origin, is divided by language, territory, and politics as a part of God's design to bring blessing to the human race.*

The expositor will probably deal as much with the context of the table as with the contents. It will be helpful to identify certain crucial names on the list (see the bibliography of this section). But it will be necessary to relate the account of Noah's oracle as a foundation for the table and the account of the dispersion at Babel as the explanation for the division. God scattered the people and confused their language because they rebelled against him and would not obey. The nations that were scattered throughout the earth, then, came from Shem, Ham, or Japheth and, we may say, were aligned with the oracle of blessing or of cursing. All the nations listed in the table are arranged with Israel and the land of Palestine at the center of the writer's thoughts, so that God's plan to bless through Israel has great bearing on Israel's relationship with these nations.

Taking this section in its context, one can see the hand of God at work in the nations of the earth. They prosper under common grace, but their diverse languages and lands are evidence of God's judgment. Israel would see all the nations arranged around them and would better understand their mission and destiny by having this map. These great nations, people who dominated the earth for centuries, or the smaller powers who plagued one another for ages, all testify to the divine will. This fragmentation was better than collective apostasy, as the story of the dispersion at Babel will show. No hope comes from powerful nations warring against one another; hope comes from the sovereign Lord who controls the nations and who will move nations to make room for his new nation.

Bibliography

Bennett, Robert A. "Africa and the Biblical Period." *HTR* 64 (1971): 483–500.

Burkitt, F. C. "Note on the Table of Nations (Genesis 10)." *JThS* 21 (1920): 233–38.

Custance, Arthur C. *Noah's Three Sons*. Grand Rapids: Zondervan, 1975.

Gibson, J. C. L. "Observations on Some Important Ethnic Terms in the Pentateuch." *JNES* 20 (1961): 217–38.

Maisler, B. "Canaan and the Canaanites." *BASOR* 102 (1946): 7–12.

Montgomery, James A. *Arabia and the Bible*. New York: Ktav, 1969.

Neiman, David. "Phoenician Place-Names." *JNES* 24 (1965): 113–15.

————."The Two Genealogies of Japheth." In *Orient and Occident: Essays Presented to Cyrus Gordon*, AOAT 22, pp. 119–26. Neukirchen-Vluyn: Neukirchener, 1973.

North, Robert. "The Hivites." *Bib* 54 (1973): 43–62.

Oded, B. "The Table of Nations (Genesis 10)—a Socio-Cultural Approach." *ZAW* 98 (1986): 14–30.

Ross, Allen P. "The Table of Nations in Genesis 10—Its Content." *BibSac* 138 (1981): 22–34.

————."The Table of Nations in Genesis 10—Its Structure. *BibSac* 137 (1980): 340–53.

Sant, C. "Links Between the Three Main Divisions, Genealogy and Chronology." *Melita Theologica* 11 (1961): 1–13; 12 (1962): 14–27; 13 (1963): 62–74; 15 (1965): 41–49.

Simons, J. "The 'Table of Nations' (Gen. 10: Its General Structure and Meaning." *OTS* 10 (1954): 155–84.

Speiser, E. A. " 'People' and 'Nation' of Israel." *JBL* 79 (1960): 157–63.

Van Seters, John. "The Terms 'Amorite' and 'Hittite.' " *VT* 22 (1972): 64–81.

Wilson, Robert R. "The Old Testament Genealogies in Recent Research." *JBL* 94 (1975). 169–89.

Wiseman, D. J. "Genesis 10: Some Archaeological Considerations." *Journal of the Transactions of the Victoria Institute* 87 (1955): 14–24, 113–18.

―――――― , ed. *Peoples of Old Testament Times.* Oxford: At the Clarendon Press, 1973.

Yamauchi, Edwin. "Meshech, Tubal, and Company: A Review Article." *JETS* 19 (1976): 239–47.

Youngblood, Ronald. "Cuneiform Contributions to Old Testament Interpretation." *Bethel Seminary Quarterly* 10 (1962): 8.

17

The Dispersion of the Nations at Babel
(Gen. 11:1–9)

The narrative in Genesis 11:1–9 reports the divine intervention among the human family to scatter them across the face of the earth by striking at the heart of their unity—their language. The predominant idea of the account is not the tower of Babel but the scattering. This passage will explain to the reader how the many nations came to be divided in the earth.

Theological Ideas

The story concerns God's judgment on the sin of the Shinarites. Their major error was not the building of a city or a tower but the attempt to unite and live in one place. Since this decision was open rebellion against God's original commission, their sin as well may be labeled hubris, that is, immense pride that leads to disobedience to God. In addition to identifying their proud ambition, the story also reflects their anxieties. According to the Lord's evaluation, their desire to enhance their unity and strength had potential for the greatest evil. It thus appears that the hu-

233

man family was striving for unity, security, and social immortality (making a name) in defiance of God's desire for them to fill the earth (9:1).

It is important to keep in mind that the judgment was the destruction not of the city but of the language that united the people. It was shattered into a multiplicity of languages, so that the common bond was destroyed. The text thereby demonstrates that the present number of languages that form national barriers is a monument to sin.

Since the people's purpose was to make a name for themselves and to achieve power through unity, the apostasy of the human spirit would shortly bring the race to the brink of another catastrophe such as the deluge. Instead God frustrated their communication and divided them into nations. It is evident, as Stigers says, that "it is the will of God, so long as sin is present in the world, to employ nationalism in the reduction of sin" (*Commentary on Genesis*, p. 129).

For ages people have restricted themselves to native manners and customs and have regarded diverse languages of foreigners with great horror. We find that Israel was delivered from a people of "a strange language" (Ps. 114:1) and was frequently warned of destruction by a fierce nation whose language would not be understood and whose deep speech could not be comprehended (Deut. 28:49; Isa. 28:11; 33:19; Jer. 5:15). The language barrier brought sudden fear and prevented unification.

Ringgren summarizes the twofold aspect of the Lord's intervention in Genesis 11 as divine reaction to pride.

> Theologically, the building of the tower in Gen. 11 is interpreted as an act of human arrogance and rebellion against God; accordingly, Yahweh intervenes against its builders and scatters them over the whole earth. This action of God is both punishment and a preventive measure; it prevents men from going too far in their pride. ["Babhel," p. 467]

Later prophets would draw on this narrative, recording the very beginnings of the divisions as they looked to the end of days when God himself would unify humankind once again. Zephaniah 3:9–11 appears to be constructed antithetically to this passage with its themes in common with Genesis 11:1–9: the pure speech (i.e., one language), the gathering of the dispersed people (even from Cush), the removal of pride, and the service in the holy mountain. The miracle on the day of Pentecost is often seen as a harbinger of that end time (Kidner, *Genesis*, p. 110).

Structure and Synthesis

Structure

The literary style of the narrative shows an artistic hand ordering the material in such a way as to mirror the ideas from the Babylonian background of the story as well as to contrast by means of antithetical parallelism the participants in the story. To such literary art, repetition and parallelism are essential.

In the antithetical parallelism of the narrative, ideas are balanced against their counterparts. The story begins with the report of the unified situation at the beginning (11:1) and ends with a reminder of that unity and its resultant confusion for the scattering (v. 9). This beginning and ending picture is reflected in the contrast of the dialogues and actions: verses 2–4 describe what the humans proceeded to do; verses 5–8, beginning with the contrastive "But the LORD . . .," describe how the Lord turned their work aside.

Within these balanced sections many elements support the antithetical arrangement (see chart 13). As seen in the Hebrew, verse 1 is balanced with 9, 2 with 8, and 3 with 7, and the narrative turns at verse 5. (For a full treatment, see Fokkelman, *Narrative Art*, p. 22.)

This structural design is enhanced even more by the literary devices that the writer used. First, the writer enhances the meaning of his last word play (*bābel*/*bālal*, "Babel"/"confuse") by the frequent use of the letters *b, l,* and *n.* Verse 3 reads *hābâ nilbᵉnâ lᵉbēnîm . . . lāhem hallᵉbēnâ lᵉʾāben.* Verse 4 has *hābâ nibneh-lānû.* In verse 5 are the words *bānû bᵉnê,* and verse 7 has *wᵉnābᵉlâ.* In verse 8, the sounds continue with *wayyaḥdᵉlû libnōt.* And in verse 9 is the anticipated culmination of the sounds in *bābel . . . bālal.* There also appears to be a play on *pûṣ* ("scatter"), the key word of the passage. The word is frequently followed by the phrase *pᵉnê kol-hāʾāreṣ* ("across the face of the whole earth"), which,

Chart 13. Antithetical Structure of Genesis 11:1–9

A All the earth had one language (*kol-hāʾāreṣ śāpâ ʾeḥāt*) (1)

  B there (*šām*) (2)

    C one to another (*ʾîš ʾel-rēʿēhû*) (3)

      D Come, let's make bricks (*hābâ nilbᵉnâ lᵉbēnîm*) (3)

        E Let's make for ourselves (*nibneh-lānû*) (4)

          F a city and a tower (*ʿîr ûmigdāl*) (4)

            G And the Lord came down to see (*wayyēred YHWH lirʾōt*) (5)

          F' the city and the tower (*ʾet-hāʿîr wᵉʾet-hammigdāl*) (5)

        E' that the humans built (*ʾăšer bānû bᵉnê hāʾādām*) (5)

      D' Come, let's confuse (*hābâ . . . wᵉnābᵉlâ*) (7)

    C' everyone the language of his neighbor (*ʾîš śᵉpat rēʿēhû*) (7)

  B' from there (*miššām*) (8)

A' (confused) the language of the whole earth (*śᵉpat kol-hāʾāreṣ*) (9)

interestingly, begins with the letter *p* and ends with ṣ, thus reflecting *pûṣ*. Other alliterations involve *hall^{e}bēnâ*/*le$^{\,}$āben*, *pen*/*p^{e}nê*, and *šām*/*šēm*.

Second, the word plays in the passage strengthen the ideas. E. W. Bullinger calls such word plays "paronomasia," which he describes as the employment of two words that are different in origin and meaning but similar in sound and appearance to emphasize two things by calling attention to the similarity of sound (*Figures of Speech Used in the Bible*, [London: Eyre and Spothiswoode, 1898; reprint, Grand Rapids: Baker, 1968], p. 307). One is placed alongside the other and appears to be a repetition of it. Once the eye has caught the two words and the attention concentrated on them, then one discovers that an interpretation is put on the one by the other.

While this description gives the general nature of word plays, it is too broad for distinguishing the types of word plays within the group known as paronomasia. To be precise, it should be said that paronomasia involves a play on similarity of sound and some point in the meaning as well; those that have no point of contact in meaning are best classified as phonetic word plays such as assonance, rhyme, alliteration, or epanastrophe (the repetition of words from the end of one sentence at the beginning of another).

This distinction becomes necessary in the exegesis of the narrative. In verse 3 is the exhortation *nilb^{e}nâ l^{e}bēnîm*, "let us make bricks" (lit. "let us brick bricks"). Immediately there follows a second exhortation: *niśr^{e}pâ liśrēpâ*, "let us burn them hard" (lit. "let us burn them for burning"). These phrases are paronomasias in the strict sense, since they offer a sound play *and* are etymologically connected.

The key play in the passage is not strictly paronomasia, since there is no connection etymologically between *bābel* and *bālal*. It is a phonetic word play. The people said that the name was called *bābel* because the Lord "made a babble" (*bālal*) of the language.

All these devices enhance the basic antithetical structure of the passage. Fokkelman illustrates this pattern by connecting the paronomasia of verse 3, *nilb^{e}nâ l^{e}bēnîm*, with the response of God in verse 7, *nāb^{e}lâ*, in a sound chiasmus (*Narrative Art*, pp. 13–16):

$$
\begin{array}{ccc}
\text{L} & \text{B} & \text{N} \\
 & \times & \\
\text{N} & \text{B} & \text{L}
\end{array}
$$

"let us make bricks"

"let us confuse"

The reversal of the order of the sounds reveals the basic idea of the passage: The construction on earth is answered by the destruction from heaven; men build, but God pulls down. The fact that God's words are also in the form of man's words (both are cohortatives) adds a corroding irony to the passage: God sings *with* the people while working *against* them (ibid., p. 14).

Fokkelman stresses the same point with šēm, šām, and šāmayim. To bring everlasting fame (šēm) they unite in one spot (šām) as the base of operations for their attainment of fame, which they make conditional on the encroachment of heaven (šāmayim), the abode of God. What drives them is hubris. What calls out the nemesis of the Lord from heaven (šāmayim) and scatters them from there (miššām) is also hubris. The "brackets" on the text illustrate this connection poignantly: what "all the earth" sought to avoid, namely, dispersion "all over the earth," actually happened (cf. v. 1 and v. 9).

Summary Message

When the human race settled together to preserve their unity and develop their fame by building a grandiose city-tower, the Lord interrupted their collective apostasy and scattered them across the face of the earth by confusing the language that united them.

Exegetical Outline

    I. Prologue: The human race was united by one language (1).
   II. Human endeavor: Migrating to the land of Shinar, the people resolved to build a grandiose city and tower to preserve their identity and their unity (2–4).
      A. Event: The people migrated to, and settled in, Shinar's fertile valley (2).
      B. Resolution: The people resolved to make bricks and build a city and a tower so that they might preserve their name and their unity (3–4).
        1. Ingenuity: They resolved to make bricks out of the materials available to them (3).
        2. Ambition: They resolved to develop a tower-city to make a name for themselves and to prevent scattering (4).
          a. Purpose: They wished to preserve their name (4a).
          b. Fear: They did not want to be scattered abroad (4b).
  III. The Lord's intervention: Investigating the enterprise of the human race and knowing the dangerous potential of their unified pride, the Lord confounded their speech and scattered them abroad (5–8).
      A. Event: The Lord descended to investigate their building (5).
      B. Resolution: Knowing their potential was dangerously evil, the Lord resolved to scatter them across the face of the earth (6–8).

1. Observation: The Lord concluded that nothing would be withheld from their designs (6).
2. Resolution: The Lord resolved to destroy their unity (7).
3. Solution: The Lord scattered them across the face of the earth so that their project ceased (8).

    IV. Epilogue: The human race was disunited and scattered by the Lord's making a babble of their one language at Babel (9).

Development of the Exposition

It will be helpful in the exposition to provide a certain amount of background material for this little story.

The Babylonian Background

That this passage has Babylon in mind is clear from the explication of the name "Babel" in verse 9. The first appearance of this term is in Genesis 10:10 in the Table of Nations, which records the beginning of the kingdom in the exploits of Nimrod from Cush. Not only is there this direct reference to proud Babylon, but also other evidences show that the background of the story was Mesopotamian. Speiser says, "The episode points more concretely to Babylonia than does any other portion of Primeval History, and the background that is here sketched proves to be authentic beyond all expectations" (*Genesis*, p. 75).

Babylon was a thing of beauty to the pagan world. Every important city of Babylonia was built with a step-tower known as a ziggurat (*ziggurratu*). In Nebuchadnezzar's Babylon, in the area of Marduk's sanctuary known as *E-sag-ila*, "the house of the lifting up of the head" (Kraeling, "Earliest Hebrew Flood Story," p. 282), there was a seven-story tower with a temple top that was known as *E-temen-anki*. This structure, measuring ninety meters by ninety meters at the base as well as being ninety meters high, became one of the wonders of the world (Cassuto, *Commentary on Genesis*, vol. 2, pp. 227–30). The tower was a symbol of Babylonian culture and played a major role in other cultures influenced by it (Gressmann, *Tower of Babel*, pp. 15–19).

The first of such towers must be earlier than Nebuchadnezzar's, for his were rebuildings of ancient patterns. Cassuto (*Commentary on Genesis*, vol. 2, p. 229) maintains that this reference must be to *E-temen-anki*, although he suggests that the occasion for the tradition giving rise to the satire would come from an earlier time, from the Hittite destruction of Babylon. Speiser does not agree. He points out that the reference here cannot be *E-temen-anki*, which cannot antedate the seventh century. Therefore this account must be centuries earlier than *E-temen-anki* (*Genesis*, p. 75). Since Esarhaddon (seventh century) and Nebuchadnezzar (sixth century) were the first since Hammurabi to build such works, the biblical reference in Genesis 11 must be to a much earlier Babylon. While the actual architecture of the Neo-Babylonian Empire *cannot* be the inspiration for this account, one must conclude that their buildings were rebuildings of some ancient tower located in the same area (Speiser, "Word Plays," pp. 317–18).

When the literary parallels concerning this architecture are considered, some very significant correspondences to the narrative are noted. First, there is a specific connection of this story with the account of the building of Babylon, recorded in the Akkadian *Enuma Elish*, tablet 6, lines 55–65.

> When Marduk heard this,
> Brightly glowed his features, like the day:
> "Construct Babylon, whose building you have requested,
> Let its brickwork be fashioned. You shall name it 'The Sanctuary'."
> The Anunnaki applied the implement;
> For one whole year they molded bricks.
> When the second year arrived,
> They raised high the head of Esagila equaling Apsu.
> Having built a stage-tower as high as Apsu,
> They set up in it an abode for Marduk, Enlil, [and] Ea.
> In their presence he was seated in grandeur.
> (*ANET,* pp. 68–69).

Within the passage are several literary parallels to the biblical narrative. Line 62 reads, "They raised high the head of *Esagila* equaling Apsu," *ša Esagila miḫrit apsî ullū rēšīšû*. Speiser notes the word play of *ullū rēšīšû* with *Esagila*, which means "structure which raises the head," explaining that it evokes a special value for the Sumerian name, giving it a significant meaning in Babylon ("Word Plays," p. 319). He thus concludes that *rēšam ullûm* became a stock expression for the monumental structures of Babylon and Assyria.

Speiser shows that *apsû* is a reference to the heavens (ibid., p. 320). He allows that it often means "the deep" but explains that the word cannot have that meaning here in the light of line 63, which says, "when they had built the temple tower of the upper *apsu*." In line 62, then, *miḫrit apsî* must be "toward heaven," and *apsu* must be celestial and not subterranean (see also Heidel, *Babylonian Genesis*, p. 48).

A second important element is the bricks. The Hebrew text in Genesis 11:4 describes the brickmaking with a cognate accusative construction. After the bricks are made, the tower is made. Speiser observes that the bricks figured predominantly in the Babylonian account, where there is a year-long brick ritual ("Word Plays," p. 321). The Babylonian account not only records a similar two-step process (making bricks in the first year and raising the tower head in the second), but it also has a similar construction, using a cognate accusative, *libittasu iltabnū* (Heb. *nilbᵉnâ lᵉbēnîm*). In fact, the Hebrew and Akkadian words are cognate. The similarity is striking.

In *Enuma Elish* and Genesis there are at least three solid literary connections: the making of the tower for the sanctuary of the gods, with Genesis reporting the determination to build the tower and city in rebellion against God; the lofty elevation of its head into the heavens, with Genesis recording almost the same reference; and the making of the bricks before the building of the city, with Genesis describing the process with the same grammatical construction.

Another correspondence is reflected in the great pride of the builders. One of the purposes of the Babylonian creation epic at its composition was to show the preeminence of Babylon over all the cities of the country, and especially the supremacy of Marduk over all deities. They were so pleased with themselves that they considered Babylon to be a celestial city, prepared by the Anunnaki gods and made for Marduk on behalf of his victory over Tiamat. It then became the pattern for the earthly city (*Enuma Elish*, tablet 6, lines 113–15; *ANET*, p. 69). In fact, Babylon, that metropolitan city for so many peoples, claimed to be the origination of society, their city having descended from heaven (see also Ringgren, "Babhel," p. 467). Herein was the immense pride of Babylon.

In light of the claim by this world-famous city and tower culture to be the heavenly plan and beginning of creation, the record in Genesis 11 is a polemic. To communicate this tone most forcefully, the text employs literary elements of the ancient, traditional theme preserved in the Babylonian culture. The content and thrust of the message, however, differ remarkably.

The differences are pointed out in part by Vos (*Genesis and Archaeology*, p. 47). First, Genesis implies that nothing similar had ever been built before by man, but the ziggurats represent traditional workings. Second, Genesis presents the building as evidence of the people's disobedience, but the Babylonian work was for the purpose of worshiping a local deity. Third, Genesis describes this effort as the work of one united race of people that became the basis of the scattering and confusion into languages and tribes, but the ziggurats were man-made mountains of a national group (their towers were the symbol of *their* culture). Also these towers developed gradually over the centuries after the diffusion and scattering.

Genesis, in setting forth the account of the divine intervention at Babel in the ancient past, deliberately alludes to the arrogance of Babylon that was represented in their literature. The result is a satire on the thing of glory and beauty of the pagan world. The biblical writer, having become familiar with the vainglorious words in the traditions of Babylon, weaves his account for the purpose of deriding the literary traditions of that ancient city and establishing the truth. In fact, traditions from Mesopotamia recorded the ancient division of languages as well. The Sumerians had recorded that there was originally one language, since everyone came to worship Enlil with one tongue (*Enmerkar Epic*, lines 141–46; see Kramer, "Babel of Tongues," p. 109).

Cassuto suggests a collection of satirical ideas that would have given rise to the Genesis narrative, and he paraphrases them as follows:

> You, children of Babylon . . . you called your city Babel—*Bâbili*, "Gate of god," or *Bâb-ilani* "Gate of the gods"—and your tower you designated "House of the foundation of heaven and earth." You desired that the top of your tower should be in *heaven*. . . . you did not understand that, even if you were to raise the summit of your ziggurat ever so high, you would not be nearer to Him than when you stand upon the ground; nor did you comprehend that He who in truth dwells in heaven, if He wishes to take a closer look at your lofty tower, must needs *come down*. . . . Your intention was to build for yourselves a gigantic city that would contain all mankind and you forgot that it was God's will to fill the whole earth with human settlements, and that God's plan would surely be realized. . . . You were proud of your power, but you should have known that it is forbidden to man to exalt himself, for only the Lord is truly exalted, and the pride of man is regarded by Him as iniquity that leads to his downfall and degradation—a punishment befitting the crime. . . . On account of this, your dominion was shattered and your families were scattered over the face of the whole earth. Behold, how fitting is the name that you have given to your city! It is true that in *your* language it expresses glory and pride, but in *our* idiom it sounds as though it connoted confusion— the confusion of tongues heard therein, which caused its destruction and the dispersion of its inhabitants in every direction. [*Commentary on Genesis*, vol. 2, pp. 229–30]

Babylon was the prototype of all nations, cities, and empires that raise themselves in pride. They would be brought down in confusion; herein was the warning to the new nation of Israel: any disobedient nation would be abased and brought low in spite of her pride, ingenuity, and strength.

The Babylon motif became the common representation for any antitheocratic program. Later writers drew on this theme and used the name as a symbol for the godless society with its great pretensions. Isaiah 47:8–13 portrayed Babylon's pleasures, sins, and superstitions. Isaiah 13:19 pictured her as "the glory of kingdoms, the beauty of the

Chaldeans' pride," and Isaiah 14:13 describes her sinful arrogance in exalting her throne above the Most High in the heavens, only to be brought low. Jeremiah also predicted the cup of vengeance on this arrogant city (chap. 51). Daniel recorded her persecutions against Judah (chap. 3). And Revelation 17–18 applies the theme to the spiritual Babylon in the eschaton, showing that it was her *sins* that reached heaven and brought the catastrophe to her, thus preparing the way for the true celestial city to come down to earth (see Kidner, *Genesis*, p. 111).

The Setting in the Primeval Narratives

The present story of the scattering is part of the primeval events of Genesis that give a picture of men and women in open rebellion against God and of God's intervening in judgment on each situation. The scattering of the race from Babel forms the capstone to the primeval history of the human race (von Rad, *Genesis*, p. 143). This development of humankind is accurately described by Kidner.

> The primeval history reaches its fruitless climax as man, conscious of new abilities, prepares to glorify and fortify himself by collective effort. The elements of the story are timelessly characteristic of the spirit of the world. The project is typically grandiose; men describe it excitedly to one another as if it were the ultimate achievement—very much as modern man glories in his space projects. At the same time they betray their insecurity as they crowd together to preserve their identity and control their fortunes. [*Genesis*, p. 109]

With this story the common history of all humankind comes to an abrupt end, as the human race is hopelessly scattered across the face of the entire earth. This fact makes the present narrative so different from those preceding it. In each previous judgment there was a gracious provision for hope, but in this judgment there is none. It does not offer a token of grace, a promise of any blessing, a hope of salvation, or a way of escape. There is no clothing for the naked sinner, no protective mark for the fugitive, no rainbow in the dark sky. The primeval age ends with judgmental scattering and complete confusion. The blessing is not here; the world must await the new history.

In view of this development, the story of the scattering of the nations is actually the turning point of the book—from primeval history to the history of the blessing. From this very confused and dispersed situation, nations developed in utter futility until God made a great nation through one man who himself would be "scattered" from this alluvial plain to the land of Canaan. The blessings of final redemption and unification would come through his seed.

The beginning of Genesis 11 presupposes a linguistic unity and localization comparable to the beginning of Genesis 10. Since the Table of Nations in Genesis 10 describes the many families of the earth "after their families, after their tongues, in their lands, in their nations" and Genesis 11 describes the divine intervention to scatter them, the question is how this story of the dispersion is compatible with the table. They appear to be reversed chronologically.

The Table of Nations gives absolutely no explanation for the scattering, but "that the author was intending right along to treat of this confusion of tongues appears from 10:25" (Leupold, *Exposition of Genesis*, vol. 1, p. 381). There it is stated that, in the days of Peleg ("Division"), the earth was divided. It is worth noting that the root word occurs in Psalm 55:9 for a moral division: "Destroy, O LORD, and divide [*pallag*] their tongues." The prayer is that God would break apart their counsel into contending factions, an end that is comparable to the story of the division of the nations.

The point of contact between the two chapters appears to be the birth of Peleg (and thus his naming) in Genesis 10. At that point the incident of chapter 11 may have happened, causing the people to spread out into the earth until they settled in their tribes as described in chapter 10. Chapter 11 is the cause; chapter 10 is the effect.

The passages are arranged in a manner consistent with Genesis. The broad survey is given first, and then the narrowing and selection or explanation. The order is thematic and not chronological. The choice of this reversed order is a stroke of genius. B. Jacob stated it well: "The placement of chapter 10 before this one is a special refinement. The absurdity of the undertaking becomes obvious if we know the numerous nations into which mankind should grow" (*First Book of the Bible*, p. 80). It should be clear by now that the story of the dispersion is a thematic sequel to the Table of Nations and is designed to explain how the nations speak different languages in spite of their common origin and how they found their way to the farthest corners of the earth. The major theme of the passage is the dispersion of the nations because of their rebellious pride and apostasy in uniting at Babel. But the story is more than an explanation of the scattering; it is an explanation of the problems due to the existence of nations.

It was at Babel—that city founded by Nimrod, a descendant of Ham through Cush; that city known for its pride and vanity; that seat of rebellion toward the true God and pagan worship of the false gods—that the Lord turned ingenuity and ambition into chaos and confusion so that the thing the people feared most came on them and that their desire to be people of renown was suddenly turned against them. For the Israelite nation the lesson was clear: If she was to survive as a nation, she must obey God's will, for the nation that bristles with pride and refuses to obey will be scattered. The account of the scattering at Babel thus has a theological significance for God's people.

The Bible teaches that those who exalt themselves shall be abased (Matt. 23:12). In this little story the proud rebellion was met by God in talionic judgment. What they feared the most came upon them, and the fame they craved came in the form of notoriety. By such justice God demonstrates his sovereignty over the foolish plans of mortals, turning their rebellion into submission to his will.

This account provides a profound and lasting example of such a judgment on ambitious pride. Moses records this event for a warning to the new nation of Israel: *God will subjugate the proud who rebel against his will.* Nothing short of dispersion across the face of the earth would await a people who refused to obey God.

I. Immense pride (hubris) is rebellion against God (2–4).

The first verse, a short prologue to the account, informs the reader that the entire race had a common language, thus showing that this beginning is parallel to 10:1. Knowing the previous arrangement of the scattered nations in chapter 10, Jacob observes that a tone of irony is already sounded in this verse (*First Book of the Bible*, p. 77).

The whole earth (i.e., the inhabitants) had one "lip" (*śāpâ*, to indicate speech) and one vocabulary (*dᵉbārîm*, to indicate the content of what was said). The point of this prologue is clear: The entire race was united by a common language.

A. Pride leads to disobedience to God's Word (2).

The narrative records that the human family migrated "off east" (*miqqedem*) and settled in the region of ancient Babylon. The verb used to describe their journey (*nāsaʿ*) carries the sense of Bedouins moving tents by stages. This wandering continued in an easterly direction from Armenia until they settled (*wayyēšᵉbû*) in Shinar, where they found a plain. This "valley of the world," as the Talmud calls it, became the designated place for the nomads-turned-settlers.

B. Ingenuity strengthens proud ambition (3).

The resolve of the race comes in two stages: in verse 3, they made bricks, and in verse 4, motivated by their initial success, they moved to a grander scale by building a city with a tower. Bush (*Notes*, vol. 1, p. 183), following Josephus (*Antiquities* 1. 4. 2), designates Nimrod as the leader of this founding of Babylon.

In their zeal for societal development, alliance, and fame, and with all the optimism of a beginning people, they began to organize their brick-making. They were an ingenious lot, for they lacked the proper stone and clay and had to make do with makeshift materials. The writer's attitude toward this ingenuity comes across in an appropriate pun: they had no clay (*hōmer*), but they used asphalt (*hēmār*). Jacob suggests that the effect of this assonance sounds like a child's play song (*First Book of the Bible*, p. 77).

Met by initial success, they advanced to a greater resolution: "Come, let us build. . . ." Couched in the same grammatical construction as the preceding resolve, their words indicate that they would use the materials made to build a city "with a tower."

The circumstantial clause draws the reader's attention to the tower. Once built, this tower would provide the pattern for fortresses and acropolises for others. Building it with its top in the heavens may reflect the bold spirit of the workers, even though it is hyperbolic language used to express security (cf. Deut. 1:28).

C. Ambition and fear motivate pride (4).

The purpose of their building venture was fame. They wished to find security by arrogantly making a name—a desire that is satirized in verse 9. But their desire to be renowned was betrayed by their fear of the oblivion of dispersion. Richardson observes this motivation:

> The hatred of anonymity drives men to heroic feats of valour or long hours of drudgery; or it urges them to spectacular acts of shame or of unscrupulous self-preferment. In its worst forms it tempts men to give the honour and glory to themselves which properly belong to the name of God. [*Genesis I–XI*, p. 128]

The basic characteristics of culture are thus seen here: underlying anxiety (the fear of being separated and disconnected) and the desire for fame (a sense of security in a powerful reputation).

II. God will not permit proud rebellious acts to succeed (5–8).

A. God investigates the activities of arrogant mortals (5).

The second half of the passage reflects the first, beginning with the Lord's investigation of the city and the tower that the humans had begun to build. The description, written very anthropomorphically, describes the Lord's close interest and participation in human affairs. He did not need to come down to look at their work—in fact, his coming down implies prior knowledge. In the words of Cassuto, one could say that, no matter how high they towered, the Lord still had to descend to see it (*Commentary on Genesis*, vol. 2, pp. 230, 244–45). The Lord's coming down does not alone strike this note of satire. The parallel construction of the cohortatives (11:7) reflects their plans made earlier. The point clearly is that the tower that was to reach the heavens fell far short.

The purpose of his coming down was "to see" the work. This is the second anthropomorphic expression in the line and announces that he will give the city a close investigation. The narrative is filled with condescension. In referring to them as *bᵉnê hā'ādām* ("sons of man"), he shows them to be earthlings. This view strikes at the heart of the Babylonian literature, which credited the work to the Anunnaki gods. According to Genesis, the work was terrestrial, not celestial.

B. God knows the danger of collective apostasy (6–7).

Verse 6 records the results of that investigation: "And the LORD said, 'If as one people all having one language they have begun to act this way, now nothing that they propose to do will be out of their reach.'" The similarity of style and wording to Genesis 3:22 is most striking. The potential for calamity is dangerous to the race, and God will prevent it. They will nullify the purposes of God in favor of their own purposes, which are within reach. They will be at liberty for every extravagance if they can think only of their own confederation.

Continuing to speak, the Lord says, "Come, let us go down and confound their language so that they cannot understand one another." The internal difficulty concerns the relationship of the word *nērᵉdâ* ("let us go down") with *wayyēred* ("but [the LORD] came down") of verse 5. The critical approach is to divide the two elements into strata, but such a solution is not satisfactory. A. Dillmann saw simply a return to heaven first, then a reflection (comparing 3:22), and then the coming in judgment (*Genesis, Critically and Exegetically Expounded* [Edinburgh: T. & T. Clark, 1897] p. 393). This understanding may be the simplest. Cassuto takes *wayyō'mer*, "and he said," as an explanatory connection of contemporaneous actions: "But the LORD came down ... thinking [*wayyō' mer*, lit. 'saying']: ... Behold, they are one people ... let us go down" (*Commentary on Genesis*, vol. 2, p. 247).

The second verb describes the actual purpose: "let us confound." This confusion (*bālal*) led to the diversity of their understanding and thus to their dispersion. Bush explains this process:

> This [confusion] was to cause a dispersion of the multitudes congregated at Babylon; an end which did not require for its accomplishment the instantaneous formation of new languages, but simply such a confusion in the utterance of the old, as should naturally lead to misapprehension, discord, and division. The dialectic discrepancies, however, thus origi-

nating, though perhaps not very great at first, would become gradually more and more marked, as men became more widely separated from each other, and by the influence of climate, laws, customs, religion, and various other causes till they finally issued in substantially different languages. [*Notes*, p. 179]

Once the understanding of one another was confounded, the division would be effected.

C. God cuts off the expectations of such pride (8).

"So the LORD scattered them from there across the face of the whole earth, and they ceased building the city." Their greatest fear (v. 4) came on them (cf. Exod. 1:10, 12). The place of unity (*šām*, "there") became the place of dispersion (*miššam*, "from there"). Their view was toward centrality; God moved them universally. The result of this dispersion meant that the city was unfinished as they had planned it. The rebellious race as a unified people did not fulfill their goal.

III. Epilogue (9).

In a marvelously clever etymological word play, verse 9 announces, "Therefore [that is why] its name is called Babel, because there the LORD confused the lip [language] of all the earth and scattered them across the face of the whole earth." The formula *'al-kēn* with *qārā'* is quite common as an explanatory inference from a reported event and is used most often with place names. Here it introduces the meaning given by the Israelites for Babylon. The word *bālal* provided a satirical meaning of "confusion" for the proud Babylonians' name. The story shows how this gate of the gods fell far short of expectations, ending in confusion and chaos.

The Lord thus scattered them across the face of the earth. The text need not imply that the confusion was immediately reached, or the scattering instantaneous. The narrator fixed this point from which the division of the peoples and the languages would begin and move ever further.

Irony may be seen in the beginning and the ending of this passage. The group at Babel began as the "whole earth" (v. 1), but now they were spread over the whole earth (v. 9). By this contrast the lesson was made clear: God's purpose (9:1) would be accomplished, in spite of the proud defiance of humankind.

The significance of this short account is great. It explains to God's people how the nations came to be scattered abroad. The import, however, goes much deeper. That it was Babylon, the beginning of kingdoms under Nimrod from Cush, adds a rather ominous warning: Great nations cannot defy God and long survive. The new nation of Israel need only survey the many nations around her to realize that God disperses and curses the rebellious, bringing utter confusion and antagonism among them. If Israel would obey and submit to God's will, then she would be the source of blessing to the world. Unfortunately, Israel also raised her head in pride and refused to obey the Lord. Eventually, she too was scattered across the face of the earth.

On the personal level the text reveals the necessity of submissive obedience to the Word of the Lord and warns against resisting through pride. Those who humble themselves in this way before God, God will exalt; but those who exalt themselves, God will abase.

Bibliography

DeWitt, Dale S. "The Historical Background of Genesis 11:1–9: Babel or Ur?" *JETS* 22 (1979): 15–26.

Fokkelman, J. P. *Narrative Art in Genesis.* Assen: Van Gorcum, 1975.

Gowan, Donald E. *When Man Becomes God: Humanism and Hubris in the Old Testament.* Pittsburgh: Pickwick, 1975.

Gressmann, Hugo. *The Tower of Babel.* New York: Jewish Institute of Religion Press, 1928.

Heidel, Alexander. *The Babylonian Genesis.* 2d ed. Chicago: University of Chicago Press, 1951.

Kraeling, Emil G. "The Earliest Hebrew Flood Story." *JBL* 66 (1947): 279–93.

Kramer, S. N. "The 'Babel of Tongues': A Sumerian Version." *JAOS* 88 (1968): 108–11.

————. *The Sumerians.* Chicago: University of Chicago Press, 1963.

Laurin, Robert B. "The Tower of Babel Revisited." In *Biblical and Near Eastern Studies,* edited by Gary A. Tuttle, pp. 142–45. Grand Rapids: Eerdmans, 1978.

Ringgren, Helmer. "Babhel." *TDOT,* vol. 1, pp. 466–69.

Ross, Allen P. "The Dispersion of the Nations in Genesis 11:1–9." *BibSac* 138 (1981): 119–38.

Speiser, E. A. "Word Plays on the Creation Epic's Version of the Founding of Babylon." *Or,* n.s. 25 (1956): 317–23.

Vos, Howard F. *Genesis and Archaeology.* Chicago: Moody, 1963; rev. ed. Grand Rapids: Zondervan, 1985.

18

The Genealogy of Shem
(Gen. 11:10–26)

T his section is designed to trace the ancestry of Abram, the son of Terah, back to Shem, the son of Noah. The genealogy is a vertical list, the kind used in the ancient Near East to document legitimate claims to thrones or inheritances. Apart from such needs, lineage was not important. In this section the writer is providing the connecting links between Abram the patriarch and Noah the second Adam.

True to the style in Genesis, the material narrows the general survey to the specific individual. Genesis has just traced the families of the earth that came from Noah's sons, explaining how they came to be scattered across the face of the earth. The Table of Nations gave the general sweep of civilization in the ancient world; the present genealogy prepares the reader for the call of Abram, a descendant of Shem.

Theological Ideas

This genealogy from Shem to Abram seems on the surface to be an uninteresting list. Its meaning comes from its purpose in the book, especially the first eleven chapters. By the two vertical genealogies (Gen. 5 and 11), Abram was connected to Adam. This link was important in

the argument of the writer because of the divine purpose and commission for Adam: Adam was blessed; he was to rule and have dominion in
the earth; his seed was to restore peace and righteousness through a
bruising conflict with evil. And now, Abram was shown to be the heir
of the promises and the commission. The genealogy thus authenticates
the direct link to the blessing at creation.

The call of Abram (12:1–3) was a demonstration of sovereign grace
in which the Lord singled out one man from the scattered nations and
promised to build a nation from him, through which he might channel
his blessing to the world. But that selection was not arbitrary. The way
was prepared from antiquity through Adam, Seth, Enosh, Noah, and
Shem. The genealogy links that blessing to a man whose ancestors represented faith in the Lord and to whom the promise of blessing had been
extended.

Structure

The pattern of the genealogy is parallel to the one in Genesis 5; both
lists have ten names (if Noah is included in chap. 11), and the last-named
person on each list has three sons (see chart 14).

Several observations are in order. First, the name of Noah is not actually a part of the genealogy in Genesis 11:10–26. In order to have the
balanced lists of ten names for each, his name must appear on both
lists. Second, the order of the three sons in each list is not chronological.
"Shem, Ham, and Japheth" was the common expression, probably be-

Chart 14. **The Genealogies
of Shem and Abram**

Genesis 5	Genesis 11
Adam	[Noah]
Seth	Shem
Enosh	Arphaxad
Kenan	Shelah
Mahalalel	Eber
Jared	Peleg
Enoch	Reu
Methuselah	Serug
Lamech	Nahor
Noah	Terah
Shem, Ham, Japheth	Abram, Nahor, Haran
Canaan (9:18)	Lot

cause of the remoteness of Japheth to the writer's message. But a close study of the references indicates that Ham was the youngest. Also, 10:21 indicates that Japheth was older than Shem. In the listing of "Abram, Nahor, and Haran," Abram was placed first because of his importance, but he was not the firstborn. Terah was 70 when he became a father (11:26) and was 205 when he died (v. 32), at which time Abram was about 75 (12:4). Abram thus could not have been born when Terah was 70. Third, one additional descendant was added to each list, and each proved to be an antagonist to Israel. To Ham was born Canaan, and he was singled out for special attention in chapter 9; to Haran was born Lot, who became the father of the Moabites and Ammonites (chap. 19).

Commentators generally view these lists as selectively arranged, formed with a deliberate pattern and effective symmetry and omitting other names. If there was a deliberate selectivity in forming the lists, however, it is hard to sustain it exegetically. To show that there are gaps in the genealogy, we would have to interpret each verse to read: "X lived so many years and begot [the line that culminated in] Y." Positing such an ellipsis in each panel would be hard to support, especially when it is clear that some of the names on these lists are actual fathers and sons. A consistent rule for interpreting the genealogies to allow for gaps must be employed if that approach is to be taken.

This study will involve textual criticism within the genealogy in the Gospel of Luke (3:36), for that record includes the additional name Cainan. A good case can be made for that name being a scribal addition in the Greek—but each exegete will have to sort through that problem separately.

Whether there are gaps or not, there is a balanced symmetry between the lists. The obvious purpose must be to draw the parallel between the line from Adam to Noah, and from Noah to Terah. By extension through the three sons, the text equates Abram with Shem as recipients of the blessing.

Development of the Exposition

It is very unlikely that an expositor would devote an entire exposition to this genealogy, even if there were the luxury of an unlimited number of expositions. It would be best to explain it as a connecting link between Shem and Abram but to relegate it to introductory remarks for another exposition.

Should someone attempt an exposition of the chapter, the study of the Hebrew text would not be as fruitful as in other passages, even in comparison to Genesis 5. A topical approach could be used, incorporating ideas about the genealogical formulas, the types of genealogy, and the purpose of connecting Abram to Adam.

The genealogy is remarkably different than the one in chapter 5, a fact that must be noted. It does not have the total number of years tallied and does not close the sections with "and he died." Of course they died, but this section has a different emphasis. Genesis 5:1–6:8 stressed that death prevailed in the race; but *Genesis 11:10–26 stresses a movement away from death toward the promise, and it stresses life and expansion, even though longevity was declining.* The tone of this list, then, is different. It actually starts with Shem, who was blessed, and concludes with Abram, who was called to receive the blessing. The line that possessed the blessing flourished for centuries under God's good hand.

Bibliography

Albright, W. F. "Contributions to Biblical Archaeology and Philology." *JBL* 43 (1924): 363–93.

———— . "The Names *Shaddai* and *Abram.*" *JBL* 54 (1935): 173–210.

Gibson, J. C. L. "Light from Mari on the Patriarchs." *JSS* 7 (1962): 44–62.

Gordon, Cyrus H. "TRH, TN, and NKR in the Ras Shamra Tablets." *JBL* 57 (1938): 407–10.

Hartman, T. C. "Some Thoughts on the Sumerian King List and Genesis 5 and 11b." *JBL* 91 (1972): 25–32.

Malamat, A. "Mari," *BA* 34 (1971): 2–22.

Unger, Merrill F. *Archaeology and the Old Testament.* Grand Rapids: Zondervan, 1954.

Youngblood, Ronald. "Cuneiform Contributions to Old Testament Interpretation." *Bethel Seminary Quarterly* 10 (1962): 8.

3

The Patriarchal Narratives About Abraham

With the beginning of the narratives about Abraham, the reader observes a significant change in the message of Genesis. The record now concentrates on God's promises to the fathers to bring blessing to all the families of the earth. The motif of cursing is still present, but it does not play the predominant role that it did in the primeval events. From this point on, the writer's primary concern is to trace the development of God's resolution to bless.

Several themes are important to this development. Most important is the covenant made with Abraham and his descendants. This theme builds on the idea of covenant introduced through Noah in Genesis 9:1–17; but, whereas that covenant was universal in its benefits, this covenant centered on the family of Abraham. The covenant with Noah promised peace and safety for all creation, but the covenant with the patriarchs promised descendants, land, fame, and blessing (for them and those in the world who shared the blessing). The sign of the Noachian covenant was the rainbow, a sign that God gave to all creation; but the sign of the Abrahamic covenant was circumcision, a rite that became a requirement for the covenant people. With the Abrahamic covenant the program of God focused on one man and his descendants as the channel for bringing blessing to the families of the earth.

Connected with the idea of the Abrahamic covenant are the themes of birth and death. If the promises included progeny, then the birth of an heir, of descendants, would be a chief concern. The narratives are accordingly concerned with marriage, birth, inheritance right, and transmission of the blessing. Conversely, the motifs of death and burial are present throughout the narratives, slowing the pace of the fulfillment of the promises. These troubling themes remind the reader of the presence of the curse. The promises of God and the faith of the covenanter must struggle against great obstacles.

Another related theme that works through the stories is the heightened conflict between good and evil. While God's blessing provides the good gifts of life and fertility within the fulfillment of the promises, the curse and its effects are a constant reminder of evil. This evil takes many forms in the patriarchal narratives, but the most pronounced is the theme of deception that frequently threatens the program of blessing. Another form that evil takes is the open conflict between people, whether they are foreign armies, pagan potentates, or selfish relatives. The story of the development of the covenantal promises is the story of the triumph of good over evil.

The section of the patriarchal narratives that is devoted to Abraham— that is, the "$tôl^edôt$ of Terah," Genesis 11:27–25:11—forms a substantial portion of the book and deserves attention as a literary unit in itself. The central focus of this material is certainly the establishment and development of God's promises to Abraham, but the way it is presented also indicates that the narrator intended to develop the character of the family. It is the story of the family's struggle to gain the promised blessings, but that struggle was made difficult by strife within the family and by threats from outside. The reader might wonder how the promised blessings from God could have derived from such tentative beginnings. The narrative takes up this very point, tracing how the promises were carried forward and confirmed with each successive strengthening of the faith of the patriarch. Ultimately, the patriarch proved himself to be a man of faith and guaranteed the future of the promise through the sacrifice of Isaac. Faith in the promises of God enabled the ancestor and his family to overcome the conflict with evil and receive the blessing of God. The nation of Israel could see themselves in the person of Abraham, facing the same kinds of tensions and learning to persevere in their faith.

The Abrahamic stories include an introduction to the cycle (11:27–32) and then the narrative proper (12:1–22:18), in which the tensions were faced by the man of faith. This narrative section begins with the obedience of Abram to the initial calling (12:1–9) and ends with the obedience of Abraham to the testing of God (22:1–18), the two units framing the other narratives. The stories between these two accounts concentrate on the development of the promise of the land (12:10—15:21) and then the promise of the seed in the land (chaps. 16–21). Then Genesis 23:1–25:11 develops the transition to the next section; this section portrays Abraham's efforts to see that the covenant continued in successive generations.

Bibliography

Albright, W. F. "Abram the Hebrew: A New Archaeological Interpretation." *BASOR* 163 (1961): 36–54.

————— . "From the Patriarchs to Moses." Part 1, "From Abram to Joseph." *BA* 36 (1973): 5–33.

Blythin, I. "The Patriarchs and the Promise." *StTh* 21 (1968): 56–73.

Clifford, Richard J. "The Word of God in the Ugaritic Epics and in the Patriarchal Narratives." In *The Word in the World*, edited by R. J. Clifford and G. W. McRae, pp. 7–15. Cambridge, Mass.: Weston College Press, 1973.

Cross, F. M., Jr. "Yahweh and the God of the Patriarchs." *HTR* 55 (1962): 225–59.

Fisher, Loren R. "The Patriarchal Cycles." In *Orient and Occident: Essays Presented to Cyrus H. Gordon on the Occasion of His Sixty-Fifth Birthday*, AOAT 22, edited by H. H. Hoffner, Jr., pp. 59–65. Neukirchen-Vluyn: Neukirchener, 1973.

Holt, J. M. *The Patriarchs of Israel.* Nashville: Vanderbilt University Press, 1964.

Knox, Laurence W. "Abraham and the Quest for God." *HTR* 28 (1935): 55–60.

McKane, William. *Studies in the Patriarchal Narratives.* Edinburgh: Handsel, 1979.

Manley, G. T. "The God of Abraham." *TynB* 14 (1964): 3–7.

Meyers, J. M. "The Way of the Fathers." *Interp* 29 (1975): 121–40.

Millard, A. R., and D. J. Wiseman, eds. *Essays on the Patriarchal Narratives.* Leicester: Inter-Varsity, 1980.

Muilenburg, J. "Abraham and the Nations: Blessing and World History." *Interp* 19 (1965): 387–98.

Muntigh, L. M. "Some Aspects of West-Semitic Kingship in the Period of the Hebrew Patriarchs." *OTWSA* 9 (1966): 106–15.

Parrot, André. *Abraham and His Times.* Translated by J. H. Farley. Philadelphia: Fortress, 1968.

Rowley, H. H. "Recent Discovery and the Patriarchal Age." *BJRL* 32 (1949–1950): 46–79.

Selman, M. J. "Published and Unpublished Fifteenth Century B.C. Cuneiform Documents and Their Bearing on the Patriarchal Narratives of the Old Testament." Ph.D. diss., University of Wales, 1975.

————. "The Social Environment of the Patriarchs." *TynB* 27 (1976): 114–36.

Wagner, N. E. "A Literary Analysis of Genesis 12–36." Ph.D. diss., University of Toronto, 1965.

Westermann, Claus. *The Promises to the Fathers: Studies on the Patriarchal Narratives*. Translated by David E. Green. Philadelphia: Fortress, 1980.

Wiseman, Donald J. "Abraham in History and Tradition." Part 1, "Abraham the Hebrew"; part 2, "Abraham the Prince." *BibSac* 134 (1977): 123–30, 228–37.

————. "They Lived in Tents." In *Biblical and Near Eastern Studies*, edited by Gary A. Tuttle, pp. 195–200. Grand Rapids: Eerdmans, 1978.

Wolff, H. W. "The Kerygma of the Yahwist." Translated by W. A. Benware. *Interp* 20 (1966): 131–58.

Zimmerli, Walther. "Abraham." *JNWSL* 6 (1978): 49–60.

19

The Record of Terah and Abram's Obedience
(Gen. 11:27–12:9)

The record of Terah forms the introduction to the whole cycle of Abraham stories. The title "these are the generations [tôlᵉdôt] of Terah," it may be recalled, indicates that what follows is what became of Terah. This report begins with the birth and marriage of Abram, the son of Terah, and continues through the life of Abraham, until the next tôlᵉdôt section. Rather than form an exegetical exposition by itself, this little subunit would best serve as part of the introductory material for Genesis 12:1–9.

That the passage forms a subunit in itself may be gathered from its beginning and ending. Verse 27 is the title introducing the story of Terah (as well as the entire section about Abram); verse 32 is the end of the account of Terah, for his story must end with his death. These two verses frame the story of Terah.

What is said within this little Terah report is restricted to what concerns Abram and his future sojourn in the Promised Land. There is the report of the birth of Abram and his brothers, the marriages of the two surviving sons, Abram and Nahor, with a note about Sarai's barrenness, and the pilgrimage of the family (including Lot) toward Canaan through Haran. This information provides the necessary lineage and background for the stories to follow.

The information in this section is parenthetical to the main narrative sequence. Genesis 11:26 reports the end of the genealogy of Shem: "Now Terah lived seventy years, and begot Abram, Nahor, and Haran." Then Genesis 12:1 begins, "And the LORD said to Abram." It is not really necessary to translate 12:1 "the LORD *had* said"—even though such a translation is one way to resolve the apparent discrepancy of the location of the call (cf. Gen. 11:31–12:1 with Acts 7:2–4). The narrator was not concerned with presenting a strict chronology for the call and the move; he provided the information about Terah's move to Haran as a parenthesis to the main idea. Genesis on occasion traces one line through to a culmination before returning to the main theme (cf. chaps. 37–39). We may reconstruct the chronology as follows: Abram received the word from God in Ur, the family left Ur to go to Canaan (11:31) by going through Haran (apparently the ancestral home), Terah died in Haran (v. 32), and Abram continued on to the place that God had promised (12:4). The record of the Word of the Lord to Abram (vv. 1–3) was placed at the beginning of the Abraham stories proper, after the report of the death of Terah.

It would be helpful to study the religion of Ur as background to the calling of Abram to see what he abandoned. According to Joshua 24:2, Terah served pagan gods beyond the Fertile Crescent. But according to Genesis 31:53, Abraham and Nahor as well as their father (Terah) worshiped the true God. It may be that a knowledge of the Lord (i.e., Yahweh) was retained in the family but that the worship of pagan gods had dominated. Then, with the word from the Lord, the family together followed the true God and migrated back to Haran. Thereafter, only Abraham continued on to the Land of Promise.

There is some discussion in the commentaries about the pagan gods. Westermann, for example, notes that the names Sarah and Milcah properly derive from titles meaning "princess" (or lady) and "queen." These definitions may not be exact, for in Babylonian *šarratu* means "queen" and *malkâtu* "princess." More to the point, *Šarratu* was the name of the wife of the moon god Sin, and *Malkâtu* was a name or title of Ishtar, daughter of the moon god. Westermann concludes that we have no indication of the link between these titles from pagan religion and the names of the two women, for nothing in the stories mentions these gods (*Genesis*, vol. 2, p. 138). Yet, if the family worshiped pagan gods and if the names parallel names of deities, it is possible there was some connection. Of course, that connection would say nothing about the beliefs of Sarah or Milcah, only of those who gave the names.

Haran died in the lifetime of Terah (11:28), and his son, Lot, journeyed with the family to the north. In all probability, when Terah died in Haran, Lot was then in the charge of one of his uncles—Abram, as it turned out. Here again we may only speculate as to Lot's interest in the word from God. It appears that the oracle did indeed quicken the knowledge of the Lord in Terah, his sons Abram and Nahor, and perhaps in Lot.

The exposition of Genesis 12:1–9 must articulate its importance in Genesis and in the Bible. It is the central passage of the book, the foundation of the Abrahamic promises, and the beginning of the nation of Israel as a worshiping community. It is somewhat surprising, then, to see how many works do not give much emphasis to this narrative unit. Westermann is correct in observing that most exegesis has put all the emphasis on 12:1–3, without noting how it fits into the broader context. He adds that the whole text requires attention, each part having something important to say on the subject of Abraham (*Genesis*, vol. 2, p. 145).

If the exegesis of this passage is thorough, then the subsequent stories about Abraham will also be clarified. The unit reports the foundational promise of blessing, the migration to Canaan, the appearance of the Lord, and the building of the altar. A pattern is set in this narrative for the history of the family.

Theological Ideas

The starting point of the narrative is the divine word to Abram, calling him to leave his homeland and found a new nation that would bring blessing to the world. Israel would learn by this account that their very existence as a nation was by God's election of one man who responded by faith. It would affirm to the nation that their beginnings were rooted in the will of God. Thus, as they heard their call to leave Egypt and go with Moses to the land of Canaan to inherit the promises to the fathers, they would know that faith in the promises would be demonstrated by obedience to the call.

The message is, indeed, that faith is demonstrated by obedience, but the circumstances in the story make this message especially powerful. Abram's obedience was not a simple act of faith (if we dare speak of such); his was the conversion of a pagan. Abram was advanced in years, probably prosperous and settled, but in a thoroughly pagan world. The Word of the Lord came to him—although we do not know how or in what form—and he left his world and his relatives to follow the Lord's command. Consequently, he has become the epitome of faith in the Bible. The exposition of this unit should therefore not trivialize the message, speaking only of everyday acts of faith by believers (although

that point could be included in the broader discussion of the principle
of faith); it must reflect the message of the text in context, namely, a
life-changing act of faith.

The narrative unit includes other theological themes that also need
to be developed. One is the revelation of God, first by word, and then by
an appearance to Abram in the land. Although the idea of revelation
may not fit too well with some scholars' idea of history, it is absolutely
essential to a theological interpretation of history. To separate it from
the report of Abram's journey would destroy the meaning. The patriarchal narratives are characterized by the revelation of the Lord in the lives
of people in a way that has not been frequently or regularly repeated.

Another theme is worship. The building of the altar and the proclaiming of the name of the Lord are critical to this story; they show that the
covenant people in the Land of Promise have as their task the proclamation of their faith through worship.

Structure and Synthesis

Structure

The passage includes the poetic arrangement of the Word of the Lord
to Abram and then the report of the itinerary. Within the itinerary the
narrative makes use of parenthetical clauses to stress the significance of
the travels of Abram. The two major parts of the unit cannot be separated
in the exposition, for the report of Abram's travels is based on, and
explained by, the word from God.

The structure of the first three verses directs the interpretation, for
it is arranged in a sequence with parallel themes (see chart 15). The
Word of the Lord is a twofold command, represented by two imperatives—Abram was to leave his land and to be a blessing. Each imperative
is followed by three promises from God. The sequence may be paraphrased as follows: You go out, and when you do, I will do three things
for you, and I will do these three things in order that you might be a
blessing; and when you are a blessing, I will do these three things as
well.

It is also interesting to observe the pattern of the narrative sequence
in the nine verses. Abram is the subject throughout the whole story,
except for verse 1 ("and the LORD said") and verse 7 ("and the LORD
appeared unto Abram and said"). In both sections where the Lord is the
subject of the sentence, speeches follow (vv. 2–3 and v. 7). In all the
other verses, where Abram is the subject, there is only action—he went,
he took, he entered, he built, he journeyed, and so on. The only breaks
in the report of Abram's itinerary come with the circumstantial clauses,
one reporting his age (v. 4) and the other reporting the presence of the

Chart 15. **The Structure of Genesis 12:1–3**

Get (you) out [imperative]	*lek-lᵉkā*
from your land	*mēʾarṣᵉkā*
and from your kindred	*ûmimmôladtᵉkā*
and from your father's house	*ûmibbêt ʾābîkā*
to the land that I will show you	*ʾel-hāʾāreṣ ʾăšer ʾarʾekkā*
and I will make you into a great nation	*wᵉʾeʿśkā lᵉgôy gādôl*
and I will bless you	*waʾăbārekkā*
and I will make your name great	*waʾăgaddᵉlâ šᵉmekā*
that you be a blessing [imperative]	*wehyēh bᵉrākâ*
and I will bless those blessing you	*waʾăbārăkâ mᵉbārᵉkeykā*
but must curse the one cursing you	*ûmᵉqallelkā ʾāʾōr*
and in you shall all the families of the earth be blessed.	*wᵉnibrᵉkû bᵉkā kōl mišpᵉḥōt hāʾădāmâ*

Canaanites (v. 6). On the basis of the structural organization we may anticipate the thrust of the passage: Abram was obediently acting on the basis of the revelation he received, in spite of his age and the presence of Canaanites.

Summary Message

Abram obeyed the commandment of the Lord (1) to forsake his homeland for the promise of a new land, a new nation, and personal greatness, by journeying to the land of Canaan, and (2) to be a blessing, by making proclamation of his new-found faith through worship.

Exegetical Outline

I. Call: The Lord called Abram to forsake his homeland for the promise of a new land, a new nation, and personal greatness, and to be the means of blessing for the world (1–3).
   A. Abram was to leave his homeland for a promised land (1).
   B. God promised Abram great personal blessings in order that he might be a blessing (2).
   C. The people of the world would be blessed if they shared in Abram's blessing (3).
II. Obedience: Although advanced in years, Abram journeyed to the land of the Canaanites with his wife, his nephew, his possessions, and his proselytes (4–6).
   A. Abram obeyed the Lord and went to Canaan, even though he was seventy-five years old (4).
   B. Abram took his wife, his nephew, his possessions, and the proselytes he made at Haran (5).

    C. Abram entered the land of the Canaanites and stopped at a shrine near Shechem (6).

  III. Confirmation: The Lord appeared to Abram and promised to give the land to his descendants (7a).

  IV. Obedience: Although he had to journey on toward the South, Abram made proclamation of his faith in the Lord at his altars (7b–9).

    A. In response to the Lord's appearance, Abram made an altar (7b).

    B. When he settled between Bethel and Ai, he made another altar and made proclamation of the Lord by name (8).

    C. Abram continually journeyed on toward the South (9).

Development of the Exposition

The passage provides a paradigm of the obedience of faith. It shows a faith that left everything and obeyed the word of the Lord; but it also portrays a believer who proclaimed his faith. The narrative develops these ideas nicely in two cycles: the Word of the Lord and Abram's response to it, and then the appearance of the Lord and Abram's response to it.

I. God calls people to leave all and receive his blessing (12:1–3).

The first part of the narrative is the poetic record of God's Word to Abram—a calling out to a new beginning with God's blessing. This call is the Word of the Lord to the pagan, inviting him to become a Yahwist and enjoy divine blessing.

The promises in these verses were given to Abram for his benefit primarily, but ultimately for the benefit of Israel and all the families of the earth. What is recorded here is not the Abrahamic covenant, although the blessings offered here will be ensured by the covenant. At this point the promises are conditioned upon Abram's obedient faith.

A. God's calling requires faith (1).

The divine imperative simply instructed Abram to leave. He was told very specifically what he was to leave—his land, his relatives, and his father's household (note the repetition of *min*, "from"). But he was told nothing of the land that God would show him. Indeed, divine imperatives seldom give the details of what is to happen, although they often specify what is not to be done.

All of this calling required faith in the Lord. This passage does not state that Abram believed, but Genesis 15:6 affirms it, and Hebrews

11:8 confirms it. The evidence of Abram's faith was his obedience to the Word of the Lord, which is stressed here. If he had not believed he would not have obeyed, and the promises of God would not have been fulfilled.

B. Obedience to God's call brings blessing (2–3).

The expositor must display the pattern of the passage: the initial imperative is followed by three promises, and those promises lead into and enable the second imperative (to be a blessing), obedience to which in turn leads to three more promises. The symmetry strengthens the meaning that God's calling has a purpose and that Abram's obedience brings a blessing.

Of course, a great deal of attention may be given to the individual promises that were made. Central to them is the idea of blessing; it occurs five times and is obviously the key word. It is not too hard to understand "I will make you into a great nation" or "I will make your name great," but "I will bless you" is less specific. If the word "bless" (bārak) essentially conveys spiritual and physical enrichment and, within the narratives of Genesis, the gift of fertility in accord with God's program, then this cohortative is closely bound up with the other two promises in verse 2. God would give Abram fame and fertility. Here the promise of blessing counteracts the crisis of Sarai's barrenness (11:30). Obedience would bring God's blessing, first to the patriarch, and later to Israel.

The Lord would send blessing in order that Abram himself might be a blessing. (The imperative with the wāw is in sequence with the preceding cohortatives; it retains an imperatival force—he must be a blessing—but it stresses the purpose of God's blessing.) It appears that at this point a more spiritual significance of "blessing" is in mind. Abram would be responsible for opening the blessing of the Lord to the families of the earth. This Word probably meant that, along with the promises of God that granted enrichment, Abram would share the knowledge of God. The blessings given to Abram could never be dissociated from the relationship with the Lord through faith and obedience. It thus became Abram's responsibility to transmit this message wherever he went. If an Abimelech or a Laban shared in the bounty, they had to know that it was the blessing from the God of the fathers.

Because the Lord was binding himself to Abram with these promises, he would safeguard his servant. Those who blessed Abram would receive blessing from God; that is, those who supported and endorsed him in his faith would actually find enrichment. Conversely, if anyone treated Abram lightly, he must be cursed. Note the precise wording of the text with the change of vocabulary, the change of the number in the participles, and the change from a cohortative to an obligatory imperfect: "I will bless those who bless you, but the one who treats you lightly I

must curse [wa'ăbārăkâ mᵉbārᵉkeykā ûmᵉqallelkā 'ā'ōr]." The two
words for "curse," 'ārar and qālal, are synonyms and thus overlap in
their meanings. But 'ārar, the stronger of the two, means to impose a
barrier or a ban, a paralysis on movement or other capabilities, or to
remove from the place and power of blessing. Qālal, "treat lightly,"
means to hold in contempt, speak lightly, or curse. Anyone who disre-
spects and treats Abram and his faith lightly will thus be removed from
the place of the blessing. The wording records this threat as a necessary
part of the outworking of the promises.

Consequently, Abram would be the channel of blessing for the whole
world. No one would find divine blessing apart from the blessings given
through Abram and his seed. The range of verse 3 extends far beyond
Israel to "all the families of the earth." In view of the preceding verse,
the line could be interpreted to read, "All the families of the earth will
bless themselves" (depending on how they treat Abram and his seed).
The form of the verb (a niphal) can also be taken as a passive ("will be
blessed in you"), which has been the choice of most translations. The
Septuagint translated the verb with a passive, and this version was taken
over by the New Testament (Acts 3:25; Gal. 3:8). This interpretation
harmonized better with the idea that salvation would go to the world
through Abram's seed, Jesus Christ. But the original expression may
have had a much broader range of meaning before this specific application came out of it (see the use of the hithpael in Gen. 22:18; 26:4;
Ps. 72:17). The promise of Genesis 12:3 is still worded in a general sense,
allowing for a wider meaning. In any case, the point of the passage is
clear; as Westermann says, "God's action proclaimed in the promise to
Abraham is not limited to him and his posterity, but reaches its goal
only when it includes all the families of the earth" (Genesis, vol. 2,
p. 152).

II. Whoever believes God's Word will follow him obediently
   (12:4–6).

The central point to be stressed in this section is the obedience of Abram
to the call. Abram's faith may be inferred from the context, but this passage
simply reports that, when Abram heard the call and the promises, he obeyed.

A. Faith obeys (4–5).

The key word used to stress this obedience is the verb at the beginning
of verse 4, wayyēlek, variously translated "went," "got out," or "departed." It corresponds to the primary verb of the call, "get (you) out"
(lek-lᵉkā). In fact, the same verb, hālak, is used again in verse 5 ("to go

to the land of Canaan"), and at the end of the narrative ("*continually* journeyed to the Negev"). The repetition of this common verb reflects the central point of the story—Abram's obedience to the call.

There are a few qualifications about Abram's pilgrimage that are important to the understanding of his faith. First, the text records that Abram departed "as the LORD had spoken [*dibber*] to him." The clause calls to mind the obedience of Noah, even though in that section of the book the expression was "as the LORD had commanded him" (6:22; 7:5, 16). The point is clear: Abram went as an act of obedience to the Word of the Lord, not as a natural migration.

Second, the text includes a parenthetical clause about Abram's age. The advanced age of Abram and Sarai, as well as the barrenness of Sarai (11:30), provides tensions through the following narratives.

A third qualification of Abram's obedience is that he took his possessions and people with him (12:5). Cassuto observes a "leaving formula" in this verse: so-and-so (the head of the family) took so-and-so (members of the family) and such-and-such possessions and went (*Commentary on Genesis*, vol. 2, p. 278). Parallel passages that employ this construction are Genesis 11:31 (Terah), 36:6 (Esau), 46:5–6 (Jacob), and Exodus 18:2–4 (Jethro). The formula shows that the report of this departure with its participants follows a normal pattern.

Tucked away in this verse, easily overlooked, is the expression "and the people [*nepeš*] whom they had acquired [*ʿāśâ*] in Haran." This expression probably does not refer to the acquisition of slaves, for the Hebrew word *nepeš* would not likely be used for that. And it certainly does not refer to their children, because Sarai was barren until Isaac's birth (21:1–7). Cassuto argues that this expression probably refers to proselytes (ibid., p. 320). If he is correct, then the narrative implies that, already in Haran, Abram had been sharing his faith in the Lord.

B. Obedience encounters opposition (6).

The text informs us that Abram passed over as far as (ʿ*ad*) Shechem, as far as (ʿ*ad*) the terebinth tree of Moreh. The mention of the "terebinth of Moreh" (ʾ*ēlôn môreh*) provides an ominous note that must be brought into the discussion. Moreh in Hebrew means "teacher." It may describe this place as some ancient shrine where instruction was given (a terebinth tree was often used for idol worship; see Hos. 4:13) or a place where oracles were declared by Canaanite priests or simply the tree itself. The pilgrim thus found himself in alien territory where pagan ideas were handed down.

That Abram's presence there formed a tension finds support in the clarifying parenthetical clause: "Now the Canaanites were at that time dwelling in the land." Throughout the Book of Genesis the Canaanites are the antagonists; even though their mention seems harmless at this point, the association with the other passages discussing their practices is inescapable. The reader already knows that an oracle of cursing lies over them. This additional clause, then, informs the reader that (1) the land promised to Abram was inhabited by others and (2) those who inhabited it were pagan (and perverse, as subsequent passages would show). The situation in Canaan revealed that the reception of the promises would not be without difficulty.

III. God confirms his promises to the faithful (12:7a).

According to this verse, the Lord appeared to Abram, once he was in the land, to confirm the promises and to reward his faith. Previously Abram had only a word from God; now he witnessed an appearance with the word. The expression "and the LORD appeared unto [*wayyērā' YHWH 'el*]" occurs again in Genesis 17:1; 18:1; 26:2, 24; and 35:9. The expositor will have to explain the nature and significance of divine appearances in the patriarchal stories. This heavenly visitation was sufficient to sustain Abram in the land of the Canaanites. He now received personally the direct word from the Lord that the land would belong to his descendants.

The interpretation of this verse must include the question of application, a frequent question in expounding narrative literature. Abram received direct revelation, an appearance of the Lord who spoke to him, in the confirmation of the promises. What may the modern believer expect as a confirmation of the promises of God? We must recognize that the incident in Genesis 12:7 is a part of the ancient record of the early stages of revelation; it reports what happened to Abram. All that the text would say to us today is that *God can appear to people;* it does not say that he will or that we must experience such an appearance for confirmation. Probably the New Testament believer will find confirmation in the sure Word of God, the Holy Scriptures, and the demonstrative appearance of the Lord in human flesh once and for all—the Christ event. The New Testament writers teach that the resurrection of Jesus Christ confirms the promises God has made to us who share this new faith (Rom. 1:2–4).

IV. God's obedient servants proclaim their faith through worship (12:7b–9).

There are two emphases in the last few lines of this passage: Abram's continual journey toward the great southern region, the Negev, and

Abram's response to God's revelation through worship. In other words, the land did not belong to him, and so he had to continue to journey as a sojourner in the Land of Promise; but he was convinced that the Word of the Lord to him was true.

The response to God's confirming appearance was worship. The idea of sacrifice, presumed here with the building of an altar, continues the ancient form of expressing gratitude and devotion. But at the second mention of his building an altar to worship the Lord is the report that he "made proclamation of the LORD by name [*wayyiqrā' beᵉšēm YHWH*]." This expression, first used in Genesis 4:26, refers to the public proclamation of faith in the Lord. The expression is used in the Bible for prayer or for praise, but in the Mosaic material it seems to be broader (although a public proclamation of the faith could include prayer and praise). Martin Luther translated it "preached" (*predigte*), a good rendering in this context.

The interesting feature about this proclamation at the altar is the substance—the name of the Lord (i.e., the attributes and activities of the Lord). When Abram's proclamation is combined with the wording of the call, we can see something of the nature of true faith. The Lord promised to make Abram's *name* great, to make him famous, and Abram responded by proclaiming the *name* of the Lord—making the Lord famous in Canaan, as it were. When we recall that the Shinarites were involved in their disobedient enterprise in order to make a *name* for themselves (11:4), we can see how different the man of faith was. Those who seek fame through disobedience will be given an infamous name, but those who seek to exalt the name of the Lord through their obedient service will be made famous.

Abram's worship and proclamation show clearly that he was the proper choice to be the channel of blessing for all the families of the earth. Because his obedience extended to both commands, he could anticipate all the promises, even though their fulfillment seemed often delayed.

This brief narrative provides a powerful portrayal of faith. Against a thoroughly pagan background and with very little information, Abram simply took God at his Word and went to the land of Canaan and became a blessing. The subsequent chapters show the struggles he faced in his new calling, tracing the development of his new faith as well as the realization of the promised blessing.

For Israel, the call of their great ancestor was instructive. It demonstrated that the promises they lived for were indeed from God—the promises of a great nation, a land, sovereign protection, and future blessings. The Lord's appearance and confirmation proved that Canaan was their destiny. Moreover, the pilgrimage of Abram provided them with their central march. He came to Shechem, Bethel, Ai, and the Negev; they would go up from the Negev to Bethel, Ai, and Shechem, where the covenant would be enacted (Josh. 24). But God required faith for any generation that wished to share in those promised blessings.

Israel thus shared the same call that their founding ancestor received—to go on a pilgrimage by faith to the Land of Promise and to worship and proclaim God there. They would have to believe in the promises in order to go, and their going and serving would be evidence of their faith. The lesson has many areas of application: *Those who truly believe the Word of the Lord will forsake all else to become worshipers of the Lord and to serve in his program to bring blessing to the world.*

In carrying this theological message across to the New Testament audience, two clarifications will have to be made. First, the expositor will need to find what promises God has made to Christians. They may be called blessings as well, and they may even overlap with some of the blessings given to Israel, but there will be notable differences. Of course, the blessings promised to people today who leave their worldly existence and follow the Lord are first and foremost spiritual—forgiveness, salvation, and eternal life. But the New Testament also makes other promises to the modern believer for this pilgrimage.

Second, the expositor will have to clarify the New Testament usage of the Abrahamic promises, especially the interpretation of the seed and the bringing of salvation to the world through the seed of Abraham. It should be noted that the specific interpretation in the New Testament does not nullify the broader application in the Old. With the advent of Christ, however, the promise of the seed and the blessing find their fullest meaning in the plan of God.

Bibliography

Barr, J. "Theophany and Anthropomorphism in the OT." *VTS* 7 (1960): 31–38.

Burrows, E. "Note on Moreh, Gen XII 6, and Moriah, Gen XXII 2." *JThS* 41 (1940): 161.

Emerton, J. A. "The Origin of the Promises to the Patriarchs in the Older Sources of the Book of Genesis." *VT* 32 (1982): 14–32.

Freedman, D. N. "Notes on Genesis." *ZAW* 64 (1952): 190–94.

Habel, N. C. "The Form and Significance of the Call Narratives." *ZAW* 77 (1965): 297–323.

Holladay, W. L. "The Covenant with the Patriarchs Overturned: Jeremiah's Intention in 'Terror on Every Side' (Jer. 20:1–6)." *JBL* 91 (1972): 305–20.

Lindblom, J. "Theophanies in Holy Places in the Hebrew Religion." *HUCA* 32 (1961): 91–106.

———— . "Die Vorstellung vom Sprechen Jahwes zu den Menschen im Alten Testament." *ZAW* 75 (1963): 263–88.

May, James C. "God Has Spoken." *Interp* 14 (1960): 413–20.

Payne, Philip B. "A Critical Note on Ecclesiasticus 44:21's Commentary on the Abrahamic Covenant." *JETS* 15 (1972): 186–87.

White, Hugh C. "The Divine Oath in Genesis." *JBL* 92 (1973): 165–79.

Wright, G. R. H. "Shechem and League Shrines." *VT* 21 (1971): 572–603.

20

The Promised Blessing Jeopardized
(Gen. 12:10–20)

The story presented here has much more to it than a lesson on honesty—although the teaching of the story does warn against deceit. When the narrative is compared with other passages of Scripture, it becomes clear that it has several implications within the Abrahamic cycle of narratives.

The story is essentially about the threat to the ancestress, and thereby a threat to the fulfillment of promises in 12:1–3. It simply but adequately traces this plot through the tension of the fear and deception of Abram to its resolution by the Lord's intervention. The writer uses speech as well as narration to develop the story, but he never strays far from the main point of interest concerning the blessing. On the one hand, God had promised to bless Abram, and so the patriarch came away from this incident a wealthy man. On the other hand, God had promised to defend Abraham from those who harmed the blessing, and so the Pharaoh was prevented from interfering with Abram and his blessing. The interesting point in the story is that it was Abram who endangered the ancestress, but it was the Lord who delivered her.

270

There are three such sister stories in the book (12:10–20; chap. 20; and 26:1–11). Although critical scholarship has been concerned with determining which story was the original and how the others developed from it, there is no compelling reason to doubt that three incidents occurred that were very similar. Genesis 20:13 indicates that it was Abram's plan to call Sarai his sister in dangerous situations. For Isaac his son to have attempted a similar ploy comes as no surprise. More important to the point of exegesis is the question why the writer saw fit to include three similar stories when one would apparently have done just as well. In this regard it may be observed that repetition is the essential feature of Hebrew rhetoric, which extends also to repetition of motifs and stories. Within the development of the book's message, however, there does seem to be a plausible explanation for the threefold repetition of this motif. In all three cases we have similar features: (1) the family sojourns in a land ruled by foreigners, (2) the ancestress is endangered by the deception of the ancestor, (3) a ruler takes her into his harem (except chap. 26), (4) divine intervention or human observation uncovers the error, and (5) the ruler confronts the ancestor. But it will also be observed that there are major differences between the stories as well (see chart 16).

For the present I shall set aside the Genesis 26 passage. In the discussion of the Isaac stories I shall suggest that the many parallels between Genesis 26 and the Abraham stories are carefully chosen and worded to show that Isaac was the true seed and that the promise had indeed passed to him.

The differences between Genesis 12 and Genesis 20 are significant enough to support the point that we have two similar but different incidents. Both have the theme of the deception by the patriarch and the

Chart 16. **Comparison of the Sister Stories**

Gen. 12:10–20	Gen. 20:1–18	Gen. 26:1–11
famine in the land (10)	—	famine in the land (1)
beauty of Sarai (11)	—	beauty of Rebekah (7)
deception as sister (13)	deception as sister (2)	deception as sister (7)
fear of death (13)	fear of death (11)	fear of death (7)
Egyptians saw her (14)	—	men of that place asked (7)
taken by Pharaoh (15)	taken by Abimelech (2)	—
wealth to Abram (16)	wealth to Abram (14–16)	—
plagues (17)	warning dream (3–7)	observed by Abimelech (8)
Abraham rebuked (18–19)	Abraham rebuked (9–10)	Isaac rebuked (9)
expulsion (20)	prayer of Abraham and healing of wombs (17)	—

preservation of the ancestress by divine intervention. But the first incident occurs in Egypt and the second in the Land of Promise, in Gerar. Since Abram had decided to lie about his relationship to Sarai wherever he went (20:13), we should not be surprised to find two accounts; but since God had determined to bless Abram with a seed in the land, we should not be surprised to find repeated deliverances by plagues and warning dreams to protect Abram's marriage. Outside the land, God would protect the blessing, in spite of Abram's deception; inside the land, God would also preserve the purity of the ancestress, in spite of Abram's deception.

The theme of powerful rulers' taking women for themselves occurs elsewhere in the Bible. We have already seen it with the "sons of God" in Genesis 6:1–4. Samuel warned Israel of how a king would take from them whatever he wished (1 Sam. 8:11–18). Indeed, David himself took another man's wife when he was captivated by her beauty (2 Sam. 11). Powerful rulers tended to overstep God's bounds and take what they fancied. In the Genesis stories, however, the patriarchs' deception about their wives provided the kings with the opportunity to take them.

Theological Ideas

The basic point of the story in Genesis is the divine preservation of the purity of Sarai for the sake of the promise. It is an account of God's protecting the future of the covenant. Israel would learn that, even when they were unfaithful, there were aspects of the promise that God would not relinquish through their failure. This deliverance in no way condoned the deception; rather, it embarrassed it.

This deception is a recurring theme in the book, a theme that will become more and more pronounced in the lives of the patriarchs. When God had to deliver his people from trouble, there usually was some failure or weakness that had brought it on. In this story, then, the exposition must be concerned with honesty and deception. People might think that, to escape from some difficult situation, they may scheme deceptively, albeit bordering on the truth so that it is not an outright lie. But from this passage we learn that, in such deception, the blessing of God may be jeopardized.

This tension is at the heart of the conflict of good and evil. In fact, the motif of good is used in this story to show the irony of the situation. Abram, recognizing that he was entering a life-and-death situation, told his wife to lie about her status "in order that *it might go well* [yîṭab]" for him on her account. He probably intended that he should be spared alive so that they might preserve the promise. But the story turns when the wife was taken into Pharaoh's household. Then the text says, "He treated Abram well [*hêṭîb*]" and enumerates all the wealth he was given. The good that he wanted was the promised blessing; the evil that he did jeopardized that blessing but brought him other good things. But what good did it do to have all the wealth and lose the wife?

Structure and Synthesis

Structure

The story has a clear structure to it: report of the situation (v. 10), the complication (vv. 11–16), the resolution by divine intervention (vv. 17–19), and the conclusion (v. 20). The narrative is also framed within the context, for 12:9 says that Abram journeyed on toward the Negev (South), and 13:1 reports that Abram and his family returned to the Negev.

The story includes two speeches that, when juxtaposed, clearly make the moral point of the story. In verses 11b–13 we have Abram's speech to Sarai, expressing his fears and advising her to lie. Then, in verses 18–19, we have the Pharaoh's speech, rebuking Abram for lying to him and expressing his fear that he might have taken her as a wife. The narrator thus emphasizes the opening and closing dialogues; the rest of the narration sets up, sustains, and resolves this tension.

When the basic structure of this little story is compared with the later experience of the nation, one can discern obvious parallels. Note the corresponding motifs in chart 17.

This parallelism is close and must be more than a coincidence. Moses has carefully worded the account of Abram's sojourn in, and deliverance from, Egypt with the greater sojourn and deliverance in mind. The effect was the demonstration that the great deliverance out of bondage by the plagues that Israel experienced had previously been accomplished in the

Chart 17. **Parallels Between Abram's and the Nation's Experiences**

Incident	Abram	Israel
Severe famine in land	Gen. 12:10	Gen. 43:1; 47:4
Sojourn in Egypt	Gen. 12:10	Gen. 47:4
Killing of the males	Gen. 12:11–13	Exod. 1:16
Bondage	Gen. 12:14–15	Exod. 1:11–14
Great wealth	Gen. 12:16	Exod. 12:36
Plagues on Egypt	Gen. 12:17	Exod. 7–11 (see 11:1)
Summons: "Take . . . go"	Gen. 12:19	Exod. 12:32
Use of *šillaḥ* ("send")	Gen. 12:20	Exod.—"Let my people *go*"
Journey to the Negev	Gen. 13:1	Num. 13:17, 22

life of the ancestor of the nation. Knowing this history would have been a comfort and an encouragement to the people under Moses, for if God, who made the promise to Abram, delivered Abram from Egypt to return to the land, then God, who confirmed the promises to the descendants of Abram, could surely deliver them as well. Even Abram's bringing the dilemma on himself through deception would also be encouraging, for the people could see that the program of God was too important to let anyone bring it to ruin.

Summary Message

When Abram passed his wife off as his sister, fearing that otherwise the Egyptians would kill him for her, he jeopardized the promise of blessing by losing his wife to Pharaoh, but the Lord intervened with plagues to deliver him and his wife from Egypt.

Exegetical Outline

   I. When Abram traveled to Egypt to escape the famine, he feared that the Egyptians would kill him for Sarai and so asked her to say that she was his sister (10–13).
      A. Abram went to sojourn in Egypt because of the famine (10).
      B. Recognizing that Sarai was very beautiful and fearing that the Egyptians might kill him to get her, Abram told her to say she was his sister (11–13).
  II. When Pharaoh's officials praised Sarai's beauty to him, she was taken into Pharaoh's harem, and Abram was paid generously for her (14–16).
      A. The princes praised the woman to Pharaoh, who took her into the harem (14–15).
      B. Pharaoh paid Abram a generous dowry for her (16).
 III. When the Lord intervened by inflicting Pharaoh's household with plagues, Pharaoh rebuked Abram for his deception and expelled him from Egypt (17–20).
      A. In order to prevent sexual defilement, the Lord plagued the house of Pharaoh (17).
      B. Pharaoh rebuked Abram and expelled him from his country (18–20).

Development of the Exposition

I. God's people often respond to danger by deception (10–13).

To understand the message of the passage, we have to look closely at what Abram did wrong and how God turned it about. In a word, Abram's scheme, born out of fear, backfired on him, so that the Lord had to intervene. This scheme, although having good motives, was nothing but deception.

A. The tension (10–12).

The occasion for the deception began with the journey into Egypt. Faced with a severe famine, which in itself formed a difficulty for the promise of the land, Abram went to sojourn in Egypt. One cannot fault Abram for this decision, for the verb "sojourn" (gûr) indicates that he had no intention of abandoning the promise but was going to Egypt for a temporary stay while the famine lasted. There are no indications in the narrative, however, that faith was operative.

The speech of Abram reveals the tension that grew out of this occasion: "I know that you are a very beautiful woman, and when the Egyptians see you they will say, 'This is his wife,' and they will kill [wᵉhārᵉgû] me and let you live [yᵉhayyû]." The knowledge of Sarai's great beauty and the fear of the Egyptians' desire for her presented Abram with what seemed an insurmountable problem. If he died, that would surely be the end of the promised blessing.

B. The scheme (13).

The scheme that Abram concocted came not from faith but from his Bedouin background (see 20:13). He wanted Sarai to deceive the Egyptians into thinking that she was his sister, possibly to buy time to escape, since anyone wanting to marry a sister would have to make negotiations. But the deception was a very subtle thing, for she was his half-sister. He could satisfy his own conscience by knowing that she was indeed a sister, but he would also know how the Egyptians would understand what he was conveying.

The motivation for the deception is expressed in two complementary purpose clauses: "in order that it may go well with me [lᵉmaʿan yiṭabli]" and "that I may live [wᵉhāyᵉtâ napši]." He was already convinced that they would spare her life, but he was concerned that they would kill him. For the *good* of their marriage and for the *good* of the promise of God, they would deceive the Egyptians to protect Abram's life.

II. Deception may jeopardize the promised blessing (14–16).

A. The complication (14–15).

The narrative reports that the Egyptians were indeed taken with Sarai's beauty, using the same words it used in Abram's speech: "that she was a very beautiful woman [ki-yāpâ hiʾ mᵉʾōd]." The complication arose when the princes of Pharaoh saw her and praised her (*wayhal^{e}lû*) to their ruler. Consequently, she was whisked away to the royal harem.

The wording of the last part of verse 15 is powerfully simple: "And the woman was taken into Pharaoh's household." Sarai is both silent and passive. The text offers no details or explanation. And Abram is powerless to prevent the seizure. His scheme might have worked with those who would negotiate for Sarai, but here was one who had no need to negotiate.

B. The reward (16).

The ironic twist to the story comes in verse 16, with the repetition of the verb *yāṭab*: "and it went well for Abraham [*ûl^e'abrām hêṭib*]." Not only did Abram stay alive, he gained wealth in exchange for Sarai. The list of his gain in the verse is itself a stereotype, used to portray the very wealthy. Now Abram stood in a different relationship to Pharaoh: whereas he had come as a mere stranger sojourning in the land, now he was an honored guest due to the generosity of his host.

The notice of Abram's wealth over the transaction serves to heighten the primary element of the complication—the loss of Sarai. The wealth would be a perpetual reminder that Sarai was no longer in his household, but in Pharaoh's.

Once again in Genesis, through fear and disobedience, the intimacy of the man and the woman is broken; once again someone has taken that which God had put off limits. But this time God would prevent it from going further, for his word of promise was in jeopardy.

III. The Lord at times must intervene to protect the promised blessing (17–20).

A. The resolution (17).

"But the LORD plagued Pharaoh and his house with great plagues." Without any clarification of the nature of the plagues or how they knew they were there because of Sarai, the text reports the divine intervention. The construction of the Hebrew stresses the severity of the plagues (note the cognate accusative: *waynagga^c ... n^{e}gā^{c}im g^{e}dōlim*), so that it is reasonable to assume that Pharaoh's household was overwhelmed by them and Sarai was untouched.

The Israelites living in Egypt at the time of the great plagues, who knew about this incident in Abram's life, certainly could have identified with the situation very well. God's plagues on Egypt under Moses not only brought ruin to the nation of Egypt but they protected and preserved the Israelites in their houses.

Divine intervention alone could deliver the wife of Abram untouched from the harem of Pharaoh. There were times in the experience of the nation of Israel, however, when God did not deliver his people from their predicaments, especially if their sin had been prolonged and rebellious. For this reason the expositor must be careful in wording the point— God at times may deliver his people, but he may not. In this passage the predicament was such that, if there was to be any deliverance, any way out, the Lord would have to provide it. And he did it because his Word was at stake. In a similar way Ezekiel described the divine motivation for the restoration of God's people. "Thus says the LORD God, 'I do not do this for your sake, O house of Israel, but for my holy name's sake, which you have profaned among the nations wherever you went' " (36:22).

B. The rebuke (18–20).

Pharaoh summoned Abram and rebuked him for the deception. The initial statement by the ruler is reminiscent of the Word of the Lord to Adam and Eve in the garden: "What is this you have done to me [mah-zōʾt ʿāśitā lî]?" Such a connection to the earlier disobedience is sufficient to inform the reader of Abram's guilt and of the fact that the error had repercussions.

The words of Pharaoh need not be interpreted to mean that there had been sexual contact. He simply stated that he took her for a wife. In a royal household, it would take time for her to come before the monarch (note the twelve months for Esther's preparation [Esther 2:12]). Moreover, the statement "Here is your wife" strongly suggests that she was returned unharmed, as his wife.

Finally, Pharaoh had Abram and his possessions escorted to the border—he expelled him. His final command, "Take and get out [qaḥ wālēk]," recalls the divine commission to Abram at the beginning of the chapter (lek-lᵉkā), but this second command to leave was occasioned by disobedience and characterized by shame. C. H. Gordon says that the ignominious dismissal of the couple is a fitting end to a most unheroic episode (Before the Bible [London: Harper & Row, 1962], p. 133). Now the relationship between Abram and Pharaoh was severed. As Coats says, "A foreigner who has called down the plagues of Yahweh by his relationship with the wife of this blessed man must separate himself from the source of divine blessing" (Genesis, p. 111).

The narrative has to be considered at two levels, the human and the divine. The overall theological message of the context of these stories deals with God's program to raise a nation through Abram and Sarai that will bring blessing to the world. But this story is worked out on the human level against that framework, for it reports how Abram stumbled through a difficult situation in his deceptive scheme. Moses would have his readers learn how *God graciously protects his plan through divine intervention when his people complicate it with deception.* But Moses would also have them learn that *it is foolish to try to deliver oneself from threatening situations by means of deceptive schemes.* To put it another way, sinful acts cannot save God's people from threatening situations. Evil cannot bring about good.

The passage also has relevance for the preservation of marriage. The purity of Sarai was in danger, and the future of the covenant in jeopardy. God prevented harm coming to either at this point, thus showing himself to be a protector of the marriage. Just as the marriage of Abram and Sarai was important to the promises that God made to them, so too the preservation of marriage has been important to all of God's covenant people down through the ages, whether in ancient Israel or in the church. If God went to these lengths to save such an integral part of the covenant, then so must God's people make every effort to preserve it.

It appears in the story that Abram prospered from his deception. He did get away rather rich, but all those riches might have become a diversion from his possession of the one person who mattered. It is worth mentioning that his ill-gotten gain plagued him with problems for years to come, first in the strife with the herdsmen of Lot, and then through the tension over an Egyptian maid named Hagar, who very possibly was included among the maidservants mentioned in verse 16.

Bibliography

Coats, G. W. "Despoiling the Egyptians." *VT* 18 (1968): 450–57.

Culley, Robert C. "Structural Analysis: Is It Done with Mirrors?" *Interp* 28 (1974): 165–81.

Emerton, J. A. "A Consideration of Some Alleged Meanings of ידע in Hebrew." *JSS* 15 (1970): 145–80.

Freedman, D. "A New Approach to the Nuzi Sistership Contract." *JANES* 2 (1970): 77–85.

Greengus, Samuel. "The Patriarchs' Wives as Sisters—Is the Anchor Bible Wrong?" *BAR* 1:3 (1975): 22–24.

————. "Sisterhood Adoption of Nuzi and the 'Wife-Sister' in Genesis." *HUCA* 46 (1975): 5–31.

Jepsen, A. "Amah und Schiphchah." *VT* 8 (1958): 293–97.

Maly, E. H. "Genesis 12:10–20; 20:1–18; 26:7–11 and the Pentateuchal Question." *CBQ* 18 (1956): 255–62.

Marcus, D. "The Verb 'to Live' in Ugaritic." *JSS* 17 (1972): 76–82.

Miscall, Peter D. "Literary Unity in Old Testament Narrative." *Semeia* 15 (1979): 27–44.

Muilenburg, J. "The Linguistic and Rhetorical Usages of the Particle כִּי in the Old Testament." *HUCA* 32 (1961): 135–60.

Mullo-Weir, C. J. "The Alleged Hurrian Wife-Sister Motif in Genesis." *Glasgow Oriental Transactions* 22 (1967–70): 14–25.

Petersen, D. L. "A Thrice-told Tale: Genre, Theme, and Motif." *Bib Res* 18 (1973): 30–43.

Polzin, R. " 'The Ancestress of Israel in Danger' in Danger" *Semeia* 3 (1975): 81–98.

Speiser, E. A. "The Verb šhr in Genesis and Early Hebrew Movements." *BASOR* 164 (1961): 23–28.

————— . "The Wife-Sister Motif in the Patriarchal Narratives." In *Oriental and Biblical Studies, Collected Writings of E. A. Speiser*, edited by J. J. Finkelstein and Moshe Greenberg, pp. 62–81. Philadelphia: University of Philadelphia Press, 1967.

Wacholder, B. Z. "How Long Did Abram Stay in Egypt?" *HUCA* 35 (1964): 43–56.

21

Faith's Solution to Strife
(Gen. 13)

This story demonstrates how faith can resolve strife. Faced with an insurmountable problem of survival, the two tribal chiefs Abram and Lot had to separate from one another in order to avoid open strife over the land. One might have expected that in the separation Abram, the recipient of the promise, would have protected his rights and chosen first. But he magnanimously offered the first choice to Lot, who promptly chose the best territory for himself. Abram was left with the less fertile land but also with the reassurance from the Lord that it all would be his.

The narrative is another little story that develops from a setting with complications to a tension that must be resolved. It may be classified as a part of the Abraham-Lot cycle of stories, which form a subplot in the Abrahamic narratives. In this unit the resolution to the tension placed Lot in jeopardy, for his settling in Sodom foreshadowed a greater tension to follow (13:13). The Abraham-Lot cycle is a narrative of contrast, but it is not a narrative of conflict like the Jacob-Esau cycle. Abram defused any conflict that might have started and then remained aloof from Lot's plight, except for his rescue and intercession.

280

Theological Ideas

The story continues the theme of the promise of the land. It begins with Abram's return to the land, concentrates on the tension over the land, and concludes with the promise of all the land for Abram. The point that the land was not able to sustain the two of them certainly provides a tension for the understanding of the promise—was this the land Israel expected to be flowing with milk and honey? At this time, however, the only land open to them was not able to sustain them. Moreover, the luxuriant quality of the land over by the Jordan provided a subtle test, for although it appeared to be the better land, it veiled deeper problems for the one who would go that way.

Within the setting of the land theme there is also the emphasis on choices. Lot's choice was selfishly motivated and based on appearance only. But Abram's choice to let Lot choose first was magnanimous and unthreatened. The recipient of the promise did not need to guard his future possessions jealously; rather, he could deny himself and relinquish the better part to Lot. Here we have an early example of the contrast between those who walk by faith and those who walk by sight. The idea that Abram was operating by faith finds support in the emphasis on his worship at the beginning (v. 4) and ending (v. 18) of the narrative.

Those who walk by sight eventually learn that seeing may be misleading. In describing what Lot would find in the region of the Jordan, the narrative brings forward one of the book's predominant theological ideas: evil. The people of Sodom were very evil people, as the later episodes of Genesis make clear. Dwelling in the best of the land may therefore not be the best choice after all. It certainly was not the best thing for a man of Lot's character to do.

Helyer ("Separation of Abram and Lot") suggests another major theological idea for this story, one that fits the theme that Abram has no heir. Since Lot would have been the heir, his departure left Abram without an heir. But this suggestion is unconvincing, for at least two reasons: (1) there is no mention of this concern in the chapter at all (cf. Gen. 15, where Abram is concerned that his servant will inherit his estate), but there is an emphasis on the land, which is mentioned seven times; (2) Lot's choice of the best part of the land did not remove him from the land (as Helyer contends) and thereby disqualify him from inheritance; the cities of the plain are in the Promised Land, according to 10:19. To take an idea that the text nowhere mentions and make it the main point of the story is not the way of sound exegesis. There is no indication that Lot was ever in the running as an heir of Abram. Besides, it is not impossible that Lot may have been older than Abram, if Abram was born so many years after his brothers. A careful reading of the text shows that it is concerned with the peaceful settlement of strife over the Promised Land.

Structure and Synthesis

Structure

The structure of the chapter is uncomplicated. It consists of three major sections: the itinerary (vv. 1–5), the account of the tension and resolution (vv. 6–13), and the reaffirmation of the promise of the land to Abram (vv. 14–17). It is helpful to note that all three sections are different literary forms. The first is a simple report, the second is a legal controversy, and the third is an oracle.

Throughout the chapter the narration makes good use of clauses and phrases to offer the interpretive emphases. The expositor must thus concentrate on the parenthetical clauses, the qualifying phrases, and the dialogue in order to understand the significance of the narrative sequence. The following sketch traces these qualifying ideas through the narrative sequence (signaled by the preterites):

```
 1   And Abram went up . . .
 2     (Now Abram was very wealthy . . .)
 3   And he journeyed by stages . . .
         to the place where he had pitched his tent . . .
 4         where he had built the altar . . .
     And he made proclamation of the LORD . . .

 5     (Now Lot, who went with Abram, also had . . .)
 6     And the land could not bear them . . .
 7   And there was strife between . . .
         (Now the Canaanite and the Perizzite were . . .)
 8   And Abram said
           Let there be no strife . . .
             for we are brothers.
 9     Is not all the land before you?
         Separate . . . if . . .
10   And Lot lifted up his eyes and saw all the region of the Jordan
         that it was well watered
             (before the LORD destroyed Sodom and Gomorrah)
             like the garden . . .
11   And Lot chose . .
     And Lot journeyed . . .
     And brothers were divided . . .
```

12   Abram dwelt in the land of Canaan,
        but Lot dwelt . . . and camped next to Sodom . . .
13   (Now the men of Sodom were wicked sinners . . .

14   So the LORD said to Abram
           after Lot had separated . . .
        Lift up now your eyes and see . . .
15   because all the land . . . I give . . .
16   and I will make your seed . . .
17   Arise, walk to and fro . . .
18   And Abram camped . . .
        and he built an altar there . . .

Within the structure of the narrative there are notable parallels. For example, Abram's speech gives Lot the choice land, and God's speech gives Abram the whole land; Lot lifted up his eyes and saw the land, and God told Abram to lift up his eyes to see the land. There is also a parallel use of parenthetical clauses: after the strife the narrative mentions the Canaanites, and after the choice it mentions the Sodomites. Then, there is also the inclusio of Abram's worship (v. 4 and v. 18).

Summary Message

When a strife about the land broke out between the herdsmen of Abram and the herdsmen of Lot after they returned to the place where the altar had been built at first, Abram settled the dispute by magnanimously giving Lot his choice of the best land—which was inhabited by wicked sinners—and in return received the reaffirmation of God's promise.

Exegetical Outline

    I. When Abram and his family returned to Bethel, where he had first built an altar, a strife broke out between Lot's herdsmen and Abram's herdsmen over the land (1–7).

       A. Abram journeyed back to the place of his altar, but now he was very wealthy (1–4).

          1. Abram returned to the land a wealthy man (1–2).

          2. He returned to the altar at Bethel and proclaimed his faith (3–4).

       B. Lot, who journeyed with Abram, was also very wealthy, so that the land could not sustain them both (5–6).

          1. Lot was also very wealthy (5).

          2. The land could not bear all their possessions (6).

    C. A strife broke out between the herdsmen, among the Canaanites who dwelt in the land (7).

  II. Abram settled the strife by offering the first choice of the land to Lot, who chose the beautiful Jordan valley (8–13).

    A. Abram stopped the quarrel because they were relatives, offering Lot his choice of all the land (8–9).

    B. Lot chose the region of the Jordan valley because—before the Lord destroyed it—it was well watered and beautiful (10–11).

    C. Lot settled near Sodom—where wicked sinners lived—but Abram stayed in Canaan (12–13).

  III. The Lord reaffirmed his promise of the land and of innumerable descendants to inhabit it and invited Abram to investigate his land (14–18).

    A. God reaffirmed the promises to Abram (14–16).

    B. God invited Abram to investigate his land (17).

    C. Abram settled near Hebron and built an altar (18).

Development of the Exposition

I. The prosperity of God's people may bring strife (1–7).

A. God's people may enjoy prosperity (1–5).

The first part of the narrative, verses 1–7, basically provides the setting for the parts to follow. The first few verses stress Abram's return to the place where he had been before, to the place where he had built the altar (the relative clauses stressing the points, and the words "formerly" and "beginning" recalling the previous context of 12:1–9). The passage begins with a return to the land and a return to worship (cf. the formula of 12:8 with the one in 13:4). The experience in Egypt was now behind the patriarch; he was making a new beginning.

Significant to this section are the reports about the wealth of the men. Verse 2 provides a parenthetical note about Abram's great wealth (*kābēd*), and verse 5 gives the parenthetical note about Lot (who went with Abram—*hahōlēk 'et-'abrām*). Verse 5 specifically mentions Lot's tents because they will be a motif later in the account. With the notice of the return to the land and to the altar, there is thus also the report of the great substance that the two had accumulated.

B. The attendant needs of wealth may lead to strife (6–7).

The tension that comes in the story is strife (*rîb*) between the herdsmen of Abram and Lot because the land was not able to support the two.

Note the repeated explanation in the text: "The land was not able to bear them that they might dwell together [*wᵉlō'-nāśā' 'ōtām hā'āreṣ lāšebet yaḥdāw*]", and "they could not dwell together [*wᵉlō' yākᵉlû lāšebet yaḥdāw*].*" Clearly, the text is stressing the great tension of dwelling together because of their great substance.

The expositor must note that this is *the* land that could not sustain their living together. This fact has implications for the hope of the promise. The reason for this inability of the land to sustain them is in the final parenthetical clause: "Now the Canaanite and the Perizzite were dwelling at that time in the land." These original inhabitants of the land probably occupied the better parts, so that Abram and Lot had to scrap for their water and food in the remaining sections. But the clause also signifies that a strife between Abram and Lot made them vulnerable to these warrior tribes.

The two were thus faced with a serious dilemma because of their great wealth. The natural response was strife. The word *rîb*, ("strife"), signifying claim and counterclaim, was used later in Israel for legal disputes. But it also is repeated in Genesis for similar disputes, notably Isaac's strife with Abimelech's men over the wells of water (chap. 26) and Jacob's strife with Laban over his wages (chap. 31). Ironically, the word is also used of the Israelites' strife with God over the lack of water in the wilderness (Exod. 17). When it came to water, the natural instinct was to strive for it.

II. Strife can be settled by the generous actions of those living by faith (8–13).

A. Those who walk by faith can be magnanimous (8–9).

The second section of this passage shows Abram's solution to the strife: he magnanimously gave Lot the best choice. One might expect Abram to cling to the land as his rightful possession, but he offered it all to Lot ("Is not all the land before you [*hᵃlō' kol-hā'āreṣ lᵉpāneykā*]"?). The one who believed that God promised to give him the land did not have to reserve it for himself. Rather, as the clan leader, he had the primary responsibility for maintaining peace, and he used the land to do so.

It is important that the expositor develop the motivation of Abram for this offer. In verse 8 he cautioned, "Let there be no strife [*'al-nā' tᵉhî mᵉrîbâ*]." These words must have struck a responsive note in the hearts of Israel when they read them in conjunction with what happened in the wilderness at Meribah (Exod. 17:1–7). In that desolate spot was no water to drink, and so the people strove with the Lord before Moses smote the rock. Forever the names Massa ("testing") and Meribah ("striving") were to become ominous names because the people out of unbelief provoked the Lord and were sent to wander in the wilderness until they died. The warning in Psalm 95:8 is almost like Abram's, "Let there be no *mᵉrîbâ*."

The reason that there should be no strife, according to Abram, is that they were relatives. Their common bond shared over such a long period of time was to Abram something worth saving. To keep their relationship intact, they must separate. Westermann says, "Responsibility for one's brother can express itself in a solution to a quarrel which results in a peaceful separation" (*Genesis,* vol. 2, p. 177). We may recall how Cain in his anger repudiated any responsibility for his brother (Gen. 4:9). Abram thus offered Lot the choice of all the land that rightfully belonged to him.

B. Those who walk by sight can be deceived (10–13).

The tenth verse elaborately describes how Lot chose the best for himself. "Lot lifted up [*nāśā'*] his eyes and saw [*rā'â*]" reflects his intense survey of the region of the Jordan. The description of what he saw is lavish; the area was well watered. As if this description were not sufficient, the writer compares it to the garden of God, probably a reference to the rivers in the garden that went out and watered all the region (Gen. 2:10–14), and to the land of Egypt, which was always well watered because of the Nile. There would be no difficulty finding water and vegetation in that lush area.

The narrator places such an emphasis on what Lot saw that the reader can understand how it aroused his desire. Just as the tree in the garden of Eden had awakened Eve's desire, so the fertile valley of the Jordan attracted Lot. With such an appeal to the senses in both passages, other considerations were forgotten.

Tucked away in the description of the valley, however, is an ominous note: "before the LORD destroyed [*šaḥēt*] Sodom and Gomorrah." This clause is poignantly inserted right after the comment that the land was well watered and before the comparison to the garden and to Egypt. The writer does not want the reader to miss the point that for some reason the Lord did not allow that region to stay as it was and that Lot's choice on the basis of sight was a temporary benefit.

Lot made his choice without any concern for Abram, a choice that would prove to be the greatest mistake of his life (note the three verbs in the sequence for Lot: "he lifted up his eyes," "he saw," and "he chose for himself"). The report that Lot pitched his tent "next to Sodom" (*'ad-sᵉdōm*) provides another significant note to anyone familiar with Sodom. Lot was not the man to be in that location, which the narrative explains with another parenthetical clause: "Now the men of Sodom were extremely wicked sinners before the LORD." The motif of evil (ra') is compounded in this note about Sodomites; the construction uses it adverbially (the hendiadys translates "wicked and sinners" as "wicked sinners"), as if to say that these sinners were a step below the normal sinners. Moreover, their sin was "against the LORD." Indeed, all sin is, but this notice goes out of its way to say that God was offended. Finally, the adverb $me^{\,\prime}\bar{o}d$ ("exceedingly") is added, as if the previous descriptions were not sufficient. Few passages in Genesis describe the wickedness of a people so strongly.

The use of "evil" in the plural ($r\bar{a}$'$\hat{\imath}m$) provides a link to the earlier account of the flood (6:5 and 8:21). The use of the plural confirms the point of both passages—the whole generation is corrupt. Moreover, in both places the corruption is wiped out (šaḥēt, in 6:12–13 and 13:10) by a catastrophe (chaps. 7 and 19), and in both places one person and his family are saved (see Westermann, *Genesis*, vol. 2, p. 178).

Calvin's comments on Lot's selfish choice are instructive:

> Therefore, seeing that he was led away solely by the pleasantness of the prospect, he pays the penalty of his foolish cupidity. Let us then learn by this example, that our eyes are not to be trusted; but that we must rather be on our guard lest we be ensnared by them, and be encircled, unawares, with many evils; just as Lot, when he fancied that he was dwelling in paradise, was nearly plunged into the depths of hell. But it seems wonderful, that Moses, when he wishes to condemn the men of Sodom for their extreme wickedness, should say that they were wicked before the Lord; and not rather before men; for when we come to God's tribunal, every mouth must be stopped, and all the world must be subject to condemnation; wherefore Moses may be thought to speak thus by way of extenuation. But the case is otherwise: for he means that they were not merely under the dominion of those common vices which everywhere prevail among men, but were abandoned to most execrable crimes, the cry of which rose even to heaven (as we shall afterwards see) and demanded vengeance from God. That God, however, bore with them for a time: and not only so, but suffered them to inhabit a most fertile region, though they were utterly unworthy of light and of life, affords, as we hence learn, no ground to the wicked of self-congratulation, when God bears also with them for a time, or when, by treating them kindly, and even liberally, he, by his indulgence, strives with their ingratitude. Yet although they exult in their luxury, and even become outrageous against God, let the sons of God be admonished not to envy their fortune; but to wait a little while, till God, arousing them from their intoxication, shall call them to his dreadful judgment. [*Commentaries on Genesis*, vol. 1, pp. 373–74]

III. The generous actions of the faithful receive the approval of the beneficent Lord (14–18).

A. God's promise remains with the faithful (14–17).

The final section of the story provides the solace: there is confirmation of the promises to Abram after Lot departed. The section begins with a strong break in the narrative sequence, marking the new beginning here: "Now the LORD [waYHWH]. . . ." With the episode of Lot resolved, Abram received the reaffirmation of the promises. Indeed, this section explains how he could offer the land to Lot—he believed in God's promises to him. The inclusion of the promises at this point thus provides a lesson that those who believe can be magnanimous. Abram had the sense that in God he had abundant possession; as Dods says, "There is room in God's plan for every man to follow his most generous impulses" (Book of Genesis, p. 117). Abram knew that God meant what he had said, and so it mattered little what Lot chose for now.

This section contrasts sharply with the preceding, as if to offset what Lot had done. The repetition of the words between the sections is striking. God told Abram, "Lift up your eyes [śā' nā' 'êneykā]," whereas Lot had "lifted up his eyes [wayyiśśā'-lôṭ 'et-'ênāyw]"; God told Abram, "Look" (r°'ēh); whereas Lot "saw" (wayyar'); and God told Abram "All the land [kol-hā'āreṣ] which you are seeing will I give to you and your seed forever," whereas Lot chose "all the region of the Jordan [kol-kikkar hayyardēn]" in response to Abram's "is not all the land before you [hălō' kol-hā'āreṣ l°pāneykā]?" The Lord thus reworded the ideas in his instruction to Abram. In other words, Abram was told to do it, but Lot simply did it; Abram was waiting for God to give it, but Lot simply took it for himself. Better that God gives it than that an individual takes it.

Linked to the promise of the land is the promise of the seed, for the seed will be the ultimate possessors of the land. In affirming the promise of the seed, God ties it to the land—" like the dust of the ground [ka'ăpar hā'āreṣ]." As Abram walked about in the land he would realize the extent of this promise—his seed would be innumerable.

The expositor may wish to include the theme of "walking to and fro" in Genesis. This verb (hithallēk) occurred earlier in the expression of Enoch's and Noah's walking with the Lord. Now the Lord used it to instruct Abram to walk about in his land.

B. The faithful continue to worship (18).

The chapter closes the way it began, with Abram's building an altar to the Lord. From beginning to end in this story, Abram was a man of devotion to the Lord. As a worshiper he could respond correctly to the strife; as a worshiper he would wait patiently for the Lord to fulfill his promise.

Here, then, is the picture of faith functioning in a conflict. The situation was right for strife and conflict and, at other times, would have naturally turned into such. But Abram's faith showed that there was a better way of solving a potential conflict, the way of self-renunciation. In the biblical revelation Abram was far ahead of his time. This idea came to its full form only with the promise of a king of peace, when wars and conflicts had run their futile course.

The solution is a choice made in the midst of difficulty. It is a story about choices. Lot, walking by sight, chose on the basis of what appealed to him. His choice was selfish, self-seeking, and self-gratifying. As the text indicates, such a choice was dangerous and short-lived, for all was not as it appeared on the surface. Walking by sight provides no cautious perception of the evil and no awareness of God's plan. Abram, on the other hand, was walking by faith—as the final instruction and promise for him in verses 14–17 affirms—and he generously allowed Lot to choose first. He was unselfish and magnanimous because he trusted the promises of God. He had learned that it was not by his own plan or power that he would come into his possession, not by jealously guarding what he thought was his. God would give it to him, even if he gave it away a hundred times. Abram, therefore, had the freedom to act generously, righteously, and mercifully in his resolving the dispute. *Those who believe the promise of God's provision may be generous with their possessions.* But those who are greedy, anxious, or covetous have not understood the nature of God's covenant.

Bibliography

Boer, P. A. H. de. "יהוה as Epithet Expressing the Superlative." *VT* 24 (1974): 233–35.

Driver, G. R. "On עלה 'Went Up Country' and ירד 'Went Down Country.' " *ZAW* 69 (1957): 74–77.

Fishbane, M. "The Treaty Background of Amos 1:11 and Related Matters." *JBL* 89 (1970): 313–18.

Gemser, B. "*Be'ēber hajjardēn*: In Jordan's Borderland." *VT* 2 (1952): 349–55.

———. "The *rîb*—or Controversy—Pattern in Hebrew Mentality." *VTS* 3 (1955): 120–37.

Helyer, Larry R. "The Separation of Abram and Lot: Its Significance in the Patriarchal Narratives." *JSOT* 26 (1983): 77–88.

Moor, J. C. de. "Lexical Remarks Concerning Yaḥad and Yaḥdaw." *VT* 7 (1957): 350–55.

Rabinowitz, J. J. "The Suza Tablets." *VT* 11 (1961): 56–76.

Ramsey, G. W. "Speech-Forms in Hebrew Law and Prophetic Oracles." *JBL* 96 (1977): 45–58.

Simons, J. "Two Notes on the Problem of the Pentapolis." *OTS* 5 (1948): 92–117.

Weinfeld, Moshe. "The Covenant of Grant in the Old Testament and in the Ancient Near East." *JAOS* 90 (1970): 184–203.

22

The Blessing of Victory for God's People
(Gen. 14)

The record of the battle of the four kings against the five is an interesting section for the development of the promise to make Abram great and to bless those who bless him and curse any who curse him. The chapter describes in great detail a typical "international" skirmish in the ancient world, in which powerful city-states formed a coalition to subjugate rebellious vassals living on the edge of the land promised to Abram.

In the aftermath of the great victory the text records two of the most fascinating encounters of the Old Testament. Two kings came out to meet Abram on his return from the battle, and they could not possibly have been more different. In explaining the contrast between the king of Sodom and Melchizedek, the king of Salem (whose very title suggested a righteous rule and who occupied the office of priest), the expositor must not overlook how wicked the people of Sodom were (13:13). Melchizedek was the one person that Abram recognized as his spiritual superior, and so he accepted the blessing from him and paid him tithes. Abram did so with perfect perception of what he was doing. He knew

The Patriarchal Narratives About Abraham

that both the victory and the blessing came from God and must not in any way be tarnished through the offer from the king of Sodom.

Archaeological information is helpful for understanding the details and events of this chapter and may be checked with the standard works on the subject (Merrill F. Unger's *Archaeology and the Old Testament* [Grand Rapids: Zondervan, 1954] is an adequate place to begin; see also R. K. Harrison, "Chedorlaomer, *ISBE*, vol. 1, pp. 638–39). The names of the foreign kings, the nature of city-states banding together in coalitions, the subjugation and rebellion of vassal states, and the line of march of the invaders all fit the world of the patriarchs. So far, however, it has not been possible to identify any of the individual kings mentioned in the lists.

Critical scholarship is inclined to view the entire chapter with a good deal of skepticism. A common view argues that, since we know of no such kings in those eastern lands and no such subjugation of the cities of the plain and since there are late words and ideas in the account, the chapter is a composition from the exilic period, showing Abraham to be a hero. Westermann concludes that the composite text was the work of a scribe from the late postexilic period, to be compared with other Jewish writings of that period, and that verses 18–20 arose during the Davidic monarchy (*Genesis*, vol. 2, p. 192).

Conservative scholarship would agree that the chapter presents Abraham as "a great and powerful prince who encounters victoriously the united kings of the great kingdoms of the east" (ibid.), but would not share the skepticism about the historicity of the material. Rather, the conservative would say that Abraham is presented as a saving hero because he was a saving hero.

Conservative scholarship would also find the reasons for dating the material late to be unconvincing. Westermann lists three basic reasons. First, the intention to elevate Abraham to a worldwide political significance conforms with an attitude that is well known from the postexilic period (cf. the Book of Judith). Second, this is the only period in which the setting of verses 12–24 into the framework of verses 1–11 is comprehensible. The bizarre synthesis of such diverse elements, to use his wording, can be understood only from a time that no longer had any sensitivity to such diversity. Third, verses 1–11 "obviously smack of the scribe's desk; the clumsy way in which the lists have been worked in betrays this, and has given occasion to describe it as 'midrash.' " This lack of style, he says, goes hand in hand with the complete lack of historical perspective (ibid.). These arguments present one major critical view. For a more balanced survey of conservative and critical views, see Roland de Vaux, *The Early History of Israel*, translated by David Smith (London: Darton, Longman & Todd, 1978), vol. 1, pp. 216–20. De Vaux does not accept the historicity of the chapter either, but primarily for the reason that archaeology has not identified the kings and the subjugation.

This story is, of course, all a part of the larger issue of the historicity of the patriarchs and their times. One may agree that different traditions about the patriarchs may have been drawn into the composition, but to date it later because it seems to fit a later period or to say that it never happened because we cannot confirm it from outside sources is unacceptable. This chapter comes to the center of the debate, since it offers lists of kings and places and events that seem very credible.

It would be possible to treat this chapter in two separate expositions, the first covering the battle and Abram's victory, and the second covering the meeting with the two kings and the blessing from Melchizedek. However, the two main sections are interdependent; to take them separately would weaken the impact of the whole narrative. The report of the battle provides the foundation for the meeting, and the meeting with Melchizedek explains the source of the victory.

Theological Ideas

The main consideration is the significance of the section in the book. In the narrative Abram is identified as "the Hebrew" (note the gentilic ending on 'ibrî, v. 13)—he was a clansman like other tribal chiefs. It may be too much to say that he had now achieved worldwide political significance, but he had become a force to be reckoned with (which may be the main reason for including this account in the narratives). We thus learn from the chapter that God blessed Abram with a great victory over foreign nations that invaded the land, and Abram responded with loyalty and devotion to the God who promised that Abram would become a great nation and enjoy God's blessing.

In addition to this manifestation of the promised blessing, we find the related idea that those who blessed Abram shared in the blessing. Abram did not fight this battle alone; he had the help of the Amorites who had made a covenant with him. These people were permitted to take their share in the spoils of war because they fought with Abram.

The capstone of the narrative comes with the covenant blessing offered by Melchizedek, enabling Abram to perceive what lay behind the offer from the king of Sodom. Reminded of the blessing of the Lord, Abram was able to resist the deal and wait for the proper enrichment from the Lord.

This figure Melchizedek naturally commands a good deal of attention, especially in view of the interpretation the New Testament offers on the basis of his nature and activity. Abram recognized this king-priest as a

spiritual brother, one who believed in the true High God who created
the universe. This incident shows how limited our thinking often is.
While our attention is focused on Abram as the one who carried the
spiritual hope of the world, there emerged out of an obscure Canaanite
valley a man nearer to God than Abram was, and he blessed Abram.

The message of this chapter has four major features. First, the land
promised to Abram was plundered by invading armies who took tribute
(cf. the later history of Israel and the tributes and captivities brought by
eastern kings). Then, Abram conquered the invading armies by the power
of God, chasing them to Dan (the northern frontier of the land) and
rescuing Lot and the other captives. Third, Abram's victory was an outworking of the promises of God (12:1–3), showing that he had indeed
become a powerful tribal leader on the international scene and that
those who shared his mission would share his blessing. Finally, Abram
chose to wait for the blessing of God rather than accept anything from
the king of Sodom, for he would not be satisfied with the spoils of war,
especially if it put him in debt to this pagan king.

Structure and Synthesis

Structure

The first part of the chapter, verses 1–12, provides the report of the
campaign. It tells of an eastern king who made a campaign against
subjects who had rebelled against him by failing to send their tribute.
The procedure was common for Mesopotamian feudal lords and their
vassals.

The second part of the chapter, beginning with verse 13, is the narrative about Abram's victory. Many scholars have noted how the account
of the battle parallels other stories in the period of the judges or the
monarchy. We may think of Gideon, taking his 300 warriors (as compared with Abram and his 318) and courageously going to battle (Judg. 7),
or David, taking 400 men and chasing the Amalekites who had taken
his two wives among the prisoners (1 Sam. 30).

On the human level the story seems clear enough: Abram was drawn
into a conflict in order to rescue his relative, and with the help of his
confederates and by means of a surprise attack, he was victorious. But
the blessing of Melchizedek added another dimension—God had given
Abram the victory, and so God could be counted on to complete the
promise.

The third section begins with verse 17. Here we may observe that the
account of the meeting with the two kings is set out in a chiasm:

17 And the king of Sodom went out (*wayyēṣē' < yāṣā'*) to meet
    him . . .

18   And Melchizedek, king of Salem, brought out (*hôṣî'* < *yāṣā'*) . . .
19   And he blessed him and said,
           Blessed be Abram . . .
           Blessed by El 'Elyon . . .
20   And the king of Sodom said to Abram
           Give me the people
           but the possessions take for yourself.

In this sequence we have the king of Sodom going out, the king of Salem bringing out, the king of Salem blessing, and the king of Sodom bartering (Sodom—Melchizedek—Melchizedek—Sodom). The central thrust of the story is clearly the action and speech of Melchizedek—it separates the action and the speech of the king of Sodom. Abram was far more prepared to resist the offer from Sodom after receiving the blessing of Melchizedek.

Summary Message

When powerful eastern kings swept through the land, destroying and plundering the cities of the Jordan and taking Lot captive, Abram and his federation of retainers pursued and defeated the invaders in a surprise night attack, rescuing Lot and the possessions; and when he was blessed by the king of Salem, Melchizedek, and then offered riches by the king of Sodom, Abram swore that he would take nothing from the king of Sodom, lest the blessing should be tarnished.

Exegetical Outline

  I. The military campaign: In an effort to put down rebellion, powerful eastern kings invaded the Jordan valley, defeating all the military forces in the region, plundering the Jordanian kings, and taking Lot captive (1–12).
     A. The eastern kings, in an effort to put down rebellion, invaded the Jordan valley and defeated all the powers in their way (1–7).
        1. Four kings waged war against five kings (summary statement) (1–3).
        2. Four kings swept through the region to put down the rebellion (4–7).
     B. The eastern kings defeated the Jordanian kings and plundered their towns, taking Lot captive (8–12).
        1. The kings of the region of the Jordan set the battle in Siddim against the invading kings (8–9).
        2. The Jordanian kings fell in battle at Siddim and fled to the mountains (10).

3. The invading kings plundered the goods from the city and took Lot captive (11–12).

II. Victory of Abram: Upon hearing of the invasion and the capture of Lot, Abram mustered his trained men and, together with his allies, pursued and defeated the invaders in a night attack, rescuing Lot and all the possessions (13–16).

A. Abram, while dwelling in Hebron with his allies, learned of the capture of Lot from one of the fugitives (13).

B. Upon hearing the report, Abram mustered his trained men and pursued the enemies to Hobah, winning a surprise attack at night (14–15).

C. Abram brought back all the goods and all the people—including Lot (16).

III. The untarnished blessing: When Abram was blessed by the king of Salem and then offered riches by the king of Sodom, he swore that he would take nothing from the king of Sodom, lest the blessing be tarnished (17–24).

A. Abram met two kings after his military victory, one offering him the blessing of the Most High God, and the other offering him a deal (17–21).

1. The king of Sodom came out to meet Abram after the battle (17).

2. The king of Salem came out to meet Abram after the battle and brought him bread and wine (18).

3. The king of Salem blessed Abram and God and then received a tithe (19–20).

4. The king of Sodom offered Abram wealth in exchange for the people (21).

B. Abram swore before the Most High Lord God, who blessed him with victory, that he would take nothing that belonged to the king of Sodom, lest Sodom take the credit (22–24).

1. Oath: He swore to take nothing that belonged to Sodom (22).

2. Motive: He wished to avoid allowing Sodom to take the credit for the blessing, although his allies could take what they wished (23–24).

Development of the Exposition

Since this passage is about Abram's victory over the invading armies, we may summarize the point theologically: God gave Abram victory over military enemies who plundered the Promised Land. It could be reworded with Abram as the subject: Abram, under the blessing of God, defeated military enemies who plundered the Promised Land. To make this idea more generally applicable, we could substitute corresponding ideas in the wording: God gives Israel, his chosen race, victory (in accord with the promises to Abram) over enemies who plunder the Promised Land. The Israelites could see that Abram represented the nation and that God, who chose Abram and gave him the blessing of the land and the nation, was the real subject of the victory. This message would have encouraged God's people in times of battle in the period of the judges and the monarchy, when foreigners invaded and plundered the land promised to Israel.

To make the message relevant to the New Testament audience involves a few more corresponding changes. Fortunately, the New Testament itself, especially Ephesians, helps us immensely by its use of military terminology. In fact, the Book of Ephesians seems to parallel the Book of Joshua in its major motifs: (1) the election of the people of God, (2) the apportioning of the promised inheritance, and (3) the conquest with the distribution of the gifts (spoils of war). An integral part of the continuing conflict is the list of the weapons of warfare (Eph. 6:10–18). But this passage, as well as others, makes it clear that in the present age the battles are primarily spiritual ("we wrestle not against flesh and blood"), the weapons are spiritual, and the promises are ultimately heavenly and eternal. In the Old Testament they were physical and spiritual—actual battles were fought as a part of the spiritual conflict between the Lord and the forces of evil. The expositor must clarify from the New Testament what the church should be fighting, why it should be fighting, and how it should be fighting. Using a military story in the exposition will force the expositor to make these distinctions.

According to Ephesians, Christ is the military conqueror who "ascends on high leading captive a host of captives"—the victory is his. The conqueror then distributes gifts to people, just as kings would distribute the spoils of war among their loyal subjects (as Abram did with those who went with him). In Ephesians, since Christ's victory was spiritual (he conquered sin, death, and the grave), his gifts were spiritual gifts for the spiritual service of his subjects. With these spiritual gifts, and armed with spiritual weapons and armor, Christians continue the fight against the forces of evil, spreading the kingdom of Christ throughout the world, championing truth, righteousness, and justice.

With this kind of warfare continuing in the church age, and with God's promised blessing of victory, the military passages in the Old Testament provide an effective metaphor for New Testament teaching. If we concentrate first on 14:1–16, we might word the basic idea as follows: *God gives his chosen people victory over the world in accordance with his promises to bless and to curse, using his servants who know his high calling and will engage the enemy with courage.* This statement is worded so that it fits the context of Genesis, the experiences of Israel, and the New Testament application. We must be very careful in wording the expository idea, for to state it in terms of spiritual warfare alone would be to eliminate the very passage being explained. Genesis 14 does not teach us about spiritual warfare in a Christian context. But the theological idea of Genesis 14 corresponds to the New Testament teaching on that subject in a number of ways. The expositor must explain the meaning of Genesis 14, articulate the theology behind it, and then show how that theological idea manifests itself in the New Testament.

It may be easier in the exposition of the chapter to divide the material into two sections, verses 1–16 and verses 17–24.

I. The people of God may be confident of victory over those who threaten God's program of blessing (1–16).

This section of the exposition will be concerned with showing how Abram instinctively came to the rescue of Lot and chased the invaders out of the land. The account presents him as the saving hero for the land and its inhabitants.

A. Believers will face conflict in their pursuit of the blessing (1–12).

This part of the exposition could survey the account of the battle and its parallels in Israel's experience, showing that such invasions and skirmishes and subjugations were frequent activities for Mesopotamian kings. The expositor will have to explain the situation: the kings of Jordan served Chedorlaomer for twelve years (meaning that they sent him tribute—produce and money), but they rebelled in the thirteenth year (meaning that they did not send anything that year), and in the fourteenth year he came to subjugate them. It was not uncommon for such campaigns to be held annually for the purpose of controlling vassal city-states.

The text mentions pits of bitumin in verse 10 (note the repeated word to stress that the region was full of pits: $w^{e^c}\bar{e}meq\ ha\acute{s}\acute{s}idd\hat{i}m\ be\ \breve{e}r\bar{o}t\ be\ \breve{e}r\bar{o}t\ \hbar\bar{e}m\bar{a}r$). This product was mentioned earlier in the book in the construction of the tower at Babel (11:3). Bitumin was perhaps one of the things that the eastern kings sought for their building projects.

In the campaign Lot was taken captive along with the people and the food of the cities of the plain. The circumstantial clause in verse 12 points out the reason very clearly—"now he was dwelling in Sodom." Apparently Lot had moved rather soon from tenting next to Sodom ('*ad* s^edōm) to dwelling in it (bisdōm). The point the text is making is that, if he had not been dwelling there, he might not have been captured, and Abram might not have been drawn into the war.

B. Believers must use what God has given them to champion the cause of righteousness (13–16).

The story of Abram's victory is one of implementing all the resources available and planning an attack with shrewdness. The section begins with the news reaching Abram, but the important point in verse 13 is made with circumstantial clauses again: "He was dwelling [šōkēn here, not as permanent as Lot's yōšēb] in the oaks of Mamre, the Amorite, brother of Eshcol, and brother of Aner; and these possessed a covenant with Abram." Apparently, to settle even temporarily in this region Abram had to make a treaty with these Amorites. In this case it worked to Abram's advantage; because he had to go to battle, they would be bound to go with him. (In the same way, it appears that Chedorlaomer was not the overlord of the invading armies, for the war took place "in the days of Amraphel," who appears more important; under a feudal system the covenanters were obligated to join in the battle.) The significance of introducing these allies of Abram is that he would probably have had far more than his 318 men to lead. Any suggestion that 318 men could not rout an army thus misses the point.

A sizable force of fighters from the four tribal chiefs' ranks and a surprise night attack from different sides were more than sufficient to terrorize the invaders and drive them far beyond Damascus. Here, then, is a man of faith and courage, using the help that God had given to him and using wisdom in the confrontation, enjoying the victory over the forces that threatened this land and its peaceful anticipation of the divine promise.

II. The victorious people of God may be assured of discernment to distinguish God's blessing from worldly treasure (17–24).

After the great victory, when the conqueror might be most vulnerable to entangling arrangements, Abram met another challenge to the promises and came away unscathed. This part of the story shows how easily the spiritual victory could be lost, but it also shows how Abram was able to avoid the loss.

A. God's blessing and the world's benefits are easily confused (17–21).

When expounding this section it will be necessary to give some description of the two kings that came out to meet Abram. The king of

Sodom is mentioned first, but there is little information about him. A glimpse at his kingdom, however, would give some indication of his life—he ruled over a city that was so wicked that God eventually destroyed it.

The other king was Melchizedek, the king of Salem (or Jerusalem, according to the ancient references). It would not be possible to be exhaustive in discussing the material on this figure, for that would involve a digression through Psalm 110 to the Book of Hebrews. Suffice it to say that in Genesis he stands as a type of Jesus Christ, uniting the offices of high priest and king in the city of ancient Salem. When the Book of Hebrews says that he was without father and mother, it may mean that, in a book given over to genealogies, this man appeared on the scene without any such notice. In the record he remains a high priest, but since he preceded Abram (and Levi), he was not a Levitical priest. When David, the first Israelite king to sit on Melchizedek's throne, declared that his great descendant would be a priest after the order of Melchizedek, it was prophetic, for the Levitical order of the priesthood would have to be done away with before a king-priest like Melchizedek could emerge.

The point of the story in Genesis concerns this priest's blessing prior to the king of Sodom's offer, an offer that was a challenge to Abram's faith in the Lord to grant the promised blessings. The encounter came at a high point, a vulnerable time; the king of Sodom offered Abram all the possessions if Abram would return the king of Sodom's people to him. Such an offer might be construed as a blessing from God, for God could bring wealth to Abram in such a way. Prior to this offer, however, there was the blessing of Melchizedek. This king of righteousness, as his title indicates, brought out refreshment for Abram and pronounced a blessing on Abram and on the one true God. The expositor must concentrate on the wording of the blessing with the specific epithets used—'ēl 'elyôn, "the Most High God," the Creator of heaven and earth. Abram had here found a true spiritual brother, one who believed in the Spirit God who created matter, the sovereign God who had given Abram the victory, the true God who had promised Abram the blessing. The words of this marvelous priest surely inspired the patriarch in his anticipation of the promise of God. Herein lies the strength for Abram's discernment of the Sodomite's offer: with a fresh reminder of the nature and promise of the Lord, the appeal from the pagan was shown to be nothing more than a confusing digression from the true faith.

B. God's blessing is untarnished by the world (22–24).

Abram clearly and solidly refused the offer of the king of Sodom. He did not want Sodom to take the advantage to say that he was the one who made Abram rich, especially knowing what he did about the people of Sodom. Abram wanted something far more enduring than the spoils of war—he wanted the fulfillment of God's promise that would be miraculous and enduring. Melchizedek's renewal of the word of blessing must have excited Abram's faith, so that he could resist this easy opportunity for "blessing." The priest's words reminded Abram that he would rise in prosperity and indicated by whom he would rise. Abram thus resolved to receive all from God and not a thread from Sodom. The people of God frame their life so that, for all success, joy, comfort, and prosperity, they depend on God—but it must be a faith like Abram's that will be able to discern what is from God and what is from the world.

The exposition will have to include a word about divine blessing. God does want to bless his people today as he did back then, not just with heaven but with good gifts as well. How, then, may believers discern when a blessing is from God and when it is not? This type of discernment is never easy, but I think that the principle in this passage is that Abram knew the wicked nature of the people of Sodom and the man over them, and he discerned that his motive might be dangerous to the reputation of God's program in the future. He wanted this man to have no occasion to claim the responsibility for the blessing. A discernment of the nature and motive of those who give or offer to give is basic.

But Abram was not so much interested in material possessions; he was interested in the specific fulfillment of the promise—the seed in the land. And that could come only through the miraculous intervention of the Lord. A test for evaluating the source of blessings would then follow: if we call something in our lives a blessing, a provision from the Lord, can it be explained in no other way than from God—miraculous, spiritual, enduring? Abram was simply not willing to say that the best that Sodom had to offer was the blessing of God!

The expositor must develop the idea of victory in battle as the foundation of the subtle offer from the king of Sodom. The point for Abram in his battle is the same for us in ours—God gives the victory to his faithful servants. There is no army, no weaponry, and no surprise night attack that can defeat spiritual wickedness, whether powerful invaders or spirit forces. The people of God must champion righteousness in the way that God has instructed them to do so, which today requires spiritual weapons. The church cannot defeat spiritual wickedness by overthrowing corrupt governments or legislating better laws and ordinances. The conflict is far greater than such efforts and calls for divine power for the victory. This passage shows that God is fully able to give his people victory over the world. They must faithfully obey his Word and contend for his cause.

In this narrative the more subtle threat came after the success in the conflict and was an offer that would confuse worldly benefits and divine blessing. In many ways, the tension that Abram faced with the king of Sodom was far more critical than the battle, for the reputation of the Lord was at stake. The people of God may win spiritual struggles, but in the limelight of their success they may give away all the glory to some pagan pretender who would be delighted to rob God of the credit for spiritual success. While believers must use all the resources God has given to them to fight their spiritual battles, they must also keep in mind the true source of their victory and their blessing so that they may discern the confusion from the world. The words of Melchizedek are thus central to the message of the whole chapter. *The realization that both victory over the world and the promised blessings come from God alone enables the believer to discern the danger of accepting worldly benefits and to wait for the untarnished blessing.*

Bibliography

Aharoni, Y. "Tamar and the Roads to Elath." *IEJ* 13 (1963): 30–42.

Albright, W. F. "The Historical Background of Genesis XIV." *JSOR* 10 (1926): 231–69.

Cornelius, Friedrich. "Genesis XIV." *ZAW* 72 (1960): 1–7.

Delcor, M. "Les attaches littéraires, l'origine et la signification de l'expression biblique 'Prendre à témoin le ciel et la terre.'" *VT* 16 (1966): 8–25.

Demarest, Bruce A. "Hebrews 7:3, a Crux Interpretum Historically Considered." *EvQ* 49 (1977): 141–62.

Emerton, J. A. "The Riddle of Genesis XIV." *VT* 21 (1971): 403–39.

————. "Some False Clues in the Study of Genesis XIV." *VT* 21 (1971): 24–47.

Fisher, L. R. "Abraham and His Priest King." *JBL* 81 (1962): 264–70.

Fitzmyer, Joseph A. "Further Light on Melchizedek from Qumran 11." *JBL* 86 (1967): 25–41.

Freedman, David Noel. "The Real Story of the Ebla Tablets: Ebla, and the Cities of the Plain." *BA* 41 (1978): 143–64.

Gammie, John. "Loci of the Melchizedek Tradition of Genesis 14:18–20." *JBL* 90 (1971): 385–96.

Gardner, W. R. W. "Genesis XIV (עד דן)." *ExT* 26 (1915–16): 523–24.

Gerleman, G. "Die Wurzel ṣlm." *ZAW* 85 (1973): 1–14.

Gevirtz, S. "Abram's 318." *IEJ* 19 (1969): 110–13.

Gray, J. "The Rephaim." *PEQ* 81 (1949): 127–39.

Grelot, Pierre. "Ariok." *VT* 25 (1975): 711–19.

Habel, Norman C. "Yahweh, Maker of Heaven and Earth: A Study in Tradition Criticism." *JBL* 91 (1972): 321–37.

Harland, J. Penrose. "Sodom and Gomorrah." In *The Biblical Archaeologist Reader*, vol. 1, edited by G. Ernest Wright and David Noel Freedman, pp. 41–75. Garden City, N. Y.: Doubleday, 1961.

Higgins, A. J. B. "Priest and Messiah." *VT* 3 (1953): 321–36.

Janitz, Kurt. "Wer ist Amraphel in Genesis 14?" *ZAW* 70 (1958): 255–56.

Kamhi, D. J. "The Root *ḥlq* in the Bible." *VT* 23 (1973): 235–39.

Levi Della Vida, K. "El ʿ*Elyon* in Genesis *XIV 18–20*." *JBL* 63 (1944): 1–9.

McCullough, John C. "Melchizedek's Varied Role in Early Exegetical Tradition." *Theological Review* (1978): 52–66.

Noth, M. "Arioch—Ariwuk." *VT* 1 (1951): 136–40.

Reif, S. C. "Dedicated to חנך." *VT* 22 (1972): 495–501.

Simons, J. "Topographical Elements in the Story of Abimelech." *OTS* 2 (1943): 35–78.

Towner, W. S. " 'Blessed Be YHWH' and 'Blessed Art Thou YHWH': The Modulation of a Biblical Formula." *CBQ* 30 (1968): 386–99.

Willesen, F. "The *Yālīd* in Hebrew Society." *StTh* 12 (1958): 192–210.

23

The Trustworthiness of the Lord's Promises
(Gen. 15)

Walter Brueggemann clearly summarizes the point of Genesis 15 by writing:

> The text of Gen. 15, taken as a unit, asks whether Abraham can, in fact, *trust*. And it asks if Yahweh can, in fact, *be trusted*. It is faith which permits Abraham to trust and God to be trusted. It is unsure faith that wonders about the delay. The issues are set here. The remainder of the Abrahamic narrative explores the answers. [*Genesis*, p. 150]

The entire chapter is given over to the Lord's confirmation of the promises to Abram, first by his specific Word, and then by a solemn ceremony of the covenant in which the Lord guaranteed the fulfillment of the promises. In the first place, the specific word from the Lord was necessary because of the complaint of the patriarch—he continued childless. But then the solemn ceremony of the covenant was necessary because of the oppression that lay ahead for the seed of Abraham. The expositor must see the promise in light of the doubts and the dangers and, conversely, must see the doubts and the dangers in light of the promise.

Theological Ideas

Central to the entire chapter is the report of Abram's belief in the Lord and the Lord's crediting him with righteousness (v. 6). This statement is the chapter's explanation of Abram's obedience and the solution for Abram's tensions. Abram received the specific word from God as well as the solemn guarantee that his seed would inherit the land; but the fulfillment of those promises seemed to lag far behind—he had no son, and then he learned that there would be a longer delay when his descendants would be oppressed for four hundred years in a foreign land. It would take faith to wait for the promises; but faith was what God was looking for, and faith made Abraham acceptable to God.

The central theological idea thus concerns Abram's faith in the Lord. A word study of "believed" ($he'\check{e}m\bar{\imath}n < {}'\bar{a}man$) is essential to the exegesis of this chapter, especially since the New Testament makes use of the verse in the discussion of saving faith. But the exegesis must also give proper attention to "righteousness" ($\dot{s}^ed\bar{a}q\hat{a} < \dot{s}\bar{a}daq$) to determine precisely what God credited to Abram.

In addition to this important theological study, the expositor will have to spend time with the idea of the covenant, that is, its nature, how it was ratified, and what it signified. Up till now the text has recorded and reiterated the divine promises to Abram; from this point on, those promises may be looked upon as covenant promises, for God now establishes the covenant and guarantees the fulfillment by this solemn swearing.

But more is involved in this chapter than the straightforward ratifying of the covenant. There is the prophetic announcement of opposition to the covenant, first through the symbolism of birds of prey, and then through the prediction of the oppression. On the one hand, we must learn of the sovereign nature of God, who controls the destiny of people in enslavement and deliverance, in judgment for sin, and in reward for faith. On the other hand, we must consider the purpose of God in charting a course of enslavement and persecution for his chosen people.

Structure and Synthesis

Structure

The chapter contains two parallel sections of the Lord's promises to Abram, verses 1–6 and 7–21. The essential substance of the chapter is dialogue between Abram and the Lord, and so Coats classifies the genre as promise dialogue. Most critical scholarship sees the chapter as a collection of Abrahamic promises from different periods of time. Although there is some debate, it is generally accepted that verses 7–21 form the earlier tradition because of its primitive cultic acts and that the famous sixth verse surely must come from a later period because of its advanced theology. Verse 6 is a theological explanation added to the traditions, but there is no compelling reason to deny that Moses might have written it. The present form of the chapter is unified on the theme of the Abrahamic promises, even though its parts may have come from different traditions and may not be chronological. Excessive divisions within the chapter are simply unwarranted.

The structure of the chapter may be charted as follows:

1. First dialogue: direct word of confirmation from the Lord (1–5).
   a. The Lord's speech: self-revelation and promise of reward (1).
   b. Abram's speech: request and complaint (2–3).
   c. The Lord's speech: specific promise of a son, instruction, and promise of innumerable descendants (4–5).
2. Conclusion and transition: report of Abram's faith and righteousness (6).
3. Second dialogue: divine guarantee of the promise (7–21).
   a. The Lord's speech: self-revelation and promise of land (7).
   b. Abram's speech: request for assurance of the promise (8).
   c. The Lord's speech: instruction (9–11).
      (1) Instruction for Abram (9).
      (2) Obedience of Abram (10–11).
   d. The Lord's speech: assurance of the promises (12–21).
      (1) Cycle one: circumstances (12) and promise (13–16).
      (2) Cycle two: circumstances (17) and promise (18–21).

The structure of this chapter does isolate it from the Abrahamic narratives in the sense that this chapter does not develop a plot in stages as the other narratives do. The chapter takes as its significance the covenantal guarantee of the promises to believing Abram. Up to this point the narratives have been predominantly interested in the land and tensions relating to that promise—famine, strife, and invasion. With this chapter the focus turns to the seed in the land, and so the subsequent narratives will be concerned more and more with that fulfillment. Chapter 15 forms a transition between the cycles of narratives and gives unity to all the Abraham stories.

Summary Message

In response to Abram's request for confirmation of his faith, the Lord specifically promised to give him innumerable descendants; and in response to Abram's request for assurance of the promise, the Lord solemnly and symbolically ratified the covenant in the midst of thick

darkness that signified the enslavement that would precede the fulfillment.

Exegetical Outline

I. In response to Abram's request and complaint, the Lord specifically promised that one from his loins would receive his inheritance and begin an innumerable seed (1–5).
   A. Oracle: The Lord declared his protection and provision for
   Abram (1).
   B. Lament: Abram expressed his concern that the promise had
   not been fulfilled and that his servant was about to inherit
   his estate (2–3).
   c. Assurance: The Lord declared that Abram's own son would
   be his heir and that his descendants would be innumerable
   (4–5).
II. Abram's faith in the Lord made him acceptable to God (6).
III. In response to Abram's request for evidence, the Lord ratified a
covenant guaranteeing the fulfillment of the promises, even
though there would be a period of enslavement before the fulfillment (7–21).
   A. In response to Abram's request, the Lord instructed Abram
   to prepare the animals for the ratifying of the covenant (7–11).
      1. The Lord identified himself and reiterated the promise (7).
      2. Abram requested some evidence to assure him of the ful-
      fillment of the promise (8).
      3. The Lord instructed Abram to prepare the animals for the
      ceremony (9–11).
   B. In the midst of Abram's horrifying thick darkness, the Lord
   revealed that, before his descendants inherited the land, they
   would be enslaved four hundred years but that Abram himself would die in peace (12–16).
      1. The Lord prepared Abram for the revelation of the
      oppression (12).
      2. The Lord disclosed that the seed of Abram would be en-
      slaved and oppressed for four hundred years before re-
      ceiving the promises (13–14).
      3. The Lord assured Abram that he would die in peace (15).
      4. The Lord explained that he would return the seed to the
      land to execute justice on the sinful Amorites (16).
   C. In the darkness the Lord symbolically ratified the covenant
   promises with the firepot and the blazing torch, assuring
   Abram of the ultimate fulfillment of the promise (17–21).

1. The Lord guaranteed the certainty of the promises by unilaterally ratifying the covenant (17).
2. The Lord clarified the promise by naming the boundaries of the land and the dispossessed people (18–21).

Development of the Exposition

The expositor could divide the chapter into two parts, Abram's trust in the word from God, and God's guarantee of the trustworthiness of his Word. In that arrangement, verse 6 would become a subpoint under the first section. The difficulty here would be in preserving the distinct point of verse 6 in the chapter. It might be better to make a separate point out of that verse.

I. God promises his people that the blessing will be supernatural and enduring (1–5).

A. God promises protection and provision (1).

The first verse is parallel to the seventh verse in that both have the self-revelation of the Lord and the promise. In verse 1, the Lord used the metaphor of the shield (*māgēn*) to promise protection, and a general word "reward" (*śākār*) for the promise of provision (note the precise emphasis of the Hebrew: "your reward shall be great," rather than "I am your reward").

This section has been linked to the preceding narrative by the introductory formula "after these things." This connection is strengthened by the use of *māgēn* ("shield"), which is cognate to the verb *miggēn* in the Melchizedekian blessing (14:20). We may conclude that the Lord's instruction for Abram not to fear may have arisen from second thoughts Abram had in the aftermath of the preceding battle.

B. Believers are often impatient for the promises (2–3).

The speech of Abram, which also parallels his speech in verse 8, is similar to a lament—he asked what God would give him, since he was childless. It is clear that Abram interpreted God's reward (*śākār*) as a child (cf. Ps. 127:3, which states that children are a heritage from the Lord, and the fruit of the womb his *śākār*).

The absence of a child complicated the matter of the inheritance. Under the prevailing customs, if Abram died childless his household servant would become his heir. This concern is expressed by means of a forceful word play on his household servant's origin: Eliezer of Damascus (*dammeśeq*) is the heir (*ben-meśeq*). Abram evidently was trying to stress to God that the *omen* was in the *nomen*, as if he saw the writing on the wall, that this man was about to inherit him. (For a discussion of this passage, see M. F. Unger, *Israel and the Arameans of Damascus* [London: James Clark, 1957], pp. 3–4.)

C. God gives his Word that his promise will be fulfilled (4–5).

The wording of the Hebrew text in the Lord's reply strongly overrules Abram's fear. The report is introduced by the formula "the Word of the LORD came to him saying," and then the point is emphasized by the Lord's making no reference to the servant's name (*"This one* shall not be your heir"). And then, to signify how great the fulfillment of the promise would be, the Lord took him outside to gaze at the heavens, for his seed would be as innumerable as the stars of the heavens. This comparison now joins the one in 13:16 ("the dust of the earth") to convey the abundance of the promise and also to call for greater faith from the one who is childless. God's answer to the troubled patriarch has all the force of an oracle of salvation.

II. God credits faith in his promises with righteousness (6).

On the surface it may appear that this report of Abram's faith was a result of the preceding assurance from God—several English translations begin "and Abram believed in the LORD." The NIV leaves the conjunction "and" untranslated to avoid the implication that verse 6 resulted from or followed verse 5 chronologically. A close study of the Hebrew construction "and he believed" reveals that the writer did not intend this verb to be understood as a result of the preceding section. The construction is not the normal sequential construction ($w^e he$'$ěm\bar{i}n$ is a perfect tense with the $w\bar{a}w$ prefixed; the $w\bar{a}w$ thus cannot be a $w\bar{a}w$ consecutive, otherwise the translation would have to be future); if the writer had wished to show that this verse followed in sequence the preceding, he would have used the normal structure for narrative sequence ($wayya$'$\bar{a}m\hat{i}n$, "and [then] he believed"). We must conclude that the narrator did not want to show sequence in the order of the verses; rather, he wished to make a break with the narrative in order to supply this information about the faith of Abram. (Of course, this whole discussion presupposes that the chapter was intended as a unified composition in its final form.)

There are several ways to explain the significance of this construction in the chapter—apart from the idea that Abram's meritorious faith resulted from the word of assurance in the preceding verses. The verse may be a summary statement of Abram's faith, or a transitional note between sections. It could be translated parenthetically, as disjunctive clauses often are ("Now Abram believed . . ."). The verb could be explained as having a characteristic nuance ("now Abram believed," in the sense that he was a believer). In other words, the text does not necessarily mean that Abram came to faith here. Hebrews 11:8 asserts that he left Ur by faith. Genesis 15:6 simply reports at this point the fact that Abram believed, and for that belief God had credited him with righteousness. The verse is placed here as a conclusion to the dialogue in which Abram questioned God about the promise, and prior to the enacting of the covenant. Abram's status as a believer to whom God imputed righteousness is reported here—now God will bind himself by covenant to Abram the believer.

The two important words to be studied in this verse are "believed" (he'ĕmîn < 'āman) and "righteousness" (ṣᵉdāqâ). Both are rich theological terms. The first is related to words conveying reliability, steadfastness, and dependability. The verb "believe" may have the idea of considering something dependable (a declarative use of the hiphil) and acting on it. The second word has the meaning of conformity to the standard, to what is right in God's eyes. Righteousness is the correct action and attitude before God; it forms the (imputed) description of the members of the covenant as well as their covenantal responsibility. Abram accepted the Word of the Lord as reliable and true and acted in accordance with it; consequently, the Lord declared Abram righteous, and therefore acceptable.

III. God guarantees his promises by his covenant, in spite of the prospects of death and suffering (7–21).

A. The Lord desires to reassure his people when they are in doubt about his promises (7–11).

Not only does this section parallel the beginning of the chapter, it parallels the Sinaitic covenant as well: "I am the LORD who brought you out [hôṣē'tîkā] from Ur of the Chaldees" forms the parallel beginning to Exodus 20:2. The Lord revealed himself to be the great Deliverer and Benefactor of the people of the covenant in both passages, but here the specific promise mentioned is the land.

The mention of the land raised doubts in Abram's mind. He wanted assurance: "Whereby shall I know ['ēda'] that I shall inherit it?" This question prompted the enacting of the covenant for the guarantee of the Word of the Lord. The following verses describe how meticulously the Lord prepared to assure Abram and how Abram participated in the preparation. A study of covenants and the symbolic acts that accompany them would be helpful here.

B. The fulfillment of the promises will be preceded by suffering and death (12–16).

This section makes two points clear: the fulfillment of the promises is sure, but there will first be a long period of enslavement and opposition. This revelation is presented both symbolically and verbally. The horror of darkness that came upon Abram may have been prompted by the coming deity or by the thought of the birds of prey coming down on the animals for the offering (an ominous thought, since the birds were unclean and were attacking the sacrifice for God.) The announcement of the enslavement, however, clarified the meaning of the symbols. The family would be enslaved and oppressed by a foreign nation for four hundred years. The word "oppressed" (ʿinnû < ʿinnâ) is the same word used in Exodus 1:11 to describe the oppression of Egypt. Between the symbol and the prediction Abram would know that, before the fulfillment, there would be suffering (cf. God's "know of a surety [yādōaʿ tēdaʿ]" with Abram's "whereby shall I know" in v. 8).

The prophecy of the four-hundred-year time period is significant. Of course, Israel at the time of Moses could note the years and see that the time of deliverance was at hand. More important, though, this period of time was tied in part to the divine longsuffering for the Amorites, whose sin was not yet full (v. 16). God was holy and just, wishing the sin of the Amorites to be full before he would judge them—and the fulfillment of the promises to Abram required retributive judgment on Egypt and the inhabitants of the land of Canaan. Abram's seed would surely get the land—but "not one hour before absolute justice requires it" (Dods, *Book of Genesis*, p. 143). Four hundred years! God had much to do before all things worked together in the promise, including the discipline to make the nation fit for the promises. But for Abram to see all this history in advance was horrible. It was, however, helpful to see it. Abram and his descendants would know that such oppression and enslavement was not a threat to the fulfillment of the promises—it was part of the divine plan.

Abram, however, would die in peace, that is, in peace of mind, untroubled (note the word play between šālôm, in v. 15, and šālēm, "full," in v. 16), at a ripe old age. He would not experience the oppression that was laid out before him. And his personal anxiety would be set at ease, for in the ancient world it was left to the son to ensure a restful interment and burial. God's promise of a son and prediction of a peaceful death no doubt set Abram's mind at ease.

C. The Lord swears by himself that his promises will be realized (17–21).

The Lord revealed himself with the image of the oven and the torch, two elements that seemed to have been connected with sacrificial ritual in the ancient world. Speiser says,

> The smoking fire pot (literally "oven") and flaming torch (to keep the fire going in the brazier) were not just fanciful inventions by the author or his immediate source. Both these details are recorded in Akk.[adian] texts pertaining to magic. They are listed together in an incantation against witches: "I sent out against you repeatedly a 'going' (i.e., lighted) oven (*āliku tinūru*), a fire that has caught." . . . The combination is almost exactly the same as in the present instance. It was evidently believed to be highly efficacious, which may explain the archaic use of "oven" in the sense of "brazier," since no detail of an occult practice, or of the wording that goes with it, must be disturbed; actual ovens would not have the required mobility. Very likely, therefore, Heb. *tannūr* in this particular context was due to similar considerations, if not directly to the use of *tinūru* in Akkadian. And a combination that worked so well against witches would be no less impressive as an ominous feature in a covenant. [*Genesis*, pp. 113–14]

These images are part of the fire, or burning, motif to describe the related ideas of God's zeal and his unapproachable holiness. With the darkness present, nothing else was seen in the vision except these fiery elements passing between the animals. Skinner says that "Yahwe[h] alone passes (symbolically) between the pieces, because He alone contracts obligation" (*Commentary on Genesis*, p. 283). In forming such a covenant, the one who passed through was binding himself by the symbolism, under punishment of death, to fulfill the oath or promise. The holy God would thus be zealous to fulfill his promises, notably concerning the land. He had come down to make this formal covenant, and since he could swear by none greater, he swore by himself. The promises were forever sure.

According to this chapter, Abram, troubled by the apparent failure of God to provide him with a child, requested that God would guarantee the promise to him. God did so through his own covenant. However, a period of enslavement and suffering would precede fulfillment of the promises.

For Abram the message was clear: In spite of having no proof of the fulfillment, and in spite of the prospects of death and suffering, his descendants would receive the promises—God assured it. Israel could be encouraged by this guarantee at the exodus as well as at subsequent times of distress and captivity: *By his solemn covenant the Lord guar-*

antees his people that his promises will be fulfilled, in spite of the prospects of their death and suffering. Essential to this statement is the understanding of "his people." That designation is reserved in the Bible for those who believe in the Lord and his Word and for those to whom the Lord imparts righteousness. For this reason, verse 6 is so essential.

The principles in this chapter are essentially the same for any age. Today people become the people of God by faith as well, and their faith brings righteousness before God (Rom. 4:3; Gal. 3:6). To New Testament believers God has also made great promises (Heb. 9:15 et al.), but those promises seem to be greatly delayed in the face of suffering and death (2 Peter 3:9). By his covenant which he made by his own blood, however, our Lord has guaranteed that his Word is sure and that neither death nor oppression can destroy his promises (Heb. 7:20–25; Rom. 8:31–39).

Bibliography

Anbar, Moshe. "Genesis 15: A Conflation of Two Deuteronomic Narratives." *JBL* 101 (1982): 39–55.

Cazelles, H. "Connexions et structure de Gen xv." *RB* 69 (1962): 321–429.

Dion, H. M. "The Patriarchal Traditions and the Literary Form of the 'Oracle of Salvation.' " *CBQ* 29 (1967): 198–206.

Dion, Paul Eugene. "The 'Fear Not' Formula and Holy War." *CBQ* 32 (1970): 565–70.

Durham, J. I. "שָׁלוֹם and the Presence of God." In *Proclamation and Presence: Old Testament Essays in Honour of Gwynne Henton Davies,* edited by John I. Durham and J. R. Porter, pp. 272–93. London: SCM, 1970.

Ginsberg, H. L. "Abram's 'Damascene' Steward." *BASOR* 200 (1970): 31–32.

Gordon, Cyrus H. "Biblical Customs and the Nuzu Tablets." In *Biblical Archaeologist Reader,* vol. 2, edited by David Noel Freedman and Edward F. Campbell, Jr., pp. 21–33. Garden City, N.Y.: Doubleday, 1964.

Gordon, Robert P. "Preaching from the Patriarchs: Background to the Exposition of Genesis 15." *Themelios* 11 (1975): 19–23.

Hasel, Gerhard F. "The Meaning of the Animal Rite in Genesis 15." *JSOT* 19 (1981): 61–78.

Ishida, Tomoo. "The Structure and Historical Implications of the Lists of Pre-Israelite Nations." *Bib* 60 (1979): 461–90.

Kessler, Martin. "The 'Shield' of Abraham." *VT* 14 (1964): 494–97.

Kline, Meredith G. "Abram's Amen." *WTJ* 31 (1968): 1–11.

McCarthy, D. J. "*Berît* and Covenant in the Deuteronomistic History." *VTS* 23 (1972): 65–85.

————. "*Berît* in Old Testament History and Theology." *Bib* 53 (1972): 110–21.

————. "The Symbolism of Blood Sacrifice." *JBL* 88 (1969): 166–76; 92 (1973): 205–10.

————. "Three Covenants in Genesis." *CBQ* 26 (1964): 179–89.

Millard, A. R. "For He Is Good." *TynB* 17 (1966): 115–17.

Muilenburg, J. "The Form and Structure of the Covenantal Formulations." *VT* 9 (1959): 347–69.

Petersen, David L. "Covenant Ritual: A Traditio-Historical Perspective." *BibRes* 22 (1977): 7–18.

Robertson, O. Palmer. "Genesis 15:6: A New Covenant Exposition of an Old Covenant Text." *WTJ* 42 (1980): 259–89.

Snijders, L. A. "Genesis xv: The Covenant with Abram." *OTS* 12 (1958): 261–79.

Tawil, H. "Hebrew צלח/הצלח, Akkadian *ešēru/šūšuru*: A Lexical Note." *JBL* 95 (1976): 405–13.

Unger, Merrill F. "Some Comments on the Text of Genesis 15:2–3." *JBL* 72 (1953): 49–50.

Weinfeld, M. "The Period of the Conquest and of the Judges as Seen by the Earlier and Later Sources." *VT* 17 (1967): 93–113.

Weingreen, J. "הוצאתיך in Genesis 15:7." In *Words and Meanings: Essays Presented to David Winton Thomas,* edited by Peter R. Ackroyd and Barnabas Lindars, pp. 209–15. Cambridge: Cambridge University Press, 1968.

24

Ishmael: The Rebuke of Weak Faith
(Gen. 16)

The narrative in Genesis 16 is the first in a series of stories that portray the tension over the delay of the promise. God had told Abram that his own son would be his heir (15:4)—which had not happened yet. In the first verse of this narrative, this issue is restated— "Sarai, the wife of Abram, was barren" (cf. 11:30). The exposition must capture the intensity of the difficulty: with very little information and with very little time left, Abram and Sarai longed for the fulfillment of the promise.

Several commentators see this story as part of an older collection of Sarah-Hagar stories constituting a novella. Coats suggests that the plot was the struggle between wife and maid, a tension that begins in chapter 16, abates in chapter 18 with the announcement of the birth, and rises again in chapter 21 with the final resolution in the expulsion of the maid and her son. In the closing of the story the exiles were rescued by an angel (*Genesis*, p. 127). Westermann suggests that Genesis 29 and 30, the sequence of the conflicts between Rachel and Leah with their maids, could be part of a sequence of several conflict scenes (*Genesis*, vol. 2, p. 237). Of course, there is no way of knowing how the old family traditions were first collected (as opposed to our knowledge of earlier collections of portions of the Psalms), and such suggestions carry no support other than that the stories have similar motifs. The benefit to be derived from such observations is the awareness of a recurring motif in the present form of the collection of Abrahamic stories. In Genesis 16, the first such conflict occurs, and while Hagar is certainly at the center of the story, the subtle point in the context of the Abrahamic narratives concerns the promise to the fathers: human assistance to the fulfillment of the divine promises only complicated the matter.

Theological Ideas

The clear revelation about God that provides the lesson for the narrative is found in the speeches of the angel of the Lord and is summarized in the names at the end of the record. By the names—one given by the angel to Hagar, one given by Hagar to the angel, and one given to the well—the passage offers to resolve the distress of the handmaid and to rebuke the impatience of the man and his wife: Ishmael (God hears—the needs and afflictions of his people), and El Roi and Beer Lahai Roi (God sees—that is, provides for their needs).

There is also the theological idea of the divine encounter in the wilderness. The angel of the Lord met the distressed woman in the wilderness and rescued her at the well of water and promised her a future with blessing. This theme anticipates the story of Israel's leaving Egypt and wandering in the wilderness, for many of these motifs appear throughout those narratives (Egypt, slaves, oppression, fleeing to the wilderness, the angel of the Lord, and water).

Structure and Synthesis

Structure

The passage is generally divided into two parts, verses 1–6 and 7–16, although verses 15 and 16 serve as a summary to the entire account, uniting the two main sections. These two sections fit together as a unit because the tension of the first part is not resolved—Sarai still did not have an heir, and her plan turned on her.

The structure of the first six verses develops in two parallel movements. The first movement (vv. 1–4a) opens with the tension that Sarai was barren, records Sarai's speech in which she blamed the Lord for her barrenness and instructed Abram to take her maid, reports Abram's obedience, and concludes with the narration of Sarai and Hagar: Sarai took her and gave her to Abram, and Hagar conceived. The second movement (vv. 4b–6) opens with the new tension that Sarai was despised by Hagar, records Sarai's speech in which she blamed Abram and called for a decision, reports Abram's relinquishing the maid to Sarai's pleasure, and concludes with the narration about Sarai and Hagar: Sarai dealt harshly, and Hagar fled. The narrative thus traces two tensions, the one growing out of the other, but resolves neither. Sarai still was barren, and Hagar simply fled. In both movements Abram is remarkably passive (cf. Jacob at the hands of Rachel and Leah).

The second part of the narrative (vv. 7–14) is the account of Hagar in the wilderness. Dialogue is also the essential element for the interpretation of this section, but the dialogue in this section informs the interpretation of the first section. The seventh verse provides the new beginning—the angel of the Lord found Hagar by a well in the wilderness. There follows, then, a series of speeches: the angel interrogated Hagar, and she explained her plight; the angel then instructed her to return, promised her many descendants, announced that she would have a son, gave him the meaningful name Ishmael, and predicted his destiny, to which Hagar responded by naming the well Beer Lahai Roi. It is clear that the names provide the key to the interpretation, and the speeches give the significance for the names within the narrative.

The last two verses record the conclusion of this narrative, with the birth report and naming of Ishmael (vv. 15–16).

Summary Message

When Sarai and Abram generated tremendous complications by their attempt to obtain an heir through the social customs of the day—complications that caused Hagar to flee to the wilderness—the Lord showed himself faithful by responding to Hagar's affliction, providing for her needs, and promising her progeny through Abram's son, Ishmael.

Exegetical Outline

I. Prologue: Sarai, the wife of Abram, was barren, but she had an Egyptian handmaid named Hagar (1).

II. Human faithlessness: Sarai and Abram carried out their own plan to obtain an heir through the social customs of the day, but succeeded only in complicating matters with a conflict (2–6).
A. Sarai's plan (2–4a):
  1. Sarai, blaming the Lord for her barrenness, instructed Abram to take the maid as a wife (2a).
  2. Abram obeyed his wife and accepted Hagar from her (2b–3).
  3. Hagar conceived (4a).

B. Sarai's tension (4b–6):
    1. Sarai, blaming her husband for the tension between Hagar and herself, called for judgment (4b–5).
    2. Abram complied with his wife's wishes (6a).
    3. Hagar fled when she was treated harshly (6b).
III. Divine faithfulness: The angel of the Lord found Hagar in the wilderness, instructed her to return, and promised to bless her with Ishmael and his descendants, thus prompting Hagar to commemorate the spot where God heard her affliction and saw her needs (7–14).
    A. The angel of the Lord found Hagar in the wilderness and instructed her to return (7–9).
        1. The angel found Hagar and interrogated her about her dilemma (7–8a).
        2. Hagar explained that she was fleeing from Sarai (8b).
        3. The angel instructed her to return to her mistress (9).
    B. The angel of the Lord foretold Hagar's progeny through Ishmael (10–12).
        1. He promised many descendants from her (10).
        2. He announced the birth of her son Ishmael (11).
        3. He predicted the destiny of her son's tribe (12).
    C. Hagar responded in faith to this gracious visitation by calling on the Lord and naming the well to commemorate the deliverance (13–14).
IV. Epilogue: Hagar, the handmaid of Sarai, bore Ishmael to Abram when he was eighty-six years old (15–16).

Development of the Exposition

I. The attempt to accomplish God's plans by worldly methods inevitably produces complications (1–6).

A. The problem (1).

Sarai was barren, and so by all human calculations the heir of the promises could not come through her at all. The first verse provides the reader with this reminder of the continuing problem (cf. 11:30)—and also introduces Hagar.

In the arrangement of the narratives in Genesis, this chapter is parallel to Genesis 12. In that passage the Lord called Abram to go to the *land* of promise, but that land had a severe famine (recall that this motif is part of the curse and not the blessing). Now, with the specific promise of an *heir* of his own, Abram had a barren wife (again incompatible with blessing). Just as the famine provided a test for Abram's faith in the promise, so did this barrenness of his wife. But it set in motion the dubious activities of Abram and Sarai. It is interesting to observe that Abram's failure in Genesis 12 may have contributed to his failure in Genesis 16—he may have acquired Hagar in that trip to Egypt.

The barrenness motif is important in the stories of the patriarchs: Sarai, Rebekah, and Rachel all were barren until God opened their wombs and enabled them to bear important sons. The motif stresses the sovereignty of God in bringing into the world famous ancestors. (See also the birth of Samuel.)

B. The human solution (2–3).

Sarai's solution to the problem of not having a child incorporated social customs of the day as a means of fulfilling the promise. Legal customs made it clear that a barren wife could give her maid to her husband as a wife and that a son born of that union could be the heir if the husband ever declared him to be so. Sarai's plan, then, was unobjectionable from the custom and law of the ancient Near East. It would seem to all concerned a reasonable option for the divine plan to follow. For a discussion of the Hurrian customs, see Speiser's commentary on this passage (Genesis, pp. 120–21), as well as law number 146 in Hammurabi's code (see ANET, p. 172).

There is, however, a note of frustration in Sarai's speech, as she placed the blame on the Lord for her barrenness (cf. Adam and Eve in Gen. 3:12). Her words were true, in a measure, and set the tension between God's promise of an heir and God's prevention of such by her barrenness. The parallel with the account of the fall is made stronger with the report of Abram's compliance with his wife's plan: "and Abram obeyed Sarai [wayyišmaʿ 'abrām lᵉqôl śārāy]." Earlier, God had rebuked Adam because he had obeyed his wife (šāmaʿtā lᵉqôl 'ištekā in 3:17). A plan was thus offered and accepted, but in the telling of this arrangement, there was already a hint that the pair had overstepped a boundary, that faith should have taken them a different way.

C. The tension (4).

This impatient solution soured when Hagar became pregnant and despised her mistress. The verb translated "despised" (wattēqal) is critical to the account. It is the same verb used in the first recording of the promises to Abram—"the one who treats you lightly [< qālal] I must curse" (12:3). It is too strong to say that Hagar cursed Sarai or treated her with contempt. She may have looked on her mistress insolently. The word probably describes an unavoidable response to the situation, a response developing from the maternal pride of Hagar in her new status.

In using this strong word to describe her attitude, the narrative is underscoring how much of a problem it was now going to be to fulfill the blessing.

D. The attempted resolution (5–6).

Once again there is a speech by Sarai and a surrendering agreement from Abram. Here, however, Sarai cast the blame for the tension on Abram and demanded that something be done about it. With his permission she began to treat Hagar harshly. The verb "treat harshly" or "afflict," 'innâ, was used in 15:13 in the prediction of Israel's enslavement in Egypt. Trible says, "It characterizes, for example, the sufferings of the entire Hebrew population in Egypt, the land of their bondage. Ironically, here it depicts the torture of a lone Egyptian woman in Canaan, the land of her bondage to the Hebrews" ("Hagar," p. 13). Undoubtedly, Sarai was attempting to maintain her status by treating Hagar as a slave, trying to remind the Egyptian girl that she was Hagar's mistress.

It is important to note that, when Abram said, "Your maid is in your hand," he was returning Hagar to her status as Sarai's servant. She was not to be on a par with Sarai.

The point of this turn of events is that God was not permitting this "solution" to be the way the promise should be fulfilled. Throughout the patriarchal stories God regularly repudiated social custom for his miraculous provision. In this case, once Hagar fled to the wilderness the question surfaced again regarding what was to become of Abram's seed.

All who study this chapter see this part as the dark side of the narrative—the bright side is Hagar's rescue in the wilderness. The dark chain of Sarai and Abram's disobedience works to produce a complication, from which emerge Hagar's pride and Sarai's harsh treatment. There is little difficulty in seeing what went wrong. Once the way of faith was abandoned and the way of human calculation was engaged, the family was caught up in a continuing chain of cause and effect that troubled them for ages. Von Rad says, "How muddled the situation has become by the application of right and wrong!" (Genesis, p. 192). Once patient waiting was abandoned for human calculations, then natural impulses and right conduct became entangled. The participants had no control once this process was set in motion, for it led to conflict. Unfortunately, the history of Israel and of the church shows that those who are called of God repeatedly follow the forbidden calculation of a Sarai and experience the conflict of a Hagar. Rather, as the subsequent narratives will show, Abram and Sarai should have waited patiently on the Lord.

II. God requires patient hope and fervent prayer for the realization of his promises (7–16).

The last half of this narrative does not specifically mention prayer nor instruct a patient waiting on the Lord. A close examination of the text, however, reveals that this response is indeed the point within the revelation. Verses 7–12 record the Lord's meeting with Hagar in the wilderness and his promises to her, verses 13 and 14 record her faith response, and verses 15 and 16 conclude the narrative with the birth report.

A. The divine intervention (7–12).

It is important in studying narrative literature to concentrate on the dialogue, especially the speeches from the Lord, for they usually underscore the point of the narrative. In this passage the story itself is not the message; the Word from the Lord is the message, and the story is the setting for the Word. Interventions and revelations such as we find in this section often come at the end of the narrative, after the story has unfolded its plot or raised its tension. Into the crisis in Genesis 16 came the messenger, declaring what would be, but also interpreting by that declaration what should have been.

The exegesis of this unit will have to study the angel of the Lord. Many commentaries conclude that this was a manifestation of the Lord himself, but each expositor must study the different contexts to see if this view can be substantiated. The important point of the designation is that the speech is the Word of the Lord (mal'āk, "messenger," signifies a message was to be communicated).

At the heart of the dialogue is the divine promise of a son and the designation of his name as Ishmael (yišmā'ē'l), with the explanation "because the LORD has heard your affliction [ki-šāma' YHWH 'el-'onyēk]." Popular etymologies of names often are used to capture and retain the significance of narratives (cf. the explanation of Reuben's name, "the LORD has looked on my affliction," and of Simeon's, "the LORD has heard my cry" [29:32–33]). They are rhetorical devices that draw from the experience in the account the explanation for the name. Accordingly, the name becomes an aid for remembering the events and their significance. The name Ishmael would thus forever recall how the Lord responded to the cry of Hagar in the wilderness. That response, of course, included the promise of blessing for Ishmael, for he too would be known as a son of Abram.

The name Ishmael conveys a significant religious idea. It means "God hears" or "may God hear." The name is a common Semitic name, attested in a number of different texts, including those of Mari (Ya-aš-ma-ah-AN) and Ebla (iš-ma-il and iš-ma-Ya). The idea "God hears" was popular in the giving of names in the ancient world. No doubt it reflects the lamentation motif, for we encounter this *šāmaʿ* ("hear") very often in prayers. Such a name attests to the misery of people who stand in need of God's help, requesting God to hear and help in distress. The name Ishmael (*yišmāʿēʾl*) represents the belief that God hears (see further *PN*, p. 198; and G. Pettinato, *The Archives of Elba* [Garden City, N.Y.: Doubleday, 1981], pp. 249, 276). This common Semitic name was chosen for Hagar's child because it measured and answered the distress of the woman. The son was to bear a name that would commemorate her having a helper in God, who heard her cries in distress.

In the story the motif of "hearing" thus becomes important. The child was to be called Ishmael because the Lord heard Hagar's affliction. (The word "your affliction," *ʿonyēk*, brings to mind the harsh treatment from Sarai in 16:6 [*wattᵉʿannehā*].) The motif of hearing reappears in Genesis 17:20, when the promised child was born—Ishmael would not be forgotten by God (*šᵉmaʿtîkā*). Genesis 17:20 is not a naming account; rather, it is an oracle that confirms the promise to Ishmael by alluding to the name's motivation. A third passage employing the motif of hearing is Genesis 21:17, where "God heard" the voice of the lad in the wilderness. In the first passage God heard Hagar, in the second he heard Abraham, and in the third he heard the lad.

An important point to be made in the exposition is found in the report of the birth at the end of Genesis 16. *Abram* named the lad Ishmael. We may presume that Hagar carried the instructions from the Lord, and the report of the circumstances, back to Abram, saying essentially, "God hears." Abram and Sarai had ignored the proper source for the fulfillment of the promise—Ishmael's name would forever be a reminder. Isaac did not make that same mistake; rather, when his wife was barren, he prayed (25:21).

God also bound himself to Ishmael in promise. The blessing in verses 10 and 12 is reminiscent of (but it is not) the Abrahamic blessing. The descendants through Ishmael would be innumerable, but their destiny would be filled with tension and strife. Nevertheless, the point should not be missed: God did not exclusively commit himself to Abraham; he delivered people who stood outside that family as well. The tension remained, however, because the child who reminded them of the Lord's concern for people in distress would also be a threat to the chosen line.

B. The faithful response (13–14).

Hagar's response to the Word of the Lord is significant and demands a careful exegesis in the Hebrew text. The text is difficult, but surely

Brueggemann is wide of the mark when he says that the disclosure of the meaning of this name, Beer Lahai Roi, "was not greatly valued in the tradition and is best left in its obscurity" (*Genesis*, p. 153).

According to the text, Hagar said, "You are a God who sees me [*'attâ 'ēl rŏ'î*]." Then she said, "Have I also looked after him who sees me [*hăgam hălōm rā'îtî 'ahărê rō'î*]?" The well was therefore called Beer Lahai Roi (*bᵉ'ēr lahay rō'î*).

The name Beer Lahai Roi seems to mean "the well of the living one who sees," even though modern scholars occasionally suggest that *Lah* was the name of some old Canaanite god, and the well an ancient shrine. But the passage gives no such motivation for the name.

The name *rō'î* is a participle with a suffix, and *lahay* could be either a substantive or an adjective modifying *rō'î*. These possibilities yield either "the well of the living one who sees me" or "the well of the living sight." The RSV translates it "well of one who sees and lives." The name probably preserves a general reference to the living God and a specific reference to a divine intervention.

Many commentators attempt to alter Hagar's words prior to the name to gain the motivation for the idea of "living." For example, Dillmann suggests: "Have I seen God and remain alive after my seeing?" (*Genesis*, vol. 2, p. 74). He then translates the well's name as "He lives who sees me."

The Masoretic Text as pointed does not yield such an interpretation. Moreover, the connection between Hagar's words and the name was not intended to be exact. In her first statement, "You are a God of seeing" (*rŏ'i* is a substantive out of pause; it means "seeing"), the text could be interpreted in a subjective or objective sense. Such an ambiguity lends itself nicely to the story. He is a God who sees all things and manifests his providence accordingly; and by his manifestation he can be seen.

The use of "after" (*'ahărê*) with "see" (*rā'â*) in her next statement probably means that she did not see him directly but only realized that he had been present (cf. Exod. 33:23, *wᵉrā'îtā 'et-'ăhōrāy*). One sees only what God leaves behind. Dillmann says that it refers to Hagar's vision, not of God, but of his aftereffects (ibid.). Lindblom translates it, "Have I here really seen the back of Him who has seen me?" ("Theophanies," p. 102, n. 21). God thus left Hagar the message of hope and the perception of the well.

The key to the explanation of the well's name is the repetition of the sounds and meanings of the words related to *rā'â*, "see." The well was evidence of the divine provision for Hagar's needs (God sees), and the provision was evidence that he is the living one. Hagar could attest to this truth because she had experienced the effects of his presence.

C. The obedient compliance (15-16).

The last two verses report the birth and naming of Ishmael. That Abram named the boy testifies to the fact that Hagar related to him all that God had done for her and said to her. For Abram to give the boy the name Ishmael would have been a lesson in itself—God hears!

The culmination of the story provides the lesson for the whole unit. It records God's direct revelation and Hagar's faith response. God sees distress and affliction and hears the cry for help. Abram and Sarai should have known this. God knew that Sarai was barren. She knew that God knew she was barren. She should have cried out to the Lord as Hannah later did (1 Sam. 1:5, 10). Instead, Sarai had to learn the hard way—from the experience of the despised slave wife who came back with the faith experience and the word from God—Ishmael. Sarai did not cry out but took human calculations; Hagar thereby benefited from God's provision instead of Sarai, so that she came to know more of God's presence in distress than did Sarai. The Lord sent her back to the tense situation from which she fled, but he sent her with a message and with hope.

Thus, *in great distress* (here it was barrenness, and then affliction) *believers should pray to the Lord because he hears the afflicted, he sees them in their need, and he will miraculously fulfill his promises.* They cannot be fulfilled by human intervention. Abram and Sarai had further to go yet in their faith.

It would be effective to develop the exposition with the narrative's natural suspense. When the story is finished, the lesson is made clear—applicable to all ages and all circumstances—God sees and God hears. This message, then, was carried back by the Egyptian slave. How Sarai must have been humbled every time she heard that boy's name—Ishmael, God hears.

Of course, the lesson calls for more faith. The major tensions in the story have not been resolved by the intervention. Sarai is still barren, and the relationship between Hagar and Sarai did not improve. But the divine word pointed to a better way as they waited for the fulfillment of the promise.

The message is timeless. It may be paralleled to situations where God's people are impatient and turn in their anxieties to careless plans and calculations rather than crying out to the one who sees and hears, the only one who can help. The lesson would be clear for Sarai, Abram, and Hagar, for Israel, and for us today: trust God's Word and patiently wait for his promises. Foolishly to adopt worldly customs and expedients will only complicate matters and bring in greater tensions. Any people who owe their existence to divine creation and election must live by faith. The good news from Hagar is that, no matter what the affliction is or how it came about, God sees and God hears.

Bibliography

Blenkinsopp, J. "Structure and Style in Judges 13–16." *JBL* 82 (1963): 65–76.

Booij, T. "Hagar's Words in Genesis 16:13b." *VT* 30 (1980): 1–7.

Dahood, M. "The Name *Yišmāʿeʾl* in Genesis 16, 11." *Bib* 49 (1968): 87–88.

Dozeman, Thomas B. "*Sperma Abraam* in John 8 and Related Literature: Cosmology and Judgment." *CBQ* 42 (1980): 342–58.

Ephʿal, I. " 'Ishmael' and 'Arab(s)': A Transformation of Ethnological Terms." *JNES* 35 (1976): 225–35.

Fensham, F. Charles. "The Son of a Handmaid in Northwest-Semitic." *VT* 19 (1969): 312–21.

Grayson, A. K. "The Childless Wife in Assyria and the Stories of Genesis." *Or* 44 (1975): 485–86.

Lindblom, J. "Theophanies in Holy Places in Hebrew Religion." *HUCA* 32 (1961): 91–106.

McEvenue, Sean E. "A Comparison of Narrative Styles in the Hagar Stories." *Semeia* 3 (1975): 64–80.

Neff, R. W. "The Annunciation in the Birth Narrative of Ishmael." *BibRes* 17 (1972): 51–60.

————. "The Birth and Election of Isaac in the Priestly Tradition." *BibRes* 15 (1970): 5–18.

Trible, Phyllis. "Hagar: The Desolation of Rejection." In *Texts of Terror: Literary-Feminist Readings of Biblical Narratives,* pp. 9–35. Philadelphia: Fortress, 1984.

Van Seters, J. "The Problem of Childlessness in Near Eastern Law and the Patriarchs of Israel." *JBL* 87 (1968): 401–8.

Vriezen, T. C. (Dedicata) *Studia et Semitica.* Wageningen: H. Veenman, 1966.

White, H. C. "The Initiation Legend of Isaac." *ZAW* 91 (1979): 1–30.

————. "The Initiation Legend of Ishmael." *ZAW* 87 (1975): 267–305.

Wilson, Clifford A. "The Problem of Childlessness in Near Eastern Law." *Buried History* 5 (1969): 106–14.

25

The Pledge of the Promise and the Sign of the Covenant
(Gen. 17)

Thirteen years passed since Abram heard from the Lord. He settled down with his family and with Ishmael his son. But the seed that God had promised to him was to be someone other than Ishmael. This chapter records the Lord's pledge of the promise to Abram and Sarai by changing their names, and the Lord's instruction for the sign of the covenant. Both the new names and the new sign called for faith on the part of the patriarch.

The nature of this chapter is almost entirely direct revelation; accordingly, it may be classified as a divine disclosure with narrative reports of Abram's response. The chapter begins with the report of the Lord's appearance to the patriarch, and the divine speeches end with a note of the Lord's departure (v. 22), the two verses framing the discourse. This chapter, with its emphases on divine appearance and divine discourse, is comparable to other passages in the patriarchal stories, notably Genesis 18 in the immediate context.

Theological Ideas

The initial mention of the Lord's appearance and self-disclosure to Abram as El Shadday (*'ēl šadday*), as well as the subsequent discourse, calls for a careful consideration of the nature of revelation. The etymology of the name *šadday* is probably still uncertain—although we do not lack for suggestions—and the nature of the appearance is not specified. Comparisons with other passages that include this designation may provide some general indications of the meaning. More specific, though, is the content of the revelation in this chapter concerning the covenant (*b**rît*, used thirteen times). The Lord guaranteed not only that a child would be born to Abram and Sarai but that kings would come from them. Moreover, the Lord instituted the sign of the covenant in order to bring about conformity to the covenant.

Within the divine discourse we have two predominant elements. The first is the changing of the names of Abram and Sarai. The expositor encounters many namings and changings of names in Genesis and so will have to understand the point. To change a name usually meant to change a person's status or circumstances. Coats says, "To give a name is to express suzerainty [lordship]" (*Genesis*, p. 134). In this passage, the new names served as reminders of God's pledge of the promise.

The second idea is circumcision, the sign of the covenant. Signs were attached to covenants as reminders of the participants' obligations and privileges under the covenant. In Genesis 9, the rainbow was the Lord's sign of the covenant with Noah; it was a perpetual reminder that there would never again be a flood to destroy the race. In this chapter the ritual of circumcision was the sign to be performed by the people of the covenant as evidence of their participation in it.

In conjunction with these theological ideas in general, there is the specific instruction for Abram to walk before the Lord and be perfect (17:1). Some attention must be given to the meaning of these terms in view of their being placed directly at the beginning of the divine discourse. Herein lay Abram's basic covenantal responsibilities. The law later repeated the requirement: "You shall be perfect" (Deut. 18:13; see also Matt. 5:48; Col. 1:28; 4:12; 2 Tim. 3:17).

Structure and Synthesis

Structure

The passage can be divided into four general sections: God's assurance of the promise by the changing of Abram's name (vv. 1–8), God's requirement of obedience by the institution of circumcision (vv. 9–14), God's specific word on the fulfillment of the promise through Sarah

(vv. 15–22), and then Abraham's compliance with the sign of the covenant by faith (vv. 23–27). God is dominant in the first three sections: he promises the son and names him Isaac, he renames Abram and Sarai to reflect the nature of the promise, and he legislates the sign of the covenant. The promise has grown more and more magnificent through the several revelations. Now it includes kings from the womb of Sarah.

Westermann says, "The division of the chapter is carefully thought out right down to the finest detail; it is an artistic composition." He clarifies this statement by showing that God's speech, set between the notice of his appearance (v. 1) and his withdrawal (v. 22), may be divided between the preamble (vv. 1b–3a) and the speech proper (vv. 3b–21). The elements in the short preamble are unfolded in the speech proper. This speech can be divided into three parts: the promise (vv. 3b–8), the command (vv. 9–14), and the promise (vv. 15–21). This arrangement, Westermann concludes, "is meant to tell us that the promise is dominant and all-embracing in what God says; the command is given to one who has received the promise; the command rests on the promise" (*Genesis*, vol. 2, p. 255).

The narrative that concludes the chapter reflects the faith of Abraham in the use of the new name and in his obedience in practicing circumcision. Whatever the nature of Abram's laughter might have been (v. 17) or whatever hopes he might have had for Ishmael as the heir (v. 18), by the end of the divine discourse the patriarch knew the certainty of the promise.

Summary Message

The Lord confirmed his covenant with Abram by establishing the rite of circumcision as the sign of obedient faith and attested to its promises by changing his name to Abraham and his wife's name to Sarah, all of which prompted Abraham to comply with the ordinance of circumcision.

Exegetical Outline

I. When the Lord appeared to Abram to confirm the covenant, he called for a life of faithful obedience and changed the patriarch's name to Abraham as a pledge of the promise (1–8).
   A. The Lord, appearing as El Shadday, called for a life of obedient faith as he prepared to confirm the promises of the covenant (1–2).
      1. Narrative framework: The Lord appeared to Abram (1a).
      2. Preamble: The Lord revealed himself as El Shadday and called for a perfect walk as a basis for receiving the promises (1b–2).

  B. Abram fell on his face before the Lord (3a).

  C. The Lord, reiterating his promises to Abram, changed the patriarch's name to Abraham as a pledge (3b–8).

    1. Name change: He named him Abraham because he would become the father of a multitude of nations (3b–5).

    2. Promises: He reiterated the covenantal promises of fruitfulness and inheritance (6–8).

 II. The Lord instituted the rite of circumcision as the sign of the covenant (9–14).

  A. The Lord identified the sign of the covenant (9–11).

  B. The Lord specified the regulations concerning the sign (12–13).

  C. The Lord set the consequences for disobedience (14).

 III. The Lord changed Sarai's name to Sarah as a pledge that the seed would come from her and would not be Ishmael, even though he too would be blessed (15–22).

  A. Name change: The Lord changed Sarai's name to Sarah as a pledge that she would be fruitful (15–17).

    1. He renamed Sarai Sarah (15).

    2. He promised that she would be blessed as the mother of nations and kings (16).

    3. Abraham laughed over the prospects (17).

  B. Promises: In response to Abraham's plea for Ishmael, the Lord promised to bless him too but affirmed that the promise would come through Isaac (18–21).

    1. Abraham pleaded for Ishmael (18).

    2. The Lord promised that Sarah would bear a son, Isaac, who would be the heir (19).

    3. The Lord promised to bless Ishmael with abundant fruitfulness, including twelve princes, but reserved the covenant for Isaac (20–21).

  C. Narrative framework: The Lord withdrew after speaking (22).

 IV. Abraham obeyed the Lord's instructions to circumcise every male in his household, being circumcised himself on the same day as Ishmael, his son (23–27).

The Development of the Exposition

The expositor could treat the first two verses as a separate section, stressing how the Lord wants his people to be obedient. Such a section would form a nice inclusio with the last part of the chapter about Abraham's obedience. In the arrangement to follow, however, I have left those verses within the first major section of the chapter because they are part of the Lord's promise to Abram that is developed in that section (cf. v. 2 in the preamble with v. 6 in the promise).

I. God guarantees his promises to his faithful people (1–8).

A. God calls the recipients of the covenant to be faithful (1–3a).

In this first part the expositor will have to clarify the possible meanings of the name El Shadday as well as the explanation of the appearance. The traditional understanding, "God Almighty," came from the translation of Jerome. That translation, however, could be a substitution for the name, much like the rabbinical use of Name (šēm), Place (māqôm, meaning the Omnipresent One), or Eternal One (ʿôlām) to represent the tetragrammaton (YHWH). Modern studies have suggested etymological connections with "mountain," and "breast" (which may be connected etymologically). If such connections could be proved, then the name would mean something like "the One belonging to the mountain"; it would designate the high God (as, for example, at the revelation of the Lord on Mount Sinai). But this meaning, as well as the numerous other suggestions, has not found clear support from any contextual usages. The epithet occurs forty-eight times in the Old Testament, thirty-one of them in Job. In the passages in Genesis (17:1; 28:3; 35:11; 48:3), the name occurs with the promise of posterity. Power could be included in the meaning; at least the name is associated with promised blessing and increase.

The divine discourse begins with two imperatives that lead into the promise. The structure of this section can be compared with the initial call in Genesis 12:1–4. The former passage contains the report that the Lord said something to Abram, and this passage has the report of his appearance and speaking to Abram; in the former passage the imperatives were "go" (lek < hālak) and "be a blessing" (wehyēh beʾrākâ), and in chapter 17 they are "walk" (hithallēk < hālak) and "be perfect" (wehyēh tāmîm); in the former the promises included "I will make you into a great nation," and here it is "I will multiply you exceedingly"; and in the former Abram's response was noted ("and Abram departed"), and here his response is noted ("and Abram fell on his face"). The chapter seems to be following that pattern to show the Lord's pledge of the promise is to one who was called to obedient faith.

The expositor will have to take some time in developing the meaning of the two imperatives: "walk before me" and "be perfect." These two imperatives could be interpreted sequentially (as with the imperatives in 12:1–3): "Walk before me in order that you may be perfect." Driver says that, by these commands, Abram was called to lead a righteous and holy life; he explains: "To 'walk before' any one is to live and move openly before him (1 S. xii. 2); esp. in such a way as (a) *to deserve,* and (b) *to enjoy,* his approval and favour. Here the thought of (a) predominates, the meaning being to comport oneself in a manner pleasing in God's sight (so xxiv. 40, xlviii. 15)" (*Book of Genesis,* p. 185). The discussion by Benno Jacob on this passage is also helpful. He writes:

> If you want to become whole, which is my request for you, you must walk before me; you must place yourself under my exclusive supervision, guidance, and protection. The image is taken from the shepherd who walks behind his herd directing it by his calls (48, 15), or from the father under whose eyes the child walks. It is more than the walking "with" God of Enoch and Noah who were practically lead [*sic*] by the hand.
>
> When questions arise you shall take directions only from God and be devoted to him without reservation. This word does not refer to moral conduct, for that would be too insignificant in this situation and is self-understood. The high demand corresponds to God's, "Be you mine, and I will be yours." [*First Book of the Bible,* pp. 109–10]

Of course, these general comments must be validated by a careful examination of the usage of the terms in the text. More can be said about the meaning of "perfect" (*tāmîm*). A study of this word is essential, for its meanings include "without fault" and "complete" or "whole." Westermann adopts the view that the text says that "belonging to God is in proper order only when it is without reservation and unconditional" (*Genesis,* vol. 2, p. 259).

B. God pledges his promises to the faithful by giving a new name (3b–8).

With the reiteration of the covenantal promise, the Lord gave Abram a personal sign. He would no longer be called Abram, but Abraham (*'abrāhām*), because he would be the father of a multitude of nations (*'ab-hămôn gôyim*). By renaming the founder of the nation, God gave a pledge of the promises.

The name Abram (*'abrām*) was a good, old West Semitic name made from two elements, *'āb* ("father") and *rām* ("exalted"). Samples of the use of *rûm* in the perfect tense may be found in the texts from Mari, Ugarit, and Ta'annek (see Speiser, *Genesis,* p. 124, and T. L. Thompson, *The Historicity of the Patriarchal Narratives* [Berlin: Walter de Gruyter, 1974], pp. 22–36). In the patriarch's name, the element *rām* probably referred to Terah, for Abram was not yet a father. It would signify, "He is exalted with respect to father"; that is, he was of distinguished lineage and high birth.

The etymology of the new name, the point of the story, is popular—
'abrāhām only sounds like 'ab-hămôn, "the father of a multitude." In
other words, the biblical explanation of the name is a sound play on the
name rather than an exact etymology. The name 'abrāhām is probably
a dialectical variant of 'abrām, with no appreciable difference in meaning. Its significance is from the word play.

The patriarch thus originally bore a name that spoke of his noble
lineage. But when the Lord confirmed the promise of posterity without
number, he signified it by the new name. This new name, 'abrāhām,
was to be a perpetual reminder of the promise that the patriarch would
be 'ab-hămôn, "father of a multitude." There would now be a looking
away from the noble lineage to the anticipation of progeny. Dods well
captures the significance of this change.

> Two seals were at this time affixed to the covenant: the one for Abram
> himself, the other for every one who shared with him in his blessings of
> the covenant. The first consisted in the change of his own name to Abra-
> ham, "the father of a multitude," and of his wife's to Sarah, "princess"
> or "queen," because she was now announced as the destined mother of
> kings. And however Abraham would be annoyed to see the hardly sup-
> pressed smile on the ironical faces of his men as he boldly commanded
> them to call him by a name whose verification seemed so grievously to
> lag; and however indignant and pained he may have been to hear the
> young Ishmael jeering Sarah with her new name, and lending it to every
> tone of mockery and using it with insolent frequency, yet Abraham knew
> that these names were not given to deceive; and probably as the name
> Abraham has become one of the best known names on earth, so to him-
> self did it quickly acquire a preciousness as God's voice abiding with
> him, God's promise renewed to him through every man that addressed
> him, until at length the child of promise lying on his knees took up its
> first syllable and called him "Abba." [*Book of Genesis,* p. 165]

There is a similar renaming in the promise of Jesus to build his church
(Matt. 16:16–18). Jesus said, "You are Peter [*petros*], and on this rock
[*petra*] I will build my church" (v. 18; see also Luke 6:14). With the
promise of the church came a name change for Simon that included a
play on the meaning of the name to preserve the significance of God's
work. By renaming the apostle, God gave us all a pledge of the promises.

II. God demands that his people be set apart to the covenant (9–14).

A. The Lord institutes the sign of the covenant (9–11).

The second section of the discourse records the Lord's instructions
concerning circumcision, the sign of the Abrahamic covenant. This sign

would apply to all who shared faith in the promise, for it carried a meaning of identification with the covenant. The fact that circumcision existed in the ancient world before it was instituted as the covenant sign does not detract from its meaning (cf. Jesus' investing bread and wine with symbolic meaning at the Last Supper). The sign of circumcision would be a reminder to God of the promises that he had made, and it would be a reminder to the seed of Abraham to live in loyalty to the covenant.

The rite of circumcision was appropriate to the nature of the covenant. With this symbol God instructed his people regarding the joining of faith with the act of reproduction. The sign was sexual—the promise was for a seed. The covenanters would be reminded (1) that human nature alone was unable to generate the promised seed if God was not willing to grant such fruitfulness, and (2) that impurity must be laid aside, especially in marriage. The sign formed a constant reminder for the people to preserve the purity of marriage in order to produce a godly seed (see Mal. 2:10–17).

Like all covenantal signs, circumcision could easily become an empty ritual. It had to be coupled with faith to have genuine meaning. The performance of the rite simply meant that the participants were identiified with the seed of Abraham. To be identified with the "spiritual seed of Abraham" required that spiritual circumcision accompany the physical act, that is, that faith and commitment to the Lord be the motivation. The law said that God would circumcise the heart so that the people would be devoted to him (Deut. 30:6). Already in the time of the lawgiver, circumcision was thus a symbol of separation, purity, and loyalty to the covenant. In Psalm 118:10, there is a hint that circumcision (generally translated "destroy" or "cut off") was the means by which the nations would be joined to the faith. Paul later said that only circumcision of the heart, that is, being set apart by the Spirit, was praiseworthy before God (Rom. 2:28–29). In both Testaments the true seal of fellowship with the Lord would be "circumcision of the heart." The lesson behind the physical rite was that one must live by faith in the Lord and his promises, for unbelief is described as a fleshly heart.

Many commentaries correlate this sign of the Abrahamic covenant with baptism as the sign of the New Covenant, showing that it was performed once at the initiation into the covenant community and could be performed on infants and adults alike. But a good case can be made for the Lord's Supper being the sign of the New Covenant, for it is expressly identified as such: "This cup is the new covenant in my blood" (1 Cor. 11:25). Moreover, remembrance, the key element of a sign, is associated with the cup: "Do this in remembrance of me." As the believer takes the cup of communion, the New Covenant is perpetuated in the community of the faithful. Naturally, even this ritual (as well as baptism) can be empty if it is not accompanied by faith.

B. The Lord warns against disregarding the sign (12–14).

In this section attention is given to the rules for keeping circumcision and especially the penalty for disregarding it. Since its significance was that the Lord's covenant would be in their flesh, anyone not complying with the rite was in effect annulling (hēpar < pārar) the covenant. The punishment was that such should be "cut off from his people [w^enikr^etâ hannepeš hahî° mē°ammeyhā]." This expression appears to be a general threat of divine punishment that could come about in a number of ways. A survey of its usages will provide the exegete with the possible meanings.

III. God plans to fulfill his promises in ways that seem impossible (15–22).

A. God pledges his promise by giving a new name (15–17).

As a sign that God would bless Sarai, that is, make her fruitful, he changed her name to Sarah. Both names probably mean "princess"; the old name Sarai (šāray) is more difficult to evaluate but may be an archaic form with an old feminine termination. In that case the change would be a modernization to mark this new beginning.

It is also possible that Sarai may be a different word entirely. The Septuagint doubles the r for Sarah (Sarra) but not for Sarai (Sara), which would suggest that the name Sarai was related to the verb "strive" or "persist" (šārâ), and Sarah to the verb "rule" (šārar). This distinction, however, may have been only in the mind of the Greek translator. It would be hard to imagine a daughter being named with a concept of striving or contending. That meaning might have significance in the story about the strife with Hagar but would be irrelevant in considering the naming at her birth. For a new name to be a pledge of the promise, it does not need a radical new meaning—it only needs to mark a new era or status. "Sarah" was thus probably a dialectical variant of "Sarai."

The thought of Sarah's having children, let alone nations and kings, prompted Abraham to laugh. Verse 17 says, "And Abraham fell on his face and laughed [wayyiṣḥāq]." The interpretations of this laughter vary between commentators. Brueggemann says, "Abraham completely doubts the promise, laughs a mocking laugh, and appeals to the son already in hand" (Genesis, p. 156). But B. Jacob says, "Abraham's questions do not imply doubt and still less that this cannot happen. Abraham, who had abandoned all for such a promise, cannot possibly now question the power of Almighty God and disbelieve the promise" (First Book of the

Bible, p. 112). Jacob adds that great happiness is often hidden behind exclamations of doubt (e.g., Can this really be true?) and that God speaks only to a soul that is receptive and makes promises only to a believer.

Both of these views seem worded too strongly. Abraham's laughter can represent doubt without being a mocking laugh and without ruining his general belief. Westermann's description seems more plausible.

> The gesture of reverence is Abraham's first and, in any case, required reaction. But then he laughs. . . . Sarah's laughter (18:10–15) at the singular announcement is understandable. But Abraham's laughter in 17:17a has something of the bizarre about it in immediate confrontation with God who is making a marvelous promise to him. . . . God, in responding, does not pursue it. God has promised to act; he continues along his majestic way, which is "above all understanding," beyond Abraham's laughter and doubt. The name of his son, which is a play on Abraham's laughter, will attest this marvelous action of God. [*Genesis,* vol. 2, p. 268]

B. God specifies the miraculous nature of the promise (18–22).

In response to Abraham's concern over Ishmael, his son, the Lord specified that the future child of Sarah would be the heir. The name of that child should be Isaac (*yiṣḥāq*), the motivation for the name coming from the verb "and he laughed" (*wayyiṣḥāq*). The naming of the child Isaac was to be a reminder of Abraham's laughter, which brought belief and unbelief very close (von Rad, *Genesis,* p. 203).

The form of the name is the common verbal pattern (imperfect or jussive) of the root *ṣāḥaq,* "to laugh." The name could be a shortened form of *yiṣḥāq-ʾēl,* "may God laugh," signifying divine approval. It could also be a shortened form of *yiṣḥāq-ʾāb,* "the father laughs." (A Hurrian story translated into Hittite has a father smiling at a newborn son placed on his lap.) If "God" was the understood subject, the name Isaac (*yiṣḥāq*) would express the popular wish that God's favor be granted.

The motif of laughter was preserved in the stories to reflect the doubts of Abraham and Sarah. Because the child was named Isaac, a name attesting to divine favor at a birth, the narrator freely used the same verb (*ṣāḥaq*) to describe the reactions of Abraham and Sarah to the promise. The point would be that God's laughter would be superimposed on theirs; his pleasure in bestowing the son would be greater than their doubts. The word play between the name and the narrator's choice to use the verb in the stories, then, serves to stress both God's blessing and their doubts.

Because Ishmael also was a son of Abraham, the Lord promised to bless him (note the word play on his name as well in v. 20: "And as for Ishmael [*ûleyišmāʿēʾl*], I have heard you [*šemaʿtîkā*])." The Lord promised to increase Ishmael into a great nation (cf. vv. 2 and 6). The promise of twelve princes would be fulfilled in the record of Genesis 25:12–18. God thus granted his blessing to other tribes as well; he did not restrict his blessings to the covenant people of Israel.

IV. The pledges of God's promises prompt the believer to obey the stipulations of the covenant (23–27).

The final section records how Abraham circumcised those in his household according to God's instructions. The expositor need not spend as much time on these verses but will have to show the relationship between Abraham's obedience and the pledges of the promise just given. Undoubtedly, the sure Word from God prompted his compliance.

The new names assured the coming of the promise, and the sign of the covenant reminded the participants that they were to live in compliance with the Lord's covenant. The chapter, which is essentially a divine discourse on the covenant, would have been most reassuring to Abraham and Sarah as well as to the later nation of Israel, which shared that covenant's bounty and kept its sign. Even in times of calamity their faith in the covenant would find reassurance as they kept the sign and rehearsed the promises.

Much is said in the New Testament about God's promises to us as well in the new covenant. The divine discourse here, however, came through Jesus Christ, who by his Word and in his ordinances assured us of the fulfillment of the promise, even though it seems impossible. In God's discourses on the covenants, the names and the signs become pledges of the ultimate fulfillment and encouragements to faith. In the area of the divine assurances through symbol and name, I would look for the word of encouragement.

Within the exposition, however, we must include the essence of the rite of circumcision. The spiritual reality behind the rite seems to remain unchanged in the two Testaments. The message could thus be summarized from this chapter as follows: *God requires a sanctified, believing life* (involving proper use of the ritual and a perfect walk before him) *of those who walk in anticipation of the promise and keep the rites of the covenant.* On the one hand, we have the pledges of the Lord to fulfill the promises; on the other hand, we have the covenantal responsibilities to be set apart to the covenant and to obey its stipulations faithfully.

Bibliography

Albright, W. F. "The Names *Shaddai* and *Abram*." *JBL* 54 (1935): 173–210.

Eissfeldt, Otto. "Renaming in the Old Testament." In *Words and Meanings,* edited by Peter R. Ackroyd and Barnabas Lindars, pp. 70–83. Cambridge: Cambridge University Press, 1968.

Fox, M. V. "The Sign of Covenant: Circumcision in the Light of the Priestly 'ōt Etiologies." *RB* 81 (1974): 557–96.

Gordis, R. "The Biblical Root *šdy-šd.*" *JThS* 41 (1940): 34–43.

Koch, K. "*Šaddaj.*" *VT* 26 (1976): 229–32.

Mitchell, John J. "Abram's Understanding of the Lord's Covenant." *WTJ* 32 (1969): 24–48.

Moeller, H. R. "Four Old Testament Problem Terms." *BiTr* 13 (1962): 219–22.

Speiser, E. A. "Background and Function of the Biblical *Nāśi'.*" *CBQ* 25 (1963): 111–17.

Westermann, C. "Genesis 17 und die Bedeutung von *berit.*" *TLZ* 101 (1976): 161–70.

White, Hugh C. "The Divine Oath in Genesis." *JBL* 92 (1973): 165–79.

26

God's Marvelous Work for His Covenant People
(Gen. 18:1–15)

T his passage has two basic parts, the appearance of the visitors to the gracious host Abraham (vv. 1–8), and the annunciation of the birth of the child (vv. 9–15). While one may be justified in seeing lessons in the first part about hospitality, it can scarcely have been for the sake of inculcating hospitality to strangers that the text reports the events in the first section. Rather, the visitation is a prelude to the annunciation, and so the purpose of the whole narrative is greater than a portrayal of a gracious host. Although the narrative is rather unusual in its composition, it nonetheless has a distinct development toward the point of the passage. It is not a narrative that moves from tension to resolution. The skeptical response to the promise provides a tension at the end of the story, but it is resolved quickly with the Lord's rebuke.

Most peculiar about this passage is the inordinate detail and apparent importance given to the first scene, all of which forces the expositor to explain why the Lord appeared to Abraham in this manner. The Lord perhaps meant a visit from strangers to be a test of Abraham in this chapter and of Sodom in the next, for the moral state of people may have been indicated by their treatment of strangers. Abraham certainly contrasts sharply with the people of Sodom in this regard. But there must be a greater connection between the hospitality and the promise of the covenant. In fact, there is a foreshadowing of the tension in the words of the visitor, "Where is Sarah your wife?" This question in the first scene would then anticipate the annunciation in the second and show the purpose of the visit.

Theological Ideas

The essence of the message comes in the word of rebuke over the disbelief in the promise: "Is anything too marvelous for the LORD?" (v. 14). The exposition of this account must stress the incomparable nature and works of the Lord (a word study on $p\bar{a}l\bar{a}$', "be wonderful," is in order). For the Lord, who created the universe, destroyed it by the flood, and confounded the languages at Babel, bringing a child from the womb of Sarah was not impossible. That the visitor knew that Sarah laughed within herself also reveals that this heavenly visitor had abilities beyond measure. These truths, of course, must be related to the point that the Lord is able to keep his promises, in spite of apparent difficulties and barriers.

In addition to this main point there is the motif of the meal provided for the visitors. The expositor must give serious thought to the significance of the Lord's appearance to eat in Abraham's tent. The point has a certain affinity with the idea of shared communal meals as signs of fellowship. The motif of eating would then signify that the promise was reiterated to one who was in covenant fellowship with the Lord.

Structure and Synthesis

Structure

The structure of the passage is fairly simple. The first section is essentially *narrative*. It has an introduction reporting the appearance of the Lord to Abraham (v. 1). This part is followed by the narrative about the reception of the visitors, which includes the visitation (v. 2), the dialogue (vv. 3–5), and the meal (vv. 6–8). The second major section is the *dialogue* concerning the annunciation of the birth. It includes interrogation (v. 9a), response (v. 9b), annunciation of the birth (v. 10a), skeptical response (vv. 10b–12), rebuke and reiteration of the annunciation (vv. 13–14), denial of laughter (v. 15a), and final correcting rebuke (v. 15b).

Coats suggests that 2 Kings 4:8–17 parallels this material (*Genesis*, p. 138). The prophecy there about the birth of the Shunammite's son

includes the following motifs: the recognition of the problem of barrenness and the aged husband (v. 14), the annunciation of the birth of a
child in about a year (v. 16), the expression of doubt by the woman (she
says, "No my lord; don't mislead your servant, O man of God!"), and the
fulfillment of the announced birth (v. 17). The narrative in Genesis 18
parallels the first three parts of the story in Kings; the last part is paralleled in Genesis 21 after the interlude about Sodom and Abimelech.

Summary Message

After sharing a meal prepared by the household of Abraham, the Lord
announced the fulfillment of the promise, declaring, in rebuke of Sarah's
laughter, that nothing is too hard for the Lord.

Exegetical Outline

    I. The Lord appeared to Abraham at Mamre and shared a com-
munal meal prepared by the patriarch and his household (1–8).
      A. Three visitors appeared at Mamre and received rest and re-
freshment from Abraham (1–5).
        1. Narrative introduction: The Lord appeared to Abraham (1).
        2. Report of the reception of the guests: Abraham received
the three visitors and persuaded them to rest with him
(2–5).
      B. The three visitors enjoyed a meal prepared hastily by Abra-
ham and his household (6–8).
    II. The Lord announced the time of the fulfillment of the promise,
declaring, in rebuke of Sarah's laughter, that nothing was too
hard for the Lord (9–15).
      A. Interrogation and annunciation: The Lord announced that
the fulfillment of the promise was imminent (9–12).
        1. The Lord inquired about Sarah, and Abraham responded
(9).
        2. The Lord announced that the birth was imminent, but
Sarah laughed over the prospects (10–12).
      B. Rebuke and annunciation: The Lord rebuked Sarah for
laughing and reiterated the annunciation (13–14).
        1. The Lord rebuked Sarah for laughing (13).
        2. The Lord reiterated the annunciation, declaring that
nothing was too hard for the Lord (14).
      C. Denial and rebuke: In response to Sarah's denial that she
laughed, the Lord affirmed that she did indeed laugh (15).

Development of the Exposition

I. God assures his people (by communal meal) that a covenant of peace exists between them (1–8).

A. The Lord visits his people (1–2).

The narrative opens with the report that "the LORD appeared to him [*wayyērā' 'ēlāyw YHWH*]." That Abraham is not mentioned (cf. 17:1) suggests that this account builds on the previous one, in which Abraham was the subject. The report sets the tone for the entire chapter: here is a narrative that will lead directly into divine discourse.

This visitation is a little more complicated in that it involves three visitors who came and ate Abraham's meal. The three could have been the Lord and two angels, a view that finds support from chapter 19 (assuming that it is a continuation of chap. 18), or a threefold manifestation of the Lord himself. The point is clear, though, that the Lord visited Abraham and that the visitation was part of the blessing.

Any reading of the commentaries will discover that there are parallels to this event in other ancient literature, especially the Greek literature. Delitzsch was probably the first to point out the comparable texts, but others have expanded the discussion. The samples most often cited are from the *Odyssey* (17.485–87), which mentions that gods in the guise of strangers from afar put on all manner of shapes and visited the cities, and Ovid (*Fasti* 5. lines 494–544), which reports that Zeus, Poseidon, and Hermes visited Boeotian and after the meal granted him his wish for a child, Orion. The commentators' explanations of these similarities will vary, but it seems logical to argue that, if the Greek stories came later and from a different culture, their connection must be indirect. If the motif of heavenly visitors was indeed widespread in the ancient world, some event such as this one might have inspired it. At the least we may say that the point of this narrative would be understood in the ancient world in view of that motif: the visitors came from another world to bring a message to Abraham. Accordingly, the writer to the Hebrews advised us to show kindness to strangers because some have thereby entertained angels (13:2).

B. The faithful respond graciously to the visitation of the strangers (3–8).

One of the issues that the expositor will have to settle is whether or not Abraham knew the identity of the visitors, or, if he did not at the outset, when he began to understand who they were. The discussion must consider the activities of Abraham in his haste to serve the visitors, as well as the use of *'ădōnāy* in verse 3. This word *'ădōnāy* is usually reserved for addressing the Lord, whereas 'ădōnî, "my lord," would be used in addressing another person. Perhaps the spelling in the Masoretic Text, 'ădōnāy, represents an adjustment to the narrative report of verse 1 that this visitor was the Lord (YHWH). Consequently, we would say that, at the outset, Abraham may not have known who his visitors were but sensed that they were worthy of honorable treatment. He even granted them the respect that is due to those higher in rank: "My lord, if I have found favor in your sight, do not pass by your servant" (v. 3). Abraham may have suspected that these were messengers of the Lord, but only with the dialogue would he know that it was the Lord.

In order to understand the reason that this visitation unfolded as it did, the exegete must survey other passages that deal with eating a meal. A good case can be made that the visitation to eat in Abraham's tent was meant to convey intimate fellowship, and on the basis of such a close relationship, the Lord would guarantee the imminent birth of the child of promise. Covenants in the ancient world were often arranged with meals (see the treaty with Abimelech in 26:28–30). To eat together was important for peaceful agreements in covenants and treaties. And so, at the ratification of the covenant at Mount Sinai, the people of the covenant ate and drank in peace before the Lord (Exod. 24). Then, in the Levitical code, the peace offering was intended to signify that the worshiper enjoyed a peaceful relationship with the Lord (Lev. 3; 7:11–21). This sacrifice was a meal to be eaten by the congregation in the sanctuary as a celebration of the Lord's provisions for them in his blessings. But it was not simply a communal meal—it was a holy meal. No one could eat it if defiled or in sin. It was a meal that brought people together who shared one thing—peace with God.

Gideon also received a visitation of peace from the angel of the Lord in which he was instructed to prepare a meal and lay it out on the rock. In a manner similar to the sacrifices, the fire of the Lord consumed the meal. The message from the Lord was "Peace!" prompting Gideon to name the altar, "The LORD is peace" (Judg. 6:14).

That the sacrifices were integrally bound up with the symbolism of eating and drinking was confirmed by Jesus' teachings on his own sacrifice. He taught that union with him would be based on eating his flesh and drinking his blood (John 6:53–58), meaning, of course, the appropriation by faith of his sacrificial death. The church's celebration of this union with Christ takes the form of eating and drinking at the Lord's table (Matt. 26:26–30). This dramatic reenactment of believers' acceptance of Christ's death on their behalf is parallel to Israel's peace offering, for only those at peace with God may eat and drink.

Elsewhere in the New Testament Jesus used the imagery of staying in someone's home to represent fellowship with him. To Zacchaeus

Jesus said, "Make haste, come down, for today I must stay at your house." And when he entered his house, he said, "Today salvation has come to this house" (Luke 19:5, 9). The imagery is also used in the letter to the Laodiceans: "Behold, I stand at the door and knock. If anyone hears my voice and opens the door, I will come in to him and dine with him, and he with me" (Rev. 3:20).

The full fellowship in the world to come is also expressed in the imagery of the banquet, specifically, a marriage supper of the Lamb (Rev. 19:7), for which the participants must prepare. The rabbis also saw that the age to come was like a banquet hall and that this life was the vestibule (*Pirqe Aboth* 3:16; 4:15). Jesus' teaching on the age to come included this well-known imagery, for eating together had become the sign of peaceful union.

There is, then, great significance in the Lord's making a special visit to Abraham's tent to announce the birth—Abraham was the friend of God, the recipient of the covenant. The Lord would use this event as the occasion for revealing the specific fulfillment of the promise. When the time was at hand, we may say, the Lord came personally and ate in Abraham's presence. Nothing could more effectively communicate the close relationship upon which the promises were based. As the true identity of the visitors dawned on the patriarch, he would have been moved by the nature of the visit.

The next time that the Lord established a covenantal meal with the family of Abraham was at Sinai at the eve of the fulfillment of the covenant (Exod. 24). On the basis of that relationship with the living God, the people of Israel knew that the promises would be fulfilled, that nothing was too hard for the Lord, even though it seemed impossible to them at the time. There the Lord united with his people in fellowship to confirm that he was with them.

II. God expects his people to believe his promises because nothing is too difficult for him (9–15).

The second part of the passage is the divine discourse on the fulfillment of the promise. Here any uncertainty about the visitors' identity would have been resolved—the voice declared that the birth would happen and that Sarah did laugh.

A. The promise of the Lord seems incredible to his people (9–12).

The discourse began with the interrogation "Where is Sarah your wife?" The question seems rhetorical, for the visitor that knew her name would probably know her whereabouts. The question served to focus attention on the point of the visit—it concerned Sarah, whose new name spoke of the promise.

The promise is emphatically and specifically worded in verse 10: "I shall surely return [šôb 'āšûb] to you this time next year, and Sarah your wife shall have a son." The promise of a son from the Lord or his spokesman occurs again in Judges 13:2–5, 1 Samuel 1:17, 2 Kings 4:8–17, and Luke 1–2. In this passage, although there are three visitors, the verb form is in the singular, showing that the word is from the Lord. His return, meaning his intervention to bless, signifies that the birth will be a divine provision.

But Sarah laughed within herself (wattiṣḥaq śārâ beqirbâ, in v. 12). This subdued laughter is reported with the same verb used in chapter 17 (wayyiṣḥāq), but here it is the feminine form and does not form as close a word play on the name Isaac (yiṣḥāq). Verse 11 offers the narrator's parenthetical explanation of the situation that made the words of the visitor seem absurd—they were old and Sarah was beyond childbearing. Then, in verse 12, the narrator reported Sarah's thinking on the matter: "After I have grown old, shall I have pleasure, my lord also being old?" (A. A. McIntosh ["Third Root עדה"] suggests that 'ednâ, usually translated "pleasure," should be interpreted "conception.") Sarah's reaction is what would be expected, given these circumstances; she looked at the promise from her side—and laughed.

B. The ability of the Lord is beyond human comprehension (13–15).

The Lord immediately rebuked Sarah's doubt with the rhetorical question, "Why did Sarah laugh [lāmmâ zeh ṣāḥăqâ śārâ]?" The rebuke is kind but forceful in its construction. What made the laughter amazing to the visitor was the ability of the one making the promise.

Verse 14 expressed this ability in the form of a rhetorical question: "Is anything too hard for the LORD?" The verb yippālē' (< pālā') must be studied thoroughly for its significance here. It basically means "to be wonderful, extraordinary, surpassing." A survey of its uses will illustrate the point. For example, it is used in Psalm 139:6 to describe the extraordinary knowledge—omniscience—of the Lord, and it is used in Isaiah 9:6 as one of the titles for the promised King (pele' yô'ēṣ, "wonderful counselor"; see Isa. 28:29). In this passage the message is that, for the Lord, nothing is too extraordinary—he delights in doing that which is impossible, marvelous, even surpassing. The rhetorical question signifies that there is nothing that is too difficult for the Lord to do. Westermann catches the point well by noting, "The messenger thus counters Sarah by saying that the announcement she has heard comes from God" (Genesis, vol. 2, p. 282).

With this point made, the Lord then repeated the promise, only now it was an appointed time (mô'ēd). The birth of Isaac was a scheduled event, as far as the Lord was concerned.

Sarah's denial of her laughter was probably an attempt to retract her laughter, now that she realized the source of the annunciation and her hasty response. She would have preferred to cancel the laughter, but the Lord's "No, you did laugh [lō' kî ṣāḥāqt]" preserves it. Moreover, leaving on that note was particularly instructive, for Abraham and Sarah were to remember their response to the promise until the child Isaac was born—they laughed. The Lord chose to do the impossible because the promised seed was to be known as the Lord's provision.

The remembrance of the laughter preserves the divine rebuke for mistrusting the Lord's omnipotence. Sarah had not renounced the Lord in unbelief; rather, she had found his specific word incredible. As von Rad states, "The unquestionable, decisive fact both for narrator and reader is that a word of Yahweh was laughed at" (Genesis, p. 207).

In this incident, then, the Lord of creation came in person to announce the time of the fulfillment of the promise. His words were laughed at, however, because they promised that which was humanly impossible. Nevertheless, the Lord had set the time for the supernatural birth, for nothing was too incredible (if we may use that word in the popular sense) for the Lord.

Basically the passage forms an exhortation for the covenant people to believe that God can do the impossible. The promise to Sarah was the annunciation of an impossible birth. At the annunciation of the birth of Jesus, Mary likewise could not understand how such a thing could be—and it was more difficult in her case. God miraculously provided the long-awaited seed to her as well.

When something similarly extraordinary is announced, our response is consistent with Sarah's—we are taken off guard; we wonder how these things can be; we look at it from the human side and laugh; and then out of fear we deny that we laughed at a word from the Lord. But God knows we laughed, if we staggered over what he said he was about to do.

The message could be summarized in this way: *Nothing is incredible for those in covenantal fellowship with the Lord, because nothing is too marvelous for him.* The New Testament parallels this story in Genesis in many ways, confirming that the nature of the Lord does not change. First, the Lord fellowships with his people (Christ established the covenantal meal in the upper room, and it remains today as the symbol of covenantal fellowship with him). Second, the Lord promises his people that which on the human level seems totally impossible (whether a supernatural birth, divine intervention, or a bodily resurrection and glorification). In it all the Lord expects his people to respond by faith and not doubt, for his Word is based on his nature. If the people of God, who enjoy covenantal fellowship with him, fully believed what he said he would do—now or at any time in the history of the faith—their lives, their world, would be very different.

Bibliography

Ap-Thomas, D. R. "Notes on Some Terms Relating to Prayer." *VT* 6 (1956): 225–41.

Kolenkow, Anitra. "The Ascription of Romans 4:5." *HTR* 60 (1967): 228–30.

McIntosh, A. A. "A Third Root עדה in Biblical Hebrew?" *VT* 24 (1974): 454–73.

Otwell, J. H. *And Sarah Laughed: The Status of Women in the Old Testament.* Philadelphia: Westminster, 1977.

Thomas, D. W. "Some Observations on the Hebrew Root חדל." *VTS* 4 (1957): 8–16.

Xella, Paola. "L'episode de Dnil et Kothar (KJU 1.17[=CTA 17] v 1–31) (KTU 1.17 [CTA 17 v 1–31] et Gen. XVIII 1–16." *VT* 28 (1978): 483–88.

27

The Justice of the Righteous Judge
(Gen. 18:16–33)

This passage has most frequently (and legitimately) been treated for its emphasis on intercession; the predominant theme of the whole section, however, is justice. This motif grows out of the preceding narrative, which stressed that God was able to do whatever he chose to do. But would it be just? The answer to this question was a foregone conclusion, which Abraham's intercession demonstrated. It is clear from the outset of the story that Abraham's intercession was not going to alter the situation, for Sodom and Gomorrah deserved judgment. The narrator thus used the intercession to show that the destruction of the cities of the plain would be just.

It is a fairly common view that the contents of this unit are not based on any historical event but are a creative product of the Yahwist's imagination. The writer, this view continues, probably had the account of Genesis 19 before him and wrote this piece as an introduction to that narrative. Accordingly, the substance of the material would have come from the postexilic period, when the people were dominated by the idea of God's righteousness, especially in his judgment of the nations. Such

347

a view was undoubtedly prompted by the circumstances of the story, that is, that the Lord appeared to Abraham and that Abraham stood and bartered with him about Sodom. But it is unreasonable to say that it could not have happened, especially if we grant that divine intervention took place in Israel's history.

The passage may best be described as the report of speeches of three kinds: soliloquy, annunciation, and negotiation (or intercession, although the term "intercession" does not adequately describe the conversation in this passage). The report comes between the departure of the men from Abraham's tent (18:16) and their arrival at the gate of Sodom (19:1). The passage does not center on the promises to Abraham but is related to them only indirectly. The concern of the speeches is with surrounding nations that might share in the promised blessings unless they disqualify themselves.

The unit provides a digression from the main line of the narratives, just as the account of the spreading evil and the destruction of the flood did earlier. In fact, Genesis 18:16–33 may be compared with Genesis 6:1–4 in that it records the Lord's contemplation of the wickedness of the people and the necessity to destroy them. The ideas about how the righteous remnant preserve the city or how the Lord seeks to avoid judgment for the sake of the righteous are certainly present in the text. But the main point is that Sodom is a wicked city without ten righteous people, and therefore God is just in destroying it.

Theological Ideas

The central theological idea in this passage is the righteousness of God in relation to the righteousness of people. This study will involve the evaluation of the key words used in the text, "righteousness" ($s^e d\bar{a}q\hat{a}$) and "justice" ($mi\check{s}p\bar{a}\underline{t}$), and the contextual information about how God's righteousness works in life. This passage shows the need for teachers of righteousness to know the mind of God as well as to participate in demonstrating God's righteousness, especially in times of judgment. Foundational to such involvement is the confidence by the faithful that the Judge of all the earth will do right. But there must also be the concern that, in any situation, this conviction be confirmed.

The biblical teaching on the remnant of the righteous first surfaces here. A nation may be preserved because of a righteous remnant. And people have a right to pray for deliverance for their sake, for God is willing to spare the wicked for the sake of the righteous.

Structure and Synthesis

Structure

The structure of this unit is fairly straightforward—it may be divided between the Lord's speeches and the negotiation dialogue. The Lord's speeches can be divided into a soliloquy expressing the divine interest in Abraham (vv. 17–19) and an announcement expressing the divine interest in Sodom (vv. 20–21). The dialogue that follows records a series of petitions and concessions (vv. 23–32). The speeches and dialogue are framed and divided by narrative reports of the movement toward Sodom (vv. 16, 22, 33).

Summary Message

After contemplating the reasons for telling Abraham of his plans for Sodom, the Lord announced that he was about to investigate the wickedness of Sodom that cried out for judgment, an announcement that prompted Abraham to intercede for the city for the sake of the righteous.

Exegetical Outline

I. Divine speeches: After the visitation at Mamre, the Lord contemplated the reasons for telling Abraham about his investigation of the wickedness of Sodom (16–21).

A. Narrative transition: After the visitation, Abraham escorted the three men on their way (16).

B. Soliloquy: The Lord contemplated the reasons for telling Abraham of his plans for Sodom (17–19).

1. Abraham would be the means of blessing for the world (18).

2. Abraham would be a teacher of righteousness (19).

C. Announcement: The Lord declared that he was about to investigate the great sin of Sodom that cried out for judgment (20–21).

II. Negotiation: Questioning God about the justice of destroying the righteous with the wicked, Abraham interceded for the city for the sake of the righteous in it, prompting the concession that it would not be destroyed if there were ten righteous people there (22–33).

A. Abraham questioned the Lord's justice in destroying the righteous with the wicked (22–25).

B. Abraham interceded for Sodom for the sake of the righteous, drawing the concession from the Lord that the city would be spared if there were at least ten righteous people there (26–32).

C. Abraham returned to his place when the Lord departed (33).

Development of the Message

I. The Lord reveals his plans to the righteous (16–21).

A. *The Lord wants the righteous to understand his righteous decisions (16–19).*

The narrative follows immediately the events of the visitation at Mamre, for once that discussion ended, the men looked toward Sodom (*wayyašqīpû ʿal-peê sedōm*). This statement is followed by two disjunctive clauses: the first reports that Abraham accompanied them in the direction of Sodom, and the second introduces the Lord's soliloquy concerning Abraham. This second clause forms a new beginning of the series of speeches to be reported: "Now the LORD said [*waYHWH ʾāmār*]. . . ."

There is a double motivation for revealing the judgment to Abraham. First, Abraham was going to be a blessing to the nations, so an account should be given to him when one nation was to be removed from that opportunity. Second, Abraham would teach justice and righteousness to his descendants. Verse 19 calls for closer examination; it reports how Abraham will command his household to keep the way of the Lord, to do righteousness and justice, that they might enjoy God's blessing. The statement in verse 19 that the Lord knew Abraham ("I know him," *yedaʿtîw*) confirms that the patriarch stood in a special relationship to the Lord and that, when he received further revelation of the righteousness of God, he would instill it in the way of his descendants. To live in conformity with the will of God (righteousness) and to make the right decisions based on his will (justice) now become the conditions for inheriting the blessings of the promise (see also Ps. 33:5; Prov. 21:3). The expositor must show how these ideas fit within this context as well as in similar situations in Israel's history when people might question God's righteousness and justice.

B. *The Lord's judgment of the wicked will be just (20–21).*

The second section of the Lord's speech is the revelation about his investigation of Sodom's wickedness. The description is very anthropomorphic: the outcry against their grievous sin was so great that the Lord would go down and see if it was that bad. Several things serve the exposition well. First, the word for outcry is *zeʿāqâ* (*zaʿăqat sedōm*), forming a word play on the theme of the passage, righteousness (*sedāqâ*). The *cry* from Sodom will speak of evil, and the response from the Lord will be *righteous*. Second, the Lord announced that he would go down (*ʾērădâ-nāʾ*) and see (*weʾerʾeh*) if it was that bad. The point is that the Lord's judgment is based on full and accurate information. But the wording alludes to a previous judgment passage, the confounding of the languages in Genesis 11:1–9. There the Lord went down to see (*wayyēred YHWH lir'ōt* in v. 5, and then *nēr'dâ* in v. 7) the city that the people were building and concluded that nothing would be withheld from them if they were allowed to continue. Third, there is an emphasis on the completeness of the evil of Sodom that reflects the concern in 15:16 that judgment on the Amorites would come when their sin was full (*šālēm*). Here the noun "completeness" (*kālâ*) is used: "to see if they have done completely as the cry of it." If their deeds were as bad as the cry indicated, they would be judged.

II. The Lord responds to intercession on behalf of the righteous (22–33).

The final unit records what has become known as Abraham's intercession for the city of Sodom. Since the format is one of question and answer, however, it is different from all subsequent intercessions. Through the questions and the answers the righteousness of the Lord in his judgment is probed. Abraham was convinced that there were righteous people in Sodom, and so he appealed for the city on the basis of God's justice. He was not simply praying for Lot to be rescued; the resolution to the negotiation, however (i.e., that the righteous would not be destroyed with the wicked), finally came by the rescue of Lot. God had the right to destroy (lit., "sweep away" [*sāpâ*]; see also 19:15 and 17) the wicked, but if he destroyed the righteous with them, he would not be just.

Throughout the negotiations we find the contrast between the righteous (*saddîq*, or *hassaddîqîm*) and the wicked (*rāšā'*). The expositor must clarify the difference between the two. Certainly in the Old Testament and already in Genesis 15:6, the concept of righteousness is related to the covenant. Accordingly, those who are joined to the Lord by faith and follow his standards in obedience are called "the righteous"; those who have no part with the covenant and have no interest in obeying the Lord are "the wicked." The psalms use this distinction repeatedly, showing that the wicked are destined for judgment because they stand outside the covenant and its stipulations. In this text Abraham's concern is that God's people not suffer the same fate as the wicked (cf. Ps. 1:5–6).

The theme of God's justice predominates. Those who would enjoy God's blessing must promote righteousness and justice; in so doing they may appeal to God for just judgment to preserve the righteous, knowing that God would withhold the judgment for the sake of the righteous remnant. Israel, and all people in general, would learn that through righteousness they would continue in God's favor. In this interchange between Abraham and the Lord, people would be reminded of God's righteousness as well as the fruits of unrighteousness. Righteous people—ten of them—would have preserved unrighteous Sodom. The Judge of all the earth will thus certainly do right (*ya'áśeh mišpāṭ*, in v. 25), in preservation or in judgment.

Abraham's character is demonstrated here through his humility and his intercession. He had personally rescued these people (Gen. 14) and now pleaded for their deliverance with boldness and perseverance. What jars the reader is that his argument seems to be an "audacious beating down of God" (Dods, *Book of Genesis*, p. 181). His appeal was made in genuine humility and reverence, however, for he pleaded for justice.

The expository idea may be expressed this way: *The righteous may be confident that the righteous Judge of the earth will not destroy the righteous with the wicked.* Since Sodom was shortly destroyed, it would be clear that they deserved divine judgment; and since Lot and his family were rescued, it would be understood that they were members of the covenant.

Israel would continue to believe that God is a righteous Judge, that righteousness exalts a nation, and that righteous people preserve society. What, then, should the righteous do—in any age? According to this passage they must live righteously before the Lord in order to enjoy his benefits, they must teach righteousness to their children, and they may entreat the Lord that the righteous not be swept away with the wicked in judgment. It became a fundamental idea among God's people to pray according to God's will; here, it was the will of God to destroy the wicked but to preserve the righteous.

It is interesting to note that, even though the cry of Sodom's sin was great, the Lord appeared willing to spare it for the sake of the righteous. Brueggemann suggests that God was free to break the death grip of the indictment-judgment scheme: "The capacity to break that scheme (which condemns us all and every city) is the substance of God's holiness. . . . God is not an indifferent or tyrannical distributor of rewards and punishments. Rather, God actively seeks a way out of death for us all" (*Genesis*, pp. 174–75). "Holiness" may not be the best word to use here, and this observation may need qualification. But the point is helpful: God was willing to spare even the wicked for the sake of the righteous. As Driver says, "The truth is established that the God of justice is also a God of mercy" (*Book of Genesis*, p. 196). We may say that the presence of the righteous in the world benefits the wicked because the justice of the Lord will not destroy the righteous with the wicked.

Bibliography

Ackroyd, P. R. "Hosea and Jacob." *VT* 13 (1963): 245–59.

Blenkinsopp, Joseph. "Abraham and the Righteous of Sodom." *JJS* 33 (1982): 119–32.

Brueggemann, W. "From Dust to Kingship." *ZAW* 84 (1972): 1–18.

Crenshaw, J. L. "Popular Questioning of the Justice of God in Ancient Israel." *ZAW* 82 (1970): 380–95.

Falk, Z. W. "Hebrew Legal Terms." *JSS* 5 (1960): 350–54.

Harrisville, Roy A. "God's Mercy—Tested, Promised, Done." *Interp* 31 (1977): 165–78.

Hoftijzer, J. "The Nominal Clause Reconsidered." *VT* 23 (1973): 446–510.

Rodd, C. S. "Shall Not the Judge of All the Earth Do What Is Just?" *Ext* 83 (1972): 137–39.

Ward, Ray Bowen. "The Works of Abraham." *HTR* 61 (1968): 283–90.

Weiss, A. "Some Problems of the Biblical 'Doctrine of Retribution.' " *Tar* 31 (1961–62): 236–63.

28

The Judgment of Sodom
(Gen. 19)

T his passage records the judgment of God on a morally
bankrupt Canaanite society, but in so recording it for Israel it also provides a stern warning against becoming like them. The reader is amazed
at the catastrophic judgment that God brought on the cities of the plain
but is also surprised at how difficult it was to get Lot and his family out
of Sodom, or to get the mentality of Sodom out of Lot's family.

Genesis 19 is an interlude in the narratives about Abraham, for the
patriarch is only briefly mentioned in verses 27–29. There the narrative
attributes the rescue of Lot to Abraham's plea not to destroy the righteous with the wicked. This passage, then, parallels chapter 14, for both
center on Sodom and its sister cities, and both attribute the rescue of
Lot to Abraham.

The passage lends itself to a comparison with the other major catastrophic judgment in Genesis, the flood (6:1–9:17). In the first part of
the story Lot stands in contrast to the wicked men of his generation,
which corresponds to Noah's being a righteous man in his wicked world.
Lot's righteousness is not stressed as Noah's was, but he was the righteous inhabitant of the city and would be delivered before the judgment.
In the second part of the chapter Lot received the announcement of the

coming destruction, which corresponds to 6:11–22. Unlike Noah, Lot was not able to convince his whole family that the warning was serious. In the third part there is some discussion over the deliverance of the family, but this element has no counterpart in the story of the flood. In the fourth part, the narrative describes the great conflagration, which reflects 7:6–12. Chapter 19 also has the report about Abraham (vv. 27–29), joining the passage to the Abrahamic stories. And finally, the episode of Lot and his daughters in the cave ends the chapter; this section goes far beyond the account of the sin of Noah's drunkenness.

Critical commentators may be led by these comparisons to suspect that the original tale of the destruction of the cities must have been universal in its scope, but as it was connected with Lot, it was restricted to the cities of the region of the Jordan. This view is supported, in part, by the observation that Lot's daughters in the cave thought they were the last survivors on earth. Coats recognizes that this reconstruction lacks convincing support (*Genesis*, p. 147). Westermann allows for some historical basis to the report: "It follows from the study of the form that the core of the tradition, the account of the annihilation of the cities of Sodom and Gomorrah, was autonomous and independent of the Abraham story, which had its origin in the experience of a catastrophe that actually happened" (*Genesis*, vol. 2, p. 299). This great catastrophe, the text explains, was a judgment from God on the wicked cities, and the escape of Lot from that judgment was the Lord's deliverance of the righteous in response to Abraham's concern.

Theological Ideas

The basic themes in this chapter are destruction and deliverance—the two counterbalance each other and retain the tension of the narrative, as in the account of the flood (ibid., p. 297). In its emphasis on destruction, the story provided Israel with a clear indication of what God thought of the wickedness of the Canaanites. The passage served as a harbinger of the judgment to come, especially, for example, in the battle of Jericho (Josh. 6) or in the battle against Sisera (Judg. 5:19–22). That the judgment was just is self-evident from the story.

Balancing the theme of judgment is the emphasis on the deliverance of the righteous—although the chapter never so describes Lot or his family. What is amazing in the rescue theme is their resistance—the family would rather not go. At the heart of the tension was the family's assimilation into the life of Sodom, as the final episode in the cave illustrates. Israel had to be warned again and again against the folly of living as the Canaanites did.

A number of other theological ideas will also surface in the exposition: the visitation of angels, the striking of oppressors with blindness, the sinfulness of Sodom and the attitudes of Lot's family toward moral impurity, and the incestuous origin of Israel's perennial enemies.

Structure and Synthesis

Structure

The passage falls into several distinct sections that trace the progress of the narrative through the tension to its resolution, only to find the creation of a further tension. The first section deals with the visit of the angels and their announcement of imminent destruction (vv. 1–14). This section includes several speeches and their responses, first of the host to the visitors, then between the host and the people of the city, then between the visitors and the host, and then between the host and his family. Westermann traces the comparison between the first eleven verses and the account in Judges 19:15–25, for there is a good deal of agreement between the two passages in structure, construction, and word usage (see chart 18).

The story in Judges 19 continues with the judgment pronounced on the city where the crime was committed, and Genesis 19 continues with the destruction of the wicked cities. Emphasis on the deliverance of the individual is missing from Judges 19. Westermann observes that the Genesis story is closer to the narratives of the primeval period in that God brings the judgment, whereas in Judges 19, a historical narrative from the early period of the settlement, people exact the punishment.

The second section of Genesis 19 reports the rescue, telling how the angels almost had to drag Lot and his family out of the city (vv. 15–22). This section includes dialogue as well: instructions, objections, concessions, further instructions, and then a commemorative naming.

The third section describes how the Lord destroyed the entire area and how Lot's wife perished (vv. 23–29). It also explains how Abraham

Chart 18. **Parallels Between Genesis 19 and Judges 19**

Incident	Genesis 19	Judges 19
Arrival and reception	1–3	15–21
Attack and repulse of attack	4–11	22–25
Attack, demand to hand over	4–5	22
Offer by householder	6–8	23–24
Rejection and threat	9	25a
Repulse of attack by guests	10–11	25b

stood in relation to the catastrophe and the rescue of Lot, verse 29 providing a summary statement for the narrative so far.

A fourth section, should it be included in the exposition, concerns the episode in the cave (vv. 30–38). The structure of this section is symmetrical: there is an explanation of the situation, a decision, the execution of the decision by the elder daughter, then by the younger, and then the result. The section concludes with the report of the births and the namings.

While the structure of the story traces a development of events, it also portrays the character of Lot. The dialogues and the narrative reports contrast him with Abraham as well as with the angels. Lot is first a hypocrite, then a buffoon (as Coats describes him), and then passive (see chart 19).

The passage is so rich in its description of Lot that the exposition could construct a character sketch to introduce the material. The following suggestion illustrates how contemporary such a sketch could appear:

Genuine faith is often hard to detect.

Here was an upright citizen, hospitable and generous, a leader of the community who was a judge—meaning that he would screen out wickedness from his town and advise on good living. He knew truth and justice, righteousness and evil. He was nicknamed the Censor.

Yet, in spite of his denunciation of the lifestyle of his people, he preferred the good life of their society. He preferred living comfortably in the city to living in the hills, where there might be no filthy living—but no good life either.

The hour of truth came when the Lord interrupted this life. His true loyalty was revealed as godly—but in the process his past hypocrisy was uncovered. The Saint had pitched his tent near the evil city, but the evil

Chart 19. **Contrasts in the Behavior of the Angels and Lot**

The Angels	Lot
The angels were reluctant to dwell in Sodom.	Lot begged the angels to stay with him.
The angels struck the wicked people with blindness and warned Lot.	Lot tried to warn the wicked people but appeared to be a mocker; he tried to offer his daughters.
The angels dragged Lot and his family out, warning them to flee to the mountains.	Lot lingered in Sodom and then, for a concession, pleaded for Zoar in the mountains.
The angels rescued the righteous so that the Lord could destroy the corrupt cities.	Lot escaped in fear, but his wife was destroyed; Lot's corruption in the cave preserved the evil of Sodom.

city had controlled his life. Oh, he was moral. He knew great, great evil when he saw it—he opposed sodomy and homosexuality. Ironically, though, he would sacrifice his daughters' virginity to fend off the vice of evil men. He would escape the judgment by the grace of God, but his heart had become part of this world. His wife was just too attached to the city to follow the call of grace, and his daughters were not uncomfortable with immorality with their father.

Hypocrisy was revealed by the visitation from on high. As long as the Lord left him alone, he would hold to his faith but live in Sodom. Ultimately, he could not have both; Sodom would destroy him if the Lord did not destroy Sodom.

Summary Message

When the Lord destroyed the cities of the plain with fire and brimstone, he delivered Lot by means of two angels who had to protect themselves from the wicked people of the city, drag the reluctant Lot from the doomed place, and agree to give him a little town in the hills—a place that subsequently proved to be the birthplace of the ancestors of the Moabites and Ammonites.

Exegetical Outline

I. When the angels visited Lot in Sodom, they repelled the threat from the wicked townspeople by striking them with blindness and warned Lot to gather his family and flee from the doomed city (1–14).

A. Visitation: The angels visited Lot, who received them with hospitality (1–3).

B. Protection: The angels prevented the wickedness of the townspeople by striking them with blindness (4–11).

1. Challenge: The men of the town wanted Lot to give them the visitors in order that they might know them (4–5).

2. Counteroffer: Lot offered his two virgin daughters in their place (6–8).

3. Renewed challenge: The men of the town ridiculed Lot's hypocrisy and pressed harder for the men (9).

4. Prevention: The angels struck the men with blindness (10–11).

C. Announcement: The angels announced their mission to Sodom and warned Lot to flee with his family (12–14).

1. The angels announced the destruction of the city and warned Lot to flee (12–13).

2. Lot appeared to his sons-in-law to be a hypocrite and a mocker (14).

II. When the angels dragged the hesitating Lot from the doomed
city, they agreed to spare the little town of Zoar for him (15–22).
   A. The angels had to drag Lot out of the city when he hesitated
      at their exhortation to flee (15–16).
   B. The angels granted Lot the little town of Zoar when he ne-
      gotiated for the concession before fleeing for his life (17–22).
III. When the Lord destroyed the cities with fire and brimstone—
and Lot's wife who looked back—he spared Lot for the sake of
Abraham (23–29).
   A. The Lord destroyed the cities and everything in them with
      a great conflagration (23–25).
   B. Lot's wife perished when she looked back to the city (26).
   C. The Lord delivered Lot for Abraham's sake (27–29).
      1. Abraham saw the great destruction from far away (27–28).
      2. The Lord remembered Abraham and delivered Lot (29).
IV. Epilogue: The daughters of Lot, thinking that they were the last
survivors on earth, arranged to be impregnated by their father
and consequently produced the ancestors of the Moabites and
Ammonites, Israel's perennial enemies (30–38).
   A. Setting: Lot and his two daughters left Zoar to dwell in the
      cave because they were afraid (30).
   B. Scheme: The daughters of Lot, realizing that there were no
      husbands, succeeded in becoming impregnated by their fa-
      ther (31–36).
   C. Significance: The sons that were born to them were the
      ancestors of the Moabites and the Ammonites (37–38).

Development of the Exposition

I. God warns his people that he will destroy their world because of its grievous sin (1–14).

A. God sends his messengers to the wicked cities (1–3).

The first fourteen verses are concerned with God's sending a warning
to his people that a swift and just judgment was coming. The narrative
begins with the report of the angels' encountering Lot in the gate (where
judges sat). In analyzing these beginning verses the expositor needs to
compare Lot with Abraham (18:1–8). Lot also showed great hospitality
by encouraging the visitors to spend the night in his residence. The
angels would have preferred to lodge in the street, perhaps hesitating
because of the evil reputation of Sodom.

The visitors eventually turned in to Lot's dwelling when he pressed
them further (v. 3). The verb "pressed" (*pāṣar*) foreshadows the pressing

in of the men of the city in verse 9: Lot pressed them to stay, but the men of the city pressed them for their vile pursuits. By such devices the narrative begins to contrast Lot and his world.

B. The wicked seek to corrupt God's messengers (4–11).

The expositor must capture the growing tension through the narrative until the great judgment. It begins to mount with the report that the men of the city sought out the visitors for their vile purposes ("that we might know them" [$w^e n\bar{e} d^{e^c} \hat{a}$ '$\bar{o} t \bar{a} m$], in v. 5). The theme of evil in Genesis takes a violent and repulsive turn in this account (note the motif expressed in the verb in v. 7: "do not do so wickedly" [$t \bar{a} r \bar{e}^c \hat{u}$]).

Along with the building tension the exposition should point up the contrasts as well. At first Lot contrasted sharply with the men of Sodom (v. 7), but in his alternative offer he appeared to be a hypocrite (v. 8). The men wanted to exploit the visitors sexually, and Lot was willing to sacrifice his two daughters' virginity instead. Ironically, Lot offered them his daughters to do whatever seemed "good" ($t \hat{o} b$) in their eyes, but even this perverted good was rejected by those bent on evil. At this moment of crisis the angels rescued Lot; they stretched out their hands and pulled Lot inside (cf. v. 16, where they seized him and his family by the hand and dragged him out of the city) and then struck the men with blindness, so that they were not able to find the door.

The picture thus begins to emerge of Lot as a man who had some righteous standards but who was ready to sacrifice the intimacy of the family. His actions led to his rejection as a foreigner by the people whom he had chosen for neighbors (Coats, *Genesis*, p. 144). Consequently, Lot became helpless in the midst of the vile society he had embraced. According to von Rad,

> It is therefore a bit comical when this heroic gesture [Lot's attempt to buy off the men] quickly collapses and the one who intended to protect the heavenly beings is himself protected when they quickly draw him back into the house and strike his assailants with a miraculous blindness. [*Genesis*, p. 219]

C. God's messengers warn of the judgment that is coming (12–14).

The visitors now delivered their message of judgment with a sense of urgency, for the wickedness of the city was every bit as great as the cry had indicated. The expositor should note that the verb used in verse 13 for "destroy" is the same that was used in reference to the flood ($\check{s} \bar{a} \hbar a t$, used twice in the verse). Here its object is "this place," that is, wicked Sodom. The motif of "their cry" ($\d{s} a^c \bar{a} q \bar{a} t \bar{a} m$) is repeated from 18:21—

it was an accusing cry, the crime crying out for judgment (cf. 4:10, where Abel's blood was crying out from the ground). In contrast to the message of blessing that the visitors gave to Abraham, the message of the visitors to Sodom is one of judgment: "The LORD has sent us to destroy it [*lᵉšaḥătāh*]."

When Lot attempted to relay the message to his family, he betrayed another difficulty that resulted from his ambiguity in Sodom—he seemed like a mocker (*mᵉṣaḥēq*) to them. This verb (*ṣāḥaq*) figures prominently in the stories about the birth of Isaac with the motif of laughing and significantly in Genesis 21:9, where Ishmael was mocking Isaac. The point here is that Lot's sons-in-law did not take him seriously. The motif of Sarah's laughter (18:12) may be reflected here; but whereas she had laughed only at a word from the Lord that promised a gracious provision of life, they mocked a word from the Lord that warned of death.

II. The influence of the world is alluring to the believer but contemptible to God (15–22).

A. God's messengers must drag the worldly believer from the evil city (15–16).

With the second major section the urgency of the story is rekindled. The angels implored the family to get out quickly, lest they should be destroyed ("swept away," *pen-tissāpeh*; see 18:23 for the use of the same verb in Abraham's concern that the righteous not be destroyed with the wicked). But Lot lingered (*wayyitmahmāh*; note the uses of the verb *māhah*, "to linger, tarry, wait"). The exposition can thus demonstrate how much Sodom had become a part of Lot. Kidner says appropriately, "Not even brimstone will make a pilgrim of him" (*Genesis*, p. 135). The angels thus seized them by their hands and took them out of the city.

Important to this section is the little explanatory clause "the Lord being merciful [*bᵉḥemlat YHWH*] to him." A study of the usage of this word and its cognates will show that it stresses a compassion that leads to delivering or sparing from danger.

B. The worldly believer wrings a concession from the messengers (17–22).

Even as the moment of judgment drew near, Lot negotiated with the messengers of the Lord for a little city. In this incident we have another contrast between Abraham and his nephew: Abraham had unselfishly interceded for Sodom, but Lot pleaded for a little city for himself. Lot thought that, if the Lord was going to destroy Sodom, then perhaps he would grant him something in consolation. Lot's prayer, if we may call it that, has all the appropriate expressions: he acknowledged that they

had shown him grace (*ḥēn*) and magnified loyal love (*ḥesed*) toward him
by saving him; but he also feared that evil (*hārāʾâ*) would befall him and
he would die. He thus asked for refuge in Zoar.

The text includes a little etymological play on the name Zoar (*ṣôʿar*)
to heighten the idea that Lot thought he was not asking for much. The
etymology of Zoar given here, "a little one" (*miṣʿār*), was used to enhance
the humble nature of the request. Conversely, it remained in Israel's
memory as a witness to Lot, who lingered and negotiated, even as he
was being dragged to safety.

III. God will preserve the righteous from the destruction of their world (23–29).

A. The Lord finally destroys the wicked in their place (23–26).

In a few short lines the expected catastrophe is narrated, and the
tension of the story subsides. The expositor will probably consider some
of the suggestions that have been offered for the conflagration of fire and
brimstone. The text, however, simply emphasizes that, whatever means
were used, it was the Lord who rained this judgment on them (note the
beginning construction of v. 24: "Now the LORD" [*waYHWH*]). Everything associated with the evil society was overthrown, even Lot's wife,
who gazed intently (< *nābaṭ*) back toward the city. The interpretive word
of the catstrophe is "overthrew" (*hāpak*)—by the fire and brimstone the
Lord overthrew the entire area (the mention of *kol-hakkikkār*, "all the
plain," in v. 25 recalls Lot's choice in chap. 13). Quickly it was reduced
to ruin (see the earlier *šāḥat*), and Lot's wife to a monument of
disobedience.

B. When the Lord destroys the wicked he remains faithful to the righteous (27–29).

Within this last section of the main narrative, verse 29 serves as a
summary: "When God destroyed [*bᵉšaḥēt*] the cities of the region, God
remembered [*wayyizkōr*] Abraham and sent Lot out of the midst of the
destruction [*hahăpēkâ*] when he destroyed [*bahăpōk*] the cities." In
sparing Lot (see the use of *ḥāmal* in v. 16), the Lord was remembering
Abraham's intercession. The verb *zākar*, "remember," is important in
terms of God's covenantal faithfulness and warrants some examination
in the study of this verse (cf. 8:1a). Sodom was evil enough to be destroyed, but the Lord was faithful to his promise to Abraham and spared
"righteous Lot" (2 Peter 2:7–8).

Bush draws a parallel between this deliverance through intercession
and the final deliverance at the end of the age.

In the fearful catastrophe of the last day, when a favored countless multitude shall be seen emerging and soaring to the mountains of salvation from the midst of a still more countless multitude left to their fate in the flames of a burning world, their deliverance shall be owing to the efficacy of his prevalent intercession and atoning blood. [*Notes*, vol. 1, pp. 329–30]

IV. Those who have grown comfortable in the wicked city may retain its corruption (30–38).

If this last section is included in the exposition, it will provide an afterthought to the narrative proper, showing that, even after the destruction of Sodom, the mentality of Sodom remained. Even though the writer does not explicitly condemn the incestuous relationships as evil, it is clear that the connection between the Moabites and the Ammonites and the corruption of Sodom is enough to cast the whole episode in a bad light. By recording this incestuous origin of the tribes the writer has described their nature.

The story is clear enough. Faced with the appearance of extinction after the catastrophic judgment, Lot's daughters devised a plan by which they would be able to continue their family's line. Coats accurately describes the nature of Lot in this story:

The impact of the unit focuses more directly on a characterization of the father. The one who offered his daughters for the sexual gratification of his wicked neighbors now becomes the object of his daughters' incestuous relationship. If the story in 19:1–29 represents Lot as a buffoon, a passive object whose retardation in the movement of the story appears somewhat comic, then the same buffoonery certainly returns here. Lot not only reverses the direction of his fear, v. 30, but in the hills loses his sensibilities to the wiles of his daughters. To be seduced by one's own daughters into an incestuous relationship with pregnancy following is bad enough. Not to know that the seduction had occurred is worse. To fall prey to the whole plot a second time is worse than ever. [*Genesis*, p. 147]

The significance of the story is bound up in the popular etymologies on the names at the end of the chapter. The one child is called Moab (*mô'āb*), a play on the word "father," as if the name meant "from our father" (*mē'ābînû*). The name was probably derived from an unknown root *m'b* rather than from a compound word (*min* + *'āb*). But it lent itself to the interpretive play to reflect the incident. The name of the second child, Ben-Ammi (*ben-'ammî*), also reflects such a play. Besides the common meaning "people," the word *'am* can also mean "kinsman."

This meaning would fit the context by forming a parallel idea with 'āb, "father." Both sons were named after being fathered by Lot; Moab was the son of their father, and Ben-Ammi was the son of the nearest kinsman.

The ambiguity of these ancient names provided the narrator with the motifs that he needed to make his point. Zimmermann writes: "It could be further explained to all those who were curious to hear that Ben Ammi as a name must have been quite appealing to Lot's daughter because she could employ it quite playfully for her son, diplomatically for her father, and innocently before strangers" ("Folk Etymology," p. 320). With the name Moab, however, there is a phonetic word play within the narrative (v. 34); yet, the name would retain its ambiguity apart from the story.

This report provided Israel with a glimpse into the origin and nature of their rivals, the Moabites and the Ammonites. The writer could develop a feeling of disdain for these tribes by including this account. The story justified the belief that lewdness (Num. 25) and the lack of natural feeling (2 Kings 3:26–27)—which appear to be fundamental to the character of both nations—were inherited from their ancestors. Moreover, the connection of the story to the judgment of Sodom prompted the proper response to such characteristics.

Four major themes surface in this chapter: the Lord's swift judgment on the vile Canaanites of Sodom, the close attachment that Lot had for the wicked society, the merciful sparing of Lot and his family from the destruction, and the rebirth of Sodom in the cave.

The exposition could be correlated with the teachings on the final eschatological judgment of the world, when the Lord of the harvest sends his angels to rescue the wheat and burn the tares (Matt. 13:30), but it must not exclude the historical point that this was a destruction by God in time, not at the end of time. The exposition must thus be concerned with how God destroyed wickedness in the world through catastrophic judgments and how these individual acts of judgment foreshadowed the final judgment. Today the church does not need a visit from angels to warn of coming judgment, for that announcement has already been recorded in God's revelation. The instruction can then focus on the preparation for that day, using Lot as the sample of the hypocritical and worldly individual who will be rescued, but not altogether willingly.

There are two expository ideas that come to mind for this passage: (1) *Love not the world, neither the things that are in the world, for the world and its lusts await the sudden, swift judgment of God;* (2) *it is dangerous folly to become attached to the present corrupt world system because it awaits God's swift and sudden destruction (and it will infect our life and jeopardize our future).* Either one would serve to capture the essence of the message of Genesis 19 and relate it to the New Testament teachings on the same theme.

Jesus used this story to warn of the destruction to come on Israel, as he urged people to "remember Lot's wife" (Luke 17:32). Jesus warned against looking back as she did and becoming entombed where she stood. Her heart was apparently in Sodom. Driver says that she is the type of those who look back with "regretful longings upon possessions and enjoyments which are inconsistent with the salvation offered to them" (*Book of Genesis*, p. 202). One may say that, if people crave the best of this world along with the world to come, they may receive neither. One's loves often betray one's loyalties.

Jesus also made it clear that, if his miracles had been done in Sodom, those people would have repented. As it was, it would be more tolerable for Sodom in the day of judgment than for the cities of Galilee (Matt. 11:20–24). This passage teaches that the judgment of ancient Sodom was not their final judgment. It also reveals that God judges according to knowledge and that there are degrees of punishment in his judgment. Although the subject of divine judgment on sinners is not a popular one, the biblical record affirms that divine judgment is just.

Israel would learn from this chapter that God judges a people severely only because of their great wickedness. But Israel would also be warned of the folly of becoming too attached to the wickedness of Canaan, for such wickedness cried out for swift judgment.

How should one live, then, knowing how God will judge the corrupt world? The point was clear to Israel; it should be clear today. No good can come of loving a society so morally bankrupt that it awaits the swift judgment of God—if not in a temporal judgment, certainly at the end of the age.

Bibliography

Alexander, T. Desmond. "Lot's Hospitality: A Clue to His Righteousness." *JBL* 104 (1985): 289–300.

Baumgarten, Albert. "A Note on the Book of Ruth." *JANES* 5 (1973): 11–15.

Cassuto, U. "Hosea and the Pentateuch." In *Biblical and Oriental Studies*, vol. 1, *Bible*, pp. 79–100 (esp. pp. 80–82). Jerusalem: Magnes, 1973.

Fensham, F. C. "The Obliteration of the Family as Motif in the Near Eastern Literature." *AION*, n.s., 10 (1969): 191–99.

————. "Salt as Curse in the Old Testament and the Ancient Near East." *BA* 25 (1962): 48–50.

Gevirtz, S. "Jericho and Shechem: A Religio-Literary Aspect of City Destruction." *VT* 13 (1963): 52–62.

Harland, J. Penrose. "The Destruction of the Cities of the Plain." *BA* 6 (1943): 41–54.

————— . "Sodom and Gomorrah: The Location of the Cities of the Plain." *BA* 5 (1942): 17–32.

Lods, A. "La caverne de Lot." *RHR* 95 (1927): 204–19.

Miller, P. D. "Fire in the Mythology of Canaan and Israel." *CBQ* 27 (1965): 256–61.

Mitchell, T. C. "The Meaning of the Noun ḥtn in the Old Testament." *VT* 19 (1969): 93–112.

Reider, J. "Etymological Studies: ידע or ידע and דעע." *JBL* 66 (1947): 315–17.

Roth, Wolfgang. "What of Sodom and Gomorrah? Homosexual Acts in the Old Testament." *Explor* 1 (1975): 7–14.

Shalem, M. "Earthquakes in Jerusalem" (in Hebrew). *Jerusalem* 2 (1949): 22–54.

Sutcliffe, E. F. "Simultaneity in Hebrew, A Note on 1 Kings 1:41." *JSS* 3 (1958): 80–81.

Van Zyl, A. H. *The Moabites*. Leiden: E. J. Brill, 1960.

Zimmermann, Frank. "Folk Etymology of Biblical Names." *VTS* 15 (1966): 311–26.

29

The Preservation of the Purity of the Marriage
(Gen. 20)

Throughout the Abrahamic narratives threats to the promise frequently arise. Now, just on the eve of the fulfillment of the promise, such a threat appears again. It is a variation of an old theme; just as before, so here, unless God providentially intervened in the matter, everything would be lost. Once again Abraham passed his wife off as his sister, and once again she was taken by a powerful ruler for a wife; this time, however, it was the ruler of Gerar within the land promised to Abraham.

This story conveys the message of God's providential protection of his covenant people, but the emphasis is on preserving the purity of marriage. God had a plan for Abraham and Sarah, and it was foolish for them to jeopardize it with this deception. Their participation in God's promised blessings demanded their preservation from corruption or impurity.

This account is parallel to, but not exactly the same as, the former incident (12:10–20). Here there is a greater development toward theological interpretation by the writer. The exposition must capitalize on these insights within the narrative, for while the chapter has a plot and a story line, its theological emphases form the message.

Theological Ideas

The predominant theological motif seems to be the tension between life and death. At the center of the story is the warning that Abimelech is a dead man because he has taken another man's wife. The king was warned that, if he did not return the woman, he would surely die. The seventh commandment from the law thus figures prominently in the interest of the narrative. Developing out of this tension is the king's plea of innocence: he asked whether the Lord would slay a righteous man. The resolution came with the Lord's instructions for Abraham to pray for the king so that he might live. Along with the clear mention of life and death, there is the subtle indication of the Lord's power over life by his closing up the wombs of the women of Gerar and then opening them again. The story makes it very clear that life is in the hand of God, and for any violations God can interrupt life or the life-giving process.

This entire issue came about because of Abraham's and Sarah's deception. Here again we have the theological point that deception jeopardized the blessing but that the Lord intervened to preserve his plan.

The narrative is also about guilt and innocence. Abimelech found himself in trouble because of his violation of another man's marriage, even though he was innocent. His plea of innocence matches those found later in the ritual of Israel—he had done it in the integrity of his heart and the innocence of his hands. Even though his claim to innocence was acknowledged by the Lord, it was still necessary for restitution to be made to maintain integrity before all concerned. The Abimelech-Abraham dialogue, an inquiry followed by a self-defense, develops the motif of Abimelech's innocence in the face of a potential punishment of death for guilt.

Structure and Synthesis

Structure

This narrative is largely made up of dialogue, interspersed with narrative reports (vv. 1–2, 8, 14, 17–18). After a short report that tells of the complication (vv. 1–2), there is dialogue between the Lord and Abimelech through a dream in which the Lord warned of the violation. Abimelech made his self-defense, and the Lord acknowledged his integrity and gave him instructions for clearing himself of guilt (vv. 3–7). Next is the dialogue between Abimelech and Abraham, in which Abimelech made his accusation and Abraham his self-defense (vv. 9–13). The final set of speeches belongs to Abimilech, in which he invited Abraham to dwell in his land and explained the matter to Sarah (vv. 15–16). Most of the dialogue is concerned with the question of blame that lies behind the complication, but in the end the situation was made right and the king exonerated. At the end of the story Abraham and Sarah stand rebuked for their deception as well as their lack of faith that the fear of the Lord could protect them in Gerar.

Summary Message

When Abimelech took Sarah into his harem because of Abraham's deception, God intervened to preserve Sarah's purity, warning Abimelech to restore the woman to her husband, make restitution for the offense, and ask for intercession from Abraham the prophet.

Exegetical Outline

    I. Complication: Abimelech took Sarah into his household when Abraham said she was his sister (1–2).

   II. Intervention: God alerted Abimelech in a dream that he had taken another man's wife and, acknowledging the integrity of Abimelech's actions, instructed him to restore her to her husband (3–7).

     A. Accusation: God informed Abimelech that he was under the sentence of death because he had taken another man's wife (3).

     B. Self-defense: Abimelech protested that he had acted with integrity in the matter (4–5).

     C. Instruction: Acknowledging Abimelech's integrity and stating that he had prevented him from sinning, God instructed the king to restore the woman to her husband and ask him to intercede for him (6–7).

       1. God had prevented Abimelech from sinning because he knew that the man had acted in integrity (6).

       2. God instructed Abimelech to restore the woman to Abraham, who would pray for the king (7a).

       3. God warned that, if Abimelech did not restore her, he would surely die (7b).

  III. Vindication: Abimelech immediately obeyed God's instructions by restoring Sarah to her husband and making restitution to this couple who had brought him into great danger (8–16).

     A. Narrative transition: Abimelech reported this message to his household (8).

     B. Accusation: Abimelech remonstrated with Abraham over

the deception that brought a great sin on him and his nation (9–10).
C. Self-defense: Abraham explained his fear of death at their hands, adding that Sarah was indeed his half-sister (11–13).
D. Restitution: Abimelech restored Sarah to Abraham, making payment for the offense and granting permission to live in the land (14–16).
1. Abimelech gave Abraham a large payment to make restitution for taking Sarah (14).
2. Abimelech gave Abraham permission to dwell in the land (15).
3. Abimelech gave payment of silver for Sarah and explained it in a rebuke to her (16).
IV. Intercession: Abraham interceded for the house of Abimelech, so that the divine judgment was withdrawn (17–18).

Development of the Exposition

I. The foolish acts of God's people may jeopardize God's program (1–2).

The first two verses set out the complication. Kidner observes that "on the brink of Isaac's birth-story here is the very Promise put in jeopardy, traded away for personal safety. If it is ever to be fulfilled, it will owe very little to man. Morally as well as physically, it will clearly have to be achieved by the grace of God" (*Genesis*, p. 137). Besides the motifs of deception and the taking of the woman (see the comments for 12:10–20), there is the setting for this story in Gerar. The patriarchal connection with this place runs through chapter 21 and then is repeated in chapter 26, when Isaac reestablished the dwelling place there. A word play in verse 1 strengthens this point: "and [Abraham] sojourned [*wayyāgor*] in Gerar [*bigrār*]." The verb of the word play is repeated at the end of the Abraham-Abimelech cycle in 21:34 (*wayyāgor*).

II. God must intervene to preserve his program when his people jeopardize it with foolish deception (3–7).

A. God warns of the punishment for committing adultery (3).

In Genesis 12, God delivered Abram from Egypt with great plagues; here he warned Abimelech in a dream to set Sarah free. Both deliverances preserved the purity of Sarah and safeguarded the promise. The first incident was outside the land and reflected more closely the life-and-death struggle of the nation in Egypt, as God saved them alive and delivered them through mighty plagues. But this passage reports an event in the land promised to the patriarch, demonstrating that God would continue to preserve his people even after settlement and instructing Israel about the importance of preserving their purity there as well. In this chapter God also intervened directly—he controlled birth, closing wombs and then opening them again. If Abraham had fully realized God's power, he would have preserved his integrity without fear of what Abimelech might do. No mere human potentate could thwart God's plan (cf. Ps. 2).

The Word of God came to Abimelech in a warning dream (cf. Gen. 31:24). The communication is striking in its suddenness: "You are a dead man [hinn⁽ᵉ⁾kā mēt] because of the woman you have taken, for she is another man's wife [w⁽ᵉ⁾hî᾽ b⁽ᵉ⁾ʿulat bāʿal]." The inevitability of Abimelech's death is pointed out with the particle hinnēh and explained by the causal clauses that follow. In addition, the choice of words that describe Sarah as Abraham's wife underscores the barriers of such a relationship—she is the possession of her owner. To abduct a married woman was to destroy another man's home.

B. Those who are innocent may protest their integrity (4–5).

The response of Abimelech shows that he was, contrary to Abraham's fears, a God-fearing individual. He had been implicated in a guilty offense by Abraham's deception and so protested his case to God. Such is the right and the responsibility of all who may be accused of a crime or who are in danger of committing such a crime.

Abimelech's initial response recalls the justice of God so thoroughly probed in chapter 18: "Lord, will you slay also a righteous nation [hăgôy gam-ṣaddîq tahărōg]?" It had earlier been established that God would not destroy the righteous with the wicked. Similarly, Abimelech appealed to God's justice before making his defense.

Such declarations of innocence may be found in the psalms. Most striking in its comparison is Psalm 24:4, which records the liturgy at the gate. In response to the question concerning admission at the gate, the psalmist requires that those who wish to ascend the temple mount have "clean hands and a pure heart [n⁽ᵉ⁾qî kappayim ûbar-lēbāb]." Here Abimelech protested his innocence by saying, "In the integrity of my heart and the innocence of my hands [b⁽ᵉ⁾tām-l⁽ᵉ⁾bābî ûb⁽ᵉ⁾niqyōn kappay] have I done this."

C. God instructs people how to preserve their integrity (6–7).

Two points need to be stressed here: God's acknowledgment of the king's integrity and his instruction to preserve it. The strengthened verb "I know" (᾽ānōkî yādaʿtî) and the repetition of "integrity of your heart"

(b^{e}tām-l^{e}bāb^{e}kā) form the substance of God's acknowledgment of his
innocence. God knew that Abimelech was blameless in his choice of
Sarah. Consequently, he did not allow Abimelech to sin against him
(mēḥāṭô-lî, "from sinning against me," rather than "from sinning against
her"). The means of this prevention is not fully explained in the text; at
this point the narrative simply reports that God did not allow him to
touch (lingōa') the woman.

Nevertheless, Abimelech was still in mortal danger. If he did not
restore the woman to her husband, he must know that he would surely
die (da' kî-môt tāmût). The expression recalls the warning against disobedience issued by the Lord God in the garden (Gen. 2:17). But even if
Abimelech did restore the wife to her husband, more was needed to
make things right. Abraham, designated here as the prophet (nābî'),
would pray for Abimelech so that he might live (w^{e}yitpallēl ba'adkā
weḥyēh). The expositor will have to spend some time on the relationship between the designation of Abraham as a prophet and this intercessory prayer. Abraham was distinguished here as a man of God, and
his intercession would be effectual in restoring things to their rightful
places.

This section of dialogue between Abimilech and God forms the central issue of the passage. The narrative report prior to it simply sets out
the circumstances that brought on the issue of guilt and innocence. The
remainder of the passage now traces how Abimelech made things right
and vindicated himself.

III. People must make restitution in order to demonstrate their integrity (8–16).

A. The uncovering of shameful acts brings reproach to God's program (8–13).

It would be effective to unite Abimelech's accusation and Abraham's
defense in the first section, for the two speeches together show how the
deception brought reproach to God's program in the eyes of this king.
Through it all, Abimelech appeared more righteous than Abraham. God
had not rebuked him but did give him the sternest of warnings not to
sin. But now Abimelech rebuked Abraham and Sarah through his prob-
ing questions and acts of restitution.

After a brief narrative transition in which Abimelech reported the
matter to his household, possibly to forewarn others, the account turns
to Abimelech's questions put to Abraham (vv. 9–10). The verbs "to do"
and "to sin" play a prominent role in the interrogation: "What have you
done ['āśîtā] to us? How have I offended you [ḥāṭā'tî] that you have
brought on me and my kingdom a great sin [ḥāṭā'â g^{e}dōlâ]? You have
done ['āśîtā] deeds [ma'aśîm] to me that ought not be done [yē'āśû]."

The violation was Abraham's; but that violation put Abimelech and his people into the place of guilt as well. Therefore, the expositor must examine the range of meanings for the verb "to sin" (ḥāṭāʾ) and its related nouns. For example, the teaching on the sin offering in Leviticus shows that even sins of ignorance required clearance and reparation before God was satisfied. Abimelech sensed the danger he was in, even though it was not brought on by his own intentional sin.

Abraham's self-defense had less to commend it than did Abimelech's self-defense before God. The latter could plead integrity at best and ignorance at the worst. But Abraham could explain his plan to deceive only as a means of self-protection, justifying it with the knowledge that Sarah was indeed his sister. Abraham's defense presupposed an acknowledgment of his guilt, and so all he could do was offer a plausible reason for his actions.

B. Making restitution demonstrates compliance with God's Word (14–16).

These verses confirm that Abimelech had integrity. He restored the woman in good conscience to her husband and made reparation payments to ensure release from the threat of death. Those who have integrity are eager to prove it by their actions. Such passages would prove instructive for Israel when they were confronted with the requirements of entrance into the sanctuary, requirements that called for full reparation as demonstration of their purity.

The reparation here involved the payment to Abraham of animals and servants, the permission to dwell wherever he pleased (ṭôb), and the payment of silver in Sarah's name. The statement of Abimelech to Sarah served as a rebuke and an explanation, for it was intended to preserve her honor as Abraham's wife—whom Abimelech referred to here as her "brother." The exact meaning of "the covering of eyes" is problematic; it may carry the idea of a justification of her honor in the eyes of those who would know of the situation.

IV. Full restoration comes through prayer (17–18).

Intercessory prayer was the divinely appointed means for having the barrenness removed, either in the family (cf. chaps. 16 and 25) or, as here, when inflicted by God as a preventive measure (for the Lord had completely closed [kî-ʿāṣōr ʿāṣar YHWH] the wombs). Abraham's deception had provided the occasion for the violation, but Abraham's God alone could restore life to its normal state. B. Jacob observes how this chapter prepares for the next: "God can certainly not refuse Abraham what he had given others through Abraham's intervention and could

Abraham show himself more worthy of a son than by asking the same for others?" (*First Book of the Bible*, p. 135).

After all was said and done, Abimelech would know two things about this man: he was a powerful man of God, but he had attempted to defend himself through deception. In such a situation Abimelech rightly did everything in his power to set things right.

God's prevention of an adulterous destruction of marriage was a didactic reinforcement of the commandment that Israel should prevent such. The meaning of this story goes beyond the idea of intermarriage with the Canaanites—a theme to be developed in the book—to that of adultery. To take the wife of another man, even if done innocently enough, is a life-and-death issue. God would not tolerate it. Nothing short of restitution and prayer would set things back to their normal conditions.

God required faith and obedience on the part of his people to fulfill the promised blessings. At times he had to intervene and protect his people from others as well as from themselves; at times his people lost out because he let their failures and schemes run their course. This little story warns: *God desires the purity of the marriages of his covenant people—preserve them; God withholds or grants children—fear him and live in integrity.* Preserving the purity of marriage involves fearing the Lord as well as maintaining integrity with others.

Bibliography

Aharoni, Y. "The Land of Gerar." *IEJ* 6 (1956): 26–32.

Greengus, Samuel. "Sisterhood Adoption at Nuzi and the 'Wife-Sister' in Genesis." *HUCA* 46 (1975): 5–31.

Moran, W. L. "The Scandal of the 'Great Sin' at Ugarit." *JNES* 18 (1959): 280–81.

Petersen, D. L. "A Thrice-told Tale: Genre, Theme, and Motif." *BibRes* 17 (1972): 30–43.

Rabinowitz, J. J. "The Great Sin in Ancient Egyptian Marriage Contract." *JNES* 18 (1959): 73.

Soggin, Alberto J. *Old Testament and Oriental Studies*, pp. 173ff. Rome: Biblical Institute Press, 1975.

Stoebe, H. J. "Gut und Böse in der jawwistischen Quelle des Pentateuch." *ZAW* 65 (1953): 188–204.

Vawter, B. "Intimations of Immortality and the Old Testament." *JBL* 91 (1972): 158–71.

Walker, N. "What Is a *Nabhi*?" *ZAW* 73 (1961): 99–100.

30

The Fulfillment of the Promise and the Removal of the Threat
(Gen. 21:1–21)

Genesis 21:1–21 tells of the long-awaited fulfillment of the promise of a son as well as the removal of the threat, real or perceived, from the child of the bondwoman Hagar. These sections belong together, even though it would be possible to treat them individually.

The first section, verses 1–7, may be classified as a birth report. The paragraph forms the culmination of the preceding narratives, especially those that include the motif of laughter. The connection comes with the very first verse, linking the fulfillment to the promise. But the fulfillment of the promise also lays the foundation for the crisis that follows.

The second section, verses 8–21, is a narrative report of the expulsion of Hagar and Ishmael. It is a continuation of the tension that surfaced in Genesis 16 rather than a doublet of it—there are too many differences. The tension now takes the form of Ishmael's posing a threat to the promised inheritance. The narrative stresses this issue by a word play on the theme of laughter, a word play that takes a troubling twist. The tension is resolved with the expulsion of Hagar and Ishmael and their subsequent rescue in the wilderness.

Theological Ideas

The prominent idea of the passage is the Lord's provision of the promised seed. The expositor must show how the birth report stresses that the birth fulfills God's Word, confirming that his Word is reliable. Even in the Word of the Lord that endorsed the expulsion of Ishmael, we find confirmation of the promise, for the Lord was ensuring that Isaac would be the heir.

On the human level we may make theological observations concerning how people respond to the fulfillment of the promise. On one side, we find great joy, renewed obedience, and concern for the future developments; on the other side, we realize that some may at the least detract from it, and at the most may oppose it. There is also the emphasis in the narrative on the Lord's protection and provision for the outcasts in the wilderness, another theme that began in the Genesis 16 story.

Structure and Synthesis

Structure

The structure of each section stresses the meaning. In the birth report (vv. 1–7) there is the narrator's initial report that the Lord fulfilled his Word (vv. 1–2). The repetition of the motif of the Lord's Word ("said ... spoken ... spoken") must not be missed in the exposition. Next comes the record of Abraham's compliance with the Word of the Lord—he named the child and circumcised him, as he had been commanded (vv. 3–4). This record of the patriarch ends with a notice of his age (v. 5). The final part of the birth report is the record of Sarah's announcement of joy over God's gift to her (vv. 6–7). This section displays a powerful unity through repeating the name Isaac and through recalling the theme of laughter.

Then, in the narrative of the expulsion (vv. 8–19), we find two crises, the second growing out of the first. There is the crisis of competition between Ishmael and Isaac (vv. 8–9), with its resolution by expulsion (10–13). Then there is the crisis of survival in the wilderness (vv. 14–16), with its resolution by God's provision (vv. 17–19). It is structurally significant that each resolution ends with an oracle from the Lord: in the first crisis, he instructed Abraham to listen to the voice of Sarah (šᵉmaʿ bᵉqōlāh) and send out Ishamel, promising to make him a nation (lᵉgôy ʾăśîmennû); in the second, he told Hagar that he had heard the voice of the lad (šāmaʿ ʾĕlōhîm ʾel-qôl hannaʿar), promising to make him into a great nation (lᵉgôy gādôl ʾăśîmennû).

The last two verses (20–21) provide a conclusion for the section.

Summary Message

When the Lord fulfilled his Word by providing Isaac, the child of promise, Abraham and Sarah responded with obedience and praise, but Ishmael became a threat to the promised heir, prompting his expulsion into the wilderness, where God provided for him and his mother.

Exegetical Outline

I. The Lord provided the child of promise to Abraham and to Sarah, who responded in faith by naming him Isaac, circumcising him according to the covenant, and praising God for this amazing fulfillment (1–7).
  A. The Lord fulfilled his promise by providing the child for Sarah and Abraham in their old age (1–2).
  B. Abraham obeyed God's Word by naming the child Isaac and by circumcising him (3–5).
  C. Sarah rejoiced over Isaac, God's gift of laughter to her (6–7).
II. God approved of Sarah's instinct to protect the child of promise by expelling Ishmael and Hagar and then provided for the outcasts when they were in distress in the wilderness (8–19).
  A. First crisis: Sarah realized that Ishmael posed a threat for the true heir (8–9).
  B. Resolution: With God's approval, Abraham and Sarah decided to send away the slave woman and her son (10–13).
    1. Sarah's speech: Sarah told Abraham to send them away (10).
    2. Abraham's response: The matter grieved Abraham (11).
    3. God's oracle: God approved the plan to protect Isaac, promising to fulfill his promises to Ishmael (12–13).
  C. Second crisis: When Hagar and Ishmael were sent out into the wilderness, they soon came to the point of perishing (14–16).
  D. Resolution: God rescued Hagar and Ishmael in the wilderness (17–19).
    1. God's oracle: God exhorted Hagar not to fear, for he had heard the cry and would fulfill his promise to Ishmael (17–18).
    2. God's provision: God directed them to water (19).
III. Epilogue: God was with Ishmael, and he prospered in the wilderness (20–21).

Development of the Exposition

I. The spontaneous response to the fulfillment of God's promises is renewed obedience and jubilation (1–7).

A. The Lord fulfills his promises at the appointed time (1–2).

The point to stress in the first two verses must be the fulfillment of the promise, or, to put it another way, the reliability of the Word of the Lord. Three times this point is stated to qualify the birth: "just as he had said" (ka'ăšer 'āmār), "as he had spoken" (ka'ăšer dibbēr), and "at the set time of which God had spoken to him" ('ăšer-dibber).

The first verb in the section also calls for some consideration. Traditionally translated "visited," pāqad here describes a divine intervention in someone's life that shapes or alters destiny. A survey of its range of usages will show that it can describe appointments to new positions, mustering of troops, intervening for blessing or for judgment, and a number of other activities as well (see appendix 4). It is significant in the Book of Genesis that this verb is used here to announce the fulfillment of the promise of the seed and then used again in 50:24 to announce the future fulfillment of the promised deliverance from Egypt: "God will surely visit [pāqōd yipqōd] you." In this context the verb pāqad signifies a divine intervention to bless Sarah, an intervention that would change the destiny of the people of God.

B. The fulfillment of the promise provides opportunity for obedience (3–5).

Here the exposition should stress the reintroduction of the motif of the name Isaac, for the name is repeated three times in the three verses. Note that, in conjunction with the repetition of the name yiṣḥāq, the qualification "his son" (benô) appears three times.

Both the naming of this son and the performance of the rite of circumcision were acts of obedience to the Lord's previous commands, a fact that the narrative report stresses: "just as God had commanded him [ka'ăšer ṣiwwâ 'ōtô 'ĕlōhîm]." This clause reflects the three earlier clauses: just as the Lord had provided the child in accordance with his Word, so too did Abraham circumcise that child in accordance with his Word.

C. The fulfillment of the promise prompts great rejoicing (6–7).

These two verses display how those who waited in great expectation for the fulfillment of the Lord's promise rejoiced when the time arrived. Here the expositor can develop again the theme of laughter, but now with a new turn. Sarah said, "God has made me to laugh [ṣeḥōq 'āśâ lî 'ĕlōhîm]; all who hear will laugh with me [yiṣḥaq-lî]." The child's name would be a reminder of God's faithfulness rather than of the parents' unbelief—although the latter would never be totally forgotten in the name. The word plays in this verse reflect the earlier naming motifs in chapters 17 and 18, but here they express the great jubilation of the mother over the birth and the anticipation of joy for all who hear about it. In contrast with the doubting laughter described in 18:12, Sarah's laughter here was full of praise and admiration for the Lord—she now was exonerated and could leave the former things behind.

It should not be too difficult to find corresponding passages for these ideas—passages that portray the joy and dedication of believers when God fulfills his promises. It would be helpful to list some of the promises that God has made to his people down through the ages and show how their fulfillment brought great joy. For the New Testament writers, the coming of the promised seed, Jesus Christ, paralleled the birth of Isaac as no other fulfilled promise could. With the long-awaited and supernatural birth of this greater Seed came a far greater visitation from on high (Gal. 3:19; Luke 1:68).

II. The necessary response to opposition to God's program is the removal of the threat (8–21).

A. God approves the removal of the threat to the promise (8–13).

The interpretation of the first crisis, the threat from Ishmael, involves some careful exegetical work in the text. The motif of laughter (ṣᵉḥōq) has already been introduced in the jubilation of Sarah over the birth (v. 6). That laughter was the display of gratitude and astonishment at how God kept his Word to provide the promised heir. But in verse 9 the text reports that Ishmael was mocking (mᵉṣaḥēq, the piel participle from the same root). What exactly Ishmael was doing is not clear. The commentaries follow either the traditional view that Ishmael was mocking the young child or the view that Ishmael was simply playing with Isaac on equal footing and that Sarah perceived a threat in that relationship. The meaning may lie somewhere in between these two interpretations.

The usage of the word mᵉṣaḥēq in Genesis proves helpful. It was used in 19:14 to describe Lot as he attempted to warn his family—he seemed a mocker or jester; it occurs in 26:8 to describe Isaac's conjugal playing with Rebekah; it appears in 39:14 and 17 in Potiphar's wife's accusation of Joseph as one who trifled, or mocked them. In each case the verb describes an activity that had been misinterpreted: the words of Lot seemed to differ from his previous words, the actions of Isaac showed a different relationship with his "sister," and in the false accusation Joseph's alleged rape differs from his good behavior. Also in the "playing" of Ishmael with Isaac, another attitude may have been very visible to Sarah.

We may also note that the verb is used in Exodus 32:6 for the "playing" of the people in the camp when Moses was on the mountain, and in Judges 16:25 when the Philistines brought out the blinded Samson to entertain or play for them. In all the uses there is the idea of a less-than-serious toying with someone, a trifling with someone or something, and possibly a deceptive play that could prove harmful. The use of the word in Genesis 21:9, then, is more complicated than children's play. On the surface the activity may have seemed harmless but Ishmael probably did not take the child or the promise seriously. The English word "mock" thus suits the context here, if the mocking is subtle. "Mock" has a wide range of meanings, including deride, scorn, ridicule, and imitate. Moreover, its etymology indicates it imitated laughter.

The Septuagint translated this verb with "give way to hilarity" (paizonta), apparently an attempt to intensify the meaning for the piel mᵉṣ-aḥēq. Paul used a stronger word in relating the event: "persecuted" (ediōk), as it has been generally interpreted (Gal. 4:29). The Greek verb (diōkō) basically means "to pursue, put to flight, chase away," usually in a hostile sense, and thus the translation "persecute" has been used. But even in Liddell and Scott's Greek lexicon, "persecute" is a very rare translation. Driver suggests that Paul was using some well-known Haggadah in his interpretation ("Ishmael," Dictionary of the Bible, vol. 2, p. 503). In the midrash on Genesis, Genesis Rabba, Ishmael was accused of unchastity, idolatry, and shooting, among other things. Whether Paul was influenced by prevailing Jewish interpretations of Ishmael would be hard to prove. But Paul's interpretation of Hagar and Ishmael does follow the method of a midrash (see also his treatment of Moses' covering his shining face in 2 Cor. 3). Paul used the biblical record analogically to make his point about the Judaizers who were trying to undermine the truth of the gospel. His choice of words to describe what Ishmael was doing is interpretive—it attempts to express what Sarah perceived to be the real threat to Isaac. Ishmael may have been playing with Isaac, but if he was permitted to continue, his real effort would have been to supplant this new heir.

In Genesis 21, then, the "laughter" was the response of faith to the promise of God, but the "mockery" signified the response of unbelief in God's plan that Isaac should be heir. The story illustrates the truth that faith and unbelief are incompatible. That which trifles with God's work must be removed so that the faith can prosper under God's blessing.

Sarah's plan was to expel Hagar and Ishmael. The precise use of words in this section is significant. First, Sarah lowered the status of Hagar from handmaid (šipḥâ in Gen. 16:1) to slave ('āmâ). Second, she distinguished Ishmael as "her [Hagar's] son" from Isaac as "my son, even Isaac." Abraham, however, was grieved over the matter because of "his son" Ishmael. But God approved of Sarah's plan, referring to Ishmael only as "the lad," but to the heir as "Isaac." The tension surfaced over sonship, but the text resolved the issue by identifying the true son as Isaac. Moreover, in verse 13 God referred to Ishmael as Sarah had, "the son of the slave woman" (also describing Hagar as Sarah had). Third, the motif of evil surfaces again here as the result of the crisis: "[It] was very grievous [*wayyēra'*] in Abraham's sight" (v. 11). But God said, "Let it not be grievous [*yēra'*] in your sight" (v. 12). The crisis and its resolution was a serious problem, but God alleviated its impact for Abraham through the wisdom of sending them away, with the promise that he would protect and provide for them.

B. God protects and provides for the outcasts in the wilderness (14–21).

The divine approval of sending away Hagar and Ishmael was a sign not of divine abandonment of Ishmael but of protection for Isaac. Once again at the end of his life Abraham sent away all his other sons in order to preserve the inheritance for Isaac (25:6). Twice in this chapter God declared that he would make Ishmael into a (great) nation, once in comforting Abraham (v. 13), and once in comforting Hagar (v. 18). God had not abandoned Ishmael; he had provided for the resolution of a tension that could have no other resolution. In the wilderness God therefore heard the voice of the lad, directed the woman and her son to water, and renewed his promise of a great future for this son of Abraham.

God desires to be the God of the outcast, the rejected, the abused, the dying. The plight of Hagar should draw sympathy from the reader, for she was an unfortunate woman caught in the web of Abraham and Sarah and their faltering efforts to achieve their destiny, and she was the abused and rejected woman who, with the birth of Isaac, was suddenly very much in the way. The deliverance of Hagar and Ishmael should evoke hope in the reader, for God did not let them die in the wilderness but gave them a new life and a great future (see Trible, "Hagar," pp. 20–29). Nothing, of course, is known of the personal faith of these individuals. From the glimpses we may catch in Genesis 16 and 21, however, we would conclude that they had faith because they cried to the Lord and he delivered them. The statement that "God was with the lad" (v. 20) surely indicates that God's blessing remained with Ishmael.

Hagar and Ishmael provide a foreshadowing of Israel in the wilderness. They too would be sent out (*šālaḥ*) of Egypt and face tremendous needs in the barren wasteland. God would honor his Word to Israel and preserve them for their destiny, just as he honored his Word to Ishmael (16:10–12; 21:18) and preserved him through the wilderness experience.

The passage clearly demonstrates God's faithfulness in fulfilling his Word, first in providing Isaac as the heir and protecting his sonship, and then by protecting Ishmael in the wilderness. Looking at the story from the human side, we may observe that, once the promised child was given, Abraham and Sarah, rejoicing in God's miraculous provision, wished to avoid any possible threat to the inheritance of Isaac. The son of the slave wife, even though a son of Abraham whom God would bless, could not remain with the child of promise. *When God provides the fulfillment of the promise, one that evokes jubilation and renewed obedience, the people of God must remove anything that poses a threat to his work of blessing.*

Paul's spiritual lesson based on this narrative helps us see one predominant New Testament principle that corresponds to this point (Gal. 3–4). We may chart the levels of correspondence in the transition from Genesis to Galatians to see how the ideas of the story could be used in Paul's treatise (see chart 20).

Paul uses the story to illustrate his point. Ishmael was born according to the flesh through the slave wife, but Isaac was born according to the promise and was the heir. By analogy, the first represents the bondage at Sinai and Jerusalem; the other, the freedom when the promise finally came. Christ was the promised Seed (Gal. 3:16); and the law was meant to bring us to Christ (v. 24). Once the promise was fulfilled, the old order was done away with.

But then we see a second step in Paul's development: those who believe in Jesus Christ also become children of the promise, for Paul says we are "like Isaac" (Gal. 4:28), the son of the free woman. Therefore, we must get rid of the son of the slave woman (note that in Gal. v. 30, Paul paraphrases the words of Sarah as the authoritative lesson). Now that the promise has come in Christ, we who believe are joint heirs, we are children of the promise, we are the spiritual seed of Abraham. To go back under the law would be to deny the fulfillment of the promise and to live according to the flesh. The spiritual seed has been set free from

Chart 20. **Paul's Analogies Between Isaac and Ishmael**

Isaac (laughter)	Ishmael (mockery)
Recipients of the promise: believers	Wanderers, in bondage: unbelievers
Spiritual seed: promise fulfilled in Christ, the Seed	Physical seed: awaiting the promise under the law
Spirit: Christians growing in grace	Flesh: Judaizers living under the law

the bondage of the law. In the Christian experience, the flesh struggles against the spirit, making a mockery of it at times, for unbelief will attack belief. Paul then advises us to cast out those things of the flesh that undermine and threaten the freedom in Christ, the promised Seed.

This analogical application of the story harmonizes with the point of Genesis 21 very well, but it is by no means taught in Genesis 21. Paul saw the principle of removing the threat to the fulfillment of the promise, and so drew the analogy between the Christian experience and the patriarchal experience.

Bibliography

Cogan, M. "A Technical Term for Exposure." *JNES* 27 (1968): 133–35.

Fensham, F. C. "The Son of a Handmaid in Northwest Semitic." *VT* 19 (1969): 312–21.

Gehmann, H. S. "ἐπισκέπτομαι in the Septuagint in Relation to פָּקַד and Other Hebrew Roots—a Case of Semantic Development Similar to That of Hebrew." *VT* 22 (1972): 197–207.

Rabinowitz, Isaac. "Sarah's Wish (Gen. XXI: 6–7)." *VT* 29 (1979): 362–63.

Reines, C. W. "Laughter in Biblical and Rabbinic Judaism." *Judaism* 82 (1972): 176–83.

Trible, Phyllis. "Hagar: The Desolation of Rejection." In *Texts of Terror*, pp. 9–35. Philadelphia: Fortress, 1984.

White, Hugh C. "The Initiation Legend of Ishmael." *ZAW* 87 (1975): 267–306.

31

The Covenant at Beersheba
(Gen. 21:22-34)

T his brief passage presents Abraham as making a covenant with a Philistine king named Abimelech. The striking feature about
the story is its culmination in the explanation of the name Beersheba,
the place that became Abraham's dwelling. This name would always
recall the covenant that the patriarch made with these early residents
of the land, enabling him to dwell in peace and prosperity there.

This story fits well in the progression of the events in the Abrahamic
narratives. It is linked to its context by its common location and common participants (see Gen. 20), as well as by the narrative transitions in
verse 22 ("it happened at that time") and verse 34 ("he sojourned"
[wayyāgor] recalls 20:1). It is also part of the gradual progression of the
narratives toward the test in chapter 22: in the earlier Abimelech story
the birth of Isaac was promised and the protection of the Lord was on
the patriarch; in 21:1-21, the child was born to Abraham and Sarah,
and the rival was expelled; and in this chapter a covenant was made
with Abimelech, allowing Abraham to settle in the land in peace. Abraham's receiving the child and settling in the land all lays the foundation
for the test in chapter 22.

The sequence of the stories may also foreshadow Israel's experience.

384

The Lord appeared to Israel to assure them of the imminent fulfillment of the promise (cf. Gen. 18), destroyed the Canaanites in the land for their great sin (chap. 19), preserved the purity of the seed in the land (chap. 20), and separated various threats to the promise from within and caused them to dwell in peace and prosperity in the land (chap. 21).

Theological Ideas

The story is about the making of a peace treaty in which the participants swear to uphold their part of the agreement. The occasion for this treaty was the dispute over a well, a motif that appears frequently in the literature and that must have been common in nomadic life. The importance of oaths and covenant agreements would be appreciated by Israel in their national experience, and so this foundational passage would have been instructive—Abraham, the founding father, made a treaty to live in peace in the land. Israel was exhorted to make peace with the non-Canaanitish groups in the land so that those people might share in the blessings of the covenant.

There is also a point to be made about the designation of God in verse 33—he is the "everlasting God" ('ēl 'ôlām). The designation calls for an exegetical examination, including a consideration of the parallel expression in Canaanite literature. The epithet signifies, at the least, that Abraham's God endured perpetually.

Structure and Synthesis

Structure

The narrative's structure unfolds easily enough. The first movement reports Abimelech's request for the oath. Next is the covenant ritual that not only provided Abimelech with the treaty but attested to the resolution of the disputation. The last four verses conclude the narrative with the report of the naming of Beersheba, adding a detail about the planting of a tree. If we charted the development, we would have the request for the oath (vv. 22–23) and the response (v. 24), the complaint over the well (v. 25) and the response (v. 26), the making of the covenant (vv. 27–28) and the response (v. 29), followed by the oath itself (v. 30). Then, the conclusion notes the naming (v. 31), the making of the covenant (v. 32), the planting and worshiping (v. 33), and the sojourning (v. 34).

The literary analysis of the passage shows that the explanation of the name Beersheba is indeed central to the story, for words related to the root šāba' are repeated throughout. The verb "to swear" occurs three times in the passage (hiššābe'â in v. 23, 'iššābēa' in v. 24, and nišbe'û in v. 31), the numerical adjective "seven" occurs three times (šeba' is in

vv. 28–30), and the name Beersheba is used three times (b^e'$\bar{e}r$ $\check{s}\bar{a}ba$' is in vv. 31–33). Along with these occurrences of the important word, there is the repetition of the verb for making a treaty ($k\bar{a}rat$ occurs in vv. 27 and 32). The emphasis of the narrative is thus on the oath made at Beersheba.

Summary Message

When Abraham prospered under the blessing of God, he agreed to make a treaty with Abimelech at Beersheba for peaceful coexistence, thereby enabling him to serve God in the Land of Promise.

Exegetical Outline

    I. Abraham, who prospered under the blessing of God, agreed to make a treaty with Abimelech (22–24).
       A. Request: Abimelech recognized that God was with Abraham and so asked for a treaty (22–23).
       B. Response: Abraham agreed to make a treaty (24).
   II. Abraham accused Abimelech of stealing his well, but Abimelech exonerated himself before the covenant was made (25–27).
       A. Complaint: Abraham charged that Abimelech's servants took his well (25).
       B. Response: Abimelech protested that he knew nothing about it (26).
       C. Resolution: They made a covenant (27).
  III. Abraham solidified his right to the well by making an oath for the covenant (28–30).
       A. Preparation: Abraham set seven animals apart from the rest (28).
       B. Response: Abimelech inquired about the significance of the animals (29).
       C. Oath: Abraham explained that they were for a testimony that he had the rights to his well (30).
  IV. Abraham concluded the agreement with Abimelech by naming the place Beersheba and by planting a tree at the spot where he would worship God (31–34).
       A. Commemorative naming: He named the place Beersheba because they swore in agreement (31).
       B. Peaceful coexistence: Abimelech and his people returned to their home after the covenant was made (32).
       C. Established worship: Abraham planted a tree and proclaimed the name of the Lord, the everlasting God, in the land of his sojournings (33–34).

Development of the Exposition

I. Believers should agree to the request for peaceful relationships (22–24).

The first section of the story portrays Abraham in an enviable light—God was with him in everything he did (*'ĕlōhîm 'imm^ekā b^ekōl 'ăšer-'attâ 'ōśeh*). This acknowledgment by the Philistine ruler formed the reason that he wanted to have a covenant with Abraham; but it also proved that God's determination to bless Abraham was being fulfilled in the presence of others. The motif of the presence of God, whether a reported fact or a promise, is an important theological idea. It is found, for example, in Genesis 39:2, 21, and in Exodus 3:12, for Joseph and Moses respectively. The promise of divine presence ensures protection and provision for those who enjoy it (see also Ps. 46:7, 11; and the prophecy of Immanuel in Isa. 7:14).

Abimelech also wanted an oath from the patriarch so that he would not deal falsely with him (*'im-tišqōr lî*). It is ironic that the two things Abimelech knew about Abraham were that God was with him and that he was not altogether trustworthy (recall chap. 20). The desire for this oath may have been motivated, in part, by the previous deception. But he wanted a covenant that would reciprocate his kindness (*ḥesed*) to Abraham (21:23).

With such an appeal Abraham was eager to comply. As long as the oath was occasioned by a recognition of what God had done for him and would be reciprocal, it was to Abraham's advantage to make it. Later, Israel's foreign policy included the encouragement of peaceful coexistence with other tribes (Deut. 20:10).

II. Believers should try to restore peace when it is disrupted (25–27).

Here the motif of the dispute over Abraham's well is prominent. Before any peaceful covenant was made, Abraham rebuked the ruler for letting his servants steal the well. A survey of the meanings of the verb *gāzal*, "to steal, take violently, rob," will indicate that Abraham made a formal, legal complaint, for the word came to be used in the law for the violation of another person's property. Abimelech's protestation of innocence reflects his earlier appeal to God (20:4–5).

Such disputes can be settled peacefully, as this story shows. After the open confrontation on the issue, Abraham provided the animals for the covenant. The covenant would now ensure that such disputes would not be repeated by the parties involved. The New Testament frequently enjoins such a peaceable settlement of disputes, wherever possible (Mark 9:50; 2 Cor. 13:11; 1 Thess. 5:13).

III. Believers should strive to ensure that peaceful relationships continue into the future (28–30).

By taking this oath at the enactment of the covenant, Abraham secured his legal right to the well and his permission to dwell in the land in peace. With his present of the seven animals to make the oath, Abraham convinced Abimelech that he had dug the well. Consequently, by securing his right to the well, Abraham was securing the continued enjoyment of God's blessing to him, so significantly represented by the well. The king of Gerar seems to have gained a pact with this man of God only to ensure the future stability between them.

The relationship between the number "seven" and the idea of swearing must be examined closely. Here the motif of the seven animals seems to be part of the process of swearing. Elsewhere it may be simply that the person taking the oath would do something seven times, or merely make an oath using the word for "seven." Whether the two words "seven" and "swear" should actually be related is uncertain; in this passage the narrative relates them so strongly that each offers significance for the other.

IV. Believers must use their peaceful, prosperous life to serve God (31–34).

Among the features of this section of the passage, three things call for greater attention: the commemorative naming, the planting of the tree, and the calling out in the name of the everlasting God. The place was named Beersheba ($b^e{}^\circ\bar{e}r$ $\check{s}\bar{a}ba^\circ$) because the two of them swore there ($k\hat{\imath}$ $\check{s}\bar{a}m$ $ni\check{s}b^e{}^\circ\hat{u}$). There is some question over the exact motivation of the name in the narrative, for there seem to be two things developing. One part of the story emphasizes the covenant that *they swore*, and the other part stresses the arbitration by oath in which *seven lambs* were presented. Does the name reflect the swearing, or the seven, or in some way both elements? The name Beersheba, possibly meaning "the well of the seven," is also explained in Genesis 26:32–33 as the well of the oath ($\check{s}ib^\circ\hat{a}$). But this latter passage seems to be a renaming of the ancient spot. In Genesis 21, the primary motivation for the name is the popular etymology "they swore," and the secondary motivation is a word play on the number "seven." A dispute over a well between men of an oath was resolved by a treaty that was solemnized by seven lambs, which in turn symbolized a mutual oath (see Speiser, *Genesis*, p. 159). The point of the commemorative naming is that it would preserve for future generations the record of how that property was secured.

The second idea that needs attention is the report of Abraham's planting the tree. To plant a tree in Beersheba presupposed a constant supply of water and indicated a determination to stay in the region. Here, then, was faith and security. The tree was meant to be a lasting landmark to God's provision and a focal point of Abraham's worship. God would continue to bless with water, and Abraham would continue to call on the name of the Lord. Israel would later understand this symbolism to mean dwelling peacefully in their land (Zech. 3:10).

The third important element in this section concerns the calling out in the name of the Lord (see Gen. 4:26; 12:8). The prosperity from God's presence was evident to all, the peaceful coexistence with the people of the land was ensured through the covenant—now began the responsibility to use both to the honor of the Lord, the eternal God.

The passage anticipates Israel's peaceful coexistence in the land with other tribes who would respond to the message of peace and who would desire to share in the blessing. Westermann observes:

> The reason a king has to petition Abraham's good pleasure is that God is with him. But Abraham also emerges from the dispute as the superior. This is the way in which it was told in an era when Abraham was regarded and celebrated as the representative of Israel. As God was with him, so may he be with his people Israel so that it may wrest recognition from the kings of the nations and face them as superiors. [*Genesis*, vol. 2, p. 350]

With rest and recognition from her neighbors, Israel could more readily become the channel of blessing that God intended her to be. Likewise, the New Testament instructs believers to pursue peace with all people, insofar as it is possible (Heb. 12:14). The message of this text is useful for believers in all periods of time: *Peaceful relationships with those who recognize the blessing of God will allow the faithful believer to proclaim his name freely.* Or we may say it this way: *The blessings of peace and prosperity facilitate the believer's proclamation of the faith.*

There is also a subtle rebuke in the story. Abimelech pressed for the treaty because he did not want Abraham to deal falsely with him. Unless in this case the real culprit was placing the danger onto the other party (cf. Laban in chap. 31), the sensing of this need could be an embarrassment to God's people. But in many cases the only thing that could guarantee there was no falsehood (*šeqer*) would be an oath (Exod. 22:11). Ideally, believers should be trustworthy so that they do not need to swear that they are telling the truth, but such is not always the case. At any rate, in this story a point can be made that guaranteed truthfulness is essential for maintaining peaceful relationships. The task of being a blessing and witnessing to the fact of God's provision flourishes in times of peace—provided that God's people do not selfishly horde his blessing or deal deceptively with the world.

Bibliography

Aharoni, Y. "Nothing Early and Nothing Late: Re-writing Israel's Conquest." *BA* 39 (1976): 55–76.

Barr, James. "Seeing the Wood for the Trees? An Enigmatic Ancient Translation" [of Gen. 21:33]. *JSS* 13 (1968): 11–20.

Falk, Z. W. "Forms of Testimony." *VT* 11 (1961): 88–91.

Grintz, Y. M. "The Immigration of the First Philistines in the Inscriptions." *Tar* 17 (1945): 32–42.

Matthews, Victor H. "The Wells of Gerar." *BA* 49 (1986): 118–26.

32

The Sacrifice of Isaac
(Gen. 22:1–19)

The greatest test in the life of Abraham came after he had finally received the promise—he was to give his son back to God through sacrifice. It was one thing to trust the Lord while waiting for the promise; but it was quite another thing to continue to trust the Word of the Lord when it called for the patriarch to do that which seemed unreasonable. Would Abraham cling to the child that God had given him, the child on which the future was based, or would he continue to obey? The test was designed to see to what extent he would obey.

This emphasis readily suggests a workable idea for the modern exposition. The passage is about a test, but not the kind of tests that we frequently find in Scripture that introduce some adversity so that the believer must respond in faith. This is a test of obedience to a clear commandment of the Lord. Those who believe in the Lord claim to obey God's Word, or at least agree to obey God's Word—but to what extent will they obey? When the Lord commands his people to make some costly sacrifice, to do some task that seems unreasonable or impossible, how willing to obey are they?

The narrative is thus essentially a testing narrative; it has three major

391

parts that fit such a type: presentation of the test, compliance with the instructions, and approval (or disapproval) of the compliance. In this narrative, though, the reader is alerted at the very outset that it was a test, thus removing from the story the tension about the ultimate danger to Isaac. The primary emphasis seems to fall on the depiction of Abraham's faith. The basic point of tension in the story, then, concerns Abraham's faith. From the beginning of the narrative, however, it is obvious that Abraham will obey the command and demonstrate that he feared God—the point of the text. There is not the slightest hint in the story that he wavered in his faith or doubted. As a result, the narrative provides a fitting climax to the Abrahamic narratives, demonstrating the unparalleled faith of the patriarch.

Modern critical attempts to see a tale about child sacrifice behind the story in Genesis are unconvincing. Coats suggests that there was an ancient story that developed a plot about the sacrifice and its resolution in the substitution of the ram and that that story was appropriated by the Yahwist to provide an example of Abraham's faith (Genesis, p. 161). There is no convincing evidence or compelling argument to support this view, however; certainly the idea that such an independent account would have a better plot than the present narrative is not sufficient.

Theological Ideas

The narrative provides us with an important teaching about the Lord's dealings with his people—he tests them. A study of the word nāsâ ("to test") in its semantic field (cf. bāḥan, ṣārap, ḥāqar) would prove most helpful in the exegesis. It can be demonstrated that, when God tested his people, he was determining the quality of their faithfulness (cf. Exod. 15:22–27). Conversely, when human beings put God to the test, they were acting out of a weakened faith or a lack of faith (cf. Exod. 17:7; Num. 14:22). From Genesis 22, we learn that God may examine the faith of his people by calling them to obey him in ways that seem inexplicable.

On the human side of this test we discover the proper response, for Abraham exhibited his faith through obedience, showing that he feared God. James L. Crenshaw says of the passage:

In short, it answers the important question What does it mean to fear God? Perhaps the simplest way of describing the answer it offers is this: For some people, true worship means to walk alone into God-forsakenness, or worse yet, to discover the Lord as one's worst enemy. [Whirlpool of Torment, p. 28]

Abraham walked that path successfully because he feared God.

The occasion for the test is the idea of sacrifice, and this passage forms an important part of the understanding of that subject. Although the commandment was to sacrifice Isaac as an offering to the Lord, the real point of the act was Abraham's sacrifice of himself, that is, of his will and his wisdom with regard to his son Isaac. For the one who brought the victim was making the sacrifice to his God. When the angel of the Lord stopped Abraham's sacrifice and pointed out the ram caught in the thicket, he signified that Abraham's sacrifice was acceptable. In truth, Abraham had made the sacrifice. In the actual outworking of his obedience, however, an animal would be substituted for the lad. All Israel would offer substitutionary animals to the Lord, but their sacrifices would be for sins as well as for worship. Leviticus unquestionably assumes this idea of substitution in sacrificial worship. By making such an offering, the worshiper found acceptance with God.

Yet it is clear that Genesis 22 is not teaching the doctrine of substitutionary atonement in the way that other passages would. It is portraying an obedient servant worshiping God in faith at great cost, and in the final analysis, God provided for the sacrifice. The passage shows that the faithful worshiper will hold nothing back but will obediently give to God whatever he asks, trusting that "the LORD will provide." This idea that the Lord will provide forms the essential motif of the story and is commemorated in the explanation of the name *YHWH yir'eh* ("Jehovah-jireh" in KJV), "The LORD will provide" (v. 14).

In Romans 8:32, Paul alluded to this passage exactly this way by using a verb from the same root as the one used in the Septuagint (*pheidomai*). Taking as an example Abraham's not sparing his beloved son, Paul reasoned about the generosity of God, "who did not spare his own son, but delivered him up for us all, how shall he not with him freely give us all things?" The sacrifice of Isaac, then, prompts the Christian expositor to think of this greatest act of divine provision—through the sacrifice of Jesus Christ.

Structure and Synthesis

Structure

The passage is a mixture of dialogue and narrative once again. After the introductory exposition of the story (v. 1a), the narrative records the Lord's instructions for the test (1b–2). This part is developed in the form of a divine call of Abraham, Abraham's response, and the divine instructions. The significant part about the construction of this speech is that it parallels the call in Genesis 12:1–3. There the Lord had said, "Get you out [*lek-lᵉkā*] . . . to the land that I will show you." Here he said,

"And get you [$w^e lek$-$l^e k\bar{a}$] to the land of Moriah ... upon one of the mountains which I will tell you." The repetition of these motifs forms an inclusio in the narrative structure of the Abrahamic narratives, pointing out the complete cycle in the patriarch's experience. The allusion to the former call would also have prompted obedience to the present one, in many ways a more difficult journey in God's direction.

The second major section of the narrative concerns Abraham's compliance with the divine instructions (vv. 3–10). This portion is made up of narrative report (vv. 3–4), instructions to the servants (v. 5), narrative report (v. 6), dialogue with Isaac (vv. 7–8), and narrative report (vv. 9–10). In the reports of the events we have a picture of the faithful servant of the Lord, proceeding methodically and inexorably toward the moment of truth. The dispatch with which his obedience began in verse 3 recalls his obedience in the previous account in sending Ishmael away (cf. 21:14, "and he rose early in the morning"). This repetition provides the reader with a point of comparison between the two passages.

The speeches within this section add the full meaning to the events unfolding. In verse 5, Abraham explained that his mission was to worship the Lord; and in verse 8, Abraham explained that the Lord himself would provide a lamb for the sacrifice. With the motifs of sacrificial worship ($hi\check{s}tah\check{a}w\hat{a}$ in verse 5) and divine provision ($r\bar{a}$'$\hat{a}$ in verse 8), we begin to see the point of the story taking shape.

The third section of the narrative reports the divine approval of Abraham's actions along with the provision of an animal for the offering and a restatement of the promised blessings (vv. 11–18). The dialogue in this section is predominantly the divine Word. The first words are the urgent, divine call to Abraham and his response, paralleling the beginning of the story (cf. vv. 11 and 1). Next come the instructions not to kill the lad (cf. vv. 12 and 2) and the reason for it.

Following this deliverance we have the narrative report of the animal sacrifice. The animal was present, and Abraham sacrificed it—although there was no instruction to do so. That Abraham considered this animal the Lord's provision (v. 8) is evident from the commemorative naming that followed. The confirmation section closes with another divine speech from heaven, guaranteeing the fullness of the blessing to Abraham. The narrative then closes with a report of the return journey to Beersheba (v. 19).

The basic narrative reports thus provide the structure of the story, but the speeches give it the meaning. The initial speech of God lays out the test, and the speeches of Abraham tell how he interpreted the instructions (worship) and how he resolved the tension (God would provide). Then the subsequent speeches from heaven reverse the initial instructions and approve the patriarch's faith.

Summary Message

In obedience to the command of the Lord, Abraham took his beloved son to the land of Moriah in order to sacrifice him to the Lord, but because of Abraham's obedience the angel of the Lord restrained him from making the sacrifice and swore to bless him, all of which prompted the patriarch to commemorate the place of sacrifice as "the LORD will provide."

Exegetical Outline

I. Prologue: The narrator explains that the ordeal to follow was a test from God (1a).

II. Ordeal: God commanded Abraham to offer his only and beloved son as a sacrifice on one of the mountains of Moriah (1b–2).

    A. Call: God called to Abraham (1b).

    B. Instruction: God commanded Abraham to take his son and offer him as a sacrifice on one of the mountains of Moriah (2).

III. Obedience: Abraham responded to God's instructions in obedient faith by journeying to the place of worship and preparing Isaac for the sacrifice (3–10).

    A. Abraham traveled to the place that God had told him and took Isaac alone up to the mountain to worship (3–5).

        1. Report: Abraham and his company traveled three days to the place that God had said (3–4).

        2. Speech: Abraham instructed the servants to wait while he and Isaac went up to worship (5).

    B. Abraham prepared to offer Isaac on the mountain as a sacrifice to God (6–10).

        1. Report: Abraham and Isaac went together up the mountain (6).

        2. Dialogue: In response to the question of Isaac about the animal, Abraham explained that God would provide the animal (7–8).

        3. Report: Abraham bound Isaac as the sacrifice and prepared to slay him on the altar (9–10).

IV. Resolution: The angel of the Lord prevented Abraham from killing his son when the angel saw that he feared God, prompting the patriarch to sacrifice an animal instead of his son and to name the place in commemoration of the provision of the Lord, after which he received a solemn promise of God's blessing (11–18).

    A. Call: The angel of the Lord called Abraham (11).

B. Instruction: The angel of the Lord instructed Abraham not to kill his son, because he had demonstrated that he did fear God (12).

C. Report: Abraham responded to the divine intervention by sacrificing a ram that the Lord had provided and by commemorating the place with the name "the LORD provides"— to which a proverb was added (13–14).

1. Abraham offered the ram instead of his son (13).

2. Abraham named the place, "the LORD provides" (14a).

3. A proverb was added to this incident: "In the mount of the LORD it will be seen" (14b).

D. Blessing: The angel of the Lord swore to fulfill the promises to Abraham and his seed because he did not withhold his son from God (15–18).

V. Epilogue: Abraham and his company returned to Beersheba (19).

Development of the Exposition

I. God tests the faithfulness of believers by asking them to surrender to him the best they have (1–2).

In the initial phase of the exposition full consideration must be given to the nature of this test. It must be reiterated that the prologue is the narrator's interpretation of the event, that is, that Abraham did not know that it was a test. Had he known that God was testing him to see if he would obey, the value of the test would have been diminished. To be effective as a test, the divine command had to be both sudden and surprising.

There is no reason to approach the narrative apologetically. To defend God by saying that he has the right to take the life of any human because all are sinners or to say that he never intended to let Abraham go through with it is surely beside the point. From Abraham's perspective, God was calling him to do something that he would have never imagined. Not only was he asking him to make a child sacrifice, but he was asking for the child who would be the heir to the promises. This unpredictability made it all such a staggering test—God seemed to be totally out of character and completely destroying his program. Or as Crenshaw says, God seemed to become Abraham's worst enemy. This aspect made Abraham's faith so great—he was willing to sacrifice to God this son who had everything in the world to live for, whom God had provided as the hope of the future.

The exposition must concentrate on the precise wording of the Lord's instructions for Abraham. In using the terminology of Genesis 12:1–3,

God may have been reminding the patriarch of the original promissory call in order to encourage his obedience. In his choice of descriptions for Isaac, however, God was also reminding Abraham of the joyous fulfillment of the promise, and such reminders made the task difficult: "Take your son [binkā], your only son [yᵉḥîdᵉkā], whom you love ['ā-habtā], Isaac [yiṣḥāq]." With each description the commandment would have become more painful. The designations are repeated in verses 12 and 16, forming a major motif in the story. Moreover, the use of "his son" in verses 3, 6, 9, and 10, and "my son" in verse 7, points to the force of the test—the long-awaited son of Abraham would be the victim.

The emphasis on the son may indicate a connection between this test and the preceding account of the expulsion of Ishmael, also a son of Abraham. In that account Abraham was grieved over the thought of losing "his son" (21:11), but God encouraged him to send him away, promising to make him into a great nation. Abraham obediently sent Ishmael away into the wilderness—to die, unless the Lord fulfilled his Word concerning that son. Now, in this passage, the Lord instructed him to kill his "only son" Isaac. Relinquishing Ishmael was made easier by the knowledge that Isaac was still there and would be the true heir. God now tested Abraham to see if he would relinquish Isaac as willingly as he did Ishmael.

God's command for Abraham to sacrifice Isaac would have had a greater impact in his world than we may perceive. Human sacrifice was known throughout the ancient world, and so the call might have seemed appropriate, except for the fact that Abraham had come to believe that the Lord was the true and righteous God. Delitzsch says,

> In fact, the God who requires Abraham to sacrifice his only son after the manner of the Canaanites (2 Kings iii. 27; Jer. xix. 5), is only apparently the true God. The demand was indeed only made to prove that Abraham was not behind the heathen in the self-denying surrender of his dearest to his God, and that when the demand had been complied with in spirit, the external fulfillment might be rejected. [New Commentary on Genesis, vol. 2, p. 91]

The command also involved a journey to a chosen mountain in the land of Moriah (hammōrîyâ). The designation occurs again in 2 Chronicles 3:1: the mountain on which the temple stood in Jerusalem. Commentators frequently claim that this name is a later addition to Genesis in order to claim the mountain of sacrifice for Jerusalem. But there is no reason to doubt that the mountain chosen actually was in that area. Accordingly, the proverb included in verse 14 would convey the abiding significance of what took place on this mountain to generations of subsequent worshipers.

The expositor will have to think of corresponding requirements that God demands of believers today. For example, Jesus' requirement of forsaking one's family, leaving all, and following him (Luke 14:26–27) is similar to the test of obedience that was taught in Genesis 22. If anyone is inclined to be a true worshiper of the Lord, it will involve the willingness to sacrifice whatever is dearest and most treasured, even if such should be considered a gift from God.

II. Faithful believers are willing to surrender the best they have to God, trusting that the Lord will provide (3–10).

A. The faithful obey God's call to worship (3–5).

The response of Abraham to God's instructions is truly amazing—instant, unquestioning obedience. The narrative report traces his journey of three days to the appointed place with an elegant simplicity. There is no mention of his feelings or thoughts, only the report of instant compliance with the hard instructions.

In the mention of the three days there may be a foreshadowing of the three-day journey of Israel into the wilderness to sacrifice to God (see Exod. 3:18; 5:3; 8:27). The emphasis on three days signifies a period of preparation for the most important event (see Gen. 31:22; 34:25; 40:20; 42:18).

The first part of the report of Abraham's obedience concludes with his speech to the young servants that he was leaving behind: "Stay here with the donkey; and I and the lad will go up there and will worship and return to you [wᵉništaḥăweh wᵉnāšûbâ ʾĕlêkem]." The expositor must try to determine what was going through Abraham's mind with this resolution to return after the sacrificial worship. From the context we can conclude only that Abraham knew that (1) God planned the future around Isaac and (2) God wanted him to sacrifice Isaac. He could not reconcile the two but would obey what God had instructed him to do.

In the final analysis Isaac would be brought twice from the dead, once from Sarah's dead womb and once again from the high altar. The Book of Hebrews suggests that Abraham concluded that God was able to raise Isaac from the dead (11:19). Whether Abraham had actually worked out the details of a bodily resurrection would be hard to say. People in the ancient world believed that life would continue beyond the grave, but a clear understanding of resurrection to this life began to unfold only later.

B. The faithful trust God to provide (6–10).

After Abraham's statement of his intent to worship, the narrative report continues, telling how the patriarch took the wood, the fire, and the knife and went off together with his son (cf. the verbs of v. 6 with those in 2). Here, too, there is a dialogue that interprets Abraham's faith. The father's response to his son's question about the animal provides the motivation for the later commemorative naming: "God himself will provide ['ĕlōhîm yir'eh] a lamb for a burnt offering" (v. 8). Then the motif of their shared journey is repeated—"they went both of them together."

That statement of faith did not hinder Abraham from completely obeying the call to sacrifice his son, for at the place he bound Isaac (wayya'ăqōd) and raised his hand to slay him on the altar. (Jewish tradition named the event the Aqedah, after this verb.) Abraham's explanation that God would provide was ambiguous enough to allow for this act. In telling Isaac that God would provide the sacrifice, Abraham actually deferred the answer to his son's question to God, gave God a way out of the ominous event that lay ahead, and covered his own intent to slay the son that God had provided. At the moment of truth Abraham did not look around for an animal or wait hesitatingly for God to intervene; he raised his hand to slay his son. Kierkegaard writes:

> There was many a father who lost his child; but then it was God, it was the unalterable, the unsearchable will of the Almighty, it was His hand took the child. Not so with Abraham. For him was reserved a harder trial, and Isaac's fate was laid along with the knife in Abraham's hand. And there he stood, the old man, with his only hope! But he did not doubt, he did not look anxiously to the right or to the left, he did not challenge heaven with his prayers. He knew that it was God the Almighty who was trying him, he knew that it was the hardest sacrifice that could be required of him; but he knew also that no sacrifice was too hard when God required it—and he drew the knife. [Fear and Trembling, p. 36]

III. Faithful believers receive God's provision for worship (11–14).

A. God approves sacrificial obedience (11–12).

The divine intervention came when the sacrifice was made—in the mind of Abraham, if not in fact. The call from heaven reflects the initial call of verse 1, but now with an intensity through the repetition of the name. Now the divine instructions prevented Abraham from doing any harm to the lad, in contrast to the instructions of verse 2. Here it became clear to Abraham that the episode was a test, and here it became clear to Israel that God took no pleasure at all in child sacrifice.

The expression "now I know" (v. 12) is significant. Westermann points out that it was usually the joyful cry of a person who experienced the effects of God's action on his behalf (Pss. 20:6; 56:9; Exod. 18:11; 1 Kings

17:24). But here it was transferred to the joyful knowledge of God gained through testing the pious man (Genesis, vol. 2, p. 361).

The knowledge gained by the test is that Abraham feared God (yᵉrēʾ ʾĕlōhîm ʾattâ) and did not withhold his son (wᵉlōʾ ḥāśaktā ʾet-binkā). That Abraham feared God, the positive statement of the result of the test, was signified by his not withholding his son, the negative expression. The one who truly feared the Lord reckoned that compliance with the Word of God, no matter what the cost, was the primary responsibility. The expositor must explain the concept of the fear of God, for it is at the heart of this test, and it is a predominant theme in the biblical narratives about worship and service. The true worshiper fears the Lord; that is, the true worshiper draws near the Lord in love and adoration and reverence but shrinks back in fear of such an awesome deity. For the motif of the fear of God, see Genesis 20; 42:18; and Exodus 20:18b–21, among the many other passages in which such a study would surface.

B. God provides for his worshipers (13–14).

The commemorative naming of the place by Abraham indicates that the discovery of the sacrificial ram was not interpreted by the patriarch as mere chance; rather, the Lord provided the animal for the sacrifice. The expositor will have to concentrate on this naming, for it expresses the central lesson of the passage. Belief that the Lord will provide enables the true worshiper to sacrifice without reservation.

He named the place YHWH yirʾeh, "the LORD sees" or "the LORD provides." The motivation for this name came from verse 8: "God will provide [ʾĕlōhîm yirʾeh]." The act of naming preserved in the memory of the people the incident that occurred here and established the place as a shrine.

The naming is complicated by the little proverb that follows it: "As it is said to this day, In the mount of the LORD it shall be seen [ʾăšer yēʾāmēr hayyôm bᵉhar YHWH yērāʾeh]." This statement seems to reflect a later saying that grew up in Israel on the basis of this event in Abraham's life. The last verb (a niphal) could be rendered either "it shall be seen (provided)" or "he (i.e., the Lord) will appear." The support for this latter interpretation comes from 2 Chronicles 3:1, where the temple is on Mount Moriah (har hammôrîyâ), where the Lord "appeared" (nirʾeh) to David. In Genesis 22, however, the motivation for the name is the provision of an animal for the sacrifice by God. The better translation would thus be "it will be seen (i.e., provided)"—although the niphal nowhere else has this sense (the qal does in Gen. 41:33).

In the verse, then, there are two referents: the name points back to the saying of Abraham in verse 8, but the explanation of the name links the point to temple worship. The significance of this place named YHWH yirʾeh, "the LORD provides," would be lived over and over again in the acts of the worship of Israel. The Lord sees (*yir'eh*) the needs of those who come to worship (cf. *yērā'eh kol-zᵉkûrᵉkā* in Exod. 23:17) him in his holy mount (*hammôrîyâ*) and is seen (*yērā'eh*) by them, that is, reveals himself to them by answering their prayers and providing their needs (*yir'eh*)—his seeing takes practical effect in being seen (Driver, *Book of Genesis*, p. 219). The ambiguity involved in the use of the verb in the *qal* and then in the *niphal* shows that the narrator was playing with the concepts in this way. The word plays within the passage point to the central lesson that he was making: "God will provide," *'ĕlōhîm yir'eh*; "fear God," *yᵉrē' 'ĕlōhîm*; "saw a ram," *wayyar' wᵉhinnēh 'ayil*; and so on.

By virtue of the word plays, the essence of the narrative and the significance of the place could easily be recalled. That essence concerned sacrificial worship in which the faithful came to appear before the Lord with their best offering, trusting that the Lord would continue to provide their needs as his people. Through his provision, God appeared to his worshipers.

IV. Faithful believers enjoy the assurance of God's blessing (15–18).

After the event was finished the angel of the Lord (i.e., the Lord himself) called out from heaven to Abraham, reiterating the promised blessings but now adding the solemn oath. The reassurance of the promises was given, but only after the sacrifice of the substitute.

It is helpful to note the emphases of this statement of the promises in comparison with the previous ones. Here the abundant fulfillment was based on Abraham's obedience—"because you have done this." But there is also an addition to the promise of blessing: not only would Abraham's descendants be numerous, they would triumph in the gate of their enemies. In practical terms for the nation, Abraham's seed would dispossess the Canaanites, just as the way of faith in fearing God would be victorious over the Canaanitish way.

The test for Abraham was designed to determine whether he feared God or not. It was important for Abraham's faith to pass this test and know that God was pleased with him. The test carried him to the limits of his emotions, for it called for him to surrender to God the one person he loved the most and had waited so long for—the heir of the promises. Abraham's obedience demonstrated that he recognized that God was the Lord of the promise. Abraham could have no power over the fulfillment of the promise, no power over life and death, apart from God's granting it to him or requiring it from him. Here Abraham demonstrated what it meant to fear God; here readers learn what is at the heart of true worship.

In understanding this sacrifice it is important to remember that God asked him to sacrifice something that he was sure was the will of God for him to have. The principle of sacrifice is thereby revealed here, for God does not ask worshipers to give him that which they do not treasure or that which they no longer care for or need. Rather, God requires that his worshipers offer him the best that they have, even their firstborn. In the law God demanded that the firstborn be given to him (Exod. 22:29); also in the law God made provision for the redemption of the firstborn (Exod. 13:13; 34:20). The offering of the best animal of the firstborn (recall Gen. 4:4) signified a substitution that was being made for a life. True worship in Israel was indeed sacrificial worship, and in sacrificing the first and the best to God, the believing worshiper was demonstrating submission to the will of God.

In the teaching of the New Testament it was easy for the apostle to make the comparison of the sacrifice of Jesus with the Israelite system. By using Genesis 22, Paul could identify the sacrifice that God the Father made by not withholding his only Son but by delivering him up for us all (Rom. 8:32). But then Paul turned the use of the narrative slightly to capture the point of Genesis 22, namely, that if God did not spare his Son, he would certainly provide all things for us. The act of sacrifice, both Abraham's and God's, thus ensures further provision from heaven.

If we think of the comparison between Abraham's obedience and the obedience of New Testament worshipers, we may approach this message from another direction. The test of obedience for the Christian would not differ essentially. The Lord calls believers to obey his instructions, including sacrificing themselves and their possessions to him in fear and devotion. This step may require relinquishing some personal possession, ambition, or direction that seems clearly to be God's design. Although we cannot completely approximate the patriarchal event, the sacrifice of something dear to the heart could be as difficult and demonstrable as Abraham's sacrifice. Christ's requirements for disciples allowed no rival loyalties and no holding back. The Christian life became a life of worship in which the true worshipers feared the Lord and surrendered themselves to him.

Taking the message in the direction of the test of true worship (for that is exactly what the motifs and the lesson of Gen. 22 reveal), we may word the expositional message as follows: *The one who fears God, that is, the faithful worshiper, will obediently surrender to God whatever he asks, trusting in God's promises of provision and blessing.* At the heart of God's program of blessing is sacrifice, and although that may seem the way of failure, in God's marvelous dealings it is the way of victory.

Bibliography

Ben-Shabbetay, D. "Why Did the Earth Open Its Mouth and the Ram Get Caught in a Thicket by Its Horn?" *Tar* 28 (1958–59): 236.

Cassuto, U. "Jerusalem in the Pentateuch." In *Biblical and Oriental Studies*, translated by Israel Abrahams, pp. 71–78. Jerusalem: Magnes, 1973.

Childs, Brevard. "A Study of the Formula 'Until This Day.' " *JBL* 82 (1963): 279–92.

Chilton, Bruce D. "Isaac and the Second Night: A Consideration." *Bib* 61 (1980): 78–88.

Coats, George W. "Abraham's Sacrifice of Faith: A Form-Critical Study of Gen. 22." *Interp* 27 (1973): 389–400.

Crenshaw, James L. "A Monstrous Test: Genesis 22." In *A Whirlpool of Torment*, pp. 9–30. Philadelphia: Fortress, 1984.

Daly, Robert J. "The Soteriological Significance of the Sacrifice of Isaac." *CBQ* 39 (1977): 45–75.

Danielou, J. "La typologie d'Isaac dans le christianisme primitive." *Bib* 28 (1947): 363–93.

Davies, Philip R. "Passover and the Dating of the Aqedah." *JJS* 30 (1979): 59–67.

————. "The Sacrifice of Isaac and Passover." In *Studia Biblica, 1978: Papers on Old Testament and Related Themes*, pp. 127–32, *JSOT* Supplement, vol. 11. Sheffield: Sheffield University Press, 1979.

Golka, F. W. "Die theologischen Erzählungen im Abraham-Kreis." *ZAW* 90 (1978): 186–95.

Gowan, D. E. "The Use of *ya'an* in Biblical Hebrew." *VT* 21 (1971): 168–85.

Hopkins, David C. "Between Promise and Fulfillment: Von Rad and the 'Sacrifice of Abraham.' " *BZ* 24 (1980): 180–93.

Kierkegaard, Soren. *Fear and Trembling* and *The Sickness unto Death*. Translated by Walter Lowrie. Princeton: Princeton University Press, 1953.

Landes, G. M. "The 'Three Days and Three Nights' Motif in Jonah 2:1." *JBL* 86 (1967): 446–50.

Lawlor, John I. "The Test of Abraham (Gen. 22:1–19)." *GTJ* 1 (1980): 19–35.

McCormick, Scott. "Faith as Surrender (Genesis XXII 2)." *Interp* 17 (1963): 302–7.

McKenzie, J. L. "The Sacrifice of Isaac." *Scr* 9 (1957): 79–84.

Peck, William Jay. "Murder, Timing, and the Ram in the Sacrifice of Isaac." *AThR* 58 (1976): 23–43.

Polish, D. "The Binding of Isaac." *Judaica* 6 (1957): 17–21.

Pope, Marvin H. "The Timing of the Snagging of the Ram, Genesis 22:13." *BA* 49 (1986): 114–17.

Rosenberg, R. A. "Jesus, Isaac, and the 'Suffering Servant.' " *JBL* 84 (1965): 381–88.

Sayce, A. H. "Wnat Was the Scene of Abraham's Sacrifice?" *Ext* 21 (1909–10): 86–88.

Schoeps, Hans Joachim. "The Sacrifice of Isaac in Paul's Theology." *JBL* 65 (1946): 385–92.

Swindell, Anthony C. "Abraham and Isaac: An Essay in Biblical Appropriation: The Offering." *Exp* 87 (1975): 50–53.

Watson, J. "Isaac, the Type of Quietness." *Exp* 11 (1905): 123–32.

Weyermann, Andrew M. "Process of Preparation: Gen. 22:1–14: From Text to Proclamation." *CTM* 43 (1972): 752–65.

White, Hugh C. "The Initiation Legend of Isaac." *ZAW* 91 (1979): 1–30.

Zerapa, P. "The Land of Moriah." *Ang* 44 (1967): 84–94.

33

The Descendants of Nahor
(Gen. 22:20–24)

Τhis little section records the expansion of the family in the eastern regions by listing the descendants of Nahor, the brother of Abraham. The inclusion of the name of Rebekah indicates the primary interest of the narrator in including this material here—it prepares for the choosing of a bride for Isaac (Gen. 24). By placing the genealogical information here, rather than just before Genesis 24, the writer signals a change in the direction of the narratives. Now that Abraham had proven faithful, attention would begin to turn to the next generation. Accordingly, everything in the subsequent narratives about Abraham is transitional: the report of the family in the east with Rebekah, the death and burial of Sarah, the choosing of a bride for Isaac, and the death of Abraham after he had ensured that Isaac would receive the inheritance.

The passage includes a transitional sentence, a genealogy of eight sons and one granddaughter (Rebekah), a conclusion of the genealogy, and then a second list of names from a secondary wife. It is interesting to note that, between the two wives of Nahor, there were twelve sons, eight from Milcah and four from the secondary wife. Later, Jacob had twelve sons, eight by his two wives and four by his two secondary wives.

The list of descendants establishes several connections between Abraham and his kin in the east, the most important of which will be Rebekah and her immediate family. With this news of the expanding family of Nahor, Abraham would know how to ensure that the promise of God would continue after he and Sarah were gone.

Bibliography

Maisler, B. "The Genealogy of the Sons of Nahor and the Historical Background of the Book of Job" (in Hebrew). *Zion* 11 (1946): 1–3.

34

The Purchase of the Cave of Machpelah
Gen. 23

The first major event in the transition section is the account of the death and burial of Sarah. It is the first in a number of death reports that the writer to the Hebrews would summarize by saying, "These all died in faith, not having received the promises" (11:13).

Theological Ideas

The major issue underlying this chapter concerns the fulfillment of the promises. Although the chapter does not make any overt theological point, the fact that the narrator included this tradition in the book gives it a theological significance. The tension arises because, with the promises of many descendants and of the land yet unfulfilled, the recipients of the promises began to die. What, then, became of the promises? It became clear that the promises would not be fulfilled within the lifetime of Abraham and Sarah. Consequently, Abraham had to prepare for the future.

This preparation introduces a second major theological theme—burial within the land of Canaan. The inclusion of the genealogy of Nahor just prior to this chapter reminds the reader that the ancestral home was in the east; but the account of the burial in the Land of Promise informs the reader that there was no going back for Abraham. The future was in Canaan, even though the first recipients of the promise would die before that promise could be realized. Consequently, Abraham secured some of the land for an ancestral burial spot.

Structure and Synthesis

Structure

This chapter is essentially a report of a death (vv. 1–2) and burial (vv. 19–20) that frames a negotiation over the burial spot. The negotiation, essentially a dialogue, takes on the tone of a legal transaction. The negotiation dialogue includes Abraham's proposal (vv. 3–4), the response (vv. 5–6); Abraham's specific proposal (vv. 7–9), the response (vv. 10–11); Abraham's request for the price (vv. 12–13), the response (vv. 14–15); and the conclusion of the transaction (vv. 17–18).

Summary Message

When Sarah, the wife of Abraham, died, Abraham purchased a family burial site in the land of Canaan from its owners, demonstrating his intention to remain in the place that God had promised.

Exegetical Outline

    I. Abraham mourned over the death of Sarah his wife (1–2).
      A. Death report: Sarah died at the age of 127 (1–2a).
      B. Mourning: Abraham mourned for Sarah his wife (2b).
    II. After obtaining permission to purchase a family burial spot in the land of Canaan, and after negotiating with the owners for the precise area, Abraham secured the field and the cave at Machpelah for a possession (3–18).
      A. Abraham received permission from the Hittites who owned the land to bury his dead in the best grave they had (3–6).
      B. Abraham obtained Ephron's agreement to sell the cave of Machpelah to him in which to bury his dead (7–11).
      C. Abraham legally acquired the field and the cave of Machpelah for four hundred shekels (12–18).
        1. Abraham urged Ephron to sell him the territory (12–13).
        2. Ephron agreed to sell it for four hundred shekels (14–15).
        3. Abraham purchased the territory from Ephron in the presence of all those who were sitting in the gate (16–18).

III. Abraham buried Sarah in the cave in the land of Canaan—his newly acquired possession (19–20).

Development of the Exposition

I. God's people must suffer loss before receiving the promises (1–2).

The main idea to be developed from these two verses is that the early recipients of the promises began to die without receiving the promises. Sarah was the first, but her death reminded Abraham of his mortality as well. This death report sets the scene for the rest of the chapter. It would be natural to find a death report followed by the report of the burial, but here a major incident comes between the two.

A significant point in the first two verses is the location of the death: "in Hebron in the land of Canaan." This place is repeated in the burial report in verse 19. The fact that Abraham was a stranger and a sojourner in Canaan (v. 4) necessitated the purchase in order to bury Sarah in the land of Canaan, where she died. The place thus figures prominently in the chapter.

The expositor should have little trouble correlating this incident with countless others just like it, in the Bible and in human experience today. Believers have often looked at their lives and their griefs and wondered what now would become of God's promised blessing. Sarah died; a life of patient waiting for the promises now faded. Others would follow. It would have been natural for the patriarch to mourn his wife and then return to the ancestral home for burial. For this man of faith, however, Sarah's death provided another situation in which faith could operate.

II. God's people believe that the promises of God extend beyond this life (3–18).

The major theme of this section is the securing of the cave and the field as a possession in which to bury the dead. Several key words heighten the theme. First, the simple expression "and he stood up" (wayyāqom) occurs twice (vv. 3, 7), preparing for the notice that the transaction was "made sure" (wayyāqom, in v. 17). Abraham's polite humility is expressed by his bowing down (wayyištaḥû, in vv. 7 and 12). The pattern is as follows: in verse 3 he stood up and spoke, in verse 7 he stood up and bowed himself down and spoke, in verse 12 he bowed himself down and spoke, and then in verse 17 he made sure of the transaction.

Another key word in the development of the theme is "possession" ('āḥuzzâ). In verse 4, Abraham asked permission to obtain a "possession" for a burial place; in verse 9, he pressed for the acquisition of this "possession" from Ephron; and in verse 20, the narrative concludes that he obtained the territory as a "possession." Although the text does not specifically mention the promises to Abraham or any specific theological interpretation, the use of this word within the Abrahamic narratives suggests the connection to the promises. Abraham did not want death to interfere with the promise of the land.

A third important motif that reminds the reader of the tension of the story is developed by the expressions about the death: "Sarah died [wattāmot]" in verse 2; "Abraham stood up from before his dead [penê mētô]" in verse 3; "that I may bury my dead [we'eqberâ mētî]" in verse 4; "bury your dead [qebōr 'et-mētekā]" in verse 6; "from burying your dead [miqqebōr mētekā]" in verse 6; "that I should bury my dead [liqbōr 'et-mētî]" in verse 8; "bury your dead ([qebōr mētekā]" in verse 11; "I will bury my dead [we'eqberâ 'et-mētî] there" in verse 13; "bury your dead [we'et-mētekā qebōr]" in verse 15; and finally, "Abraham buried [qābar] his wife" in verse 19. It should be clear that Sarah's death is the central theme of the narrative, and the primary concern of the patriarch. The elaborate detail of the dialogue and the repetition of the theme obviously indicate that the narrator wanted to press the point home to the readers. With all this emphasis on death within the Abrahamic narratives about the promised blessings, the tension becomes clear.

Many scholars have seen similarities between these elaborate details of the narrative and the Hittite laws of trade recorded at Hattushash, or Bogazköy (see *ANET,* pp. 188–91, paragraphs 46–48, 169; paragraph 46 deals with feudal obligations for the whole field; paragraph 47 with gifts that nullify these obligations). Lehmann tries to show how the issue in the negotiations centered on feudal responsibilities, that is, by receiving the territory from Ephron ben Zohar, Abraham would have become the feudatory. He writes:

> Abraham's answer in v. 13—an almost desperate accession to Ephron's ultimatum—could be translated freely, "If you would only listen? (However,) I will pay the price for the (entire) field, take it from me. . . ."
>
> In the light of this legal interpretation, the argument of the two men thus did not revolve around an attempt to extract an excessive price, nor did Ephron ever make a false tender of a free gift to entice Abraham. It rather concerned the question of who would render the services due the king as a result of principal ownership of the land. ["Abraham's Purchase," pp. 16–17]

Several scholars have disagreed with this connection, arguing that there are parallels to the transaction in other cultures as well, notably in the Neo-Babylonian documents (see Tucker, "Legal Background," for one discussion). While such arguments may be correct, there still seem to be points of contact with the Hittite laws. First, the people are called Hittites in the passage, possibly referring to a pocket of Hittite people who had migrated far south, for the Hittite Empire never extended this far south. Second, even though the Hittite laws do not come from the same period of time, the laws could have codified earlier legal traditions and customs and so explain the customs in the narratives (cf. the Hebrew laws of the levirate marriage and reports of the custom in Gen. 38 and the Book of Ruth).

Whatever connections there may be between this chapter and legal customs of Hittites, the point remains that a legal transaction was being completed. Abraham bought a field and a cave in the presence of witnesses in the gate (note the key motifs of possession, field, cave, trees, borders, making sure, giving, and those in the gate). Whether he also acquired feudal responsibilities or whether he avoided such by paying the four hundred shekels is debatable. Investigation into such possibilities may produce a plausible explanation for the elaborate detail and unusual dialogue in the chapter.

The point of the story is that Abraham went through these elaborate negotiations to purchase a possession in which to bury his dead. This purpose is significant, for burial was usually in one's native land. It seems clear enough that he was making this portion of the land the ancestral home. There would be no going back to Haran.

When Abraham bought Machpelah, he was renouncing Paddan Aram (which was just brought to the reader's attention in 22:20–24). Canaan was the land his descendants would inherit. It is interesting to observe here that the only portion of the Promised Land that Abraham ever received, he bought—and that was a grave. But this grave bound them to the land, for later patriarchs would die and be gathered to their ancestors—in Canaan (see 50:13).

The point for biblical theology is that Abraham and Sarah had not exhausted God's promises in their lifetime. They had only Isaac as their son and heir, and their prosperity in their sojournings fall far short of the promise of the land. Abraham knew it and made plans for the future. Dods says, "But buying land for his dead he is forced to enter upon it from the right side, with the idea that not by present enjoyment of its fertility is God's promise to him exhausted" (Book of Genesis, p. 236). God would do far more for them than he had done in this life—which is the hope of all who die in the faith.

The promise of the land is one of the major themes of Genesis—but so is death. Death entered the race by sin, and the death of the patriarchs was a harsh reminder of the presence of evil. It brought out the mourning. But death in this passage became the reason for hope. In life the patriarchs were sojourners; in death they were heirs of the promise and occupied the land.

The purchase of the cave and the field around it did not guarantee the whole Land of Promise to Israel, but it did give the patriarch and his descendants a tie to the Promised Land. As B. Jacobs says, "The purchase does not create a legal title in the eyes of the world, but it binds the heart" (*First Book of the Bible,* p. 153).

III. God's people demonstrate their faith by reconciling death with the abiding promises (19–20).

This final section stresses again the major themes of the chapter: Abraham buried Sarah his wife in the land of Canaan, the land promised to Abraham and his descendants, in the burial spot that he had acquired as his possession. The actions of Abraham were evidence that he believed that the promises were not in vain.

Whatever lessons the expositor wishes to make about death, mourning, burying, and legal contracts must be subordinate to the main point of the passage, namely, that *God's promises are not exhausted in this lifetime.* Just as Abraham bought the cave in hope, we too have a hope for the full benefits of the promise of salvation beyond this life. We may reword the statement to make it more instructive: *The time of death (when the natural inclination is to mourn as the world mourns) should be the time of our greatest demonstration of faith, for the recipient of God's promises has a hope beyond the grave.* Applications of this idea could focus on strength and comfort in times of distress (even death), as well as how we must live in view of our understanding that what God has in store for us is far greater than what we now experience.

Naturally, times of sadness and grief come to the believer. But the eternal hope enables the believer to endure. Kierkegaard says that "despair is precisely to have lost the eternal and oneself" (*Sickness unto Death,* p. 195). A focus on things eternal kept Paul from despairing in the trials of life (2 Cor. 4). If a person takes that which is earthly so much to heart, as Kierkegaard explains, such an attitude introduces a weakness to despair, for when that which is earthly is taken away from that person, despair rushes in. In times of grief only a living faith in the eternal will keep one from despair.

Von Rad says that "an indirect prophetic moment is especially clear, as it is in all patriarchal stories, namely, the foreshadowing of future benefits of salvation (Heb. 10.1). The chapter contains a preview of our relationship to the saving benefit promised to us, the new life in Christ into which we also bear" (*Genesis*, p. 250). When Jesus was talking to the Sadducees about the resurrection, he referred to God's being the God of Abraham, Isaac, and Jacob—not the God of the dead, but the God of the living (Mark 12:26–27). His point was that the promises to the fathers were not exhausted in their lifetime. Rather, the promises of God extend into the life to come, demanding a resurrection for their fulfillment. The Book of Hebrews observes that they all died not receiving the promises—yet they died in faith.

Bibliography

Evans, G. " 'Coming' and 'Going' at the City Gate: A Discussion of Professor Speiser's Paper." *BASOR* 150 (1958): 28–33.

Fensham, F. C. "Ugaritic and the Translator of the Old Testament." *Bible Translator* 18 (1967): 71–74.

Gordon, Cyrus. "Abraham and the Merchants of Ura." *JNES* 17 (1958): 28–31.

Gottstein, M. H. "נשיא אלהים (Gen XXIII 6)." *VT* 3 (1953): 298–99.

Heidel, Alexander. "Death and the Afterlife." In *The Gilgamesh Epic and Old Testament Parallels*, pp. 137–223. Chicago: University of Chicago Press, 1963.

Kierkegaard, Søren. *Fear and Trembling* and *The Sickness unto Death*. Translated by Walter Lowrie. Princeton: Princeton University Press, 1953.

Kitchen, K. A. "Historical Method and Early Tradition." *TynB* 17 (1966): 63–96.

Lehmann, M. R. "Abraham's Purchase of Machpelah and Hittite Law." *BASOR* 129 (1953): 15–18.

Petschow, H. "Die neubabylonische Zwiegesprächsurkunde und Genesis 23." *JCS* 19 (1965): 103–20.

Reviv, Hanoch. "Early Elements and Late Terminology in the Description of Non-Israelite Cities in the Bible." *IEJ* 27 (1977): 189–96.

Rin, S. "The מות of Grandeur." *VT* 9 (1959): 324–25.

Speiser, E. A. " 'Coming' and 'Going' at the City Gate." *BASOR* 144 (1956): 20–23.

Tucker, G. M. "The Legal Background of Genesis 23." *JBL* 85 (1966): 77–84.

Westerbrook, R. "Purchases of the Cave of Machpelah." *Israel Law Review* 6 (1971): 29–38.

35

The Choosing of a Bride for Isaac
(Gen. 24)

The purpose of Genesis 24 is to explain how Isaac acquired his wife, Rebekah. The focus of the narrative is not on Abraham; after commissioning his servant he recedes into the background and does not even come on the scene for the marriage. Rather, the focus is on the servant of Abraham as he follows God's guidance to the wife of God's choosing. The emphasis of the chapter, then, is on the providential work of God in the circumstances of the faithful servant.

The story is a little different than the other patriarchal narratives; it is closer to the Joseph stories in that it fully develops its plot through its speeches and events. Coats classifies it as a novella, or more specifically, an example story (*Genesis,* p. 170). Westermann classifies the story as a "guidance narrative," that is, "a narrative whose purpose is to attest the hand of God in the life of a small community and thus in personal life" (*Genesis,* vol. 2, p. 382.). And Eichrodt explains that "it was particularly in the stories of the Patriarchs that the Israelite story-tellers loved to provide their people with illustrations of divine Providence" (*Theology of the Old Testament,* translated by J. A. Baker [Philadelphia: Westminster, 1961], vol. 2, p. 168). This story, then, demonstrates how the Lord providentially ensured the continued development of the promise by guiding the faithful servant in the acquisition of a bride for Isaac.

Theological Ideas

Central to the development of the story is the idea of covenantal loyalty (*ḥesed*), both from the divine perspective and the human. Abraham acted with *ḥesed* in preparing for the future of the covenant through the marriage, Eliezer acted with *ḥesed* in faithfully carrying out his responsibilities, and God demonstrated his sovereign *ḥesed* by guiding the servant to the proper place and ensuring that the mission did not fail. Any exposition of this chapter must include a thorough study of this word.

With this concept at the heart of the story, the direction of the message is clear: it is about the providence of God in the lives of faithful people, ensuring the perpetuity of the covenant. Two considerations are important here. First, God is declared to be the sole cause of the events in the narrative. The characters in the story voice the narrator's convictions on this point. Verse 27 records the theme clearly: "He has led me." Even Laban recognized this guidance and would not dare contest providence. Second, God is deliberately behind the scenes, yet directing the acts. In this respect the account is very similar to the Book of Ruth. The story records no word from God, no miracle, no cultic contact, and no prophetic oracle; it does not even restate the Abrahamic covenant. It reports the hidden causality of God, sovereignly working through the circumstances of those who are acting in faith. The role of faith, expressed in personal prayer, trusting for divine guidance through the circumstances, and acting responsibly in anticipation of God's faithfulness, is predominant because God is not visibly active.

The narrative is more than an object lesson in divine guidance, however. It is a major part of God's program for covenantal blessing. Accordingly, many potential setbacks are avoided: the servant could have failed (vv. 5–8), the sign could have been missed (v. 21), Laban could have disagreed (v. 49), or Rebekah could have refused (vv. 54–58). But the Lord triumphed over all potential hazards and brought about a compliance of all persons concerned.

Structure and Synthesis

Structure

The narrative can be divided into four major sections that trace the development of the plot through a series of complications and resolutions. First, there is the *commission* (vv. 1–9), in which Abraham, confident in the promise of the Lord, bound his servant by oath to find Isaac a wife. This section includes the oath dialogue—instruction, objection, reassurance—as the major part of the commissioning. Second is the *trust* (vv. 10–27), in which the faithful servant trusted the Lord to grant him specific guidance and then witnessed the answer to his prayer. This section includes the prayer of the servant at the well, a prayer to resolve the complication of uncertainty (vv. 12–13), the answer to the prayer, and the dialogue between the servant and the girl that resolved the complication. The section closes with the servant's praise (vv. 26–27). Third, there is the *success* (vv. 28–60), in which the servant recounted the providence of God to Rebekah's family and gained their permission to take her to Isaac. This section includes the narrative exposition in which the servant is welcomed, the speech of the servant (vv. 33–49), and the agreement of the family (vv. 50–60). And finally there is the *completion* (vv. 61–67), in which Rebekah returned with the servant to become Isaac's wife. This section begins with the family's blessing but concentrates more on the meeting with Isaac (vv. 62–67).

The passage is predominantly composed of speeches: dialogue, prayer, report, blessing. Once again, the content of the speeches gives the interpretation for the narrative events.

Each unit within the chapter includes a point of tension that must be resolved. In the first it is the servant's concern that the woman may not be willing to go with him (v. 5); this issue was resolved by Abraham's instructions (vv. 6–8). In the second section the complication comes with the identification of the woman at the well, whether she actually was the one the Lord chose (v. 21); this matter was resolved with the inquiry and identification (vv. 22–27). In the third section the tension comes first in obtaining the approval of the family, and so the servant offered his lengthy explanation (vv. 34–49); it was resolved by the family's agreement (vv. 50–51). A second tension in the section is the request that Rebekah remain a few days (v. 55); this matter was resolved by the servant's perseverance (v. 56) and Rebekah's decision to go (v. 58). In the final section there is only a hint at a tension in the meeting of Rebekah and Isaac (v. 65); it was quickly resolved in the marriage (v. 67).

Summary Message

Entrusted with the responsibility of finding a bride for Isaac and trusting in the Lord's covenantal faithfulness to prosper his way, the servant of Abraham faithfully and resolutely carried out his task under the providential guidance of the Lord, so that he acquired Rebekah to be Isaac's wife.

Exegetical Outline

I. Abraham solemnly entrusted the responsibility of finding a wife for his son to his servant (1–9).
   A. Introduction: Abraham was old and enjoyed the blessing of God (1).
   B. Commission: Abraham solemnly entrusted the finding of a wife for Isaac to his obedient servant (2–8).
     1. The patriarch instructed the servant to swear to the task (2–4).
     2. The servant hesitated, fearing that she might not be willing (5).
     3. The patriarch reassured the servant that he would be free of the oath in that case, but under no circumstances should he take Isaac out of the land (6–8).
   C. Oath: The servant took the oath (9).
II. When the faithful servant arrived in the land of the relatives, he prayed for a sign of God's guidance and then praised God for sending Rebekah as the chosen one (10–27).
   A. Introduction: In the region of the relatives, the servant settled down by a well (10–11).
   B. Prayer: The servant prayed that the Lord would show his faithful love by sending out a young girl to give him drink and to water his camels (12–14).
   C. Resolution: The Lord sent out Rebekah to the well as the answer to the servant's prayer, for she showed kindness and kinship (15–25).
     1. Rebekah showed kindness in her activities, fulfilling the test set by the servant (15–21).
     2. Rebekah identified herself as the daughter of Bethuel and welcomed the servant to their lodging (22–25).
   D. Worship: The servant acknowledged the Lord's faithfulness in leading him to this place (26–27).
III. When the servant was welcomed into Laban's household, he faithfully discharged his duty to secure Rebekah as Isaac's wife before enjoying their hospitality, recounting in the process how the Lord had led him there (28–60).
   A. Introduction: The girl hurried to tell her family (28–29).
   B. Complication: Laban extended hospitality to the servant so that he might rest and receive refreshment (30–33a).
   C. Resolution: The servant refused to accept hospitality until he had discharged his duty to acquire a wife for Isaac (33b–53).

1. The servant reported how the Lord had demonstrated faithfulness by leading him to Rebekah (33b–48).
2. The servant obtained the family's approval to take Rebekah (49–51).
   a. The servant pressed for the betrothal (49).
   b. The family consented, in view of the Lord's providence (50–51).
3. The servant worshiped the Lord for allowing him to complete the betrothal (52–53).

D. Complication: Laban and Rebekah's mother stalled over the time of departure (54–55).
E. Resolution: The servant's perseverance and the girl's willingness to go resolved the complication (56–60).
   1. The servant protested the delay, since the Lord had prospered (56).
   2. The girl's willingness to go settled the matter (57–60).

IV. Rebekah returned with the servant and became Isaac's wife (61–67).
   A. Introduction: They journeyed with the servant back to the land (61).
   B. Meeting: Rebekah met Isaac when he was out in the field meditating (62–65).
   C. Culmination: Rebekah became the wife of Isaac through the providential dealings of the Lord (66–67).
      1. The servant related all that had happened (66).
      2. Isaac took Rebekah as his wife (67).

Development of the Exposition

The exposition of this passage has the difficulty of length. The expositor will have to be selective in the detailed discussions within the narrative in order to cover it all. However, a simple retelling of the story without these selected discussions would run the risk of missing the theological impact of the story.

I. Believers have the responsibility of ensuring that God's program continues to the next generation (1–9).

The first section of the story stresses the activity of Abraham in this period of his life. By endeavoring to provide a wife for Isaac who would be appropriate for the covenant program as they had it, the patriarch was discharging his responsibility to see that the divine plan for blessing could continue to the next generation. This is the second major narrative in the transition period of the Abrahamic stories. The reports that Abraham was old (*zāqēn*) and that God blessed (*bērak*) him provide the significance for this activity within the argument of the book.

Abraham's commission of the servant takes the form of a solemn oath by which the servant had to swear to find a wife from among the relatives who would be appropriate to the continuation of the covenant. The servant's concern was that such a woman might not be willing (*'ûlay lō'-tō'beh*) to go with him to Canaan (cf. the hesitancy of Moses in Exod. 3:11 and 4:1). This tension will build throughout the narrative until the story is completed. The preliminary resolution to the servant's hesitancy is found in Abraham's conviction that God's angel (*mal'āk*) would be sent before him. In short, he placed the success of the mission on divine intervention. With the success or failure of the mission left up to the providence of God, the servant executed the ancient oath, swearing to do his part in the quest.

II. Believers may be confident that the Lord will lead them in their faithful activities (10–27).

Here the exposition would stress the servant's faith as he obeyed his master by going on the journey and trusted the Lord by praying for guidance. The confirmation of his prayer came in the activities of the young Rebekah at the well (vv. 17–21) and in her identification (vv. 23–24), for which the servant acknowledged the Lord's faithfulness in the climax of the section (v. 27).

In the introduction to this section, which reports the servant's arrival at the well, there is a subtle word play connecting this section with the first. The text says that he made his camels kneel down (*wayyabrēk*, in v. 11), a detail that would not otherwise be necessary in the story. But this verb is a homonym of *bērak*, "to bless," which introduced the first section (v. 1). The word intimates that the arrival at the proper place was all a part of the divine blessing.

Faced with the uncertainty of finding the proper young woman, the servant prayed that the Lord would show covenantal faithfulness (*'ăśēh-ḥesed*) to his master Abraham (vv. 12–14). The details of the servant's prayer were then repeated in the narrative report (vv. 15–21), showing clearly the divine choice of the woman. The details of his test were not arbitrarily chosen; they would indicate a kind and industrious nature in the woman.

Within the narrative report is a description of Rebekah. She was very beautiful in appearance (*ṭōbat mar'eh mᵉ'ōd*), a trait that was reported earlier for Sarah (12:11). She was also a virgin (*bᵉtûlâ*).

In spite of this clear indication of divine intervention, another complication arose in the mind of the servant: the servant wondered if the Lord had indeed made his journey prosperous (hahiṣlîaḥ < ṣālaḥ). Until the woman and her family recognized and accepted the sign of the Lord's guidance, the mission was far from successful. But the matter was resolved in the servant's mind with the dialogue that followed (vv. 22–25). Here the young woman identified herself and extended hospitality to him.

The high point of this section comes with the servant's response to how the matter turned out (vv. 26–27). The servant bowed (wayyiqqōd) and worshiped the Lord (wayyištaḥû laYHWH), offering a most significant word of praise to the Lord: "Blessed be the LORD [bārûk YHWH] God of my master Abraham, who has not forsaken his loyal love [ḥasdô] and his faithfulness [wa'ămittô] from my master: I, being in the way, the LORD led me [nāḥanî] to the house of my master's brethren." His praise was based on the fact of the Lord's guidance (nāḥâ; cf. the use in the psalms, esp. Pss. 23 and 139); and the Lord's guidance was evidence that he had not abandoned his faithful loyal love (the two words may be a hendiadys here). The earlier questions about the success of the mission seemed to dissolve with this praise for the Lord's providential guidance to the proper woman. Israelite believers again and again found comfort in the Lord's guidance in their lives when they were discharging their covenantal duties in faith and in faithfulness.

III. Believers must give priority to completing God's work (28–60).

The point of this lengthy section is that, before he would indulge himself in the hospitality of the relatives, the servant of Abraham faithfully discharged his duty and secured the betrothal of Rebekah. The leading of the Lord was such an important part of his task that it became the primary motivation for his resolution to settle the matter. This point can be demonstrated by the lengthy retelling of the events by the servant. The narrative is not satisfied to state simply that he told all that had happened (as in v. 66), but rather repeats all the major parts of the events leading up to this moment.

The section opens with the servant's receiving all the hospitality by the family (cf. Gen. 29:13–14 and Exod. 2:19–20). Laban's welcome continues the emphasis on the Lord's blessing: "Come in, O blessed one of the LORD [bô' berûk YHWH]." But Laban's hospitality was delayed until the servant could complete his business.

The servant's speech (vv. 34–48) retraced the events that had transpired. Here the exposition should repeat the significant motifs as well, for the repetition in the narrative was deliberately designed to emphasize them. The servant stressed the blessing on Abraham (v. 35), the inheritance of Isaac (v. 36), the oath to take a wife other than a Canaanite (v. 37), the provision of the angel to prosper his way (v. 40), the prayer at the well for the Lord to prosper him by signifying whom the Lord appointed to be Isaac's wife (vv. 42–44), the identification of Rebekah as the one, and the praise to the Lord for leading him in the right way (v. 48).

On the basis of this impressive report of the Lord's providence in leading him to Rebekah, the servant implored the family to indicate their approval. In his request he asked for them to deal kindly and truly with him, the same expressions used in describing how the Lord had dealt with him (*'ōśîm ḥesed we'ĕmet*, in v. 49). Faced with such a powerful display of providence, the family could only acquiesce. The wording of Laban's response is striking: "The thing proceeds from the LORD; we cannot speak to you good or evil [*lō' nûkal dabbēr 'ēleykā ra' 'ô-ṭôb*]." Here the theme of good and evil reappears in the book, but in this case the providence of God was obvious enough that it prevented Laban from speaking either good or evil. Later in the book, Laban would be prevented in a dream from doing good or evil to the fleeing Jacob (31:24). Since the matter was so clearly decided by providence, the family agreed to the betrothal. Their instructions to take Rebekah and go (*qaḥ wālēk*) recall an earlier divine intervention in which the beautiful Sarah was restored to her husband in Egypt (12:19).

Once again the servant of Abraham responded to the prosperity of the mission by worshiping the Lord (*wayyištaḥû 'arṣâ laYHWH*, v. 52). This response clearly demonstrated that the servant's faith was in the Lord, who had accomplished this mission (cf. v. 27).

A second tension arose when the family sought to delay the departure of Rebekah (v. 55). The servant asked them to let him depart with her (*šalleḥûnî*) to his master, but they expressed their wish that she abide (*tēšēb*) with them and then leave. The resolution in this crisis came when the decision was made by Rebekah—"I will go" (*'ēlēk*, in v. 58).

The section ends with the blessings at the departure of the company (vv. 59–60). The blessing offered to Rebekah harmonized rather closely with the actual Abrahamic blessing of which she was to become a part (cf. 22:17b).

IV. Believers may rest assured that the Lord will complete the good work he has begun (61–67).

This final section brings the narrative to its intended conclusion. The travelers entered the land of Canaan, Isaac came on the scene, and the couple became husband and wife. There is a slight building of tension when Rebekah first prepared to meet Isaac, but it dissolved as a matter of course. The Lord had guided the servant in all his ways, and so this culmination of the mission could only be cause for further praise and satisfaction—as no doubt the servant's report would have stressed again (v. 66).

It is important to note that Rebekah actually replaced Sarah by entering the tent of Sarah. She would be the new matriarch of the clan, as Isaac would be the new patriarch (see v. 36). The fact that Abraham neither appears on the scene at this point nor is mentioned as the master (Isaac is now referred to as the servant's master in v. 65) suggests that this story formed a very important part of the succession of patriarchal and matriarchal figures. The theological significance of this succession is that Rebekah was the new matriarch *by God's own choosing.*

The exegetical exposition of this story could be stated in the following way: *Believers may trust the Lord to give them guidance and success through his covenant faithfulness as they act responsibly in obedience to the covenant.* It must be stressed that this guidance and success concerns the matter of the program of God. It is the program of God's blessing that God prospers through this choice of a wife; it is the responsible pursuit of covenant obligations that God guides to completion.

Both sides of the matter of guidance are present in this story: human faithfulness (*ḥesed*) and divine guidance based on divine faithfulness (*ḥesed*). The entire event concerned the Lord's guidance for a wife, but not just any wife—this marriage was essential to the work of God in the world. Perhaps the question that should be asked today by those who seek guidance in such matters of life is not whether God will lead a person to the right partner but of what value to God such a marriage would be. Prayer for guidance through the circumstances cannot come from a selfish motive; it must be for the will of God. If there is thus the commitment to do the will of God faithfully, to subject all action to his purpose, to praise and worship him for every indication of his presence and leadership, then we may speak of trusting his guidance in such matters. Of course, the exposition of this passage will have to explain when signs are legitimate for discernment of divine leading today. We may at least say that God's will cannot be divined but may be discerned by those who prayerfully and righteously fulfill their covenantal obligations.

Of the characters in the story, the servant certainly stands out as exemplary: he was loyal to his sacred commission to participate in God's program for blessing humankind, faithfully carrying out his part before receiving benefits for himself; he trusted God implicitly, looking for God's guidance as he carried out his task; his predominant motivation was covenantal faithfulness (ḥesed); and he offered praise to God whenever there was any indication of divine intervention.

The choice for the bride was God's choice. The sign confirmed it. Laban recognized it. Rebekah complied with it. Likewise in other situations, those who do the will of God prayerfully and obediently may be confident that they were led by God (Prov. 3:5–6)—but they may not perceive *how* they were led until after they act by faith.

Bibliography

Crenshaw, J. L. "*YHWH Ṣeba'ôt Šemô:* A Form-Critical Analysis." *ZAW* 81 (1969): 156–75.

Freedman, David. "A New Approach to the Nuzi Sistership Contract." *JANES* 2 (1970): 77–85.

Freedman, R. David. "Put Your Hand Under My Thigh—the Patriarchal Oath." *BAR* 2 (1976): 3–4, 42.

Garcia-Lopez, Felix. "Del << Yahvista >> al << Deuteronomista >> Estudio Crítico de Genesis 24." *RB* 87 (1980): 514–59.

Glueck, Nelson. *Ḥesed in the Bible.* Translated by Alfred Gottschalk. Cincinnati: Hebrew Union College Press, 1967.

Gordis, R. A. "A Note on Gen. 24, 21." *AJSL* 51 (1934–35): 191–92.

Gottstein, M. H. "A Note on צנח." *VT* 6 (1956): 99–100.

Hals, Ronald M. *The Theology of the Book of Ruth.* Philadelphia: Fortress, 1969.

Nicholson, E. W. "The Problems of צנח." *ZAW* 89 (1977): 259–66.

Rabinowitz, L. "A Study of Midrash—Gen. 24." *JQR* 58 (1967): 143–61.

Roth, W. M. W. "The Wooing of Rebekah: A Tradition-Critical Study of Genesis 24." *CBQ* 34 (1972): 177–87.

Speier, S. "The Targum Jonathan on Gen 24:56." *JQR* 28 (1937–38): 301–3.

Steinmueller, J. E. "Etymology and Biblical Usage of 'almāh." *CBQ* 2 (1940): 28–43.

Wernberg-Møller, P. "A Note on לָשׂוּחַ בַּשָּׂדֶה in Gen. 24:63." *VT* 7 (1957): 414–16.

36

Abraham's Death and Isaac's Inheritance
(Gen. 25:1–11)

In this little section the life of Abraham comes to a close, and God's blessing transfers to Isaac, Abraham's "only" son. The passage is made up of two sections, a genealogy of the other sons of Abraham (1–6) and a death report of the patriarch (7–11).

It should be noted in passing that this unit is placed here to provide a fitting closing to the Abrahamic narratives but is not actually in chronological order. The subsequent account of the birth of Jacob and Esau appears to follow the death of Abraham. If, however, Abraham died at the age of 175 and Jacob and Esau were born when Isaac was 60, then they were born fifteen years prior to the death of Abraham.

Theological Ideas

The fulfillment of the promises is one theological motif that can be derived from the passage. Abraham was promised many nations (chap. 17) and a death at a ripe old age (chap. 15). The genealogy traces nations that came from him, and the death report indicates that he died at a good old age.

The safeguarding of the covenant is also evident here. Abraham acted responsibly to ensure that Isaac would receive the heritage of the promise. His other sons were thus awarded their inheritances and dismissed.

Structure and Synthesis

Structure

The first section of the passage, the genealogical report, includes the notice of Abraham's marriage to Keturah (v. 1), the record of his sons (vv. 2–4), and then the preservation of the inheritance for Isaac (vv. 5–6). The list of the descendants through Keturah includes three generations of names.

In the second part of the passage, the death report, we find the normal motifs: the summary of Abraham's years (v. 7), the death notice (v. 8), and the burial notice (vv. 9–10). The unit is completed with a report that, after his death, the Lord blessed his son Isaac (v. 11).

It is clear, then, that the passage was intended to join the report of Abraham's descendants with the report of his death and burial, forming a transition in the patriarchal succession. Although many tribes rightfully claimed to be the descendants of Abraham, only one line continued the covenant.

Summary Message

Before he died, Abraham ensured that the covenantal blessing would belong to Isaac by sending away his concubine's sons; after he died, the Lord confirmed this decision by blessing Isaac.

Exegetical Outline

 I. After Sarah's death Abraham fathered sons who became ancestors of several Arabian tribes, thus fulfilling the promise that he would be the father of many nations (1–4).
 II. Abraham gave the family inheritance to Isaac, but he gave gifts to the sons of the concubines and sent them away (5–6).
 III. Abraham died in peace, enriched by the Lord's blessing, and was buried by Isaac and Ishmael in the cave of Machpelah (7–10).
 IV. After Abraham's death, the Lord blessed Isaac as he dwelt in Beer Lahai Roi (11).

Development of the Exposition

This passage is a little more difficult to handle than the last few and perhaps may best be used as a summary for the Abrahamic narratives.

It does have a message of its own, however, and could be treated as follows.

I. Believers must ensure that the blessing of God passes on to the next generation (1–6).

Abraham had the responsibility of ensuring that the blessing, as God planned it, would pass to Isaac. The message in this part is straightforward: believers will die, and so they must ensure that the work begun in them by God will continue as God desires. It may be through their children, or it may be through some other means; but no one may personalize the program so that no thought is given to the next generation.

There is no way to tell for sure when Abraham married Keturah, but the verbs imply that it was after the death of Sarah. In that case there could have been thirty-eight years for the births of six sons, who were sent away before the death of Abraham. The problem in this section concerns the genealogical connections. Tribes in Sheba and Dedan, as well as Midianites, came from Abraham through Keturah. Others living in Sheba and Dedan and Midian did not come from Abraham (Gen. 10:7). But the passage bears witness to the fact that God truly made Abraham the father of many nations and tribes.

Abraham loved all his sons and gave them gifts before he sent them away—as he had done with Ishmael. This step was necessary to establish Isaac as the true heir, for these sons of the concubine could not be allowed to pose a threat to the heir of the promise.

II. Even though faithful believers die, the program of God to bless the world continues (7–11).

No one is indispensable in God's program. Good people die, and others take up the task to continue God's program.

Abraham died at the age of 175 and was gathered to his people (i.e., he left the land of the living). His sons united to bury him in the cave of Machpelah, just as Jacob and Esau would do for Isaac, and the patriarchs for Jacob. Death seems to remain the most sobering element in the human struggle for the blessing of God. But the work of God to bless the world continues from generation to generation, as the report about Isaac indicates (v. 11).

This final verse reports two significant things about Isaac. First, God blessed him. This statement must be connected to the initial promise of blessing in Genesis 12:1–3 and then traced through the narratives. The blessing was passed on to Isaac; the God of Abraham was to be the God of Isaac as well. Second, the verse also reports that Isaac dwelt near

Beer Lahai Roi. God had heard Hagar here and delivered her. And here Isaac had come to meditate when he awaited Rebekah. In the next section of the book Isaac prays here for his barren wife. Isaac thus dwelt in a place where prayer was effectual, where God could be found—and God blessed him.

The passage as a whole shows that, by sending away all the other sons, Abraham by faith provided for the transference of the blessing to Isaac. Abraham would be gone, but God's program would continue through Isaac. No leader of the covenant is indispensable, for God's program to bless the world will continue to grow and expand from generation to generation. *God's servants must do all they can to ensure that God's program of blessing continues from generation to generation without interruption.*

Bibliography

Dumbrell, W. J. "Midian." *VT* 25 (1975): 327–29.

Winnett, F. V. "The Arabian Genealogies in Genesis." In *Translating and Understanding the Old Testament: Essays in Honor of Herbert Gordon May.* Edited by Harry Thomas Frank and William L. Reed. Nashville: Abingdon, 1970, 171–96.

4

The Patriarchal Narratives About the Descendants of Abraham

The last four *tôlᵉdôt* sections of the Book of Genesis follow a definite pattern: the lines in each generation that are not chosen lines are traced before the narrative returns to the chosen line. Immediately after the death report of Abraham we have the *tôlᵉdôt* of Ishmael, which is a brief listing of names (25:12–18). Once this account has been completed, the narrative returns to the main line, the *tôlᵉdôt* of Isaac (25:19–35:29). This section concerns the record of Isaac, how the blessing had in fact passed to him, but essentially focuses on Jacob.

After the Jacob stories come to their intended conclusion, that is, reporting how Jacob with his family and his flocks settled in the Land of Promise, the narrative turns to the next generation. First we have the *tôlᵉdôt* of Esau (two *tôlᵉdôt* headings for a complete tracing of the Edomites), in which the descendants and vassals of Edom are listed (36:1–8 and 36:9–37:1). Once this line has been surveyed, the narrative returns to the main line, to the *tôlᵉdôt* of Jacob (37:2–50:26). This last section of the book is essentially the story of Joseph, although Jacob figures in it at the beginning and the end.

Since the Joseph story is unique within the Book of Genesis, I treat that section in a separate part. In this part I consider the rest of the patriarchal narratives.

37

The Record of Ishmael
(Gen. 25:12–18)

These few verses provide the *tôlᵉdôt* section of Ishmael, the son of Abraham by Hagar. The passage has two parts, the genealogy (12–16) and the death report (17–18). In recording the family records of the patriarchs, the narrative must include what became of this son of Abraham.

Once again the genealogy records twelve names (see Gen. 22:20–24). These twelve princes provide further evidence of how the promises were fulfilled—God had promised to make of Ishmael a great nation, to give him many descendants (16:10; 21:18), and so this report attests to God's faithfulness. But it also must be connected to the promises to Abraham, for many nations and kings were to come from him (17:6).

This genealogical record also fits harmoniously in the chapter, for in the preceding section there is the account of the descendants of Abraham through Keturah, and here there is the record of the sons of Ishmael through Hagar. All of these sections are important, for they record the Bedouin tribes that trace their ancestry to Abraham.

The only other point that the narrative notes about Ishmael is the death report. The verses have the summary formula of his years, the report of the death and burial, and then an explanation of the patriarchal succession of his descendants.

431

It is unlikely that anyone would devote a full exposition to these verses. Rather, the material can be easily used as transitional information in tracing the message of the book.

38

The Creation and Election of the Seed
(Gen. 25:19–26)

With this account of the births of Jacob and Esau, the tôlᵉdôt of Isaac begins. In the final collection of the traditions, these patriarchal narratives have been arranged to explain what became of Isaac, but that explanation centers primarily on Jacob. Isaac's stories (chap. 26) form an interlude to establish that the promises did indeed transfer to him.

Genesis 25:19–35:29 is not a self-contained short story, as is Genesis 37:2–50:26. The narrative complex includes a variety of types of literature that have been woven together to develop the grand theme of the tôlᵉdôt, the acquisition of the blessing and its development and protection by the Lord. On the divine side, we learn how the blessing was guaranteed to Jacob; on the human side, we learn how the conflict between brothers threatened the blessing for Jacob. The arc of tension in the collection of stories concerns the flight and the return of Jacob, a flight that began with deception and a return that ended with reconciliation with Esau. The narrative of the conflict between Jacob and Laban is set within the Jacob-Esau cycle; it also begins with deception and ends with reconciliation. Within these narratives about life in Paddan Aram, we also find the conflict between Leah and Rachel. Tying the cycles together is a series of divine revelations and manifestations, the most important ones being at Bethel (28:10–22), at the time of Jacob's flight out of the land, and Mahanaim and Peniel (32:1–2, 24–32), at his return.

These narratives, then, confirm the ancient conflict between good and evil. Deception attaches itself to the conflict between the brothers, a deception that brings pain and separation. In spite of the conflict and deception, the blessing becomes Jacob's possession and begins to develop in his stay with Laban, first in the blessing of his family, and then in the blessing of his cattle. Finally, when Jacob is reconciled with Esau, he can point to all his family and his possessions as God's good blessing.

The account of the births of Jacob and Esau in the present passage (Gen. 25:19–26) provides a fitting introduction to the Jacob-Esau cycle, for the struggle for supremacy is foreshadowed by the struggle of the infants. Moreover, the oracle that accompanied the pregnancy sets the tone for the narratives that follow, for it is clear from the outset that Jacob was the heir by divine election.

Michael Fishbane observes how this initial composition foreshadows the subsequent developments:

> The prologue hints at themes and issues which recur in the Jacob narrative and thereby provides it with cohesion and tension. The oracle . . . is the principal foreshadowing statement of the prologue. However, three instances of anticipation appear before it. The first is the brief reference to Rebekkah as both daughter of Bethuel and sister of Laban, who lives in Padan Aram (v. 20). . . . The second instance involves Rebekkah's being barren ('aqarah, v. 21) before the birth of Jacob. . . . The third case of foreshadowing is the reference to Rebekkah's difficult pregnancy, "when the sons struggled within her." [*Text and Texture*, pp. 44–45]

Fishbane shows how these themes—Laban in Paddan Aram, barrenness, and struggles—reappear through the Jacob narratives. Clearly this first unit prepares the reader for the others.

John Goldingay adds this observation of parallels back to the Abrahamic narrative:

> As in the Abraham narrative, a word from Yahweh is set at the beginning of the Isaac story. But whereas the word to Abram includes the promise that he will be made a great nation, the word to Isaac's wife speaks of her mothering two nations. In the event, the word to Abram (though often imperilled) also received a double fulfillment, through Ishmael and Isaac; it was the younger of the half-brothers who was to be preferred

(17:21; 21:12), but there is no suggestion of rivalry between them—though there was tension between their mothers (16:4–6; 21:9–10). The word to Rebekah, however, already speaks of the preferment of the younger of the two sons she is to bear, and hints at the trouble there will be between them (25:23). ["The Patriarchs in Scripture and History," in *Essays on the Patriarchal Narratives,* edited by A. R. Millard and D. J. Wiseman (Leicester: Inter-Varsity, 1980), p. 17]

Theological Ideas

The predominant theological element of this passage is the oracle of the Lord. Not only does this oracle represent one of the ways that God revealed himself in the Old Testament age, but it also reveals the divine prerogative for election, that is, the electing of the younger over the elder. While the passage reports a birth of twins, that birth carried greater significance because of the divine interpretation. The expositor will have to consider both the nature of this oracle and its message.

The concept of God's answering prayer also figures prominently in this story. Both Isaac and Rebekah prayed, and God responded to both. Prayer was thus established as the means by which God chose to grant his promised blessing. The commemorative naming at the end of the story is a recognition by the parents of God's oracle as the answer to their prayers.

Another theological motif that needs mention is that of God's provision of children from the barren womb. Psalm 113 elevates this divine activity to a standard example of God's gracious intervention. It would be understood that, when the Lord God opened the barren womb and enabled the woman to become pregnant, the child was to be considered a provision from the Lord, whether it be Jacob, Isaac, Joseph, or Samuel. They each were men of destiny because they had births that were considered to be supernatural because of the impossibility of natural childbirth.

Structure and Synthesis

Structure

This passage includes a birth report and an oracle, as can be easily seen in the structure. Following the heading for the entire section of the Jacob stories (v. 19), we have the account of the birth (vv. 20–26). Within this account, and as an integral part of it, is the oracle (v. 23). In fact, the meaning of this oracle probably influenced the commemorative naming (vv. 25–26).

The narrative includes two tensions, which develop the structure. The first is the motif of barrenness in the patriarch's wife, and the second is the struggle of the children within her womb. The first tension is not very prominent, for it is only mentioned in a causal clause that explains Isaac's prayer for his wife. The second is prominent, becoming a major motif in the Jacob-Esau cycle; it therefore forms the major point of tension in the narrative and is resolved only by an oracle from God. In fact, the divine intervention in the first tension brought on the second tension.

The entire narrative is bracketed by reports of the age of Isaac. He was forty years old when he married Rebekah (v. 20), and he was sixty years old when the children were born (v. 26). Fokkelman illustrates the passage with this bracketing in mind in order to show the concentric structure (see chart 21).

Fokkelman admits that the concentric structure is not "everywhere compelling" but notes that the structure does indicate what is at the heart of the matter—the oracle (*Narrative Art,* p. 93). It should be noted as well that the structure of the oracle follows poetical parallelism:

> Two nations are in your womb,
> > Two peoples shall be separated from your body;
> One shall be stronger than the other,
> > And the older shall serve the younger.

Summary Message

After twenty years of barrenness God answered Isaac's prayers and gave Rebekah two sons, Esau and Jacob, declaring that two nations would come from them and that the elder would serve the younger.

Chart 21. **Chiasmus of Genesis 25:20–26**

A Isaac was forty years old when he took to wife Rebekah (20).

  B Rebekah was barren; prayer for children was answered (21a).

    C ⎰His wife Rebekah conceived (21b).
       ⎱The children struggled together within her (22a).

      D Rebekah asks for (22b) ⎫
                                ⎬ an *oracle.*
      D' Yahweh grants her (23) ⎭

    C' ⎰Her days to be delivered were fulfilled (24a).
       ⎱And behold, there were twins in her womb (24b).

  B' Jacob and Esau are contrasted in birth and appearance (25–26a).

A' Isaac was sixty years old when Rebekah bore the twins (26b).

Exegetical Outline

Title: This is what became of Isaac (19a).
  I. Prologue: Isaac, the son of Abraham, was forty years old when he married Rebekah, a relative from his father's homeland (19b–20).
  II. In response to Isaac's diligent prayer concerning his wife's barrenness, the Lord enabled Rebekah to become pregnant (21).
      A. Isaac prayed earnestly for Rebekah (21a).
      B. The Lord answered the prayer (21b).
  III. In response to Rebekah's inquiry concerning the turmoil in her womb, the Lord revealed that her two sons, like the two nations that would come from them, would struggle against each other and that the elder would serve the younger (22–23).
      A. Rebekah went to inquire of the Lord concerning the turmoil she felt in her womb (22).
      B. The Lord gave an oracle concerning the destiny of her offspring (23).
  IV. When the twins were born, the first was named Esau because of his appearance, and the second was named Jacob because of his activity (24–26a).
      A. Rebekah gave birth to twins (24).
      B. The parents named the children (25–26a).
          1. The first was named Esau because he was reddish and hairy (25).
          2. The second, the one promised the greater destiny, was named Jacob because of his action of grabbing the heel (26a).
  V. Epilogue: Isaac was sixty years old when the boys were born (26b).

Development of the Exposition

It would be effective to use the three middle points of the exegetical outline in forming the exposition, leaving the prologue and the epilogue for transitional comment. In this way the main exposition would deal with the provision of a son for Isaac (vv. 19–21), the selection of the younger over the elder (vv. 22–23), and the births of the twins, in which the parents observe and commemorate the active younger son (24–26).

I. God sovereignly provides the recipient of the promises (19–21).

The first few verses show Isaac's connection to Abraham and the family, compare Isaac to Abraham by mentioning the barrenness of his wife, and show how the promise moved to the next stage by the answer to prayer. In this narrative the reader learns that the birth was a supernatural provision. The seed of Abraham, as it came to be called, existed because the Lord miraculously brought it out of a barren womb. It was therefore a creative act.

The expositor would also think of the spiritual seed of Abraham in the New Testament. The people of God do not exist by natural birth but are born of the Spirit. They exist because God brought them into existence as his people.

It is important to observe how this section stresses the family connections. The heading mentions that Isaac is the son of Abraham (ben-ʾabrāhām), a point that would seem unnecessary within the context of the book. But then the narrative proper begins on that same point—Abraham begot (hôlîd) Isaac. The usage of the Hebrew terms marks this material out as genealogical report, but the repetition of the point stresses Isaac's connection to the one who received the promise. The following accounts continue that connection, beginning with the barrenness of Rebekah and the prayer of Isaac.

There is also repetition concerning the family of Rebekah. The text identifies both her father and her brother as Aramaeans (hāʾărammî). This information not only links this story to Genesis 24 but also lays the foundation for the Jacob-Laban cycle, in which Israel and Syria conflict in their ancestors.

There is also a theological observation to be made within the context of this birth report. Although Isaac was the son of Abraham, the heir of the promise, and although Rebekah was of good stock, carefully chosen to be the bride, these facts are not sufficient to produce the next heir of the promised blessing; it would still take divine intervention. (For a development of this idea, see Brueggemann, *Genesis*, p. 212).

The main didactic element of this first section, however, comes from the report of the prayer of Isaac. Abraham earlier had prayed for the barren wombs of Gerar (20:17)—but not for Sarah's. Isaac knew that the only recourse for such a problem was to entreat the Lord. That this is the predominant point may be seen from the repetition of the verb: "Isaac entreated [wayyeʿtar] the LORD . . . and the LORD was entreated [wayyēʿāter]." The verb ʿātar thus warrants a closer study as part of the exegetical procedure. Such a study will discover that the verb occurs frequently in the narratives of the plagues of Egypt (Exod. 8–10), in which Moses entreated the Lord to remove the plagues. There may not be sufficient evidence to determine all that went into Isaac's supplication, but it is interesting to note that the Arabic cognate of the verb meant "to slaughter for sacrifice," and the Hebrew cognate noun (ʿātār) was used in Zephaniah 3:10 to describe worshipers or suppliants who would bring offerings. Some form of ritual perhaps accompanied Isaac's prayer. At any rate, a study of the verb's usage shows that God is always the one being entreated for deliverance or relief. Here, the result of the entreaty was that Rebekah's barrenness was removed.

These verses indicate, then, that God sovereignly and graciously removed Rebekah's barrenness so that she could have children, notably the recipient of the promises.

II. God chooses the recipient of the promises by sovereign election (22–23).

The second section introduces the major tension of the narrative, the turmoil within the womb of Isaac's wife. The tension intensifies because Rebekah's pregnancy was an answer to prayer; something was wrong in the divine provision. The verb $rāṣaṣ$, used to describe the children's struggling in her womb, warrants further study. Since it normally signifies crushing or oppressing, this was apparently not a mild discomfort. The verb appropriately lays the foundation for the greater conflicts the brothers later engaged in.

Once again the recourse was prayer. The sentence "and she went to inquire [$lidrōš < dāraš$] of the LORD" suggests the activity of seeking an oracle. At least such a meaning of the verb is common. But the narrative does not indicate where Rebekah went or what she did. The choice of the verb $dāraš$ by the narrator is sufficient in itself to provide a didactic interpretation for the readers—when faced with such turmoil, inquire of the Lord. Other Scriptures that use this verb will provide clarification of how Israel sought the Lord.

The report of the tension and the seeking of the Lord lead up to the main point of the passage: the oracle from the Lord. God revealed that two nations ($gôyīm$ // l^e'$ummîm$) would come from her womb—meaning that the two sons would be the founders of great tribes—and that they would have conflict, with the elder becoming servant (ya'$ăbōd$) to the younger. Like the oracle of Noah, here was a declaration based on a simple family event that eventually had far-reaching effects on national relations. Down through her history Israel recalled that the Lord had given her priority over Edom, one of her perennial enemies.

By sovereign election, God declared that the promised line would belong to Jacob, the younger son. Jacob thus owed his supremacy not to natural order or to human will but to divine election. The theological motifs of creation and election thus figure prominently in the development of the chosen people of God.

The divine choice of Jacob also would become a source of the conflict the patriarch would face. When God chose the younger over the elder, he upset the natural order of society and prepared the way for opposition and antagonism (see Matt. 19:30; 20:16). Moreover, Jacob and his mother would cling to this oracle and attempt to achieve presumptuously what it had promised, thus adding to the conflict. Those who claim to be the chosen of God cannot expect the world to congratulate them (cf. John 15:18–19).

III. The faithful acknowledge the outworking of the sovereign plan (24–26).

The central thrust of the third section concerns the naming of the twins. The parents observed the unusual circumstances of the births—especially in view of God's oracle—and commemorated them in the naming. In these acts of naming we may perceive that the parents acknowledged the oracle of God.

In view of the report of the namings in this story, Driver suggests that the oracle in the context may be the verdict of history, thrown back in poetical form to the ideal beginnings of the two nations, reflecting how Edom was subjugated by David (2 Sam. 8:12–13; prophesied in Gen. 27:40), because the naming identifies Esau with Seir and Edom (*Book of Genesis*, p. 245). The characteristics and events about Jacob and Esau picture the natures of, and the relationship between, Israel and Edom. However, I would say that the narrator selected those traditions about the ancestors that best explained what became of their descendants.

Esau's appearance—more like an animal of the field than an ordinary baby—prompted his naming. The narrative here establishes the qualities that are essential in Genesis 25:29–34 and in chapter 27. It is important to observe that the child is described using only nouns. This style provides a static effect as opposed to the description of Jacob, who comes engaged in action (Fokkelman, *Narratve Art*, p. 90). The first child was red-brown (ʾadmônî), a description that significantly formed the basis of the sons of Esau, the Edomites. With the description of "hairy" (śēʿār), there is an allusion to Mount Seir, where Esau later dwelt (Gen. 36:8). The narrator could have used other words to describe the child but, knowing his destiny, chose to capture the ominous condition of his birth.

The younger twin followed on the heels of his brother—"his hand was seizing the heel [baʿāqēb] of Esau" (v. 26). The name Jacob (yaʿāqōb) was apparently chosen to retain the memory of the unusual activity of the infant. In time the name came to suggest "take by the heel, trip up, defraud." The word ʿāqēb ("heel") is used in passages describing oppo-

sition, perhaps an attack from behind (Gen. 3:15; Job 18:19). But as
Driver states, the sense of defrauding came to be known to the narrator
after the later actions of Jacob revealed the true significance of his dive
for the brother's heel (see Hos. 12:3). In the view of the parents, the
seizing of the heel would have conveyed an affectionate thought. On
later reflection they would realize that the child was in essence struggling for the best starting position. The name naturally lent itself to the
interpretation by Esau (Gen. 27:36).

The name Jacob likely had a positive connotation at the time of the
naming. There is evidence for a meaning "protect" rather than "overreach, assail" (see *PN*, pp. 177–78; Albright, *From the Stone Age to
Christianity* [Garden City, N.Y.: Doubleday, 1957], p. 237). The name
may have been contracted from *ya'ăqōb 'ēl*, "may God protect." Its
connection with "heel" probably was that of the following at the heels
as a rearguard—but it would not be necessary for the parents to know
the actual etymology when they chose the name.

The name seems to have been in existence from an early stage. Because the name sounded like the word for heel, the parents chose it to
commemorate the unusual event, the grabbing of the "heel" (*'āqēb*).
Later events then showed how his name took on the negative significance of assailant or overreacher. Tradition loved to tell of those incidents that verified his name, as Driver puts it. It is quite unlikely, however,
that parents would have named a baby "assailant, overreacher," or
"deceiver."

The names were thus chosen to reflect the appearance and activity
at birth, but in both cases the names were ominous, anticipating the
natures and activities of the two and their descendants. The narrator
wished to reflect that significance by his choice of words. For this reason
the narrative is not interested in relating an amusing and unusual event
about the births of two boys; rather, the narrator wished to portray that
the destiny of two nations, Israel and Edom, was evident from the births
of their ancestors, in harmony with the divine oracle.

The passage clearly teaches that Jacob and Esau were supernaturally
provided at birth to the barren woman and that Jacob was unexpectedly
elected over his older brother. We thus may say that the fulfillment of
the promise was supernaturally provided by creation and election. Those
who enjoy participation in God's program of blessing do so because they
are the creation and the elect of God.

On the human side, faith is essential. Faith is exemplified in this
story by the prayer of Isaac, the inquiry of Rebekah, and the naming by
the parents. God apparently used the barrenness and the struggle to
prompt their faith. It says to Israel, and to us, that the promises will not

be achieved except by faith in God's supernatural dealings. God later gave Israel, his elect, the promised blessing. It did not come without a struggle, however, because God's supernatural dealings reversed the natural order. Israel would learn that their status as God's elect would require faith in God's supernatural provisions, both realized and expected.

The beginning of two nations was thus acknowledged in the birth and naming of the twins. From the oracle and the birth we learn that the nation of Israel was supernaturally superintended. The primary emphasis is on sovereign grace, in that God was providing for the accomplishing of his program. Paul in Romans 9:11–12 used this passage in his discussion of election, explaining that the younger was chosen over the elder before their births. In election God reverses the natural order—for his ways are not our ways (1 Cor. 1:27–29).

God's program in our day, although very different from the patriarchal age, still develops on the same theological principles. Today God is building a nation from among the nations, an elect people (1 Peter 2:9), his new creation (2 Cor. 5:17). Since it is his program, it is supernatural throughout. God elects to use the things that are weak to confound the mighty, the things that are not to confound the things that are.

We are a part of his current program to bless the world because we have become recipients of the promised blessings. On the one hand, it is easy to look back and see how God worked supernaturally through events to bring us to himself—he elected us and made us his new creation; but on the other hand, today and tomorrow we must walk by faith, discerning how the Lord will work through apparent tensions. Just as Isaac and Rebekah acknowledged the revelation of God's plan through the difficulties, so too must believers today! We may not know what God will do with the troubling and the trivial things that come our way. But *those who owe their existence to sovereign creation and divine election must be able to acknowledge the hand of God in the circumstances of life.* If we know his will, we will look at circumstances differently, for everything has significance that must be retained in the memory of the people of God.

Bibliography

Coats, G. W. "Strife Without Reconciliation—a Narrative Theme in the Jacob Traditions." In *Werden und Wirken des Alten Testaments*, edited by R. Albertz, Hans-Peter Müller, Hans Walter Wolff, and Walther Zimmerli, pp. 82–106. Göttingen: Vandenhoeck & Ruprecht, 1979.

Fishbane, Michael. "Composition and Structure in the Jacob Cycle (Gen. 25, 19–35, 29)." *JJS* 26 (1975): 15–38.

Fokkelman, J. P. *Narrative Art in Genesis,* pp. 86–94. Assen: Van Gorcum, 1975.

Freedman, D. N. "The Original Name of Jacob." *IEJ* 13 (1963): 125–26.

Fretheim, T. E. "The Jacob Traditions: Theology and Hermeneutics." *Interp* 26 (1972): 419–36.

Hauge, M. R. "The Struggles of the Blessed in Estrangement." *StTh* 29 (1975): 1–30, 113–46.

Kardimon, Samson. "Adoption as a Remedy for Infertility in the Period of the Patriarchs." *JSS* 3 (1958): 123–26.

Kraft, R. A. "A Note on the Oracle of Rebecca (Gen. XXV 23)." *JThS* 13 (1962): 318–20.

Luke, K. "Two Birth Narratives in Genesis." *IndThSt* 17 (1980): 155–80.

Maag, V. "Jakob—Esau—Edom." *ThZ* 13 (1957): 418–29.

Miscall, P. D. "The Jacob and Joseph Stories as Analogies." *JSOT* 6 (1978): 28–40.

Thomas, D. W. "The Root אָהֵב 'Love' in Hebrew." *ZAW* 57 (1939): 57–64.

Thompson, T. L. "Conflict of Themes in the Jacob Narratives." *Semeia* 15 (1979): 5–26.

Williams, James G. "The Comedy of Jacob: A Literary Study." *JAAR* 46 (1978): 208.

39

The Sale of the Birthright
(Gen. 25:27–34)

This passage forms a self-contained unit describing the transfer of the birthright from Esau to Jacob. The story develops the motif given in the previous narrative, showing how the divine oracle began to express itself in the lives of the boys. What had appeared to be a trivial event at the birth of the twins became more ominous with this development. Here Jacob and Esau developed according to their initial characteristics. The "redman" was overcome by his physical appetites for the "redstuff" and sold his birthright. The "heel-grabber" cunningly overtook his brother and gained the birthright.

The narrative is primarily interested in explaining how the birthright became Jacob's possession. But the story carries with it moral lessons as well. There are no winners in this encounter, even though Jacob comes away with the birthright. Neither man is exemplary. On the one hand, we have the profane man, Esau, who considered the spiritual heritage of little value and traded it for the lentil soup. On the other hand, we have the shrewd man, who, although he regarded spiritual things highly, made the cause serve him through manipulation. The two are played off of each other, for the point of tension in the story comes when the two brothers meet and exchange what they have. But the entire narrative is

444

slightly slanted against Esau's profanity, for it characterizes Esau, or Edom, according to his impulsive nature and ends with a report of his despising the birthright.

The story does not actually come to a resolution, even though there is a transference of possessions—there is no lasting resolution and no divine approval. Consequently, there is some hesitancy to classify the unit as a narrative. Coats prefers to call it an anecdote, a report of an incident in the life story of the two people (*Genesis*, p. 187). But if the unit explains how the younger obtained the birthright, then it forms a complete unit in itself, albeit a unit that now forms part of the major plot of the conflict between the brothers that will be resolved only at their reconciliation (33:15–20). In the Jacob stories we do not find individual episodes such as formed the Abrahamic narratives; rather, these events develop a major plot through to its resolution.

Theological Ideas

Central to this unit is the nature of the birthright as the portion of the heir who will carry on the line of the promised seed. The passage is not filled with theological concepts, but it does present a forceful study of how the birthright—the abiding, spiritual heritage—was perceived. Here we must analyze Esau's despising the birthright as the subtheme in the theological point of the story.

Another motif in this story, although not a theological idea in the strict sense of the term, is an important part of the instruction of the Torah. In this passage we are introduced to the favoritism of the parents that threatens to divide the family with irreconcilable differences. This theme is part of the conflict that constantly threatens the blessing of the family.

Structure and Synthesis

Structure

As with previous narratives, this passage blends narrative report and dialogue in its structure. The first two verses report the different natures of Jacob and Esau as well as the favoritism of the parents. Verses 29–34 report the event with the dialogue: narrative report about Esau's hunger and Jacob's food (v. 29), dialogue (business transaction) between Jacob and Esau (vv. 30–33a), and narrative report about the culmination of the trade (vv. 33b–34).

The dialogue has an interesting contrast: Esau asked to be fed (the imperative *hal'îṭēnî*) because he was famished (*kî 'āyēp 'ānōkî*), but Jacob responded with the demand of the birthright (the imperative *mikrâ*,

"sell"); Esau responded by asserting that he was about to die (hinnēh
ʾānōkî hôlēk lāmût) and would have no use of the birthright, but Jacob
pressed the matter for the sale (the imperative hiššābeˁâ, "swear"). Esau's
preoccupation with himself (both speeches using ʾānōkî, "I") and Jacob's
demands (two imperatives pressing Esau to comply) focus the attention
on the nature and activity of Esau. The repeated use of "birthright"
(bekōrâ is used four times) shows the focus of the attention. Esau was
oblivious to what he had because he was preoccupied with the way he
was; Jacob was occupied with obtaining what Esau had and planned to
capitalize on the way Esau was. The last part of the narrative report with
its rapid succession of verbs—"and he ate, and drank, and arose, and
went out"—provides the climax to the description of the profane Esau.

Fokkelman diagrams the structure of the story to show that the turning point is Esau's disregard for the birthright (see chart 22). Referring
to chart 22, Fokkelman writes,

> Esau is hemmed in by his brother's cunning design. The Centre, X, is
> the highest point, or rather the lowest point, for it shows (and there-
> fore it is also the turning-point) Esau toppling (over), a prey to his
> craving for strengthening food, because he is dead tired. He exchanges
> his own pride and dignity, the ornament of the birthright for . . . a mess
> of pottage. It is a concrete thing, the short-term man thinks, and Jacob,
> the long-range-planner, has scored his first hit. [Narrative Art, p. 95]

There is also a slight parallel with the story of the fall in Genesis 3.
In both accounts there is a confrontation between the shrewd and the
naive. In both passages the birthright is traded for food. And in both
passages after the exchange, the narrative reports the development with

Chart 22. Chiasmus of Genesis 25:29–34

A   Jacob was boiling pottage (29a).

   B   Esau came in from the field; he was tired (29b).

      C   *wayyōʾmer ˁēśāw:* Let me eat some of that red pottage . . . , I am so tired! (30).

         D   *wayyōʾmer yaˁāqōb:* First sell me your *bkrh* (31).

            E   *wayyōʾmer ˁēśāw:* I depart; I die! Of what use is a *bkrh* to me? (32).

         D'   *wayyōʾmer yaˁāqōb:* Swear to me first. So he swore to him and sold his *bkrh* to Jacob (33).

      C'   Jacob gave Esau bread and pottage of lentils; he ate and he drank (34aα).

   B'   He rose and went his way (34aβ).

A'   Thus Esau despised his birthright (34b).

a series of verbs in rapid succession. At the heart of each narrative is the dialogue that invites the naive to surrender the spiritual blessing for the satisfaction of the natural desires.

Summary Message

Without regard for the benefits of the firstborn, Esau, the cunning hunter, swore to sell the birthright to the crafty Jacob for a meal of red stuff, a description that was appropriate to his nature.

Exegetical Outline

    I. Esau became a cunning hunter and the favorite of his father, who enjoyed wild game, but Jacob became an even-tempered man, loved by Rebekah (27–28).

       A. Esau grew up to be a skillful hunter, whereas Jacob became a settled nomad (27).

       B. Isaac loved Esau because he brought him game, but Rebekah loved Jacob (28).

    II. When Esau came in from the open country famished and found Jacob preparing red soup, he greedily asked for some "red stuff" to eat—the designation of which food was appropriate to his character and that of his descendants (29–30).

       A. Esau, famished from a futile hunt, found Jacob cooking red soup (29).

       B. Esau greedily asked for some of the red stuff (30a).

       C. Esau's descendants shared his impulsive nature (30b).

    III. Esau swore to give Jacob his birthright in exchange for the red soup (31–33).

       A. Jacob forced Esau to sell him his birthright before he would give him the soup (31).

       B. Esau considered his birthright worthless at this point (32).

       C. Jacob forced Esau to confirm the sale (33).

    IV. Having sworn to relinquish his birthright, Esau gulped down the food and left, thus demonstrating his disdain for the birthright (34).

Development of the Exposition

There are a number of ways that this passage could be developed. One could contrast both men in a discussion of the tension over the birthright—with neither man being viewed as exemplary. But Esau seems to be the focus of the writer in this story, so much so that the popular etymology is applied to him in a summary of his nature, and the conclusion is concerned with how he despised the birthright. It may therefore be best to center the exposition on Esau as the sample of the profane person, using Jacob's actions as the occasion for the disclosure of Esau's true nature.

I. The profane person lives a life of worldly freedom that is pleasing to the natural man (27–28).

This point is drawn from the description of Esau in contrast to his brother Jacob, and represents the reason for the favoritism of Isaac. Esau was the outdoorsman, a cunning hunter roaming the fields. The text does not condemn this activity but uses it to show that Esau lived for the best of this life. Isaac favored Esau because he loved the taste of Esau's game. The favoritism was thus based on natural senses rather than enduring qualities. By way of contrast, Jacob was even-tempered and resolute. He had things under control.

A. *The profane person lives free (27).*

In describing the two men now grown, the narrative contrasts their characters by means of a chiastic arrangement: Esau was a cunning hunter (*yōdēaʿ ṣayid*), a man of the field (*ʾîš śādeh*); but Jacob was a man of even temperament (*ʾîš tām*), dwelling in tents (*yōšēb ʾōhālîm*). The couplet is framed by the use of the participles—cunning hunter and dweller in tents—and parallels antithetically field and tents. We thus meet the aggressive hunter versus the reflective nomad. Esau is the sportsman, rough, wild, free, boisterous, and exciting; Jacob is the settled man, stable, quiet, thoughtful, and civilized. It will be important to study the use of *tām*, "even-tempered," in the description of Jacob. The word usually means "perfect, blameless, without blemish" but seems to have a different meaning here. Commentators generally interpret it to mean "even-tempered," but that meaning will have to be verified to the satisfaction of the expositor. It may also be helpful to note the significance of "dwelling in tents." In the ancient Sumerian king list, many named early on the list are said to dwell in tents, apparently signifying that they were honorable and civilized.

In this regard some scholars have seen a greater significance lying behind this story, a contrast between the hunter and shepherd. Maag ("Jakob—Esau—Edom") attempts to demonstrate that this story is part of an ancient tradition that showed the shepherd replacing the hunter in the development of civilization, because the shepherd could plan and control economic life. He contends that the story was applied to Jacob and Esau to show that the rivalry extends to all civilization. It seems to me, however, that, while this is an interesting theory, there is no compelling evidence that the narrative ever was anything other than what it now is, a record of the transference of the birthright.

The point of the contrast of occupations lays the foundation for the transaction. Esau, whose profane nature gradually unfolds, lives with the freedom and the risk of the hunt—he is a skillful hunter. Jacob is steady, settled, awaiting the time to make his move for the birthright.

B. The profane person appeals to the natural senses (28).

In verse 28, the parental favoritism is introduced in a way that contrasts Jacob and Esau (cf. the contrast of Cain and Abel). The text first reports that Isaac loved Esau "because the game was in his mouth [kî ṣayid bepîw]"—he loved the taste of game. Here is introduced a weakness in Isaac that will be fully exploited in Genesis 27—he made his choices on the basis of his senses. Because he loved what Esau gave him to eat, he loved Esau. The causal clause stresses Isaac's self-gratification.

No such explanation is provided for Rebekah's love for Jacob, but in view of her concern in chapter 27 that the wrong son not receive the blessing, we may suspect that the oracle of the Lord raised her interest in the younger son. The text does stress the contrast between the parents ("but Rebekah") as part of the conflict between the brothers. And the change to the participle ('ōhebet) from the preterite (wayye'ĕhab) may signify the more durative and persevering nature of Rebekah's love for Jacob.

II. The profane person acts on impulse for the gratification of the natural appetites (29–33).

In this section the narrator effectively depicts the animallike nature of Esau and the superior hunting ability of Jacob. The cunning hunter fell into a better hunter's trap, becoming prey to his own appetites.

A. The profane person is the victim of personal appetites (29–30).

In a brilliant narration we read of the clever hunter laying a trap for the hungry animal. Word plays stress this turnabout within the verses: the verb and the noun chosen to describe Jacob's activity of boiling pottage (wayyāzed ya'ăqōb nāzîd [< zîd]) recalls the sounds of the word used to describe the hunter (ṣayid). Esau might have been a cunning hunter, but Jacob also knew how to catch game.

The verb zîd may also give another connotation to the action. Although it certainly means "boil" in this passage, elsewhere it was used to describe presumptuous actions. Jacob's boiling the pottage seemed a simple act, but by the choice of this word the narrator implies that Jacob was hunting his prey and that he was acting presumptuously.

Esau, faint from a fruitless effort in the field, appeared and demanded to be fed with some of the food that Jacob was preparing. The expositor needs to look closely at Esau's first speech. The verb used in his initial appeal is a colorful one—"feed me" (hal'îṭēnî [< lā'aṭ]). It conveys the basic idea of gulping down food. The rabbis used it to describe the activity of cramming food down the throat of an animal. The paraphrase "let me gulp down" might better capture his mood.

Esau wanted to gulp down the reddish lentil soup Jacob boiled. The repetition of the "red stuff" (hā'ādōm) also characterizes Esau's impulsive nature: "Let me gulp down some of this red stuff, red stuff [min-hā'ādōm hā'ādōm]." The picture is one of a wild and blustery man pointing and gasping, "Red stuff, red stuff," explaining that he is faint from hunger.

The narrator's choice of the word for red ('ādōm) was deliberate, for it is etymologically related to the word for Edom ('ĕdōm). By the choice of this word in the telling of the story, the narrator sought to describe the Edomites as impulsive and profane as their ancestor. Esau did not take the name Edom; rather, the descendants of Esau were known as Edomites. The interest of the writer extends beyond the simple report of what happened between brothers; it affirms that the Edomites share the nature of their ancestor and have no interest in the birthright.

B. The profane person relinquishes things of value for the satisfaction of appetites (31–33).

This was the moment that Jacob had been waiting for, and perhaps had observed on prior occasions as his best chance. Rather than give his brother the food, he betrayed his real interest: "Sell me today your birthright." This birthright (bᵉkōrâ), so central to the Jacob stories, probably represents the priority in the inheritance (but see the literature on it). Jacob apparently interpreted the oracle to mean that, if he obtained the birthright, he would occupy the place of the elder son as heir. Being farsighted and calculating, he pressed the matter on his famished brother.

Esau's response was desperate—"I am about to die, what good is the birthright to me?" Here again we catch another glimpse of the profane person, who lives for the moment, showing no concern about the cost. Besides, the conclusion to the story shows that he was nowhere near the point of death. He meant that he was dying of hunger, but in his impassioned response he saw no value in the birthright.

Jacob wished to ensure the agreement for the exchange, and so he demanded that Esau swear that very day. Esau quickly—and not unexpectedly—forgot this oath, for in chapter 27 he went to hunt in order to receive his father's blessing. But the transaction was completed. At the beginning Jacob had lentil soup and Esau had the birthright; and through the exchange Esau obtained the soup, and Jacob the birthright.

The narrative does not offer any moral judgments on Jacob. It simply explains that Esau sold his birthright to Jacob. There was no deception on the part of Jacob, only the calculated manipulation of his impulsive brother. The act no doubt added to the growing animosity that Esau had for Jacob. But God would use it as a part of his elevation of Jacob to the place of supremacy.

III. The profane person has no regard for the things of God (34).

Here the statement that Esau despised his birthright forms the central point of the verse. Kidner observes that the chapter "does not comment 'So Jacob supplanted his brother,' but 'So Esau despised his birthright'; and Hebrews 12 shares its standpoint, presenting flippant Esau as the antithesis of the pilgrims of Hebrews 11" (Genesis, p. 152).

The rapid series of verbs prior to the report that Esau despised the birthright both lead up to and explain his despising. That is, by eating and drinking and rushing out, Esau showed that he had no interest in the birthright. He was more interested in feeding himself, like a brutish beast of the field. The report that he despised the birthright seems to summarize the entire event. "To despise" (bāzâ) something means to treat it as worthless or to hold it in contempt. The word often describes an attitude of contempt for the things of God, such as the law, the sacrifices, or the temple. In this passage the object is the birthright. Not only did Esau consider it worthless—a fair trade for lentil soup—but afterward he came to despise it, perhaps looking back in angry remorse over his foolish act.

The narrative thus explains how Jacob, the younger son, came to possess the birthright. The quiet, calculating man recognized the value of the birthright and manipulated his profane brother into relinquishing it. Israel might appreciate the tenacity of their ancestor in obtaining what was eventually to be his, but they would also learn that God would not allow the promises to be obtained that way.

Israel would also be warned by the profane nature and activity of Esau. The lesson certainly concerns more than a worldly, free lifestyle. It concerns the sacrificing of spiritual provisions for the satisfaction of physical appetites, of relinquishing eternal things for momentary pleasures. It is thus a matter of priorities and values. The primary lesson would concern the profane person: *Profane people are willing to relinquish*

*things of lasting spiritual value because they live to satisfy their basic
appetites.*

Esau was portrayed as very emotional. He was fainting, gasping, gulping, and then despising. He was not here a skillful hunter; he was more
like the animals that he must have trapped with a morsel of bait. To live
on this level is tragic, for living to satisfy the appetites inevitably leads
to despising things of value, especially when they become the possession
of others. Delitzsch writes:

> Esau's forfeiture of these privileges is, according to Rom. IX (comp. Mal.
> i.2 sq.), a work of free Divine election, but not without being at the same
> time, as this narrative shows, the result of Esau's voluntary self-degra-
> dation. As Ishmael had no claim to the blessing of the first-born, because
> begotten κατὰ σάρκα [according to the flesh], so does Esau, though not
> begotten κατὰ σάρκα forfeit the blessing of the first-born, because minded
> κατὰ σάρκα. [*New Commentary on Genesis*, vol. 2, pp. 136–37]

A secondary lesson may be derived from this passage concerning what
Delitzsch calls the "unbrotherly artifice" of Jacob. Jacob knew that Esau
was profane and often came in famished, and so he planned to take
advantage of his brother and obtain what the oracle said would be his.
The fact that what Jacob strongly desired was worth desiring makes him
the more pleasing of the two. But there is a danger in such spiritual
ambition. The lesson for the household of faith should be to seek the
things of spiritual value, to be sure, but *those who earnestly desire
spiritual possessions must not seek to attain them through base means.*

Bibliography

Fokkelman, J. P. *Narrative Art in Genesis,* pp. 94–97. Assen: Van Gorcum,
  1975.

Maag, V. "Jakob—Esau—Edom." *ThZ* 13 (1957): 418–29.

Saydon, P. P. "Some Unusual Ways of Expressing the Superlative in Hebrew
  and Maltese." *VT* 4 (1954): 432–33.

Sharp, Donald B. "In Defense of Rebecca?" *BThB* 10 (1980): 164–68.

40

The Preservation of the Faith
(Gen. 26:1–11)

T his story concerns Isaac's deception of Abimelech. It
rehearses first how Abraham was obedient in the faith to preserve and
pass down the promise and then reports how God preserved the promise
by his intervention in the life of Abimelech.

Genesis 26, with its concentration on Isaac rather than Jacob, does
not seem to be closely connected to its context. Without it, Genesis 25
and 27 would form a smooth continuation for the Jacob stories. In a
parallel way Genesis 34 (the story of the rape of Dinah) seems to interrupt Genesis 33 and 35. But chapters 26 and 34 form interludes in the
development of the Jacob stories: the first interlude is about the father
of Jacob, and it comes just prior to the major break with Esau; the second
interlude is about the sons of Jacob, and it comes just after the reconciliation with Esau. The two chapters, then, bracket the concentration
on the Jacob and Esau conflict, linking the stories to the ancestry and
progeny. Fishbane writes:

The symmetry between Genesis 26 and 34, together with their parallel
functions as interludes, thus preclude any assumption of haphazard editorial arrangement. Moreover, they are linked to each other and to their

453

respective contexts by the common themes of deception and strife. The first section of chapter 26, in which Isaac deceives Abimeleck with regard to Rebekkah (v. 7) involves a case of strife wherein a wife is called a "sister" ('ahot) and there is fear of intercourse (stem: shakhav) with a member of an uncircumcised ethnic group. In its second section, in which Isaac charges the Philistines with deception (v. 27), there is a case of strife among the shepherds (v. 20) as well as an issue of covenantal malfeasance in which the treaty partners are called "brothers" ('ahim). In a parallel way, Genesis 34 also reports an event involving deception (mirmah, v. 34; cf. 27:35; and 29:25)—but now because of an actual case of intercourse (stem: shakhav) between the "uncircumcised" Schechem ben Hamor and Dinah, the sister ('ahot) of Simeon and Levi. The deception also involves covenantal malfeasance (v. 10) and considerable strife.

While the interludes in chapters 26 and 34 divert the pace of the Jacob Cycle, they also enlarge our sense of the lives of the patriarchs. From the outset the issues of entangling relations and marital complexity are expressed. The interludes, while suspending the main action, mirror these issues along a broader familial continuum. They are witnesses to the creative-artistic imagination which synthesized the multiple traditions of the Jacob Cycle as a whole. [Text and Texture, pp. 47–48]

As an interlude, Genesis 26 has another point to make—that the blessing of Abraham had indeed passed to Isaac (and so Jacob could obtain that for which he struggled). Goldingay lists the parallels between Isaac and Abraham found in this chapter that show God was with Isaac:

The original blessing theme is explicitly resumed in chapter 26. Here Yahweh appears, commands, and promises, as he had to Abraham (26:2–5; cf. 12:1–3). Although Isaac made mistakes very like his father's (26:6–11; cf. 12:10–20; 20:1–18), he also received blessings very like his father's (26:12–14; cf. 13:1–4). He was involved in strife like his father (26:15–22; cf. 13:5–13; 21:25–32), but he was reassured by Yahweh and he worshipped like his father (26:23–25; cf. 13:14–18; 21:33) and was acknowledged by the nations like his father (26:26–33; cf. 14:19–20; 21:22–24). Indeed, it is explicitly because Yahweh committed himself to Abraham, because Abraham obeyed him, and as the God of Abraham, that Yahweh appears to Isaac (26:3, 5, 24). Nevertheless, there is one distinctive motif characteristic of the Isaac narrative, the promise "I will be with you" (26:3) or "I am with you" (26:24). It reappears in the form of Abimelek's acknowledgment of Isaac, "Yahweh is with you" (26:28), as it had featured in Abimelek's acknowledgment of Abraham (21:22). It reappears in the Jacob material in the chapters that follow (28:15, 20; 31:3, 5, 42; 35:3), and constitutes the distinctive aspect to the promise and experience of Yahweh's blessing as this is portrayed in the Isaac narrative. ["Patriarchs," pp. 17–18]

The story in the first half of Genesis 26 parallels the stories in 12:10–20 and 20:1–18 (see the earlier discussions for the parallels). But in this account the event occurs in the land of Gerar in the lifetime of Isaac and his wife. Moreover, in this account the king does not take the beautiful woman, and the source of discovery is not divine. The marriage was thus kept intact from the threat of intermarriage with a pagan king. Coats says, "Thus, in this story the intimacy between husband and wife is never broken by the husband's foul deed, though the potential is there. Isaac offered, but no one took up his offer, and the family remains intact" (*Genesis*, p. 190).

Theological Ideas

It is helpful to recall that these stories have a theological interest over and above the simple details of the story. They frequently foreshadow the fulfillment of the promises to the covenant people. Motifs and events were selected with that theme in view. But often this significance is not easy to detect. In that case we must fit the story into the general purpose of the patriarchal narratives. These narratives were written down to show how Israel came into existence and why. Accordingly, they stress the divine creation and election as well as supernatural preservation of the family. All this material was didactic; Israel could compare the points of these stories with the clear teachings of the law to confirm the lessons. In fact, the emphasis on the law in this unit is rather pronounced.

When the story of Isaac was told, many pietistic lessons could legitimately be drawn from it. But the central point of the story concerned the development of the promise, the continuation of the blessing. In Genesis 26, Abraham was gone! He was dead! What would happen to the promised blessings? The promise in fact continued after his death to his son. Genesis 26 convincingly reveals that the promises extended to Isaac. Even though he failed as his father failed, the Lord preserved him and blessed him.

But the promises did not come without responsibility. The corresponding theological lesson in this section thus concerns obedience. Abraham is held up to Isaac (and to the reader) as the epitome of obedience to the laws of God. His faith in God's promises not only engendered unparalleled obedience but cast out fear. Conversely, where faith is weak, people cower in fear and often endanger the work of God. Here is where Isaac comes in. This narrative teaches Israel—and us—to be strong in the faith in order to live in obedience to God's laws rather than act shamefully out of fear.

Structure and Synthesis

Structure

The structure of this story is somewhat similar to the preceding sister stories. The narrative transition is found in verse 1, which reports a famine in the land and alludes to the famine in the days of Abraham (the writer was thus aware of the previous incident). The second section of the passage records a theophany and so is without parallel in the previous stories (vv. 2–5). In this theophany the Lord instructed Isaac on his course of action and then related the promised blessings to him. Verse 6 reports how Isaac complied with the instructions.

The rest of the section is a narrative about Isaac's deception and the discovery. Isaac's plan of deception is narrated in verse 7, and the truth is discovered in verses 8–10. Much like the preceding stories on this theme, the dénouement works through a dialogue of accusation and self-defense. Finally, there is a warning given to the people of Gerar (v. 11) that serves to remind the reader of the law that preserves the marriage.

Summary Message

When God prevented Isaac from leaving the land promised to Abraham, his obedient father, God renewed the covenant with him but then had to protect Rebekah from Abimelech when Isaac lied about her.

Exegetical Outline

    I. The Lord prevented Isaac from abandoning the land in the famine, by confirming to him the covenant promises he had made with his father, Abraham (1–6).

        A. Narrative introduction: When a famine began, Isaac left Canaan and went to Abimelech, king of the Philistines, at Gerar (1).

        B. Theophany: The Lord appeared to Isaac and commanded him not to leave Canaan, in order that the Lord might confirm the covenant made with Abraham his father (2–5).

           1. Instruction: The Lord commanded Isaac to stay in the land so that he might be with and bless Isaac (2–3a).

           2. Promise: The Lord reiterated the promises of the land and of descendants on the basis of the obedience of Abraham (3b–5).

               a. Blessing: The Lord promised to confirm the covenantal blessings of the land and descendants (3b–4a).

               b. Effect: The Lord affirmed that the blessing would go to the whole world through Isaac's descendants (4b).

        c. Reason: The Lord based the fulfillment of the covenant promises on the obedience of Abraham (5).
    C. Isaac obeyed the Lord by remaining in Gerar (6).
II. After Isaac deceived the men of Gerar about his wife's true identity, Abimelech discovered the deceit, rebuked Isaac for putting his people in moral jeopardy, and forewarned his people not to touch them (7–11).
    A. The plot: Isaac hid the true identity of Rebekah by representing her as his sister because he feared a personal attack (7).
    B. The detection: After a long time Abimelech discovered the deceit when he saw Isaac engaging in conjugal play with Rebekah (8).
    C. The rebuke: Abimelech confronted Isaac and rebuked him for his deceit (9–10).
        1. Abimelech confronted Isaac and expressed shock that he had hidden the truth so long (8a).
        2. Isaac explained his action by relating his fear of being killed on account of Rebekah (9b).
        3. Abimelech rebuked Isaac because his action could easily have allowed someone inadvertently to bring guilt on the nation (10).
    D. The resolution: Abimelech commanded his people not to harm Isaac or Rebekah, on the penalty of death (11).

Development of the Exposition

The passage can be treated in two parts, the promise of the blessings and the deception that endangered the promises. The first part records how the obedience of one man brought blessings to his descendants.

I. The obedience of the faithful brings blessings to those who follow in the faith (1–6).

A. God requires obedience (1–3a).

The occasion for the Lord's instructions to Isaac was a famine in the land (cf. Gen. 12:10). The additional explanation that this famine was beside that earlier famine in the lifetime of Abraham not only attests to the existence of the two events but invites comparison between Abraham and Isaac. In the earlier account Abraham went down to Egypt to sojourn, only to endanger his wife through fearful deception. At this time the Lord appeared to Isaac to prohibit his going down to Egypt ('altērēd miṣrāyᵉmâ; cf. wayyēred 'abrām miṣraymâ in 12:10). Rather, Isaac was to sojourn (gûr) in the land (cf. lāgûr in 12:10). In this instruction there seems to be a word play on the place name Gerar (*g^erārâ*, in v. 1) with the verb "sojourn" (*gûr*). More important, though, there is an allusion to the initial call of Abraham in the words "in the land which I shall tell you [*bā'āreṣ 'ăšer 'ōmar 'ēleykā*]." Such an allusion would encourage Isaac's faith in following the Lord's instructions.

This appearing and these words form a parallel with Genesis 12. At the beginning of the Abraham stories the Lord appeared to Abram with instructions and promises pertaining to the land and the seed. The Lord also makes such an appearance to Isaac at the beginning of this chapter. The parallels reinforce the point of the continuation of God's program to this second generation.

B. Obedience brings blessings (3b–6).

Following the instructions for Isaac to remain in the land are the promises—in fact, the promises show the purpose of the commands ("Sojourn in this land *in order that* I may be with you"). Here the promises first made to Abraham were reiterated to Isaac, promises of the land and of numerous descendants. Several advances, however, can be seen here. First, these promises would be fulfilled because of the covenant made with Abraham. In other words, the fulfillment was guaranteed because the Lord swore to do it. Any contingency-based obedience would refer to participation in the promises, not the fulfillment itself. Second, the promise of the land was broadened to the plural—"all these lands" (*hā'ărāṣōt*) would be given to Isaac and his descendants. This phrase probably referred to territory possessed by other tribes living in the Promised Land, since in this chapter Isaac was dealing with the Philistines in Gerar. Third, the promises now included the presence of the Lord. As mentioned above, this promise remained with the family through the time of Isaac and Jacob. And it became particularly significant in the revelation of the Lord to Moses (Exod. 3:12).

In the transferring of the Abrahamic promises to Isaac, the presentation of Abraham as the obedient servant is remarkable. The basis of the promise is in verse 5: "because Abraham obeyed my voice and kept my charge, my commandments, my statutes, and my laws [*'ēqeb 'ăšer-šāma' 'abrāhām b^eqōlî wayyišmōr mišmartî miṣwōtay ḥuqqōtay w^etôrōtāy*]." The allusion must be to Genesis 22, specifically verse 18 ("because you have obeyed my voice"), but probably encompasses more generally the life of obedience Abraham led. The terminology used to describe his obedience is striking—the words are legal designations from the law and presuppose a knowledge of Deuteronomy. The use of these words to describe Abraham's obedience has led some to explain that Abraham obeyed the entire law before it was given (see *Kiddushin* 4:14 in the Mishnah ["We find that Abraham our father had fulfilled the whole Law before it was given"]) and others to conclude that "this can have been pronounced and written only in a period when Israel's relationship to God was centered on its obedience to the law; that would be the post-Deuteronomic period, as the language of v. 5 clearly shows" (Westermann, *Genesis*, vol. 2, pp. 424–25). Perhaps the simplest explanation is that the lawgiver himself elaborated on the simple report that Abraham obeyed the Lord, by using a variety of legal terms with which the readers would be familiar. By offering this interpretive paraphrase of the tradition, he raised Abraham as the model of obedience to the law, as if to say that, had Abraham had the laws, statutes, and commandments, he would have obeyed them.

At any rate, the point of the speech is clear: Isaac and his family enjoyed the blessing of God because Abraham was obedient; therefore, Isaac and his family should obey what God instructed in order that they might enjoy further blessings from the Lord that would in turn be passed on to the next generation. The section ends with a note of Isaac's obedience (v. 6).

II. The blessings of God should (but often do not) engender obedience to the faith (7–11).

These verses record how Isaac deceived and was rebuked by a pagan king who knew that the penalty for adultery would be death. Such a legal note would remind Israel of the importance of preserving marriage for future generations, for if that mainstay went, society would soon deteriorate (indeed, if Isaac's marriage broke up, there would be no society of God's chosen ones).

A. Deception endangers the blessing (7).

The deception of Isaac followed the pattern of the deception of Abraham, showing that the scheme was retained by the son: the wife was very beautiful, the man feared for his life, and the plan was to identify her as the sister. Whereas in Abraham's deception that identification was partially true, in Isaac's it was not.

It is surprising that fear motivated Isaac's plan. One would think that the recent theophany with its instructions for obedience and its promise of blessing as well as the divine presence would have engendered courage in the patriarch, but ironically it did not. When faced with a possible life-threatening situation, Isaac fell back on the plan to deceive the men of Gerar about his wife. Although he did not lose his wife to a royal harem, the lie made her available to others.

B. Detection of the deception ends the threat to the blessing (8–11).

In this story the detection comes by the observation of the king, not by divine intervention. He observed Isaac "playing" with his wife in a way that signified she was not his sister. In reporting this observation the writer used a significant word play on the name of Isaac: "and Isaac was playing [w^{e}hinnēh yiṣḥāq m^{e}ṣaḥēq]." The participle is etymologically related to the name Isaac and forms an interpretation on the nature of the patriarch. This participle was used earlier in the story of Ishmael's mocking play with Isaac; it would be difficult to ignore the meaning of the participle in that passage when studying this one. The choice of the word is significant. On one level it simply reports that he was playing with his wife, but on another level there is an implication that his lapse of faith in deceiving the men of Gerar made a mockery of the great promise embodied in his name. In fact, Isaac had made a mockery of Abimelech and his men by the deception. He should have taken the covenant promises seriously, but he failed and was discovered. His "playing" thus not only betrayed his claim to be her brother, it revealed that he had acted in bad faith with the men of Gerar.

Abimelech's rebuke, then, provided the moral teaching on the matter. He appraised Isaac of the danger that he almost put Gerar in: "You might have brought guiltiness ['āšām] upon us" (v. 10). If someone had taken the woman for a wife, then guilt would have been brought on the nation, and reparation would have been required insofar as it was possible. The law of Israel fully developed the teachings on guilt and the guilt offering ('āšām) in Leviticus 5. The warning to Israel in this narrative is that deception may give occasion for sin to others, making them guilty before God.

Recognizing the seriousness of the matter, Abimelech instituted a protective law for Isaac and his wife. Through this law God protected the marriage of Isaac from the people of Gerar, and from Isaac himself. The wording of the penalty for violation recalls the warning of the Lord in the garden: "He shall surely be put to death [môt yûmāt]." Here, as well as in Israel, the warnings of the law kept the marriage safe.

In the story we learn that Isaac, like Abraham, received the great promises and the instruction for obedience, but in fear he deceived the men of Gerar and in effect made a mockery of his faith. In playing with Rebekah he was detected (his nature was uncovered as well), and he was rebuked by a king with a sense of morality and justice.

The lesson of the entire passage may be worded as follows: *A mature faith in God's promises engenders a fearless walk with him, but cowering in fear endangers the blessing and makes a mockery of faith.* Faith boldly faces danger, but fear is a mockery of faith. The one who truly believes God's promises of his presence and of his blessing will obey his statutes, precepts, and laws. But when the servant of God falters in faith and jeopardizes the promise, God must intervene to preserve his plan. Here, the preservation of the family came through the exigency of a pagan king who also feared what might happen to his people if they became guilty of an offense such as adultery.

Believers today also have a sure covenant that is based on the obedience of one man, but their enjoyment of the blessings of that covenant requires obedience to the Word of the Lord. Sin, such as deception, can tarnish the reputation of the household of faith and endanger the promised blessings. The expositor could very well use the same subject matter for a sample of how deception can endanger the blessing, for the sanctity of the marriage is also linked to enjoyment of blessings in the new covenant. Any deceptive practices by believers, however, could have far-reaching effects that might endanger their participation in God's blessings.

Bibliography

Fishbane, Michael. *Text and Texture*, pp. 46–48. New York: Schocken, 1979.

Goldingay, John. "The Patriarchs in Scripture and History." In *Essays on the Patriarchal Narratives*, edited by A. R. Millard and D. J. Wiseman, pp. 11–42. Leicester: Inter-Varsity, 1980.

Lutz, D. A. "The Isaac Tradition in the Book of Genesis." Ph.D. diss., Drew University. *Dissertation Abstracts* 29 (1968–69): 2135A.

Schmidt, G. "Zu Gen. 26:1–14." *ZAW* 85 (1973): 143–56.

Snaith, N. H. "The Meaning of the Hebrew אָךְ." *VT* 14 (1964): 221–25.

41

The Blessing of Water in the Wilderness
(Gen. 26:12–33)

T his section continues the preceding unit; the two passages have common characters (Isaac and Abimelech), a common place (Gerar), and a common theme (the blessing of the Lord on Isaac). In the last narrative the blessing of the Lord was promised to Isaac as it had been to his father Abraham; in this passage the blessing of the Lord was extended to Isaac as it had been to Abraham, for here Isaac received water in the wilderness from the wells that Abraham had dug—much to the envy of the men of Gerar—and reestablished Beersheba as the place of blessing.

Of the development of the theme of blessing in the chapter as a whole, Brueggemann writes:

> The movement of chapter 26 compresses the sojourn of Isaac into a brief account. But even in brevity, it spans a movement from *famine* (v. 1) to *water* in Beersheba (vv. 32–33). At the beginning, the life of this son of promise is precarious. At the end, Isaac is safely settled and richly blessed. And Isaac knows, as the narrative announces, that "every good endowment and every perfect gift is from above . . ." (James 1:17). Like his

father, Isaac calls on the name of and relies only on Yahweh (v. 28). Yahweh is one who is known in the blessing of sowing (v. 12), in the prosperity of flocks and herds (v. 16), in war and in peace (v. 27). In a quite understated way, this narrative uses the formula of promise (vv. 3–4, 24) to announce the goodness of a blessed world. The narrative provides a theological nuance different from that of the father before or the son after. The Isaac narrative invites reflection on a world teeming with generously given life. The abundant life is recognized as blessing to those who will receive and share it. The chapter presents a world-view in which *affirmation of the world* and *gratitude to God* are held integrally together [*Genesis*, pp. 225–26]

The blessing recorded in Genesis 26 is a little more specific than what Brueggemann envisions. That it was given to Isaac, in the wilderness and to the envy of Abimelech, underscores its uniqueness. The passage recounts how Isaac sojourned in the land with both divinely given prosperity and Philistine opposition, the latter being caused in part by the former. The point of the narrative is that, no matter where Isaac was forced to dig, and no matter how often the Philistines stopped up his wells, he found water in the wilderness—because God was with him.

The narrative as a unit follows the form of an itinerary with events at the various locations. The common motif in the itinerary concerns the digging of wells, and so Coats has classified the larger portion of the unit (vv. 17–33) as a "well itinerary."

Theological Ideas

The confirmation of the blessing to Isaac is certainly the central topic here. All the blessings—the crops, the possessions, the servants, and especially the water from the wells—confirmed that Isaac was the true recipient of the Abrahamic blessings. Any exposition of this section must recall the original blessings and compare the events here with the events in the life of Abraham.

A related theological theme introduced in this chapter is the reason for the blessing, so clearly recognized by Abimelech: "We have surely seen that the LORD is with you" (v. 28). The blessing was thus evidence of God's presence.

This narrative also restates the idea of living in peace with other nations (see Deut. 20:10). Here Isaac made a treaty to live in peace with the Philistines because these Philistines recognized the blessing of the Lord on him and wished to live in harmony with him.

Structure and Synthesis

Structure

The narrative is organized around the itinerary of the wells, some of which are given etymological explanations on the basis of the narrative reports. An introduction to this itinerary asserts that the blessing of the Lord rested with Isaac (vv. 12–16). But this introduction also lays the foundation for the power struggle between Abimelech and Isaac. There then follows a series of well-diggings and namings (vv. 17–22), in which the namings reflected the conflicts as well as the final resolution. The last section records the events at Beersheba: the theophany (vv. 23–25a), the digging of a well (v. 25b), the treaty with Abimelech (vv. 26–31), and the completion of the well at Beersheba (vv. 32–33). The contents of the unit are thus rather diverse, but they have the common theme of digging wells and resolving the conflict with Abimelech.

A predominant motif in the section is the explanations of the names of the wells—Esek, Sitnah, Rehoboth, and finally Beersheba. Such popular etymologies contribute not only to the organization of the passage but also to the memory of the themes.

Summary Message

The Lord confirmed his promise to bless Abraham's seed by providing crops, flocks, servants, and especially water in the wilderness wells that Isaac dug, in spite of the unjust opposition from Gerar, ultimately enabling him to dwell in peace in Beersheba.

Exegetical Outline

I. The Lord's abundant blessing on Isaac brought opposition from the men of Gerar, hindering him from living peacefully among the people of Gerar (12–16).
   A. The Philistines envied Isaac because of the great prosperity that the Lord gave him (12–14).
   B. The Philistines had stopped up all the wells that were dug in the days of Abraham (15).
   C. The Philistines drove Isaac away because he was becoming mightier than they (16).
II. Isaac's attempts to reclaim the wells of his father met strong opposition until he moved from the Gerar river basin and dug an uncontested well (17–22).
   A. Isaac attempted to settle in the Gerar valley but met with conflict over the water rights (17–21).
      1. The wells in the basin of Gerar that had been stopped up

by the Philistines were reopened by Isaac, who gave them the names that Abraham had given them (17–18).

2. Two wells that Isaac dug were forfeited to the herdsmen of Gerar, who quarreled about the ownership of the water (19–21).

a. Isaac named the first well Contention when he had to forfeit it to the men of Gerar (19–20).

b. Isaac named the second well Hostility when a dispute forced him to relinquish that well also (21).

B. After leaving the Gerar basin, Isaac opened an uncontested well and named it Room because the Lord had given them a place (22).

III. Isaac's faith in the Lord's promise at Beersheba was confirmed by an oath of peace with his enemies and the discovery of another well of water (23–33).

A. The Lord appeared to Isaac at Beersheba to renew the promise of blessing, prompting Isaac to worship the Lord and make preparations to dwell there (23–25).

1. The Lord appeared to Isaac and reaffirmed his promise to bless him for the sake of his father Abraham (23–24).

2. Isaac responded to the Lord's appearance by worshiping him and by settling in Beersheba (25).

B. The people of Gerar obtained an oath of peace from Isaac because they recognized that the Lord was with him (26–31).

1. After seeing the blessing of the Lord on Isaac, Abimelech came to Beersheba to make an alliance of peaceful relations (26–29).

2. Isaac and Abimelech made a peace covenant through a great feast and an exchange of oaths (30–31).

C. When his servants found water that same day, Isaac named the well Oath—the event from which the city of Beersheba in part derived its name (32–33).

Development of the Exposition

Although the first section of this passage forms a little introduction to the entire section, it includes enough of the common theme of opposition from the Philistines to make it an integral part of the second section. In the exposition I would thus treat verses 12–22 together—still distinguishing the two sections in the discussion, but as subpoints now.

I. The blessing of God may excite envy and opposition from the world (12–22).

A. God may richly bless his people (12–14a).

The first part of this passage describes God's abundant blessing on Isaac—the text explains: "and the LORD blessed him [*waybārăkēhû YHWH*]." This explanation sets the tone for the entire section; its affirmation is finally recognized by the king of Gerar: "You are now blessed of the LORD [*'attâ 'attâ berûk YHWH*, in v. 29]."

In the exposition of this section one cannot fail to note the great stress in the wording of verse 13. The Jewish Publication Society's translation captures the idea well: "And the man grew richer and richer until he was very wealthy." A literal reading of the text shows the repetition of the word "great" (root *gādal*): "And the man became great [*wayyigdal*], and he continually became greater [*wayyēlek hālôk wegādēl*], until he became very great [*'ad kî-gādal me'ôd*]." This greatness is then explained by the subsequent verse, which enumerates his possessions— flocks, herds, and servants—and by the statement of the king that Isaac had become mightier (*kî-'āṣamtā mimmennû*) than they (v. 16). The text thus gives a picture of a man growing wealthier and more powerful all the time because God was blessing him.

The expositor must be careful in applying a passage such as this one. A narrative report that God blessed someone in a certain way is no guarantee that he will do so for all. In fact, wisdom literature later dealt with the problem of why the righteous at times suffer and face poverty and famine. Narrative literature allows us to say that, since God prospered Isaac, he is *able* to do it. For this reason I have worded the point to say that God *may* richly bless his people.

B. The world may envy the blessing (14b–22).

This section begins with the report that the Philistines envied Isaac and then incorporates five scenes of well-digging, the first four of which are followed by opposition. A study of the word for "envy" is in order in this exposition. The verb *qānā'* describes intense jealousy, an impassioned zeal, that leads to some action. The same word can mean "to be jealous" or "zealous," the difference being one of motivation: envy is selfish but zeal (such as zeal for the Lord and his cause) is unselfish. The simple point in this passage is that the Philistines strongly desired what Isaac had and attempted through conflict to obtain it.

The first scene is the conflict over the wells that Abraham had dug (vv. 15–16). We are led to believe that, in an attempt to hinder the prosperity of Isaac, the Philistines had caved in these wells and hindered Isaac's access to the water. The scene concludes with Abimelech's expulsion of Isaac with words that are similar to the Egyptians in Exodus: "for you are mightier than we" (*'āṣamtā mimmennû;* cf. *'āṣûm mimmennû* in Exod. 1:9).

The second scene records how Isaac dug the wells of Abraham in Gerar and renamed them with the names that Abraham had given them (vv. 17–18). The opposition in this scene is again the stopping of the wells by the Philistines. They apparently thought that, once Abraham had passed off the scene, their treaty with him ended and that his son should not get the wells.

The third scene continues the strife over wells (vv. 19–20). This controversy is marked out with an etymological word play: he called the name of the well Esek (*'ēśeq*) because they strove with him (*hit'aśś^eqû*). The idea of contention is conveyed by the verb *'āśaq* in the causal clause as well as by the verb *rîb* in the main clause.

The fourth scene reports the strife over another well (v. 21). Here they strove (*rîb*) over another well and so named it Sitnah (*śiṭnâ*). This name is to be related to the verb *śāṭan*, "to oppose" (cf. *śāṭān*, "adversary"). No causal clause is given for the name, but its significance can be clearly seen in the passage.

The fifth scene draws the conflict to a close (v. 22). Isaac moved farther away and dug another well; since he received no opposition over it, he named it Rehoboth (*r^eḥōbôt*), saying, "For now the LORD has made room [*hirḥîb*] for us, and we shall be fruitful in the land." The name is cognate with the verb in the causal clause, forming the etymological word play. The name means "room" or "open place"; the meaning is enhanced by the plural.

By reporting the constant provision of water, the narrative thus emphasizes the intervention of the Lord in accordance with the promises of the covenant. The naming signified that the Lord had ended with conflict, and now they would be "fruitful in the land" (*ûpārînû bā'āreṣ*).

II. The confident faith of God's people will triumph over worldly antagonism (23–33).

Once the conflict over the wells had ended and it was obvious that Isaac would prosper in everything that he did, Abimelech sought a treaty with him in order that they might live in peace together. This final section shows how the people of God, avoiding the hostilities of the world and enjoying God's blessing, can realize an end to such antagonism.

A. God's people have the word of promise (23–25).

At Beersheba, the ancient home of Abraham, the Lord appeared (*wayyērā'*) to Isaac and reiterated the promises. But this time the theme of the Lord's presence predominates: "Fear not, I am with you, and I will bless you." Once again the blessing was linked to Abraham (ba'ăbûr 'abrāhām 'abdî, "for the sake of my servant Abraham"; cf. 26:3–5).

Isaac's response to this reassurance parallels Abraham's faith activities—he made an altar and made proclamation of the Lord (for wayyiqrā' bešēm YHWH, see the discussion in Gen. 12:8). With the promise of blessing now restated, Isaac also settled in and dug another well.

B. God's presence may be acknowledged by the world (26–31).

The second part of this section shows how Abimelech and his men came to make a treaty with Isaac. The whole enterprise surprised the patriarch, for he had thought that they hated him (śenē'tem 'ōtî, in v. 27). They claimed, however, that they had done nothing but good for Isaac (an ironic use of ṭôb in v. 29, for ṭôb is one of the major themes of Genesis). Their hostility and opposition was winked at in their pressing for the peace treaty, because, at the heart of the matter, they recognized that God was blessing him. "We have surely seen that the LORD is with you" in verse 28 is the climax of the message of the passage, for Isaac's enemies now had to acknowledge that this prosperity came from God. In spite of their efforts to hinder his prosperity, they had to admit that Isaac was blessed of the Lord (berûk YHWH, in v. 29). They simply could not hinder the blessing of God (cf. Exod. 1).

Isaac thus entered into a covenant of peace with them, and they departed in peace (šālôm). Here is an early example of how the Lord makes one's enemies to be at peace with him (Prov. 16:7).

C. God's people continue to enjoy his blessing (32–33).

On the same day, the servants of Isaac struck water in the well they had been digging. Isaac named it Shebah (šib'â) because of the treaty they had made at the well, much after the manner of the earlier treaty Abraham had made when he had settled at the place. The text has already indicated in verse 18 that he customarily named the wells with the names his father had used. It therefore comes as no surprise that, when he made a treaty at Beersheba with the king of Gerar as his father had done, he renamed the place to commemorate that event.

The similarities between Genesis 26 and Genesis 21 show a deliberate attempt by the writer to parallel Isaac and Abraham. It would be surprising if Abimelech and Phicol were the same individuals that were there earlier; the names may have been titles or commonly used names. Most modern scholarship sees these names as evidence that one story got told twice, but other solutions are possible. Besides, given the life expectancy of people at this time, is it impossible that Abimelech and Phicol were in Gerar for a span of seventy-five years? However the apparent tensions between the stories are explained, their parallel elements demonstrate that the blessing had passed to Isaac, the son of Abraham, because the Lord was with him.

Because the Lord was with Isaac and blessed him, the blessing would thrive, no matter how much opposition came. The more the Philistines attempted to seize the water, the more water Isaac's servants found. In the final analysis these people, and other nations at other times, had to acknowledge that God's hand was on the seed of Abraham. The only recourse for the Philistines was to seek peace and share the blessing. Thus it was with Isaac, and thus it would be with the nation of Israel when they were obedient worshipers enjoying God's blessing, and thus it is with God's people of all ages.

Isaac's responsibility was to continue to pursue the blessing by living by faith in the promises and worshiping the Lord at the altar. We may thus word the lesson of the whole unit as follows: *In spite of the envy and hostility from the world over the Lord's blessing, the people of God must maintain their confident trust in the Lord's promise of his presence and his provision.* In this passage Isaac never wavered in his confident trust. He quietly and resolutely went about his business of obtaining water for his flocks and his crops, and God abundantly blessed him. Moreover, when he received the word of reassurance from the Lord, he made proclamation of the Lord through worship. By his living in God's provision and by his proclamation in worship, he left no doubt that God was with him. The people surrounding him could only acknowledge this presence and seek peaceful relations.

The blessings that Isaac received were material, but they were proof of the spiritual heritage he had received from his father. In the New Testament also, believers often enjoy God's blessings. It is their responsibility to live in the expectation of divine provision for the needs of this life and, when enjoying them, to proclaim the divine presence. If opposition should come, believers can take the lead from the example of Isaac on how to live in peace with all people. If believers were truly confident that God would supply all their needs no matter what hostility they faced from the world, their proclamation of the faith would be far more substantive and convincing.

Bibliography

Limburg, J. "The Root ריב and the Prophetic Lawsuit Speeches." *JBL* 88 (1969): 291–304.

McCarthy, D. J. "Three Covenants in Genesis." *CBQ* 26 (1964): 179–89.

Selms, A. van. "The Origin of the Title 'the King's Friend.' " *JNES* 16 (1957): 118–20.

Speiser, E. A. "Akkadian Documents from Ras Shamra." *JAOS* 75 (1955): 154–65.

Wyatt, N. "The Problem of the 'Gods of the Fathers.' " *ZAW* 90 (1978): 101–4.

42

The Deception for the Blessing
(Gen. 26:34–28:9)

God has always provided direction and enablement for his people to carry out their responsibilities in his covenantal program. Unfortunately, many people persist in handling them in their own earthly way, often complicating matters greatly. Genesis 27 gives us a detailed look at an entire family living this way. On the surface it is the familiar story of how Jacob got the blessing by deceiving his father Isaac into thinking that he was Esau; but it is also the story of a family that fragments over the pursuit of spiritual blessing. This aspect makes it relevant to all who seek God's blessing.

Hebrews 12:16 and 17 simply declare that Esau sold his birthright and traded away the blessing. But the details of this act weave a tangled web. In fact, all the participants were at fault. Isaac, whether he knew of the earlier sale of the birthright or not, did know the oracle of God that the elder would serve the younger; yet he set himself to thwart it by blessing Esau. Esau, in agreeing to the plan, broke his oath to Jacob (25:33; Hebrews implies that, when he sold the birthright, he lost the blessing too). Rebekah and Jacob, with a just cause, went about achieving it by deception, with no faith or love. Theirs would be the victory—although they obtained only what God declared they would receive anyway—but they would reap the appropriate fruit of hatred and separation (Rebekah never saw her beloved Jacob again).

The conflict in the lifelong struggle between Jacob and Esau was greatly intensified with Jacob's grasping. He wanted what he believed belonged to him, but the manner in which he achieved the goal destroyed their relationship completely. Yet the story is not just about Jacob; he alone did not destroy the family. Parental preference actually did. More-over, the entire scheme was made possible by the base level on which the family lived. Kidner observes:

> All five senses play a conspicuous part, largely by their fallibility, in this classic attempt to handle spiritual responsibilities by the light of nature. Ironically, even the sense of taste on which Isaac prided himself gave him the wrong answer. Rebekah had not the slightest doubt that she could reproduce Esau's gastronomic masterpiece—had she often smarted under this?—in a fraction of Esau's time. But the real scandal is Isaac's frivolity: his palate had long since governed his heart (25:28) and silenced his tongue (for he was powerless to rebuke the sin that was Esau's downfall); he now proposed to make it his arbiter between peoples and nations (29). Unfitness for office shows in every act of this sightless man rejecting the evidence of his ears for that of his hands, following the promptings of his palate and seeking inspiration through—of all things—his nose (27). Yet God put these very factors to work for Him. [*Genesis*, p. 156]

In spite of the efforts of some scholars to divide this passage into two sources and obtain differing accounts (see Coats, *Genesis*, pp. 199–200), the arguments have been far from convincing (see Westermann, *Genesis*, vol. 2, p. 436). Part of the difficulty in the narrative is the fact that, while the story develops a plot around the conflict between the brothers, the tension is not actually resolved. It is only postponed by removing Jacob from the scene. But the plot development is sufficient to classify this as a story, at least in the sense of a part of the longer account of Jacob. Or it may be described as Fokkelman describes it, an act from a play, which consists of six scenes. He adds, "It has indeed a theatrical preciseness because the moments exclude each other mutually and the transitions come about by the entrance of other characters" (*Narrative Art*, p. 97).

Theological Ideas

The central theme of this story is the transference of the blessing to the (presumed) firstborn. From beginning to end, the concern for the blessing predominates. Isaac sought to bestow it, and Esau wanted it. Rebekah heard about it and ensured that Jacob got it. Isaac unwittingly gave it to Jacob, and Esau was furious over having lost it. And finally, Isaac restated the blessing on Jacob in terms of the Abrahamic covenant.

The expositor should contrast the importance of the blessing to the program of God with the varied human activities designed to gain it. Once again, unfortunately, the exposition will be limited to negative models for the household of faith. Evil in its many manifestations—here we have the disobedience to the oracle, disregard for the oath, deception, and blasphemy—cannot be the way to discharge spiritual responsibilities. Discord, hatred, and separation consequently result from this mixture of good and evil.

Structure and Synthesis

Structure

The story cannot be limited to chapter 27, for there are other structural indications that broaden it. First, the reports of Esau's wives, while not actually part of the main story, serve to frame the entire account. Genesis 26:34–35 thus forms a brief prologue to the story, and 28:6–9 an epilogue. That this material should be connected to the story can be seen from Rebekah's use of the marriages of Esau within the story and from Isaac's instructions for Jacob not to marry a Canaanite woman (27:46 and 28:1).

Within these framing notices we have six scenes. Fokkelman illustrates the development in chart 23. He then explains the symmetrical composition of the story as follows:

> Its main purpose is to arrange the material (four main characters; a complicated action which occurs partly in the absence of the first-born; vehement emotions) clearly in six scenes of almost equally bright lighting. In the middle the dramatic centre: C + C'; Esau's visit and the anti-blessing he receives are the exact antipole of Jacob's visit which renders him the true blessing. Around it, central between the ascent (A-B-C) and the descent (C'-B'-A') of the story, is the scheming mother who shows her son the way, B and B'. Around that is again the ring formed by A and A', most revealing for the exchange of parts between Jacob and Esau. [*Narrative Art*, p. 101]

It is interesting to note that in the six scenes the family is never together: in the first it is Isaac and Esau; in the second, Rebekah and Jacob; in the third, Isaac and Jacob; in the fourth, Isaac and Esau; in the fifth, Rebekah and Jacob; and in the sixth, Isaac and Jacob. In fact, Jacob and Esau never meet in the story; nor do Rebekah and Esau. In four of the six scenes we find the parent with his or her favorite son.

Chart 23. **Chiasmus of Genesis 27:1–28:5**

A   Isaac and the son of the *brkh/bkrh* (= Esau) (27:1–5).

  B   Rebekah sends Jacob on the stage (27:6–17).

    C   Jacob appears before Isaac and receives blessing (27:18–29).

    C' Esau appears before Isaac and receives antiblessing (27:30–40).

  B' Rebekah sends Jacob from the stage (27:41–45).

A' Isaac and the son of *brkh/bkrh* (= Jacob!) (27:46–28:5).

Summary Message

In swift reaction to Isaac's disobedient plans to bless Esau, the disqualified son, Jacob, in conspiracy with Rebekah, deceptively took the blessing by passing himself off as his brother, an act that resulted in the bitter anger of Esau, who could only be given a lesser blessing and who therefore planned to kill Jacob, and the flight of the deceiver—albeit with his father's blessing.

Exegetical Outline

    I. Prologue: Esau continued to show his disregard for the divine oracle and for his parents by marrying into the Canaanite line (26:34–35).

   II. Deception within the family (cause): In disobedience Isaac prepared to bless his older son Esau, prompting Rebekah and Jacob to take matters into their own hands by deceiving Isaac for the blessing (27:1–29).

    A. Scene one—the disobedience of Isaac and Esau: Believing that he was about to die, Isaac prepared to bless his older son, contrary to the oracle, but Rebekah overheard the plan (1–5).

      1. Narrative introduction: When Isaac was old and going blind he called in Esau, his oldest son (1).

      2. Plan: Isaac instructed Esau to prepare him a meal of game so that he could bless Esau (2–4).

      3. Transition: Rebekah overheard the plan (5).

    B. Scene two—the deception of Rebekah and Jacob: Having found out about Isaac's plans, Rebekah and Jacob conspired to gain the blessing through deception (6–17).

      1. Introduction: Rebekah reported Isaac's plan to Jacob (6–7).

      2. Plan: Rebekah instructed Jacob to bring two kids that she might prepare a meal for Isaac, convincing him that, if anything went wrong, it would be on her head (8–13).

      3. Transition: Rebekah prepared the meal for Jacob to take to Isaac and dressed him up like Esau (14–17).

C. Scene three—the theft of the blessing: Impersonating Esau, Jacob passed Isaac's tests and received the blessing of the firstborn (18–29).

   1. Deception: Jacob deceived his father into thinking that he was Esau (18–25).

   2. Blessing: Isaac, thinking that it was Esau, gave the blessing of the firstborn to Jacob (26–29).

III. Distress within the family (effect): When Esau, filled with bitter anxiety over being tricked out of the blessing, plotted to kill his younger brother, Rebekah persuaded Isaac to send Jacob away to get a wife in Paddan Aram (27:30–28:5).

A. Scene four—the distress of Isaac and Esau: After Esau returned with the game, he and his father were distressed to learn that Jacob had deceptively taken the blessing, leaving only an antiblessing for his brother (27:30–40).

   1. Introduction: Esau returned with the meal for Isaac (30–31).

   2. Plan discovered: Esau and Isaac were filled with anxiety over the fact that Jacob had deceived his father for the blessing (32–35).

   3. Antiblessing: Isaac gave a lesser blessing to Esau (36–40).

B. Scene five—the distress of Rebekah and Jacob: As a result of the stolen blessing Esau threatened to kill Jacob, prompting Rebekah to advise him to leave for a while (27:41–45).

   1. Introduction: Esau's hatred was turned into a plan to kill his brother after Isaac died (41).

   2. Plan discovered: Rebekah heard of the plan and told Jacob (42).

   3. Instruction: Rebekah advised Jacob to go and live with Laban until his brother's anger subsided (43–45).

C. Scene six—the giving of the blessing: Isaac sent Jacob to Paddan Aram to get a wife, giving him the full Abrahamic blessing (27:46–28:5).

   1. Introduction: Rebekah convinced Isaac to send Jacob away to get a wife (27:46).

   2. Instruction and blessing: Isaac sent Jacob away with the full Abrahamic blessing (28:1–4).

   3. Conclusion: Jacob left for Paddan Aram (28:5).

IV. Epilogue: Esau, realizing his error with his parents, remarried into the line of Ishmael (28:6–9).

Development of the Exposition

It would be very effective to arrange the exposition according to the six major scenes in the story. The expositional outline could be arranged in two sets of three scenes (as above) or in a straight series of six points. I have chosen the latter here because it simplifies the structure of the exposition.

I. God's people create tensions by attempting to set aside God's will for their will (27:1–5).

The first scene creates the tension for the rest of the story: Isaac in his old age decided to bless Esau. Whether the old man had forgotten the oracle or never took it to heart is difficult to say. In either case, his intent to bless the older son, the one who had sold his birthright to the younger son, created a major crisis.

The details of the first scene are important for the entire story. In his old age—he was at least one hundred, because at last report Esau was forty (26:34)—Isaac was losing his sight, a fact that would enable the plan of Rebekah to work. Isaac wished to bestow the blessing at this time because he thought that he had not much longer to live. He actually lived at least twenty more years, because he did not die while Jacob was in Paddan Aram.

The significant point in this section is the motivation for giving the blessing—a tasty meal. Isaac instructed Esau to take his bow and go out into the field (hassādeh) and hunt him some venison (wᵉṣûdâ lî ṣayid), and then prepare him a savory meal (maṭʿammîm) just like he loved (ʾāhabtî). The expressions used in Isaac's instructions recall the narrative of the sale of the birthright, for there it was reported that Isaac loved Esau because the taste of venison was in his mouth—he loved the food. In this story, that love for savory meat from the hunt controlled the old man's will—"Bring it to me that I may eat and bless you before I die" (v. 4).

It is interesting to note in this story that "soul" (as it is translated in some versions) is the subject of the verb "bless" (tᵉbārekkā napšî). Four times the text says, "nepeš may bless" (vv. 4, 19, 25, 31). The point is that Isaac wanted to bless Esau with all his resources—with all the blessing that he had received and with all his desire and vitality. It is more than saying that he wished "with all his heart" to bless Esau; it would be passing on his lifetime of blessing.

The scene closes with a note that Rebekah overheard the plan of Isaac. This comment forms the transition to the next scene (v. 5a).

A sense of urgency is then transmitted by the report that Esau went to hunt game. The words repeated in this verse (wayyēlek ʿēśāw haśśādeh lāṣûd ṣayid) bring forward the motifs of Esau's nature and Isaac's misguided choices. It was, after all, going to be for the satisfaction of a physical appetite that Isaac would give the cherished blessing to his favorite son.

II. God's people often attempt to ensure God's plan for blessing by deceptive, manipulative measures (27:6–17).

This section records the immediate reaction of Rebekah: through deception Jacob would gain the blessing from Esau. Rebekah apparently thought that the desperate situation demanded desperate measures. We might think that the better approach would have been to confront Isaac— but the family was not that close, and favoritism had ruled for some time. What would have happened if Rebekah had not heard, or if she had done nothing? We may only speculate; but since the oracle of God had reserved the birthright for Jacob, any attempted blessing would have come to naught. Perhaps, as with Balaam, the Lord would have overruled the effort by some unusual means.

It is important to note that, in the first part of this scene, Rebekah told Jacob exactly what Isaac had said (v. 7). The repetition of the motifs of venison (ṣayid) and the savory meat (maṭʿammîm) extends the theme of Isaac's weakness and makes that weakness the occasion for the deception. Rebekah obviously felt that she could reproduce the taste, for she instructed Jacob to bring her two kids of the goats so that she could make the savory meat (maṭʿammîm) that he loved (ʾāhēb). Her plan simply replaced Esau in the process, for Jacob would take it to Isaac in order that Isaac might eat and bless Jacob.

Jacob's hesitancy (vv. 11–12) was based not on moral grounds but on fear of being detected. His concern that Esau was hairy (śāʿīr; cf. 25:25) and he smooth (ḥālāq) put the difficulty in focus. The wording of Jacob's fear in verse 12 is significant to the theme of the story: "Perhaps my father will feel me, and I will appear to him as a mocker [kimtaʿtēaʿ], and I shall bring a curse [qᵉlālâ] upon myself and not a blessing [bᵉrākâ]." The risk was truly great; in his quest for the blessing, Jacob would be conducting himself in a manner that deserved a curse.

With the assuring words of his mother ("your curse be upon me"), Jacob obeyed and fetched the animals. Moreover, Rebekah dressed Jacob in Esau's finest clothes and covered his arms and neck with animal skins. Her constant pressuring of Jacob to obey her voice had brought about his compliance and set his fears at ease. The deception was prepared.

There is something symbolic in Jacob's being clothed with Esau's robes. It is as if the younger son was indeed replacing the older son in the anticipation of the blessing. And then, with the repetition of the motif of the savory meat (maṭʿammîm, in v. 17), the substitution was completed.

III. God's people may appear to achieve success through their manipulative measures (27:18–29).

The third scene moves us to the center of the story: Jacob deceived his father and received the blessing. The expositor needs to take some time developing the theme of deception, for the text reports this in eight verses. Two lies are recorded in this deception, the first pertaining to his identity ("I am Esau your firstborn" [bᵉkōrekā], in v. 19), and the second crediting the Lord with expediting the hunt ("because the LORD your God brought it to me" [kî hiqrâ YHWH ʾĕlōheykā lᵉpānāy], in v. 20). The first lie was enough to deceive, but the second was blasphemy.

In spite of the claims of his son, the old man was not sure that it was Esau. The deceiver was thus put to a closer scrutiny, that of feeling and smelling, before the patriarch was ready to bless him (waybārᵉkēhû at the end of v. 23 should be translated "and he was about to bless him"). Once again he asked to be sure, and the lie was repeated. Only after eating the venison and smelling the clothing did the father give the blessing.

The blessing that Isaac bestowed on his son had four main parts. The first element built on the smell of the field that Isaac smelled, which became the symbol of fertility for the blessing of the Lord. The second element called for the Lord's blessing of fertility in the field. The third element, and perhaps the most important, made Jacob lord (gᵉbîr) over his brethren and over the nations (yaʿabdûkā). The fourth part reiterated the protection of the blessing first given to Abraham—"cursed be those who curse you, and blessed be those who bless you" (cf. 12:3).

The deceiver was successful in gaining what he set out to obtain. It is important to explain that, while God used this incident for the bestowal of the blessing on the proper son, he did not condone it. Dods writes:

The fate of all such attempts to manage God's matters by keeping things dark, and misrepresenting fact, is written for all those who care to understand in the results of this scheme of Rebekah's and Jacob's. They gained nothing, and they lost a great deal, by their wicked interference. They gained nothing; for God had promised that the birthright would be Jacob's, and would have given it him in some way redounding to his credit and not to his shame. And they lost a great deal. The mother lost her son; Jacob had to flee for his life, and, for all we know, Rebekah never saw him more. And Jacob lost all the comforts of home, and all those possessions his father had accumulated. He had to flee with nothing but his staff, an outcast to begin the world for himself. From this first false step onwards to his death, he was pursued by misfortune, until his own verdict on his life was, "Few and evil have been the days of the years of my life." [*Book of Genesis*, p. 274]

IV. God's people eventually realize how wrong their actions were and how the Lord overruled (27:30–40).

The fourth scene records the other half of the center of the story. In this section the tension shifts dramatically, for the blessing has been given and Jacob has gotten away free. But now when Esau came and presented his venison to his father, the deception of Jacob became painfully clear—but it was too late. Isaac trembled violently (*wayyeḥĕrad yiṣḥāq ḥārādâ gᵉdōlâ*) over what had happened, and over what he had just done in attempting to bless Esau (v. 33). He knew that he had blessed his other son, and there was no going back on that now (*gam-bārûk yihyeh*, in v. 33). If he had simply blessed Jacob under false pretenses, that would be one thing; but the blessing of that son fulfilled the oracle of God, which was another matter. It was done.

Isaac's trembling was exceeded by Esau's great and bitter cry (*wayyiṣʿaq ṣᵉʿāqâ gᵉdōlâ ûmārâ ʿad-mᵉʾōd*, in v. 34; the verb may form a word play on the name of Isaac, uniting Esau's cry and Isaac's folly). Still, in his anguish, he sought a blessing from his father as well. But Isaac's explanation made it clear that little was left for him: "Your brother came in deceptively [*bᵉmirmâ*] and took your blessing [*birkātekā*]." Here is the dark side of the story of Isaac's blessing of Jacob.

The expositor will have to spend some time with the word play on the name of Jacob in verse 36, for it indicates that Esau began to understand the true nature of his brother. He said, "Is he not rightly named Jacob [*yaʿăqōb*], for he has supplanted me [*wayyaʿqᵉbēnî*] these two times." The verb is used primarily in conjunction with this event and signifies "to overreach, supplant" in the sense of tripping up or deceiving. Jacob had been named to commemorate his grabbing his brother by the heel, but in the opinion of Esau that playful act now took on ominous proportions. The real significance of the name would now become "overreacher" or "deceiver."

Another word play in Esau's complaint concerns the birthright and the blessing ("my birthright" is *bᵉkōrātî*, and "my blessing" is *birkātî*). They both belonged to the firstborn, but Esau had traded them to Jacob in an earlier moment of weakness. But now Esau lamented his double loss to his deceiving brother. Hebrews 12:16–17 unites the birthright and the blessing when describing how Esau regretted selling them.

All that was left for Esau was the antiblessing, a "blessing" that would reiterate that the real blessing went to Jacob, for as Isaac said, "I have made him your lord [$g^e b\hat{\imath}r$]" (v. 37). The blessing for Esau was that he would live off the fat of the land and serve his brother until he would break Jacob's yoke from his neck. It was a blessing from God to be sure, but it restricted Esau's descendants to a subservient role under Jacob's descendants—Jacob would be Esau's lord ($g^e b\hat{\imath}r$), and Esau and his brethren would serve ($ta\,{}^c\bar{a}b\bar{o}d$) their brother Jacob.

V. God's people may even bring danger on themselves by such deceptive deeds (27:41–45).

Although Jacob apparently got what he sought, he also incurred the wrath of Esau. It was perhaps to be expected that, sooner or later, Esau would have occasion to bear a grudge ($wayyi\acute{s}\d{t}\bar{o}m$) against Jacob in view of the parental favoritism. After all, if the father loved one son and the mother, the other, harmony between the sons would be impossible. But the occasion recorded here of the blessing brought Esau's animosity to the boiling point—he vowed to slay ($h\bar{a}rag$) his brother over the blessing.

A comparison can be made between Cain and Abel and Esau and Jacob. In both cases the older brother became angry over the younger brother's possession of God's blessing. In the story of Cain and Abel, Abel's actions were completely righteous, and yet Cain slew him. In the story of Jacob and Esau, Jacob's actions were anything but righteous, but Esau only threatened to kill him. According to Rebekah (v. 42), this plan to slay Jacob was Esau's way of consoling himself ($mitnah\bar{e}m$).

Rebekah's plan was simple. Jacob should flee to Paddan Aram and stay with her brother Laban for "a few days" until Esau settled down (vv. 43–45). She based her instructions to Jacob on the great urgency she sensed from Esau's anger ($h\d{a}mat\;{}^{\prime}\bar{a}h\hat{\imath}k\bar{a}$, and then ${}^{\prime}ap\text{-}{}^{\prime}\bar{a}h\hat{\imath}k\bar{a}$). The situation was critical. In what must have been surprising to Jacob, Rebekah placed the responsibility for the crisis on Jacob—"until . . . he forgets that which *you* have done to him."

For Jacob to remain in the land was certain death. His only recourse was to leave and stay with Laban for "a few days," a period that would actually turn into twenty years.

VI. God's people retain the promise of the blessing in spite of the predicaments they bring on themselves (27:46–28:5).

In the final scene of the story Rebekah prevailed over Isaac—by a subtle deception again—to send Jacob away to Paddan Aram. In so doing, Isaac confirmed the blessing of his father Abraham on his son Jacob (vv.

1–4). This time he was fully aware of what he was doing and of what the will of God was. The bestowal of this blessing was in no way a divine approval of how Jacob had obtained the blessing; it was a recognition that the younger son was the one that God chose to carry on the Abrahamic blessing. The point of the scene is clear enough—Isaac blessed him (*waybārek*) and invoked God to bless him (*w^e'ēl šadday y^{e}bārēk*).

Rebekah and Jacob thus won, although in achieving their goal they were losers. The fact that their success was soured by fearful separation reveals that their deceit and highhandedness were guilt not simply against others but against God.

Their activities succeeded in doing only what God declared in his oracle, and so their success was not really *their* success. The deceiver can take no credit for accomplishing the divine will. God's program triumphs, often in spite of the activities of people living on such base levels. To word a positive, theological lesson from this passage, we must begin by thinking in terms of the negative example in Jacob. We may say, *God's people who know God's will must not stoop to deceptive, manipulative schemes to gain spiritual success but must strive to achieve God's will righteously.*

It is tragic that those who seek to handle spiritual responsibilities think it necessary to stoop to such means. This story is based on the earlier note of parental favoritism, but it quickly forms a description of spiritual insensitivity at the mercy of overwhelming deception. Reliance on the senses for spiritual discernment not only proves fallible but often complicates life needlessly. At least Jacob realized that to live by deception is to walk a thin line between blessing and cursing; and at least Isaac had enough spirituality to tremble at what he had done and come to his senses.

People still live on these base levels. It seems to be the natural response to difficulties and crises. It may even seem necessary at the moment for the fulfillment of God's will. But Paul instructed believers to renounce such hidden things of shame and live honestly and transparently before all people, without deception or craft (2 Cor. 4:2). The reason is timeless: God will not permit his people to secure his blessings through deceptive and manipulative schemes.

Bibliography

Bright, J. "The Apodictic Prohibition: Some Observations." *JBL* 92 (1973): 185–204.

Fishbane, Michael. *Text and Texture,* pp. 48–51. New York: Schocken, 1979.

Fokkelman, J. P. *Narrative Art in Genesis,* pp. 97–121. Assen: Van Gorcum, 1975.

Gevirtz, S. "Isaac's Blessing over Jacob." In *Patterns of the Early Poetry of Israel,* pp. 35–47. Chicago: University of Chicago Press, 1963.

Gordon, C. H. "Indo-European and Hebrew Epic." *ErIs* 5 (1958): 10–15.

Hoffner, H. A. "Symbols for Masculinity and Femininity: Their Use in Ancient Near Eastern Sympathetic Magic Rituals." *JBL* 85 (1966): 326–34.

Kselman, J. S. "Semantic-Sonant Chiasmus in Biblical Poetry." *Bib* 58 (1977): 219–23.

Levene, A. "The Blessing of Jacob in Syriac and Rabbinic Exegesis." *StPat* 7 (1966): 524–30.

Luke, K. "Isaac's Blessing: Gen. 27." *Scr* 20 (1968): 33–41.

Mendelsohn, I. "On the Preferential Status of the Oldest Son." *BASOR* 156 (1959): 38–40.

Miscall, Peter D. "The Jacob and Joseph Stories as Analogues." *JSOT* 6 (1978): 28–40.

Speiser, E. A. "I Know Not the Day of My Death." *JBL* 74 (1955): 252–56.

Thomas, D. W. "A Note on the Meaning of מתנחם in Gen. 27, 42." *ExT* 51 (1939–40): 252.

Thompson, Thomas L. "Conflict Themes in the Jacob Narratives." *Semeia* 15 (1979): 5–26.

43

Jacob's Vision: The Founding of Bethel
(Gen. 28:10–22)

The clear revelation of God's gracious dealings can transform a worldly individual into a worshiper. Such a drama has been repeated again and again throughout the history of the faith. Perhaps no story in Scripture illustrates this transformation so vividly as does Jacob's dream at Bethel. Before this experience Jacob was a fugitive from the results of his sin, a troubled son in search of his place in life, a shrewd shepherd setting out to find a wife. After this encounter, however, he was a partner with God as a recipient of his covenant promises and a true worshiper. The transformation was due to God's intrusion into the course of his life.

The story unfolds quickly and dramatically. Being persona non grata in Canaan after deceiving Isaac and receiving the blessing, Jacob fled to Haran until things settled down. At sundown he stopped at a place and, taking one of the stones there, prepared to spend the night. In a dream the Lord appeared to him from the top of an angel-filled stairway and confirmed that the blessing was indeed his. When Jacob awoke he was afraid because he realized that the Lord was in that place; at dawn he set up the stone as a memorial, named the place Bethel, or "House of God," and vowed to worship there when he returned to his father's house in peace.

Theological Ideas

The two most significant events in the life of Jacob were nocturnal theophanies. The first was this dream at Bethel, when he was fleeing from the land of Canaan—which, ironically, was his by virtue of the blessing. The other was his fight at Peniel, when he was attempting to return to the land. Each divine encounter was a life-changing event.

The location of these episodes in the Jacob stories is strategic. The Bethel story forms the transition from the Jacob-Esau cycle to the Jacob-Laban cycle, and the Peniel story forms the connection back to the Esau story. In each of the encounters with God there is instilled in the patriarch great expectation for the uncertain future. In this incident at Bethel Jacob's vow expresses his anticipation for the future. God would now be with him and help him, even though he might be slow to realize it. The promise of God's presence and protection would bring continued encouragement during the twenty years with Laban.

The parallels between this story and the beginning of Genesis 32 are striking, showing that the story of Jacob's sojourn in Aram is deliberately bracketed with supernatural visions (see Fishbane, *Text and Texture*, pp. 53–54). In this story Jacob saw the angels of God (*mal'ăkê 'ĕlōhîm*) on the stairway, but in 32:1 the angels of God (*mal'ăkê 'ĕlōhîm*) met him (Houtman, "Jacob at Mahanaim," p. 39). These are the only two places in the Book of Genesis where reference is made to the "angels of God." In addition, in both passages (28:11; 32:1) the construction of the verb "encountered, met" is the same, a preterite form of *pāga'* with the preposition *b* and the object. In 28:16–17, *zeh* is used four times, the last two being in the statement "this is the house of God, this is the gate of heaven"; in 32:2, it reappears in the clause "this is the camp of God." Also in both accounts Jacob names the spot, using the same formula for each: "and he named that place [*wayyiqrā' ('et-)šēm-hammāqôm hahû'*]." Finally, Jacob's journeying (*wayyēlek* in 28:10 and *badderek* and *hôlēk* in 28:20) is reflected in 32:2 (*hālak lᵉdarkô*).

The stories about Jacob's encounters with God or his angels also form an interesting contrast with the other Jacob stories. Jacob is usually working against another individual in the narratives, first Esau in the Jacob-Esau cycle of chapters 25–27, and then Laban in the Jacob-Laban cycle of chapters 29–31, and then Esau again in 33. The account in chapter 34 of the defilement of Dinah also shows a crisis, though Simeon and Levi figure more prominently in that narrative. But in the encounter passages (28:10–22 at Bethel, 32:1–2 at Mahanaim, 32:22–32 at Peniel, and 35:1–7, 14–15 at Bethel again, the latter forming a conscious liturgical conclusion to the whole complex [see Westermann, *Promises to the Fathers*, p. 90]), Jacob alone is mentioned. Neither Esau nor Laban are with him. In fact, Esau never experienced any divine appearance, and Laban received only a warning dream. But when Jacob had these appearances he participated in liturgical acts. The narratives, then, heighten what the Bethel story declares, namely, that Jacob's life functioned on two levels—his conflicts with individuals and his encounters with God. The encounters assured Jacob that he would prevail in the conflicts.

This liturgical motif forms the climax in the Bethel story. Westermann calls the whole story a sanctuary foundation narrative (ibid., p. 85). It explains how Bethel came to be such an important center for the worship of the Lord. Because God actually met the patriarch on this spot, it was holy ground. Here, then, was a place where worship was appropriate.

Structure and Synthesis

Structure

The literary devices in the passage are designed to show that the vision inspired the manner of Jacob's worship and gave new meaning to the place of his vision. The repetition of key terms throughout the narrative ties the whole account together and explains the significance of Jacob's response (see Fokkelman's discussion of these points in *Narrative Art*, pp. 65–81). In his dream Jacob saw a stairway standing (*muṣṣāb*) on the earth, and the Lord standing (*niṣṣāb*) above or by it. This repetition suggests that the stairway functioned to point to the Lord. Then, in view of what he saw, Jacob took the stone he had used and set it up as a *maṣṣēbâ* ("pillar"), this word recalling the previous two. By setting up the stone in this way, Jacob apparently wanted to establish forever that he had seen the Lord standing over the stairway. The word plays then focus the reader's attention on Jacob's vision of the Lord—the standing stairway pointing to it, and the standing stone being a reminder of it.

The repetition of the word *rō'š* also confirms this connection between the two parts. Jacob had seen the stairway with its top (*rō'šô*) in the heavens, and so he anointed the top (*'al-rō'šāh*) of the stone that he set up in commemoration, a stone he had used for the place of his head (*mera'ăšōtāyw*).

Moreover, the key words in verses 11–12, the last part of the vision, are reversed in their order in the first part of Jacob's response. Jacob saw the stairway reaching to *heaven*, on it the angels of *God*, and above it *the Lord.* That the central focus is on the Lord is clear from the inversion; what came last in the vision is the first thing Jacob was concerned with. He exclaimed, *"The* LORD *is in this place. . . . This is the house of God; this is the gate of heaven!"* (vv. 16–17).

The story deliberately emphasizes the place's insignificance, which leads up to its naming in verse 19. The word "place" (*māqôm*) is used six times in the story. Verse 11 reports that Jacob came upon a *place* to spend the night, took one of the stones from the *place,* and lay down in that *place.* In the second half of the narrative, after the theophany, Jacob said, "Surely the LORD is in this *place,*" and "How terrifying is the *place!*" Then "he named that *place* Bethel," though it was formerly called Luz (v. 19). It was not an anonymous place after all; there was a city nearby called Luz. For the sake of this story, however, it was just a "place" until it became Bethel.

The literary features, then, strengthen the development of the motifs of the narrative to show how a place became a shrine, a stone became an altar, and a fugitive became a pilgrim—God in his grace revealed himself to Jacob in that place.

Summary Message

After the Lord appeared at the top of an angel-filled stairway, restating the Abrahamic promises and further promising to bless and protect him, Jacob fearfully acknowledged God's presence and then at dawn set up the stone as a memorial, named the place Bethel, and vowed that, if God did indeed bless and protect him, he would worship him in that place.

Exegetical Outline

    I. Appearing in a dream at the top of an angel-filled stairway to the weary traveler Jacob, who had stopped at an unnamed place, the Lord confirmed the Abrahamic promises to him and promised to bless and protect him during his journey (10–15).

    A. On his journey from Beersheba to Haran, Jacob stopped at sundown at an unnamed place and, after preparing a stone for his sleeping place, went to sleep (10–11).

        1. Jacob departed from Beersheba on the lengthy journey to Haran (10).

        2. Forced to stop at an unnamed place by the darkness of sundown, Jacob prepared to sleep (11).

    B. Appearing to Jacob in a dream, the Lord confirmed the Abrahamic promises to him and further promised to bless and protect him on his journey (12–15).

1. The Lord appeared to Jacob in a dream, standing at the top of an angel-filled stairway (12–13a).
2. The Lord restated the Abrahamic promises of the land, the innumerable seed, and the subsequent universal blessings (13b–14).
3. The Lord promised Jacob that he would bless and protect him (15).

II. Awakening from his dream, Jacob fearfully acknowledged the Lord's presence; at dawn he set up the stone as a memorial, named the place Bethel, and vowed that, if God did indeed bless and protect him, he would worship him in that place (16–22).

A. Awakening from his dream, Jacob fearfully acknowledged the Lord's presence in that holy place (16–17).

B. Arising at dawn, Jacob set up the stone as a memorial, poured oil on its top, and named the place Bethel (18–19).
1. Jacob set up the stone as a memorial and anointed it with oil (18).
2. Jacob commemorated the event by naming the place Bethel—although it was formerly called Luz (19).

C. Jacob vowed that, if the Lord did indeed bless and protect him, then he would worship the Lord in that place (20–22).
1. Jacob's vow was based on the Lord's promises of blessing and protection (20–21).
2. Jacob vowed to worship the Lord in that place (22).

Development of the Exposition

I. God's revelation to his people assures them of his protection and provisions (10–15).

A. The occasion (10–11).

The story begins with Jacob's departure from Beersheba for Haran. The preceding narrative in Genesis explains the reason for this trip— Esau was threatening to kill him for stealing the blessing. As Kidner says, Jacob was thrust from the nest he was feathering (*Genesis*, p. 155).

To be sure, Jacob had obtained the blessing by deception at first but then had it confirmed by the shaken Isaac (28:1–4), who, realizing what had happened, was powerless to change it (27:37). But were the promises actually his? If he truly was the heir, why must he flee from the land? Would God's blessing be his as it had been Abraham's and Isaac's before him? Nothing less than a sure word from God would ease his doubts and give him confidence for the future.

The narrative unfolds in a disarmingly casual manner. Jacob came upon a place where he would stay for the night, for the sun had set. The only detail that is mentioned is that he took "one of the stones" at random to lay by his head while he slept. (It is unlikely that the stone was his pillow; rather, it was placed at the place of his head [cf. 1 Sam. 26:7].) But this casual finding of an anonymous place and taking one of the stones in the darkness of night begins to build suspense.

B. The revelation (12–13a).

With an abrupt change of style that brings the vision into the present experience, the narrative introduces the dream. Up to this point the narrative sequence has employed preterites (*wayyēṣēʾ*, *wayyēlek*, *wayyipgaʿ*, *wayyālen*, *wayyiqqaḥ*, *wayyāśem*, *wayyiškab*, and *wayyaḥălōm*), but this pattern is now abruptly replaced with the repetition of *hinnēh* followed by participles. Jacob was surprised by what he dreamed, a reaction that the reader is vividly made aware of. Fokkelman points out that the particle *hinnēh* functions deictically; it is pre- or paralingual. It goes with a lifted arm and open mouth: "There, a ladder! oh, angels! and look, the Lord Himself!" (*Narrative Art*, pp. 51–52).

The arrangement of the clauses also narrows the focus to the central point of the vision—the Lord. Each clause in Hebrew is shorter than the preceding; the first has seven words, the second six, and the third four: "There was a stairway standing on the earth with its top reaching the heavens, and there were angels of God ascending and descending on it, and there was the Lord standing over it." Attention is focused first on the setting, then narrowed to the participants, and then to the Lord.

The first thing noticed is the stairway. The word *sullām*, translated "ladder" or "stairway," is a hapax legomenon. It has been traditionally connected to the root *sālal*, "to heap up, cast up." Related nouns are *mᵉsillâ*, "paved way" (but not of a street in a city), and *sōlᵉlâ*, "a bank, siege-ramp" (2 Sam. 20:15). These suggested etymological connections, however, do not clarify the meaning. The Septuagint translated *sullām* with *klimax*, Greek for "ladder" or "staircase." The Latin *scala* is also ambiguous. The same uncertainty of meaning prevails with the versions.

Several specific interpretations have been offered for *sullām* (Houtman, "What Did Jacob See," pp. 337–52), but the one that has the most to commend it is the view that connects *sullām* with the Mesopotamian temple towers. The Akkadian word *simmiltu*, cognate to *sullām*, provides the link. It is used to describe the "stairway of heaven" extending between heaven and the netherworld, with messengers ascending and descending on it. (See Cohen, *Biblical Hapax Legomena*, p. 34). The comparison is certainly an attractive one. Another possible connection is with the celestial ladder found in the Pyramid Texts of Egypt (see

Griffith's articles in the bibliography for this section), although differences exist. Pyramid text 267, for example, shows that the function of the stairway was to lead the deceased (king) to heaven.

The connection to Akkadian *simmiltu* with the Mesopotamian background is the most probable view. In the myth of Nergel and Ereshkigal, communication between the netherworld and heaven takes place via the long stairway of heaven that leads to the gate of Anu, Enlil, and Ea (see Millard, "Celestial Ladder," pp. 86–87; for the text, see Gurney, "Myth"). The idea of a ziggurat with its long staircase to the temple top would be behind the idea. Nothing in Genesis 28, however, describes a ziggurat. The most that can be said is that a word used in ziggurat settings is cognate to the word used here, a word that fits the way of communication between heaven and earth. Hebrew *sullām* is thus appropriate to the point of the story—here was a place that heaven and earth touch, where there is access to God. (Note that Jesus compared himself to the stairway in John 1:51.)

The second feature of the vision is the angelic hosts "ascending and descending" on the stairway, suggesting their presence on earth along with their access to heaven. Driver writes, "The vision is a symbolic expression of the intercourse which, though invisible to the natural eye, is nevertheless ever taking place between heaven and earth" (*Book of Genesis*, p. 265).

Nothing is said here about the function of the angels, nor can a hint be found in the corresponding episode at Mahanaim, which simply reports that the angels "met him." Other references to angels in Genesis are more helpful. The cherubim in 3:24 guard the way to the tree of life. In chapter 18, three visitors come to Abraham, and in chapter 19, two go on to meet with Lot in Sodom. In 18:2, they are simply called "three men." The context suggests that this incident may be a manifestation of the Lord, a view that is reinforced by the use of *niṣṣābîm ʿālāyw* in 18:2, which corresponds to 28:13. In 19:1, however, the two who went to Sodom are called *šnēh hammalʾākîm*. Their task was to rescue Lot before the judgment on the city.

The expression *malʾak YHWH*, "the angel of the Lord," is used interchangeably with "the Lord" in 22:11, 15. In 48:16, Jacob apparently was referring to the Lord when he said, "The angel [*hammalʾāk*] who protects me from all evil bless the lads." The activities in these passages are guarding, communicating, rescuing, and protecting. In this vision, then, the angels of God communicated God's protection for Jacob, the recipient of the promises.

The third and central feature of the vision, however, was the Lord, who was standing over the stairway. Later, in Genesis 48:3, Jacob identified the Lord as God Almighty (*'ēl šadday*), explaining that God had given him the blessing at Bethel.

C. The promise (13b–15).

The Word of the Lord in this vision took the form of a covenantal communication and extended the patriarchal promises to Jacob. The message begins with the identification of the Lord as the covenant God: "I am the LORD, the God of Abraham your father, and the God of Isaac." This pattern of self-revelation was used in Genesis 15:7 for Abraham; it also appears in Exodus 20:1 at the beginning of the covenant and throughout the law when God stressed his covenant relationship to his people. The identification of Abraham as the "father" of Jacob shows the latter's continuity with the covenant.

The first part of the revelation guaranteed that Jacob would receive the blessings at first promised to Abraham. The wording of the promises is close to that in Genesis 13:14–16 and 22:17–18. Prominence is attached to the promise of the land, for it is mentioned before the seed promise and stressed by the word order: "The land, upon which you are lying, to you I will give it and to your seed." The mention of the seed here would have been encouraging to Jacob, who was going to find a wife, and is further elaborated by the statement that the seed would "break out" and settle in every direction in this Promised Land (cf. 13:12–18). Finally, the promise that all the families of the earth would be blessed in Jacob shows that the Abrahamic blessing had indeed been carried forward to Jacob (cf. 12:3).

These promises given to Jacob so dramatically would have provided him with confidence. Though Jacob had been deceitful in gaining the blessing, God in grace gave it to him; and even though he was fleeing from his land, God promised to give him the land.

The second part of the revelation guaranteed protection for Jacob in the sojourn. It begins with the promise of God's presence: "Indeed, I will be with you [*wᵉhinnēh 'ānōkî 'immāk*]." The promise of the divine presence carried God's chosen people through many times of danger and difficulty. It assured them that they did not have to accomplish his plan by themselves. Moses, for example, drew great comfort from this assurance in his early career. When he was afraid to go to deliver the people, God said, "Surely I will be with you [*kî 'ehyeh 'immāk*]" (Exod. 3:12). The writer of Psalm 46 also realized the benefits of God's presence: "The LORD of hosts is with us ['*immānû*], the God of Jacob is our refuge" (vv. 7, 11). This passage also brings to mind Isaiah's oracle that promises "God is with us ['*immānû 'ēl*]" (7:14).

That God's presence would guarantee safety is verified by the next verb, "and I will keep you." His presence, then, meant that God would be Jacob's "Keeper," so that no harm would come to him wherever he should go (see Gen. 31:24). Joshua also reminded the people how God had protected them on their sojourn (Josh. 24:17). Psalm 121 develops this theme for pilgrims on their way to Jerusalem, where they would hear the high-priestly blessing announce the same divine intent: "The LORD bless you and keep you" (Num. 6:24). The promise of divine protection does not exclude conflict and tension, but it does guarantee the outcome for the good of the covenant and its recipient.

The promise concludes with the statement that God will restore Jacob to the land to receive the promises. The statement "I will not forsake you *until* I shall have done" need not imply that, once God fulfills the blessing, he will abandon Jacob; rather, it provides assurance that the promises just made will be fulfilled. God's protective presence will work toward the fulfillment of the promise.

II. The response to God's revelation should be one of worship and commitment (16–22).

A. The realization of the revelation (16–17).

When Jacob awakened he was overwhelmed with the fact that the Lord was "in this place" (v. 16). He had never imagined that this rather ordinary place could be a holy place. Jacob here realized what God had promised—God's presence was with him.

Jacob's attitude of fear was appropriate for such a meeting with the Lord. The term "fear" is used in the Bible to describe a mixture of terror and adoration, a worshipful fear (cf. Exod. 19:16). All worshipful acts must begin with and be characterized by reverential fear at the presence of the Lord (Exod. 3:6; 19; Ps. 2:11). Of Jacob, Bush says, "His feelings upon awakening were those of grateful wonder mingled with emotions of reverential awe, bordering close upon dread" (*Notes*, vol. 2, p. 109).

Jacob realized that this place was holy: "How frightening is this place! This is none other than the house of God, and this is the gate of heaven." Here the motif of "house" is first introduced (bêt 'ĕlōhîm, "house of God"). By using this term Jacob designated the place as a shrine. No literal house was there, nor was an actual gate. But it would now be known as a place where people could find access to God, where God could be worshiped. He had seen God in the heavens, and so God's house on earth was the gate to the heavens.

B. Worship and commitment (18–22).

1. Devotion (18). Early in the morning Jacob arose and stood the stone up as a pillar at which he could express his submission through worship. The preparation for worship by setting up a pillar raises questions about the custom. Graesser ("Standing Stones") shows how such stones in the ancient world served as markers, arresting the attention of the onlooker because they were not in their natural position. Such a standing stone had to have been put that way; it could mark a grave (Rachel's pillar in 35:20), form a boundary (the treaty with Laban in 31:45), note some important event (Samuel's Ebenezer in 1 Sam. 7:12), or, as here, mark out a sacred area where God could be found, where prayer could reach him. This pillar would commemorate the vision, recalling the stairway to heaven.

Jacob's offering took the form of oil poured on top of the stone, perhaps pointing to the Lord at the top of the stairway. Pouring the oil before the Lord was a gift to God, for it conveyed much the same attitude as making a sacrifice. It was a symbolic ritual act by which Jacob demonstrated his devotion to the Lord and consecrated the spot as holy to him. Later, oil was used in worship to sanctify the holy places and holy things (Lev. 8:10–11). This duly consecrated altar thus served to commemorate the appearance, express the patriarch's devotion, and guarantee the seriousness of the oath of the worshiper (cf. Gen. 12:8; 13:18; 26:25).

2. Commemoration (19). According to the story, Jacob named the place Bethel because God had come near to him there. This naming actually transformed the place from being merely a Canaanite town called Luz into God's "house" for Jacob and his descendants to use for worship.

Modern scholarship suggests that this spot was originally a Canaanite shrine or sanctuary city, founded before the time of Abram and dedicated to the god El. Von Rad says that Bethel must have been known as a cult center before the time of Israel because a god named Bethel was worshiped there (*Genesis*, p. 286). The name Bethel indeed does not always seem to be a place name but at times is a divine name, perhaps developing metonymically through association with a shrine (see Hyatt, "The Deity Bethel," and further bibliography in Ross, "Jacob's Vision"). The evidence for this deity does not, however, include Phoenician or Ugaritic literature, and so the presentation of such a deity for the second millennium B.C. in Canaan cannot be convincingly defended. As far as the Hebrew account is concerned, the name Bethel derives its significance from the fact that the Lord appeared to Jacob there.

This part of the passage develops the theme of "house." The key is the patriarch's exclamation "This is the house of God!" He then preserved the vision by naming the place "House of God." The word *bêt* is repeated two more times in verses 21 and 22, as though this fugitive was saying that, when he returned to settle in the land, God would settle with him. God would go with him and bring him back to his father's "house" in peace. When he returned, there would be a "house" for God in the Promised Land.

3. Dedication (20–22).   Jacob's promise to worship God at Bethel was solemnized by an oath. Vows were not made to induce God to do something he was not willing to do. They were made to bind the worshiper to the performance of some acknowledged duty. Jacob made his vow on the basis of what God had guaranteed to do. He was thus taking God at his Word and binding himself to reciprocate with his own dedication.

The oath then must be divided between a protasis ("if") and an apodosis ("then"), although it is not easy to determine just where to make this division. The protasis should form the foundation for his promise and should include what God had promised to do. The apodosis should record what Jacob wanted to do for God. The most appropriate place to start the apodosis may be in verse 22. The vow would then read:

> *If* the LORD God is with me
> and keeps me in this way in which I am going
> and gives me bread to eat and clothing to wear,
>   so that I return in peace to the house of my father
> and the LORD becomes my God,
> *then* this stone which I set up as a pillar
>   will be the house of God,
> and all which you give me a tenth I will give you.

God had promised to be with him, keep him, bless him, and return him in peace—in short, to be his God; consequently, Jacob promised that the spot would be a place of worship and that he would tithe.

The vow to tithe is the only part of Jacob's promise that is a concrete action. Moreover, the structure of the speech changes to the second person in a personal address to God directly. His gratitude and submission to God would be expressed through the paying of a tithe.

Jacob thus did more than consecrate Bethel as a place of worship for the nation of Israel. He himself was moved to worship there, and his acts formed a pattern for later worshipers to follow in the offering of their devotion and their substance to God.

This brief account tells how God suddenly and unexpectedly broke into the life of the deceiver, who was fleeing for his life, and assured him of the covenantal promises and God's protective presence. But the point of the narrative is the effect on Jacob's life—he worshiped and prepared for the worship of his descendants at this "house of God."

The didactic level of the story for Israel would be clear. Jacob, who represents Israel in the story, who was anything but obedient at the outset, would spend a number of years outside the land (cf. Gen. 15:13–16). During that time God would protect and bless him (cf. Exod. 1:7, 12, 20) and ultimately return him to his inheritance. Such covenantal blessings should inspire worshipful devotion from God's people (cf. Exod. 5:1; 14:29–15:21; Josh. 4:19–24; 8:30–31).

The effectual revelation of God's protective presence and promised blessings will inspire devout and faithful worship. Those who fully realize God's gracious provision, those whom the Word of God has powerfully impressed, will respond with consecration and commitment. Where there is no reverential fear, no commitment or no devotion, there is probably very little apprehension of what the spiritual life is all about. Like the revelation to Jacob, the written revelation of God makes believers aware of the Lord's presence and prompts them to a higher level of living.

Bibliography

Barackman, Paul F. "The Hard Pillow." *Interp* 9 (1955): 41–50.

Barth, Christoph. "Jakob in Bethel—ein neues Buch zur Vätertradition." *TLZ* 104 (1979): 331–38.

Cohen, Harold R. *Biblical Hapax Legomena in the Light of Akkadian and Ugaritic.* Missoula, Mont.: Scholar's, 1978.

Couffignal, Robert. "Le song de Jacob: Approches nouvelles de Genèse 28, 10–22." *Bib* 58 (1977): 342–60.

Dumbrell, W. J. "The Role of Bethel in the Biblical Narratives from Jacob to Jeroboam I." *AJBA* 2, no. 3 (1974–75): 65–75.

Fishbane, Michael. *Text and Texture*, pp. 53–55. New York: Schocken, 1979.

Fokkelman, J. P. *Narrative Art in Genesis*, pp. 65–81. Assen: Van Gorcum, 1975.

Glenn, M. G. "The Word לוז in Gen. 28:19 in the LXX and in the Midrash." *JQR* 59 (1968–69): 73–76.

Graesser, C. F. "Standing Stones in Ancient Palestine." *BA* 35 (1972): 34–63.

Griffiths, J. G. "The Celestial Ladder and the Gate of Heaven (Gen. 28:12 and 17)." *ExT* 76 (1964–65): 229–30.

———. "The Celestial Ladder and the Gate of Heaven in Egyptian Ritual." *ExT* 78 (1966–67): 54–55.

Gurney, O. R. "The Myth of Nergal and Ereshkigal." *Anatolian Studies* 10 (1960): 105–31.

Henderson, A. "On Jacob's Vision at Bethel." *ExT* 4 (1882): 151.

Houtman, C. "Jacob at Mahanaim: Some Remarks on Genesis 32:2–3." *VT* 28 (1978): 37–44.

————— . "What Did Jacob See in His Dream at Bethel? Some Remarks on Genesis 28:10–22." *VT* 27 (1977): 337–52.

Hyatt, J. Philip. "The Deity Bethel and the Old Testament." *JAOS* 59 (1939): 81–98.

————— . "A Neo-Babylonian Parallel to *Bethel-šar-eṣer*, Zech. 7:2." *JBL* 56 (1937): 387–94.

Keller, C. A. "Über einige alttestamentlichen Heiligtumslegenden I." *ZAW* 67 (1955): 141–68.

Maxwell-Mahon, W. D. " 'Jacob's Ladder': A Structural Analysis of Scripture." *Semitics* 7 (1980): 118–30.

Millard, A. R. "The Celestial Ladder and the Gate of Heaven (Gen. 28:12, 17)." *ExT* 78 (1966–67): 86–87.

Moscati, S. *An Introduction to the Comparative Grammar of the Semitic Languages*, p. 63. Wiesbaden: O. Harrassowitz, 1964.

Patrides, C. A. "Renaissance Interpretations of Jacob's Ladder." *ThZ* 18 (1962): 411–18.

Ross, Allen P. "Jacob's Vision: The Founding of Bethel." *BibSac* 142 (1985): 224–37.

Stockton, E. "Sacred Pillars in the Bible." *ABR* 20 (1972): 16–32.

Westermann, Claus. *The Promises to the Fathers*, pp. 84–94. Translated by David E. Green. Philadelphia: Fortress, 1980.

44

Jacob's Marriages and Laban's Deception
(Gen. 29:1–30)

The Bible demonstrates repeatedly the principle that people reap what they sow. This truth has been called poetic justice, or irony. It is, furthermore, a form of divine retribution, a talionic justice in which there is a measure-for-measure turn of affairs, where the punishment fits the crime. Believers do not view such turns of affairs as mere coincidences; rather, believers recognize that God orders the affairs of human beings in order to remind them of their sins and to set things right.

Genesis 29 provides us with an example of this divine ordering. The climax of the story comes with the deception of Jacob on his wedding night—the deceiver was deceived. Kidner writes,

> In Laban Jacob met his match and his means of discipline. Twenty years (31:41) of drudgery and friction were to weather his character; and the reader can reflect that presumably Jacob is not the only person to have needed a Laban in his life.
>
> Through this man he also drank deeply of his own medicine of duplicity; yet even as the loser he displayed qualities that were lacking in

Esau. The tenacity that showed at his birth and, supremely, at Peniel, enabled him to regard the defeat over Rachel as only a setback. [*Genesis*, pp. 159–60]

This chapter forms the introduction to the Jacob-Laban episode; it describes Jacob's arrival at Haran and his service for his wives. Along with chapter 31, where there is the departure from Haran and the deception (by Rachel) of Laban, Genesis 29 frames the Jacob-Laban episode. In between these two chapters we have the development of the blessing—the fruitfulness of the family and the flocks.

Theological Ideas

The story does not expressly make any theological points. There is no vision, no oracle from God. Rather, the narrative unfolds its theological lessons in a subtle way.

In the first half of the chapter we have the account of Jacob's arrival at the well and his meeting of Rachel. The significance of this event is greatly clarified by observing the parallel in Genesis 24:11–33 (see also Exod. 2:15–22). Just as Abraham's servant had met Rebekah at the well (it could have been the same well), so now Jacob met Rachel there. In all probability Laban would have remembered that earlier incident, especially how the Lord had led the servant to that spot. The parallel is more than coincidence. Yet this narrative does not emphasize divine leadership—it simply implies that providence was at work in Jacob's life. Here was a man who received a marvelous vision at Bethel. He knew God's plan to bless and protect him. And then he came to the spot in the vicinity of Laban's place and just happened to meet Rachel. The parallel with Genesis 24 and the emphasis of this chapter in its immediate context strongly suggest that God brought him to Rachel—and to Laban.

A recognition of this theological implication leads directly into the major idea of the story, namely, the deception by Laban. If Jacob sensed that God was controlling his destiny, then Laban's explanation that his *younger* daughter could not be married before the *firstborn* would have been sufficient to make Jacob realize that his sin had come back to haunt him. If Esau would forever remember how he was deceived out of his birthright and blessing, Jacob would have to live with the results of this deception for the rest of his life. He would realize that this deception was designed by God to make him, the deceiver, know that such devices were repugnant to God.

Structure and Synthesis

Structure

The story can be divided into two parts, the meeting at the well (vv. 1–14) and the deception in the marriage (vv. 15–30). The structure of the first part draws attention to Rachel by the repeated use of the particle *hinnēh*, traditionally translated "behold." Its threefold usage in this story parallels its threefold usage in the preceding narrative: the first use pointed to the setting, the second to those attendant upon it, and the third to the focal point in the story (see chart 24).

The situation at the well with the shepherds provided the occasion for Jacob's magnanimous act to provide water for the sheep of Rachel. The invitation to the hospitality of Laban (vv. 13–14) then forms a transition to the Jacob-Laban meeting and the first part of their rivalry. While the first part builds to the meeting with Rachel, that meeting rapidly gives way to the next scene, which is the episode in Laban's house.

The second half of the chapter forms a discrete unit. The story moves from the hospitality of Laban to the business transaction (vv. 15–19). The business transaction, however, was complicated by the deception, and the deception resolved by a second marriage. The report of the complication through deception can be charted in a chiasm (see chart 25).

In this section of the chapter the narrative centers on the dialogue between Jacob and Laban at the point of crisis—Jacob accusing Laban

Chart 24. **The Parallel Use of *hinnēh* in Genesis 28 and 29**

Element Introduced by *hinnēh*	28:12–13	29:1–6
Setting	There was a ladder (12).	There was a well in the field (2).
Attendants	Angels of God, ascending and descending (12).	Three flocks of sheep were lying by it (the shepherds were lazy) (2).
Focus	The Lord was standing above it (13).	Rachel was coming with the sheep (6).

Chart 25. **Chiasmus of Genesis 29:20–30**

A   Jacob's payment for his wife (20)
   B   Consummation of the marriage to Leah by deception (21–24)
      C   Jacob's accusation against Laban (25)
      C' Laban's defense (26)
   B' Consummation of the marriage to Rachel by negotiation (27–30a)
A' Jacob's payment for his wife (30b)

of deceiving him, and Laban explaining that the younger cannot be married before the firstborn. When we consider that everything in the first part of the chapter focuses on the meeting with Rachel and that that meeting leads to the business transaction with Laban, we can see that this central dialogue forms the climax to the chapter. Here the lesson may be found.

Summary Message

After meeting Rachel at the well, where, in spite of its strictly regulated use and the reluctance of the shepherds to accommodate him, he moved the stone and watered the flocks, and after serving Laban seven years for Rachel, Jacob was deceived by Laban into marrying Leah, the firstborn, and had to serve another seven years for Rachel.

Exegetical Outline

I. Jacob met Rachel at the well, where, in spite of its strictly regulated use and the reluctance of the shepherds to accommodate him, he moved the stone and watered her flocks (1–14).
   A. Encouraged by God's blessing, Jacob traveled until he came to a well where three flocks were waiting to be watered (1–3).
   B. Jacob learned from the shepherds that his journey was almost over and that his cousin Rachel was coming with her flock (4–6).
   C. Jacob failed to get the shepherds to remove the stone and water the sheep, and so when Rachel arrived he removed the stone himself, watered the sheep, and, in an emotional outburst, kissed her (7–11).
      1. Jacob could not get the shepherds to remove the stone and begin watering the sheep (7–8).
      2. When Rachel arrived Jacob removed the stone himself and watered the sheep (9–10).
      3. Jacob kissed Rachel in an emotional outburst (11).
   D. Jacob revealed his identity to Rachel and was warmly welcomed into the house of Laban (12–14).
II. After serving Laban seven years for Rachel, Jacob was deceived by Laban and found himself married to Leah, the firstborn, and was able to marry Rachel only when he agreed to serve seven more years (15–30).
   A. After being welcomed into Laban's household, Jacob agreed to serve seven years for Rachel, whom he loved (15–19).
   B. After completing the seven years of service, Jacob claimed

his bride but was deceived into marrying Leah and had to serve seven more years for Rachel (20–30).

1. Jacob completed the seven years of service and asked for his bride, Rachel (20–21).
2. Laban deceived Jacob at the marriage feast by bringing Leah to him in the place of Rachel (22–24).
3. Jacob accused Laban of deceiving him, but Laban defended his actions by appealing to custom (25–26).
   a. In the morning Jacob discovered the deception and accused Laban (25).
   b. Laban claimed that the custom of the land was to marry off the older daughter before the younger (26).
4. After completing the marriage week, Jacob married Rachel as well, having agreed to serve Laban seven more years for her (27–30).
   a. Laban advised Jacob to complete Leah's week, after which he could have Rachel as well—for seven more years of service (27).
   b. Jacob received Rachel—whom he loved—and served for seven more years (28–30).

Development of the Exposition

The first half of the narrative shows how Jacob prospered in his search for a wife, and the second half relates the harsh deception brought on the unsuspecting Jacob. The first part builds toward the deception in that Jacob appears unsuspecting, almost naive, in his apparently successful mission for a wife. He was not aware that God had also led him to Laban.

I. Those who believe that God is working in their lives will be inspired to magnanimous and enthusiastic service to others (1–14).

A. The recipients of the promise find that God prospers their way (1–6).

It is important in developing the message to show the parallels between this chapter and Genesis 24, for such a comparison suggests how the writer was understanding Jacob's swift success. This passage may not explicitly refer to the Lord's leading, but the parallelism suggests that, just as the Lord guided the servant to Rebekah, so did he guide Jacob to Rachel. Moreover, the parallelism between the three clauses beginning with *hinnēh* in chapter 28 and the threefold use of *hinnēh* in chapter 29 also indicates how Jacob's success was to be interpreted—the vision at Bethel was the promise, and the meeting at the well was the beginning of the fulfillment.

How did Jacob respond to the promise that he received at Bethel? A literal translation of the first verse will clarify his attitude: "And Jacob *picked up his feet* and went to the land of the people of the east." After the vision at Bethel there was a new spring in Jacob's walk. Esau no longer concerned him; now he was on a mission with the Lord's promise of protection and provision. This clue strongly suggests that Jacob's confidence in the Lord's direction to Laban's house was very high.

B. The recipients of the promise can magnanimously and enthusiastically serve others (7–14).

The picture we gain of Jacob in this section of the story is vastly different from that of chapters 25 and 27. Here he was magnanimous in his eagerness to remove the stone and water the flock. Of course, he was riding the crest of the vision and of his success in finding the proper location and of his meeting Rachel. It all seemed to come together so quickly.

That the encounter took place at a well is significant in the story, for wells were signs of God's blessings (water provided for life; see Gen. 26). Moreover, Jacob's watering of Laban's flocks foreshadowed the subsequent stories in which Laban and his flocks would prosper with Jacob's care.

Jacob must be contrasted with the lazy shepherds. He was generous, zealous, and industrious—spurred on to a magnanimous act. He had a mission, a quest. That burning goal implanted by previous experiences had lightened his step and driven him to success.

The first half of the chapter closes with Jacob's being welcomed into Laban's house (vv. 13–14). It is interesting to make another comparison between the last chapter and this one: after the vision of the Lord, Jacob vowed to return to worship in the house of God, but after the meeting with Rachel he entered the house of Laban. As the story unfolds, Jacob becomes so entrenched in Laban's house that the Lord has to remind him of the vow to return to the house of God, to Bethel (31:3).

Laban's greetings for his relative were warm and enthusiastic. In referring to Jacob as his bone and flesh (ʿaṣmî ûbᵉśārî), Laban acknowledged their close blood ties, reminding us of the earlier use of these terms in the joyous words of Adam over finding one with whom he could form a marital union (2:23). Indeed, Jacob had found the family from whom he was instructed to take a fitting bride.

II. God will effectively discipline his people by making them painfully aware of their sins (15–30).

In the first part of the story Jacob was convinced that the Lord was at work in his life, putting a new swiftness to his step and prospering his way to the house of Laban. But the Lord was also at work in Jacob's life in another way, for there were matters yet unsettled in his life.

A. God's people often pursue his blessing naively, forgetting their unresolved sins (15–19).

In this section Jacob seized the opportunity to acquire Rachel for a wife, thus fulfilling his mission (28:2) and beginning to realize the divine blessing promised to him at Bethel (vv. 14–15). But an ominous note surfaced, perhaps so subtle that Jacob was blind to it—Laban had two daughters, the *elder* was Leah, and the *younger* was Rachel (29:16). Here the motif of the two brothers, the elder Esau and the younger Jacob, reappears. Jacob desired to marry the younger—but he would soon realize that the elder daughter stood in the way of his plans.

B. God's people often find their sin coming back on them to discipline them (20–30).

The story passes over the years of service for Rachel (except to note Jacob's love) until it comes to the critical point, the complication at the marriage. In this event a real nemesis was at work, as Laban exhibited a different side to his nature than previously seen. The narrative's simplicity adds to the drama: when the time came for the marriage union, the feast was arranged for the celebration; hearts were merry, and spirits high. Over seven years Jacob's love for Rachel had grown, but in one night it would be forever marred by the substitution of Leah. This account provides, as Kidner says, "the very embodiment of anti-climax, and this moment a miniature of man's disillusion, experienced from Eden onwards" (*Genesis*, p. 160). Or, as von Rad says, "That Laban secretly gave the unloved Leah to the man in love was, to be sure, a monstrous blow, a masterpiece of shameless treachery. . . . It was certainly a move by which he won for himself far and wide the coarsest laughter" (*Genesis*, p. 291). But what pain it caused! Such treachery lies at the heart of the message of Genesis: on the eve of another stage in the fulfillment of the blessing, treacherous deception brought pain and apparent disaster.

Jacob's protests were to no avail. Now he would understand how Esau had felt. Now he would have to serve seven more years and receive a divided family, a loved wife and an unloved wife who had shared in the deception.

The dialogue provides us with the point of the story: it was not right to marry the *younger* before the *firstborn*. How these words must have brought back Jacob's own deception! If social convention was to be set aside, it should be not by deception but by God. Laban's stinging words are left without any editorial comment—the event itself was God's rebuke and discipline of Jacob.

The expositor must pick up the three important allusions to previous stories in this section, for they greatly enhance the point of the story. First, in verse 25, Jacob accused Laban of deceiving him: "Why have you beguiled me [*rimmîtānî*]?" The verb *rimmâ* is cognate to the noun used in Genesis 27:35 that described Jacob's deception (*mirmâ*). Second, when Laban offered his explanation to Jacob, he used the word "firstborn" (*bᵉkîrâ*) to describe his older daughter. This word would recall the major motif of chapter 27, the blessing of the firstborn. And third, the motif of serving figures prominently in this chapter—Jacob served (*wayyaʿăbōd*) Laban for his daughters. The blessing that Jacob had gained by deception from Isaac said that his brothers would serve him (27:29); but here was one brother (29:12) that beat Jacob at his own game and seemed to nullify the benefits of that stolen blessing. This painful experience was God's rebuke of Jacob for deceiving his father to obtain the blessing.

The narrative all works to develop the point that Jacob's marriages to Leah and Rachel, the two women who built the household of Israel, were the result of deception and prolonged service. But Israel could still be encouraged, for here an ancestor of the Syrians dealt underhandedly with their ancestor, but their ancestor made the best of it. After all, it was not merely a match-up between two crafty men; in spite of all that Jacob might face, God had promised to protect and bless him.

In spite of the promise—which Jacob perhaps assumed naively would come his way unopposed—God brought the patriarch-to-be to Laban for discipline that would bring his deception before his eyes. The lesson is that, *even though God's people may experience God's blessing on their endeavors, God will effectively discipline them by making them painfully aware of their unresolved sins.* In short, we may say that they will reap what they have sown—even though they seem to be making progress by God's provision. God may wait patiently before disciplining his people, but discipline he will, often using means similar to the offense to correct them. If they sowed iniquity, they will reap sorrow (Prov. 22:8; see also 11:18); if they sowed the wind, they will reap a whirlwind (Hos. 8:7; see also 10:12–13); whatever they have sown, they will reap (Gal. 6:7).

If we use the story of Jacob as a sample, we may say that, when we are thrown together with people who are crafty, arrogant, deceitful, contentious, gossipy, or a host of other human frailties, before we lament that we have to be around such people, we perhaps should take a long look at ourselves. It may be that some of those traits characterize us and that other people may be part of God's means of disciplining us.

Bibliography

Ackroyd, Peter R. "Hosea and Jacob." *VT* 13 (1963): 245–59.

Carney, Frederick S. "The Virtue-Obligation Controversy." *JRE* 1 (1973): 5–19.

Daube, D., and R. Yaron. "Jacob's Reception by Laban." *JSS* 1 (1956): 60–62.

Diamond, J. A. "The Deception of Jacob: A New Perspective on an Ancient Solution to the Problem." *VT* 34 (1984): 211–13.

Fokkelman, J. P. *Narrative Art in Genesis*, pp. 123–30. Assen: Van Gorcum, 1975.

Frankena, R. "Some Remarks on the Semitic Background of Chapters xxix–xxxi of the Book of Genesis." *OTS* 17 (1972): 53–64.

Gordon, C. "The Story of Jacob and Laban in the Light of the Nuzi Tablets." *BASOR* 66 (1937): 25–27.

Kornfeld, W. "Mariage dans l'Ancient Testament." *Dictionnaire de la Bible. Supplement* 5, pp. 905–26.

Van Seters, John. "Jacob's Marriages and Ancient Near Eastern Customs: A Reassessment." *HTR* 62 (1969): 377–95.

45

The Mishandling of God's Blessing
(Gen. 29:31–30:24)

The desire for affectionate approval often leads people down dangerous paths. Unrequited love, lack of recognition, or complete disregard is difficult to endure. One recourse is to pursue love and recognition by any means, without regard to the cost in terms of the long-range effects. Such a direction is life on the earthly level; it is not the way of faith.

The contest of childbearing between Rachel and Leah shows just such a struggle within the family. The nature of the section is a dispute between the wives of Jacob, which is a part of the broader series about the dispute between Jacob and Laban. This account of the dispute is in part narrative and in part genealogical report, the two types of literature being linked by the etymological word plays throughout the section. By recording the genealogical information with the word plays on the names, the narrator stressed simultaneously the rivalry between the women and the way that the Lord blessed Jacob with children.

Theological Ideas

The unit reports the births of the ancestors of the Hebrew tribes as part of the fulfillment of the promises. God's blessing on Jacob is thus the predominant theme. This unit along with the next forms the central focus of the Jacob stories; here the tribes of Israel took shape, and in the next unit they flourished. The emphasis in this text is on God's sovereign provision of the seed, which can be seen from the frequent recognition by the participants in the rivalry that God opened or closed wombs and gave the women children.

Something of the nature of God can also be gathered from the sentiments that accompanied the namings, for they expressed the popular beliefs of the people. In these sayings the women acknowledged that God championed the needy and the afflicted when he saw their trouble and heard their cries; but they also acknowledged that God was the giver of bountiful blessings, especially in the fulfillment of the covenant promises. The exposition must capture these popular religious beliefs.

The tension caused by the rivalry between the wives is not actually a point of theology, but it is symptomatic of weak faith. Apparently without realizing the significance of their bearing these children, and without wisdom in their dealings with one another, the members of the family struggled against one another for affection and recognition. What could have been a rich experience in God's blessing was greatly tarnished by the tensions that divided the family—a division that remained in the tribes through the divided monarchy.

Structure and Synthesis

Structure

The narrative reports a series of twelve births, most of which contain explanations of the names. The passage begins and ends with the note of Rachel's barrenness; in between there are many births—but none to Rachel. The first set belongs to Leah, the second to Rachel's maid, the third to Leah's maid, the fourth to Leah, and finally the last birth belongs to Rachel. The force of the struggle remains before the reader, with several critical links such as Rachel's desperate complaint to Jacob, the employment of the maids to bear children, and the hiring of Jacob with the mandrakes. The narrative reaches its climax in verses 22–24, when the barrenness of Rachel was removed and the conflict between the wives subsided.

Summary Message

God formed the family of Jacob, the founders of the tribes of Israel, in fulfillment of his promises at Bethel, even though Jacob and his wives lived in envy and friction over how God chose to bless them.

Exegetical Outline

I. God responded to Leah's plight with the births of four sons, all the while withholding the blessing from Rachel because of Jacob's unfair treatment of Leah (29:31–35).

A. God took note of Leah's plight and opened her womb but withheld the blessing from Rachel (31).

B. God gave four sons to Leah, who responded appropriately in faith (32–35b).

1. Leah recognized that Reuben was the blessing of the Lord and expressed her desire that her husband would love her (32).

2. Leah acknowledged that Simeon was the blessing of the Lord in response to her unfavored status with Jacob (33).

3. Leah expressed the hope that Jacob would be joined to her because of her fruitfulness in bearing a third son, Levi (34).

4. Leah bore Judah and consoled herself with the praise of the Lord (35a–b).

C. Leah ceased bearing children (35c).

II. Filled with envy over her sister's fruitfulness, Rachel complained to Jacob and then competed with Leah by bearing children through Bilhah, which she correctly recognized as God's blessing (30:1–8).

A. Rachel complained of her barrenness to Jacob (1–2).

1. When Rachel saw her barrenness in contrast to Leah's fruitfulness, she blamed Jacob (1).

2. Jacob angrily reminded her that it was God who made her barren (2).

B. Rachel competed with Leah by giving her maid, Bilhah, to Jacob to bear children for her (3–8).

1. She gave her maid to Jacob in her place (3–4).

2. She expressed the sentiment that God had taken her side and granted her Dan in response to her prayer (5–6).

3. She received a second son through Bilhah, Naphtali, and claimed victory in her bout with Leah (7–8).

III. Responding to Rachel's use of her maid, Leah continued the competition by giving her maid, Zilpah, to Jacob and finding success in the births of two more children (30:9–13).

A. Leah gave Jacob her maid (9).

B. Leah received two sons through Zilpah and expressed pleasure in her success (10–13).

IV. Rachel and Leah both expressed their discontent and continued

to seek to outdo each other in having children; God responded
to Leah by granting her two more sons and a daughter (30:14–21).
A. Rachel and Leah expressed their discontent and arranged for
the acquisition of Jacob with the mandrakes (14–15).
1. Rachel indicated her discontent with her barrenness by
seeking an aphrodisiac from Leah (14).
2. Leah expressed her discontent by accusing Rachel of
stealing her husband (15a).
3. Rachel exchanged a night with Jacob for Leah's aphrodisiac (15b).
B. God blessed Leah with three more children (16–21).
1. God honored Leah with a fifth son, Issachar (16–18).
2. God blessed Leah with a sixth son, Zebulun; Leah expressed her wishes that Jacob would now exalt her (19–20).
3. Leah bore Dinah (21).
V. God remembered Rachel and ended her barrenness with the
birth of Joseph—which prompted her to pray for another son
(30:22–24).

Development of the Exposition

In order to do justice to the exposition of this section, the expositor
will have to discuss the word plays on the names. Many expositors do
not like to discuss such technical things in the exposition. There is no
other way, however, to capture the meaning and the tone of the material.
To explain this material accurately and yet clearly will call for a certain
amount of skill in addition to the preparation.

I would organize the narrative in four major sections, joining the second and third sections in the exegetical outline because they make a
similar point in the overall message. Throughout the exposition I would
stress the growing intensity and frustration in the competition as well
as the progression of the work of God. The two themes can then be
joined to form a lesson.

I. God, in his justice, blesses the oppressed and the despised as he builds his program (29:31–35).

The narrative is rather bare. The developing themes are based on the
contrasts between the two wives: Rachel was barren, but Leah had four
sons in rapid succession. The record of these births is sad because of the
conditions; but the underlying message that God was building his nation
provides the consolation.

A. Reuben: The Lord sees affliction (31–32).

The name Reuben (*r^e'ûbēn*) looks like a combination of "look" (*r^e'û*) and "a son" (*bēn*). The name however, is explained by the expression *rā'â b^e'onyî*, "has looked on my affliction." This statement was worded to reflect the sounds of the name, not to give the actual meaning of the name (Driver, *Book of Genesis*, p. 273). A second word play occurs with the verb "love me," for the sounds of "son," *bēn*, can be heard in *ye'ĕhābanî*. A name was thus selected for the firstborn, and then two sentiments were expressed that played on the sounds of the name—a lament and a wish. Whatever the name Reuben actually meant (and "look, a son" is not an impossible analysis, only unparalleled in Hebrew names), the expression that the Lord looked on her affliction expressed the significance of the birth to Leah. The name would form a perpetual reminder of this truth.

B. Simeon: The Lord hears (33).

Leah's second son was named Simeon (*šim'ôn*) because the Lord heard (*šāma'*) that she was hated. The word play catches the true significance of the name, for it is one of many names etymologically related to the verb *šāma'*, "to hear." "Simeon" could be a form from the verb with a nominal ending -*ôn*. The old idea that it was related to an Arabic word for "hyena" was correctly discarded long ago because it was not found in Northwest Semitic. But the verb "to hear" is well attested in names, a fact that reflects how much in need of divine help people have been.

Like Reuben, Simeon owed his existence to providential dealings in the face of antagonism. And his name would be a reminder of the truth that God hears his people in need.

C. Levi: Hope for attachment (34).

Leah named her third child Levi (*lēwî*), with the hope that her husband would now be drawn to her (*yillāweh*). The verb in the sentiment is from *lāwâ*, "to join." It was used again in Numbers 18:2 and 4 in a similar word play on the name of the tribe, expressing how the Levites would be joined to Aaron in the service of the shrine. That word play has contributed to the interest in the name by scholars because it suggests that the name reflects a priestly tribe. Yet Genesis presents Levi, the ancestor of the Levites, without any hint of their later priestly function.

Many suggestions have been made concerning the etymology of the name Levi. Hommel connected the name with *lavi'u*, "priest," from the Minaean inscriptions (*Auf-sätze u. Abhandlungen*, pp. 30–31). But

"Levite" is not used in the Old Testament with the primary meaning of "priest." Albright connected the name with the Egyptian word *ra-wi-'i-ra* (= *lawi'el*), meaning "client of El" (*The Vocalization of the Egyptian Syllabic Orthography* [New Haven: American Oriental Society, 1934]). This idea is close to the view that the name signifies a person pledged for a vow (see "Levi" in *IDB*). And then Nöldeke, following Wellhausen, argues that the name is a gentilic of the mother's name—*lēwî* from *lē'â* ("Review of *Kinship and Marriage in Early Arabia* by W. Robertson Smith," *ZDMG* 40 [1886]: 186).

It is entirely possible that one of these etymological connections may be correct and that the name Levi, or something close to it, was common in the ancient world, or even signified a priestly class. The name was chosen by Leah, however, because its sounds harmonized with her wish— or she formed her wish to harmonize with the sounds of the name. A gentilic explanation would fit the story very well.

Later the name took on a greater significance when the tribe was attached (*weyillāwû*) to the ark. This word play in Numbers 18:2 alludes to the origin of the tribe but suggests another meaning for Leah's words.

D. Judah: Praise for the Lord (35).

The births of the first two sons encouraged Leah because they obviously meant that the Lord had responded to her unhappy lot. She had hoped that the birth of the third son would strike a responsive chord in her husband, but it apparently failed to do so. With the fourth son Leah thus resolved—or resigned herself—to praise ('*ôdeh*) the Lord for his provision of a son. She called him Judah (*yehûdâ*). The names in sequence suggest that this son would be the consolation of the unloved wife.

The name Judah has also received much attention by interpreters. Perhaps Albright's analysis that the name is a verbal formation and not a compound name makes the best sense ("Names 'Israel' and 'Judah,'" p. 172). He shows that the uncontracted *hophal* forms of the verb *yādâ* would include *yehûdeh* for the imperfect, and *yehûd* for the jussive. The name is closest to the imperfect but could have been shortened from *yehûde'ēl*, "God be praised." Albright offers an explanation of the final vowel *ā* as a lengthening under the influence of the *aleph*.

The narrative thus reports that Leah's resolution to praise the Lord came with the birth of the founder of this important tribe. Possibly, again, an existing name was chosen and the sentiment expressed to form the word play. Since the name meant "he will be praised," or "let him be praised," it carried some ambiguity. This fact permitted another play on the name in Genesis 49:8, in which Jacob prophesied that Judah's brothers would praise him (*yôdûkā 'aheykā*, "your brothers will praise you"), meaning that the tribe of Judah would rise to prominence. Neither Leah's "I will praise" (*'ôdeh*) nor Jacob's "your brothers will praise you" (*yôdûkā*) is the exact meaning of the name; they are merely plays on the name, expressing anticipated praise because of Judah.

II. God, in his grace, blesses his people even through their faulty human efforts (30:1–13).

In the next two sections of the narrative, the women gave their maid-servants to Jacob. This was the custom used by Sarah that brought such trouble to Abraham's household; but since these events all preceded the law, moralizing would be beside the point. God used this custom to continue building the tribes of his nation.

A. Dan and Naphtali: Success in strife (1–8).

The namings of Rachel's sons born through her maid Bilhah do not reflect a strong faith like Leah's. Rather, they reflect Rachel's bitter struggle with her sister for vindication.

Dan (*dān*) was the first son born to Bilhah. The sentiment expressed at the naming was "God has vindicated me [*dānannî*]." The name itself could be a perfect tense ("he judged, vindicated") or a participle ("judge") and is thus very closely related to the explanation. This birth indicated to Rachel that God was beginning to set things right for her, that he was vindicating her cause.

The name of the second son, Naphtali (*naptālî*), emphasizes the conflict motif more than any other of the names (vv. 7–8). Rachel said, "A mighty struggle [*naptûlê 'ĕlōhîm*] have I waged [*niptaltî*] with my sister." According to this explanation, the name carries the meaning "my wrestling."

The expression of the popular etymology raises some interpretive questions that will have to be studied. With whom did Rachel actually fight, and how? Gunkel suggests that Rachel struggled with God to obtain a son, because a victory over her sister, who already had four sons, would be superfluous (*Genesis*, p. 334). But the use of *'ĕlōhîm* in the etymology probably indicates the superlative degree: "A mighty struggle" is better than "a veritable God's bout" (Skinner, *Commentary on Genesis*, p. 387). It could be that *naptûlê 'ĕlōhîm* is a figurative expression that has its background in ordeals settled by gods, a plausible view in light of this family's familiarity with household gods (see Anne E. Draffkorn, "Illāni/Elohim," *JBL* 76 [1957]: 216–24). According to this meaning, her expression reflects the mentality that the justice of the gods was to her advantage but that it came through ordeal.

Whatever origin lay behind the name or the expression explaining it, the narrative stresses by the repetition of sounds in the connected words the ongoing struggle between the wives. Although Leah was outdistancing Rachel in childbearing, the birth of Naphtali provided a token of satisfaction for her struggle. By naming this child Naphtali, Rachel may have thought that divine justice was rewarding her tenacity.

B. Gad and Asher: Prosperity and happiness (9–13).

Leah responded by giving her maid, Zilpah, to Jacob. The first son born was Gad (gād), meaning "fortune." Leah's exclamation at the birth was appropriate for the source of the name: "what fortune [bāgād]."

The name Gad may go back to an early name of a god of fortune found in Aramaean and Phoenician inscriptions (equivalent to the Greek tychē, a word for luck that was later deified—like the Latin fortuna). If the name was used for a pagan god, there is no indication in the text that Leah so thought of it or used it. (Gunkel says that beḡād earlier would have meant "with Gad's help" [Genesis, p. 334]). All that can be concluded about Leah's expression is that she sensed that fortune had smiled upon her.

The second son was named Asher ('āšēr); she said, "What fortune [be'ošrî], for women will consider me fortunate ['iššerûnî]." The basic meaning of 'āšēr is "go straight, go right, advance," with the developed ideas of "set right" and "pronounce happy, blessed" in the piel. The name could mean something like "happy one"; Dillmann qualified it further by saying "one of even tenor," that is, both "fortunate" and "propitious lucky" (Genesis, vol. 2, p. 242 [343]). The expression that Leah offered at the birth, be'ošrî, means something like "I am in luck; everything is right." The sense is further explained in the causal clause that women will consider her fortunate. Leah thus rejoiced over yet another indication of her happy lot and even anticipated the supportive praise of other women.

III. God, in his justice, blesses his people by contraverting superstitious and jealous practices (30:14–21).

Leah's family continued to increase with three additional children. The birth of Issachar underscores the message that birth is given by God. Reuben found some "mandrakes," which were supposed to be some sort of an aphrodisiac, and Rachel thought they might help her cause. Leah traded them to Rachel for Jacob—and she had the child; Rachel, even with the help of the mandrakes, remained barren.

The name Issachar (yiśśā[s]kār) was explained in commemoration of this incident: "God has given me my hire [śekārî]." The actual etymology of the name is uncertain, partly because of the spelling in the Ben

Asher text, in which it is pointed as though there is no second letter *sin*. The Ben Naphtali text is pointed *yiśśākār* (see Spurrell, *Notes*, p. 262). There are several possibilities for the meaning of the name. The Ben Asher text has it pointed like a *niphal* imperfect, "got for hire." Albright suggested that the original name was *yašaśkir*, "may he favor" ("Northwest Semitic Names," p. 222). Another possibility is that the name could mean "there is recompense" (*yēš śākār*) or "man of recompense" (*'īš śākār*). Spurrell notes that Ben Naphtali may read *yiśśā' śākār* (*Notes*, p. 262).

Whatever the exact meaning of the name was, the connection between the name and the explanation is unmistakable. The sounds (and perhaps the meaning) stress the reward (*śākār*) Leah received from God. This word was used elsewhere of the Lord's provision of children (Ps. 127:3; Gen. 15:1). The name reminds the reader of the divine intervention in the struggle to bear Jacob's children. The word play also reflects Leah's statement, *śākōr śᵉkartîkā* (v. 16), and by this irony provides an ethical comment on Rachel's efforts through the mandrakes.

The next son was Zebulun. Leah said, "God has endowed me [*zᵉbādanî*] with a good dowry [*zebed*]; now will my husband honor me [*yizbᵉlēnî*], because I have born him six sons." Here the anxiety over the struggle surfaces again.

In this instance there are two motivations for the name. The first one, *zᵉbādanî*, is loosely connected. *Zābad* means "to endow with" (a dowry). This verb is strengthened in the verse by its cognate accusative. The second word play appears to be based on this recognition of providence. *Yizbᵉlēnî* expresses Leah's expectation (or wish) for honor. The verb *zābal*, translated "dwell" in the KJV, actually means "exalt, honor" (see also *zᵉbūl*, "elevation"). Speiser suggests that the link is in the Akkadian *zubulla*, a bridegroom's gift. This proposal makes sense, for it supplies a natural semantic basis, it accounts for the form, and it accords with the other motivation for the name (*Genesis*, p. 231). The difficulties would be the strangeness of her longing for a bridegroom's gift after her sixth son, the duplication of the former motivation, and the dependence on Akkadian. Besides, the word *zābal* occurs in Hebrew with the idea of "honor" or "exalt," which makes very good sense here. With the gift of another son, Leah thus hoped that her husband would honor her. The name Zebulun would therefore remind her of divine justice in the face of human injustice. Leah received the divine justice; but she still had not found human justice.

Finally, Leah gave birth to Dinah. The text makes no play on this name, for the girl would not be a tribal ancestor. Etymological word plays are the narrator's way of stressing the significance of the individuals who were important to the formation of the nation.

IV. God, in his compassion, blesses his people by removing their reproach (30:22–24).

Finally, Rachel had a son of her own—Joseph. The report expresses a major triumph in Rachel's struggle: the birth of a son after a long period of unfruitfulness displayed divine intervention on behalf of the favorite wife.

With this name there is also a double word play, the first being an expression of joy loosely connected to the name by sound (*'āsap*), the second forming the motivation for the name Joseph (*yôsēp*): "May the LORD add [*yōsēp*] to me another son." Rachel, earlier haughty and impatient, now gave praise to God for taking away her reproach and prayed for another son from the Lord. After all, if a birth had broken the barrenness, more could follow. The name thus meant "may he add," or "may he increase."

The passage is a combination of all small narratives accenting the plays on the names. Each name was interpreted to reflect the concrete family conditions (in contrast to the plays on the names given at Jacob's blessing in Gen. 49), instead of simply repeating the pious substance that they had as testimonies to God as the Giver and Protector of life.

Certainly the passage shows how God prospered Jacob and started to form his great nation. But it was sad that they could not adjust to unfavorable situations and avoid the hatred and the conflict, for that pressure only further split the family and the nation. All Israel could look back to this tradition and see their ancestry in Jacob—and in the conflict between the women. They were brothers, sons of Israel, and should not, like their mothers, waiver in their faith and bitterly compete for God's blessing. Prosperity is dispensed to people by the sovereign will.

We thus have the rivalry between the two women. Leah, a woman of strong faith, was earnestly longing for the affection of her husband but was being blessed by God in childbirth. Rachel does not appear so strong in the faith; she possessed the affection of her husband but anxiously desired the blessing of God in childbirth. In it all, the message was clear to Israel. God chose the despised mother, Leah, and exalted her to be the first mother. The kingly tribe of Judah and the priestly tribe of Levi were traced back to her, in spite of Jacob's love for Rachel and his later favoritism toward Rachel's son Joseph.

We can learn many lessons from this struggle in Jacob's family. Although having two wives was not immediately Jacob's fault (the law only later prohibited such a marriage [Lev. 18:18]), through it God taught the nation about his wisdom and justice and compassion. We can learn the danger of favoritism in family relationships, a recurring theme in the patriarchal narratives. We can also learn about the danger of thwarting human affection. The tragedy comes when we, striving for love and recognition, either within the family or not, live our lives on such an earthly level that only temporal things mean much to us. To sacrifice things spiritual for things physical—to trade things that are above trade value—is tragic in the long run. This loss may happen when we are filled with anxiety and envy over the apparent inequity of God's dealings with his people. *God's people must put away envy and strife, which lead to bitter conflicts, and accept the truth that God dispenses his blessings in sovereign wisdom, justice, and compassion.*

We learn that God's choice to bless is not made by human standards. In fact, God characteristically works for things or people that humans reject—the downcast, the afflicted, the troubled, the oppressed, and the rejected. Those who find themselves in such predicaments can by faith rely on God, who in his sovereign plan will bless them. His blessing, however, cannot be gained by bargaining or striving.

Whatever our lot in life—whether we are hated or ignored, oppressed or challenged, troubled or anxious—our attitude should not be one of jealousy, nor our efforts those of bitter rivalry. Rather, we must cultivate a wholehearted trust in God, waiting patiently for his blessing on us. Paul, in Romans 13:13–14, says, "Let us walk properly, as in the day . . . not in strife and envy. . . . But put on the Lord Jesus Christ, and make no provision for the flesh, to fulfill its lusts."

Bibliography

Albright, W. F. "The Names 'Israel' and 'Judah,' with an Excursus on the Etymology of *Tôdâh* and *Tôrâh.*" *JBL* 46 (1927): 151–85.

————. "Northwest-Semitic Names in a List of Egyptian Slaves from the Eighteenth Century b.c." *JAOS* 74 (1954): 222–33.

Anderson, Francis I. "Note on Genesis 30:8." *JBL* 88 (1969): 200.

Draffkorn, Anne E. "Illāni/Elohim." *JBL* 76 (1957): 216–24.

Eissfeldt, O. " 'Gut Glück!' in semitischer Namengebung." *JBL* 82 (1963): 195–200.

Haveli, B. "The Arrangement of the Names of the Twelve Sons in the Jacob Stories." *BetM* 55 (1973): 494–523.

Janzen, W. "ʾašrê in the Old Testament." *HTR* 58 (1965): 215–26.

Lewi, Julius. "The Old West Semitic Sun-God Ḥummu." *HUCA* 18 (1944): 429–81.

Millard, A. R. "The Meaning of the Name Judah." *ZAW* 86 (1974): 216–18.

Nicol, George G. "Reuben's Reversal." *JThS*, n.s., 31 (1980): 536–39.

Strus, A. "Étymologies des noms propres dans Gen. 29:32–30:24." *Sal* 40 (1978): 57–72.

46

The Blessing of Prosperity
(Gen. 30:25–43)

Prosperity can have one of two effects on people. Some view their success as a trust from God and put it to good use for him. Others, however, see it as a personal accomplishment and the means to personal power. Such an independent, self-sufficient attitude is harmful to the faith, for it robs God of his honor by attributing the prosperity to human ingenuity. Sooner or later, believers—even those caught up in this worldly attitude—will acknowledge that their prosperity came from God.

In Genesis 30, we have an unusual story about Jacob's acquiring great wealth at the expense of Laban. This clever man outwitted another opponent—or so it seemed. But Jacob owed more to God in this successful venture than he realized at the time.

This narrative complements the narrative about the increase in the family. The two passages together form the center of the Jacob stories, for in the blessing of Jacob's family and then Jacob's possessions, God's promises began to develop rapidly. In addition, the two passages come at the center of Jacob's journeys; prior to the last narrative was the account of his journey out of the land to Paddan Aram, and subsequent to this narrative is the account of his journey home. The Jacob stories in effect describe a patriarch who came to the land of the Aramaeans to receive God's blessing. In that account there is a similarity with the history of Israel, for the abundant blessing of God that turned the family of Jacob into a great nation occurred in the land of Egypt.

This unit does not specifically explain, though, that the success was the work of God—that conclusion will be affirmed in 31:9. Rather, the narrative portrays Jacob as outwitting Laban in what appear to be clever devices for breeding animals. In this way it forms a contrast with chapter 29: there Laban deceived Jacob in order to gain fourteen years of service from him, but in chapter 30 Jacob outwitted Laban in order to gain the larger share of the herd. Fokkelman highlights the pattern effectively: in Genesis 27, Jacob is a deceiver; in Genesis 29, Laban is a deceiver of a deceiver; and in Genesis 30, Jacob is a deceiver of a deceiver of a deceiver. Fokkelman says, "What this repeating 'fraction' shows is: whenever people like Jacob and Laban mix with each other, there is no end to it. How is this to go on? Will the two take to an escalation of deceit, will they continue *ad infinitum?* What a prospect!" (*Narrative Art,* p. 151).

Theological Ideas

The point of the story, as Jacob's own interpretation of it will say (Gen. 31:9), is God's sovereign blessing of the patriarch in accord with the promises. Jacob's blessing was far more than the expected food and clothing (28:20)—it was abundance.

On the human side of the success we find manipulation, deceit, and anxiety—all of which was so unnecessary, since it was God who was causing the animals to multiply. Yet in the manipulation Jacob beat Laban at his own game and took over his substance. Besides the theological idea of the blessing, we thus also have the idea of the justice of God in bringing Laban his due.

Structure and Synthesis

Structure

The narrative can be divided into two distinct sections. The first section, verses 25–34, is entirely dialogue; the second section, verses 35–43, is entirely narrative report.

The dialogue of the first section establishes the action in the second section. Jacob's first speech is his request to leave Laban (vv. 25–26); it stresses the service that he has given for his wives and his children. Laban's response was a plea for Jacob to stay and work for wages (vv.

27–28); it stresses Laban's acknowledgment that the Lord had prospered him because of Jacob.

Jacob's second speech builds on the words of Laban (vv. 29–30); it stresses how faithfully he served Laban, how abundantly the Lord blessed Laban, but how little he was able to provide for his own house. Laban's response was a simple inquiry into the wages that Jacob wanted (v. 31a).

Jacob's third speech sets out the plan for the breeding of the animals that would be Laban's and those that would be his (vv. 31b–33). Laban's response was one of agreement (v. 34).

The second half of the passage simply reports how this arrangement worked out. The dialogue's emphases on Jacob's diligent work and the Lord's abundant blessing suggest the underlying reasons for the success of this plan. The divine source of the blessing is indicated by the comparison of Jacob's second speech, "and it has now increased into a multitude [*wayyiprōṣ lārōb*]" (v. 30), and the conclusion of the story, "and the man increased exceedingly [*wayyiprōṣ hāʾîš mᵉʾōd mᵉʾōd*] and he had much [*rabbôt*] substance" (v. 43); the terminology that described God's blessing on Laban was used to describe Jacob's success here.

Summary Message

When Jacob agreed to continue serving Laban in exchange for the odd-colored animals of the flock, God sovereignly overruled both the deceit of Laban and the devices of Jacob in order to bless the patriarch.

Exegetical Outline

   I. When Jacob completed his service for Laban's daughters but realized that he had gained little substance for his family, he agreed to serve longer in exchange for the odd-colored animals (25–34).
   A. When Jacob wished to leave with the women and children for whom he had labored, Laban desired that he stay—so that Laban could continue to enjoy God's blessing (25–28).
      1. Jacob requested permission to return to his homeland with his wives and his children for whom he had labored (25–26).
      2. Laban offered to pay Jacob his wages if he would stay, because Laban realized that the Lord had blessed him (27–28).
   B. When Jacob complained that God had blessed Laban abundantly but that he had nothing, Laban agreed to pay his wages (29–31a).
      1. Jacob complained that very little of the abundant blessing God had given belonged to him (29–30).

       2. Laban agreed to meet his wages (31a).

   C. When Jacob set forth his plan to work for the odd-colored animals of the flock, Laban agreed (31b–34).

       1. Instead of taking wages, Jacob proposed working for the odd-colored animals that would be born in the flocks (31b–33).

       2. Laban agreed to the plan (34).

 II. Desiring to outwit the deceitful Laban, Jacob employed questionable breeding practices in order to produce odd-colored animals for himself (35–43).

   A. Laban cleverly removed all the odd-colored animals from the flock and placed them a good distance away (35–36).

   B. Jacob employed questionable breeding practices to produce the animals for himself (37–42).

       1. He placed striped rods in the watering troughs before the flocks when they were in heat (37–39).

         a. The peeled rods were placed before the animals (37–38).

         b. The flocks produced odd-colored animals (39).

       2. He separated the lambs from Laban's flocks (40).

       3. He differentiated between the stronger of the flock so that his flocks would be stronger (41–42).

   C. Jacob became more and more prosperous (43).

Development of the Exposition

The unit is difficult to develop for exposition because it reports a unique event and does not express the theological point. The following arrangement is workable: the request to leave (vv. 25–26) is followed by the development of the plan for animals (vv. 27–34); and the deceptive ploy of Laban (vv. 35–36) is followed by the prosperity of the plan (vv. 37–43). God's blessing is evident in each half of the passage.

I. Having known the blessing of God in the past, God's people can anticipate his continued faithfulness in their lives (25–34).

A. Anticipation of a new era (25–26).

The first part is Jacob's request to leave for his homeland. He had been with Laban for fourteen years of faithful service for his wives and children. He clearly had kept his part of the bargain in an unfortunate situation. The repetition of the root ʿābad, "to serve" (ʿābadtî, "I served," and ʿăbōdātî, "my service"), strengthens the point of Jacob's completing the responsibility he had to Laban. But now he was ready to return with his family to his homeland. God had given him a family; he now could look forward to the fulfillment of the promised blessing in the land.

B. Enjoyment of God's abundant blessing (27–34).

This part of the passage develops Jacob's decision to stay. Both he and Laban acknowledged that the Lord had blessed Laban because of Jacob. The acknowledgment of the Lord's blessing by the two men forms an interesting contrast. Laban observed (lit. "divined" [niḥaštî]) that the Lord had prospered him through Jacob. He had enjoyed prosperity while Jacob was with him and so concluded, through whatever means of perception he used, that God had done it. Jacob, on the other hand, simply stated that the Lord had blessed Laban because of him. The repetition of the word for bless points up the true source of the increase that Laban experienced when Jacob was living with him.

The abundance that they recognized as God's blessing led them to a new agreement. Laban wanted Jacob to stay so that Laban might continue to prosper with this man; and Jacob agreed to stay because he was confident that the Lord would now provide for him, now that his obligations toward Laban were completed. Jacob thus proposed a plan by which (ostensibly) he would gain little: he would receive the rare animals, the odd-colored and black goats. Laban agreed to this arrangement because he thought it could work only to his advantage.

Jacob's plan was risky. How could unicolored animals produce spotted animals? Nevertheless, both Laban and Jacob knew that the Lord was blessing Jacob's work—and in their own ways, each man sought to obtain additional blessings from the Lord.

II. Faced with antagonism and deception, the recipients of the promises enjoy the blessing of God—often in spite of their clever schemes (35–43).

A. Opposed by deceptive competitors (35–36).

The next part of the passage reports the ploy of Laban. For greater advantage, Laban removed all the animals of abnormal color and, as an additional precaution, placed a three-day journey between them and the others. Then he set his men over them. The point of this move is that, even though he entered into a bargain with Jacob that would provide Jacob with wages, Laban made sure that Jacob would have a difficult time succeeding. In general, Laban represents clever, deceptive opponents who ensure their own success by taking unfair advantages.

B. Successful in spite of schemes (37–43).

The final part of the chapter recounts how Jacob's plan succeeded (or so he thought) and his possessions increased greatly. Jacob placed peeled branches in all the watering troughs, directly in front of the breeding flocks. The resulting offspring were streaked, speckled, or spotted; Jacob separated the young for himself. He also selectively bred the stronger animals, so that the weaker ones went to Laban.

Behind this plan was the common belief that a vivid sight during conception or pregnancy would leave its mark on the embryo. The success of the enterprise, however, must have been due to other factors. Selective breeding may have played a large part in the success, but it would have been too slow for this story. Jacob later acknowledged what the reader suspects: God intervened to cause the animals to flourish (Gen. 31:9–12).

The exposition of this section is the difficult part because the theological point must be made in conjunction with the surrounding contexts. The expositor will have to show that the effort expended by Jacob was not the means by which the intended results were gained—Jacob's activities, then, become negative examples, or a foil for the truth. Even though the narrative traces what Jacob did, we would have to point out that the people of God must recognize that success comes from God and not from questionable customs, especially when such customs are followed in order to compete with deceptive and antagonistic people. Clues in the narrative and explanations in the contexts show that this emphasis on God's role is the writer's point.

The believer who has to live among people like Laban faces a great crisis in the faith. There is something incompatible with the acknowledgment of God's blessing for prosperity and the employment of superstitious customs in order to obtain those divine blessings. How a believer competes with a nonbeliever is important to the faith. It is not a matter of fighting fire with fire, playing his or her game, or turning the tables. Rather, it is a matter of acknowledging that the true source of success is God and then engaging in practices that are compatible with that belief. *Those who experience material prosperity must acknowledge that it is the blessing from the Lord and not the product of their own limited abilities.* If this truth is acknowledged from the outset, then the human efforts in the process will be brought into line with the faith. The lesson is not so much a rebuke for the use of superstitious practices as it is a call for acknowledging the true source of success. If God promises to bless his people, nothing can hinder him; and if God determines not to bless, nothing can alter his decision.

Bibliography

Braithwaite, Gilbert. "Expositional Problems in the Jacob-Laban Controversy Concerning Livestock Wages." Th.M. Thesis, Dallas Theological Seminary, 1972.

Finkelstein, J. J. "An Old Babylonian Herding Contract and Genesis 31:38f." *JAOS* 88 (1968): 34–35.

Fokkelman, J. P. *Narrative Art in Genesis,* pp. 144–51. Assen: Van Gorcum, 1975.

Gordon, Cyrus. "The Story of Jacob and Laban in the Light of the Nuzi Tablets." *BASOR* 66 (1937): 25–27.

47

Jacob's Flight from Laban and God's Protection
(Gen. 31)

The narratives of the Jacob-Laban cycle draw to a close with this account of Jacob's flight from Laban. The chapter forms the contrast to chapter 29, and the two frame the narratives about the blessings in Paddan Aram. Now, with all the possessions that God had given to him, the time was right for Jacob's return to the land of Canaan. Since the return was commanded by God himself, God's protection guaranteed his safety.

The major parts of this narrative are tightly bound together: Jacob's flight, Laban's pursuit, Laban's accusation, Jacob's accusation, and the treaty between Jacob and Laban. The tone of the story is tense up to the meeting of the two men but then turns to triumph with Jacob's complaint, in which he declared that God had seen his affliction and taken up his cause (Westermann, *Genesis*, vol. 2, p. 489). Consequently, Laban acquiesced to the separation and accepted his defeat silently. The treaty that they shared resolved the tension that had lasted for years, but it was a resolution in which the two men remained enemies.

Since the speeches come to the fore in this episode, greater attention must be given to them. The use of the verb *rîb* (v. 36) and the nature of the speeches with their charges and countercharges set this interaction off as a legal controversy, the kind that was found in ancient societies in confrontations in the gate. In this dispute the charges of Laban—especially over the theft of his gods—find no support; but the countercharges of Jacob were self-evidently true—and God himself had taken the side of Jacob in this dispute. The legal tone of the material finalizes Jacob's separation from Laban and solidifies his victory over Laban.

The episode has a significant parallel with Genesis 12:1–9, in which God called the patriarch to leave his relatives and go to the land that God would show him. In that chapter Abraham took all his possessions and departed for the land of Canaan. In this chapter, the Lord commanded Jacob to return to the land of his fathers and to his relatives (v. 3), and Jacob took all his possessions that he had acquired to go to his father in the land of Canaan (v. 18). The parallel use of words such as *môledet*, "kindred," *rᵉkûš*, "possessions," and *'arṣâ kᵉnā'an*, "to the land of Canaan," establish a connection between the two events. Jacob was thus repeating the obedience to the call that his grandfather had followed, only now the "tribes" of Israel made their journey to the land of Canaan, not just one man with the promise of a great nation. (For a full discussion of these parallels as a foreshadowing of Israel's conquest under Joshua, see Cassuto, *Commentary on Genesis*, vol. 2, pp. 304–6).

Theological Ideas

The two predominant themes of this story are human obedience and divine protection. The obedience was Jacob's, for he immediately set out to return to the land of Canaan when he received the call from God. He acknowledged that God had kept the promises made at Bethel and that he had to complete his vow by returning to the land of his father. Closely linked to this theme is the motif of faithfulness. Jacob appears throughout the chapter as the faithful servant who kept his part of the bargain. In his faithfulness to his master and his obedience to his God, Jacob is exemplary.

The protection came from God. Through the dream and the treaty, the Lord ensured that his obedient servant would return unscathed to the Land of Promise. Even Rachel's foolish act of stealing Laban's household gods did not controvert the Lord's protection of his people, although it threatened to do so. In fact, the resolution of that brief moment of tension served to add insult to injury as far as Laban's gods were concerned.

In the Lord's warning of Laban through the dream, we encounter two important motifs of Genesis—good and evil. God said, "Take heed that you do not speak to Jacob either good or evil [*miṭṭôb 'ad-rā'*]" (v. 24). Whatever knowledge of good and evil Laban had, the Lord God sovereignly prevented him from so much as mentioning it in his dealings with Jacob. Laban could have no power whatsoever over this servant of God. In tracing this point through the chapter, the expositor should note the repetition of the words. In verse 7, Jacob said, "God did not permit him to harm me [*lᵉhāraʿ ʿimmādî*]." After Laban received the dream (v. 24), he told Jacob, "It is in my power of my hand [*yeš-lᵉʾēl yādî*] to do you harm [*laʿăśôt ʿimmākem rāʿ*], but the God of your father spoke to me last night, saying 'Take heed that you do not speak to Jacob either good or evil [*miṭṭôb ʿad-rāʿ*]' " (v. 29). The contents of this warning dream then figured prominently in Jacob's zealous speech, for in verse 42 he interpreted the dream as God's rebuke of Laban. This event thus confirmed what he first expressed in verse 7—God was with him, protecting him from the deception of Laban.

Structure and Synthesis

Structure

There is a striking parallel structure between the two major sections of this story, the flight and the dispute, showing that the separation of Jacob from Laban was not only justly deserved but engineered by God (see chart 26).

Chart 26. **Parallel Themes in Genesis 31**

Laban's sons became hostile, and Laban's disposition changed from before (*šilšom*) (1–2).	Laban and his brethren pursued after three days (*šᵉlīšî*) and overtook Jacob in Mount Gilead (22–23).
The Lord spoke to Jacob: an instruction to return and a promise of his presence (3).	God spoke to Laban the Syrian: a warning not to speak good or evil to Jacob (24).
Jacob called Rachel and Leah to meet him in the field (4).	Laban camped near Jacob in the mount (25).
Jacob reported Laban's displeasure to his wives (5).	Laban angrily accused Jacob of fleeing away, stealing his daughters, and stealing his gods (26–35). (extended section on Rachel's theft of the household gods)

Jacob's speech:
  I served your father (6);
  he deceived me and changed my
    wages ten times (7a);
  but God protected me (7b).
	Jacob's speech:
	  I served you twenty years (36–41a);
	  you changed my wages ten times
	    (41b);
	  God has rewarded me for my affliction
	    and rebuked you (42)

Laban's daughters agreed to the separation from Laban, telling Jacob to do what God said to do (14–16).	Laban agreed to the separation from Jacob, calling on God to be the witness between them (43–54).
Jacob rose up, stole away, and fled to go to his father in the land of Canaan (17–21).	Laban rose up and kissed and blessed them and returned to his place (55).

It is clear from this parallel construction that the resolution fully reflects the tension and that Jacob's speeches are central to both parts. In the first part the story portrays an angry Laban in hot pursuit of the fleeing Jacob; and in the second part—after the Lord warned Laban off—the story portrays a defeated Laban who acts the part of a wounded father but blesses Jacob's family and leaves them in peace. The speech of Jacob is given twice, once to convince his wives to go with him, and then to break off ties with Laban once and for all. The speech basically says: I served faithfully, Laban deceived, but God was with me. These motifs—"I," "the enemy," "you" (God)—are frequently found in the psalms of lament. Jacob's speech is not a lament, but it recounts lamentable circumstances from which God had delivered. Having been through it all, Jacob was able to turn the ideas into a legal complaint. Laban had no answer for this impassioned speech and so sought a treaty.

Summary Message

Motivated by Laban's resentment and encouraged by the agreement of his wives, Jacob obeyed the Lord's command to leave for Canaan; and when angrily accused by Laban, who overtook them in Gilead, Jacob defended his record of faithful service and accused Laban of deceitful practices, thereby silencing Laban and prompting him to press for a peace treaty at the border.

Exegetical Outline

I. Because of mounting resentment from Laban's family and in obedience to the Lord's command, Jacob and his family departed secretly for the land of Canaan (1–21).

A. Jacob decided to return when he perceived the mounting resentment and received the call from the Lord (1–3).

1. Laban's family resented Jacob for taking away their possessions (1–2).

2. The Lord commanded Jacob to return to his kindred in Canaan (3).

B. Jacob's wives wholeheartedly agreed to leave with Jacob when they heard his speech, acknowledging that Laban had mistreated Jacob and robbed them of their dowries (4–16).

1. Jacob presented his case for leaving Laban, arguing that, while he had been faithful in his duties, Laban had not been faithful but that God had richly rewarded him with Laban's possessions (4–13).

2. Rachel and Leah together agreed to leave for Canaan with Jacob, explaining that their father had mistreated them (14–16).

   C. Jacob and his family secretly stole away from Laban to return to Canaan—and Rachel stole Laban's gods (17–21).

II. After hotly pursuing Jacob to Gilead and being warned in a dream not to harm him, Laban was unable to prove his accusations; but Jacob defended his record of faithful service and accused Laban of treachery, leaving Laban only to negotiate for a treaty (22–55).

   A. Laban hotly pursued Jacob to Gilead but was warned in a dream not to interfere with Jacob's migration (22–25).

   B. Laban's attempt to engage Jacob in a judicial encounter backfired when Jacob successfully defended himself and brought his counterclaim (26–42).

      1. Laban registered his accusations against Jacob (26–30).

      2. Jacob countered Laban's accusations with a plea of innocence (31–32).

      3. Laban failed to find the stolen gods and thus could not sustain his charge of robbery (33–35).

      4. Jacob registered his counterclaim against Laban, accusing his father-in-law of treachery in their business dealings and claiming that the Lord had blessed and protected him (36–42).

   C. Jacob and Laban negotiated a peace treaty at Galeed, swearing before God not to approach the other for harmful purposes (43–54).

   D. Laban departed in peace (55).

Development of the Exposition

There are several ways that a story this long and involved can be divided for exposition. I have chosen to follow the twofold division presented in the exegetical outline, that is, Jacob's return to Canaan (vv. 1–21) and Jacob's protection from Laban through legal dispute and peace treaty (vv. 22–55), giving prominence to Jacob's speech to his wives and then to his speech to Laban as the critical moment in each part.

I. God, who abundantly provides for his people, calls them to forsake their flourishing world and get on with the advancement of his program (1–21).

A. God calls his people to their obligations in his program (1–3).

1. Through circumstances (1–2). Of the two interrelated reasons for Jacob's flight to Canaan, the first was the increasing animosity he sensed from Laban's family. The word's of Laban's sons have the ring of bitterness, for they realized that all Jacob's wealth (*hakkābōd*) was taken from their father. Laban realized this imbalance too, for his countenance was not in favor of Jacob as it was before ('*ênennû* '*immô kitmôl šilšôm*, lit., "three days before yesterday," or "formerly"). In short, Jacob's prospering under God's good hand of blessing was at Laban's expense, and Laban began to resent it.

2. Through God's Word (3). With this growing danger on Jacob's mind, the Lord instructed Jacob to leave. One wonders how easily Jacob could have been dislodged from this prosperous life if there had not been the growing resentment. At any rate, the Lord's command to leave reflected the call of Abram. Whereas Abram was to leave his kindred and his father's house to go to the land of Canaan, Jacob was to go to the land of his fathers and to his kindred. This call is thus to return (*šûb*).

Along with the call came the restatement of God's presence: "and I will be with you [*we'ehyeh 'immāk*]" (see 28:15, '*ānōkî 'immāk*). The narrative just reported that "Laban's face was not with him ['*immô*]" but now records that the Lord would be with him. The former use of '*im* marked a possible threat; but the Lord's use of '*im* more than compensated for that threat.

B. God's people must be sure that they are acting in good faith (4–16).

The point of this section centers on Jacob's argument that he was both justified and wise in leaving Laban, an argument that met with approval from his wives. Jacob's speech is one of the high points in his life. As Fokkelman says, "Jacob is the keen observer and genuine believer and grateful proclaimer of God's help; his interpretation is profound and authoritative" (*Narrative Art*, p. 162).

1. God's blessing and protection (4–9). Jacob's convincing speech traces how God prospered him in his faithful service to Laban and protected him from Laban's deceit and declares that God called him to fulfill his vow that he made at Bethel. Jacob knew that it was right for him to leave Laban.

It is important to the exposition to trace the argument of this speech, especially in verses 5–9. Jacob first reported that Laban's countenance was not with him as before (repeated from v. 2) but that God was with him (*wē'lōhê 'ābî hāyâ 'immādî*, in v. 5). He then affirmed that he had been a faithful servant—with all his strength (*bekol-kōḥî 'ābadtî 'et-'ăbîken*)—but that Laban had deceived him (*wa'ăbîken hētel bî*), changing his wages ten times. Nevertheless, he explained, God had not allowed this deceptive one to harm him (*l^ehāra^c*, "to cause evil"). Even though in this context Jacob was making his case, his speech actually acknowledged God's blessing and protection.

2. God's call (10–13). Jacob told his wives the dream that he had, reminding him of his obligation to fulfill his vow, that is, to return to his homeland. God's self-revelation reminded Jacob of the vow by alluding to the place—"I am the God of Bethel [*'ānōkî hā'ēl bêt-'ēl*]." If Jacob's wives were not convinced to go by the appeal to Laban's mistreatment of him, they would be by the news of God's call. The migration to Canaan was not only a wise thing to do—it was God's will.

3. God's justice (14–16). In the response of Jacob's wives, which is united this time, God's justice emerges as another reason for the migration. Laban had apparently withheld their inheritance, having sold them and thoroughly consumed (*wayyō'kal gam-'ākól*) their money, or dowry. They therefore saw divine justice in God's taking the wealth of their father and giving it to Jacob. The word used to describe God's taking the wealth from Laban is a forceful one, *hiṣṣîl* (<*nāṣal*), which can be used for stripping away for plundering. Interestingly enough, the verb is used in Exodus 12:36 to describe how the Israelites plundered the Egyptians when they ended their slavery in that foreign land. Convinced that God was in it, Rachel and Leah were in complete agreement with Jacob's resolution to obey God's call.

C. God's people must avoid complicating their mission by petty retribution (17–21).

The flight from Laban's land was to prove more risky than it needed to be, for Rachel stole her father's teraphim (*t^erāpîm*). The expositor will have to reach some satisfactory conclusion regarding the nature of these idols. The teraphim may have guaranteed protection or the right of inheritance. Whatever their exact nature, Laban was certainly exercised to get them back. It was one thing to take his flocks and his family—but his household gods? For all he knew, Jacob might return some day and lay claim to everything he possessed.

There is a word play in verses 19 and 20 that is important to this section. In verse 19, we read that Rachel stole (*wattignōb*) the idols; and in verse 20, we read that Jacob stole away (*wayyignōb*) unawares. The first use is literal, but the second is idiomatic, for the exact expression is that "Jacob stole the heart of Laban the Syrian in that he did not tell him that he fled." To "steal the heart" (*nāgab + lēb*) means to deceive. The translation "stole away" captures the word play but not the idiomatic meaning. The point of the word play shows Rachel and Jacob to be of kindred spirit; she was, as Fokkelman says, "a true Jacoba" (*Narrative Art*, p. 163). Her theft only complicated matters. Any hope that Laban would resign himself to their departure was now out of the question.

Jacob thus arose (vv. 17, 21) and fled (v. 21). These words allude to the conclusion of the first period of his life. At that time he took the advice of his mother, who said, "Arise and flee" [$w^eq\hat{u}m\ b^erah$] (27:43); now he arose and fled from another brother (29:15), but at God's command (ibid.).

II. God, who calls his people to follow him, protects them from hostile relationships in their obedience (22–55).

A. God may intervene directly to protect his people (22–24).

The tension in the story begins with Laban's pursuit three days later ($\check{s}^el\hat{\imath}\check{s}\hat{\imath}$, "third," links the beginning of this section with the beginning of the first). The significant point in these verses, though, is the warning given to Laban the Syrian (not now the relative) in the dream: "Take heed that you speak not to Jacob either good or evil [$mi\underline{t}\underline{t}\hat{o}b\ \acute{a}d-r\bar{a}\acute{}$]." The expositor should recall that Laban had earlier told the servant of Abraham that, since God had led him to them, they could not speak to him $ra\acute{}\ \acute{}\hat{o}$-$\underline{t}\hat{o}b$, "evil or good" (24:50). God thus twice prevented Laban from interfering with his program, first by his clear providence, and now by this warning. The difference is that, in 24:50, the decision was Laban's, but in 31:24, the words are from God. In this warning dream, then, God was suspending Laban's prerogative to exert his ability to interfere in Jacob's life. The warning dream made Laban's claim that it was within his power to harm Jacob (v. 29) an empty boast.

B. Those under God's protection may boldly contend for righteousness (25–42).

In the dialogue that follows we have the central point of this section of the chapter, namely, Jacob's protesting of his innocence and of Laban's injustice. The section develops from Laban's complaint, to Jacob's claim of integrity, to Laban's accusation, to Jacob's counterclaim. The use of the verb *ríb* (*wayyāreb*, in v. 36) shows that this dispute was serious. It was a legal dispute that would settle the matter once and for all. Oswald T. Allis writes,

The meeting of Jacob and Laban is a kind of diamond-cut-diamond affair. All the bottled-up bitterness in Jacob's heart is poured out now. Laban makes it plain that fear of God's vengeance alone restrains him from his use of violence. His attempt to put Jacob in the wrong (verses 26–30) is so overdone that it makes him ridiculous, and makes Jacob righteously indignant. [*God Spake by Moses* (Philadelphia: Presbyterian and Reformed, 1951), p. 42]

In the first complaint Laban accused Jacob of robbing (*wattignōb*) him. It is interesting to note that Laban and Jacob were now enemies, for the terminology is militaristic: "fled," "overtaken," "pursuit," "pitched his tents" (*tāgaʿ* instead of *nāṭaʿ*), and carried off the women as captives of the sword (Fokkelman, *Narrative Art*, pp. 164–65). This wording all adds to the tension at the meeting. But Laban presented himself as the hurt father who was not given the chance to send off his daughters with a celebration, as well as the frustrated avenger who was not permitted to harm his enemy—physically or legally. Finally, after a lengthy accusation of Jacob's foolish and unfair acts, Laban accused him of stealing the household idols.

Jacob responded to this lengthy charge by protesting his integrity in leaving secretly and his innocence in the matter of the household gods (vv. 31–32). By the strength of his statement that whoever had the gods should not live, Jacob unwittingly put Rachel under the death penalty.

Laban was ready to take up the challenge to search for the gods but was once again deceived, this time by Rachel (vv. 33–35). Her statement that "the custom of women [*derek nāšîm*] is upon me" forms a subtle retaliation for Laban's deception of Jacob by the use of custom (29:26). Apparently Laban never dreamed that a woman in her condition would contaminate his gods. What a blow this development was to the teraphim—they were worthless gods, for a woman sat on them during her menstrual period. Leviticus 15 legislated that at such times women were to remain separate from the shrine. This passage says much about Israel's contempt for false gods—they are as unclean as can be.

With Laban's accusations being unproven, Jacob brought his stern countercharge (vv. 36–42; for a detailed analysis of this speech, see ibid., pp. 171–82). Ignorant of Rachel's theft of the idols, Jacob made his devastating attack. His words repeat those of his speech to his wives earlier, but now with a new intensity. He claimed that (1) he had served faithfully in Laban's house for twenty years and Laban benefited greatly; (2) Laban had dealt faithlessly with him, changing his wages ten times; and (3) God had been with him to ensure that he did not go away empty or fall into danger. Jacob ended his speech by pointing out that Laban's recent dream was a vindication of him and a rebuke of Laban (v. 42). Laban could not counter this argument; he could only appeal for a peace treaty.

C. Those under God's protection may welcome peaceful coexistence (43–55).

The last section of the chapter records the making of a treaty for the boundary. This event forms the climax of the story in that the tension was resolved by it—the two enemies agreed to remain apart.

Laban instigated the treaty, suggesting in his words that Jacob was the slippery one to be watched. Jacob did not need the treaty, for God had clearly protected him from Laban, but he welcomed it because it would keep Laban apart from him. In wording the agreement Laban made it sound as though Jacob was the culprit who needed to be watched; he evidently interpreted this point as some sort of victory over Jacob. But since Jacob had no intentions of ever going back to Paddan Aram, the monument was for him an "everlasting confession in stone of a man released from servitude" (ibid., p. 190).

Jacob set up a monolith, and then a heap. Laban named it in Aramaic $y^egar\ \acute{s}\bar{a}h\check{a}d\hat{u}t\bar{a}$ ', but Jacob called it $gal\acute{e}d$, both names meaning "the heap is witness." Laban also added the name $mi\d{s}p\hat{a}$, expressing the wish that the Lord would watch ($yi\d{s}ep$) between them—to keep them apart and to keep his daughters safe. This event with the namings adds the final confirmation to the message of the chapter, namely, that God delivered and protected Israel as he brought the people back into the land. It was the last step in the victory over Laban, the idolater with his idols.

The two languages in the treaty have always been seen as a key element in the story. Laban the Syrian gave it an Aramaic name, and Jacob the Hebrew gave it a Hebrew name; in the region of Gilead both languages were spoken. The location on the boundary between Israel and Syria seems to have occasioned the double designation. Any attempts to fit this treaty into a later period of Israel's history (say, the wars of David with the Aramaeans) does not find support from the context. Although Laban was hostile, he and Jacob were not at war. By all observations the report of this section reflects the time when peaceful negotiations were entered into in order to secure an existing peace. The only way that Laban and Jacob—or later, Syria and Israel—could maintain peace was to establish their boundary and agree not to infringe on one another's rights.

Genesis 31 delineates how God guided Jacob away from Laban and protected him from danger. The chapter forms the culmination of the Jacob-Laban cycle of stories, explaining that the success of Jacob in his dealings with Laban was due to the Lord's presence with him and that God's intervention in the time of crisis was his only source of strength. The lesson for Israel, and for us as well, is that *the one who has experienced the blessing of God and who is obediently following the call of God may be confident of God's protection.* It is important to emphasize in this message how the passage reveals Jacob in a good light—obedient to God's call to return, faithful in his service to Laban, protesting his innocence before God, and acknowledging God's presence with him. God's people must live on this level if they wish to enjoy God's continued protection and provision.

It is not always that way. The Laban years were sad for Jacob and his family—there was deception, dishonesty, bargaining, theft, animosity, fear, and retaliation. Mutual distrust led to estrangements; and suspicions, to angry accusations. In this chapter, however, in the final phase of the conflict, God spoke to both Jacob and Laban in order to bring about their separation. Then, after their legal dispute, God himself was invoked to watch between them.

Bibliography

Ackroyd, P. R. "The Teraphim." *ExT* 62 (1950–51): 378–80.

Burrows, M. "The Complaint of Laban's Daughters." *JAOS* 57 (1937): 250–76.

Coats, G. W. "Self-Abasement and Insult Formulas." *JBL* 91 (1972): 90–92.

Fensham, F. C. "The Stem *HTL* in Biblical Law." *VT* 9 (1959): 310–11.

Finkelstein, J. J. "An Old Babylonian Herding Contract and Genesis 31:38f." *JAOS* 88 (1968): 30–36.

Fokkelman, J. P. *Narrative Art in Genesis*, pp. 162–96. Assen: Van Gorcum, 1975.

Frankena, R. "The Semitic Background of Genesis XXIX–XXXI." *OTS* 17 (1972): 54–57.

Greenberg, M. "Another Look at Rachel's Theft of the Teraphim." *JBL* 81 (1962): 239–48.

Hillers, D. R. "Critical Note: *Pahad Yiṣḥāq*." *JBL* 91 (1972): 90–92.

Hoffner, H. A. "Hittite *TARPIŠ* and Hebrew *TERĀPHÎM*." *JNES* 27 (1968): 61–68.

Labuchagne, C. J. "Teraphim—a New Proposal for Its Etymology." *VT* 16 (1966): 115–17.

Mabee, Charles. "Jacob and Laban: The Structure of Judicial Proceedings." *VT* 30 (1980): 192–207.

McKenzie, D. A. "Judicial Procedure at the Town Gate." *VT* 14 (1964): 100–104.

Malul, M. "More on *pahad yiṣḥāq* (Genesis xxxi 42, 53) and the Oath by the Thigh." *VT* 35 (1985): 192–200.

Mauchline, J. "Gilead and Gilgal: Some Reflections on the Israelite Occupation of Palestine." *VT* 6 (1956): 19–33.

O'Callaghan, R. "Historical Parallels to Patriarchal Social Custom." *CBQ* 6 (1944): 391–405.

Ottosson, Magnus. *Gilead: Tradition and History.* Translated by Jean Gray. Lund: C. W. K. Gleerup, 1969.

Plantz, W. "Die Form der Eheschliessung im Alten Testament." *ZAW* 76 (1964): 298–318.

48

A Gift from the Camp: An Unnecessary Attempt at Appeasement
(Gen. 32:1–21)

With Laban behind him, Jacob faced the prospects of meeting another enemy of his own making—Esau! How could the patriarch return to his father's home, from which he had fled with the report of Esau's murderous threats ringing in his ears? How can God's people in general face such times of crisis with confidence? This narrative provides instruction on this theme, both by revealing God's solution for the crisis and by reporting Jacob's misguided efforts to buy off his brother with a gift.

Chapters 32 and 33 must be surveyed in their entirety in order to see the culmination of the Jacob-Esau cycle. There are four major parts: the vision of the camp of God (32:1–2), the sending of the gift to Esau in fear (vv. 3–21), the fight with the Lord at the Jabbok (vv. 22–32), and the peaceful reconciliation with Esau (chap. 33). The reconciliation with Esau came only after Jacob was crippled and blessed; after these developments, the reconciliation was surprisingly peaceful. The two chapters together show that this reconciliation was a work of God in answer to Jacob's prayer, not a result of Jacob's attempt to appease his brother with a gift.

The present narrative (32:1–21) includes different genres. At the heart of it is the prayer of Jacob (vv. 9–12). It is framed by two reports of sending embassies to Esau (vv. 3–8 and 13–21). The entire section begins with the revelation of the camp of God (vv. 1–2) and leads into the nocturnal meeting at the Jabbok (vv. 22–32).

Even though there are diverse parts in the first twenty-one verses of the chapter, they are knit together by the repetition of key words. In the first two verses Jacob was met by the "messengers of God" (mal'ăkê 'ĕlōhîm). He responded by exclaiming that the place was the "camp of God" (mahănēh 'ĕlōhîm) and named it mahănāyim ("two camps"). Immediately in the second part (vv. 3–8), Jacob sent messengers (mal'ākîm) to Esau to try to find grace (hēn) in his eyes. But when the messengers (hammal'ākîm) returned with news that Esau was coming, Jacob panicked and divided his people into "two companies" (lišnê mahănôt). He reasoned that, if one company (hammahăneh) were attacked, the other company (hammahăneh) could escape (v. 8). In the third part (vv. 9–12), he prayed desperately to the Lord for deliverance from Esau, stating that the Lord's goodness to him had made him into two companies (lišnê mahănôt).

In the fourth part of this account (vv. 13–21), Jacob attempted through his own devices to appease his brother. He prepared a "gift" (minhâ) for Esau (v. 13). He instructed his servants to explain to Esau that the animals were a gift (minhâ) sent to him (v. 18), and that by this gift (bamminhâ) he hoped to appease him (v. 20). The narrative closes by reporting that the gift (hamminhâ) went on before Jacob, but Jacob lodged that night in the camp (bammahăneh).

The repetition and interchange of the words for "messengers" (mal'ākîm), "camp" (mahăneh), and "gift" (minhâ) show that these twenty-one verses form a unified narrative. The word plays indicate that Jacob in his desperation actually sullied the magnificence of the revelation he received.

Theological Ideas

The vision of the "camp of God" is the predominant theological idea in this passage because of its place of prominence at the beginning. The meaning of that encounter sets the standard for faith in a crisis, showing that those who were for Jacob were greater than those who were against him.

A second major theological point concerns the nature of Jacob's prayer. In both form and content, this prayer makes a significant contribution to our study of prayers.

A third idea found in this chapter concerns the blessing. The exegesis will show that, in sending the gift to Esau of 550 animals, Jacob was attempting to return the blessing that he had stolen from his brother. And in constantly referring to himself as Esau's servant and to Esau as his lord, he was attempting to restore the precedence that his father's blessing had taken from Esau and bestowed on him. When one compares the previous narratives about Jacob's blessing with this misguided venture, it is clear that Jacob thought that reconciliation could be gained only through the restoration of what he had taken. But it had been the plan of God for Jacob to have the blessing.

Structure and Synthesis

Structure

As indicated above, the passage falls into four sections. The first section reports a vision and a naming. Accordingly, it has been called an etymological etiology—which is acceptable if such a designation simply means that the event reported in the section explains the name (a secondary etiology).

The second section is the account of Jacob's plan to send messengers to Esau—an idea that was probably triggered by the vision of God's messengers. These verses include dialogue and narrative report. Jacob's speech provided the message to be taken to Esau, but the speech of the returning messenger threw Jacob into a panic. The four movements in this section are: (1) Jacob sends messengers, (2) the message goes to Esau, (3) the message returns about Esau, and (4) Jacob arranges two camps. Both motifs of "messengers" and "camp" were drawn from the first section and are used here.

The third section, the prayer of Jacob, follows the pattern of prayers out of distress. It begins with the address to God (v. 9), rehearses the favor that God has shown him (v. 10), makes the petition for deliverance from Esau (v. 11a), and motivates God to answer by stressing his own helplessness (v. 11b) and God's promise to treat him well and fulfill the promises in him (v. 12).

The fourth section reports Jacob's sending the gift. This section is framed with the notice that Jacob lodged in the camp and sent the gift to his brother (vv. 13 and 21).

Summary Message

In spite of the vision of the messengers of God, when Jacob learned from his messengers that Esau and 400 men were coming to meet him, he divided his people into two camps as a precaution; even though he prayed earnestly for the Lord's deliverance, he sought to pacify his brother's anger with a gift of 550 animals.

Exegetical Outline

    I. The messengers of God met Jacob in the way, prompting him to name the place to commemorate the vision (1–2).

   II. Jacob then sent messengers to his brother Esau but, upon hearing that Esau was coming with four hundred men, divided his camp out of fear (3–8).

     A. Jacob sent messengers before him to meet Esau (3).

     B. The messengers were to report to Esau how Jacob had sojourned with Laban (4–5).

     C. The messengers brought back news that Esau and four hundred men were coming to meet Jacob (6).

     D. Jacob divided his people into two camps out of great fear (7–8).

  III. Jacob then prayed earnestly for deliverance from Esau, reminding God of his promises and expressing his own unworthiness (9–12).

     A. He addressed the Lord and reminded him of his promise (9).

     B. He acknowledged his unworthiness of the great blessings God had given him (10).

     C. He petitioned God to deliver him from Esau (11a).

     D. He motivated God to respond to his prayer by confessing his fear and reminding God of his promises (11b–12).

  IV. Hoping to pacify his brother, Jacob sent a gift of 550 animals with his servants, who were to present them to Esau (13–21).

     A. Jacob sent a gift to Esau (13–16).

       1. Jacob lodged there that night and sent a gift to Esau (13).

       2. The gift consisted of 550 animals (14–16).

     B. Jacob instructed his servants what to tell Esau (17–20).

       1. They were to tell Esau it was a gift and that Jacob was following behind (17–19).

       2. They were also to tell Esau that Jacob hoped the gift would appease his brother and that he would accept him (20).

     C. Jacob sent the gift to Esau, but stayed in the camp that night (21).

Development of the Exposition

I. Believers can take comfort from the revelation that the angels of God are present (1–2).

The first two verses of this chapter report a brief but significant experience in the life of Jacob. As Jacob was about to enter the land and face Esau once again, God's invisible world openly touched Jacob's visible world. Jacob's encounter with the angels of God is told with extreme brevity: four Hebrew words report the meeting. As von Rad observes, the absence of any explanation provides an impassable barrier for the interpreter. At least we can say that the two verses preserve a tradition about a place, one that gave rise to the name Mahanaim. But the ambiguity of the report raises several questions for the reader. Who were these messengers? Were they friendly or hostile to Jacob? Why did Jacob name the place with a dual form, Mahanaim?

One clear point is that these verses introduce the transition chapter from the Laban stories back to the Esau stories. As Jacob went on his way from Laban toward Esau, he must have wondered if God would go with him and sustain him as he had originally promised at Bethel when he was on his way to Laban's place. Then he was leaving the land; now he was re-entering it.

In fact, a comparison with that earlier encounter at Bethel proves most instructive. The expression "messengers of God" (or "angels of God") occurs here and in 28:12, and nowhere else in the Old Testament. The expression "met him" (*pāgaʿ* with *bᵉ*) occurs both here and in 28:11. The pronoun "this" (*zeh*) is used four times in 28:16–17 and is an important reference in the speech of Jacob here. In both passages Jacob interpreted what he had seen before he named the place (cf. 28:17 and 32:2). A similar expression (*wayyiqrāʾ [ʾet] hammāqôm hahûʾ*) is used in the naming of both places (28:19 and 32:2). Finally, *hôlēk + derek*, "going in the way" (28:20, in Jacob's oath), is reflected in 32:1. None of these comparisons would be very striking alone, but taken together they show a direct correlation between the two passages. We may say, then, that the same kind of event that took place at the naming of Bethel on the way out of the land took place at the naming of Mahanaim on the way back into the land. Mahanaim, like Bethel, was a spot where the heavenly world made contact with the earth, where the invisible was opened to the visible.

In this incident Jacob saw the angels of God who met him. The text does not explain how he saw them or how they met him. Such a meeting could have been in a good sense or in a bad sense. Whatever Jacob saw he explained as the "camp of God" (*maḥănēh ʾĕlōhîm*)—a designation that is a little ambiguous. *Maḥănēh* can mean an army camp; but were these messengers hostile or amicable? If the account is to be taken in the same sense as the Bethel story, then we would have to say that the meeting was amicable. As Jacob approached the Promised Land, he also approached God's encampment, where the angels of God had their encampment, or base of operations. When Jacob came along, the exceptional character of the place was revealed to him in some way.

But the Hebrew name *maḥănāyim* is also difficult, for the word appears to be a simple dual. Should it then be translated "two camps"? That rendering might harmonize with Jacob's division of his family into two camps later on (v. 7); but why would Jacob call this place "two camps"?

It follows from 32:7–8 that the pronunciation of this word as a dual is a very old tradition, for Jacob divided his camp into two camps. And in verse 2 itself a suggestion of the double camp may be found in the camp of the angels and in the camp of Jacob. In other words, the host of God met his host in the way—two hosts. There is thus evidence and reason for the dual idea.

But Houtman raises the question of whether this is a real dual or not. It is not necessary in such namings to have a perfect correspondence between the name and the sentiment; a similarity of sounds is sufficient to make the etymological word play. The Septuagint understood it as a plural, translating the word "encampments." Some scholars suggest that the original word was "camping place" and that an old ending -*am* dissolved to the dual. Accordingly, an old spelling of the name could have been *maḥăneh*, "encampment" (in accord with Jacob's expression), which could have been lengthened by mimation to *maḥănem*, which was then taken to be the dual in the later pointing.

That such a possibility exists for this and other place names in the dual is widely recognized. Yet the connection between the significance of the name and the two camps in this narrative leads me to suspect either that the name was dual or that the narrator spelled it that way to carry out the pun. The fact that Jacob used the singular ("this is the camp of God") need not detract from the possibility of its being a dual, for etymological explanations are seldom exact in the narratives.

At any rate, these two verses form an indissoluble unit, including the meaning, the sentiment, and the naming. The speech is framed in the language of the event and enforced with the use of *zeh*, referring to the camp of God. The word play in the giving of the name ties the last section with the sentiment.

After leaving one danger, Jacob thus faced another. But the glimpse he was given of the angels of God assured him, once again, of the divine protection accompanying him on his return to the Land of Promise. The reassurance came at the right time and with the right force. Jacob could depend on God's powerful presence because he had been made aware of the angelic communication between heaven and earth.

The expositor may wish to take the time to correlate other passages that reveal the same truth. At times people were permitted to see the angelic presence; most of the time, however, God's people have had to rely on his Word that they are there. Nevertheless, such knowledge is a comfort to those facing some crisis.

II. Believers must often face threatening and dangerous situations (3–8).

The tension in this section came with the anticipation of the meeting with Esau. It would be important to mention, however, that the dilemma Jacob faced was largely of his own doing, from years before. These verses tell how Jacob's apprehension led him to act and how the response to his action led him to fear.

The expositor should develop several important ideas in the text. Jacob had just seen the *mal'ăkê 'ĕlōhîm* at the *maḥănēh 'ĕlōhîm*, and so he sent his messengers (*mal'ākîm*) to Esau with a message; but when those messengers returned with their news that Esau was approaching, Jacob divided his people and possessions into two camps (*lišnê maḥănôt*). It is clear that the vision in the first two verses influenced Jacob's actions here—but his actions were on a lower plane.

It is also important to note the designations that Jacob used for himself and for Esau. Verse 4 records that he instructed his servants, "Thus you shall speak to my *lord* Esau [*la'dōnî l^e'ēśāw*], 'Your servant Jacob ['*abd^ekā ya'ăqōb*] says . . .' " (v. 4). This instruction is reiterated in verse 5: "I have sent to tell my lord [*la'adōnî*] that I may find grace [*ḥēn*] in your sight." These precautions all appear to be an attempt to minimize the blessing that Jacob had received from his father. In Genesis 27:29, the blessing made Jacob the lord over his brother and made people serve (*ya'abdûkā*) Jacob. Isaac confirmed this ranking to Esau by stating that he had made Jacob his lord (*g^ebîr*) and given all his brethren to him as servants (*la'ăbādîm*) (27:37). But now, in order to find grace from his brother Esau, Jacob appeared to be relinquishing what the blessing had given him.

This initial indication of Jacob's anxiety shows how serious he thought the situation was. But when the news came of the approach of his brother and four hundred men (v. 6), Jacob became terrified and distressed. Now, almost certain of an attack, Jacob made preparations to face the threat by dividing his people and property into two camps. It seems that Jacob had not learned the point of the vision of God's encampment, for he was willing to sacrifice part of his host—what God had given him—so that the others could escape. Genesis 33:2 makes it painfully clear which groups he was willing to sacrifice.

III. Believers may pray for protection with confidence because of God's plans for them (9–12).

In this section of the chapter Jacob followed the correct procedure in the face of imminent danger—he prayed for deliverance from Esau. He was still terrified ("for I fear him" [v. 11]), but he petitioned God for help. This is a model prayer and certainly shows that Jacob knew the correct way out of danger. Unfortunately, Jacob's faith was usually mingled with his crafty devices.

The prayer has the initial address to the God of the fathers but adds the reminder of the promise: "The LORD who said to me, 'Return to your country, and to your kindred, and I will deal well with you.' " By describing God in the address with this expansion, Jacob was reminding the Lord that he was obediently carrying out his commission. God had brought him to this point. It is worth noting, too, that the theme of "good" surfaces here in the verb "I will deal well" (w^e'êtîbâ). In the last chapter the Lord had kept Laban from harming him; in this chapter Jacob rested on God's promise to deal well with him.

Verse 10 is Jacob's confession of unworthiness, which is the correct attitude for prayer. We may note that, in the process of this confession, Jacob summarized all his possessions and his family as God's covenantal loyal love and faithfulness (mikkōl ha$h$ăsādîm ûmikkol-hā'ĕmet). Through God's bounty, Jacob had become two hosts (li$s$nê ma$h$ănôt), a reference to the two groups that he had divided earlier. But we should also note that Jacob referred to himself as God's servant ('abdekā, in v. 10). If he was God's servant, he need not be Esau's servant.

The petition proper is in verse 11a: "Deliver me [hassîlēnî]." This verb was used at the end of this chapter (v. 30), after Jacob wrestled with his unknown assailant: "I have seen God face to face, and I have been delivered [wattinnā$s$el nap$s$î]." When Jacob was blessed by God (32:29), he was delivered from Esau.

Finally, the motivation for God to act concludes Jacob's prayer (vv. 11b–12). There are two sides to the motivation: he was in a life-threatening situation, but God had promised to bless him and treat him well ('ê$t$îb). Jacob rehearsed God's promises in his prayer not simply to remind God of his Word (although that seems to be a common feature of prayers) but to build his own confidence that God would deliver him.

In spite of Jacob's dependence on God through prayer, his fear and his guilt appear to have controlled him at this point. And so his faith, demonstrated so clearly in the prayer, was tarnished by his subsequent attempt to appease Esau.

IV. Believers often attempt to extricate themselves from their difficulties rather than wait confidently on the Lord (13–21).

The final section of the story delineates Jacob's unnecessary efforts to deliver himself from Esau. He sent a large gift (minḥâ) to Esau to pacify him ('ăkappᵉrâ, in v. 20). In short, Jacob did not really want to find grace in the sight of his brother (v. 5)—he wanted to buy him off! The 550 animals that he sent were taken from the two camps that God had given him (v. 10). Jacob was thus essentially willing to relinquish his blessing to Esau. In fact, Jacob actually said to Esau in 33:11, "Please take my blessing [qaḥ-nā' 'et-birkātî]," referring to this gift.

The instructions that Jacob gave to those taking the gift to Esau include the improper use of "servant" and "lord" again (see vv. 19–20). Not only was Jacob willing to return the blessing, he was ready to nullify his place of leadership in the family. Only fear and guilt could motivate such anxious efforts.

There is also a significant use of the word "face" in this narrative and in the subsequent narratives (see 32:30 and 33:10). In verse 20, Jacob said, "I will appease him [pānāyw] with the gift that is going before me [lᵉpānāy], and afterward I will see his face [pānāyw]; perhaps he will forgive me ['ûlay yiśśā' pānāy; lit., "lift up my face"]." Then in verse 21, he sent the gift over "before him" ('al-pānāyw), but he lodged the night in the camp. The point of sending the gift was to appease (kipper) Esau's "face" so that Esau would "lift up his face" (i.e., forgive him). But Jacob sent the gift before him while he went to sleep. Brueggemann writes:

> As we shall see (in 32:22–32 and 33:1–17), the theme of "seeing the face" is an important one. Here the term is used as a posture of servility by one unworthy to look upon the face of the other. Yet Jacob hopes that the stronger party will pardon and accept, that is, "lift his face" to recognition and well-being (cf. 40:20–21). Jacob engages in an act of self-abasement. That posture is further heightened by the use of "appease," (v. 20). The term is kpr, seldom used in secular contexts and usually rendered "atone." The word suggests the gravity of the meeting. [Genesis, p. 266]

The narrative closes by repeating the unit's major word play to show how contrary the gift was to the spirit of the vision: "The gift [hamminḥâ] passed over before his face, but he lodged in that night in the camp [bammaḥăneh]."

As with Jacob, the nation of Israel often faced the threat of opposing, antagonistic forces coming to meet them—old foes approaching. This passage, corroborated by others like it, would show that, since the Lord God had committed himself to protect his people, he could be counted on to deliver them from danger, even if it meant the deployment of his angelic hosts. The lesson could thus be stated: *God's people can pray with confidence for deliverance from their enemies because of his promises to them—and they need not seek to appease their enemies by giving away God's blessing on them.* Unfortunately, even a good king such as Hezekiah stumbled in his faith under the threat of invasion and sent tribute from the temple to the foreign invaders.

The lesson is the same for the church as it was for Israel. We face a spritual conflict when we follow God, not merely a physical one. No human effort is sufficient for these things, no physical defense, no amount of money. The source of confidence and the means of victory come from God's revelation that he delivers his people by his angelic hosts. The people of God can be strengthened by such a revelation, so that they might avoid any anxious efforts to extricate themselves from crises. Their confidence must be that he who has begun a good work will complete it, no matter what dangers appear.

Bibliography

Fensham, F. C. " 'Camps' in the New Testament and Milḥamah." *RevQ* 4 (1963–64): 557–62.

Fokkelman, J. P. *Narrative Art in Genesis*, pp. 197–208. Assen: Van Gorcum, 1975.

Houtman, C. "Jacob at Mahanaim: Some Remarks on Genesis XXXII 2–3." *VT* 28 (1978): 37–44.

Rendtorff, R. "Botenformel und Botenspruch." *ZAW* 74 (1962): 165–77.

49

Jacob at the Jabbok, Israel at Peniel
(Gen. 32:22–32)

W hy do the people of God attempt to gain the blessing of God by their own efforts? Faced with a great opportunity or a challenging task, believers are prone to take matters into their own hands and use whatever means are at their disposal. In such a situation there may even be a flirtation with unscrupulous and deceptive practices—especially when things become desperate.

As we have seen, Jacob displayed these tendencies. All his life he managed very well. He cleverly outwitted his stupid brother—twice, by securing the birthright and by securing the blessing. And he eventually conquered Laban and came away a wealthy man—surely another sign of divine blessing. Only occasionally did he realize that it was God who worked through it all, but finally this truth was pressed on him most graphically in the night struggle at the ford Jabbok.

At Jabbok Jacob wrestled with an unidentified man until dawn and prevailed over him, and though he sustained a crippling blow, he held on to receive a blessing once he perceived that his assailant was

546

supernatural. That blessing was signified by God's renaming the patriarch "Israel," to which Jacob responded by naming the place "Peniel." But because he limped away from the event, the "sons of Israel" observed a dietary restriction.

Gunkel, comparing this story with ancient myths, observes that all the features—the attack in the night by the deity, the mystery involved, the location by the river, the hand-to-hand combat—establish the high antiquity of the story (*Genesis*, p. 361). It is clear that the unusual elements fit well with the more ancient accounts about God's dealings with human beings, namely, the primeval events. To be sure, something unusual has been recorded, and the reader is struck immediately with many questions—some of which probably cannot be answered to any satisfaction. Who was the mysterious assailant? Why was he fighting Jacob, and why was he unable to defeat him? Why did he appear afraid of being overtaken by the dawn? Why did he strike Jacob's thigh? Why did he refuse to reveal his own name? Why was the dietary taboo not included in the law? What is the significance of this narrative within the patriarchal traditions? A survey of the more significant attempts to understand the present form of the text will underscore the difficulties.

Several interpreters have suggested that this passage is a dream narrative. Josephus understood it to be a dream in which an apparition (*phantasma*) made use of voice and words (*Antiquities* 1.20.2). Others have given the story an allegorical interpretation. Philo saw a spiritual conflict in literal terms, a fight of the soul against one's vices and passions (*Legum Allegoriae* 3.190). Jacob's combatant was the Logos (*De Mutatione Nominum* 87); it was his virtue that became lame for a season. This allegorical approach was accepted in part by Clement of Alexandria; he said that the assailant was the Logos, but he understood that he remained unknown by name in the conflict because he had not yet appeared in flesh (*Paedagogus* 1.7.57).

From the time of Jerome, many have understood the passage to portray long and earnest prayer. Schmidt relates how Umbreit expanded this idea to say it was a prayer that involved meditation in the divine presence, confession of sin, desire for pardon and regeneration, and yearning for spiritual communion (see Schmidt, "Numen," p. 263).

Jewish literature, however, recognizes that an actual fight is at the heart of the story. R. Hama b. R. Hanina said it was a real struggle but with the prince or angel of Esau (*Midrash Genesis* 77.3). Rashi followed this explanation, and the *Zohar* (170a) named the angel Samael, the chieftain of Esau.

The passage has proved problematic for critical analysis as well. Schmidt explains that the usual criteria fail. Yahwe does not occur at all, not even on the lips of the renamed hero. Elohim is found everywhere, but in a way that would not be impossible even to a writer usually employing the name Yahwe. The words and phrases generally depended on by the analysis are not decisive. ["Numen," p. 267]

As a result, there has been little agreement among critical scholars. Knobel, Dillmann, Delitzsch, and Roscher assigned it to E. And DeWette, Hupfeld, Kuenen, Studer, Wellhausen, Driver, Skinner, Kautzsch, Procksch, and Eichrodt assigned it to J.

Gunkel attempted to muster evidence from within the narrative to show that two recensions of an old story had been put together: (1) verse 25a records that the hip was dislocated by a blow, but verse 25b suggests that it happened accidentally in the course of the fight; (2) verse 28 presents the giving of the name as the blessing, but verse 29 declares that the assailant blessed him; (3) verse 30 has Jacob victorious, but verse 31 records that he escaped with his life.

Critical scholars have also attempted to uncover an ancient mythical story about gods fighting with heroes that could have been adapted for the Jacob stories. Fraser, Bennett, Gunkel, and Kittel thought that the old story included a river god whose enemy was the sun god, which diminished the river with its rays (especially in summer). In other words, the Hebrew tradition was pure fiction and was based on an old myth about a river god named Jabbok who attempted to hinder anyone from crossing. Peniel was his shrine (see Schmidt, "Numen," p. 269).

The myth was also identified with the deity El, the god of the land of Canaan. John McKenzie suggests that the narrative followed an old Canaanite myth in which the "man" was at one time identified. When Jacob became attached to the story, he argues, the Canaanite deity so named was deliberately obscured ("Jacob at Peniel," p. 73), being replaced by a mysterious being who may or may not be taken as Yahweh. This being, McKenzie suggests, was left vague because there was a hesitancy to attribute such deeds to Yahweh. Later, the role was transferred to intermediate beings, such as the angel of Esau.

To say that the account gradually developed from some such ancient myth greatly weakens a very important point in the history of Israel in the memory of the Israelites and in reality solves none of the tensions that exist. Gevirtz cautions:

The passage cannot be dismissed merely as a bit of adopted or adapted folklore—a contest with a nocturnal demon, river spirit, or regional numen who opposes the river's crossing—to which "secondary" matters of cultic interest have been added, but is rather to be understood as bearing a distinct and distinctive meaning for the people who claim descent from their eponymous ancestor. Where, when, and how Jacob became Israel cannot have been matters of indifference to the Israelite author or to his audience. ["Patriarchs and Puns," p. 50]

Theological Ideas

Several observations will give direction to the theological interpretation of the story. First, the wrestling occurred at the threshold of the Land of Promise. Jacob had been outside the land ever since his flight from Esau but now was returning to meet Esau. Second, the unifying element of the story is the naming, or the making of Jacob into Israel. Third, the account is linked to a place name, Peniel. The names Peniel (Gen. 32:30), Mahanaim (vv. 1–2), and Succoth (33:17) are each given and etymologized by Jacob in his return to Canaan and so are important to the narratives. Fourth, the story is linked to a dietary restriction for the sons of Israel. This taboo was a custom that grew up on the basis of an event but was not part of the law.

The theme of the story is the wrestling—no one suggests anything else. However, one cannot study the account in isolation from the context of the Jacob cycle of stories. The connection is immediately strengthened by the plays on the names. At the outset we find the man *ya'ăqōb*, the place *yabbōq*, and the action *yē'ābēq*. These similar sounding words attract the reader's attention. Before a Jacob may cross the Jabbok to the land of blessing, he must fight. He will attempt once more to trip up his adversary, for at this point he is met by someone wishing to have a private encounter with him, and he is forced into the match. Fokkelman says:

> Tripping his fellow man by the heel (*'qb*) has for Jacob come to its extreme consequence: a wrestling (*'bq*) with a "man" which to Jacob is the most shocking experience of his life, as appears from the fact that thereafter he proceeds through life a man changed of name, and thus of nature, and under the new name he becomes the patriarch of the "Israelites." (This comes out even more strongly in Jacob's own confession in v. 31.) [*Narrative Art*, p. 210]

Ryle notes that the physical disability he suffers serves as a memorial of the spiritual victory and a symbol of the frailty of human strength in the crisis when God meets man face to face (*Book of Genesis*,, p. 323).

The main theological point of the narrative centers on what happened to Jacob when God blessed him at the crossing of the river. There was the blessing to be sure, for the new name signified a new status and a new direction. But there was also a defeat, for Jacob's crippled walk signified that before God he was powerless and dependent.

Structure and Synthesis

Structure

The event recorded in the narrative gives rise to two names: God renamed Jacob Israel, and Israel named the place Peniel. Everything in the narrative builds to the giving of the name "Israel"; and the giving of the name "Peniel" reflects the significance of the entire encounter as it was understood by Jacob. These names provide a balanced picture of the significant event.

In a helpful analysis of the structure of this passage, Barthes evaluates the structure as in chart 27 ("Struggle," p. 29). The parallel arrangement is instructive: The direct response of Jacob to his assailant leads to his being renamed "Israel." The indirect response of the assailant, however, leads Jacob to name the place "Peniel," for he realized that it was God who fought ("Israel") with him face to face ("Peniel"). One name is given by the Lord to Jacob, the other is given by Jacob in submission to the Lord.

The passage may be divided into three main sections, with a prologue and epilogue. Of the three sections, the first (the event, vv. 24b–25) prepares for the second (the blessing, vv. 26–29), and the third (the evaluation, vv. 30–31) reflects the first two.

Summary Message

After wrestling Jacob all night at the river Jabbok without prevailing over him, the Lord dislocated the patriarch's hip and blessed him by changing his name to Israel, prompting Jacob to name the place Peniel to commemorate his seeing God face to face and being delivered (the incident was also commemorated in Israel's dietary laws).

Chart 27. **Parallel Arrangement of Genesis 32:27–30**

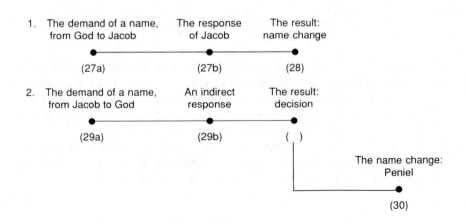

Exegetical Outline

 I. The preparation: After Jacob sent all his family and possessions across the river, he was left alone (22–24a).
  A. Summary statement: Jacob took his family across the Jabbok in the night (22).
  B. Introductory statement: Jacob sent all that he had across the river and was left alone (23–24a).
   1. Jacob sent all his possessions across (23).
   2. Jacob was left alone (24a).
 II. The fight: After wrestling with Jacob until daybreak and being unable to defeat him, a "man" touched and dislocated his hip (24b–25).
  A. A "man" wrestled with Jacob until daybreak (24b).
  B. This "man" put Jacob's hip out of joint when he could not prevail over him (25).
 III. The conversation: When Jacob clung to the man for a blessing, Jacob had his name changed to Israel but was unable to discover the name of the one who blessed him (26–29).
  A. Jacob clung to the man for a blessing (26).
   1. The visitor asked to be released, for the day was breaking (26a).
   2. Jacob refused to let go without a blessing. (26b).
  B. Jacob's name was changed to Israel because he had fought with God and man and had prevailed (27–28).
   1. The man asked Jacob his name (27).
   2. The man renamed Jacob Israel (28).
  C. Jacob attempted to discover the name of the one who blessed him (29).
   1. He asked the name of his visitor (29a).
   2. The visitor marveled that he asked his name, and blessed him (29b).
 IV. The evaluation and conclusion (30–31).
  A. Evaluation: Jacob named the place Peniel because he saw God face to face and was delivered (30).
  B. Conclusion: Jacob crossed over Peniel as the sun rose upon him, but he was limping (31).
 V. Editorial note: The children of Israel did not eat the sinew of the hip because it was touched in the struggle (32).

Development of the Exposition

It is probably simplest to divide the story into three parts—the fight, the blessing, and the response. The final part about the dietary law can be incorporated as an epilogue.

I. The Lord must on occasion "cripple" self-sufficient believers in order to bless them (22–25).

A. The prologue (22–24a).

These opening verses record the crossing of the Jabbok by Jacob and his family. Verse 22 provides a summary statement of the crossing of the river by the clan. The actual crossing is then developed, beginning with verse 23. Between the time Jacob sent his family across and the time he joined them, the wrestling and blessing occurred.

Jacob's being left alone (v. 24a) is not explained. One suggestion is that Jacob was anticipating an encounter with Esau, and so he began a night crossing of the river to establish his ground in the land. Whether he anticipated an encounter in the night or simply was caught alone is difficult to say. If Jacob remained behind to make sure everything was safely across, then the meeting came as a complete surprise (Fokkelman, *Narrative Art*, p. 211). When he was alone, he was attacked by a man and caught in the match.

At any rate, the narrative goes to great lengths to isolate Jacob on one side of the river. The question of his plans is irrelevant to the story. The important point is that he was alone.

B. The Fight (24b–25).

Only four sentences are used for the fight; no details are given, for the fight was but the foundation for the most important part—the dialogue. Yet, the fight was real and physical. Dillmann says that the limping shows that it was a physical occurrence in a material world (*Genesis*, vol. 2, p. 281). The memory of Israel's limping away from the night that gave rise to the dietary restriction attests to the physical reality.

The verb used to describe the wrestling is *wayyē'ābēq*, "and he wrestled." It is rare, being found only here and in verse 25. Since the word *'ābāq* is "dust," this denominative verb perhaps carries the idea of "get dusty" in wrestling.

Martin-Achard concludes that this very rare verb was selected because of assonance with *yabbōq* and *ya'ăqōb*, the sounds *b/v* and *k/q* forming strong alliterations at the beginning of the story ("Exegete," p. 39). The verb plays on the name of the river as if to say *yabbōq* was equal to *ya'ābōq*, meaning "wrestling, twisting" river (see Gunkel, *Genesis*, p. 326). The word play employs the name of the river as a perpetual reminder of the most important event that ever happened there.

At this spot "a man" (*'îš*) wrestled with Jacob. The Hebrew word is ambiguous, which is fitting, for the "man" refuses to reveal himself directly. The effect of the word choice is that the reader is transported to Jacob's situation. Jacob perceived only that a male antagonist was closing in on him. The reader gradually learns his identity as Jacob did—by his words and actions.

The time of the match is doubly significant. On the one hand, it is interesting that the struggle was at night. Darkness concealed the adversary's identity. The fact that he wished to be gone by daylight shows that he planned the night visit. As it turns out, had he come in the daytime, Jacob would have recognized his special authority (v. 29) and identity (v. 30b). If Jacob had perceived whom he was going to have to fight, he would never have started the fight, let alone continue with his peculiar obstinancy (von Rad, *Genesis,* p. 320). On the other hand, the fact that the wrestling lasted till the breaking of day suggests a long, indecisive bout. Indeed, the point is that the assailant could not defeat Jacob until he resorted to something extraordinary.

The turning point of the bout came when the man "touched" Jacob. This touch was actually a blow—it dislocated Jacob's hip. The text uses a mild term for it, thereby demonstrating a supernatural activity (cf. Isa. 6:7, "he touched Isaiah's lips"). The effect of this blow is clear: the assailant gave himself unfair advantage over the patriarch, for he was more than a match for Jacob. The one that might be expected to take advantage of the other was himself crippled by a supernatural blow from his assailant.

II. The Lord blesses the dependent believer with the prospect of victory (26–29).

The true nature of the nameless adversary began to dawn on Jacob as the physical darkness began to lift. It is one who has power over the affairs of humankind! He said, "Let me go, for the day breaks!" But Jacob, having been transformed from a devious fighter into a forthright and resolute one (Speiser, *Genesis,* p. 255), held on for a blessing. He said, "I will not let you go except you bless me!" Fokkelman characterizes Jacob here: "From the most miserable situation he wants to emerge an enriched man" (*Narrative Art,* p. 215). Jacob may not have been aware of all of the implications (the narrator certainly was), but he knew the source of blessing.

The blessing for which Jacob pleaded found expression in a changed name. The assailant first asked the patriarch, "What is your name?"—undoubtedly a rhetorical question. The object was to contrast the old name with the new. When one remembers the significance of names, the point becomes clear: by giving his name, Jacob had to confess his nature. This name, at least for these narratives, designated its owner as a crafty overreacher. Here the "heel-catcher" was crippled and had to identify his true nature (Jacob) before he could be blessed (Israel).

"And he said, 'Not Jacob shall your name be called from now on, but Israel, for you have fought with God and man and have prevailed.' " This renaming of Jacob is an assertion of the assailant's authority to impart a new life and new status (cf. 2 Kings 23:34; 24:17). What is the meaning of the name Israel? Both Genesis 32:28 and Hosea 12:4 describe Jacob's activity as a fight. The meaning of "Israel" would then be defined as "God contends; may God contend, persist."

Coote analyzes Genesis 32:28b ("Meaning," p. 137) and concludes that (a) the syllabic meter is 8:8; (b) the parallel pairs are śry || ykl, ʻm || ʻm, ʼlhym || ʼnšym; (c) the archaic parallelism of qtl || yqtl is present; and (d) the arrangement is chiastic (śry—twkl). The last word is isolated to combine the clause:

> ky śryt ʻm ʼlhym　　"for you fought with God
> wʻm ʼnšym wtwkl　　and with men, and you prevailed"

The root śārâ is used to explain the name yiśrāʼēl because it sounds the same, is derived from the very story, and is otherwise infrequent (see also Coote, "Hosea XII," VT 21 [1971]: 394). The verb yākōl is used to explain the outcome of śārâ.

When the narrative signifies that the name yiśrāʼēl means "God fights," the meaning involves an interpolation of the elements; that is, "God fights" is explained by "you fought with God." Thus the name is but a motto and a reminder of the seizing of the blessing that would be a pledge of victory and success (Skinner, Commentary on Genesis, p. 409). Gunkel states that this explanation of the significance of the name was affectionately and proudly employed to show the nature of the nation to be invincible and triumphant: Israel would fight the entire world with God's help and, when necessary, God himself (Genesis, p. 328).

Many have been troubled by the difficulties with this explanation. First, if the name means "God fights," then how is it reversed to say that Jacob fights with God? Second, the verb śārâ is very rare, making a clear definition difficult. Third, the versions did not understand the distinction between śārâ, "to contend," and śārar, "to rule." The problem may be traced to the pointing of the verb in Hosea 12:4—wayyāśar, probably a geminate root śārar, "rule" (Symmachus, Aquila, and Onkelos). As a result the versions and commentators follow either the idea of "rule" or "contend/oppose" (Josephus).

Various other suggestions for the actual etymology of "Israel" have been made (for a survey, see Danell, Studies, pp. 22–28). A. Haldar suggests that the root is išr/ʼšr, "happy," and that it could possibly be connected to the Canaanite god Ashera ("Israel," IDB, vol. 2, p. 765). Edmond Jacob connects the name with the root yāšār, "just, right" (Theology of the Old Testament, translated by Arthur W. Heathcote and

Philip J. Allcock [New York: Harper & Row, 1958], p. 203). He finds confirmation for this idea in the noun "Yeshurun" (Deut. 32:15; 33:5, 26; Isa. 44:2), a poetic designation of Israel, as well as the *sepher hayyashar*, the old collections of national songs (Josh. 10:13; 2 Sam. 1:18). This could be the book of Israel, the righteous one, the hero of God, according to E. Jacob. The major problem with this interpretation is that it involves a change of the sibilant.

Albright takes the name from yaśar, "to cut, saw," with a developed meaning of "heal": "God heals" ("Names 'Israel' and 'Judah,'" p. 166). He argues that the original name was *Yaśir-'el, from a verbal stem yśr, with the developed meaning of "heal" (supported by Ethiopic *šaraya* and the equation/interchange in Arabic of *našara* for *wašara*).

Coote, also using the strong letters *śr* (possibly from roots beginning with *yod* or *nun*, geminate [or reduplicated] roots, or roots ending in a weak letter), chooses the Akkadian root *wašāru* and traces a semantic development of "cutting > deciding > counseling" (Arabic *'ašāra*, "counsel," and *mušîr*, "counselor") ("Meaning," p. 139). He finds support in Isaiah 9:5–6, where there is confluence of *śar* and *śry* as in Genesis 32. The word for "government" is the key there. He concludes that the name *yiśrā'ēl* means "El judges" and is from either *yśr* or *śry*. It has the meaning of govern by rendering a decree or judgment (Ps. 82:1).

Noth, taking "Israel" to be from a third weak root *śārâ*, suggests the meaning "to rule" or "be lord over" (*PN*, pp. 191, 208). In this capacity God takes action in the world and particularly helps his own. "Israel" then would mean "God will rule" or "may God rule."

It is certainly possible that one of these Semitic roots is etymologically connected to the name and that the name meant something like "rule," "judge," or "heal" at one time, for the name occurred before this time, as the Eblaite material suggests (see G. Pettinato, *The Archives of Ebla* [Garden City, N.Y.: Doubleday, 1981], p. 249). The popular etymology in Genesis is giving the significance of the name. Most of these other suggestions, however, are no more compelling than the popular etymology given in the text of Genesis. The concept of God's fighting with someone is certainly no more of a problem than the passage itself. And the reversal of the emphasis (from "God fights" to "fight with God") in the explanation is due to the nature of popular etymologies, which are satisfied with a loose word play on the sound or meaning of the name to express its significance.

The name served to evoke the memory of the fight. It was freely interpreted to say that God was the object of Jacob's struggle. Hearing the name *yiśrā'ēl*, one would recall the incident in which Jacob wrestled with God and prevailed. Dillmann says that ever after the name would tell the Israelites that, when Jacob contended successfully with God, he won the battle with man (*Genesis*, vol. 2, p. 279). The name "God fights" and the popular explanation "you fought and prevailed" thus obtained a significance for future struggles.

III. The believer who realizes the real source of victory will become bold in the faith (30).

Jacob afterward attempted to discover his assailant's name. The "man" had acted with full powers and spoken with authority. He had gotten to the bottom of Jacob's identity; he could not be mortal. Thus Jacob sought his name.

The answer, however, was cautious: "Why do you ask my name?" On the one hand, he seemed to say to Jacob, "Think, and you will know the answer!" (Fokkelman, *Narrative Art*, p. 218). On the other hand, he was unwilling to release his name for Jacob to control. The divine name cannot be had on demand or taken in vain, otherwise it could be exposed to magical manipulation (A. S. Herbert, *Genesis 12–50* [London: SCM, 1966], p. 108).

Jacob had to be content with a visitation from a "man" whom he realized was divine. Jacob might have recalled that Abram was visited by "men" (Gen. 18) with such powers. Lot also received those men in the night and was saved alive when the sun arose (chap. 19). Apparently, such humanlike visitations represented one manner of the manifestation of the Lord in Genesis.

Jacob named the place Peniel because he had seen God face to face and had been delivered. This action forms the second part of the basic structure. First, God demanded and changed his name. Here, Jacob was not given the divine name but named the place to commemorate the event. He had power over that realm but could not overreach it. The play on the name is clear: having seen God face to face, he named the place Peniel, or "face of God."

The impact of the encounter was shocking for Jacob. Seeing God was something no one survived (Gen. 48:16; Exod. 19:21; 24:10; Judg. 6:11, 22; chap. 13). But this appearance of the man guaranteed deliverance for the patriarch. God had come as close to Jacob as was imaginable. Jacob exclaimed, "I have seen God face to face and I have been delivered [< *nāṣal*]." His prayer for deliverance (Gen. 32:10–13) was answered. Meeting God face to face meant that he could now look Esau directly in the eye.

IV. Epilogue (31–32).

Verse 31 provides the conclusion for the narrative. As the sun rose, Jacob crossed over Peniel with a limp. Ewald says that he limped on his thigh "as if the crookedness, which had previously adhered to the moral nature of the wily Jacob, had now passed over into an external physical attribute only" (*The History of Israel,* vol. 1, p. 358).

The final verse of the story is an editorial note that explains a dietary restriction that developed on account of this event. The wounding of Jacob's thigh caused the "children of Israel" not to eat of the sciatic nerve "until this day." This law does not form part of the Sinaitic code and so may have been a later custom in Israel. The fact that the reference is made to Israelites rather than the "sons of Jacob" may also suggest that the custom is post-Sinaitic.

The expression "until this day" is usually taken as indicating an etiological note. Childs concludes that, in the majority of the cases, it expresses a personal testimony added to and confirming a received tradition, a commentary on existing customs ("Until This Day," p. 292).

The special significance of Jacob's becoming Israel is the purification of character. Peniel marks the triumph of the higher elements of his life over the lower elements; but if it is a triumph for the higher elements, it is a defeat for the lower. The outcome of the match is a paradox. The victor wept and pleaded for a blessing (Hos. 12:4); once blessed he emerged, limping on a dislocated hip. How may this outcome be a defeat and a victory?

Because Jacob was guilty, he feared his brother and found God an adversary. Jacob had prepared to meet Esau, whom he had deceived, but God broke Jacob's strength. When God touched the strongest sinew of Jacob, the wrestler, his strength shriveled, and with it Jacob's persistent self-confidence (Dods, *Book of Genesis,* p. 300). His carnal weapons were lamed and useless—they failed him in his contest with God. He had always been sure of the result when he helped himself, but his trust in the naked force of his own weapons was now without value.

What he had surmised for the past twenty years now dawned on him—he was in the hands of one against whom it was useless to struggle. With the crippling touch, Jacob's struggle took a new direction. With the same scrappy persistence he clung to his opponent for a blessing. His goal was now different. Now crippled in his natural strength he become bold in faith.

Jacob emerged from the encounter an altered man. After winning God's blessing legitimately, Jacob found that the danger with Esau vanished. He had been delivered.

What, then, is the significance of this narrative within the structure of the patriarchal history? In the encounter the fulfillment of the promise seemed threatened. At Bethel a promise was given; at the Jabbok fulfillment seemed to be barred as God opposed Jacob's entrance into the land. Was there a change of attitude with the Lord, who promised the land? Or was this threat a test?

In a similar story, Moses was met by God because he had not complied with God's will (Exod. 4:24). With Jacob, however, the wrestling encounter and name changes took on a greater significance because he was at the frontier of the land promised to the seed of Abraham. God, who was the real Proprietor of the land, opposed his entering as Jacob. If it were only a matter of mere strength, then God let him know he would never enter the land (Dillmann, *Genesis*, vol. 2, p. 280).

The narrative thus supplies a moral judgment on the crafty Jacob, who was almost destroyed in spite of the promise. Judging from Jacob's clinging for a blessing, the patriarch made the same judgment on himself.

On the surface, the story appears to glorify the physical strength and bold spirit of the ancestor of the Israelites. Like so much of the patriarchal history, however, it is clearly transparent as a type of that which Israel the nation experienced from time to time with God (von Rad, *Genesis*, p. 325). The story of Israel the man serves as an acted parable of the life of the nation, in which is here presented its relationship with God almost prophetically. The patriarch portrays the real spirit of the nation to engage in the persistent struggle with God until emerging strong in the blessing. The nation is consequently referred to as Jacob or Israel, depending on which characteristics predominate.

The point of the story for the nation of Israel entering the Land of Promise would be significant: Israel's victory would come not by the usual ways by which nations gain power but in the power of the divine blessing. Later in her history Israel was reminded that the restoration to the land was not by might nor by strength but by the Spirit of the Lord God, who fights for his people (Zech. 4:6). The blessings of God come by God's gracious, powerful provisions, not by mere physical strength or craftiness. In fact, at times God must cripple the natural strength of his servants so that they might receive the blessing by faith.

We also learn from the example of Jacob. If we are to accomplish what God wants us to do, it must be accomplished by faith in him and not by the strength of the flesh. If we do not develop in our faith, God may bring us to some point—just as he did Jacob—where our self-sufficiency is proved insufficient. *To become strong in the faith, believers must be rid of their self-sufficiency.*

Bibliography

Albright, W. F. "The Names 'Israel' and 'Judah,' with an Excursus on the Etymology of *Tôdâh* and *Tôrâh.*" *JBL* 46 (1927): 151–85.

Anderson, B. W. "An Exposition of Genesis XXXII 22–32: The Traveler Unknown." *ABR* 17 (1969): 21–26.

Barthes, Roland. "The Struggle with the Angel: Textual Analysis of Genesis 32:23–33." In *Structural Analysis and Biblical Exegesis,* edited by R. Barthes et al., translated by Alfred M. Johnson, Jr., pp. 21–33. Pittsburgh: Pickwick, 1974.

Childs, Brevard S. "A Study of the Formula 'Until This Day.' " *JBL* 82 (1963): 279–92.

Coote, R. B. "The Meaning of the Name Israel." *HTR* 65 (1972): 137–41.

Danell, G. A. *Studies in the Name Israel in the Old Testament,* pp. 22–28. Uppsala: Appelbergs, 1946.

Eslinger, Lyle M. "Hosea 12:5a and Genesis 32:29: A Study in Inner Biblical Exegesis." *JSOT* 18 (1980): 91–99.

Fokkelman, J. P. *Narrative Art in Genesis,* pp. 208–23. Assen: Van Gorcum, 1975.

Gevirtz, Stanley. "Of Patriarchs and Puns: Joseph at the Fountain, Jacob at the Ford." *HUCA* 46 (1975): 33–54.

Gibble, Kenneth L. *The Preacher as Jacob.* New York: Seabury, 1985. (See especially chap. 6 for an exegesis and drama/sermon on this passage.)

McKenzie, John L. "Jacob at Peniel." *CBQ* 25 (1963): 71–76.

McKenzie, Steve. "You Have Prevailed: The Function of Jacob's Encounter at Peniel in the Jacob Cycle." *Restoration Quarterly* 23 (1980): 225–31.

Martin-Achard, Robert. "An Exegete Confronting Genesis 32:23–33." In *Structural Analysis and Biblical Exegesis,* edited by R. Barthes, translated by Alfred M. Johnson, Jr., pp. 34–56. Pittsburgh: Pickwick, 1974.

Ross, Allen P. "Jacob at the Jabboq, Israel at Peniel." *BibSac* 142 (1985): 338–54.

Roth, Wolfgang. "Structural Interpretation of Jacob at the Jabbok." *BibRes* 22 (1977): 51–62.

Schmidt, N. "The Numen of Peniel." *JBL* 45 (1926): 260–79.

Trigt, F. von. "La signification de la lutte de Jacob près du Yabboq: Gen XXXII 23–33." *OTS* 12 (1958): 280–309.

White, Hugh C. "French Structuralism and Old Testament Narrative Analysis: Roland Barthes." *Semeia* 3 (1975): 99–127.

50

Reconciliation
(Gen. 33)

Genesis 33 records the conclusion of the Jacob-Easu cycle, a story that began with Jacob's flight and now ends with his return. Since the occasion for the flight was Jacob's deception (chap. 27), before there can be any end to the cycle, there must be a reconciliation. This chapter also marks the close of the patriarch's wandering; not only did he return to the land and find reconciliation with his brother, he also built a house for himself and set up an altar to the God of Bethel.

The long-expected reconciliation with Esau finally came about, and it was marvelous. God had so turned Esau's heart that he was eager to be reconciled with his brother. He cared nothing for the birthright, for ever since Jacob had left he had enjoyed a full and productive life under God's blessing. Esau was magnanimous and gracious, but Jacob was halting and self-abasing (if not groveling). The contrast is captured nicely by Westermann:

Esau greets Jacob as one brother greets the other after a long separation (v. 4); Jacob greets Esau as a vassal greets his patron with a ceremonial which has its origin in the royal court; there is a display of solemnity as becomes rank, the seven-fold obeisance, the submissive address, the presentation of gifts of homage. These two types of greeting are so skillfully worked together that the contrast speaks for itself. [*Genesis*, vol. 2, p. 524]

Theological Ideas

The central theme of the episode is the reconciliation. But there are different interpretations for this development. One view is that Jacob was acting wisely in sending his gift to his brother, for reconciliation demanded restitution. In the process, one brother confessed his guilt and the other forgave—although neither act is specifically mentioned in the text. Essentially, this view sees Jacob as a changed person, now facing up to his responsibilities (see Fokkelman, *Narrative Art*, p. 223). Accordingly in chapter 33 Jacob considered the gift a restitution rather than an appeasement.

Another view is that, although Jacob had been made to realize that God would deliver him from danger, he still employed measures that were troubling and unnecessary—the division of the family, the bowing, and the gift. This view would argue that since Jacob's prayer for deliverance from Esau was answered in his meeting with the Lord at Peniel, the reconciliation with Esau was a work of God.

Several hints in the chapter lend support to the latter view. First, Jacob's arrangement of his family groups (32:7–8) before the approaching Esau shows his favoritism and his willingness to sacrifice the unloved members of his family. Second, as pointed out above, Jacob's approach to Esau with all the bowing and the use of the language of a servant to his lord shows an attempt to downplay if not nullify his status as Esau's lord. If it was just protocol, it is significant that Esau did not bow but embraced his brother. Third, Jacob's deceptive agreement to follow Esau to Seir shows that he still could not deal openly and honestly. It seems, then, that Jacob had not changed as much as some suggest. He may have believed that the Lord would deliver him, but he would do what he could to assist that deliverance. His actions show him to be filled with guilty fears.

Besides the theme of reconciliation, there are a few other motifs that should be noted in passing. Jacob's arrival at his destination and the establishment of the altar mark this chapter as the culmination of these Jacob stories. Two commemorative names solidify this development— Succoth and El Elohe Israel. Succoth was the name for the sheds that he built for his cattle, marking the end of his pilgrimage; and El Elohe Israel was the name of the altar, commemorating the name Israel on the occasion of his return to the land.

Structure and Synthesis

Structure

The scene opens with the statement that Jacob lifted up his eyes and saw Esau coming (v. 1a). There follow two episodes, one in which Jacob and Esau came together (vv. 1b–11), and the other in which they separated (vv. 12–17). The last three verses provide an additional itinerary note highlighting the culmination of the return.

Once again, dialogue plays a predominant role in the episodes, Jacob's speeches forming the major part and always coming in response to Esau's brief questions or comments. It is interesting to chart Jacob's responses to Esau's actions and words:

I. The brothers come together (1–11).
    A. The meeting (1–4):
        1. Jacob lifted his eyes and saw Esau coming (1a).
        2. Jacob divided his family (1b–2).
        3. Jacob bowed to the ground as he drew near (3).
        4. Esau embraced his brother (4).
    B. First question (5–7):
        1. Esau lifted his eyes and asked, "Who are these with you?" (5a).
        2. "The children God graciously [ḥānan] gave your servant ['abdekā]" (5b).
        3. The families came near and bowed down (6–7).
    C. Second question (8):
        1. Esau: "What do you mean by this drove [hammaḥăneh] that I met?" (8a).
        2. Jacob: "These are to find grace [ḥēn] in the eyes of my lord ['ădōnî]" (8b).
    D. Discussion over the gift (9–11):
        1. Esau: "I have enough [rāb] my brother ['āḥî]; keep what you have for yourself" (9).
        2. Jacob: "If I have found grace [ḥēn] in your sight, then receive my present [minḥātî]. . . . Take my blessing [bir-kātî] because God has dealt graciously with me [ḥan-nanî]" (10–11).
II. The brothers separate (12–17).
    A. Esau's suggestion that they travel together (12–14):
        1. Esau: "Let us take our journey and let us go, and I will go before you" (12).
        2. Jacob: "My lord ['ădōnî] knows that the children are tender. . . . Let my lord ['ădōnî] pass over before his ser-

vant [ʿabdô] . . . until I come to my lord [ʾădōnî] to Seir" (13–14).

   B. Esau's suggestion that he leave people to assist (15):
      1. Esau: "Let me leave some of the people who are with me" (15a).
      2. Jacob: "Why is it necessary? Let me find grace [ḥēn] in the sight of my lord [ʾădōnî]" (15b).
   C. Esau returned to Seir, but Jacob journeyed to Succoth (16–17).
  III. Itinerary of Jacob near Shechem (18–20).

From this survey we see that Jacob was very carefully responding to Esau. Jacob made it clear that God had been gracious to him, but he wanted Esau to extend grace to him as well, first by accepting his gift and then by leaving him alone on his journey. Esau treated Jacob as a brother; he cared not for the gift but offered to receive Jacob to his place and assist him on the way. Jacob was glad for the reconciliation but had no intention of following Esau to Seir. Once again, the dialogue vividly portrays how simple Esau was and how shrewd Jacob was.

Summary Message

Although Jacob was prepared to sacrifice part of his family in conflict with Esau and although he treated his brother as his lord, Esau magnanimously welcomed his brother home, reluctantly received Jacob's gift, and offered to accompany them all to Seir—an offer that Jacob deceitfully ignored as he traveled to Succoth and settled down there.

Exegetical Outline

    I. Jacob anxiously prepared for the meeting with his brother, but Esau enthusiastically and joyfully welcomed him and reluctantly accepted the large gift that Jacob had sent (1–11).
      A. In spite of Jacob's division of his family in the face of danger and his acts of obeisance to his brother, Esau warmly embraced his brother (1–7).
        1. When Jacob saw Esau coming, he divided his family in the order of their importance to him and then approached Esau, bowing to the ground (1–3).
        2. When Esau met his brother he embraced him and wept and then learned of the family that God had given Jacob (4–7).
      B. In spite of Esau's protests, Jacob pressed his brother to accept the gift that he had sent along, asserting that God had both blessed him and delivered him (8–11).

    II. Jacob agreed to follow his brother back to Seir at a slower pace but then turned and went to Succoth (12–17).

       A. When Esau offered to lead them to Seir, Jacob agreed to follow at a slower pace (12–15).

       B. When Esau went back to Seir, Jacob turned and journeyed to Succoth (16–17).

    III. Epilogue: Jacob returned to Canaan, bought land at Shechem, and established an altar there (18–20).

Development of the Exposition

If the expositor concludes that Jacob's gift to Esau was unnecessary and that his humility was overdone, then this narrative will continue the point of the Jacob stories that God frequently accomplished his plan in spite of the efforts of Jacob. Jacob truly is a comic figure, for he stumbles through life by his wits—and yet it works out. But Jacob was sensitive enough to know that God was in it. This narrative portrays the reconciliation of the brothers as an answer to Jacob's prayer (32:11). In short, reconciliation was the way God delivered Jacob from Esau.

I. God is able to bring about reconciliation, even though his people may exhibit weaknesses in their faith (1–11).

The first seven verses report how Jacob met Esau. When he saw Esau approaching with four hundred men, Jacob lined up the children and the wives in the order of their importance to him, Joseph and Rachel being at the back. This preparation was the outworking of the scheme first contrived in 32:8. But how it must have hurt the family to see which ones Jacob thought were expendable! This ranking probably fed the jealousy over Joseph that came out later (37:2–11).

The actual meeting of the brothers is recorded in verses 3–4. The exposition must concentrate on the contrast. Jacob haltingly approached his brother, bowing himself to the ground seven times (as was common in the ancient world in court protocol). Esau's approach does not follow such a ceremonial comportment—he eagerly ran to meet Jacob, embraced him, kissed him, and wept. Such is the result when "God fights" in his way. This warm welcome shows clearly that Esau had forgiven his brother and held no grudge against Jacob, either because it was all so much water under the bridge to Esau or because God had mellowed his attitude toward his brother over the years by prospering him.

It is important to emphasize Jacob's descriptions of their relationship: he referred to himself as the servant, and to his brother as the lord. As mentioned earlier, such references deny the point of the blessing that made him Esau's lord. Moreover, Jacob informed his brother that all he had gained came by God's gracious dealings. He was certainly approaching humbly and cautiously, but this posture was caused by his fear and guilt.

The second movement of this half of the chapter describes how Jacob pressed Esau to receive the gift as a token of grace (vv. 8–11). Jacob's explanation of the gift is revealing and should be analyzed closely. In this urging, Jacob called it "my blessing" (birkātî). It was impossible for Jacob to give back the blessing, but it was not impossible for him to share the fruit of the blessing with his brother. This one word would be sufficient to recall the earlier tensions over the blessing, and it would indicate to Esau that Jacob was trying to make restitution for his wrongs. At the same time, however, Jacob knew that the change in Esau was the work of God and not a result of his gift, and so he pressed Esau to take the gift as a token of their reconciliation.

Jacob explained that seeing Esau's face was like seeing the face of God. This statement refers directly to the preceding narrative, in which Jacob saw God face to face in the nocturnal struggle and was delivered. Having seen God's face, he could see Esau's. Or, Esau's favorable reaction was like God's gracious dealings just prior to this meeting.

There is a significant emphasis on the idea of grace in this section. Jacob urged Esau to accept the gift in order that he might find grace in his eyes. The family and possessions were God's bounty (= grace), but Jacob wanted Esau's forgiveness (= grace). He attempted to give of God's gracious bounty to obtain Esau's grace. But his purpose (v. 8) was derailed because the reconciliation had taken place beforehand. Now the gift could not be "to find grace"; rather, it was given "if I have found grace" (v. 10). Esau's taking of the gift convinced Jacob that they were reconciled.

II. Believers need not use deception when they must make wise decisions to follow their calling and avoid danger (12–17).

The second major section of the episode concerns the peaceful separation of the brothers. It records how Jacob smoothly, albeit deceptively, avoided traveling with Esau to Seir. Esau no doubt knew that his brother had no intention to come to Seir but would separate. The narrative shows by their separation that reconciliation need not result in communal living—they can go their separate ways in peace. Jacob was wise in not going to Seir, for such a journey would have interrupted his completing his vow; but he did not need to deceive his brother once again.

The story tells of Jacob's settlement in the land. Westermann says, "The longtime traveler makes a permanent settlement, providing housing for personnel and animals. The narrator wants to say that the wanderings of the patriarchs came to an end in Canaan and their descendants settled down to sedentary life" (*Genesis*, vol. 2, p. 527). The event was commemorated by a naming—Succoth (*sukkōt*), because Jacob made shelters (*sukkōt*) for his cattle. Many believe that a name Sukkoth existed here from ancient times as an old Canaanite place for the observance of the harvest festival that came to have the same name (see "Succoth" in *IDB*). In that event, the biblical etymology would be providing a new significance of the name in the patriarchal experience. But to say that the Canaanites had such a feast would say little about the name's origin. At any rate, the narrative with the naming contributes a significant point to the Jacob stories. It attests that the promises made at Bethel were continuing to be fulfilled—Jacob had returned in peace to the land. For Jacob to build stalls witnessed not only to his settlement in the land but also to his abundant possessions that needed care. The name *sukkōt* would be a perpetual reminder of Jacob's prosperous return and peaceful settlement in the land—by the grace of God. Fokkelman notes that this naming is the antipole of *maḥănayim*,, for protection would now come from the building of *sukkōt* (*Narrative Art*, p. 229).

III. Believers need to acknowledge that their peace and prosperity is the work of God (18–20).

Whatever guilty fears Jacob had, and however he sought to make restitution to assuage them, in the end he truly acknowledged that God had faithfully reconciled him to his brother and brought him back to the land. He did so through setting up an altar to God (cf. *wayyaṣṣeb* in v. 20 with *maṣṣēbâ* in 28:18).

This brief itinerary report tells how Jacob moved to Shechem in peace (although Westermann takes *šālēm* to be a place name), bought land from the sons of Hamor, and set up an altar. That this step too was a high point in Jacob's life can be seen from the commemorative naming: it was called *'ēl 'ĕlōhê yiśrā'ēl*. This report forms a parallel with Genesis 28, but here the stress is on the fulfillment of the promises. The name given to the altar says, in effect, "the God of Israel is an *'ēl*," that is, a strong God, a mighty one—a God who keeps his promises. The name may have been shortened from something like "the altar of El, the God of Israel."

The name was designed to signify the successful fulfillment of God's promise to bring back the patriarch to Bethel in safety. The struggle with the night visitor, in which his name was changed to Israel, ensured it. Now Jacob affirmed through worship that the God who appeared to him at Bethel and at Peniel was indeed his strong deliverer. The new man, Israel, thus declared his faith in the strong God by naming the altar. This was indeed an Israelite altar, for he purchased the land and made it his, as Abraham had done with the cave.

Reconciliation is a work of God. Jacob may have had difficulty appreciating that truth at the time he was preparing to face Esau. In the final analysis, however, he realized that God had been gracious to him and delivered him and brought him safely home—just as he had promised.

The work of grace brought a change in both men. In Jacob God brought about a spirit of humility and generosity that, although unnecessary in appeasing Esau, was useful as an expression of guilt and a token of restitution. Jacob had reconciled with God in the fight at the Jabbok; he could now expect to be reconciled with Esau. The change in Esau was from seeking bitter revenge to embracing his brother. The conflict and tension had lingered from the beginning of the Jacob-Esau stories but now was resolved by the deliverance of the God of Peniel.

The message of this chapter has to be presented as a culmination of the Jacob stories and a continuation of the last passage: *Those who have received God's grace (deliverance at Peniel and bounty of possessions) may be confident of God's promise of protection when they seek reconciliation with others.*

If people would trust the Lord to deliver them, they would not be so anxious, so willing to relinquish that which God has given to them and done for them; they would face the difficulties with the expectation that the Lord would resolve the matter; and they could look back on such times with a triumphant acknowledgment of God's deliverance. They may find it proper to make restitution for past wrongs, not in order to appease an enemy, but as witness to the faith in God's working in their lives. *Reconciliation is a work of grace, to be sought by faith and acknowledged in praise.* This point should come as no surprise to the believer; Paul announced that God was at work today, reconciling the world to himself (2 Cor. 5:16–21), and Jesus taught that we should, accordingly, be reconciled to one another (Matt. 5:24).

Bibliography

Fokkelman, J. P. *Narrative Art in Genesis,* pp. 223–31. Assen: Van Gorcum, 1975.

Vischer, W. "La réconciliation de Jacob et d'Esau." *VigChr* 41 (1957): 41–52.

51

Defilement from the Pagans
(Gen. 34)

The account of the rape of Dinah and the revenge of Simeon and Levi forms an interlude in the Jacob stories. The story is told on the level of the family but functions much more for the tribal life in the land, for it is concerned with the problem of intermarriage with the Canaanites and the decision to destroy them (Deut. 7:1–5).

The narrative develops its plot through a gradually increasing tension until the resolution by slaughter. The major issue does not seem to be the rape of Dinah so much as the ravaging of the people of Shechem by Simeon and Levi. The rape formed the basis for the unbridled revenge. The narrator uses dialogue and interpretive descriptions to contrast the Israelites and the Canaanites, until the final question of the avenging brothers in verse 31 puts the matter in perspective. According to them, to treat their sister like a prostitute betrayed the Shechemites' contempt for Israel and warranted justice on Dinah's behalf.

Some commentators suggest that, because the children of Jacob were still frail, according to the previous episode (Gen. 33:13), this narrative must be separated from the former by a lengthy period of time and probably does not belong in the sequence of events recorded in chapters 27–33. Rather, because the story seems to refer to tribes rather than individuals, many conclude that it took place much later (see, e.g., Westermann, *Genesis*, vol. 2, p. 537). It is possible that this account came from a later period of time in Jacob's family, but it most likely did not come from a period later in Israel's history. Simeon and Levi attacked the city when the Shechemite males were weakened from circumcision. Nothing is said of Simeon's and Levi's ages, or of the number of people involved. We would expect that these two men had help from their families, clans, or servants—if they had begun to develop such. At any rate, the event described in this story need not imply a wholesale tribal warfare but only a slaughter on a small scale between tribal families.

If this event took place soon after Jacob's return to the land and before Joseph's sale into Egypt, the participants would be rather young. If Reuben was born to Leah in the eighth year of Jacob's twenty-year stay with Laban, he would have been about fourteen at the return, making Simeon and Levi a couple of years younger, and Joseph possibly seven. According to Genesis 37:2, Joseph was seventeen when his first conflict with the brothers surfaced; and according to 41:46, he was thirty when he stood before Pharaoh (and thus thirty-seven after the seven years of plenty, when the brothers went to Egypt for food). If the rape of Dinah took place before Joseph was sold, the brothers would be in their early twenties; but if it took place after the sale, they could have been anywhere up to their early forties.

Theological Ideas

The law said that Israel was not to intermarry with the Canaanites or make treaties with them but was to destroy them because they posed such a threat. This passage provides part of the rationale for such laws, for it describes how immoral Canaanites defiled Israel by sexual contact and attempted to marry for the purpose of swallowing up Israel. Israel's outrage over the folly was correct, for the defilement could not be ignored. But Israel's method of seeking vengeance was wrong, for the sons used the sign of the covenant as a means of deception in planning their revenge, rather than seeking vengeance directly. For their deception and violence, Simeon and Levi were passed over in the order of the inheritance (Gen. 49:5–7).

In studying the passage the expositor must watch closely for the recurring themes of defilement and folly, circumcision and uncircumcision, anger and grief, and deception. These motifs, in conjunction with what the law later prescribed, give guidance to formulating the theological point(s).

Structure and Synthesis

Structure

The chapter can be divided into three major sections: the defilement of Dinah (vv. 1–3), the deceptive negotiations between the tribes (vv. 4–24), and the ruthless attack (vv. 25–31). The first section is a simple narrative report that lays the basis for the rest of the chapter; the final sections combine narrative reports and dialogue. By tracing the speeches we can see the argument unfold:

1. Shechem attempted to correct his folly by requesting Dinah for a wife (v. 4).
2. Hamor negotiated for intermarriage between the tribes (vv. 8–10).
3. Shechem appealed to the Israelites for Dinah as his wife (vv. 11–12).
4. Jacob's sons deceitfully agreed to intermarriage if the Shechemites became circumcised (vv. 14–17).
5. Hamor and Shechem deceitfully appealed to their people to agree (vv. 20–23).
6. Jacob rebuked his sons for their violence (v. 30).
7. The sons attempted to justify their acts by reminding Jacob of Shechem's folly (v. 31).

The chapter opens with the report of the defilement of Dinah (v. 1) and ends with the brothers' reminder of it (v. 31). In between we have a contrast between the Israelites and the Shechemites. The Israelites' first response was grief and anger over the folly that was done (v. 7). Their action began with their deceitful agreement to the negotiations (vv. 13–17) and culminated with their violent attack on the city and their justification of it (vv. 25–31). The picture of the Shechemites contrasts rather sharply, for they appear not to be disturbed by the rape but see it as an opportunity for intermarriage and eventual overtaking of the Israelites. In the end, their plan to possess everything the Israelites had was reversed because Israel looted their cities in the attack and proved not to be the peaceful family that Hamor thought they were.

Summary Message

After Dinah was defiled by the uncircumcised Shechem, the sons of Jacob gained revenge by deceitfully inducing the Shechemites to accept circumcision as the condition of the marriage, thus enabling them to slaughter the incapacitated males of the city.

Exegetical Outline

I. When Dinah went to see the Canaanite women, she was raped by Shechem, the son of Hamor, the Hivite prince (1–3).

    A. Dinah—Leah's daughter—went out to see the women of the land (1).

    B. Shechem raped Dinah but loved the girl (2–3).

II. When Hamor and Shechem bargained for the intermarriage of the people of Jacob and the people of Shechem, Jacob's sons deceitfully induced the Shechemites to accept circumcision as the condition for intermarriage (4–24).

    A. Shechem demanded that his father arrange his marriage with Dinah (4).

    B. The incensed sons of Jacob displaced the indifferent Jacob in the bargaining process (5–7).

       1. The indifferent Jacob was approached by Hamor (5–6).

       2. The sons of Jacob, incensed by the rape of their sister, returned home just as Hamor began to bargain with Jacob (7).

    C. Hamor bargained with them for the complete intermarriage of their tribes, but Shechem was concerned only for his marriage with Dinah (8–12).

       1. Hamor urged them to intermarry in order that they might gain possessions from the land (8–10).

       2. Shechem urged them to name the dowry price so that he could marry Dinah (11–12).

    D. Jacob's sons deceitfully proposed circumcision as the condition for the marriage (13–17).

       1. The sons answered deceitfully because they were incensed over the defilement of their sister (13).

       2. The sons proposed that, if the Shechemites were circumcised, then they could intermarry and become one people (14–17).

    E. Shechem and Hamor convinced their people to follow Shechem's example and be circumcised (18–24).

       1. They were pleased with the plan, especially Shechem, who delighted in Dinah (18–19).

       2. They urged their people to agree to the plan, explaining that the Israelites were a peaceful people and suggesting that, through this intermarriage, they could possess all of Israel's substance (20–24).

III. Simeon and Levi ruthlessly destroyed all the incapacitated males of the city, delivered their sister Dinah, and plundered the city, causing Jacob to fear for their lives (25–31).

    A. Simeon and Levi ruthlessly killed all the incapacitated men of the city and rescued Dinah from Shechem's house (25–26).

B. Jacob's sons plundered the city in revenge for the defilement of Dinah (27–29).
C. Jacob became afraid for their lives after such a violent attack, but his sons justified it by the violation Shechem had done (30–31).

Development of the Exposition

I. Mingling with pagans inevitably leads to defilement (1–3).

In the first part of the passage, I would stress both the danger of Dinah's interest in the women of the land and her defilement. In the first place, Jacob's family had settled in the vicinity of Shechem (33:18), rather than going on to Bethel as he had vowed, a vow he had to be reminded of (35:1). While they lived in Shechem, Dinah became intrigued by the "daughters of the land." Her excursion into their circles loosened the stone for the slide. Avoidance of the Canaanites would have been far safer. Jacob had made a commercial connection with Shechem, but this investigation of the women of Canaan was a step toward serious complications.

The report of the rape is foundational to the rest of the story. The text says that Shechem "saw her, took her, and lay (with) her, and raped her [way'annehā]." Two things should be noted here. First, the verb "he lay" uses the direct object ('ōtāh) rather than the indirect object ('immāh, "with her") to draw attention to the force used in committing the crime. Caspi notes that to use "with her" would imply permission, such as in the words of Potiphar's wife: "lie with me" (Gen. 39:7), which asked for both consent and willingness ("Story of the Rape," p. 32).

The second thing to note is the word used to describe the rape—'innâ, which means "to humble, defile, rape." It signifies a humbling affliction, even a persecution. This verb was used in Genesis 15:13 in the prediction that Abraham's seed would be afflicted for four hundred years in a foreign land (see Exod. 1:11). Here the text describes the act as a rape, with all its humiliation and violence.

The irony here, however, was that Shechem loved the girl and wanted her for his wife. The text says that he became very attached to the girl (wattidbaq napšô). Here was a strange inversion of the moral teaching on marriage provided in Genesis 2:24, namely, "a man shall leave his father and his mother and shall cleave [wedābaq] to his wife, and they shall become one flesh." By this rape, Shechem had forced the intimacy before the marriage, a clear violation of all moral law. It is probably true also that his love (wayye'ĕhab) was based on the physical desire (cf.

wayye'ĕhab in 25:28). Caspi notes here that the narrator presents the first three main verbs in opposition to the next three:

took	lay	defiled
clave	loved	spoke (kindly)

He explains that the first three verbs serve to justify the anger of the brothers and underline the immorality of Shechem. The second three, then, attempt to soften the grimness of the crime, as if to say that Shechem acted out of wild consuming love (ibid., p. 33).

II. Defilement often excites drastic reactions by those who are zealous but immature—especially when leaders are indiffferent (4–24).

The central portion of the unit develops the responses to the rape. Jacob's response is most unusual: he heard that Dinah had been defiled (*ṭimmē'*), but he kept quiet (*weheḥĕrīš*) until his sons returned. It is hard to understand Jacob's lack of action. (Some commentators [e.g., Bush and Jacob] see his silence as a proper course of wisdom.) Perhaps if it had been Rachel's daughter he might have been more decisive in seeking restitution (after all, he had been willing earlier to sacrifice Leah and her family in favor of Rachel). This initial inactivity seems to indicate a general indecisiveness. In verses 6–8, when Hamor came to speak to Jacob, Hamor had to speak to the sons—they took over the negotiations. Jacob is not heard from again until he protested the violence (v. 30) but was soundly answered by his sons (v. 31). It appears that Jacob was relinquishing his patriarchal leadership.

The sons of Jacob—Dinah's full brothers—were incensed, as one might have expected Jacob to be. The description in verse 7 is worth spending some time with, for it describes the true feelings of those who cared for Dinah and who realized the magnitude of the crime. They were grieved (*wayyit'aṣṣĕbû*) over the crime (cf. Gen. 6:6) and were very angry (*wayyiḥar lāhem me'ōd*) "because he had wrought folly [*nebālâ*] in Israel in lying with Jacob's daughter, which thing ought not to be done" (v. 7). By describing the defilement (*ṭimmē'*) as a folly (*nebālâ*), the text portrays it as a godless act that polluted the family. Such a sexual crime was an infamous deed, a sacrilege incriminating the whole community—it ought not be done. The nation of Israel (note the use of "in Israel" in v. 7) could in no way tolerate such blatant violations of God's moral law. The words of the sons thus put the crime in its true light.

The Canaanites' response was a proposal of intermarriage, apparently trying to make the best of a situation that could become a crisis. Their actions and words betrayed their characters. Shechem was a rather stormy fellow—no savoir-faire. He simply wanted the girl and would pay for her. But this attempt to pay her price only signified to the brothers that he was treating their sister like a prostitute (v. 31). Old Hamor was shrewd. He made a diplomatic speech, promising that great advantages would be gained by both sides of such an agreement to intermarry (vv. 8–10). He said, "You shall dwell with us, and the land shall be before you; dwell and trade in it, and get possessions in it." The land was indeed before them, but God would give it to them, not Hamor. Besides, Hamor had no intention of carrying through this bargain, for he told a different story to his people in Shechem: "Shall not their cattle and their substance and every beast of theirs be ours? Only let us consent to them and they will dwell with us" (v. 23). Hamor was crafty enough to tell each side a different story in order to obtain what he wanted. Clearly, no good could come from entering into covenant with the defiling Canaanites.

The brothers' response to this appeal forms the turning point in the story, for here was set in motion the major deception (mirmâ in v. 13; see also its use in 27:35, where Jacob came before Isaac deceptively). The brothers justified their deception by reasoning that Shechem had defiled (ṭimmēʾ) their sister. Their deceptive response was based on the issue that the Shechemites were not circumcised (ʿorlâ); if they became circumcised (mûl), then they could intermarry and become one people (ʿam ʾeḥād). The sign of circumcision, however, was not to be used in this manner; for the Shechemites it represented no turning to the covenant God in faith. To deceive the Shechemites was one thing; to use the sign of the covenant in the deceit was another matter entirely.

III. Excessive acts of vengeance by believers profane the faith of the covenant community (25–31).

The final scene in this story reports the tragic, yet understandable, outworking of the complication. The brothers not only slaughtered the males of the city while they were healing from their circumcision, they plundered the city for its property, wealth, women, and children. We see from verse 25 that their attack was premeditated: they each took their swords and came upon the city boldly or confidently (beṭaḥ). Thus, the deception was completed: Hamor's appeal to his people that the Israelites were peaceable (šelēmîm, in v. 21) shows how well the deception had worked.

The reason that all the males of the city, whatever number that may have been, were killed in the raid was that all the males of the city were held responsible for the defilement of Dinah (ṭimmeʾû ʾaḥôtām, "they defiled their sister," in v. 27). This guilt may have been deduced by the brothers when the Shechemites took the defilement as a matter of course without any outrage, seeing it only as a means to intermarriage.

The plundering raid that followed the slaughter, however, went far beyond the call of justice for the crime. This incident is comparable to Numbers 31:9–10, which reports the plundering of Midian after the slaughter of Midianite kings. The event recorded here, then, foreshadows the wars of the conquest of Canaan. The irony of the plundering is that those who would have taken over the wealth and assets of Jacob's family by entering into the negotiation through circumcision suddenly were destroyed and plundered, so that their possessions became Israel's (Caspi, "Story of the Rape," p. 41).

The final conversation of the chapter is between Jacob and his sons. Jacob's concern was that his reputation would become a stench in the land and that there might be recriminations from other tribes. This statement is hardly a forceful rebuke of his sons. But Jacob remembered their cruelty when he conferred his blessings (49:5–8). The sons' response, however, forms the culmination of the story, resting the case with the obvious answer to their question, "Should he deal with our sister as with a prostitute [hakzônâ]?" This point reveals that the entire negotiation was a sham, that all along vengeance was in the minds of the sons. Shechem had dealt perversely with Dinah but then compounded the crime by offering to pay for her in a dowry. The story that began with the rape and the shame thus ends with cruel retribution and some restoration of honor.

This story has much to say about defilement, deception, and vengeance. Its message centers on the response of the family to the great crime by Shechem that certainly called for justice. As Kidner says, Jacob and his sons, the appeaser and the avengers, "swayed respectively by fear and fury, were perhaps equidistant from true justice. They exemplify two perennial but sterile reactions to evil" (*Genesis*, p. 174).

The law made it clear that Israel must not play the harlot with Canaanites (Lev. 20:5; Num. 25) nor defile themselves with the abominable Canaanites, neither by intermarriage (Lev. 18:24; Deut. 7:1–5) nor by covenant treaties. Israel's policy called for the complete destruction of the abominable and defiling Canaanite tribes. The people were simply prohibited from amalgamating with those tribes—although individuals who came to faith joined Israel.

But the Israelites were not to use the covenant deceptively in their wars with Canaan, and certainly not here in seeking justice for rape. The covenant was not a ploy to be dangled in deception before the pagans. The sons' instinct for justice was correct, but their methods were ruthless and excessive.

If deception and unbridled violence were incorrect responses, Jacob's reticence to act was equally improper and, in fact, probably incited the sons to act. Unfortunately, Jacob's attitude later reappeared in the nation's tolerance of the Canaanites. On occasion, God would need to use a Simeon and a Levi, or a Jehu, even though they were extreme in their violence.

The expository idea can be worded to reflect these two responses: *When spiritual leaders are indifferent to, and fail to act decisively about pagan defilements, those who are immature may profane the covenant by their misguided zeal.* There are correct and wise ways to respond to evil and worldly defilement, and mature leaders should take the responsibility for acting decisively. Young zealots usually react correctly to evil—but their tactics may profane the covenant faith. Attempting to destroy or punish evil through lawless or unrighteous acts should not be confused with righteous indignation. Rather, the righteous must seek justice and oppose evil in a manner that brings honor to God and his covenant.

Bibliography

Ackroyd, P. R. "The Hebrew Root באש." *JThS* 2 (1951): 31–36.

Caspi, Michael Maswari. "The Story of the Rape of Dinah: The Narrator and the Reader." *Hebrew Studies* 26 (1985): 25–45.

Clements, R. E. "Baal-Berith of Shechem." *JSS* 13 (1968): 21–32.

Fensham, F. C. "Genesis XXXIV and Mari." *JNWSL* 4 (1975): 87–90.

Kessler, M. "Genesis 34—an Interpretation." *RefRev* 19 (1965–66): 3–8.

Kevers, Paul. "Étude littéraire de Genèse XXXIV." *RB* 87 (1980): 38–86.

Porter, J. R. "The Legal Aspects of the Concepts of 'Corporate Personality' in the Old Testament." *VT* 15 (1965): 361–80.

Pummer, Reinhard. "Genesis 34 in Jewish Writings of the Hellenistic and Roman Periods." *HTR* 75 (1982): 177–88.

Pury, Albert de. "Genèse XXXIV et l'histoire." *RB* 76 (1969): 4–49.

Wernberg-Møller, P. "A Note on זור, 'to Stink.' " *VT* 4 (1954): 322–25.

52

The Return to Bethel
(Gen. 35)

For some reason, God's people are susceptible to spiritual declension when they are satisfied or fulfilled in their spiritual quests. When the goal is achieved, perhaps a letdown occurs from the struggle; then a complacency sets in, and vows and commitments are forgotten (see Deut. 8). During such a relaxation it is relatively easy to drift from an earlier zealous commitment to God—and this incipient decay soon shows up in disobedience.

Genesis 35 seems to be speaking of this very problem, which believers in all ages have faced. The chapter is a complex of minor traditions, but it has two themes running through it—*completion* and *correction*. It is a record of completion because Jacob was back in his homeland with all his family and his substance: the victory was won, the goal achieved, and the promise fulfilled. In addition, one generation was drawing to a close as people died—Deborah, Isaac, and Rachel—indicating that a new generation would be coming to the fore. But it is also a story of correction, for the family had not completely maintained the faith. Idols had to be buried. Reuben's sin had to be corrected.

Since each tradition is a distinct unit, literary observations will be discussed in each section.

577

Theological Ideas

There are a few important theological matters that this chapter addresses. First, there is Jacob's vow. The payment of vows was no small matter in Israel, and so God's reminder of Jacob's vow would be instructive. It was a very important vow because it involved the worship of the Lord. Thus, no other gods could be tolerated in his household.

Second, the patriarchal promises figure prominently in the passages. Here the divine names and epithets attested to the confirmation of the promises. And the birth of Benjamin completed the twelve tribes; the listing of the tribes in the completed roster thus forms the final comment on God's promises.

Other theological ideas that surface in the chapter pertain to worship, mourning over deaths, and sin.

Structure and Synthesis

Structure

Most commentators recognize that this chapter is a conclusion to the Jacob stories and contains smaller pieces of different kinds. According to Westermann, however, "One cannot say with H. Gunkel and others that Gen. 35 is a heap of blocks. Rather it follows a carefully conceived plan" (*Genesis*, vol. 2, p. 549). Westermann points out that itinerary and genealogy once again form the framework of the chapter (see chart 28).

Summary Message

Reminded of his commitment, Jacob returned to the land to worship at Bethel, where he received the confirmation of the promises from the Lord and the completion of his family through the birth of Benjamin; but in the process he had to endure the deaths of Deborah, Rachel, and Isaac, as well as the presumptuous sin of Reuben.

Chart 28. Structure of Genesis 35

Journey	Birth and Death
Departure from Shechem (1, 3, 5)	—
Arrival at Bethel (6, 8)	Death of Deborah (8)
Departure from Bethel (16)	—
Stop near Ephrath (16–20)	Birth of Benjamin (16–18)
—	Death and burial of Rachel (19–20)
Departure, stop at Migdal Eder (21)	Sin of Reuben (22a)
—	Sons of Jacob (22b–26)
Arrival at Mamre (27)	Death of Isaac (28–29)

Exegetical Outline

I. In obedience to God's reminder of his unfulfilled vow, Jacob returned to Bethel, where he consecrated his family to worship the Lord and mourned the death of Deborah (1–8).

   A. Jacob obediently traveled to Bethel and worshiped God in recognition of the Lord's appearance at Bethel and in fulfillment of his vow to the Lord (1–7).

      1. God commanded Jacob to return to Bethel and build an altar in commemoration of the appearance there that confirmed the promises (1).

      2. Jacob obediently prepared his household spiritually for the journey (2–4).

      3. God's promised protection allowed Jacob's company to arrive safely at Bethel (5–6).

      4. Jacob built an altar, worshiped God, and acknowledged his blessing (7).

   B. Deborah, Rebekah's nurse, died and was buried outside of Bethel (8).

II. In response to Jacob's compliance, God confirmed the promises of the covenant to him (9–15).

   A. God renewed the patriarchal blessing to Jacob, prompting him to worship (9–13).

      1. God appeared to Jacob and blessed him (9).

      2. God's blessing took the form of renaming him Israel (10).

      3. God promised Jacob the patriarchal blessings—nations and land (11–12).

      4. God went up from the place (13).

   B. Jacob performed a ritual ceremony commemorating the place where God spoke to him (14–15).

      1. He erected a stone pillar and poured a drink offering and oil over it (14).

      2. Jacob called the name of the place Bethel (15).

III. When Jacob returned to the Promised Land, his family was completed with the birth of Benjamin, but he had to endure the deaths of Rachel and Isaac and the sin of Reuben (16–29).

   A. In the land promised to his father, Jacob's final son, Benjamin, was born, but Rachel died in the process (16–21).

      1. After Jacob left Bethel for Hebron, Rachel struggled in childbirth (16–17).

      2. Out of her agony Rachel named her child "son of my trouble," but Jacob named him "son of my right hand" (18).

3. Rachel died and was buried on the way to Ephrath, and Jacob erected a lasting monument to her there (19–21).
B. Reuben attempted to usurp his father's authority by having sexual intercourse with Bilhah, Jacob's concubine (22a).
C. The twelve sons of Israel composed the complete patriarchal ancestry of Israel (22b–26).
D. Jacob returned to Hebron with Esau to bury Isaac (27–29).

Development of the Exposition

It would certainly be possible (and correct) to take individual sections from this chapter for exposition, because they are individual units. But since the narrator has joined them together as a culmination of the Jacob stories, their cumulative effect can be better captured if taken together.

I. God reminds his people of their spiritual commitments (1–7).

The first seven verses record the return to Bethel as the completion of the vows. Even though Jacob had been called by God to return to Bethel (31:3), his compliance was not immediate. In fact, God had to remind Jacob not to delay fulfilling his forgotten vows any longer.

The preparation for completing the vows included a process of purification. Israel's family belonged to the Lord and so they had to make themselves holy before they could worship at his altar. They removed all false idols and buried them. The Lord would permit no rivals and no charms; he demanded single loyalty. All this preparation was solemn for Jacob, and instructive for the nation. Removing false gods (*'ĕlōhê han-nēkār*), becoming clean (*wᵉhiṭṭahărû*), and changing garments (*wᵉha-ḥălîpû śimlōtêkem*) would become necessary steps in consecration when approaching the Lord to worship him.

As the family journeyed toward Bethel, "the terror of God was upon the cities [*wayhî ḥittat 'ĕlōhîm 'al-heʿārîm*]." This protective measure of the Lord ensured his pilgrims a safe journey to the shrine. The reference may be to the previous chapter, in which the Israelites gained a reputation as a warrior tribe.

II. God's people must endure death (8).

On the journey to Bethel, Deborah died. This death, a sorrowful loss for Jacob, was but another indication that this era of the patriarchal period was ending. The naming of the place forms part of the death report, commemorating the event.

Deborah apparently became a follower of Jacob as she had been with

Isaac. This nurse was very old, apparently 180 years old or so at her death. Because of this figure, many biblical scholars suggest that the tradition has been misplaced or that an account of Deborah the judge was mixed up with the patriarchal stories. But there need be no more problem with her age than with Abraham's 175 years, or Isaac's 180.

Deborah was buried at the base of an oak tree (lit. "the oak," as if it was known); the place was called 'allôn bākût, "the oak of weeping." An oak tree was regarded as sacred in the ancient world (Amos 2:9; Hos. 4:13; Gen. 12:6). It was common to designate oaks as shrines, landmarks, or dwelling places. This one was distinguished from others by the qualification "weeping" (< bākâ). It was a memorial for the old nurse. The fact that a tree was named and that the naming was recorded in tradition shows that this person was sorely missed. A long era (two patriarchs) was bridged by her life, and her death reminded the people of the era that ended with the return of Jacob to Bethel.

III. God confirms his people's obedience with his assurance of the promise (9–15).

The third part of this collection of short traditions reports what took place at the next stage of Jacob's pilgrimage. God appeared to Jacob and confirmed the promises made at Bethel. This passage parallels the account in 17:5–8, in which Abram's name was changed to Abraham as a sign of the surety of the promise. The name change to Israel was proof of the promises, and here the promises included nations, royalty, and the land.

The passage also clearly overlaps with 28:18–19, in which Jacob stood up the stone, anointed it with oil, and named the place Bethel. Here, in verse 14, Jacob erected the pillar and poured oil on top of it—once again worshiping God. But the report that he named the place Bethel has posed a bit of a problem for scholarship, especially since it had already been named Bethel in the earlier account. One way to explain the duplication is to say that here Jacob affirmed the naming he had earlier designated. It is not likely that the traditions were mixed or duplicated, for the present narration certainly recognizes the previous experience at Bethel.

IV. In spite of death, God continues to bless his people according to his promises (16–21).

Once in the land at Bethel the family was completed by the birth of Benjamin. Rachel, however, died in childbirth, a fact that raises the question of the possible connection with Jacob's judgment of death upon the one who stole Laban's gods (31:32). At any rate, her death was the second transitional death in the chapter.

The birth of Benjamin, an answer to Rachel's prayer for another son (yōsēp, "may he add," in 30:24), completed the number of the tribes. Some have wondered why Benjamin's birth was in the land, when all the other children were born in Paddan Aram. One interpretation suggests that it means the tribe of Benjamin was already in the land when the Israelite tribes got there (taking the stories as tales about the later periods). Skinner says,

> The birth of Benjamin in Canaan is interpreted by many critics to mean that this tribe, unlike the rest, was formed after the conquest of the country (We. Sta. Guthe, al.): Steuern. goes further, and infers that the rise of Benjamin brought about the dissolution of the Rachel tribe. But all such speculations are precarious. The *name* Benjamin, however, does furnish evidence that this particular tribe *was* formed in Palestine. [*Commentary on Genesis*, p. 427]

According to the story, Rachel named her son Ben-Oni, but Jacob changed it to Benjamin. Ben-Oni (ben-'ônî) means "son of my sorrow." By this name we are to understand that Rachael refused comfort in her affliction—the birth cost her her life. Gunkel thought the name would make better harmony with binyāmîn if the plural were read: ben-'ōnîm, "son of lamentations" or "sighs" (*Genesis*, p. 382). Jacob could then have easily changed the sounds to form the new name, with a far more positive meaning for the new era.

Muilenberg draws on the material from Mari to offer an explanation of the Benjamin traditions ("The Birth of Benjamin," *JBL* 75 [1956]: 194–201). In the Mari documents the banū-yamīna are "southerners" who were rebellious; and Genesis 49 describes Benjamin as a fierce tribe. But the name in the Mari texts (DUMU.MES) could be written in Akkadian either as binū-yamīna or marū-yamīna—in which case the parallel is not so convincing. If the name Benjamin, "son of the right," signified "southerner," it may have been selected because the narrative reports the birth in Canaan and not in Aram Naharaim.

The naming was significant at this time. In contrast to the name of lamentation provided by Rachel in her suffering, Jacob's naming may have signified his sense of freedom from Laban and safe return to the God of Bethel—to the southern land of Canaan, for the completion of the tribes. Moreover, the lesson for Israel would be that the promise of progeny would continue after the nation settled in the land.

V. The evidence of God's blessing cannot be nullified by sin or death in the community (22–29).

The point to be made from this section is that the roster of the sons of Jacob was witness to God's blessing, and these sons in turn were only the first fruits, as it were, of the promise of the nation. Since the section includes reports of sin and death, the list of the tribes is all the more striking—it becomes irrefutable evidence that God's blessings continued in spite of sin and death.

The first part reports Reuben's incest, how he went and lay with Bilhah, his father's concubine. This cryptic note may be far more important than meets the eye. Perhaps Reuben was prematurely attempting to replace his father as the patriarch by some pagan custom of taking over the concubines (cf. Absalom's attempt in 2 Sam. 16:15–23). It was an offense that Jacob took note of and that figured prominently in his final words, when the birthright passed by Reuben (49:3–4).

The final part, following the listing of the tribes, reports the death of Isaac and his burial by Jacob and Esau. This note also marks the end of the tôlᵉdôt section of Isaac—which was predominantly about Jacob. The last sections of the book provide the tôlᵉdôt sections of Esau and Jacob, tracing what became of them.

Genesis 35 brings to an end the full account of the Jacob stories. Jacob appears in the last section of the book, but that portion is essentially concerned with his sons. In this chapter his self-inflicted wanderings had temporarily come to an end. He had returned in peace and prosperity to the land. But in it all he had to be reminded to keep his vow.

In organizing an expository idea of this entire chapter, we shall have to be general, for many ideas are present. There were sad deaths that marked the end of an era, but the promises continued. There was sin that ruined an inheritance, but it could not nullify the obvious blessing of God. And there were forgotten vows, but God ensured that they were kept, and when they were kept he confirmed his promises. The unifying principle of the chapter is the completion of the blessing of God and the compliance with the will of God through purified worship.

Complacency creeps in very easily when people find their lives fulfilled and successful; but there is no room for spiritual complacency in the service of God—especially in a transitional period such as this one. At such times the faith must be revitalized in order that the covenant can be carried forward from generation to generation. At a time when Deborah, Rachel, and Isaac all passed off the scene and Reuben, through sin, relinquished his right to inherit, God called for vows to be kept, idols to be removed, and worship to be purified. For those faithful ones who complied, he completed his promises and confirmed what was yet to be.

God continually calls each generation of believers to rekindle their faith, to revitalize it as if they were in the greatest of spiritual struggles— for they are and dare not let down. Each end is a new beginning, calling for a new commitment. *God's people must fulfill their commitments (that which they have vowed to do in God's program) by spiritual renewal in order that God's promises may be confirmed to them in their journey.* In this idea I would concentrate on the need for keeping spiritual commitments (because death and sin threaten the faith), the manner of fulfilling them (purification and worship), and the results (God's continuing blessing and confirmation of the promises yet to be fulfilled).

Bibliography

Daube, D. "The Night of Death." *HTR* 61 (1968): 629–32.

Fokkelman, J. P. *Narrative Art in Genesis,* pp. 231–36. Assen: Van Gorcum, 1975.

Gevirtz, S. "The Reprimand of Reuben." *JNES* 30 (1971): 87–98.

Keel, O. "Das Vergraben der 'fremden Götter' in Genesis XXXV 4b." *VT* 23 (1973): 305–36.

Nielsen, E. "The Burial of the Foreign Gods." *StTh* 8 (1954–55): 102–22.

Muilenberg, James. "The Birth of Benjamin." *JBL* 75 (1956): 194–201.

Shaanan, J. "And His Father Called Him Benjamin." *BetM* 24 (1978): 106.

Tamisier, R. "L'itinéraire spirituel de Jacob." *BTS* 47 (1962): 4–5.

53

The Extensive Prosperity of the World
(Gen. 36:1–37:1)

This chapter is complicated and difficult, both in its exegesis and in its exposition. In the first place, the structure is difficult: the chapter begins with the heading *tôlᵉdôt* with the name Esau, but then this heading is repeated in verse 9 again with the name Esau, as if a second development was added. These two headings do not seem to match the pattern of the chapter, which has two passages, verses 1–9 and 20–30, each with the order of sons and then chiefs, prefaced to the record of the kings of Edom. These parts break down into sons (vv. 1–14) and chiefs (vv. 15–19), and then again sons (vv. 20–28) and chiefs (vv. 29–30), followed by the kings (vv. 31–39) and then a summary or appendage (vv. 40–43) of eleven other names.

Not only is the organization difficult, the purpose of this chapter has been the subject of much debate. One common view is that it was an Edomite king list that came into the hands of Israel when David conquered the Edomites and that helped Israel administer the conquered land. It was then added to the patriarchal records to extend the narrative about Esau. The expositor will have to sort through the literature in studying this passage to try to determine the chapter's form and function. It is not impossible that the narrative, or most of it, could have been collected and arranged in the organization of Genesis before the time of David's conquest. Centuries passed from the time of Esau until the time of the Israelite conquest of the land, allowing for much of the expansion recorded in the chapter.

But I would not expect too many expositors to devote an entire exposition to this chapter unless they had the luxury of time and could include it in a series of lessons. But there is a poignant lesson in it, not only for Jacob, but also for all recipients of the promise.

The first major part is the tôle̱dôt of Esau (vv. 1–8). According to this section Esau had three (major) wives: Adah, Oholibamah, and Basemath. The names cannot be harmonized with the names of the previous wives (as some think they should). It seems that Esau had several wives, some more important than others (as with Jacob).

From these wives Esau had five sons: Eliphaz from Adah, Reuel from Basemath, and Jeush, Jolam, and Korah from Oholibamah. The narrative stresses two points. First, Esau had all these children in Canaan before he moved to Seir. Second, Esau *is* Edom, a point that the narrator reminds the reader of all through the chapter.

The wording of verse 6 is striking. One can only think of the similarity with Lot: the land was not able to bear them because of their great substance (13:6). Esau thus left for the East and greener land. This great substance was part of God's blessing on Esau (27:39–40).

The second heading occurs in verse 9 but seems to continue the listing of the sons and then the chieftains (vv. 9–19). This is the tôle̱dôt of Esau, the father of the Edomites in Seir. Possibly, once the family moved and settled (or conquered) Seir, a new record was kept with a new starting point, even though it continued the family history of Esau.

The sons of Esau also had sons: six from Eliphaz and four from Reuel. Esau thus had five sons and ten grandsons (either literal grandsons or tribes founded by them). Thirteen (omitting Eliphaz and Reuel) are called chiefs. The terminology speaks of the organization: they are not just sons but heads of tribes ("These were the sons of Esau, who is Edom, and these were their chiefs").

The next section, verses 20–29, lists first the sons of Seir the Horite, the inhabitants of the land, and then the chiefs. The former were the aboriginal Seirites conquered by Esau (Deut. 2:12), which formed part of the Edomite kingdom. Seven sons became chiefs, and from these seven came twenty-one sons and daughters (or tribes). Thus far a picture of Esau as a powerful overlord is emerging. Not only did his own sons become chiefs of clans, but the clans in the land were subjugated to him. And, Esau is Edom.

The fourth part lists the kings of Edom (31–39). There are eight names in this line of kings. It is not certain how the eight were related to Esau, but they were kings in Edom, and Esau is Edom. One could argue that the organization of the clans in Edom must have paralleled that in Israel, developing from the family to tribes, and from tribes to a nation choosing a king from one of the tribes and carrying a line of succession.

The point of this section is comparative: there were kings in Edom "before any king reigned over the Israelites" (v. 31). Apart from the obvious implication of the passage that Esau rapidly became powerful and wealthy, this verse states that he preceded Israel with kingship. This section, and especially this verse, seems most likely to have been written after Israel had a king.

The final section of the chapter adds the list of chiefs who came from Esau, according to their families, after their places, by their names. Eleven names appear here; they seem to be districts (Teman is the only familiar one—out of it came Eliphaz in Job). The section closes with the reminder that these are the chiefs of Edom, and this is Esau, the father of the Edomites (see chart 29).

Esau moved to Seir with his sons and then, with his grandsons, controlled the land, conquering the Horites. It was no wonder that he had four hundred men accompany him to meet Jacob. The passage shows Esau over tribes, kings, and districts. Here was the political structure of the nation. No one could doubt that Esau was flourishing: he dwelt with the fatness of the earth, he lived by the sword, and he shook off the yoke of his brother from his neck (27:39–40).

Chart 29. **Summary of Genesis 36**

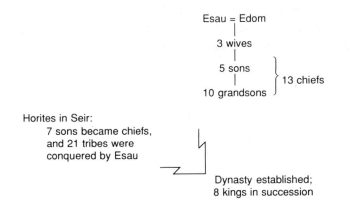

The most important thing for the exegete to note is that 37:1 is part of this section (37:2 is the heading that starts the next section of the book). In contrast to the expanding, powerful Esau, Jacob was dwelling in the land of the sojournings of his father (be᾿ereṣ meɡûrê ᾽ābîw). He had no kings, no full tribes, and no lands to govern. He too was a sojourner. Delitzsch notes poignantly that "secular greatness in general grows up far more rapidly than spiritual greatness" (New Commentary on Genesis, vol. 2, p. 238). The promised spiritual blessing demands patience in faith, and emphasizes that waiting while others prosper is a test of faithfulness and perseverance. Wisdom literature later developed this theme more fully: the unrighteous prosper in worldly power and wealth, while the righteous seem at times to lag behind such prosperity (see Ps. 49; 73). God will give the promised blessings to Jacob's seed, but only after long refining and proving of the faith.

An exposition of this section is thus very workable. It must tie in the blessings made to Esau and to Jacob, beginning in chapter 27. The first half of the exposition would deal with chapter 36, tracing the abounding fulfillment of Esau's promised blessings; the second half would then deal with the transitional note about Jacob in 37:1, showing how the narrator contrasted his lot with that of his brother. The expositional idea that Delitzsch expressed would work nicely for this discussion and could be correlated with the wisdom literature. The point to be made would be encouraging and instructive for those waiting patiently for the fulfillment of the promise.

Bibliography

Bartlett, J. R. "The Edomite King-List of Genesis XXXVI 31–39 and I Chronicles I 43–50." JThS 16 (1965): 301–14.

Beeston, A. F. L. "What Did Anah See?" VT 24 (1974): 109–10.

Driver, G. R. "Gen XXXVI 24: Mules or Fishes." VT 25 (1975): 109–10.

Horowitz, W.J. "Were There Twelve Horite Tribes?" CBQ 35 (1973): 69–71.

5

The Story of Joseph

The story of Joseph forms a unique literary unit in the Book of Genesis. In many ways this section displays a continuity with the preceding narratives about the patriarchs, but in many ways it differs. Biblical scholars have debated the form and the function of this section of the book for some time, and now there is a renewed interest in it as a piece of literature.

Anyone familiar with the story of Joseph can identify its distinctive features rather easily. Within the unit there are three sets of dreams that are symbolic, four sets of parallel relationships (Joseph and his family, Joseph and Potiphar's house, Joseph and the prisoners, Joseph and Pharaoh's household), two episodes in the pit or prison because of false accusation with clothing as the proof, repeated visits of Joseph's brothers to Egypt, and then the settlement of the family in Egypt. In addition to these motifs we have the figure of Joseph himself—righteous, wise, patient, and majestic. Even a casual reading of the story is sufficient to see that it is written differently than the patriarchal narratives.

There are clear links, however, to the preceding patriarchal narratives. The story continues the theme of God's blessing in the births and prosperity in Egypt; and the themes of good and evil come to a firm conclusion in the outworking of this story. The story also develops further the history of the patriarchal family, with its old animosities and its propensity to deceptive practices. Moreover, like the Jacob stories, the Joseph story is constructed around a journey out of the land, which was caused by deception within the family. But unlike Jacob, Joseph's return to the land is not reported in the story; rather, the story ends with a preparation for the exodus narrative. Joseph, like Jacob, endured a twenty-year period of separation from the family and ended it with a reconciliation with his brothers—they came to Egypt, however; he did not return home. Like Esau, the brothers of Joseph exhibited a profound change from their earlier hatred.

As with the preceding narratives, the story of Joseph is archetypal and didactic. It shows that, just as Joseph lived in bondage in Egypt before his deliverance and supremacy over Egypt, so would the nation. Just as suffering and the bondage formed tests for Joseph to see if he kept his faith and was worthy of the promise, so too the bondage of the nation was a means of discipline and preparation for the nation's future responsibilities. Moreover, the climax of the story showed that the Hebrew slave served a God who was infinitely superior to Egypt, who controlled the economy of Egypt, and whose wisdom outstripped the wisdom of Egypt.

This emphasis on wisdom in the story led Gerhard von Rad ("Joseph Narrative"; "Story of Joseph") to treat the material as wisdom literature. He argued that it portrayed the ideal state official, the wise ruler, and so might have been written in the time of Solomon. There are wisdom motifs throughout the Joseph story, which I will analyze more closely unit by unit. Joseph was called a wise and discerning man in Genesis 41:33 and 39, and his life certainly displayed that characteristic. Von Rad drew several parallels to wisdom literature: Joseph feared the Lord more than people (cf. Prov. 1:7; 2:5–9); he gave wise counsel (16:13; 16:21); he avoided the adulterous woman (6:24–29); he was diligent in his preparation when there was plenty (21:5; 24:27); and he did not act out of revenge against his brothers (20:22; 24:29).

Other similarities between this section and wisdom literature include (1) the emphasis on the tension between the suffering of the rightous and the apparent prosperity of the wicked; (2) the emphasis on wisdom as a life of obedience to the Lord's instructions, so that the life is productive; (3) the indirect nature of revelation through symbolic dreams and mystery without direct theophany, showing people the Word of God through events; (4) the emphasis on the Lord as the Creator and Sustainer of life, ordering the universe; (5) the contrast between the righteous and the wicked; (6) the envy and hatred of the righteous by the wicked; and (7) the ultimate blessing of the righteous.

The proposal that the Joseph material is wisdom literature has met with refining criticism. In general, scholars have concluded that von Rad's use of the designation "wisdom" is too general for so many diverse materials. Crenshaw ("Method"), for example, argued against using wisdom as the broad category just because some similarities occur. The point is that several of these motifs characterize other literature as well. But von Rad was not consistent in his treatment of the material, which several scholars have pointed out. For example, Ruppert (*Josepherzählung*) commented that Joseph's ability to interpret dreams is a polemic against Egyptian wisdom, although von Rad said that wisdom literature is nontheological. Von Rad overlooked theological asseverations and the nonwisdom themes. The major criticism of wisdom as the genre classification, however, is the very nature of the Joseph story—it is a short story (see Westermann, *Genesis*, vol. 3, p. 19).

Most modern writers follow Gunkel in classifying the material as a short story or novella. The story begins with Joseph as a boy and ends with his death, so there is the expected continuity. It has the development of a plot through conflict with the brothers that works out in their reconciliation. The story flows with several individual scenes, each with its own exposition, climax, and conclusion. Coats explains that, in contrast to the patriarchal narratives, this section is not a series of independent tales. It uses the Joseph story as the central trunk and then hangs one independent account (the Judah-Tamar story) and two dependent but distinct stories (Jacob's death report and Joseph's death report) onto its framework (*Genesis*, p. 259).

There have been other suggestions for classifying this material—a story of divine guidance, or confrontation literature, or heroic literature. This third classification, proposed by Ryken (*Literature of the Bible*), has some merit to it but is not totally satisfying. Unlike classical heroes, Joseph does not risk everything to perform a heroic act. He functions as a faithful servant of God; it is God who moves through the events to bring deliverance.

In this light Joseph is very much like Daniel. Both men had the wisdom of God, both interpreted the dreams of the king, both were imprisoned for their obedience, and both were made rulers in the land. The similarities demand that the expositor investigate the two in order to determine the significance of the parallels; the similarities need not imply though, that the accounts were written at the same time.

The structure and motifs fit the classification of a short story best (or as Westermann suggests, the family novel). The risk involved in so labeling it is that short stories are usually concerned with the individual and are identified as fiction. Westermann asserts that these distinguishing marks do not hold for the Joseph story:

> At least it is not fiction inasmuch as it tells of people who actually lived
> (R. de Vaux also emphasizes this); nor is it restricted to the individual,

inasmuch as it does not deal with the experiences or fate of Joseph
(though many think so) but of the family of Jacob, for which Joseph
acquires a particular significance. [*Genesis*, vol. 3, p. 25]

If we can think of a short story that is not a fictional piece about an
individual who is at odds with society, then we may use the designation
for the Joseph narratives. They certainly form a self-contained narrative
unit that traces a complete story through to the resolution of its plot.

The classification of the genre is important because it helps us to
understand the literary design of the material. The form of the literature
presents the ideas in a unique way; knowing the features of the literary
type helps the reader understand why things were said or not said in the
development.

Bibliography

Coats, G. W. *From Canaan to Egypt: Structural and Theological Context for
the Joseph Story.* CBQMS 4. Washington: Catholic Biblical Association, 1975.

————— . "The Joseph Story and Wisdom: A Reappraisal." *CBQ* 35 (1973):
285–97.

————— . "Redactional Unity in Genesis 37–50." *JBL* 93 (1974): 15–21.

Crenshaw, J. L. "Method in Determining Wisdom Influence upon 'Historical'
Literature." *JBL* 88 (1969): 129–42.

Fritsch, C. T. " 'God Was with Him': A Theological Study of the Joseph Narrative." *Interp* 9 (1955): 21–34.

Gnuse, Robert Karl. *The Dream Theophany of Samuel: Its Structure in Relation
to Ancient Near Eastern Dreams and Its Theological Significance.* Lanham,
Md.: University Press of America, 1984.

Hubbard, D. A. "The Wisdom Movement and Israel's Covenant Faith." *TynB*
17 (1966): 3–33.

Janssen, M. A. "Egyptological Remarks on the Story of Joseph in Genesis."
JEOL 14 (1955–56): 63–72.

Loader, J. A. "Chokma—Joseph—Hybris," *OTWSA* 17–18 (1974–75): 21–31.

Lowenthal, E. I. *The Joseph Narrative in Genesis.* New York: Ktav, 1973.

Miscall, P. D. "The Jacob and Joseph Stories as Analogues." *JSOT* 6 (1978): 28–
40.

Rad, Gerhard von. "The Joseph Narrative and Ancient Wisdom." In *Problems
of the Hexateuch and Other Essays*, translated by E. W. Trueman Dicken,
pp. 292–300. New York: McGraw-Hill, 1966.

————— . "The Story of Joseph." In *God at Work in Israel*, translated by
John H. Marks, pp. 19–35. Nashville: Abingdon, 1974.

Redford, Donald. *A Study of the Biblical Story of Joseph (Genesis 37–50)*. VTS 20. Leiden: E. J. Brill, 1970.

Richard, E. "The Polemic Character of the Joseph Episode in Acts 7." *JBL* 98 (1979): 255–67.

Ruppert, Lothar. *Die Josepherzählung: Ein Beitrag zur Theologie der Pentateuchquellen*. Munich: Kösel, 1965.

Ryken, Leland. *The Literature of the Bible*. Grand Rapids: Zondervan, 1974.

Savage, M. "The Literary Nature of the Joseph Story." In *Scripture in Context: Essays on the Comparative Method*, edited by C. D. Evans, W. W. Hallo, and J. B. White, pp. 79–100. Pittsburgh: Pickwick, 1986.

Seybold, D. A. "Paradox and Symmetry in the Joseph Narrative." In *Literary Interpretations of Biblical Narratives*, edited by Kenneth R. R. Gros Louis, with James S. Ackerman and Thayer S. Warshaw, pp. 59–73. Nashville: Abingdon, 1974.

Vergote, Josef. *Joseph en Égypte: Genèse chap. 37–50. A la lumière des études égyptologiques récentes*. Louvain: Publications Universitaires, 1959.

Ward, W. A. "The Egyptian Office of Joseph." *JSS* 5 (1960): 144–50.

White, Hugh C. "The Joseph Story: A Narrative Which 'Consumes' Its Content." *Semeia* 31 (1985): 49–70.

Whybray, Roger. "The Joseph Story and Pentateuchal Criticism." *VT* 18 (1968): 522–28.

Williams, James G. "Number Symbolism and Joseph as Symbol of Completion." *JBL* 98 (1979): 86–87.

54

The Sovereign Choice of the Wise Leader
(Gen. 37:2–11)

Genesis 37 provides the introduction to the Joseph story in that it lays the foundation for the crisis between Joseph and his brothers and foreshadows through the dreams the final resolution to the crisis. The whole chapter can be divided into three scenes, the first (vv. 2–11) and the third (vv. 31–35) taking place in the father's house, and the second (vv. 12–30) taking place in the field. While it would be possible to treat the entire chapter in one exposition (including the choice of Joseph and then his rejection), there is sufficient material for two expositions. The first scene, the subject of this exposition, traces the growing estrangement between Joseph and his brothers, caused by the father's love and the Lord's choice of Joseph.

The report of Joseph's dreams forms the divine call of Joseph, his choice by God to lead the nation. The immediate effect of this choice was hatred by his brothers. The expositor can readily see the paradigm in this scene of the story: when God chooses someone to lead, there may be envy and hatred in those who may feel more qualified to have that position of leadership. The chosen must give no one occasion to find fault.

Theological Ideas

The major theological idea of this first scene is revelation through dreams. God confirmed through two dreams that Joseph would rule over his brothers. The expositor will have to study the significance of dreams in the ancient Near East, and especially in revelation from God. Here it must be noted that the dreams of Joseph differ from other dreams in God's revelation; previously in Genesis, dreams included verbal communication, but now there were only symbols that needed interpretation. It appears that symbolic dreams were chosen because through them the wisdom of Joseph could surpass the wisdom of Egypt.

The unit also portrays human nature in response to the divine revelation. Jealousy welled up in the brothers over the choice of Joseph, a jealousy that later turned into murderous hatred. Joseph seemed rather oblivious to it all; he simply served his father faithfully, bringing back an evil report about his brothers. Biblical teachings on faithfulness in the midst of envy and hatred find their beginnings here.

Structure and Synthesis

Structure

After the heading for the final section of Genesis ("these are the generations of Jacob"), the attention turns to Joseph. The first scene has two parts: Jacob's love for Joseph (vv. 2b–4) and Joseph's dreams (vv. 5–11). The motif that ties these two parts together is the report of the brothers' hatred for Joseph (vv. 4–5, 8).

The first part includes a narrative report of Joseph's faithfulness to his father and then parenthetical information about Jacob's love for Joseph and his brothers' hatred. The second part has two dream reports that are parallel in their construction: an introduction to the dream, a dream speech, a speech in response to the dream report, and a final narration of the consequences of the report. Both dream speeches use the particle *hinnēh*, a typical form for reporting dreams.

Summary Message

When Joseph faithfully brought back the bad report about his brothers, his father demonstrated his love for this son of his old age by giving him preferential treatment, but his brothers hated him; and when the Lord confirmed Joseph's selection for leadership through two dreams, his father was perplexed, but his brothers hated him all the more.

Exegetical Outline

Title: These are the generations of Jacob (2a).

    I. Joseph, while tending the family flock with his brothers, brought back an evil report about their activity, for which he enjoyed preferential treatment from his father but endured hatred from his brothers (2b–4).

A. While tending the family flock as a youth, Joseph had occasion to bring back a report of his brothers' evil activities (2b).

B. Israel loved Joseph and gave him preferential treatment, but his brothers hated him (3–4).

   1. Jacob loved Joseph more than the others and gave him a multicolored tunic (3).

   2. Joseph's brothers hated him because they were jealous of the favoritism shown by their father (4).

II. Joseph reported two dreams that symbolically revealed he would rise to prominence over his family, causing his father to rebuke him and his brothers to hate him all the more (5–11).

A. First dream: Joseph reported having a dream that symbolically (using sheaves) foretold his rise to prominence (5–8).

   1. Introduction: Joseph dreamed a dream and told his brothers (5).

   2. Dream speech: Joseph explained the dream to his brothers (6–7).

   3. Response: His brothers asked him if he would rule over them (8a).

   4. Consequences: His brothers hated him more (8b).

B. Second dream: Joseph reported another dream that reiterated symbolically (using sun, moon, and stars) that he would rise to prominence over his family (9–11).

   1. Introduction: Joseph dreamed again and told his brothers (9a).

   2. Dream speech: Joseph explained his dream to his brothers (9b–10a).

   3. Response: His father rebuked him (10b).

   4. Consequences: His brothers envied him, but his father pondered it (11).

Development of the Exposition

I. Those who are faithful in their service will find favor from their master but hatred from individuals who are unfaithful (2–4).

The beginning of the story portrays Joseph as a faithful son among unfaithful sons. While keeping his father's flocks with some of his breth-

ren, Joseph had occasion to bring back an evil report (*'et-dibbātām rāʿâ*).
This information requires careful explanation. Grammatically, the suffix
-ām must mean that the report was about the brothers, and the adjective
"evil" (one of the important themes in Genesis) modifies this report—
he brought back a report of their evil deeds. This verse provides the first
glimpse of the evil activity of Joseph's brothers; before the story gets
very far, their evil will be turned on him.

A report such as Joseph gave about his brothers' activities, whatever
they were, has never been considered the popular thing to do. It opens
up the one who gives it to charges of being a tattletale from those who
would take evil lightly. In fact the incident shows that Joseph was faithful to his father. Those who would be leaders must prove faithful in the
smaller responsibilities. The story holds up this trait of Joseph's as
exemplary.

In a parenthetical clause—not unrelated to Joseph's act of faithfulness—the text explains that Jacob loved (*'āhab*) Joseph more than all
his children because he was the son of his old age. That he was Rachel's
son, and that he was faithful to Jacob as verse 2 indicated, greatly enhanced this love. But we cannot ignore the parallel between this report
in 37:3 and the one in 25:28. At the beginning of the *tôlᵉdôt* of Isaac we
learned of the father's greater love for one of his sons and of the subsequent discord between the sons that eventually led to deception and the
flight of Jacob; and at the beginning of the *tôlᵉdôt* of Jacob we discover
the father's greater love for one of his sons and the subsequent envy and
hatred that led to deception and the disappearance of Joseph.

The love of the father was expressed in this episode by Jacob's giving
his son a distinctive tunic. The traditional idea of "a coat of many colors"
may not be what the text means. It probably describes a sleeved coat
that reached to the wrists and ankles (cf. the apparel of a princess in
2 Sam. 13:18). Far more than being a nice gift, this tunic set Joseph apart
from the brothers as the favored one, probably indicating that he would
receive the inheritance (i.e., the leadership and the double portion). Joseph was Rachel's son after all, the son of the wife that Jacob had chosen
before being deceived by Laban, and the son of his old age.

But Jacob should have remembered from his own childhood as well
as from his early marriage days what a display of favoritism would do
to a family. It had separated him from his mother, and it would separate
Joseph from him. He probably could not avoid feelings of favoritism—
especially in a family like this one; but to display those feelings in this
way was naive.

Predictably, the brothers "hated him [*wayyiśnᵉʾû ʾōtô*]" and could not
speak peaceably to him [*wᵉlōʾ yākᵉlû dabbᵉrô lᵉšālōm*]." The reader
must appreciate the narrator's understanding of human nature; they

hated Joseph, not his father. Those who are envious often turn their hatred on the one favored, not on the one who showed favoritism. Likewise in the Cain and Abel story, Cain attacked Abel, not God (see further, Westermann, *Genesis*, vol. 3, p. 37). To capture the significance of this animosity, a study of the verbs "to love" (*'āhab*) and "to hate" (*śānē'*) is essential. They describe active emotions, choosing and rejecting, and responding favorably to and acting in hostility against.

Bush analyzed the relations as follows:

> *They hated him.* This result showed that Jacob acted unwisely in distinguishing Joseph from his brethren by this mark of his regard. It seemed to be a palpable, invidious, and premature taking away of the birth-right from Reuben and giving it to the first-born of his beloved wife. The birth-right was indeed to be Joseph's; and it was due to him as the eldest son of Rachel, when the first-born son of Leah had forfeited it. But, as might have been expected, Joseph was at once exposed to the envy of his brethren by this mark of his father's fondness; and the effects of that envy cost the good old man many years of pungent affliction. [Notes, p. 223]

The hostility in the brothers' hatred is amplified by the notice that they could not speak peaceably to him. Here was the first noticeable disruption of the peaceful existence the family now enjoyed. Probably they could not now even greet their brother in a civil fashion. Verses 19 and 20 of this chapter record the bitterness they exuded when they merely spoke about their brother.

Immediately the story opens a rift between Joseph and his brothers. They were evil, and he was faithful; he was favored, and they were not. Their intense hatred soon found expression in destructive action.

II. The Lord will use the one who is faithful in little things to have authority over greater responsibilities (5–11).

The second part of the passage poses a greater difficulty for the expositor because the ideas in the text must be transferred to an applicable level. It simply will not work to remain on the literal level of the story and make some observations about God's revelation in dreams. In wording the point from these verses, I have thus concentrated on the meaning of the revelation rather than the method.

Through these dreams God confirmed Jacob's choice of his faithful son to be the leader. In a dream with both symbolism and verbal communication, the Lord had informed Abraham of the sojourn in Egypt; in a dream the Lord had promised Jacob protection and prosperity with Laban in Paddan Aram; in a dream God spoke to Laban and kept him from harming Jacob; and so here too God used dreams to predict the rule of Joseph over his family. In all these passages the recipients were either Israelites about to sojourn in gentile lands or non-Israelites themselves. Dreams apparently were highly regarded as of divine origin in the ancient world.

Here the dreams were symbolic. They both carried the same message—the first introduced the important revelation, the second merely reiterated it. Joseph in his boyish naiveté reported the dreams to his family, and they, fully understanding their import, reacted as might be expected under the circumstances.

The first dream had an agricultural symbolism, possibly anticipating the manner by which Joseph would come to power in Egypt. The second dream involved celestial images—the sun, moon, and stars being easily recognized for their significance for rulership. These dreams symbolically represented the exaltation of Joseph over his whole family (who, incidentally, would also have positions of authority, as the symbol of stars signified—but they missed that point when they saw only the supremacy of Joseph.) The key idea in the dream is the explanation that their symbols bowed down to his, showing an act of submission and obeisance (wattištaḥăweynā and mištaḥăwîm; see 43:26, which says "they bowed themselves to him to the earth").

In response to these dream reports, the brothers hated him all the more (vv. 5 and 8) and envied him (wayqan'û, in v. 11), questioning his audacity to suggest that he would actually rule over them. Their interpretation of the dreams was correct, and their scoffing was forcefully displayed: "Will you indeed rule over us?" (or better, "You don't mean to tell us that you will rule over us, do you?") The infinitive absolute in the question heightens the doubt (hămālōk timlōk ʿālênû). This construction is then repeated, but with a different verb: "or will you indeed have dominion over us?" ('im-māšôl timšōl bānû, the particle 'im here being the interrogative particle).

They understood perfectly. A younger brother would rule over the rest. The question of who should rule, especially among brothers or equals, is a troubling matter at any time, but frequently so in ancient Israel (see, e.g., the parable in Judg. 9:9–15 and then the subsequent struggles for rulership in the monarchy). This choice of Joseph marked a change from the normal societal order but did not differ from previous narratives in which the younger son was made lord over his older brother.

Jacob's response to the dream was more tempered. At first he reacted strongly, rebuking (gāʿar) his son, but then he observed (šāmar) the saying. Surely Jacob must have seen the repetition of his own beginnings in the beginnings of Joseph's career. Surely he knew for a fact that God would select the younger over the older and could declare his choice in advance whether by an oracle (25:23) or by a dream.

The story of Joseph begins by unfolding the grand theme (Joseph would be elevated to rule over his brothers) and the major tension (his brothers' growing hatred of him). Their reaction of envy and hatred is understandable; yet, placed in contrast to Joseph's faithfulness and honesty, demonstrates why they were not chosen. The first scene of the Joseph story, then, relates how God sovereignly selected his future leader and how that choice brought out the envy of those who would have to submit. Rather than recognize God's apparent choice through their father and through the divine revelation, the brothers set themselves on a course in which they would eventually try to destroy him. There is no place in leadership for such uncontrollable hatred and envy, but leaders often must face such opposition.

The lesson is timeless: *God will choose a faithful, righteous person for a position of leadership in spite of the jealousy of others.* This statement could be turned the other way as well: *Those whom God chooses for positions of leadership may encounter jealous hatred from others.* The one who would be a leader must be faithful in discharging the duties at hand, no matter what hatred this faithfulness brings. God, and those who are spiritually mature, will honor it. And those who are called to submit to others, even though they might feel more qualified to lead, must not let their jealousy turn to cruel hatred. Even in Christianity the call to submit to others is not a popular teaching.

Bibliography

Brown, J. P. "Peace Symbolism in Ancient Military Vocabulary." *VT* 21 (1971): 1–23.

Brueggemann, Walter. "Life and Death in Tenth Century Israel." *JAAR* 40 (1972): 96–109.

Coats, G. W. "Self-Abasement and Insult Formulas." *JBL* 89 (1970): 14–26.

Fensham, F. C. "A Cappadocian Parallel to Hebrew *KUTŌNET.*" *VT* 12 (1962): 196–98.

Finkel, A. "The Pesher of Dreams and Scriptures." *RevQ* 4 (1963–64): 357–70.

Gevirtz, S. "Of Patriarchs and Puns: Joseph at the Fountain, Jacob at the Ford." *HUCA* 46 (1975): 33–54.

Gnuse, Robert Karl. "Dreams in the Biblical Tradition." In *The Dream Theophany of Samuel,* pp. 57–118 (esp. pp. 88–100). Lanham, Md.: University of America Press, 1984.

Grintz, Y. M. "Potifar—the Chief Cook." *Lesbonenu* 30 (1965): 12–15.

MacIntosh, A. A. "A Consideration of Hebrew גער." *VT* 19 (1969): 471–79.

Oppenheim, A. L. "The Interpretation of Dreams in the Ancient Near East." *TAPhs* 46 (1956): 179–373.

Peck, W. J. "Note on Genesis 37:2 and Joseph's Character." *ExT* 82 (1970–71): 342–43.

Reif, S. C. "A Note on גער." *VT* 21 (1971): 241–44.

Zeitlin, S. "Dreams and Their Interpretation from the Biblical Period to the Tannaitic Time: An Historical Study." *JQR* 66 (1975): 1–18.

55

The Selling of the Chosen into Bondage
(Gen. 37:12–36)

While the previous section showed how people envy the faithful chosen servant of the Lord, this section reveals the fruit of that hatred and envy if left unchecked—the brothers tried to get rid of Joseph. It is the Cain and Abel story all over again. For all practical considerations, the brothers did destroy Joseph, for they believed they finally got rid of him. And they did their best to convince Jacob that his son was dead. Their action shows that they did not accept God's choice of Joseph; their envy and hatred were so strong that they thought only to put an end to his dreams in the quickest way possible.

Two motifs run through this part of the story—the obedience of Joseph and the hatred of the brothers. The brothers' statement, "Let's see what becomes of his dreams," actually expresses the nature of Joseph's first test. What would happen to Joseph's faith in the dreams when those over whom he was to rule sold him into slavery? Would he despair over the loss of his destiny, or would he remain faithful to God who had chosen him?

Theological Ideas

The dominant ideas in this section deal more with human nature than with theology proper. On the one hand, we have a sample of the suffering of the righteous at the hands of the wicked; on the other hand, we see the results of unchecked hatred and jealousy. Moreover, the brothers' deception of the old patriarch once again brought pain to one who was no stranger to deception. The predominant theological idea, then, would be evil, both its employment and its effects. It is ironic that twice in the chapter the treachery was blamed on an evil beast (ḥayyâ rāʿâ).

Structure and Synthesis

Structure

This part of the story of Joseph unfolds in several small scenes that work together to develop the crisis. In each step the participants and speakers differ (see chart 30).

The actions of the family are framed by the verb "to send" (šālaḥ)—Jacob sent Joseph to his brothers, and they sent his bloodied coat back to him. In between are the details of the movement from one sending to the other; the critical point comes when the brothers debated which blood they should have to account for. By selling Joseph they were free from having to cover his blood and instead could simply use the blood of a goat. The unit ends with a transitional report of another sale, this time to Potiphar in Egypt.

Chart 30. **Literary Movement in Genesis 37:12–36**

Participants	Action
Israel and Joseph (12–14)	Israel sent (šālaḥ) Joseph to inquire of his brothers' welfare (šālôm).
Joseph and a man (15–17)	Joseph required help from a certain man in order to locate his brothers.
The brothers and Reuben (18–22)	The brothers conspired to kill Joseph, but Reuben delivered him by warning them not to lay (šālaḥ) a hand on him or shed blood (dām).
Joseph and his brothers, Judah and the Ishmaelites (23–28)	The brothers threw (šālak) Joseph into a pit. Judah advised them to sell him to the Ishmaelites rather than slay him and conceal blood (dām).
Reuben and the brothers, the brothers and Jacob (29–35)	When Joseph was sold, Reuben became anxious and tore (qāraʿ) his garments; the brothers dipped the coat in blood (dām) and sent it to their father; Jacob tore (qāraʿ) his garments and mourned.
Midianites and Potiphar (36)	The Midianites sold (mākar) him to Potiphar.

Summary Mesage

When Jacob sent Joseph to check on the welfare of his brothers, his brothers plotted to kill him and end his dreams but decided rather to sell him and deceive their father into thinking an evil beast devoured him; in spite of the painful success of their plan, however, Joseph was alive and well in Egypt.

Exegetical Outline

I. Joseph, in obedience to Israel's request, went to inquire of the welfare of his brothers in Shechem and, with the help of a certain man, found them in Dothan (12–17).

   A. Israel sent Joseph to Shechem to see about the welfare of his brothers and their flocks (12–14a).

   B. Joseph obediently traveled to Shechem and, with the help of a man, was able to trace them to Dothan (14b–17).

II. Joseph's brothers conspired to kill him when they saw him coming but ended up selling him into slavery instead at the advice of Judah (18–28).

   A. Joseph's brothers plotted to kill him to end his dreams (18–20).

      1. They conspired to kill him when they saw him coming (18).

      2. They planned to say an evil beast devoured him—and then would see what became of his dreams (19–20).

   B. Reuben urged his brothers not to kill Joseph, for practical and personal reasons (21–22).

      1. Reuben urged his brothers not to lay a hand on him or shed his blood (21).

      2. Reuben urged them not to kill Joseph, because he was planning to deliver his brother (22).

   C. Joseph's brothers stripped him and threw him into an empty cistern but then, at the advice of Judah, sold him to some Midianites who were going down to Egypt (23–28).

      1. Joseph suffered at the hands of his brothers, who stripped him and threw him into an empty cistern (23–24).

      2. Judah urged his brothers to sell Joseph for profit when Ishmaelite traders passed by their camp (25–27).

      3. Joseph again suffered at the hands of his brothers as they sold him into Egypt (28).

III. Jacob and his entire family suffered as a result of the deeds and the deception of the brothers (29–35).

   A. Reuben returned to the cistern and grieved when he failed to find Joseph there (29–30).

  B. Joseph's brothers succeeded in deceiving Jacob into believing
   that Joseph was dead (31–33).
    1. Joseph's brothers prepared his tunic by dipping it in blood
     in order to deceive their father (31–32).
    2. Jacob was deceived into believing that Joseph was de-
     voured by some evil beast (33).
  C. Jacob mourned the loss of Joseph and refused to be comforted by his family (34–35).
 IV. Epilogue: Joseph was sold to Potiphar in Egypt (36).

Development of the Exposition

The story progresses from the *faithfulness* of Joseph (vv. 12–17), to
the *treachery* of the brothers (vv. 18–28), to the *deception* of the brothers
(vv. 29–35), to the epilogue about Joseph's *well-being* (v. 36). Since
the thrust of the passage is on the evil of the brothers, I would join the
first two sections, contrasting Joseph's faithfulness with the brothers'
treachery.

I. Obedient servants who faithfully keep their charge may suffer persecution from those who are disobedient (12–28).

A. *Faithfulness (12–17).*

The first section provides the setting for the treachery. Israel naively
decided to send Joseph to Shechem to see if all was well (*šālôm*) with
his brothers. It should be noted that this incident parallels the beginning
of the preceding unit, in which Joseph brought back a report of his
brothers (37:2). Perhaps the evil report of the earlier mission prompted
Jacob to send Joseph on this one.

The repetition of the word "welfare" (*šālôm*) in the wording of this
commission provides an ominous link to the preceding section. Joseph
was sent to see about their welfare (*šālôm*), but they hated him so much
that they were not able to speak "peaceably" (*lᵉšālôm*, in v. 4) with him.
The mission seemed doomed from the start.

Joseph went in obedience to his father's commission (*šālaḥ* is used
twice to stress that he was sent). Obedience was the mark of Joseph, no
matter what prospects lay ahead of him. In contrast to other commission
speeches, Joseph offered no objections at all (cf. Exod. 3:11).

The few verses that report the meeting of the man in Shechem who
directed him to Dothan are a bit perplexing. This interlude has a brief
exposition (v. 15a), an exchange of speeches (vv. 15b–17a), and then the
resolution (v. 17b). Joseph must have said more to the man than the text
records. As B. Jacob notes, "The Bible has him speak with moving am-

biguity, *I am seeking my brothers!* A sentence which reflects the soul of Joseph and of the whole story" (*First Book of the Bible,*, p. 253).

This incident retards the progress of the narrative, showing further diligence on the part of Joseph to find his brothers—who were not where they were supposed to be—and bring back the report to his father. Perhaps this section was designed to show how helpless Joseph was away from his father—he was wandering in a field. And then, when he found his brothers, he was twelve miles farther away from his father.

B. *Treachery (18–28).*

The text moves quickly to the plot of the brothers to prevent Joseph's dreams from being fulfilled. The crisis is somewhat similar to the plans of Isaac to give the blessing to the one who did not figure in God's plan (27:2–4). This crisis was far more serious, however, for, rather than attempt to channel the blessing to the wrong person, the participants planned to destroy the brother to whom it apparently belonged.

The words of the initial plan are worth noting in some detail (vv. 19–20). The speech begins and ends with a contemptuous reference to the dreams: "Look, here comes this dreamer [ba'al haḥălōmôt]" and "we shall see what will become of his dreams [ḥălōmōtāyw]." The plan was to slay him (hārag) and throw him (šālak) into some pit and then to lie about their crime: "An evil beast [ḥayyâ rā'â] has devoured him." Except for the slaying of Joseph, this plan was carried out.

The plan was changed by Reuben, who was hoping to deliver (haṣṣîl, in v. 22) Joseph to his father. Was Reuben hoping to regain favor after his folly with his father's concubines? Whatever his motives were, his speech was a commendable corrective of the brothers' plan. He exhorted them not to kill the lad: "Do not shed blood [tišpᵉkû-dām], cast [hašlîkû] him into this pit which is the wilderness, but lay no hand on him [wᵉyād 'al-tišlᵉḥû-bô]." The speech is made memorable by the repetition of sounds between the verbs: šāpak, šālak, and šālaḥ.

The advice was accepted. The brothers stripped Joseph of the tunic his father had given him and threw him into the empty pit. Remarkably, the brothers then sat down "to eat bread." It is ironic that they had planned to say that an evil beast had devoured Joseph ('ăkālātᵉhû < ' ākal, in v. 20), and after they attacked him, they sat down to eat (le'ĕkol < 'ākal, in v. 25). The text thus signifies what evil beasts attacked Joseph.

But then a new plan came to the brothers' attention, thanks to Judah. His speech, the third of the brothers' decisions, called for the sale of Joseph. He asked, "What profit [beṣa'] is it if we slay our brother ['āḥînû] and conceal his blood?" With this first sign that they acknowledged Joseph as their brother came another, more convincing recognition of

the kinship: "He is our brother and our flesh [kî-'āḥînû beśārēnû]."
Although this speech was designed to lessen their crime by selling their
brother rather than murdering him, it ultimately underscored how wicked
their deed was—they sold their brother, their own flesh and blood.

Joseph was thus treated harshly by his brothers but was preserved
alive. The text passes over his suffering, concentrating on the brothers'
wickedness. They all were involved in the crime, even Reuben and Judah. They were all in opposition to the divine plan. The narrator later
introduces the motif of Joseph's pleas for mercy from this empty cistern
(42:21).

II. Those who would destroy the righteous find it necessary to deceive others about their sin but succeed only in causing grief (29–35).

A. Deception (29–32).

The plan of the sons to say that an evil beast devoured Joseph had to
be carried out, once Reuben discovered that they had sold the lad. His
initial response was anxiety—he tore his clothes (wayyiqraʿ 'et-begā-
dāyw) and lamented his dilemma. Apparently as the oldest of the brothers a certain amount of responsibility lay with him; more important,
though, his plan to deliver Joseph had been foiled. All that was left now
was to deceive the father.

The theme of deception thus appears once again in the family traditions: the deceiver (Jacob) was being deceived by his sons. Ironically, his
sons dipped Joseph's tunic in the blood of a "kid of the goats" (śeʿîr
ʿizzîm) to deceive the father into thinking that Joseph was dead. It was
with two kids of the goats (ʿizzîm) that Jacob deceived his father Isaac
(27:9).

The brothers "sent" (wayšalleḥû answers the initial commission of
Joseph, who was "sent" to them [vv. 13–14]) the garment to their father
and brought it in to him with a degree of callousness that could come
only from their hatred: "This have we found [māṣā'nû; cf. wayyimṣā'ēm
in v. 17]; recognize [hakker-nā'] now whether it be your son's [binkā]
tunic or not." No longer do they speak of their brother or their flesh; it
is now "your son."

B. Grief (33–35).

The response of Jacob was predictable — he recognized it
(wayyakkîrāh). His conclusion was exactly what they had conspired to
promote, perhaps under their prompting. Jacob concluded that an evil
beast (ḥayyâ rāʿâ) devoured Joseph—"Joseph was undoubtedly torn in
pieces [ṭārōp ṭōrap yôsēp]." The repetition and the construction suggest

that this outburst was a form of a lament. The text affirms such a conclusion: "And Jacob tore [wayyiqra'] his clothes" (v. 34). Jacob's cry of lament forms the low point of the Joseph story; from here on there could only be healing and reconciliation.

It is interesting to observe the extent of Jacob's mourning for Joseph, how he refused to be comforted (waymā'ēn lᵉhitnaḥēm), resigning himself to go to his grave in mourning over Joseph. One recalls how, after Isaac was deceived by Jacob, Esau sought to console himself (mitnaḥēm) by planning to kill (hārag) Jacob, the deceiver (27:42). This episode, even though sad for Jacob, is another example of reaping what was sown. A family that so easily deceives to win their way cannot hope for anything but pain and grief. The brothers succeeded in their plan—they got rid of Joseph. But they also succeeded in causing inconsolable grief and bitter pain in the family.

III. In spite of the persecution and the deception, God's program will continue (36).

The final verse of the chapter is short but critical. It reports that Joseph was sold into Egypt and was with Potiphar. He was not an ordinary field slave but had already entered a place of higher responsibility. The verse stands in remarkable contrast to the grief in Hebron and to the brothers' attempts to destroy him and end his dreams.

This chapter in the story of Joseph is one of treachery and deception; it centers on Joseph, the faithful son, but is essentially about the brothers, who sought to rid themselves of the favored son and perhaps open the way for a better status for themselves. But the blessing does not go to such as do these things. Moreover, God's choice of a leader cannot be so easily altered.

The message could be worded either from the perspective of the righteous who suffer or from the perspective of the envious brothers. Since it is all the story of Joseph, the expositor would do well to make him the focal point. The unit teaches that God's faithful servant may suffer devastating persecution from those who hate him or her, who deceive others about their persecution, and whose evil deeds cause great grief, but will survive to fulfill his or her destiny in God's program. In short, *those who faithfully serve their master often must endure grievous persecution but cannot be prevented from fulfilling their God-given destiny.* In this chapter the destiny was revealed through the dreams; when the brothers sought to kill Joseph and see what became of his dreamed destiny, a strange set of circumstances and voices of moderation worked to deliver Joseph alive to Egypt, where he eventually fulfilled this destiny. Far from preventing Joseph's dream, the brothers actually became the agents of fulfilling it.

In the New Testament Paul catalogued the persecutions and sufferings that he had to endure in his service for God (2 Cor. 4:7–18). In all his trials and tribulations, he did not lose heart, because he kept his sight on the goal that was set before him—as must every believer who desires to fulfill God's will (see Rom. 8:31). In spite of envy, hatred, and even persecution from others, the spiritual leader can rest assured that, if God has chosen him or her for a task, no amount of opposition can nullify that destiny. Rather, God may use the opposition in working out his will.

Bibliography

Brown, J. P. "Peace Symbolism in Ancient Military Vocabulary." *VT* 21 (1971): 1–23.

Coats, G. W. "Self-Abasement and Insult Formulas." *JBL* 89 (1970): 14–26.

Gevirtz, S. "Of Patriarchs and Puns: Joseph at the Fountain, Jacob at the Ford." *HUCA* 46 (1975): 33–54.

Grintz, Y. M. "Potifar—the Chief Cook." *Lĕšonénu* 30 (1965): 12–15.

Winnett, F. V. "A Brief Comment on Genesis 37:32." *BCSBS* 12 (1947): 13.

56

The Triumph of a Just Cause in a Corrupt Family
(Gen. 38)

This bizarre episode seems to intrude upon the story of Joseph, slowing the pace of that story considerably. It is a self-contained family narrative that deals with a case of family law. At issue is the distressing case of childlessness, which is common in patriarchal narratives, but in this case the young woman is a childless widow. The story has been inserted here because it forms part of the account of Jacob's family (note "these are the *tôlᵉdôt* of Jacob" in 37:2). In chapter 37, Joseph was a mere youth; but when Joseph brought his family down to Egypt (chap. 46), the sons of Tamar were included. There is no other place that this narrative would fit quite so well. Moreover, the chapter has a general similarity to the Joseph story, shares a common motif in that both Jacob and Judah are deceived and subsequently forced to give recognition to a piece of evidence, and shares certain vocabulary phrases with the Joseph story (see Donald Redford, *A Study of the Biblical Story of Joseph (Genesis 37–50)* [Leiden: E. J. Brill, 1970], pp. 17–18).

The tradition about Tamar and Judah may have served another purpose apart from its purpose within the Joseph story, for it does explain

611

developments within the tribal organization of Judah. This tradition accounted for the origin of the three principal clans of Judah by the story
of the struggle of Tamar to be mother in Judah and the struggle of Perez
to gain the precedence over his brother. Set in the formative days of the
tribe, the narrative would seek to explain Judah's isolation from the
other tribes and her amalgamation with Canaanites, the extinction of
the oldest branches of the tribe, and the rivalry of its youngest branches
(Skinner, *Commentary on Genesis*, p. 449). The tradition thus records
the beginnings of Judah's tribal history. Suggestions that the whole episode was of Canaanite origin do not hold up under close examination,
for the genealogical information makes it clear that this incident was in
the family of Judah. There are only two Canaanites in the story: one
marries into the family of Judah, and the other is subordinated to Judah
(see the articles by J. A. Emerton listed in the bibliography).

This episode was included here for its significance to the Joseph story.
J. Goldin correlates the narrative with the present structure of Genesis
by concentrating on the *breaking through of the younger* ("Youngest
Son," pp. 43–44). Joseph, the favored heir apparent and the younger son,
had apparently been removed once and for all by being sold into Egypt.
But when Judah, the new leader of the brothers, refused to give his
youngest son to the widow Tamar, she took matters into her own hands.
As a result, twins were born to Judah (with circumstances reminiscent
of Jacob and Esau [25:24]). The second infant forced his way to the fore,
signifying that the younger would rise to prominence. The repetition of
this motif here stresses that God's design for Joseph's prominence could
not be set aside as easily as Judah thought. In his own family, and in
spite of his own indifference to Tamar, Judah saw the strange outworking
of the plan whereby the younger gained priority in the family. The next
chapter of Genesis, then, presents Joseph alive and prospering in Egypt.

Tamar qualifies as a heroine in the story, for she risked everything to
fight for her right to be the mother in the family of Judah and to protect
the family. Westermann observes that, in the patriarchal narratives, re-
volts against the established order are characteristically initiated by
women. In each case the justice of such self-defense is recognized (*Genesis*, vol. 3, p. 56). But the samples Westermann lists—Hagar, Rebekah,
Leah, Rachel, Lot's daughters, and Tamar—may not all merit the ascription of justice to their self-defense. But they indeed revolted against
established order, especially Tamar, and the problem that they faced was
in a large part caused by corruption or indifference of men.

Theological Ideas

This chapter has been dubbed a secular story because it does not have
a great emphasis on God's acting or speaking in the events. The closest

that we come to a theological point is Judah's statement that Tamar had been more righteous than he (v. 26). She had fought for her right and thereby preserved the community. We may gather from the use of this story in the present context that the underlying idea is that God was providentially protecting the community from the corruption in the family, thereby ensuring the continuation of the line. The parallel of the twins' birth with the birth of Jacob and Esau also supplies a connection with the theological points of the patriarchal stories.

The event in Genesis 38 also forms a rebuke for the wickedness of Judah and his brothers in attempting to subvert God's plan to exalt the younger. The rebuke is subtle but nonetheless is talionic justice.

Condemnation for wickedness also is present in the story, for it reports that one son was evil, and God killed him. The second son used the ancient levirate custom for self-gratification, and God killed him too. These brief reports, although not the main point of the story, do warn of the consequences of evil.

Structure and Synthesis

Structure

The center of the episode is found in verses 12–26; it is framed by two sections with genealogical considerations, verses 1–11 and 27–30. The entire chapter weaves together narrative reports and speeches between the participants.

The beginning section about the family introduces the complication: Tamar became a childless widow. The final section reports how Tamar gave birth to Judah's sons, with the judicial approval of the family. In between these sections the narrator traces how the problem of childlessness was resolved.

This resolution is constructed around the deception of Judah by Tamar. The narrative reports Judah's change of location (vv. 12–14), allowing for Tamar's plan. The plan is worked out through a dialogue involving the business negotiation between Tamar and Judah (vv. 15–19) and concludes with the frustrated attempt of Judah to redeem his pledge (vv. 21–23). The dénouement of the story occurs in a legal setting where Tamar, about to be condemned because she was pregnant, produced Judah's pledge and was acquitted (vv. 24–26).

Summary Message

When Judah failed to ensure the levirate rights of his daughter-in-law, Tamar, she deceived him into having sexual intercourse with her by playing a prostitute and thereby championed her right to be the mother

of Judah's children, the younger of which displaced the older in an unusual birth.

Exegetical Outline

I. The faithfulness of Judah and his sons to God and his earthly
program led to the near destruction of Judah's family (1–11).
  A. Judah left his brothers and married a Canaanite woman, who
  bore him three sons: Er, Onan, and Shelah (1–5).
  B. Judah gave to Er and then to Onan a wife named Tamar, but
  both sons died without progeny because of evil done before
  God (6–10).
    1. The Lord took the life of Er, Tamar's first husband, be-
    cause he was evil (6–7).
    2. The Lord took the life of Onan, Tamar's second husband
    under levirate law, because he was immoral (8–10).
  C. Judah reneged on his responsibility under levirate law to give
  his third son to Tamar: he deceitfully withheld Shelah and
  placed the family lineage in jeopardy (11).
II. When Tamar realized that Judah had no intention of giving Shelah to her as a husband, she deceived him by acting like a prostitute and thereby conceived his child (12–23).
  A. Judah's wife died, and after the time of mourning ended, he
  and Hirah went up to the sheepshearing festival (12).
  B. Tamar disguised herself as a prostitute and deceived Judah
  so that she could conceive his child (13–19).
    1. Realizing that Judah did not intend to give Shelah to her,
    Tamar disguised herself as a prostitute to entice Judah
    (13–15).
    2. Judah promised the prostitute a kid from the goats and
    gave her, as pledged, his seal and his staff (16–19a).
    3. Tamar became pregnant (19b).
  C. Judah's attempt to fulfill the bargain with the prostitute failed
  when no prostitute could be found, so he decided to let her
  keep his pledge (20–23).
    1. Judah sent Hirah to regain his pledge and fulfill the bar-
    gain he made with the prostitute, but no prostitute could
    be found (20–22).
    2. Judah abandoned the effort, deciding to let her keep the
    pledge (23).
III. When Judah discovered that Tamar was pregnant, he ordered her
to be burned to death; but when she proved that he was the
father, he admitted that she was in the right (24–26).

    A. Three months later, Judah learned that Tamar was pregnant (24a).
    B. When Judah ordered her to be burned to death, she produced his pledge (24b–25).
    C. Judah admitted the wrong done to Tamar in not ensuring her rights and recognized that she had done right (26a).
    D. Judah allowed her to live but did not take her as a wife (26b).
IV. Tamar gave birth to twins, and although Zerah's hand appeared first, Perez was actually born first (27–30).
    A. Tamar gave birth to twins (27).
    B. The midwife marked the first hand to appear with a scarlet thread (28).
    C. Perez forged through to be born first (29).
    D. Zerah was born (30).

Development of the Exposition

I. God's people often complicate his program by their failure (or refusal) to fulfill their responsibilities (1–11).

The first eleven verses of the chapter present the complication that Tamar faced. Typical of such narratives, the writer had to provide the setting with genealogical information (cf. the beginning of the Book of Ruth, with its report of the family members, their move to Moab, the marriages of the sons, the deaths of the men, and the surviving widows). Here Judah separated himself from his brethren and married a Canaanite woman. This act was out of harmony with the will of the patriarchs not to marry Canaanite women (see 28:1). B. Jacob says, "He was also the first of his brothers to lower himself by seeking intercourse with Canaanites" (*First Book of the Bible*, p. 257). From this marriage Judah had three sons.

The plot develops with the account of the marriages of Judah's sons to Tamar (vv. 6–11). She was given to Er; but Er was displeasing to the Lord in some way, and the Lord slew him. No details are provided here, but the fact that he was "wicked" (*ra'*) was sufficient to warrant it untimely death. Whenever this motif appears in Genesis, it describes something deserving of divine judgment. Notably, in Genesis 6, the whole population was evil, and God destroyed them; in Genesis 19, the wicked people of Sodom were overthrown by the Lord. So whatever Er was in the custom of doing, he was in that company, and the narrative interprets his death as divine justice.

By an application of levirate marriage Tamar was given to the second son, Onan. This custom, presented here in a slightly different form than

its definition under the law (Deut. 25), had as its purpose the raising up
of the name of the deceased over his inheritance. There was no purpose
for this second marriage other than to ensure that the line of the deceased Er would continue through his widow.

But Onan had no such plan. He was willing to use the custom to
have Tamar but, since he was unwilling to raise up a child through it,
he would regularly spill (šiḥēt) his seed on the ground. Here, then, was
another wicked member of the family, one who would use the law to
gratify the flesh and, rather than take the responsibility bound up in the
custom, would destroy the seed. This attitude of gratification without
responsibility has been repeated from generation to generation in immoral people. The Lord slew Onan as well, because it displeased
(wayyēraʿ) him.

Judah then withheld his youngest son from marrying Tamar, fearing
that he might lose this son as well (v. 11). Tamar, who according to the
law had the right to be the mother of the heir, was thus not given that
privilege. She would remain a widow, and a barren widow at that. She
would have to take matters into her own hands if she was to be granted
the rights under the law, if the family line was to continue.

These first verses, then, present a picture of a corrupt family. Judah
continued his irresponsible course: he had earlier moved the sale of
Joseph, then separated from his brothers and married a Canaanite, and
now had seen the fruit of that marriage thoroughly evil and so refused
to give the younger son to Tamar. The only bright spot in his family
would be Tamar, but he would be too slow to recognize it. It is clear that
the complications were caused by the failure and the refusal of the men
in the family to live obediently to God's laws and to fulfill their responsibilities faithfully.

II. God's people often resort to desperate, deceptive actions to ensure the success of what they know to be right (12–23).

The next scene continues to paint Judah as profane, but it also portrays Tamar as taking a great risk to obtain what was her right. When
the time was right—that is, after the death of Judah's wife (when there
would be no more chance of Judah's having an heir through her) and at
the time of the sheepshearing festival (when people would be in a festive
mood)—Tamar lured Judah into what was for him an immoral union
with a prostitute (zônâ).

There is an interesting interchange in vocabulary in the chapter. According to verse 15, Judah thought that she was a prostitute (zônâ) because she had covered her face. But when he later sent Hirah to retrieve
his pledge, Hirah looked for a cult prostitute (haqqᵉdēšâ) and could

report back only that there was no cult prostitute there ($q^e d\bar{e}\check{s}\hat{a}$, in vv. 21–22). Then, when Tamar's pregnancy was discovered, it was told to Judah that she had prostituted herself ($z\bar{a}n^e t\hat{a}$) and had gotten pregnant by her prostitution ($lizn\hat{u}n\hat{i}m$, in v. 24). The cult prostitute was a higher-class woman than the prostitute, or whore. The ploy of Tamar demanded that she cover her face. By so doing, she may have satisfied the scruples of Judah, who would turn aside to the prostitute but perhaps not to the cult prostitute, for the latter might have involved Canaanite worship. Tamar's deception worked well, for Hirah went looking for the cult prostitute—who would have been present at festival time—but found none.

It is interesting to compare Tamar with Leah, who participated in the deception of Jacob on his marriage night (29:23). That deception was part of the talionic justice on Jacob the deceiver. Also through this deception was the measure-for-measure justice beginning to unfold for Judah, the deceiver of Jacob (37:31–32). But it is also interesting to compare Tamar with Ruth. Ruth, however, only claimed Boaz as her levirate husband at the festival time and did not actually engage in sex with him. Had she done so, there could have been no reason to offer her in marriage to the near kinsman first (Ruth 4:3–4).

The negotiation of Judah with Tamar took an interesting turn (vv. 16–18). The bargain was reached for a kid from the flock, a common motif in the deceptions of this family (see 27:9 and 37:31). Until Judah could send the payment, though, he had to give his pledge—his tokens of identification. The result of the transaction was that Tamar conceived. She did what justice and the death of her husband demanded of her—but by a very dangerous scheme.

The text of Scripture does not cast any moral judgment on Tamar. Delitzsch may have been too generous in calling her a saint, but she is presented in the Bible in a most favorable light (Ruth 4:12). It is not appropriate to judge her by Christian ethics, for in her culture at that time, her actions, though very dangerous for her, were within the law. She had the right to have a child by the nearest of kin to her deceased husband. She played on the vice of Judah to bear this child, and her deception worked.

III. Such desperate actions, even though drawing righteous indignation, reveal the faithlessness of those who fail in their responsibilities (24–26).

The third scene adds hypocrisy to Judah's lack of integrity. When Tamar was reported pregnant, Judah condemned her to be burned to death—until it was proven by the seal and the staff that he was the guilty party. Then, rather than include himself in any punishment, he simply exonerated her.

Tamar was exonerated by these words of Judah: "She has been more righteous than I [$ṣād^eqâ$ $mimmenî$]." This is a critical appraisal and calls for close study. Judah is at the least saying that Tamar was more in the right than he, for he did not fulfill his responsibilities. Tamar did nothing that the law did not entitle her to do, although her method was desperate. She won the right to be the mother of Judah's children and, in the final analysis, was held up as the more righteous. Brueggemann says,

> The narrative contains a radical critique of morality for those who will pursue it. The text makes a judgment about relative guilts. Tamar has committed the kind of sin the "good people" prefer to condemn—engaging in deception and illicit sex and bringing damages to a good family. For a moment, until aware of his own involvement, Judah reacts on the basis of that sort of "morality" (v. 24). . . .
>
> In that context, a new insight about righteousness comes out of the mouth of Judah (v. 26). He draws an unexpected conclusion. In the midst of this sordid story of sexuality, there is a new understanding of righteousness. The story may give us pause about the usual bourgeois dimensions of sin. What is taken most seriously is not a violation of sexual convention, but damage to the community which includes a poor, diminished female. [*Genesis*, pp. 310–11]

This scene, then, is the turning point. Tamar's risky ploy came to light, but she was exonerated as being in the right. In the process, however, Judah's reputation suffered another blow—he was immoral and hypocritical. It is often the case that a desparate act to set things right will reveal the reason for the act—someone else has been irresponsible or faithless.

IV. God may use such desparate actions to bring about his will when faithlessness appears to hinder it (27–30).

The final scene reveals the outcome. As the climax to this tangled story, these verses provide the significance of the chapter. God granted twins to Tamar—the line of Judah continued because of her.

The births, however, were unusual. The narrative reports how the second child broke out first, prompting the midwife to exclaim: "What a breach you have made for yourself [*mah-pāraṣtā ʿaleykā pāreṣ*]!" The verb *pāraṣ*, "to break through," frequently occurs with the cognate accusative *pereṣ*, "a breach." Elsewhere the expression refers to judgment breaking forth (cf. 2 Sam. 5:20; 6:8; Ps. 106:29), but here it simply describes a breaking out. This event, in turn, provided the meaningful name *pereṣ*, "he who breaks through." The naming signified the completion of Tamar's struggle and also depicted the destiny of the tribe of Perez, who later became predominant (see Gen. 46:12; Num. 26:20).

The second child was named Zerah because a scarlet thread (*šānî*) was tied to his hand before Perez forced through to be born first. Zerah became the founder of the Zerahites (Num. 26:20) and an ancestor of Achan (Josh. 7:1). The name *zārah* (*zerah* in pause) is not explained by a word play, but the emphasis on the scarlet thread implies the meaning. In western Aramaic *zᵉḥôrî* is "scarlet, scarlet thread," as is Babylonian *zaḫuritu*. If such a word was behind the meaning of Zerah, connecting the name to the *idea* of the scarlet thread (*šānî*), it would involve a metathesis (*zḥr > zrḥ*). In biblical Hebrew, however, *zerah* refers not to scarlet but to the rising dawn. Perhaps the name meant something like "God has shone forth." There seems to be no connection with an idea of "shining" in Genesis 38, unless the attempt to come out first was commemorated with a name used often for the dawn. It may be that the name referred simply to the shining string.

These births, with their commemorative namings, remind us of the births of Jacob and Esau. In both cases the younger struggled to be first. In the birth of Perez, it was as if the oracle given to Rebekah had been revived in the line of Judah. In Judah's family, in spite of his own attempts to halt Tamar's opportunity to conceive, twins were born, and the younger surpassed the elder.

The significant aspect of this incident is the connection to Joseph. Judah and his brothers had sold their younger brother into slavery, thinking that they could thwart God's plan that the elder brothers should be subservient to the younger. God worked out that principle through the births in Judah's own family, affirming that Joseph's leadership over his brothers could not be so easily set aside—as Judah would discover.

In an exposition of this story, the main point within the argument of the book will have to deal with the way that God was working on Judah through talionic justice. The central idea could be worded as follows: *Those who disregard God's plan and pursue a life of self-gratification, God will correct, often using talionic justice in the correction.* There are many ways to state this point, but this wording does convey what the point of the story is within the story of Joseph. The way that the whole event works out is ironic; the thing that Judah tried to prevent happened, and it was his means of correction. If it had been left up to Judah, the family would have assimilated with Canaanites. But Tamar retrieved the line and served as the corrective.

Of course, if the expositor wishes to focus on Tamar, then the entire idea would have to be recast along these lines: In the midst of corruption and faithlessness, the faithful may have to take risks to do what is right.

Bibliography

Aharoni, Y. "Tamar and the Roads to Elath." *IEJ* 13 (1963): 30–42.

Burrows, M. "The Ancient Oriental Background of Levirate Marriage." *BASOR* 77 (1940): 2–15.

————— . "Levirate Marriage in Israel." *JBL* 59 (1940): 23–33.

Cassuto, U. "The Story of Tamar and Judah." In *Biblical and Oriental Studies*, vol. 1, *Bible*, pp. 29–40. Jerusalem: Magnes, 1973.

Coats, G. W. "Widow's Rights: A Crux in the Structure of Genesis 38." *CBQ* 34 (1972): 461–66.

Emerton, J. A. "An Examination of a Recent Structuralist Interpretation of Genesis 38." *VT* 26 (1976): 79–98.

————— . "Judith and Tamar." *VT* 29 (1979): 403–15.

————— . "Some Problems in Genesis 38." *VT* 25 (1975): 338–61.

Goldin, Judah. "The Youngest Son; or, Where Does Genesis 38 Belong?" *JBL* 96 (1977): 27–44.

Meek, T. J. "Translating the Hebrew Bible." *JBL* 79 (1960): 328–35.

Mitchell, T. C. "The Meaning of the Noun ḥtn in the OT." *VT* 19 (1969): 93–112.

Niditch, Susan. "The Wronged Woman Righted: An Analysis of Genesis 38." *HTR* 72 (1979): 143–48.

Porter, J. R. "The Legal Aspects of the Concept of 'Corporate Personality' in the Old Testament." *VT* 15 (1965): 361–80.

Robinson, I. "*bepetaḥ enayim* in Genesis 38:14." *JBL* 96 (1977): 569.

Yamauchi, E. M. "Cultic Prostitution." In *Orient and Occident: Essays Presented to Cyris H. Gordon*, pp. 213–23. AOAT 22. Neukirchen-Vluyn: Neukirchener, 1973.

Zimmermann, F. "The Births of Perez and Zerah." *JBL* 64 (1945): 377–78.

57

How the Wise Man Resists Temptation
(Gen. 39)

Afterthe significant interlude about the family of Judah, the story line focuses on Joseph in Egypt, continuing from where it left off at the end of chapter 37. The second part of the story of Joseph concerns his advancement in Egypt and covers three scenes (chaps. 39–41). In the first scene, Joseph began his advancement in Potiphar's house, endured a great fall through false accusation, but then began to advance in prison. Each part of the scene leads into the next; at the end of the chapter, Joseph even met Pharaoh's officials there in the prison.

Chapter 39 is essentially about the temptation of Joseph in Egypt. It actually formed another test of God's leader—if Joseph was to be the leader of God's people, he had to show himself faithful to God. The example of Joseph makes an excellent study on how to overcome temptation.

Theological Ideas

The temptation by Potiphar's wife clearly forms the central motif of this passage, but the focus is on Joseph's resistance to it. The temptation came when Joseph was enjoying the blessing of God and was, perhaps, more vulnerable. His resistance to the temptation was due to his whole-hearted trust in God's purpose for him, and that purpose was being confirmed in his present experience. In other words, the evidence of God's presence strengthened his faith. Convinced that he was chosen by God to rule, Joseph would not sin against God; sure that God was with him as he faithfully served Potiphar, he would not do wickedly against his master. He knew that he could not succeed by defying God.

Resisting temptation did not bring Joseph immediate reward. Rather, he was thrown into prison, without a hearing and without justice. His rapid advancement in prison assured him that God was pleased with him, but the immediate results of his obedience were unpleasant. This observation adds an important qualification to the theological idea that God rewards obedience.

Structure and Synthesis

Structure

This unit falls into three sections: Joseph's success in the house of Potiphar (vv. 1–6), Joseph's resistance to the temptation by Potiphar's wife (vv. 7–20), and Joseph's success in the prison (vv. 21–23). The first and last sections are parallel and frame the account of the temptation. In the two framing sections the emphasis is on the Lord's presence with Joseph, Joseph's prosperity, Joseph's finding grace in the eyes of his master (first Potiphar, then the jailor), and Joseph's being given greater responsibilities.

The middle section includes two cycles: (1) temptation and refusal, continued temptation and refusal (vv. 7–12); (2) notice of his garment and first false accusation, laying aside his garment and second false accusation (vv. 13–18). The section closes with the account of Potiphar's anger and Joseph's imprisonment (vv. 19–20).

The parallelism of this event with the earlier throwing of Joseph into the pit must also have been striking to Joseph. Donald Seybold shows the following comparisons in chart 31. Seybold shows that under each "head," Joseph was placed in a position of dominance over a group of people:

He is a favorite of the head of the household (Jacob, Potiphar, prison-keeper) over others like himself, whether brothers, slaves, or prisoners; and he is in a position of dominance over the others, whether he is checking on his brothers for his father (37:12–14), presiding over the other slaves of Potiphar (39:4–5), or overseeing the other prisoners (39:21–23). . . . The robe and the cloak . . . indicate first his elevation and then a stripping away . . . and the pit/prison . . . is the place where Joseph is both condemned and saved. [D. A. Seybold, "Paradox and Symmetry in the Joseph Narratives," in *Literary Interpretation of Biblical Narratives,* edited by Kenneth R. R. Gros Louis, James S. Ackerman, and Thayer S. Warshaw (Nashville: Abingdon, 1974), p. 63]

Additionally, the pit was a result of Joseph's rejection by his brothers, as the prison was a result of his rejection by Potiphar. This pit-rejection motif appears later on in the psalms and the prophets. For example, Jeremiah was cast into a pit because the Word of the Lord that he delivered was rejected (Jer. 38:4–6)—just as was the Lord's revelation that Joseph delivered (Gen. 37:5–11).

Summary Message

While enjoying the Lord's abundant blessing upon him in Potiphar's house, Joseph repeatedly refused the seductive attempts of his master's wife, testifying that he could not sin against God and do wickedly against his master; and when he was imprisoned because of her false accusation, he once again enjoyed the Lord's abundant blessing.

Exegetical Outline

    I. After Joseph had been brought to Egypt and purchased by Potiphar, the Lord prospered everything he did and blessed Potiphar's possessions when Joseph was put in charge of them (1–6).
       A. After Joseph had been taken to Egypt, Potiphar purchased him from the Ishmaelites (1).
       B. The Lord was with Joseph and caused him to prosper in everything that he did (2).
       C. When Potiphar saw that Joseph was prospering, he put him in charge of everything he owned and thus shared in God's blessing (3–6a).
       D. Transition: Joseph was of fine appearance and handsome (6b).
    II. In the light of God's blessing on him, Joseph repeatedly refused

Chart 31. **Parallelism in Joseph's Pit and Prison Experiences**

Head of Household	Position of Subservience	Symbol of Dominance & Transition	Symbol of Ambiguity & Paradox
Jacob	Joseph	Long-sleeved robe	The pit
Potiphar	Joseph	Cloak	The prison
Prison keeper	Joseph	—	—

the seductive attempts of Potiphar's wife, only to be falsely accused by her to the servants and to her husband (7–20).
  A. First temptation: Joseph refused the repeated advances of
     Potiphar's wife because he knew that to accept would be sin
     against God, who had given him such great responsibility
     (7–10).
     1. Potiphar's wife was physically attracted to Joseph and
        tried to seduce him (7).
     2. Joseph refused her invitation, explaining that to accept
        would be to sin against God who had caused Potiphar to
        entrust him with great responsibility (8–9).
     3. Joseph spurned the continual advances of the woman (10).
  B. Continued temptation: When Potiphar's wife forcefully tried
     to seduce Joseph, he ran from her, leaving his garment in her
     hand (11–22).
  C. Potiphar's wife falsely accused Joseph to her household ser-
     vants and to her husband, so that Joseph was imprisoned
     (13–20).
     1. First false accusation: Using Joseph's coat as evidence,
        Potiphar's wife told her servants that Joseph had tried to
        seduce her (13–15).
     2. Second false accusation: She told her husband that Joseph
        had tried to seduce her (16–18).
     3. Potiphar was angry and had Joseph imprisoned (19–20).
 III. The Lord was with Joseph in prison and dealt with him in loyal
      love, causing him to prosper, so that the warden put everything
      in his care (21–23).
  A. The Lord was with Joseph and granted him favor with the
     warden (21).
  B. The warden confidently put Joseph in charge of everything
     in the prison because the Lord was with him (22–23a).
  C. The Lord prospered everything that Joseph did (23b).

Development of the Exposition

I. The purposeful blessing of the Lord is the evidence of his presence (1–6).

The first section of this passage stresses the point that the Lord was
prospering Joseph as he faithfully served in Potiphar's house. The youth
could begin to see the hand of God working in his life by means of the
favor he achieved with his master. This prosperity not only began the

advancement of Joseph, it also prepared Joseph for the temptation to follow.

The exposition must thoroughly develop the statements in the text in order to catch the emphasis. Verse 2 declares, "The LORD was with Joseph and he was a successful (prospering) man [$way^eh\hat{\imath}$ YHWH 'et-$y\hat{o}s\bar{e}p$, $way^eh\hat{\imath}$ '$\hat{\imath}\check{s}$ $masl\hat{\imath}ah$]." The theological notion of the presence of the Lord, repeated so often in the Scriptures (and epitomized in the name Immanuel, "God with us"), is the reason for Joseph's prosperity. The verse gives the cause (the presence of the Lord) and the effect (the prosperity). A study of the verb $s\bar{a}lah$, "to prosper," is important to the exegesis of this passage; its meaning is helpfully clarified in the subsequent verses.

The point to be made from this statement, and supported from verse 3, is that this was not any ordinary prosperity—it was phenomenal and unexpected, because even Potiphar had to admit that the Lord was with him, causing him to prosper. Joseph's industry and success found favor ($h\bar{e}n$) in Potiphar's eyes, and so he appointed Joseph overseer over his whole house. Because this man recognized the work of the Lord and honored Joseph, the Lord blessed ($wayb\bar{a}rek$) his household, so that the "blessing of the LORD" ($birkat$ YHWH) was upon all that he had. The text illustrates, then, the promise that whoever blessed the seed of Abraham would be blessed (Gen. 12:1–3). Potiphar trusted Joseph and enjoyed a share in the divine blessing on the lad.

The text also indicates that Joseph served faithfully. If the interpreter had any doubts about Joseph's faithfulness from studying Genesis 37, they would be swept aside here. Everything that Potiphar owned was under the care of Joseph, and it flourished. He was the faithful servant par excellence; Potiphar had no need to be concerned about anything he had—even about his wife.

The first section closes with a parenthetical transition: "Now Joseph was of fine appearance and handsome [$y^ep\bar{e}h$-$t\bar{o}$'ar $w\hat{\imath}p\bar{e}h$ mar'eh]" (or as the Jewish Publication Society translation [*Torah*, 1964] has it, "Now Joseph was well built and handsome"). The description reminds the reader of the appearance of Sarai and Rebekah (12:11 and 26:7) that made them susceptible to the sexual advances of potentates, an Egyptian in the case of Sarai, and then Abimelech, a Philistine.

II. The awareness of God's presence enables his people to resist temptation (7–20).

The second section reports Joseph's faithfulness in resisting temptation. God was apparently testing him through this woman to see whether he was obedient. After all, he was far away from his family, and it was his master's wife—to give in may have seemed an easy and expedient thing to do. But it should be pointed out that, if he had succumbed to her advances, he still might have ended up in prison—but as a failure with God.

The story unfolds in cycles: temptation and refusal, temptation and refusal; then false accusation to the men and false accusation to Potiphar; and finally imprisonment. By this repetition the narrative is heightening the issue: Joseph's determined resistance met with doubly wicked false accusation—and the latter won out.

The temptation was powerful by its boldness and directness: "lie with me [šikbâ 'immî]." The narrative tells us that she had cast her eyes on him and then, when alone in the household (Potiphar seems regularly to have been away), pressured him, day after day. As von Rad has pointed out, the passage recalls the warning of Proverbs about the seductress who casts her eyes on the young man and invites him to take his fill of love with her because her husband is away (Prov. 7:6–27).

Joseph simply refused. There was no debating, no flirtatious conversation. He refused to lie with her or to be with her. And when she grabbed his garment, he fled from her. At the center of the narrative is his explanation of his refusal: to do it would be a great wickedness (hārā'â hagg^{e}dōlâ) and a sin against God (w^{e}ḥāṭā'tî lē'lōhîm). His defense was in God, as Candlish says, "in a prompt, abrupt, instant, and, as it were, instinctive appeal to God, as in his law forbidding this sin, and all sin, peremptorily and without room for evasion, or exception, or compromise" (Studies in Genesis, p. 617). His refusal was possible because he was convinced that (1) God had chosen him for a special task and (2) God had been prospering him to give him the responsibilities that he had. He had evidence of God's plan in his rise from the pit and enjoyment of God's presence. His refusal is thus instructive: one cannot sin against God if one is convinced of becoming a significant part of God's program. Adam and Eve missed this important aspect of leadership; rather than be satisfied with the Lord's bounty and enjoy the Lord's presence, they desired forbidden fruit. No one can fulfill his or her divine destiny by disobeying God.

A significant point here is the nature of the sin and the timing of the temptation. Little sins gnaw away at a person's effectiveness in service, and at times God tolerates a person for some time until he must deal with that individual, although God can forgive and restore the sinner. In this passage, however, we have a paradigm for leaders (and therefore all who follow them): people cannot defiantly sin against what they know to be God's righteous will when they are on the verge of becoming what God wants them to be. One cannot willfully sin against God and continue to enjoy his presence and his blessing.

Equally important is the lesson that resistance to temptation does not always find immediate reward. Joseph suffered for his spiritual victory—all because of a false accusation. Potiphar's wife, humiliated by Joseph's refusal of her, accused Joseph of assaulting her. We can discern more of her nature through the discrepancy between her speeches. In verse 14, she told the men of her household, "See he has brought in a Hebrew to us to mock us"; but in verse 17, in speaking to her husband, she said, "The Hebrew servant, which you have brought to us, came in to me to mock me." Her words imply that her husband mocked them by bringing Joseph to them, even though it was Joseph who mocked her. Her words to the men of her household betray her disloyalty and bitterness toward her husband.

The verb "to mock" (l^{e}ṣaḥeq) recalls the story of Lot, who, when trying to rebuke the wicked people of Sodom, was called a mocker (19:14); it also reflects the mocking of Isaac by Ishmael (21:9). The verb in this stem seems to describe an activity that cannot be taken seriously or that does not take something seriously. It refers to holding something up to ridicule, toying with it. Potiphar's wife accused Joseph of such an offense to her husband, as if Joseph had attempted to rape her, holding her in contempt and not taking her seriously. What Joseph said to Potiphar, she contended, was a totally different side of him. And Potiphar, perhaps out of necessity, believed her and imprisoned Joseph.

Now for the second time Joseph was imprisoned for being faithful to his master. In both cases his garment was used in the false report. The first experience at the hands of his brothers must now have been of some comfort to him—he knew he had been here before. If God could raise him then, he could also do so now.

III. The renewed blessing of the Lord (in spite of the adverse consequences of obedience) confirms God's approval of the believer (21–23).

The final section repeats the motifs of verses 1–6, showing once again phenomenal and unexpected prosperity. Joseph in prison began to rise in favor because God was with him and prospered him. The chapter even repeats the motif of the master's turning over all his affairs to Joseph because God was with him, and everything he did prospered. Joseph might have been considered a failure with Potiphar, but he was a success with God, and even in prison that achievement meant more than a momentary pleasure with Potiphar's wife.

The point of this section is to confirm that Joseph did the right thing, even though he suffered for it. Joseph's phenomenal success in prison was clearly evidence of God's approval.

This event confirmed that Joseph remained faithful to his God. With the dreams in the back of his mind and being aware of God's presence, he refused to yield to temptation at his first enjoyment of power. The wise young man recognized that allegiance to God was the first requirement of the ideal ruler. Israel would learn that she too must remain faithful in spite of the consequences. The people of God would be faced with many temptations, especially while serving in Egypt; but if they wished to fulfill the destiny that God had planned for them, they would have to prove faithful. Joseph did not sin, because he was convinced beforehand that God had something marvelous for him to do. We may reflect this lesson in an expositional idea: *Dedication to the calling of God will enable the servant of God to resist temptation.* This dedication idea means that one is convinced of God's plan and committed to carrying it out—that is, shows obedience and faithfulness. Such dedication must be developed over a period of faithful service to God and enjoyment of his presence. In the moment of temptation there is no time to fortify oneself with commitment to God's plan.

Bibliography

Coats, G. W. "Despoiling the Egyptians." *VT* 18 (1968): 450–57.

————. "The Joseph Story and Ancient Wisdom: A Reappraisal." *CBQ* 35 (1973): 285–97.

Hamada, A. "Stela of Putiphar." *ASAE* 39 (1939): 273–77.

Honeyman, A. M. "The Occasion of Joseph's Temptation." *VT* 2 (1952): 85–87.

Jacobson, Howard. "A Legal Note on Potiphar's Wife." *HTR* 69 (1976): 177.

Kornfeld, W. "L'adultère dans l'Orient antique." *RB* 57 (1950): 92–109.

Ward, W. A. "Egyptian Titles in Genesis 39–50." *BibSac* 114 (1957): 40–59.

Yohannan, Y. D., ed. *Joseph and Potiphar's Wife in World Literature: An Anthology of the Story of the Chaste Youth and the Lustful Stepmother.* Norfolk, Conn.: New Directions, 1968.

58

Joseph in Prison:
An Unwavering Faith
(Gen. 40)

third test of Joseph's faith came while he was in prison. He had kept himself pure from the temptress but suffered imprisonment for it. The question to be answered was whether or not he had abandoned his dreams. That Joseph did not lose faith is proven by his willingness to interpret the dreams of the cupbearer and the baker. After all that had happened, he was still convinced of his ability to understand dreams and therefore of the meaning of his own. This passage makes it clear that God put his servant in this adverse situation to test his perseverance in the promised hope. Joseph seized the opportunity to demonstrate his faith, and when the dreams were fulfilled exactly as he had predicted, he must have been greatly encouraged in his faith.

Genesis 40 is clearly dependent on the general context of the Joseph story by virtue of the repeated motifs, which means that the surrounding chapters must be used in interpreting this chapter. The sets of two dreams, first Joseph's (chap. 37), then the cupbearer's and the baker's (chap. 40), and then Pharaoh's (chap. 41), link the passages together. Joseph's dreams predicted his destiny; the dreams of the cupbearer and the baker formed a test for Joseph's perseverance; and the dreams of Pharaoh provided the opportunity for Joseph's ascendancy.

The dreams of the cupbearer and the baker spoke of life and death, respectively. In this way their dreams anticipated the dreams of Pharaoh, which spoke of plenty before the famine, or the prospects of life before the prospects of death. The polarity of ideas in these dreams corresponded to Joseph's experiences of moving from favor to slavery (chap. 37), from bounty to bondage (chap. 39), and finally from prison to dominion (chap. 41). In all the experiences of Joseph and the dreams that he interpreted, the Lord God was demonstrating his sovereign authority over success and failure, bounty and famine, and life and death.

This chapter provides the second episode in Joseph's rise to power in Egypt. Its structure shows that it is a self-contained unit, but its substance interrelates with the surrounding context.

Theological Ideas

In its context, this chapter illustrates the endurance of faith in adversity. God prompted the demonstration of Joseph's faith by giving him dreams to interpret. Had he given up on his own dreams, he would never have offered to interpret the two in this chapter. Joseph did not waver in his faith. Moreover, his triumph here must have built up his confidence for interpreting the dreams of Pharaoh, when that call came.

Along with this major point is the clear statement of the passage that the interpretation of dreams comes from God, not Joseph. This confession should silence all ancient and modern mystics who would claim to possess such power. Joseph was asserting that the Egyptian magicians could not interpret the dreams because God had not revealed the answer to them. Without that insight they were in the dark.

A minor theological point can be drawn from Joseph's protestation of innocence, which appears here for the first time in Joseph's speeches. It opens the study to comparisons with other passages in which the innocent protest that they suffer unjustly (e.g., Ps. 44).

Structure and Synthesis

Structure

In chart 32, Westermann shows the structure of this chapter and how its symmetry unites the scene (*Genesis*, vol. 3, p. 72). The meeting of the two officials offered Joseph some hope for deliverance (vv. 1–4), but after it was all over he was forgotten in prison (v. 23). The heart of the passage concerns the dreams (vv. 5–22), but between the two explanations is Joseph's appeal to be remembered because he had been imprisoned unjustly. The central position of this request shows that it is the predominant idea in the episode and that this event is indeed the preparation for Joseph's being remembered.

Summary Message

When Pharoah's cupbearer and baker had disturbing dreams in prison, Joseph accurately foretold the cupbearer's restoration and the baker's execution, but his request to be remembered was quickly forgotten.

Exegetical Outline

    I. Pharaoh's cupbearer and baker were sent to Joseph's prison for gravely offending their king (1–4).

   II. When the cupbearer and the baker had disturbing dreams, Joseph interpreted their dreams, foretelling the cupbearer's restoration to his post and the baker's execution (5–19).

     A. The cupbearer and the baker had disturbing dreams and became dejected because no one could interpret them (5–8a).

     B. Joseph implored them to tell him their dreams, asserting that the interpretation came from God (8b).

     C. Joseph interpreted their dreams (9–19).

       1. The dream of the cupbearer (9–15):

         a. The cupbearer related his dream, in which he gave a cup of wine to Pharaoh that he had squeezed from grapes from a three-branched vine (9–11).

Chart 32. **Symmetrical Arrangement of Genesis 40**

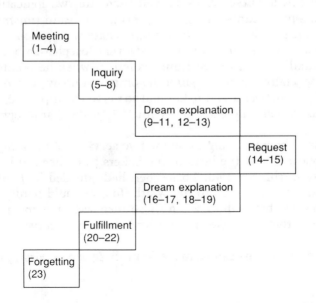

      b. Joseph explained that within three days he would be restored to his post (12–13).

      c. Joseph requested that the cupbearer help obtain his release from prison (14–15).

    2. The dream of the baker (16–19):

      a. Expecting a positive interpretation too, the baker related his dream, in which birds devoured baked delicacies for Pharaoh that he was carrying in three wicker baskets atop his head (16–17).

      b. Joseph explained that within three days the baker would be executed and hung on a stake from which the birds would devour his flesh (18–19).

III. The dreams were fulfilled three days later, when Pharaoh granted amnesty to the cupbearer but executed the baker, just as Joseph had foretold; but the cupbearer forgot to mention Joseph to Pharaoh (20–23).

Development of the Exposition

I. God's servants often find themselves in situations that can discourage their faith (1–4).

The first part of the chapter records the setting for the events, namely, the imprisonment of the cupbearer and the baker in the ward in which Joseph was imprisoned. The expositor may need to recall the situation at the end of chapter 39 in order to provide a thorough explanation of Joseph's plight. In these verses as well there are two indications of Joseph's unhappy circumstances. First, it was the ward (*mišmar*) of the captain of the guards (*śar haṭabbāhîm*, cognate with *ṭābaḥ*, "to slaughter, butcher"). And second, the text says that Joseph was bound (*'āsûr*) there. Naturally, he was freed from his fetters when he was to serve in the jail, especially when the jailor appointed him (*wayyipqōd*) to take charge of the cupbearer and baker and to serve them (*wayšāret 'ōtām*). But there is evidence here and in Psalm 105:18–19 that Joseph was kept in bonds.

Into this unhappy setting came the two servants of the king, the head of the cupbearers and the head of the bakers (*śar*, "head, ruler," is used twice more in this section). These men had offended (*ḥāṭe'û*) the king in some way and fell prey to his wrath. Joseph could hardly have suspected what lay before him when these men were put in his care. For the moment, they were two more people he had to serve in his duties in prison.

Several observations can be made from these verses. First, Joseph continued to serve faithfully and receive appointments to tasks, even though he was in a most unfavorable and discouraging place. Second, the narrative reveals that the prison was a most disagreeable place, for Joseph later appealed for help to gain release. Third, God was beginning to move to bring about Joseph's release and ascendancy, even though it was not known to Joseph. In fact, the introduction of the cupbearer marks the turning point of Joseph's career—he had fallen as far as he would.

In spite of the disagreeable conditions in which Joseph found himself, he continued to serve faithfully in whatever responsibilities he was given. The reader can certainly learn from Joseph's example of patience and obedience; but when the events of the chapter unfold, the reader can learn the reason for such patience and faithfulness—God was beginning to work.

II. God's servants must take every opportunity to demonstrate their faith, in spite of their circumstances (5–19).

A. God provides his people with opportunities (5–8a).

The opportunity for Joseph came when the two new prisoners had dreams in one night. At first the men simply looked sad. (Once again the narrative begins a dialogue section with *rā'â* and *hinnēh:* "And Joseph looked upon them [*wayyar' 'ōtām*], and behold [*wᵉhinnām*] they were sad [*zōʿăpîm*]."] In his questioning, Joseph asked, "Why do you look so sad today? [*maddûaʿ pᵉnêkem rāʿîm hayyôm*]" (lit., "Why are your faces bad today?").

They were dejected because there was no interpreter for the dreams they had. The word used here for interpreter, *pōtēr*, occurs in biblical Hebrew only in this section of the Bible. It is far more common in Aramaic and later Hebrew, as well as in the cognate languages. The word signifies the interpretation of dreams with their symbolic meanings; it eventually came to be used for secret interpretations of a special class of people. The two prisoners knew that no such interpreter would be available to them.

B. The faithful seize opportunities to demonstrate their faith (8b–19).

Joseph's response to their reason asserts that interpretations come from God: "Do not interpretations [*pitrōnîm*] belong to God?" The implication of this statement seems to be that God will tell their dreams through him. He had not lost his confidence in God or in his being one to whom God revealed interpretations. Joseph thus invited them to tell him their dreams.

The rest of this section details how Joseph interpreted their dreams.

The chief of the cupbearers had a dream that had a favorable interpretation. The dream reflected his profession and showed by the repetition of the word "Pharaoh" that he had a close relationship with the ruler. The ripening grapes signified that Pharaoh would lift up his head (*yiśśā' par'ōh 'et-rō'šekā*) and restore him to his position. The motif "to lift up the head" signified a restoration of favor (Ps. 3:3; see also 2 Kings 24:27–30).

To this favorable interpretation Joseph added his personal request (v. 14). He asked, "But remember me [*z*e*kartanî*] when it is well [*yîṭab*] with you, and show kindness [*ḥāsed*] to me, and make mention of me [*w*e*hizkartanî*] to Pharaoh, and bring me out of this house." Joseph anticipated that things would go well (< *yāṭab*) with this man (in contrast to *rā'îm* in v. 7). He thus appealed to the faithfulness (*ḥāsed*) of the cupbearer to assist him in getting out of the prison, twice using the verb "remember" (< *zākar*).

In support of his appeal, Joseph explained his plight in a rare moment of self-defense (v. 15). The construction is emphatic: "I was surely stolen [*gunnōb gunnabtî*] from the land of the Hebrews," referring to his being sold by his brothers. Then he added that he had done nothing to deserve prison now (*lō'-'āśîtî m*e*'ûmâ* being literally true), for he was falsely accused. His protesting of his innocence adds to the idea that God was testing him, for he was suffering without a cause.

The second dream interpretation was not so pleasant, although the baker anticipated that it was going to be. The baker's dream anticipated death. It reflected his profession as well, but as the birds were eating the bread he was carrying, so they would eat his flesh when Pharaoh had him hung. (For the second time now in Genesis, birds of prey are used to signify oppression, the first being in chap. 15).

In telling the interpretation to the baker, Joseph repeated the expression of the first interpretation, but with an ironic twist: "Pharaoh will lift up your head from you [*yiśśā' par'ōh 'et-rō'šekā mē'āleykā*]." The expression probably does not mean a beheading; rather, Pharaoh would hang the baker. The word *mē'āleykā*, "from you," may signify that the favor would be removed from him, for "to lift up the head" signifies a restoration to favor.

III. God's servants often find encouragement through the results of their faithful actions (20–23).

The third section reports the fulfillment of the dreams—just as Joseph had interpreted them (*ka'ăšer pātar lāhem yôsēp*). This development must have been a tremendous encouragement to the faith of this young man; it would increase his confidence that he was right, that he had not misunderstood God's revelation to him in dreams. He was sure that God would yet use him, even though he had waited eleven years.

Of course, the tension he faced in his imprisonment was not resolved by this reinforcement. The last verse stresses that the chief butler did not remember (*lō' zākar*) him but forgot him (*wayyiškāḥēhû*). The rising expectations of Joseph thus had reason to falter—he was forgotten. The knowledge that he was correct might have seemed little consolation while he was in prison. But it was consolation: others may have forgotten him, but God would not. He had a future.

Joseph's faith could not be destroyed by the circumstances, which was exactly what God was looking for in a leader. Joseph had been stolen from his land and then wrongly imprisoned, but when the opportunity arose for him to exercise his faith in God, he did. He was able to discern the interpretation of dreams correctly. His faith was confirmed. Now he was ready for greatness in public.

God tests his people's faith in the promises before he entrusts them to positions of greater responsibilities. *Those who are convinced that God desires to use them in greater capacities will demonstrate their unwavering faith in the midst of discouraging situations.*

Bibliography

MacLaurin, E. C. B. "Joseph and Asaph." *VT* 25 (1975): 27–45.

Offord, J. "The Princes of the Bakers and the Cup-Bearers." *PEFQSt* 50 (1918): 139–42.

Redford, D. B. "The 'Land of the Hebrews' in Gen XL 15." *VT* 15 (1965): 529–32.

Speiser, E. A. "Census and Ritual Expiation in Mari and Israel." *BASOR* 149 (1958): 17–25.

59

How God Controls Nations to Accomplish His Program
(Gen. 41)

When God elevated Joseph to power, in fulfillment of the dreams, he again used dreams in order to confirm the work he was about to do. If the ruler of Egypt had the dreams and obtained their interpretation through God's servant, then he would know for sure that God was sovereignly controlling his land and that Joseph was God's spokesman. Had the prisoners mentioned Joseph earlier, the ruler might have ignored them; at this time, however, the ruler was dependent upon Joseph.

This chapter forms the turning point in the Joseph story, for it tells how Joseph came to power. The story of Joseph began with the brothers' disbelief that Joseph should rule over them (Gen. 37), and in the end the fulfillment of the dream was disclosed to them (chap. 45). At the center of that development is this account of Joseph's coming to power in Egypt. When Joseph stood before Pharaoh the favor of God on him and the destiny of God for him came into sharpest focus. At the center of this dramatic moment the dialogue confirms the work of God: Joseph explained that it was all for the good of Egypt, and Pharaoh acknowledged God's power at work in Joseph.

This chapter has several similarities to the account of Daniel (as well as the extrabiblical story of *Ahiqar*). Four points of contact may be identified: (1) the Hebrew slave (in the biblical texts) is summoned before the king to resolve the problem of the interpretation of the dream, (2) the king explains the problem that has eluded the wise men of the court, (3) by the help of God the Hebrew slave interprets the dream, and (4) the king elevates the Hebrew in reward for the resolution of the problem. For both Joseph and Daniel the events took place while they were in bondage in a foreign land. In both cases the dreams that the rulers received demonstrated that God was controlling the destiny of those lands and that they and their wise men were unable to do anything other than submit to the counsel of the Hebrew interpreter, in whom the wisdom of the Spirit of God resided.

Theological Ideas

The sovereignty of God is the underlying theme of this chapter, for the economy of Egypt—in fact, Egypt's whole future—was subject to the Lord God of Israel. The Bible affirms that God raises up kings and sets them down; and he controls the destinies of empires in accord with his plans for his people. In this instance, he controlled Egypt's life source, for God had determined that his wise servant would be the means of delivering Egypt.

A major part of this theological theme is the dreams of Pharaoh. They provide God's revelation of things to come. But they also signify something more. As Brueggemann observes, the dreams took the initiative away from Pharaoh; he was not the subject, but the object, receiving messages and not generating them (*Genesis,* p. 326). Behind Joseph's rise to power was the loss of power and initiative by Pharaoh and the helplessness of his courtiers. This emphasis on the loss of power under God's sovereign plan also appears with the Pharaoh of the exodus period, who lost control and initiative to Moses. It also occurs in the New Testament with Herod, who could not stop the birth of Jesus, and with Pilate, who had only power that was given to him from above. To his credit, the Pharaoh before whom Joseph stood did not resist the revelation from the living God but recognized that God was the source of wisdom. Because this ruler wisely submitted to the more powerful sovereign, his lands were spared.

In addition to this grand theme, we have a short note at the end of the chapter about the births of Manasseh and Ephraim. Westermann states the point succinctly: "The two names, expressing the praise of God, are a witness that the great statesman in Egypt remains bound to the God of his fathers" (*Genesis,* vol. 3, p. 99). This example would be instructive for Israel in bondage or captivity: because God was sovereign over the nations, Israel can and must remain true to her heritage.

Structure and Synthesis

Structure

The chapter effectively employs repetition of motifs found in the surrounding contexts as well as in this chapter itself. It records that the king had two dreams (vv. 1–7) and that the courtiers failed to interpret them (v. 8). Then, in verses 9–13, it reports how the cupbearer recalled the events of chapter 40, thereby forming a literary connection to the preceding chapter. It then includes the king's telling of the dreams for the second time in the chapter (vv. 17–24). It breaks the pattern by telling that this time he received the proper interpretation (vv. 25–32), along with wise counsel (vv. 33–36). The chapter closes with Joseph's elevation to power and his blessing from God (37–57).

The turning point of the narrative is Joseph's interpretation and advice, followed by Pharaoh's acknowledgment of God. The reader is immediately impressed that God was sovereignly controlling both the interpretation of the revelatory dream and the response to it.

Summary Message

After Joseph faithfully interpreted the two dreams of Pharaoh, God elevated Joseph to power and demonstrated his sovereignty in controlling the economic life of Egypt as he worked to accomplish his will for Israel through Joseph's preparation for the years of famine.

Exegetical Outline

    I. Pharaoh had two dreams that greatly troubled him and could find no wise man to interpret them (1–8).
       A. Pharaoh dreamed two consecutive dreams (1–7).
          1. His first dream was of seven thin cows eating seven healthy ones (1–4).
          2. His second dream was of seven scorched ears of grain swallowing seven good ears (5–7).
       B. Pharaoh was greatly troubled and could not find a wise man to interpret for him (8).
   II. After the cupbearer remembered Joseph's abilities and told Pharaoh about them, Joseph interpreted the dreams of Pharaoh, explaining that interpretations came from God, and then advised Pharaoh regarding what he should do (9–36).
       A. The cupbearer remembered Joseph and related to Pharaoh what had happened in the prison (9–13).

    B. Pharaoh sent for Joseph from the dungeon in order to have him interpret his dreams (14–24).

      1. Pharaoh summoned Joseph to the court (14).

      2. Pharaoh explained that he had heard Joseph could interpret dreams, but Joseph explained that it was God who did it (15–16).

      3. Pharaoh told his dreams to Joseph (17–24).

    C. Joseph interpreted the dreams of Pharaoh (25–32).

      1. The two dreams were one message concerning God's future actions in Egypt (25, 28).

      2. The seven good cows and ears represented seven years of abundance in Egypt (26, 29).

      3. The seven thin cows and ears represented seven years of severe famine in Egypt (27, 30–31).

      4. The fulfillment was certain and immanent (32).

    D. Joseph advised Pharaoh regarding how to plan for the famine (33–36).

      1. Pharaoh should appoint one wise man as an overseer to store up the grain (33–34).

      2. The grain should be reserved for the famine (35–36).

  III. Recognizing that God's hand was on Joseph, Pharaoh appointed Joseph to the office of vizier over Egypt, provided him with a wife, who bore Ephraim and Manasseh, and gave him authority over the economy of the land (37–57).

    A. Joseph became the administrator over Pharaoh's house (37–45).

      1. Pharaoh chose Joseph and gave him great authority over all the land of Egypt (37–44).

      2. Pharaoh gave Joseph a new name and a new wife (45).

    B. Joseph served as minister of agriculture over Egypt (46–49).

    C. Asenath bore Joseph two sons (50–52).

      1. Joseph named the first son Manasseh, because God had made him forget (50–51).

      2. Joseph named the second son Ephraim, because God had made him fruitful (52).

    D. Seven years of famine came upon Egypt (53–57).

      1. Despite the severe famine, Egypt had food (53–54).

      2. People were sent to Joseph for food (55).

      3. The famine was severe throughout the world (56–57).

Development of the Exposition

I. The nations cannot understand the purposes of God over the affairs of people (1–8).

A. God's symbolic revelation (1–7).

The occasion for Joseph's rise to power came after two years, when Pharaoh had two dreams in one night. There is clear Egyptian coloring in the two dreams: the cows stood half-submerged in the Nile in refuge from the heat and the flies and then came up out of the water for pasture. The troubling part of the first dream came when seven other cows that were gaunt (rā'ôt mar'eh, "bad of appearance," as opposed to yᵉpôt mar'eh) and lean (daqqôt habbāśār, "thin of flesh," as opposed to bᵉrî'ōt bāśār) came up after them and devoured them. Here was the beginning of the symbolic revelation of God's control over the life-and-death cycle of Egypt.

The second dream carried a similarly disturbing theme. Seven ears on a stalk, plump and good (ṭōbôt, "good," balancing rā'ôt, "bad," in the vision of the cows), were swallowed up by seven thin ears (daqqôt being repeated here) that were shriveled by the east wind.

What must have been very troubling to Pharaoh was the depiction of the Nile in the first dream. Because of the Nile, the land of Egypt weathered famines rather well—there was usually grain in Egypt. And if there was grain, the livestock would flourish, and all life as well. These two dreams, however, repeating the basic message that poverty will destroy plenty, struck at the source of Egypt's economy. Because of the Nile itself, the prosperity of the field and the herd would cease.

B. Mankind's frustrated understanding (8).

Because of the symbolic nature of these dream revelations, Pharaoh and his magicians were unable to derive a proper interpretation. (Probably few of the covenant community could have done any better; it took one in whom the gift of interpretation resided.) The sages of Egypt, although they were skilled in handling the ritual books of magic and priestcraft, could not interpret (wᵉ'ên-pôtēr 'ôtām lᵉpar'ōh). But this limitation too was part of God's plan for using symbolic dreams rather than direct verbal communication. (See also the reasoning behind the parables in Matt. 13:10–17). God used an Israelite slave to confound the wisdom of Egypt, just as he later used another captive from Zion, Daniel, to explain the dreams to Nebuchadnezzar. God employed such communication to show that, no matter how powerful and prosperous these nations were on the face of the earth, they were still subject to his sovereign control.

II. God uses his people to explain to the nations the revelation of the divine plan for the world (9–36).

A. *The consulting of God's servant (9–24).*

Bringing Joseph to his hour took two steps in the narrative: the remembrance by the cupbearer and Pharaoh's decision to summon Joseph. In Pharaoh's disturbance over the symbolic revelation, only one avenue was open to him for the meaning—the servant of the Lord. The experience of his dreams caused the cupbearer to recall his faults that brought him into Joseph's care in the prison. Verses 9–13, then, record the cupbearer's report of what happened in chapter 40. Central to the report to Pharaoh is the cupbearer's statement: "And he interpreted [*wayyiptor*] for us our dreams, to each man according to his dreams did he interpret [*pātār*]. And it happened just as he had interpreted [*pātar*] for us" (vv. 12b–13a). Here was the missing element in the understanding of the dreams by Pharaoh; he now apparently could find an interpreter.

Joseph was thus summoned to stand before the king. But when Joseph was confronted with the evidence about his abilities ("I have heard say of you that you can understand a dream to interpret it [*tišmaʿ ḥălôm liptōr ʾōtô*]"), Joseph immediately corrected Pharaoh with regard to the true source of the meaning. He disclaimed any innate ability, saying that God would answer Pharaoh with peace. This conviction was reiterated after Pharaoh recounted the dreams to him (v. 25), because it was obvious to Joseph that God was declaring what he was going to do. This emphasis on the Lord God would have been remarkable in the courts of Pharaoh, for in Egypt Pharaoh was a god himself—but not like this God of the Hebrews. Benno Jacob writes:

> The decisive element is the form which Joseph gives his interpretation and to which the commentators have given no attention. He uses the word *God;* Joseph began, "God may give Pharaoh a favorable answer," not I. He goes from the prison to the throne of the king, and this is his first word. This speech is as pious as it is frank. He who is aware of God, is humble and fearless at the same time. Even a king is nothing compared to God. We are not told of Pharaoh's reaction to this; then after reporting his dreams, Joseph begins his interpretation with God (verse 25) and ends with God (verse 28); he emphasizes this once more by twice using "God" in verse 32. [*First Book of the Bible,* pp. 280–81]

The humility and faith of Joseph thus come through in the chapter. Because God had given Joseph the special gift and because God had singled out Joseph for this special interpreting ministry, it was Joseph's duty to give glory to God for the revelation and the meaning and to take none of the glory for himself. Those whom God calls to special service must make it a point to inform the unbelieving world that any success or ability that they have comes from God. When they explain God's revelation to the world, they must confront the world with God. The servants are not greater than the master.

B. The interpretation by God's servant (25–36).

The interpretation section begins with a reiteration of the source of the dream and its meaning—God. The dreams were a communication to this god Pharaoh from the true God, concerning what he was about to do in the earth. The seven cows and seven ears represented seven years; seven years of plenty would thus be followed by seven years of famine that would eat up the plenty. Of great importance is the statement by Joseph that the dream's coming in two forms meant that it was established (nākôn) by God and would quickly come about (v. 32). This comment perhaps applies generally to the many things in the life of Joseph that were in pairs, including his own imprisonments.

Because God revealed these things for a purpose, Joseph added wise counsel to the interpretation (vv. 33–36). Pharaoh should find a man who was discerning and wise (nābôn wᵉḥākām) and place him over the land of Egypt; this man should collect a fifth of the produce during the good (haṭṭôbôt) years so that the nation would not perish in the years of famine. The bounty of the earth—God's blessing—in this chapter is called "good" (ṭôb); if it is cared for well, it will see them through the bad (rāʿôt) years of the severe famine (rāʿāb).

This revelation was not only the means to get Joseph to power; it was also the means by which God would save Egypt and the world in the time of crisis, causing everyone to know that deliverance comes from God—if people would believe the Word from God and prepare accordingly. Wisdom literature advises that people should store up in times of plenty for times of need, which is just practical living (Prov. 6:6–11; 20:4). But here the entire event was part of God's way of making himself known to the world. Because of the dreams and because of their clear interpretation, Pharaoh and his courtiers were convinced that it would happen.

III. Believers who recognize that the success of their service is part of God's sovereign plan will not abandon their faith when they find success (37–57).

A. The reward of God's servant (37–45).

The last part of the chapter builds to a climax, starting with Joseph's meteoric rise to power in Egypt and concluding with a reminder of God's blessing and a report of Joseph's preserving his faith. It would have been easy for a young man to be taken with his success and forget his spiritual heritage. But Joseph was the faithful servant of the Lord.

The elevation to power began with Pharaoh's response: "And the thing was good [*wayyîṭab*] in the eyes of Pharaoh and his servants" (v. 37). Joseph's interpretation and his ascription of authority to his God were considered good by the court—as indeed they are. Pharaoh recognized immediately that this was the man to use, for the "Spirit of God" (*rûaḥ ʾĕlōhîm*) was in him (v. 38). He could conclude only that, since God had revealed all this interpretation to Joseph, there was none who was as discerning and wise (*nābôn wᵉḥākām*) as Joseph. Pharaoh thus decreed that Joseph would be over all the affairs of Egypt; only Pharaoh himself would be over him. Joseph had been faithful over what had been given him to do, whether Potiphar's house or the house of prison, and so God made him ruler over greater things, the house of Pharaoh. With the decree of Pharaoh the dreams of Joseph began to be realized; now Egypt was under his control, and by the royal decree everyone had to bow the knee as the chariots went past (*ʾabrēk*, "bow the knee," is a homonym of the verb *bārak*, "bless," and although unrelated in meaning, does provide an allusion by the sounds of the words).

To signify his new status, Pharaoh gave Joseph a new name, which has generally been interpreted to mean, "God speaks and lives." He also gave him a wife, the daughter of a priest of On. A novel was written in Philo's time, entitled *Joseph and Asenath*, which included the account of the conversion of Joseph's wife to Yahwism. Whether factual or not, all that can be determined from this passage is that their children were given Hebrew names.

B. The faithfulness of God's servant (46–57).

The faithfulness of Joseph is reiterated in the closing verses of this account. He was now ruler over all the land of Egypt, second only to Pharaoh. The land produced abundant crops for seven years, just as Joseph had predicted. In spite of his success and status, he did not forsake his heritage. He gave his sons Hebrew names.

The first child born to Joseph was named Manasseh (*mᵉnaššeh*); he explained this name by saying, "God has made me forget [*naššanî*] my toil and my father's house." The name forms a description of divine activity on behalf of Joseph, explaining in general his change of fortune. The name itself is in the form of a *piel* participle, suggesting the meaning "he who brings into forgetfulness." Noth says the name is the kind that would suggest compensation for misfortune or bereavement at the time of birth which overcame the blow (*PN*, p. 211, n. 1). The verb *naššanî* may have been used instead of the normal *niššanî* in Hebrew to provide a closer paronomasia with the name. The meaning of the name is an integral part of this section of the Joseph story; it presents the brighter outlook of Joseph in view of the change of fortune. The memory of toil and sorrow were replaced by the birth of this son and what he signified.

The name of the second son was Ephraim (*'eprāyim*). This name was explained by Joseph as follows: "God has caused me to be fruitful [*hipranî*] in the land of my affliction." The house of Joseph first represented a change of fortune (Manasseh) and then a new prosperity (Ephraim).

The explanation of the name Ephraim uses the verb *pārâ*, "to bear fruit," the letters *p* and *r* making the sound play. This idea of fruitfulness is also connected with the Joseph tradition in Genesis 30:2, which says that God had withheld the fruit (*p*ᵉ*rî*) of Rachel's womb—the fruit that eventually was Joseph. Genesis 49:22 announces that Joseph is a "fruitful bough" (although there are different interpretations offered for the text of this verse). Deuteronomy 33:13–17 further develops the idea. Finally, Hosea writes about Ephraim: "Though he be fruitful [*yaprî'*] ... his spring shall become dry" (13:15). The biblical traditions thus link *pārâ* with *'eprāyim* in the household of Joseph.

There is a slight difficulty in that the name is spelled with the dual ending, which usually indicates a place name. Delitzsch simply stated that the name meant "double fruitfulness," the dual being used in the superlative sense as in Egyptian (*New Commentary on Genesis*, vol. 2, p. 305), a proposal I do not find very convincing. G. J. Spurrell argues that it may be a diphthongal pronunciation of a name ending in *-an* or *-am*, often thought to be dual suffixes (see Diblaim in Hos. 1:3; *Notes*, p. 334). Many, however, associate the name with the territory of Ephraim and interpret it to mean "fertile land" (see C. Fontinoy, "Les noms de lieux en *-ayim* dans la Bible," *UF* 3 [1971]: 33–40). The dual would then be an old locative suffix. Various other views have been offered for the name, relating it to such things as "pastureland" or "embankment of earth," all with the idea that the tribal name was taken from the name of the territory in which the tribe settled.

If the name Ephraim is related to the verb *pārâ*, then its basic meaning is "fruitfulness." This idea would also be possible as a description of the territory of Ephraim, and the form of the name—now a dual—would lead us to understand it as a place name. But since it forms part of the Joseph story, it has another significance in Genesis. The name signifies that Joseph's fruitfulness (i.e., his prosperity and posterity) came by divine intervention. Because of this story, *pārâ* came to mind when one heard the name. The fact that such fruitfulness was part of the promise to be passed on to Ephraim underscores this thought. An Egyptian setting with its affliction provided a suitable contrast for the significance of the name. The name would also remind the later Israelites to hold to their heritage, for it signifies the action of God, who prospered his people under affliction (cf. Exod. 1:7, 12).

The narrator thus recorded the birth report about the ancestor of the Ephraimites and, with a precise choice of expression, perhaps changing the name to a dual, incorporated it into the Joseph story to explain the fruitfulness of Joseph—and the fruitfulness of the tribe—as a work of God. In the tradition Joseph used Hebrew names for his children that signified his faith in the Lord was as strong as ever, in spite of his suffering and in spite of his success.

Joseph's wisdom also bore fruit in the land of Egypt, for the seven years of plenty in the land came to an end, and the famine began. Everyone who came to Egypt to buy grain was sent to Joseph.

In the exposition of this passage three persons must be in view: God is the prime mover of the events, Joseph is the faithful servant and the center of the narrative, and Pharaoh is the potential antagonist who becomes the quiescent agent of God's sovereignty. The unit as a whole teaches that *God sovereignly controls the destinies of nations to protect and provide for his covenant people.* The working of the expository idea would have to be modified to fit the particular emphases of the expositions. In developing it as I do, I stress that God controlled the economy of Egypt to bring Joseph to power and thereby prepare for the migration of Israel to Egypt. In conjunction with this theologically worded idea, I would stress the faithfulness of Joseph, who serves as the model for the believer. Joseph knew God's revelation, boldly declared it to Pharaoh, and advised him to conform to what God was about to do. Here, then, is the directive for applying this story to believers in other times. It must also be added that, once Joseph was elevated to his position of responsibility, he continued to live in faith.

In order to correlate these ideas with what the later Scriptures teach on this topic, we must make the wording a bit more general. Dreams as a form of revelation may not be given now—they were part of the diverse means that God used in the Old Testament. We now possess God's full revelation, which makes it clear that God controls the destinies of nations for his purposes, and his purposes include the protection and provision of his people. How should the believer live in the light of this great truth? In great comfort, in bold faith to declare God's plans, and in responsible obedience to what he or she knows God's plan is.

Bibliography

Aptowitzer, V. "Asenath, the Wife of Joseph—a Haggadic Literary-Historical Study." *HUCA* 1 (1924): 239–306.

Fensham, F. C. "Genesis XLI 40." *ExT* 68 (1956–57): 284.

Kapelrud, A. S. "The Number Seven in Ugaritic Texts." *VT* 18 (1968): 494–99.

Kitchen, K. A. "The Term *Nšq* in Genesis 41:40." *ExT* 69 (1957): 30.

Levine, B. A. "Notes on an Aramaic Dream Text from Egypt." *JAOS* 84 (1964): 18–22.

MacDonald, J. "The Status and Role of the *Naʿar* in Israelite Society." *JNES* 35 (1976): 149–70.

Niditsch, S., and R. Doran. "The Success Story of the Wise Courtier: A Formal Approach." *JBL* 96 (1977): 179–93.

Ogden, G. S. "Time and the Verb היה in Old Testament Prose." *VT* 21 (1971): 451–69.

Saydon, P. P. "The Inceptive Imperfect in Hebrew and the Verb *hēḥēl*, "to Begin." *Bib* 35 (1954): 43–50.

Sperling, David S. "Genesis 41:40: A New Interpretation." *JANES* 10 (1978): 113–19.

Thomas, D. W. "Some Observations on the Hebrew Root חדל." *VTS* 4 (1957): 8–16.

Ward, W. A. "The Egyptian Office of Joseph." *JSS* 5 (1960): 144–50.

60

The Awakening of Conscience (Gen. 42)

Joseph's tests of his brothers were important in God's plan to channel his blessing through the seed of Abraham. God had planned to bring the family to Egypt so that it might grow into a great nation. But because the people who would form that nation had to be faithful, the brothers needed to be tested before they could share in the blessing. Joseph's prodding had to be subtle; the brothers had to perceive that God was moving against them so that they would acknowledge their crime against Joseph and demonstrate that they had changed. If they failed the test, God could have started over with Joseph, just as he had said he would with Moses in Exodus 32:10, when his wrath was kindled against Israel.

This chapter is a scene in the story of Joseph and so must be interpreted in the light of what has gone before and in anticipation of what is to follow. The scene provides a complication of the plot that parallels chapter 37: the oppressed became the oppresser, the spy accused the brothers of being spies, and the one who had been thrown into prison by his brothers put them into prison. All this pressure was applied as a deliberate test of the brothers—the text makes clear that Joseph recog-

647

nized them and remembered their deeds, and although they did not recognize him, they began to remember their deeds.

Theological Ideas

The scene shows how a wise ruler tested the faithfulness of those who would participate in the theocratic program, a testing process that was necessary because of the past actions of these men. In fact, Joseph uses the word "to test" (*bāḥan*) when he established the way that they could prove they were honest men (v. 15). This first test was meant to awaken their consciences and so was essentially a preparation for the next test.

All the activities of Joseph were designed to bring the brothers to a point of remorse over their evil. If they would not manifest guilty consciences, there would be no reason to continue. But the brothers did show such a change, because their response now to the idea of getting rid of Joseph (see 37:20) sounds very different in verse 21—they knew they had been indifferent to Joseph's cries for mercy. Then, as things gradually unfolded, the brothers sensed that God was beginning to deal with them for their crimes. In other words, guilt was present, even though there had been no punishment. The exposition must therefore capture both sides of this scene: Joseph's testing of his brothers, and the brothers' realization that God had found out their guilt.

Structure and Synthesis

Structure

This scene unfolds in three panels: (1) the brothers and Jacob in Canaan, (2) the brothers and Joseph in Egypt, and (3) the brothers return to Jacob in Canaan. The first panel (vv. 1–5) is a commission to go to Egypt and buy grain; the second is the confrontation with Joseph (vv. 6–26), and the third is the fear and lament over the situation (vv. 27–38). As with previous sections of Genesis, the narrative works primarily with speeches that are connected with narrative reports and comments (see chart 33).

Not only do the first and last panels frame the account of the confrontation, the structure of the central panel focuses attention on the brothers' imprisonment in Egypt—just as Joseph had been imprisoned at their hands (see chart 34). Having to explain that one of their brothers was dead (v. 13) put the sale of Joseph in the forefront of their thinking. Then, having to spend three days in jail in Egypt gave them time to think it through. These events awakened their consciences.

Chart 33. **Connections Between Narrative and Speech
in Genesis 42**

Narrative Itinerary	Speech
Jacob learned there was grain in Egypt (1).	Rebuke and commission of brothers (2–3).
The brothers journeyed to Egypt (3).	
Benjamin was not sent (4a).	Precaution (4b).
The brothers came to Joseph (5–6).	
Joseph recognized them (7a).	Interrogation and response (7b).
Joseph knew and remembered (8–9a).	Accusation (9b).
	Self-defense (10–11).
	Repeated accusation (12).
	Repeated self-defense (13).
	Testing instructions (14–16).
Joseph imprisoned them (17).	New testing instructions (18–20a).
The brothers agreed (20b).	Confession of guilt and indifference (21).
	Accusation by Reuben (22).
Joseph understood and wept (23–24a).	
Joseph ordered the test (24b–26).	
The brothers discovered money (27).	Bewildered realization (28).
The brothers returned (29).	Report of events (30–34).
All the brothers discovered the money (35).	Lament of Jacob (36).
	Oath of Reuben (37).
	Refusal of Jacob (38).

Chart 34. **Chiasmus of Genesis 42:7–24**

A Joseph knew his brothers and remembered (7–9a).
  B Joseph accused them of being spies, but they explained their situation (9b–13).
    C Joseph set out a test whereby they could prove they were honest men (14–16).
      D Joseph put them in prison (17).
    C' Joseph set out a new test for the brothers to prove they were honest (18–20).
  B' The brothers confessed their guilt concerning their brother, and Reuben accused them of their fault (21–22).
A' Joseph understood and wept (23–24).

Summary Message

By putting his brothers into prison as spies when they came to Egypt for grain and by keeping Simeon hostage while the others returned to bring Benjamin back, Joseph awakened his brothers' guilty consciences.

Exegetical Outline

I. When the family of Israel was out of grain, Jacob sent his sons down to Egypt to buy grain but did not send Benjamin (1–5).

A. Jacob sent his sons to Egypt to buy grain in order to preserve the life of the family (1–2).

B. Jacob's sons went to Egypt, but Benjamin did not go with them (3–5).

    1. Jacob kept back his son Benjamin, fearing that something evil would happen to him (3–4).

    2. The brothers joined a caravan and went to Egypt (5).

II. Joseph tested his brothers when they came before him, accusing them of being spies, putting them in prison, and holding Simeon while the others returned to get Benjamin to prove that they were truthful men (6–26).

A. Joseph accused his brothers of being spies and put them in prison until one could go and get Benjamin, but then he let them go while one remained in prison until they brought Benjamin (6–20).

    1. Joseph accused his brothers—who did not recognize him— of being spies (6–9).

    2. They defended themselves by explaining their family situation and then declaring that their father had sent them to buy food (10–13).

    3. Joseph put the men in prison, demanding that one of them bring down Benjamin to prove their story (14–17).

    4. Joseph allowed the men to return home, but he kept one as a hostage (18–20).

B. The brothers confessed their guilt over the way they had treated Joseph, who, having understood their words, was overcome with emotion (21–26).

    1. The brothers repented over their putting Joseph into such distress twenty years earlier (21–22).

    2. Joseph heard his brothers and was overcome with emotion (23–24).

    3. Joseph had Simeon bound and dismissed the brothers, but he put money in their sacks (25–26).

III. As the brothers returned to Jacob in Canaan, they were dismayed to find money in their sacks; Jacob, upon hearing of the events, refused to permit Benjamin to return with them to Egypt (27–38).

A. On the way home one brother found money in his sack, and they all trembled with fear (26–28).

B. The brothers returned to Canaan and related what happened to them in Egypt (29–34).

C. The family was dismayed to find money in all the sacks of grain (35).

> D. Jacob refused to send Benjamin to Egypt with the brothers, in spite of Reuben's appeal, for he was afraid that Benjamin too would die (36–38).

Development of the Exposition

I. God uses the circumstances of life to bring about his (revealed) plan for his people (1–5).

The first panel records how Jacob sent his sons to Egypt to buy grain— all except Benjamin, for he would not risk losing his other son of Rachel. Benjamin figures prominently in these testing narratives. In the first and third panels Jacob was resolute that Benjamin would not go down. In the second panel, however, Joseph demanded that they bring him down. Jacob thus stood in the way of their proving to Joseph their honesty. His refusal to send this boy reflects the attitude that everything seemed to be against him. Besides, the characteristics of the other sons may have given him cause to suspect that more trouble lay ahead.

The words of Jacob in this regard are significant. His first speech seems to have an accusing character to it: "Why do you look at one another?" These are the words of a man frustrated with his sons' inactivity. The second speech is a commission to go to Egypt and buy food that they might live and not die (w^{e}niḥyeh w^{e}lō$^\prime$ nāmût). And the third speech is the precautionary explanation at not sending Benjamin: "Lest some harm might meet him [pen-yiqrā$^\prime$ennû $^\prime$āsôn]." This last expression could be Jacob's reasoning rather than a verbalized explanation to the other sons. Jacob was concerned that they be preserved alive, especially Benjamin; but the famine created a tension for that survival.

Unwittingly the brothers began to fulfill the dream revelation of Joseph as they left for Egypt to buy grain—from Joseph. God had used many unusual and unexpected events to bring about this fulfillment. In this instance, the famine proved to be the means of bringing the family to Egypt.

In these five verses there is a hint at the underlying theme of the chapter—the awakening of their consciences. The mention of possible harm to Benjamin in the midst of the family's attempt to buy grain to live would have put the events of the past in the minds of the brothers.

II. God's chosen leaders must ascertain the faithfulness of those who would participate in God's program (6–28).

A. The effective test reminds the guilty of their crime (6–20).

The narrative begins by telling how the brothers came and bowed down to the ground before Joseph (wayyištaḥăwû-lô $^\prime$appayim $^\prime$ār^{e}ṣâ)—

a direct fulfillment of the dreams recorded in 37:7 and 9. The text notes that Joseph recognized them (*wayyakkīrēm < nākar*) but pretended not to know them (*wayyitnakkēr*) and spoke to them harshly (*qāšôt*). After the initial inquiry of their purpose in Egypt, this editorial note is repeated: "Joseph recognized [*wayyakkēr*] his brothers, but they did not recognize him [*lō᾿ hikkīrūhû*]." Moreover, the narrative reports that Joseph remembered (*wayyizkōr*) the dreams; that is, he was ready to begin doing something about his guilty brothers. With this information and advantage, Joseph was very much in control and able to test his brothers.

The initial testing by Joseph was designed to apply pressure to his brothers by reminding them of their crimes. Joseph began with a false accusation that they were spies (he had been falsely accused by Potiphar's wife, and he had been sent by his father to check on their conduct). Now Joseph was turning things around to put them into situations similar to those that he had faced. He appeared on the surface to be handling them roughly, but underneath the severity there was affection, as witnessed by the emotional responses (the first is in v. 24).

Seeing his brothers bowing down before him must have dramatically confirmed the truth of the dreams Joseph now remembered—but not the fulfillment until the entire family came to Egypt. Joseph's task was to get Israel to Egypt, but not until he was sure they were ready. Thus, to establish that the men were honest and faithful, he demanded that they bring their youngest brother down to Egypt. Joseph would be risking the life of Benjamin, as far as he knew, but the purpose was great. He gave his brothers three days in prison to think about it.

Putting the brothers in prison for three days would have continued to work on their consciences. The threat to Benjamin had surfaced twice now, and this imprisonment would have given them a taste of what Joseph must have experienced. But Joseph's words upon their release from prison were designed to focus their thoughts on God, not just on the dilemma they faced over Benjamin. He said, "Do this and live [*wiḥyû*], for I fear God [*᾿et-hā᾿ĕlōhîm ᾿ănî yārē᾿*]." The motif of the fear of God was thus brought into the perplexing events that reminded them of their crime.

Joseph's new plan was presented as the means to confirm (*wᵉyē᾿āmᵉnû*, in v. 20) their words and prove them to be reliable men (*᾿im-kēnîm ᾿attem*, in v. 19). One brother would be kept in prison in Egypt until the rest returned with Benjamin. If they returned with their youngest brother, then Joseph would know their word was good.

B. God awakens the consciousness of guilt in his people (21–28).

The circumstances and the test by this governor immediately evoked guilt feelings in the brothers: "We are certainly guilty [*᾿ăbāl ᾿ăšēmîm*] concerning our brother" (v. 21). They confessed to each other that, because they heard Joseph's cries for mercy (*b*e*hithan*e*nô*) and would not respond, this distress had come upon them. There is a word play in verse 21 that shows the link between their crime and this dilemma: they had seen the anguish (*ṣārat napšô*), and now distress (*haṣṣārâ*) had come on them. Their infliction of anguish was the crime; this trouble was the just punishment. At this point their spiritual discernment was correct.

Reuben's remonstration further expressed this guilt (v. 22). He protested that he had warned them not to sin against the lad (*'al-teḥeṭ'û*), but they would not listen. (The brothers thus ignored first Joseph's cries and then Reuben's warnings.) Consequently, Reuben warned, the blood of Joseph would be required (*w*e*gam-dāmô hinnēh nidrāš*), a warning that more anguish lay ahead for the guilty. The demand for blood from the guilty recalls the ancient oracle of God to Noah that the one who sheds blood will be so punished (9:5–6). The brothers had not actually shed blood, but for all they knew they had, and they had certainly passed the matter off to Jacob as if blood had been shed.

The second phase of Joseph's testing was to plant their money in the sacks to compromise them and quicken the fear of God in them. At the stop at the inn the brothers discovered the money in one sack. The sense of guilt already aroused made the group quick to see the hand of God in the ruler's actions. The rhetorical question "What is this that God has done to us [*mah-zō't 'āśâ 'ĕlōhîm lānû*]?" has a note of irony to it. So far in Genesis this kind of expression had been used to interrogate the guilty ("What is this you have done?" in 3:13; 4:10; 12:18). Here the guilty brothers expressed their fear of events by the question. It was all an ominous note of foreboding. The words may imply ignorance at what God was doing, but inwardly the brothers knew that he was bringing their guilt out into the open.

III. God's people who know their sins will be willing to prove themselves before God and other people (29–38).

The last few verses of this scene record the report of these events to Jacob, including the requirement of bringing Benjamin to Egypt to prove themselves honest and to retrieve Simeon. They could not return to Egypt for more grain without Benjamin; they could not even go for Simeon without Benjamin.

Before Jacob's response is recorded, the narrative inserts the notice of the discovery of more money in the sacks (v. 35). Once again the brothers, and now also the patriarch, were afraid when they saw the money. The money in the sacks had now become an omen that something— God or fate—was menacing their lives. The brothers, who knew they were guilty, could perceive that it was God's retributive hand, for this was the second time they had come home with money, having abandoned a brother to prison in Egypt.

The scene ends with the discussion over Benjamin's accompanying them to Egypt on the next trip. Jacob, seeing the ominous nature of all the events, lamented the loss of Joseph and Simeon and the imminent loss of Benjamin—everything seemed to be against him. The verb *šik-kaltem* "you are making me childless," (v. 36), was probably meant to say that the brothers had twice brought back news of the loss of a brother. But it probably carried a greater meaning for the guilty brothers.

Reuben, representing the brothers, was determined to return and see the matter through (v. 37). His oath, even though a foolish way to guarantee the safety of Benjamin (would Jacob actually kill Reuben's sons?), demonstrated his concern for the safety of Benjamin—as if Benjamin were his own son. The brothers, and especially Reuben, were willing to comply with the Egyptian governor's test, for they had changed.

Jacob refused for the present, saying that Benjamin's brother was dead and that, if any harm should fall on Benjamin (*ûqᵉrā'āhû 'āsôn*), he would die in sorrow. Jacob's reference to himself by the figure of gray hairs (metonymy) indicates his grief and sorrow already over the loss of Joseph. The loss of Benjamin would be the death of him.

This chapter provides a complication for the family of Jacob over Benjamin's fate. Using this theme, the chapter forms an inclusio with the words of Jacob in Canaan: in verse 4, Jacob refused to let Benjamin go, lest some harm fall upon him; and in verse 38, he continued to refuse, lest some harm fall upon him. In between the events in Canaan is the meeting in Egypt, in which Joseph demanded that the brothers prove themselves by bringing Benjamin down to Egypt. The complication, then, put the brothers in a dilemma. By focusing on the problem they began to see that God was at work, bringing them to face their past crimes. Only when they began to have their consciences awakened could they perceive their guilt, and only then would they be willing to prove themselves honest and protect their brothers at the same time. *If believers have unresolved guilt in their lives, God will stir up their consciences to see if they are spiritually sensitive enough to share in his program.* He may do this through deliberate testings by his wise administrators. If such people are fit for service, they will have to prove that they are sensitive to their guilty consciences, that they have changed to become honest people, and that, if put in similar circumstances, they can be trusted to act righteously.

Bibliography

Canney, M. A. "The Hebrew מליץ (Prov IX 12; Gen XLII 23)." *AJSL* 40 (1923–24): 135–37.

Greenfield, J. C. "The Etymology of אֲמַתַּחַת." *ZAW* 77 (1965): 90–92.

Heaton, E. W. "The Root *š'r* and the Doctrine of the Remnant." *JThS* 3 (1952): 27–39.

Lehmann, M. R. "Biblical Oaths." *ZAW* 81 (1969): 74–92.

Richardson, H. N. "Some Notes on ליץ and Its Derivatives." *VT* 5 (1955): 163–79, 434–36.

Scott, R. B. Y. "The Shekel Sign on Stone Weights." *BASOR* 153 (1959): 32–35.

Speiser, E. A. "The Verb *šḥr* in Genesis and Early Hebrew Movements." *BASOR* 164 (1961): 23–28.

61

The Testing for Jealousy
(Gen. 43)

The famine continued, and the family needed more grain. But Benjamin would have to go with the brothers to Egypt if they were to be received by the ruler of Egypt. Jacob was reluctant but had to entrust Benjamin to his brothers if they were to get grain and live. This step, of course, was the precise plan of Joseph, even though it involved some risk to Rachel's second son.

This chapter forms a link between chapters in that it builds on the first journey to Egypt by the brothers (Gen. 42) and prepares for the resolution of the matter (chap. 44). The tension in this scene appears to ease when the brothers were greeted with peace in Egypt and when their honest explanation about the money was set aside with the attribution of the gift to God's intervention. And yet, within their peaceful and joyous visit to Joseph's house, they were uneasy over the seating and the gifts. There seemed to be a nemesis at work. Indeed, Joseph was deliberately favoring Benjamin over his brothers, providing them with reason for jealousy and preparing them for the opportunity to rid themselves of Benjamin as they had Joseph.

Theological Ideas

Joseph continued to demonstrate wisdom in leadership. Other kings and judges would learn from Joseph's example that they were responsible for preserving righteousness in the nation. Envy and hatred among God's people would be disastrous to the unity of the nation and so could not be left unchecked.

In this chapter Joseph continued his efforts to evaluate his brothers by testing them for jealousy. Accordingly, the episode centers on Benjamin and how the brothers would respond to his being favored. Benjamin's favored status appears early in the chapter with Jacob's hesitancy to let him go, and it is prominent at the end in the treatment by Joseph.

The motif of favoritism is balanced by the emphasis on God's mercy (v. 14), God's provision (v. 23), and God's grace (v. 29). The first came in Jacob's prayer as the brothers were leaving; the second, in the steward's response to their explanation about the money; and the third, in Joseph's blessing of Benjamin. In view of this emphasis, and because of the apparent changes in the brothers, the favoritism of Benjamin did not seem to pose a problem for the brothers.

Structure and Synthesis

Structure

Genesis 43 parallels chapter 42 very closely in that it is constructed around the brothers' departure, their stay in Egypt, and their return. The difference between the two accounts is that this second return to Canaan is interrupted by the arrest and return to Egypt for the resolution of the matter (chap. 44). The entire narrative of the second journey frequently refers to the first journey, showing how this one parallels it.

The structure once again is largely dialogue interspersed with narrative comments. The first dialogue is between Jacob and his sons, notably Judah, over the taking of Benjamin to Egypt. It includes the brothers' refusal to go without Benjamin (vv. 3–5), Israel's perplexity about their telling the ruler about Benjamin (v. 6), their explanation (v. 7), Judah's impassioned appeal (vv. 8–10), and Jacob's reluctant agreement, advice, and prayer (vv. 11–14). The second part has the dialogues in Egypt: Joseph's instructions that they be taken to his home (v. 16), the brothers' expression of their fears (v. 18), their explanation to the steward (vv. 20–22), the steward's comforting reply (v. 23), and Joseph's interrogation and blessing (vv. 27–29). The last section is entirely narrative report without speeches or dialogue, except for the instruction to set food on the table (v. 31). The importance of the passage must thus be seen through the speeches and dialogue; the contrast will be clear between the fears in the family and the comfort from Joseph's household.

Summary Message

After an impassioned dialogue with Jacob about taking Benjamin, the brothers brought Benjamin to Egypt; when they attempted to repay the money from their sacks, they received gracious and peaceful treatment from Joseph, which included lavish favoritism of Benjamin over the elder brothers.

Exegetical Outline

I. In an impassioned conversation with Jacob, the brothers, with Judah as their spokesman, gained permission to take Benjamin to Egypt in order to buy more grain (1–15).
   A. The famine continued in the land, necessitating another trip to Egypt (1–2).
   B. Judah and his brothers repeated the conditions of their return (3–10).
      1. Judah repeated the ruler's demands for their return to Egypt (3–5).
      2. Israel expressed his perplexity over their telling the man about Benjamin (6).
      3. The brothers explained that they had no idea that the ruler would make this demand (7).
      4. Judah appealed to his father to entrust Benjamin to his care (8–10).
   C. Israel reluctantly agreed to send Benjamin with them, instructing them to take a gift to the man and entrusting them to the protection of God Almighty (11–14).
      1. Israel instructed them to take the man a rich gift and money (11–12).
      2. Israel agreed to send Benjamin, entrusting them to God Almighty (13–14).
   D. The brothers returned to Joseph with their gift and with Benjamin (15).
II. In a tense and emotional meeting the brothers offered their explanation of the money, only to find a peaceful and gracious response by the steward and Joseph (16–30).
   A. Before meeting Joseph again, the brothers fearfully but honestly explained the presence of the money in their sacks, only to be treated peacefully and graciously by the steward (16–25).
      1. Joseph instructed his steward to prepare a feast and take

the men to his home; when the men were in Joseph's home, they became afraid (16–18).

2. When the brothers explained that they had been given back their money from the first visit, the steward comforted them by declaring that their God had given them the money (19–23).

3. When the brothers were brought into Joseph's house, they prepared their gift (24–25).

B. When Joseph met the brothers at his house, he inquired of their welfare, but when he blessed Benjamin, he was moved with compassion (26–30).

1. The brothers paid homage to Joseph and informed him of their father's welfare (26–28).

2. Joseph blessed Benjamin but, moved by his intense compassion, hurried away to weep (29–30).

III. In a prepared banquet for his brothers, Joseph seated the men in the order of their births and favored Benjamin over the others with extra servings (31–34).

A. Joseph prepared the banquet (31–32).

B. The brothers were amazed that they were seated in order (33).

C. Joseph favored Benjamin over them all (34).

Development of the Exposition

I. Those who would participate in God's program must demonstrate responsibility (1–15).

A. The faithful must take responsibility in order to discharge their duties (1–10).

After the notice of the first verse regarding the famine, the passage records the discussion of Jacob and his sons over the return to Egypt. Judah now succeeded where Reuben had failed (42:37–38); he intervened with a forceful but warmly personal initiative. What is surprising in this section, though, is the sons' refusal to go to Egypt without Benjamin. The reason for the refusal was repeated to Jacob twice: "The man solemnly warned [*hāʿēd hēʿîd*] us, saying 'You shall not see my face unless your brother is with you' " (vv. 3 and 5). The brothers were eager to return to Egypt, but they were convinced that they had to take Benjamin to clear themselves and free Simeon.

This forceful appeal prompted a frustrated rebuke from Jacob (v. 6). He asked, "Why did you deal so wrongfully [*hărēʿōtem* < *rāʿaʿ*] with me as to tell the man whether you had still another brother?" This question of the patriarch's continues the theme of the evil that he was to endure at the hands of others. He saw their mentioning that they had another brother as yet one more sign that everything was against him (see 42:36). His sons explained that they had acted in ignorance (43:7).

Eventually Judah prevailed in persuading Jacob to send Benjamin with him, vowing to take the blame if anything should happen to the lad. This was not a hollow promise, for Judah set stern conditions if he failed to bring Benjamin back: "then let me bear the blame forever [$w^e h \bar{a} t \bar{a}' t \hat{i}$ $l^e k \bar{a}$ kol-hayyāmîm]" (v. 9). The appeal was convincing, and time was wasting, so Jacob agreed to let Benjamin go.

B. Those who act responsibly may trust their work to God Almighty (11–15).

Jacob's words sound pitiful as he relinquished Benjamin for the journey. He had no choice. (Note the word order in v. 13: w^e'et-'ăḥîkem qāḥû.) But since they were going, he gave them instructions that might secure favor from the ruler. He wisely instructed his sons to take a lavish gift to the man in Egypt in order to obtain mercy (v. 11) and then to double the money that they found in the sacks (v. 12).

His prayer at their departure is very important to the theme of the chapter: he entrusted them to God Almighty ('ēl šadday) for mercy (raḥămîm) before the man, that he might release Simeon and Benjamin to them. But there was a resignation in his words that he might have to live with bereavement: "If I am bereaved, I am bereaved [wa'ănî ka'ăšer šākōltî šākāltî]!"

II. Those who would participate in God's program must make restitution for any appearance of wrongdoing (16–25).

A. The faithful must deal honestly where there is the appearance of wrongdoing (16–22).

The meeting between Joseph and his brothers was arranged by Joseph. He planned to entertain them with a meal in his house. This decision, although probably intended as an act of kindness in setting the men at ease before testing their jealousy of Benjamin, evoked great fear and guilt in the men. They were afraid that he was laying a trap for them because of the money. This fear hastened their attempt at making restitution for the money that had been in their sacks.

B. Those who act honestly find favor with God and man (23–25).

It is important to examine closely the response of the steward to the men's explanation of the money. He said, "Peace be with you [šālôm lākem]; do not be afraid [ʾal-tîrāʾû]. Your God and the God of your father has given you treasure in your sacks; I had your money." This communication would have set the men at ease with regard to the Egyptian ruler's anger but would have troubled them in their understanding of God's dealings with them, for they knew they were guilty. According to von Rad,

> The master of ceremonies' gracious answer is the jewel in this masterful scene. It is reassuring and intended to distract the upset men from the object of their fear; but its dark ambiguity touches the innermost mystery of the whole Joseph story: God's concealed guidance. God is at work in the events and therefore nothing is said now about money but rather about a "treasure" which God has placed for them in their sacks. This answer may at first have reassured the brothers somewhat, but they could only understand it later. [*Genesis*, pp. 388–89]

III. Those who participate in God's program must rejoice in their provisions—even when a brother receives more (26–34).

The brothers' approach to Joseph was humble; they prepared their gifts carefully and then bowed (*wayyištaḥăwû*) before him once again. Joseph's words, however, brought them comfort in what must have been a frightening moment. He asked them of their welfare (*lᵉšālôm*—what he had originally been sent to find out in 37:14) and the welfare (*šālôm*) of their father. After they responded that Jacob was alive and well, they bowed again and did obeisance (*wayyiqqᵉdû wayyištaḥăwû*).

Joseph's attention then turned to Benjamin. His blessing is significant in the scene: "God be gracious [< *ḥānan*] to you my son." But having blessed Benjamin, Joseph could not refrain from emotionally responding (*kî-nikmᵉrû raḥămāyw ʾel-ʾāḥîw*). The tender mercy for which Jacob prayed (v. 14) came naturally from one who was moved by compassion for his brother.

This exchange all led into the next testing of the brothers—the banquet feast. In what must have been a troubling display of apparent divine intervention, the brothers realized they had been seated according to their ages. But this baffling situation gave way to the real issue, the favoritism toward Benjamin. Now that Joseph had increased their uneasy sense of exposure to God's intervention, he focused their attention on Rachel's son by favoring Benjamin five times over them. If they retained any envy for this son of Rachel, Jacob's favorite of the lot, this treatment was bound to excite it. The test was calculated to give them the opportunity to rekindle the old animosity. But the men drank and were merry with him.

This episode presents the brothers in a different light than before. From Judah's kind speech to his father, in which he was willing to take the blame for any harm to the lad, to their open acknowledgment regarding the money, to their enjoyment at the feast in spite of the favoritism to Benjamin, the brothers displayed a greater maturity about their lot in life. They were aware of God's intervention more than ever before, and so they demonstrated the proper response under the testing of Joseph—but one more severe test was needed to be sure.

The strengths that the brothers manifested in this chapter were also necessary for the nation (or the church) if they were to be God's servants through whom the blessing would be continued. In this chapter the brothers promised to take the blame for any catastrophe (responsibility); they acknowledged their culpability and made restitution for the money in their sacks (honesty); they retrieved their brother from prison in Egypt (unity); they recognized that God was at work in their midst (belief); and they rejoiced in their provisions, even when a brother was receiving more than they were (gratitude). Such is the maturity of the people of God whom God will use to bless the world. *Those who would participate in God's program must be willing to take responsibility for their actions, make restitution when they are culpable, and accept their lot gratefully and without jealousy.*

Bibliography

Heidel, A. "A Special Usage of the Akkadian Term *šadû*." *JNES* 8 (1949): 233–35.

Humbert, P. "Le substantif *to'ēbā* et le verb *t'b* dans l'AT." *ZAW* 72 (1960): 217–37.

Neihaus, J. "The Use of *lûlē* in Psalm 27." *JBL* 98 (1979): 88–89.

62

The Testing for Loyalty
(Gen. 44)

Ondash ne more test was necessary before Joseph could disclose himself to his brothers and move his family to Egypt. Joseph had to see if they would abandon Rachel's other son, the favored Benjamin, if it should come to their life or his. Joseph gave them the opportunity in this calculated test. Dods says,

> Everything falls short of thorough repentance which does not prevent us from committing the sin anew. We do not so much desire to be accurately informed about our past sins, and to get right views of our past selves; we wish to be no longer sinners, we wish to pass through some process by which we may be separated from that in us which has led us into sin. Such a process there is, for these men passed through it. [*Book of Genesis*, p. 387]

This episode forms part of the account of the brothers' second journey to Egypt; it is an interruption of the return journey to Canaan that was due to the stolen goblet in Benjamin's sack. The chapter is a narrative report in the first half (vv. 1–17) that leads into Judah's speech on behalf of his brother in the second half (vv. 18–34). This marvelous speech elicits Joseph's emotional response in chapter 45. This narrative thus builds to a climax in the testing of the brothers, for the events recorded here threatened Benjamin and provided the occasion for either a new way of dealing with the matter or a repetition of the events in chapter 37.

Theological Ideas

The important theological point of the passage is the brothers' acknowledgment that God had found out their iniquity (v. 16). This motif is underscored by the fact that the verb "to find (out)" occurs eight times in the narrative. Their consciences may have been bothering them for some time, but through the testing their senses were exercised to be reminded of the loss of Rachel's son. The brothers were accused of something they had not done (spying), and Benjamin was accused of doing something he had not done (stealing). Yet they acknowledged that they had been found out for their crime against Joseph.

This theological idea of guilt over past sins informs the central point of the passage—love for the brother. The passage teaches that, in order for brothers to live together in unity, they must have self-sacrificing love for one another; but it teaches this lesson by demonstrating that those who have not possessed such love will be called on to demonstrate it. Judah's speech focuses on this point, for he appealed for Benjamin for his father's sake and willingly offered himself in the place of Benjamin. He did so because he knew that God had found out their past sins and that the present difficulty was a part of the retribution.

Structure and Synthesis

Structure

The chapter corresponds rather closely to parts of chapter 43: Joseph's commission to the steward (43:16–17 and 44:1–2, 4–6), the brothers' appeal to the steward (43:18–23 and 44:7–13), and the brothers' submission before Joseph (43:26–30 and 44:14–17, 18–34). Such parallelism in the story of Joseph is common. Here it serves to heighten the tension of the testing by Joseph before there could be any resolution.

Within the chapter itself repeated elements reinforce the message. The motif of evil occurs in verses 4, 5, and 34, stressing that the brothers had done evil and would again bring sorrow to Jacob. The preposition *taḥat*, "for," occurs in verses 4 and 33, relating their doing evil for good and Judah's desire to replace Benjamin in captivity. The expression *ḥālîlâ*, "God forbid," is used twice, once by the men when accused (v. 7), and once by Joseph when he chose to keep only Benjamin (v. 17). The verb "to die" is repeated; it is used by the brothers when they rashly put a death penalty on Benjamin (v. 9), and then by Judah when he realizes that it would kill Jacob to lose Benjamin. Finally, the verb "to find" occurs eight times (vv. 8, 9, 10, 12, twice in 16, 17, 34). Its central use is in the explanation of God's finding out their iniquity (v. 16), showing how they understood the other findings.

Summary Message

Having forced the brothers to bring Benjamin down to Egypt, Joseph tested their concern for him by framing the lad and blaming him for taking the cup, all of which prompted the brothers' acknowledgment that God was finding out their sin against Joseph, and Judah's intercessory plea on Benjamin's behalf.

Exegetical Outline

I. When Joseph tested his brothers' concern for Benjamin, the brothers acknowledged that God had found out their iniquity in the evil done to Joseph (1–17).
   A. Joseph tested them by placing his silver cup in Benjamin's sack and accusing the brothers of stealing it (1–6).
      1. Joseph commanded his servant to put his silver cup in Benjamin's sack (1–2).
      2. He commanded his servant to follow them and accuse them of stealing it (3–6).
   B. Joseph's test elicited a defensive and unified response from the brothers (7–13).
      1. They responded to the accusation by affirming their honesty in returning the money from their first visit (7–8).
      2. They responded in confidence by offering the life of the one in whose sack the cup might be found (9–11).
      3. They responded in dismay when the servant found the cup in Benjamin's sack (12–13).
   C. Joseph's test both prompted the brothers to acknowledge that God had found out their iniquity and examined the brothers' concern for Benjamin by declaring him to be a slave (14–17).
      1. Judah and his brothers bowed before Joseph (14).
      2. Joseph reiterated that he practiced divination (15).
      3. Judah confessed that God had found out their iniquity and declared that all of them were Joseph's slaves (16).
      4. Joseph declared that only Benjamin would be his slave and that the others could go free (17).

II. Judah's intercessory plea on behalf of his brother Benjamin demonstrated his concern for his father and therefore the favorite son (18–34).

A. Judah approached Joseph as the intercessor and recalled their first meeting with him (18–23).

1. Judah approached Joseph as intercessor of the group (18).

2. He recalled their first meeting, when Joseph demanded to see their youngest brother Benjamin (19–23).

B. Judah recounted how they had told their father that they could not return to Egypt without Benjamin and reported Jacob's anxiety over his favorite son (24–29).

1. Judah related how they told Jacob that they could not return to Egypt without Benjamin (24–26).

2. He reported how Jacob expressed sorrow over losing Joseph and anxiety over letting Benjamin go (27–29).

C. Judah explained that Jacob would die in sorrow if Benjamin did not return and offered himself as a slave in Benjamin's place (30–34).

1. Judah explained that, if they returned without Benjamin, their father would die in sorrow and he would bear the guilt for it (30–32).

2. He offered to remain as a slave in Benjamin's place, demonstrating his concern for his father and his brother (33–34).

Development of the Exposition

I. Because of their past failures, God may have to test his people's love and concern for others (1–17).

A. Accusation of evil (1–6).

Joseph's strategy, already brilliantly successful in creating the tensions he required through the two visits of the brothers, now produced his master stroke. He tested their concern for Benjamin by giving them the opportunity to recall their evil and not repeat it. If they should have no compassion for their brother, then they had no place in the development of the promise. The test involved placing Joseph's cup in Benjamin's sack and then pursuing them to arrest Benjamin.

The accusation of the steward is powerfully worded: "Why have you repaid evil for good [lāmmâ šillamtem rāʿâ taḥat ṭôbâ]?" and "You have done evil [hărēʿōtem]." They had been greatly favored in Egypt but now were accused of responding to that good with an evil act. On a deeper level these words would have struck a responsive chord concerning the evil they had earlier done to someone who was good.

B. Protestation of innocence (7–13).

The brothers' anxious fears found immediate expression: "God forbid" (ḥālîlâ). They protested their innocence by explaining how they returned the money they had found (māṣā'nû)—they were honest men. They were so confident of their innocence that they put a death penalty (wāmēt) on the one in whose sack it might be found (yimmāṣē'). But the steward declared that only the one in whose sack the cup might be found (yimmāṣē') would become a servant—the rest would be blameless (neqîyīm). Of course, the cup was found (wayyimmāṣē') in Benjamin's sack, much to the grief of the brothers.

C. Acknowledgment of iniquity (14–17).

The brothers then returned to Egypt and again bowed before Joseph. Judah confessed their frustration and admitted that God had found out their iniquity: "What shall we say to my lord? What shall we speak? Or how shall we clear ourselves? God has found out the iniquity of your servants [māṣā' 'et-'ăwōn 'ăbādeykā]." Benno Jacob says,

> According to a higher moral order an exact relationship exists between their distress and their crime. They acknowledge that the men who act against them are only tools of higher justice. God is the true judge. Their public profession of this and acceptance of the verdict is their repentance and greatness. [*First Book of the Bible*, pp. 297–98]

Judah then declared that they would all be his slaves. To their consternation, he said, "God forbid" (ḥālîlâ)—only the guilty would be a slave; the rest were free to go in peace (lešālôm).

II. Those who truly acknowledge their iniquity will follow a very different course when given another opportunity (18–34).

The rest of the chapter is the lengthy appeal of Judah, in which he showed himself to be a man fit for leadership. His intercession on behalf of Benjamin, a fine and moving appeal, demonstrated great love for his brother and great concern for his father. This was not the Judah of old.

The final words show that a genuine change had come about. Judah appealed to Joseph on the basis of the evil (bārā') that would come upon (yimṣā') his father if he returned without Rachel's son—he would die (wāmēt). Before, they had not considered that consequence and were overwhelmed when they could not console Jacob over his son. It appears from this verse that the anguish of the father had been felt by all. Judah, exhibiting a self-sacrificial loyalty, requested that he be kept instead of (taḥat) Benjamin.

In this final and great test the brothers thus demonstrated that they had changed, that they were repentant over their sin against their brother. There was now concern for the father and self-sacrificing love for the half-brother. No nation could long survive without such care and compassion. As Westermann says, "There is a path that leads from the Joseph story right up to the very threshold of community; the healing of a breach is possible only when there is one who is ready to take the suffering upon oneself" (Genesis, vol. 3, p. 178). Consequently, Joseph would make himself known to them.

In the testing the brothers had responded correctly and showed themselves worthy. They demonstrated that they knew what kind of spirit was needed in the family, in the nation. Sadly enough, this lesson was learned by Judah through the divine activity in his conscience—he learned first the evil that results from hating a brother and then, to prevent such evil again, he would sacrifice himself for his brother. *God requires self-sacrificing love among believers, but such loyalty may need to be fostered through the uncovering of past sins.* If believers have been envious and hateful of others in the past, then God might have to put them through stressful situations to make them realize how much they must do for their fellow believers to prevent great evil in the family of God. But once they come to the point of laying down their lives for others, they find that there is truly no greater love.

Bibliography

Glueck, J. J. "Nagid—Shepherd." *VT* 13 (1963): 144–50.

Hillers, D. R. *"Berît ʿam:* 'Emancipation of the People.' " *JBL* 97 (1978): 176–82.

Jacobs, L. "The Qal Vaḥomer Argument in the Old Testament." *BSOAS* 35 (1972): 221–27.

63

The Reconciliation of Brothers
(Gen. 45:1–15)

T his unit presents the favorable resolution to the tension of the story that began in chapter 37. It is also the turning point of the story, for now Joseph could bring the family down to Egypt and settle them in the best of the land so that they could survive as the people of God. Now that his brothers had reconciled themselves to the fact of his leadership, Joseph could indeed rule over them.

The first fifteen verses of this chapter essentially record Joseph's emotional speech, in which he made himself known to his brothers (vv. 3–13). After what had happened between them in the past, a speech of this type is the only thing that would have relieved guilt, eased their fears, and prevented bitterness. There would be no retaliation from Joseph, not just because he had seen that they had changed, but because he had a proper understanding of how God had been working in his life.

Theological Ideas

One major theological idea affirmed in this passage is that God sovereignly preserves life on the earth. He overcomes this crisis of the famine by preparing a deliverer who would be able to save his people

and all the world. This point of theology informs the entire story of
Joseph but finds expression here.

A second idea, growing out of the first, is that God uses even the evil
that people do to bring about his plan. Here is the inscrutable balance
between the sovereign will and the human will—they had sold him in
hatred, but God sent him to Egypt to save them. The righteous can
discern that God works even through the evil plans of humans (cf. Acts
2:23). Those who do evil are responsible for their actions, but God will
use even those actions for his glory.

Out of this theological point grows a practical matter. The perception
of this second truth by the righteous will enable them to forgive others,
for if God includes all in his sovereign plan, then they must give no
room to retaliation or bitterness.

Structure and Synthesis

Structure

The passage begins and ends with narrative reports. The first two
verses record Joseph's emotional revelation to his brothers and their perplexity, and the last two verses record the warm reunion with the brothers.

Joseph's speech dominates the passage. In it he explained God's purpose in all that had happpened and advised his brothers on what they
were now to do. The structure includes a double revelation in verses 3
and 4, which would be necessary under the circumstances, an explanation of his circumstances (vv. 5–8), and instruction for their migration
to Egypt (vv. 9–13). The beginning revelation and the closing instructions concern family matters. ("I am Joseph. Does my father yet live?"
And, "Now your eyes see that it is my mouth that speaks to you . . . tell
my father of all my glory in Egypt.") But Joseph's explanation of his
circumstances provides the main point of the speech; it stresses God's
sovereignty, for the phrase "God sent me" is repeated three times, affirming that the brothers did not send him—God did. His purpose in
this emphasis was to set the brothers at ease over their past guilty offense and lend support to the instructions he was about to give.

Summary Message

In a burst of unrestrainable emotion, Joseph revealed his identity to
his brothers, assuring them that it was God's sovereign purpose in sending him to Egypt and instructing them to bring his father to Egypt, and
then was warmly united with his brothers.

Exegetical Outline

  I. When Joseph could no longer restrain himself, he revealed his
     identity to his brothers and assured them that it was God's sov-

ereign purpose to send him to Egypt in order to preserve the family (1–8).

A. Joseph dismissed the Egyptians when he was moved to reveal himself to his brothers (1–2).

B. Joseph revealed his identity to his brothers and inquired about his father's welfare—all of which caused his brothers to be panic-stricken (3).

C. Joseph urged his brothers to forgive themselves for selling him, explaining that God had brought him to Egypt in order to preserve the family from starvation (4–8).

  1. He reiterated his revelation that he was Joseph, whom they sold into Egypt, but urged them not to be angry with themselves (4–5a).

  2. He explained that God had sent him to preserve them with a great deliverance (5b–7).

  3. He clarified the point that they had not sent him there— God had; and God had made him a ruler over all Egypt (8).

II. Joseph instructed his brothers to inform his father of all his glory in Egypt and to bring Jacob to Egypt so that the whole family could dwell in security with ample provision (9–13).

A. He told them to hurry home with the news that God had made him ruler in Egypt and with the instruction to come down to Egypt (9).

B. He explained that they would live in security and plenty during the rest of the famine (10–11).

C. He assured them that he was Joseph, as they could plainly see, and told them to bring his father down to Egypt (12–13).

III. Joseph reunited himself with his brothers (14–15).

Development of the Exposition

Some expositors may find it advantageous to incorporate into one exposition all the material in chapters 42 through 45:15, making this unit the culmination of the development. In that case the first scene (chap. 42) would be the awakening of guilty consciences; the second scene would be the testing for maturity (chap. 43), requiring those who would share in God's program to take responsibility, make restitution where necessary, and rejoice in God's provisions without jealousy; the third scene would be the testing for loyalty (chap. 44), calling for self-sacrificing love; and the fourth scene, the culmination of the testing, would be the reconciliation (45:1–15). Such an exposition would be arranged more like a survey of the contents of the chapters, selecting critical ideas for closer examination.

Each unit, however, has sufficient material for an exposition in its own rights, and this unit is no exception. The subject matter here is forgiveness that makes reconciliation possible.

I. A proper understanding of the sovereignty of God enables the believer to forgive others (1–8).

A. Compassion is the motivation for reconciliation (1–3).

Although this unit is largely the speech of Joseph, it begins with a narrative report about Joseph's desire to reveal his identity to his brothers. The story has previously hinted at Joseph's emotional response to his brothers (43:30); here it became too strong to control any longer (*wᵉlō'-yākōl yôsēp lᵉhit'appēq*, in v. 1), and so with an emotional outburst he made himself known to his brothers (*hitwadda'*). Joseph's weeping aloud (v. 2) and his immediate inquiry about his father (v. 3) show that he strongly desired to be reconciled with his brothers and united with his family. He now knew that his brothers were different and so made himself known to them.

The brothers' response to this sudden revelation was understandable, given all that had gone on before—they could not answer him (*wᵉlō'-yākᵉlû 'ehāyw la'ănôt*) because they were troubled (*nibhălû*) at his presence. They were confused and terrified (see *bāhal*) by the sudden revelation, unsure what it might all lead to. It is worth noting, that, in verse 1, Joseph could not (*lō'-yākōl*) restrain himself because of his emotions, and in verse 3, his brothers could not (*lō'-yākᵉlû*) speak because of their terror.

B. Forgiveness is the means of reconciliation (4–8).

The first half of Joseph's speech opened the way for reconciliation between them. It is one of the clearest statements of the sovereignty of God in Genesis. After identifying himself as Joseph, whom they sold into Egypt (this relative clause convincing them he was not a pretender), he told them not to be grieved ('al-tē'āṣᵉbû [cf. 3:16–17; 6:6]) or angry with themselves ('al-yihar bᵉ'ênêkem), because God had sent him to Egypt to prepare for the famine in order to deliver their lives. Three times he affirmed that God sent him (*sᵉlāhani 'elōhîm*, in v. 5; *wayyišlāhēni 'elōhim*, in v. 7; and *lō'-'attem sᵉlahtem . . . kî hā'elōhîm*, in v. 8). The use of this verb reminds the reader of commission narratives in which the leader could announce that God had sent him (see Exod. 3:15).

Not only had God sent Joseph to Egypt, he had made him a lord ('ādôn) and a ruler (*mōšēl*) over all the land of Egypt. This last verb recalls the response of the brothers when they first interpreted his dream that he would be a ruler: "Will you indeed have dominion [*māšôl timšōl*] over us?" (37:8).

The purpose of Joseph's being sent before them was to preserve a posterity (*šeʾērît*) in the earth and to save their lives (*ûlᵉhaḥăyôt*) by a great deliverance (*liplêṭâ*). The use of words such as "posterity," or "remnant" (*šeʾērît*) and "deliverance," the lot of survivors (*pᵉlēṭâ*), brings forward the motif of rescue that is thematically important in Genesis (see von Rad, *Genesis*, pp. 398–99). These two words, which occur predominantly in prophecy, express the expectation of salvation (see Isa. 10:20; 15:9; Ezra 9:14). Joseph's whole purpose was to ensure that the remnant of God's people would be saved in this crisis.

Joseph's speech forms a classic expression of providence; it was his conviction that God's will, not the will of human beings, was the controlling reality in the events of his life. His explanation that the brothers had not sent him to Egypt meant that they had not acted independently of God's will—they were part of God's greater plan to bring Joseph to Egypt to deliver them. They had attempted to be rid of their brother by selling him into Egypt, but as Calvin asserts, God from heaven overruled their counsels and attempts and, in short, did by their hands what he had himself decreed (*First Book of Moses*, p. 378). The act of sending Joseph to Egypt was thus attributed both to men and to God, but for very different purposes—they acted because they hated him, but God planned to use Joseph as their deliverer.

Dods correctly cautions that "the discovery that through our evil purposes and injurious deeds God has worked out his beneficent will, is certainly not calculated to make us think more lightly of our sin or more highly of ourselves" (*Book of Genesis*, p. 394). The knowledge that God overruled an evil plan may have brought great relief from years of guilt, but also fear and sadness from realizing what might have happened (cf. Isaac in 27:33). They had maliciously sold Joseph, hoping that his dreams would be put to an end; God used that means to bring him to Egypt so that they now might have a savior in the famine. God is able to bring good out of evil, as the developing message of Genesis has shown. But every sin, every failure, every self-deceiving enterprise that appears to work in one way, although evil, carries its own cost because it is sin. The brothers' life was not what it might have been, had they not sinned; nevertheless, because of their sin and its pain, they developed a deeper appreciation for one another and a greater understanding of their sovereign Lord God. Had they but obeyed and followed God's plan, they would have enjoyed his blessings to the full and spared themselves and their family the pain. In spite of their attempts to change the divine plan, eventually they found out that God's plan would triumph. Through it all they learned which side to follow—not the side of evil borne of envy and hatred, but the side that can discern the hand of God in human affairs. They might not understand God's plan, but they must accept it and promote it.

This theology is the basis of reconciliation; without it there would be only bitterness and blame, rancor and revenge. The principle is that whoever is spiritual will perceive the hand of God in the course of events and therefore be able to forgive what others have done. No one who believes in the sovereignty of God in the affairs of life can bear a grudge or take revenge. Joseph magnanimously comforted his brothers with this sound doctrine.

II. The forgiveness of others enables believers to enjoy complete reconciliation (9–15).

A. Further development is the purpose of reconciliation (9–13).

The second part of Joseph's speech records his instructions for the family. He told his brothers to return to Jacob with all the news of his glory (i.e., importance [kābôd]) in Egypt and with the instructions to move to Egypt to survive the famine. In his instructions Joseph continued to stress the sovereignty of God, instructing them to tell Jacob that God had made his son ruler over all Egypt (v. 9). And now, in order for Joseph to fulfill his destiny as the deliverer of his family, the family would have to move to Egypt, where he could nourish them (wᵉkilkaltî; see the usage of kûl in Ruth 4:15, 1 Kings 4:7, 27; 17:4, 9). To remain in Canaan would have led to poverty and death in the five years remaining in the famine.

It would not be particularly easy for the brothers to take this message to Jacob (see 45:24), for in telling the good news, the brothers would need to include the bad news—how Joseph came to be in Egypt in the first place. Hard as it might have been, such open confession was necessary for the healing of the family. But no healing would have been possible without their recognition of God's mysterious ways.

B. Unity is the reward of reconciliation (14–15).

The passage closes with a brief report of the reunion of the brothers. First Joseph and Benjamin, and then all the brothers, were tearfully united. The emotional pitch that began the unit surfaces again at the end in this tearful reconciliation. The scene is reminiscent of the reconciliation of Jacob and Esau (33:4); that reconciliation, however, was not a true one, for Jacob and Esau never did unite. Distrust and deception clouded that meeting. But here there was a new beginning.

The exposition of this passage must capture the theology, for it is applicable in any age. Far from being a piece of speculative theology, it is very practical for averting retaliation and recrimination: *Reconciliation comes through forgiveness, and forgiveness through the recognition of God's sovereignty.* When the one who has been wronged can see things as God sees them, can perceive them as God planned them, and can communicate that understanding as the basis for compassion and forgiveness, then reconciliation is possible. But anyone who bears a grudge or hopes to retaliate has not come to appreciate the meaning of the sovereignty of God. And without the forgiveness that comes with such an appreciation, there can be no reconciliation.

Bibliography

Hasel, G. F. "Semantic Values of Derivatives of the Hebrew Root š'r." *AUSS* 11 (1973): 152–69.

Vater, A. M. "Narrative Patterns for the Story of Commissioned Communication in the Old Testament." *JBL* 99 (1980): 365–82.

64

The Moving of Israel to Egypt
(Gen. 45:16–46:30)

T his section of the story extends the reconciliation theme to its completion with the family's move to Egypt. Everything about the passage is positive, from the delight of Pharaoh over the discovery to the reunion of Jacob with his lost son. Not only does the unit trace the reconciliation through to its completion, it does so within the fulfillment of the dreams as well—the family would now live together in Egypt under the rulership of Joseph. Genesis 46, then, forms the very beginning of the conclusion of the Joseph story (chaps. 46–50).

The passage comprises several different types of literature: narrative report (45:16–28), a theophany with promise, fitted into an itinerary (46:1–7), a name list (vv. 8–27), and a concluding narrative report (vv. 28–30).

Theological Ideas

As an important part of the culmination of the Joseph story, this section explains how Israel (i.e., the patriarch with his clan) found their way to Egypt. Joseph himself had said that God had sent him on before to prepare the way and save them in the time of famine. Here, then, is the report of how that plan started to come to fruition: Joseph, in power in Egypt, brought his family to Egypt, where they could survive.

676

Within the account of the trek to Egypt is the message of the Lord to Jacob. This theophany is reminiscent of the patriarchal narratives and so seems a little out of place in the story of Joseph. But it probably was intended to connect the move to Egypt with the patriarchal promises. The message reaffirmed the promises made to Abraham so long ago, in a way that parallels them. Here again God assured his believers of the ultimate fulfillment of the promises, in spite of the Egyptian sojourn.

Structure and Synthesis

Structure

Since the passage has four different types of literature, the analysis of structure needs to be restricted to the individual sections. The first section traces Pharaoh's confirmation of the invitation to the father (45:16–20), Joseph's discharging his brothers on the mission (vv. 21–24), and their arrival in Canaan with the news (vv. 25–28). This section is narrative report interspersed with speeches.

In the second section, itinerary reports (46:1 and 5–7) bracket the theophany. This revelation to Israel in the night vision follows the pattern of the patriarchal promises: God's self-revelation, his instruction not to fear, the reiteration of the promise, and the promise of his presence.

The list of names in the third section follows the order of Leah's sons, the sons of Leah's maid, Rachel's sons, and finally the sons of Rachel's maid. The closing section narrates the reunion of Joseph and his father. It bears similarity to the ending of the first narrative section (45:28) in that Israel said, "Now let me die, since I have seen your face, because you are still alive" (46:30).

Summary Message

When the brothers brought news of Joseph's survival and prosperity in Egypt, Israel went to be reunited with his son and to dwell in the land of Egypt, having been encouraged to go by the Lord, who assured him of the promises in a night vision.

Exegetical Outline

I. After the brothers returned to Canaan to tell of Joseph's survival and prosperity in Egypt, Israel decided to journey to Egypt to see his beloved son (45:16–28).

   A. When Pharaoh heard about the brothers, he commanded Joseph to have his family move to Egypt, where they could be cared for with the best of the land (16–20).

   1. Pharaoh was pleased to hear about Joseph's brothers (16).

   2. He issued an invitation for the family to sojourn in Egypt and promised to sustain them there (17–18).

   3. He reiterated the invitation (19–20).

B. In compliance with Pharaoh's commands, Joseph provided gifts and provisions for the brothers as they departed for Canaan (21–24).
   1. Joseph provided gifts and provisions (21–23).
   2. Joseph sent them on their way, instructing them not to quarrel (24).
C. After Jacob's sons told him about Joseph, Israel was stunned, but he resolved to go to Egypt to see his son (25–28).
   1. When they told their father the news, he was stunned (25–26).
   2. After seeing the gifts and provisions, Jacob revived and resolved to go to Egypt (27–28).
II. When Israel stopped on the way to worship at Beersheba, the Lord God spoke to him in a night vision, sanctioning his departure, confirming the promises, and assuring him of the Lord's continued presence and blessing on the family (46:1–7).
   A. Itinerary: Israel journeyed to Beersheba and offered sacrifices to God (1).
   B. Revelation: God spoke to Israel in a night vision (2–4).
      1. He identified himself as the God of his father (2–3a).
      2. He encouraged Jacob to go to Egypt and promised to make him into a great nation (3b).
      3. He promised that his presence would accompany them to Egypt and that they would be delivered from Egypt (4).
   C. Itinerary: Jacob, with his family and all his possessions, left Beersheba and proceeded to the land of Egypt (5–7).
III. All the descendants of Israel's household, some seventy in all, settled in the land of Egypt (46:8–27).
IV. Israel came to Egypt, where he was reunited with his exalted son, Joseph (46:28–30).

Development of the Exposition

I. Believers must be responsive to the Lord's plan, especially when it is so obvious in the circumstances of God's dealings with his chosen leaders (45:16–28).

The first section of the passage, the instructions and the decision for the move to Egypt, shows how Israel recognized that the report of the mysterious happenings was true and resolved to go to Egypt. The narrative begins with Pharaoh's delight and participation in the move of Israel to Egypt. The text states that, when he heard that Joseph's brothers had come to Egypt, it pleased (wayyîṭab) him (v. 16). Then twice in his advice on the move he declared that "the good [*ṭûb*] of the land" would be theirs (vv. 18 and 20). Here was a man, no doubt grateful to Joseph and to Joseph's God, who was blessing the seed of Abraham and in return would enjoy God's blessing on his land.

Joseph implemented the instructions of Pharaoh with a necessary counsel for his brothers not to "fall out" (*rāgaz*, "be agitated," and so quarrel) on the way (v. 24). This was not a time for accusations and recriminations, which could easily have come to blows. It was a time for joyful reunion. However, Joseph knew what lay ahead of them—a full explanation of what had happened.

In sending provisions home, it is interesting to note that Joseph again gave Benjamin far more than the others. Benjamin was, after all, his full brother, and the brother that he had subjected to danger during the testing. With the provisions he sent a gift to his father—ten donkeys loaded with the good things (*ṭûb*) of Egypt, and ten female donkeys loaded with food.

The last four verses of chapter 46 report both the brothers' arrival with the news and Jacob's response. At first he was numb (unable to move) from astonishment, but upon the arrival of the provisions his spirit revived (*wattᵉḥî rûaḥ*). He then realized that Joseph was alive and resolved to go see his son before he died ('*ēlᵉkâ wᵉ'er'ennû bᵉṭerem 'āmût*).

The royal invitation to the old patriarch near the end of his hope and to the ten brothers burdened with guilt was a turning point in their lives and a fulfillment of the prophecy to Abram (15:13–16) that they would go into a strange land for a period of time. But that prophecy also forewarned of opposition in that foreign land.

The impact on Jacob of all those developments should be stressed in this section. Everything seems to build to the final announcement that Joseph was yet alive (v. 26) and the report of Jacob's acceptance of that news (v. 28). It would now be so clear that God had worked in a marvelous, yet strange, way to bring them to this hour. Now that God's hand on Joseph could be so clearly seen, Joseph's instructions must be followed. God was obviously using his chosen and wise leader to lead others.

II. Believers need the reassurances of God's promises to be with them and ultimately to bring them to their destined place, as they make their decisions in life (46:1–7).

A. Obedience (1).

Having recognized the will of God through circumstances and the instructions from Joseph, Israel journeyed toward Egypt. His journey took him to Beersheba, where he made sacrifices (*wayyizbaḥ zᵉbāḥîm*) to the God of his father, Isaac. Not only did Israel immediately comply with the instruction that he now knew was God's plan, he began with worship at the altar in Beersheba. Such faith in God led Israel to comply.

B. Confirmation (2–4).

After he had sacrificed to the Lord at Beersheba, Israel received confirmation from the Lord about the move. In a night vision the Lord reiterated the promise that he would make Israel into a great nation (cf. 12:2) and that he would deliver his people from Egypt (cf. 15:14). This vision would have encouraged not only Israel the patriarch but also the nation of Israel later when they were preparing to leave the land of Egypt to return to Canaan. The revelation was clear: God was with them, and so the promise would be fulfilled and they would be delivered.

C. Continued obedience (5–7).

These verses report how Israel and all his family and possessions entered into Egypt.

III. Believers must respond to God's leading in anticipation of the fulfillment of the promises, because out of their number God will build his covenant community (46:8–30).

For this last point I have joined the list of names (8–27) with the narrative report about the reunion of the family in Egypt (28–30). The predominant part of this section is the listing of seventy names of the family in Egypt, from which the nation of Israel would grow. Seventy is a full number for the foundational family of God's nation. The number corresponds to the seventy nations in the Table of Nations (Gen. 10). In Deuteronomy 32:8–11, Moses explained that the nations' boundaries were established according to the number of the children of Israel (see Cassuto, *Commentary on Genesis*, vol. 2, pp. 175–78).

As a full family unit, Israel settled in Egypt. There they would become the great nation that God had promised. He had brought them to Egypt through supernaturally controlled circumstances and by wise actions of spiritual leaders who understood the meaning of the circumstances. The family entered Egypt convinced that that was where God wanted them and that the fulfillment of the promises would follow.

The concluding report in verses 28–30 is interesting from two perspectives: first, Judah seemed again to come to the fore in the patriarchal commission; second, the motifs of life and death—so common in Joseph's experiences—were reiterated in the expression of the patriarch.

Israel could die in peace (*'āmûtâ*) because Joseph was alive (*ḥāy*); when he had thought that Joseph was dead, he could have no rest.

The message of the move concerns the fulfillment of God's Word in prophecy and in dream, confirming the promises and thereby encouraging people in their faith. Through Joseph, God brought about the unity of the family and their move to Egypt according to his predetermined plan. Central to this account is the dream of Jacob, for in it God explained to the patriarch what he was doing and affirmed that the promises would yet be fulfilled. Such words of comfort and clarification in times of confusion and perplexity serve to strengthen the faith of God's people.

After twenty-three years, Joseph and Jacob were thus reunited. Jacob rejoiced to see Joseph alive, for this was the son whom he had designated as the heir and whom God had chosen to rule over the family. The gathering was more than a family reunion; it was proof that God's previously revealed plans had never been set aside.

In all ages God's people are constantly learning—and being amazed at—how God works to bring about his promises, at the same time developing faith in his people. *Believers must respond to God's supernatural dealings in the circumstances of life by making their decisions in accordance with the wisdom of divinely guided leaders, in assurance of the fulfillment of the promises, and in the knowledge that the future of the covenant will be developed from them.*

Bibliography

Coats, G. W. "A Structural Transition in Exodus." *VT* 22 (1972): 129–42.

Cody, A. "When Is the Chosen People Called a *Goy*?" *VT* 14 (1964): 1–6.

Davies, G. I. "The Wilderness Itineraries: A Comparative Study." *TynB* 25 (1974): 46–81.

Marcus, D. "The Verb 'to Live' in Ugaritic." *JSS* 17 (1972): 76–82.

Sasson, J. M. "A Genealogical 'Convention' in Biblical Chronology." *ZAW* 90 (1978): 171–85.

65

By Wisdom Kings Reign
(Gen. 46:31–47:27)

With the family now settled in Egypt under the rule of Joseph, a major phase in God's program was completed—yet the program would continue. Joseph had to ensure that his family would be taken care of and that the land of Egypt would prosper so that they could live there and flourish until God delivered them. Moreover, because Pharaoh treated Joseph's family with great kindness, Joseph would work to ensure that Pharaoh would prosper. All of these tasks by God's theocratic administrator required wisdom from above.

The present section may be divided into two spheres of Joseph's work: the presentation of the family to Pharaoh and the rule over the land. The first part accounts for Joseph's care for the family. As Westermann notes, all that was needed in the story was the short note in 47:11–12; but instead, a detailed presentation before Pharaoh was recorded, showing "the narrator's concern to base the settlement of Jacob's family and the provision made during the famine expressly on the Pharaoh's guarantee" (*Genesis*, vol. 3, p. 167). The second part of the passage seems to be an independent tradition about the administration of Joseph (Coats calls it a tax etiology [*Genesis*, p. 298]). It has been recorded in this context because it carries forward the motifs of the preceding section: in the first place, Pharaoh provided land and food for Jacob's family; in the second place, Joseph provided food for the people in exchange for their land and livestock. Both provisions are attributable to Joseph's wisdom.

Theological Ideas

In Proverbs 8:15, wisdom declares, "By me kings reign, and rulers decree justice." Joseph's administration of the affairs of Egypt during the famine exemplifies this perception of wisdom's importance. His purpose was to deliver his family, and the world as well, from the severe famine. He accomplished this deliverance through a wisdom given to him from above to discern the times and know the future. The wisdom that Joseph exemplified, and Solomon after him, was not merely human wisdom, or quick and clever decisions at the appropriate times. Rather, this quality was extraordinary perception and insight by a faithful servant of the Lord who was living in harmony with the revealed will of God. That will had been made clear to the patriarchs for generations—God would bless this family and make them into a great nation. Through his wisdom Israel was able to prosper under Pharaoh's kindness, and because Pharaoh favored the seed of Abraham, he also grew wealthy.

Structure and Synthesis

Structure

Each part of this section of the story provides a concluding note to the Joseph story: 47:11–12 expresses the completion of the family's move to Goshen under Joseph's provision and protection, just as Pharaoh had guaranteed; and 47:27 also concludes that the family was prosperous in the land of Goshen. These two concluding notes unite the two sections at the end of the story of Joseph. Genesis next returns to Jacob's activities in Egypt.

The first section (46:31–47:12) records the presentation before Pharaoh. It traces the preparation for the presentation (46:31–34), the brothers' audience with Pharaoh (47:1–6), and Jacob's audience (vv. 7–10). The climax of these audiences comes in Jacob's blessing before Pharaoh (vv. 7 and 10).

The second section relates Joseph's administrative activities in Egypt (47:13–27). The emphasis here is on Pharaoh's prosperity through Joseph as the people sold their land, their livestock, and themselves to Pharaoh for food.

Summary Message

Joseph acted wisely in presenting his family to Pharaoh so that they received the best of the land from Pharaoh, whom Jacob blessed in return; and then by wisdom Joseph bought almost all the land of Egypt for Pharaoh while saving the lives of the Egyptians and preserving Israel's prosperity in Goshen.

Exegetical Outline

I. Through Joseph's wise planning, Pharaoh provided land and food for Jacob's family in Egypt in the midst of a famine (46:31–47:12).
   A. Joseph prepared his family for their audience with Pharaoh (46:31–34).
      1. Joseph said that he would tell Pharaoh that his family had come from Canaan with all their possessions and that the men were herdsmen (31–32).
      2. Joseph instructed them to tell Pharaoh that they were herdsmen so that he would let them live in the land of Goshen (33–34).
   B. He presented his brothers to Pharaoh, who questioned them about their occupation and granted their request to live in the land of Goshen (47:1–6).
      1. Joseph told Pharaoh that his family had come to the land of Goshen from Canaan (1).
      2. Joseph presented his brothers to Pharaoh (2).
      3. Joseph's brothers told Pharaoh that they were shepherds (3).
      4. Joseph's brothers explained that they had come to Egypt because of the severity of the famine and requested permission to live in the land of Goshen (4).
      5. Pharaoh offered Joseph the best of the land, granting the brothers' request for Goshen, and requested that Joseph put any capable men among them in charge of the royal livestock (5–6).
   C. He presented Jacob to Pharaoh, and Jacob responded with a blessing (47:7–10).
      1. When Joseph presented Jacob to Pharaoh, the patriarch blessed him (7–8).
      2. When Pharaoh asked the old man how long he had lived, he explained that his days had been few and unpleasant, shorter than those of his fathers (9).
      3. Jacob blessed Pharaoh and left his presence (10).
   D. He settled Jacob and his family in the land of Rameses and provided them with food (47:11–12).
II. Joseph ruled wisely when he saved the lives of the Egyptians by providing food for them in exchange for their money, livestock,

land, and lives, thus acquiring almost all the land of Egypt for
Pharaoh (47:13–27).

   A. Joseph sold grain to the Egyptians, gathering vast sums of
      money from Egypt and Canaan into Pharaoh's household
      (13–14).

   B. He gave the Egyptians food for one year in exchange for their
      livestock (15–17).

   C. The following year the Egyptians offered to become Phar-
      aoh's slaves in exchange for food and seed so that they might
      live and cultivate the land (18–19).

   D. He bought all the land of Egypt for Pharaoh except for prop-
      erty belonging to the priests, and he enslaved the people to
      Pharaoh, requiring a fifth of all the harvests (20–26).

      1. The land became Pharaoh's because Joseph bought the
         fields (20).

      2. Joseph enslaved the people of Egypt (21).

      3. Joseph did not buy the priests' lands because they lived
         off an allotment from Pharaoh (22).

      4. Joseph required a fifth of the harvest for Pharaoh (23–24).

      5. The Egyptians gratefully acknowledged that Joseph had
         saved their lives, and they requested that they might be-
         come Pharaoh's slaves (25).

      6. Joseph made a statute that Pharaoh should have a fifth of
         the land (26).

   E. Israel lived in the land of Goshen, prospering materially and
      numerically (27).

Development of the Exposition

I. Through wisdom God's people can ensure that successive generations of believers can enjoy the blessings of God (46:31–47:12).

A. Preparation: It is wise not to offend those with authority in the world (46:31–34).

The presentation before Pharaoh was designed to ensure that the family received a good land for their dwelling so that they might not only
survive but flourish under God's blessing. The preparation by Joseph was
a cautious one: he prepared them for their audience by instructing them
to say that they were herdsmen (*'anšê miqneh*), because a shepherd
(*rō'ēh*) was an abomination in Egypt. Joseph sought to circumvent the
tension by a carefully worded answer. Joseph feared that the Egyptians
would think of his family as unsettled nomads. He wanted, as Kidner
says, "to ensure that Pharaoh's good-will would be to the family's real

The Story of Joseph

benefit, not to their detriment by drawing them into an alien way of life at the capital" (*Genesis*, p. 210).

B. Presentation: God may use those in authority to grant favor to his people (47:1–12).

When Joseph presented some of his brothers to Pharaoh, they said that they were shepherds from a long line of shepherds. Their straight-forward answer, although slightly different from Joseph's advice, was intended to achieve what Joseph's advice wanted to achieve—a separate life in the land of Goshen.

The point of this brief section is to affirm that Egypt's ruler gave the best land to Israel, in spite of any feelings he might have had about shepherds. The name Goshen has not yet been attested in Egyptian lists; 47:11 gives its later name, the district of Rameses (which could have been an earlier name after the name of the sun god). It was probably in the eastern delta.

One highlight of the audience came with the presentation of Jacob (vv. 7–10). The short unit begins and ends with the statement that Jacob blessed Pharaoh. That he was an old man, the patriarch of the clan, automatically gave more power to his blessing. Since he was the recipient of the promised blessings, his words here were more than a wish; he spoke for God in granting the blessing to Pharaoh, one that began shortly through the wise administration of Joseph.

Jacob's confession that his days had been "few and evil" (*mᵉ⁽aṭ wᵉrāᶜîm*, emphasizing the calamitous times he had experienced) must have been sobering for the family. But the description is appropriate for what Jacob had been through in his lifetime—much of it of his own doing. Here was the dilemma with Jacob: he was the channel of divine blessing to the world, but his days were few and filled with trouble. Many since Jacob have had to confess the same.

The first part of the passage closes with a statement about the family's possession of the best (*mêṭab*) of the land of Egypt (vv. 11–12). There Joseph provided all their needs, just as Pharaoh had commanded. The entire incident provided a pattern that was worked out again and again in Israel's history: the people of God proferred the blessing to others who had authority over the stations of this life, and in exchange they were afforded the good land. They did not always experience such blessing, but still they were responsible to act wisely and magnanimously before others as they extended the blessing of God.

II. Through wise leaders God will ensure that his people survive and that many share in the blessings (47:13–27).

Joseph's wise rule over the land of Egypt not only ensured the peace and prosperity of his family but also saved the people of Egypt from starvation and prospered Pharaoh abundantly. In selling food to the people, Joseph accepted first money and livestock as payment, and then finally their lands as well. Once the land belonged to Pharaoh, Joseph instructed the people to plant seed, his only requirement being that Pharaoh was to receive one-fifth of the produce. In short, the people survived, but they were in bondage to Pharaoh. Only the priests were exempt—probably due to the sanctity of the priesthood and the temple holdings over which Pharaoh had little control.

This entire situation informs the meaning of Exodus 1:8–11, which states that a new king came to power who did not know Joseph. Consequently—and ironically—that king began to enslave the Israelites to work in his projects. Had he remembered Joseph, he would have realized how loyal and faithful Israel could be in their sojourn in the land. Because this Pharaoh treated Israel well, they flourished, and he became powerful and wealthy; but because that new king treated Israel harshly, he would have none of the blessing of God, nor would he be able to hinder the prosperity of the people of God. From the beginning to the end of the Egyptian sojourn, prosperity and growth came from God's blessing. Those who acknowledged it shared in it.

It is interesting to note that the people of Egypt proclaimed Joseph as their savior—which is what God had prepared him to do (v. 25; see 45:7). So grateful were they that they willingly became the slaves of Pharaoh. Such gratitude is a model of devotion and loyalty by those saved from certain death.

Verse 27 provides a concluding statement to this section of the passage: in the land of Goshen the people of Israel prospered and multiplied greatly, for God was blessing them according to the promises made to Abraham and reiterated to Jacob as he migrated to Egypt (46:3). They were beginning to grow into a great nation. The text states that they were fruitful (*wayyiprû*) and multiplied exceedingly (*wayyirbû m^{e}'ōd*); these verbs recall the plan of the Creator (1:28) and anticipate the greater fulfillment in Exodus (1:7). Here, then, the predominant theme of blessing moves from promise to fulfillment. God blessed the seed of Abraham, and God blessed Pharaoh and his land for the sake of his people, all in accord with the promise.

The wise leader discerns that prosperity comes from God alone and so must make decisions in accordance with the will of God—that is, what God has revealed about his plan of blessing in fulfillment of the promise. Joseph exemplifies this wisdom by his faith in God's plan and by his skill in administering it. He knew that God sovereignly controlled the economics of the land in accord with his will. Joseph thus becomes the model for kings and administrators of God's people. Wisdom is essential to any ruler, but wisdom from above is required for theocratic administrators.

Also in the New Testament we learn that spiritual leaders need wisdom to guide the people of God into the place of blessing in fulfillment of the promises. Leadership cannot be oblivious to God's dealings in the past, for in them they see the outworking of God's program of blessing. Nor can leadership ignore the world around God's people, for God's people must flourish first in this world and, in so doing, bring blessing to a lost world.

Bibliography

Brueggemann, W. "The Kerygma of the Priestly Writers." *ZAW* 84 (1972): 397–414.

Childs, B. S. "A Study of the Formula 'Until This Day.' " *JBL* 82 (1963): 279–92.

Redford, D. B. "Exodus 1:11." *VT* 13 (1963): 401–18.

Shibayama, S. "Notes on *Yārad* and *ʿĀlāh*: Hints on Translating." *JBR* 34 (1966): 358–62.

Victor, P. "A Note on חק in the Old Testament." *VT* 16 (1966): 358–61.

66

Faith That Has Learned the Ways of God
(Gen. 47:28–48:22)

Out of Jacob's long career, the writer to the Hebrews selects the incident in this section as his greatest act of faith (11:21)—namely, his reaching out to the future of the promise in the face of death as he blessed the younger over the older. There is irony in the fact that this incident is comparable to the situation in which he had received the blessing over his older brother. Once more the blessing was given to the younger, but this time there was no deception or bitterness. This time the blessing was given openly, in accord with God's plan.

The exposition of the passage must take these circumstances into consideration. Here was the man of God at the brink of death, passing on the blessing—a hope for the future. But there is also Jacob's recognition that the elder would serve the younger—and so he crossed his hands in the blessing. Believers learn throughout life to accept God's crossing up of the normal conventions, for God's ways are not the ways of humankind. Death itself is part of the mysterious plan of God, for one enters the promise through death. And many of the teachings of Jesus with their apparent paradoxes exemplify this principle and call for a faith that looks beyond the grave.

This section begins a series of narratives about the death and burial of Jacob, drawing the *tôlᵉdôt* of Jacob to a close. The death of Jacob was anticipated throughout the Joseph stories (37:35; 42:38; 43:27–28; 44:22, 29–31; 45:9, 13, 28; 46:30). With so many references, the reader expects the section to close with Jacob's death. But these references raised the question of the circumstances of his death. Would matters be resolved? Would he die in peace? In the way that things worked out, the death of Jacob thus provided the culmination of the patriarchal narratives; it was a death that fit harmoniously within God's program for the blessing. The material in these last chapters includes the adoption of Ephraim and Manasseh, the last blessing on the sons, and the death and burial of the patriarch. All the events bring an age to a close and, at the same time, announce the future.

Theological Ideas

Various aspects of faith form the background of the words of Jacob in this passage. Most notable is his discernment of the will of God in blessing the younger over the elder, a concept that had taken him a lifetime to learn. Also notable is the sense of certainty that the promise will find its fulfillment in the land of Canaan. In harmony with this confidence Jacob obtained the promise from Joseph to bury him there and, in anticipation of it, gave the double portion to Joseph. The passage is fully about the faith of the patriarch who was about to die without receiving the promises but who had learned in his lifetime about the ways of God.

Structure and Synthesis

Structure

The passage has several parts that contribute to the deathbed scene, parts that are not always easily harmonized, as a check of the more critical commentaries will show. The first part of the deathbed scene is the oath dialogue between Jacob and Joseph (47:28–31). Then follows the adoption of Manasseh and Ephraim in a speech by Jacob (48:1–7). The third part records the blessing of Ephraim and Manasseh (vv. 8–20), and the last two verses, Jacob's farewell speech. Most of the passage is the words of Jacob—instructing, adopting, blessing, and promising for the future.

Summary Message

Jacob believed that God's promises to him were certain, even after death, and so he worshiped God, proving his faith by demanding to be buried in the Land of Promise; Jacob also believed that God sovereignly gave his blessing contrary to human expectations, proving his faith by blessing the younger Ephraim over the older Manasseh.

Exegetical Outline

I. Near the end of his life, Jacob by faith made Joseph swear to bury him in the cave of Machpelah and not in Egypt (47:28–31).

II. On his deathbed, Jacob gave the birthright to Joseph by raising Manasseh and Ephraim to the status of firstborn sons (48:1–7).

   A. Joseph prepared to receive Jacob's blessing by bringing his two sons to his father (1).

   B. Jacob recounted God's promise of the blessing of a numerous people and the everlasting possession of the land (2–4).

   C. Jacob gave the birthright to Joseph with his two sons (5–6).

   D. This birthright reversal was consolation for Rachel's having few sons because of her early death (7).

III. In confirming the birthright through the blessing, Jacob by faith exalted the younger Ephraim over the older Manasseh (48:8–20).

   A. Joseph reverently presented his two sons, with Manasseh in the favored position, to the nearly blind Jacob for the blessing (8–13).

      1. Joseph brought his two sons in for a blessing (8–11).

      2. He revered his father (12).

      3. He presented his sons to his father, with Manasseh in the favored position (13).

   B. Jacob blessed the sons, exalting the younger Ephraim over the older Manasseh (14–20).

      1. Jacob crossed his hands, putting his right hand on Ephraim the younger (14).

      2. Jacob pronounced the blessing: The God of his fathers, his Shepherd and Redeemer, would bless the lads with the Abrahamic blessings that they might be a multitude in the land (15–16).

      3. In response to Joseph's protest, Jacob maintained that the order of the blessing was correct, for the younger would be greater than the elder (17–19).

      4. Jacob reiterated the blessing of both sons but put Ephraim first (20).

IV. Believing that God would bring them back to the land, Jacob stated that he had just given the double portion of the birthright to Joseph (48:21–22).

Development of the Exposition

I. A mature faith does not lose sight of the promise (47:28–31).

Near the end of his life, Jacob asked Joseph to swear that he would bury him in the cave that was purchased by Abraham. Here is another indication of the hope of the patriarch, for he knew that the fulfillment of the promise was in Canaan, not in Egypt. Moreover, Jacob did not want to be buried in a foreign land but to be laid to rest in the family plot with his fathers.

The significance of the oath is the same as the one in Genesis 24:2 and 9. It stressed the solemnity of the matter and guaranteed the request. When Joseph's promise was sealed with the oath, Jacob no longer was concerned over its fulfillment. Israel then bowed himself (*wayyištaḥû*) on the head of the bed (see 1 Kings 1:47). Many commentators conclude that this was a reverent act of thanksgiving by the patriarch.

II. A mature faith knows how to develop confidence for the future from past blessings (48:1–7).

When Jacob heard that Joseph came to visit him in his sickbed, he strengthened himself to receive him. He rehearsed from his bed how the Almighty God had blessed (*waybārek*) him with the promise of a multitude of people in the land of their everlasting possession (vv. 3–4). The words of the promise had provided the patriarch with hope through all his pilgrimage, just as they would preserve the hope of the nation. It was the sure Word of God. The exposition must stress the centrality of the blessing through these passages, for the deathbed scenes recapture this main theme of the patriarchal narratives. Jacob's report of how God blessed him included God's promise to him to make him fruitful (*mapreḵā*), to multiply him (*weḥirbîtîḵā*), and to make him a multitude of people (*qeḥal 'ammîm*). The expressions not only recall the Abrahamic covenant but also reflect the original commandments at creation to be fruitful and multiply (1:28). These words are repeated in Exodus 1:7 to report how the nation had flourished in their Egyptian sojourn.

Jacob, now confident of the Lord's promise, passed the double blessing of the birthright on to Joseph by elevating Ephraim and Manasseh to the rank of heirs (vv. 5–7). The recognition of them along with Reuben and Simeon would alter the portioning of the Land of Promise. They both would have a share in the Promised Land. Of course, the granting of the double portion to them was done in full confidence that they would have something to inherit, that is, that the tribes would return to the Land of Promise. This expectation is not unlike Jeremiah's purchase of the field at the time of the captivity—he was convinced that they were coming back.

Jacob's elevation of Joseph's sons seems to have been influenced in part by the patriarch's recollection of the beloved Rachel, who died in the land of Canaan (v. 7). It seems to continue the remembrance of the revelation at Bethel (vv. 3–4), which is tied to Rachel's death in Genesis 35:16–19. With Joseph present, Jacob remembered what must have been a moving event in his experience, the burial of Rachel—especially since now he was thinking of his own burial. But the precise connection of verse 7 to the preceding announcement of the inheritance is not entirely clear. Delitzsch suggests that seeing Joseph brought back the memory of Rachel: "It is as though he wanted to lead Joseph to his mother's grave, and there to give him or receive from him a promise" (*New Commentary on Genesis*, vol. 2, p. 358).

III. A mature faith recognizes that God's ways are not man's ways (48:8–22).

The rest of the chapter is concerned with Jacob's choice in blessing Joseph's younger son first. The last two verses reiterate the theme of the double blessing to Joseph.

When Jacob pronounced the blessing on the sons, he wittingly guided his hands (*śikkēl 'et-yādāyw*) so that his right hand was on Ephraim's head, and his left on Manasseh's, even though Manasseh was the first-born (v. 14). This was Israel's decision, in spite of Joseph's displeasure. Joseph, and many others like him, expected God to work in a certain way but found that he chose to work in a different and unconventional way. Joseph had brought his two sons before Jacob so that Manasseh would receive the first blessing (v. 13), but Jacob crossed his hands. It had taken Jacob a lifetime of discipline to learn this truth about God. In his early years he had deceived his blind father for the blessing, but in his duty now of passing on the blessing, he performed in the way that God wanted, blessing the younger over the elder (see the oracle in 25:23). He would not attempt to bless the wrong one, as his father had attempted to do; nor would he handle the blessing dishonestly.

In his blessing Jacob used a threefold invocation of God as the God of the fathers (a fact that steadied Jacob's faith at times [28:13; 31:5, 42; 32:9; 46:3]), the God who shepherded (*hārō'eh*) him all the way, and the Angel who delivered (*haggō'ēl*) him out of trouble (*rā'*). (The word *gā'al* expresses the protection he had experienced during his troubles.) These remarkable descriptions reveal Jacob's faith—one that had matured through the years and that had learned to trust the Lord in the difficulties of life.

Joseph was displeased (*wayyēra'*) when he saw that his father was blessing the younger first and so held up his father's hand (v. 17). His words, "This is the firstborn [*zeh habbᵉkōr*]," would have brought back to Jacob's memory the struggles for the rights of the firstborn. His response was thus to persist in the order of blessing he had chosen and thereby to silence his son Joseph. His "I know, my son, I know" expresses the full confidence of faith. He knew that God's blessing was not to follow ordinary convention. He also knew that God's plan had to be initiated by faith.

Finally, Jacob reiterated that, when God would restore the family to the land, the double portion would go to Joseph. There is a word play in verse 22 with the word "portion" (*šᵉkem*) also referring to Shechem, the place where Joseph would be buried as a sign of the possession of his bequest. The allusion in the verse to the taking of the land from the Amorite with the bow and sword is unclear but may refer to some skirmish that took place there.

There is little wonder that the writer to the Hebrews would select this event as the epitome of Jacob's faith, for it presents one of the finest samples in Scripture of a mature faith (11:21). *Believers who have matured in the faith through a lifetime of experiences in which the covenant God has shepherded and delivered them—no matter how difficult the maturing process may have been—can discern with confidence the purpose and plan of God for the future.* This statement does not say that the believer will have the ability to predict; it merely says that the mature believer is familiar with God's ways, knows God's plans, and can prepare for the future with a certain expectation.

The epitome of Jacob's faith in this passage comes with his crossing of his hands in the blessing. Dods offers this homily:

> We meet with these crossed hands of blessing frequently in Scripture; the younger son blessed above the elder—as was needful, lest grace should become confounded with nature, and the belief gradually grow up in men's minds that natural effects could never be overcome by grace, and that in every respect grace waited upon nature. And these crossed hands we meet still; for how often does God quite reverse *our* order, and bless most that about which we had less concern, and seem to put a slight on that which has engrossed our best affection. It is so, often in precisely the way in which Joseph found it so; the son whose youth is most anxiously cared for, to whom the interests of the younger members of the family are sacrificed, and who is commended to God continually to receive His righthand blessing, this son seems neither to receive nor to dispense much blessing; but the younger, less thought of, left to work his own way, is favoured by God, and becomes the comfort and support

of his parents when the elder has failed of his duty. And in the case of much that we hold dear, the same rule is seen; a pursuit we wish to be successful in we can make little of, and are thrown back from continually, while something else into which we have thrown ourselves almost accidentally prospers in our hand and blesses us. Again and again, for years together, we put forward some cherished desire to God's right hand, and are displeased, like Joseph, that still the hand of greater blessing should pass to some other thing. Does God not know what is oldest with us, what has been longest at our hearts, and is dearest to us? Certainly He does: "I know it, My son, I know it," He answers to all our expostulations. It is not because He does not understand or regard your predilections, your natural and excusable preferences, that He sometimes refuses to gratify your whole desire, and pours upon you blessings of a kind somewhat different from those you most earnestly covet. He will give you the whole that Christ hath merited; but for the application and distribution of that grace and blessing you must be content to trust Him. You may be at a loss to know why He does no more to deliver you from some sin, or why He does not make you more successful in your efforts to aid others, or why, while He so liberally prospers you in one part of your condition, you get so much less in another that is far nearer your heart; but God does what He will with His own, and if you do not find in one point the whole blessing and prosperity you think should flow from such a Mediator as you have, you may only conclude that what is lacking there will elsewhere be found more wisely bestowed. And is it not a perpetual encouragement to us that God does not merely crown what nature has successfully begun, that it is not the likely and the naturally good that are most blessed, but that God hath chosen the foolish things of the world to confound the wise, and the weak things of the world to confound the things that are mighty; and base things of the world and things which are despised hath God chosen, yea, and things which are not, to bring to nought things that are? [*Book of Genesis*, pp. 423–25]

Bibliography

Dumbrell, W. J. "The Role of Bethel in the Biblical Narratives from Jacob to Jeroboam I." *AJBA* 2, no. 3 (1974–75): 65–75.

Goldman, M. D. "The Root פָּלַל and Its Connotation with Prayer." *Australian Biblical Review* 3 (1953): 1–6.

Holladay, W. L. "The Covenant with the Patriarchs Overturned." *JBL* 91 (1972): 305–20.

Johnson, A. R. "The Primary Meaning of the Root גאל." *VTS* 1 (1953): 67–77.

Kingsbury, E. C. "He Set Ephraim Before Manasseh." *HUCA* 38 (1967): 129–36.

Mendelsohn, I. "On the Preferential Status of the Eldest Son." *BASOR* 156 (1959): 38–40.

————— . "A Ugaritic Parallel to the Adoption of Ephraim and Manasseh." *IEJ* 9 (1959): 180–83.

Miller, P. D. "The Blessing of God: An Interpretation of Numbers 6:22–27." *Interp* 29 (1975): 240–51.

Mowvley, H. "The Concept and Content of 'Blessing' in the Old Testament." *BiTr* 16 (1965): 74–80.

Neyrey, Jerome H. "Jacob Traditions and the Interpretation of John 4:10–26." *CBQ* 41 (1979): 419–37.

Speiser, E. A. The Stem *pll* in Hebrew." *JBL* 82 (1963): 301–6.

67

The Shaping of Destiny
(Gen. 49:1–28)

It is a fundamental principle in God's economy that the actions of individuals will affect the lives of their descendants. This pattern is clear in the patriarchal narratives, for the deeds and dispositions of the patriarchs were passed on in one way or another to their children. Genesis 49 exemplifies this theme with the deathbed oracle of Jacob's blessing. We have here the last of the great sayings in Genesis. Jacob, by faith and under divine inspiration, looked forward to the conquest and the settlement of Israel in the land of Canaan and then beyond to a more glorious age, as he distributed blessings to his sons.

The oracle evaluates the twelve sons of Jacob, announcing the participation of each in the blessing of God. There are two different types of sayings used in the chapter: short epigrammatic statements that offer a brief characterization of a tribe in the form of an aphorism, and the more extensive oracles about the power and influence of a tribe (see Lindblom, "Political Background"). The more extensive oracles treat Reuben, Simeon and Levi, Judah, and Joseph, the tribes that seemed to command the most attention in the order of things.

Theological Ideas

Prophecy was given by God to sustain his people through their barren, and sometimes dismal, experiences, to show them that God planned their future. For Jacob's family, the future lay beyond their settlement in Egypt in the Land of Promise. Like their ancestors, the people of Israel would need to hear again and again the promises of their inheritance and of their participation in the continued program, in order to keep the faith. The overall theme of the oracle of Jacob is thus the blessing of the fathers that would now be handed down to the tribes.

The enjoyment of that blessing and the participation in that future program varied in accordance with the faithfulness of the participants. Accordingly, from the solemnity of his deathbed Jacob evaluated his sons one by one and carried his evaluation forward to their descendants. The theological point that surfaces in this oracle is that the sins of the fathers may be visited on their descendants, meaning that bound up in the tribal ancestors were all the potential strengths and weaknesses of the descendants. Just as the nation of Israel would see itself in Jacob, so could the tribes in the sons of Jacob.

Structure and Synthesis

Structure

This chapter records primarily the blessing of Jacob. After a brief narrative introduction (vv. 1–2), the passage moves through the oracle about the sons, but it does not proceed in the order of their births. The six sons of Leah are treated first, then Dan, the son of Rachel's maid, then Leah's two sons by her maid, then Naphtali, Rachel's other son by her maid, and then finally Rachel's own sons, Joseph and Benjamin. In giving the blessing of the birthright, Jacob passed over the first sons and gave Judah kingship; after all the sons were discussed, Jacob gave the double portion of the blessing to Joseph. For further discussion of the structure, see M. O'Conner, *Hebrew Verse Structure* (Winona Lake, Ind.: Eisenbrauns, 1980), pp. 425–43.

Summary Message

In blessing his sons, Jacob foretold what would befall each of them and their descendants in the latter days; he disqualified Reuben for the birthright because of sin and Simeon and Levi because of violence but gave kingship to Judah and extensive blessing to Joseph, while briefly declaring the other sons' fortune in life.

Exegetical Outline

    I. Prologue: Jacob called all his sons together so that he could tell them what would befall them in the latter days (1–2).

II. Reuben lost the birthright because he acted presumptuously in the struggle for succession (3–4).
  A. Jacob praised Reuben as the beginning of his strength (3).
  B. Jacob disqualified him because of his sin (4).
III. Simeon and Levi would be dispersed because of their fierce and unjustified anger (5–7).
  A. Jacob lamented how cruel and murderous Simeon and Levi were (5–6).
  B. Jacob cursed them for their wrath, dispersing them among the other heirs of the land (7).
IV. Judah would receive the kingship and anticipate a time of abundance because he would act in a valiant and praiseworthy manner (8–12).
  A. Jacob gave Judah the authority over his brothers because he would act valiantly and they would praise him (8).
  B. Using the figure of a lion with its prey, Jacob described the might of Judah (9).
  C. Jacob predicted that the rulership would remain with Judah until the rightful heir came (10).
  D. Jacob described the abundance of the time of Judah's reign (11–12).
V. Zebulun would dwell by the sea and be a haven for ships (13).
VI. Issachar would prefer ease and luxury to the hard work and freedom for which he was equipped (14–15).
VII. Dan, although small, would help his brothers against oppression (16–18).
VIII. Gad would be raided by marauding bands but would fight back (19).
IX. Asher's land would be so fertile that he could deliver delicacies to royalty (20).
X. Naphtali would be a swift messenger with a message of victory (21).
XI. Joseph would prosper abundantly and, when fiercely attacked by his enemies, would be successful because of the help of the God of his father—a blessing that gave Joseph a position above the others (22–26).
  A. Jacob declared that Joseph would be fruitful (22).
  B. Jacob predicted that Joseph would be fiercely attacked by his enemies (23).
  C. Jacob explained that the God of the fathers would continue to protect and bless Joseph (24–25).
  D. The blessings that Joseph would receive would be greater than the blessings of others (26).

XII. Benjamin will be successful and share his substance (27).
XIII. Epilogue: This is Jacob's blessing on the twelve tribes (28).

Development of the Exposition

The material in this chapter is rather difficult to develop for exposition. Of the two types of announcements in the chapter, short aphorisms and elaborate tribal sayings and predictions, the short aphorisms are almost impossible to interpret in an exposition, for so little is known about the tribal history of each. It may be best to concentrate on the major sections—Reuben, Simeon and Levi, Judah, and Joseph—and mention the others only in passing. We may understand the aphorisms but may not be able to make a theological lesson out of them.

I. Prologue: God reveals the future (1–2)

Jacob summoned all his sons together so that he could tell them what would befall them in the latter days (be'aḥărît hayyāmîm). His predictions were based on their actions and their characteristics. No doubt Jacob could discern enough of their traits to make reasonable projections, but in some cases his words went beyond his experience and were more like a prophetic oracle. The expression "in the latter days" probably should be interpreted to mean an undetermined time in the future, early or late (cf. Dan. 2:28–29, 45; Ezek. 38:16; Jer. 23:20). In Numbers 24:14 the expression probably refers to David's victory over Moab and not to an eschatological event (see 24:17–18). But the term can be used when eschatological events are meant. Here in Genesis 49, the time of fulfillment differs with each tribal saying, extending from the near future to the eschatological kingdom of Messiah.

Jacob's words, then, formed a prophetic oracle concerned with the blessing of the tribes. It is significant that this oracle comes near the end of the patriarchal stories, for it thus serves to advance the record of the blessing to the subsequent generations of the tribes. The oracle also forms a parallel with the oracle of Noah (9:25–27), who at the end of the primeval events declared the blessing and cursing of the descendants on the basis of the actions of his sons, Shem, Ham, and Japheth.

II. Sinful actions may remove people from positions of leadership (3–4).

The patriarch began with his firstborn son, Reuben, who should have been the heir of the promise. He was entitled to leadership and the double inheritance, but because he had the ungoverned impulse of boiling water, he would fail in leadership. Jacob began by heaping praise on this son (v. 3), only to change to blame when he announced that Reuben had defiled his couch (Gen. 35:22). The old sin probably was an attempt by Reuben to assume prematurely the right of succession, but it meant only that he lost the birthright.

The praise of Jacob set Reuben out as the beginning of his strength and might, one who was preeminent in dignity and strength. The idea of dignity (śe'ēt) is confirmed by the use of this word in Job 13:11, Habakkuk 1:7, and Psalm 62:5. The word is to be taken from the root meaning "to honor" (nāśā', cognate to Akkadian našû, "to honor"), and may be illustrated from the Hebrew word for prince (nāśî'). As the beginning of Jacob's strength, Reuben should have been preeminent in such dignity and honor.

Because he was "unstable as water," however, he would not excel. This expression (paḥaz kammayim) has had many interpretations. Pehlke summarizes the various views and then, after a thorough discussion of the three critical passages Judges 9:4, Jeremiah 23:32, and Zephaniah 3:4, concludes that the expression signifies that Reuben was destructive like water. He interprets the word paḥaz with the sense of disregarding the godly order and acting with pride or presumption (cf. Akkadian paḥāzu). Essentially, Reuben destroyed his right to inherit ("Exegetical and Theological Study," pp. 127–31).

Since Reuben defiled his father's bed and did not observe his father's sacred right, his own family would have no chance for the birthright. This fact is clearly attested in 1 Chronicles 5:1. Even in Judges 5:15–16, Reuben was characterized by irresolution. The family of Reuben would not have the character to lead—and this failure of character was first seen in the ancestor's sin.

III. Anarchy and violence are incompatible with spiritual leadership (5–7).

Simeon and Levi would not replace Reuben in the leadership of the nation, because they were men of anarchy and not justice. Here, then, is the moral judgment on Genesis 34: God distinguishes holy war from ruthless vengeance. As a result of the actions that characterized these families, they would be divided and scattered (ḥālaq and pûṣ, in v. 7) throughout Israel. Simeon was later swallowed up in the tribe of Judah, and Levi received an honorable dispersion as the priestly tribe.

Jacob began his oracle on these two by describing them as brothers, a word that probably stresses their similar nature, for all the sons were brothers. His expression "instruments of violence are their habitations" has been the subject of much study. This last word (mekērōtêhem) is

critical to the meaning of the line. For a summary of the various interpretations, see the commentaries by Skinner (*Commentary on Genesis*,
pp. 516–17) and B. Jacob (*Das Erste Book der Tora: Genesis*, p. 896).
Some of the more plausible suggestions are those of F. M. Cross and
D. N. Freedman, *Studies in Ancient Yahwistic Poetry* (SBL Dissertation
Series 21), 1952 ("weapons of violence are their merchandise [*mākar*])
and Edward Ullendorf, "The Contribution of South Semitics to Hebrew
Lexicography," *VT* 6 (1956): 194 ("weapons of violence are their counsels;
see James Barr, *Comparative Philology and the Text of the Old Testament* [Oxford: Clarendon, 1968], pp. 57, 270). Helmuth Pehlke ("Exegetical and Theological Study," p. 142) suggests that the noun follows
the pattern of nouns that describe tools (a *maqtil* or *miqtil* form; see
Bauer and Leander, *Grammatik*, p. 492) and takes it from the root *kārat*
to get a translation "their knives." This rendering finds support in the
use of the verb *kārat* in Exodus 4:25 for circumcision, providing a direct
link to the incident in Genesis 34. The line would then read, "Their
circumcision knives are instruments of violence." The view was also
held by M. Dahood (" 'MKRTYHM' in Genesis 49, 5" *CBQ* 23 [1961]:
54–56).

   Because of the violence of Simeon and Levi, Jacob would have nothing
to do with their deeds or thoughts. They had acted in pride and anger
and, in their pleasure (*rāṣōn* signifying they had desired to do it), destroyed the community and hamstrung oxen (ʿiqqᵉrû-šôr)—making unprofitable for others what they chose not to take for their own use. Their
anger was cursed, meaning that they were cursed (ʾārûr), or expelled,
from the community. Such ruthless violence eliminated those tribes
from the leadership of the nation as well.

IV. God entrusts leadership to those who are praiseworthy and responsible (8–12).

The oracle on Judah predicts a fierce dominance of Judah over his
brothers, who would praise him. These verses provide a miniature preview of the kingship of Judah that would span the years until Messiah
should come.

A. Judah will have the leadership (8).

The first verse in the section announced that the other tribes would
bow down to Judah. Because of the brothers' bowing to Joseph in Egypt,
the oracle is probably speaking not of the brothers in the immediate
family but of the future tribes. The text makes it clear that Judah will
earn his right by heroic deeds over his enemies and will therefore be
looked to for leadership.

There is a significant word play here. Judah ($y^ehûdâ$) means "let him be praised" or "he will be praised." In the naming narrative (29:35), Judah's mother chose this name and explained her reason with the word play, "I will praise ['ôdeh] the LORD." But here Jacob turns the significance of the name with the play, "Your brothers will praise you [yôdûkā]." The sounds in the name are further echoed in the next clause: "Your hand [$yād^ekā$] will be on the neck of your enemies." The oracle thus finds reinforcement in the name, as if to say that Judah would experience what his name meant. He would show himself powerful over the enemies and be praised for it.

B. Judah will be mighty (9).

In this verse the text employs the metaphor of the lion's cub to portray Judah as powerful. Three steps are present in the figure: seizing the prey, bringing it back to the den, and reclining over it. Judah also would be mighty in battle and kingly in repose. The figure of the lion is used for the monarchy in other cultures as well (see *ANET*, p. 384; *Ancient Near East in Pictures*, edited by James B. Pritchard [Princeton, N.J.: Princeton University Press, 1954], nos. 522 and 526; and D. Marcus, "Animal Similes in Assyrian Royal Inscriptions," *Or* 46 [1977]: 87).

C. Out of Judah will come the Messiah (10).

This verse moves into promise for the eschatological future, looking beyond the normal period of Israel's history to the dawn of the messianic age. The "scepter" was the symbol of kingship—it would be Judah's. The word is paralleled with "lawgiver's staff" to strengthen the idea that the theocratic administration would remain with Judah.

This rule would continue, the oracle says, until "Shiloh" comes. Much debate has centered on the meaning of this term (for which, see the various commentaries). Most commentators recognize that it indicates a person because of the pronouns in the context—the obedience of the nations are *his*, for example. It is not likely a personal name, or a title, although older commentators tried to translate it "his peace." The word may very well be the relative pronoun (*še*), a preposition (*l^e*), and a pronominal suffix (*ōh*), or *šîlōh*, "who to him," or "to whom it belongs." In other words, the scepter—that is, the theocratic administration—would remain in the tribe of Judah until the one comes to whom it belongs. The prophecy, although dim in its details, provides an early hint at the coming of Messiah, an interpretation that is confirmed by the *Targum Onkelos*, which reads, "until the Messiah comes, whose is the kingdom, and him shall the nations obey."

It is interesting to note that the Creator's plan for the administration

704 The Story of Joseph

of his program resurfaces after all that had happened. God had created humankind to "rule and have dominion" over the earth as his vice regent. And now, as the plan to restore that blessed estate and purpose for his creation developed, God selected one family with a view to the restoration of rulership. The New Testament affirms that the anticipated king is Jesus the Messiah, the second Adam, a son of David of the tribe of Judah.

D. It will be the dawn of a new age (11–12).

The language of blessing is used in the last two verses, showing abundance in the land. Binding a foal to a vine and washing garments in wine, whatever else they may signify, speak of a time of great plenty and paradisiacal splendor. Each expression speaks of abundance—it will be a golden age. As Kidner says, "It bids adieu to the pinched régime of thorns and sweat" for the shout of rejoicing and feasting (*Genesis*, p. 219). The similes used in verse 12 (wine and milk), used to describe the appearance of the coming one, suggest the abundance of the times. The prophecy is not detailed; it simply catches the mood of a time when the curse will have little effect and the land will have great blessing.

In John 2:1–11, Jesus turned the water into wine at the marriage of Cana in Galilee. John describes that miracle as the first sign that he did (v. 11). By the miracle Jesus was signifying that the kingdom was at hand—a message that he also declared verbally. The creation of the abundance of wine signaled that the Messiah was present. And everyone knew that Messiah would come out of Judah.

In Genesis the promise of the kingdom went to Judah because (1) the sons in line before him defaulted their right by sin and (2) Judah had shown himself responsible and praiseworthy (note Gen. 43:9 and 44:33). Participation in the blessing thus depended on obedience to God.

V. Shorter sayings: God declares the destinies of his people (13–21, 27).

In a series of short aphorisms the oracle traces through the future destinies of the tribes. Because we lack the necessary information about the ancestors of these tribes and about their tribal history, we cannot interpret beyond noting that God spoke through Jacob concerning their destinies.

A. Zebulun (13).

Jacob declared that Zebulun would be enriched by seaborne trade. Essentially the oracle declared that the tribe would border on the Mediterranean Sea and the city of Sidon. Scholars have been bothered by the mention of Sidon this early, but archaeological evidence supports the antiquity of Sidon (it could be *Zidanum* in the Ur III tablets and in Ebla). Tyre is the later city (Isa. 23:12 refers to Tyre as the daughter of Sidon). At any rate, Zebulun would dwell close to the commercial shoreline.

B. Issachar (14–15).

The oracle predicted that, because Issachar would prefer abundance and luxury, he would be too willing to trade his liberty for the material things of life. The future of this tribe seems to be forced labor, for seeing that rest was good (*ṭôb*) and the land pleasant (*nāʿēmâ*), Issachar would become a servant, lowering his shoulder to accept the burden. The words "to bear" (*lisbōl*) and "became a servant under tribute" (*mas-ʿōbēd*) describe compulsory labor of subservient people.

Issachar would be levied for corvée work like prisoners of war (cf. Deut. 20:11; Josh. 16:10; 17:13; Judges 1:28, 30, 33; 1 Kings 9:21). Jacob says that, instead of using his ability to work for himself, Issachar would work for the Canaanites for food and rest. This gain was considered a mockery by the oracle, for it was a reversal of the relationship that should have prevailed between Israel and the Canaanites (Carmichael, "Some Sayings," p. 437).

C. Dan (16–18).

The oracle sets out a high hope for the tribe. Although Dan would be smaller than the other tribes, its calling was to help its fellow tribes against the suppression of a mighty enemy. The oracle begins with a word play on the name, giving the significance for the future (cf. 30:6, in which the word play gave the significance for the mother): "Dan will vindicate [*dān yādîn*] his people, as one of the tribes of Israel." Issachar, like a large-boned ass, was equipped to get the job done but preferred a relatively easy life; Dan, born of a concubine and not as privileged as the others, would help its people get their rights.

The images in verse 17 explain how this vindication would happen. As a snake can strike at the legs of a horse and overthrow the mightier animal, so too would Dan be able to exert itself as one of the tribes. The tribes of Israel would be a minority in Canaan, as they were in Egypt, and Dan would be one of the smaller tribes. But if this blessing should come true by the power of God, as verse 18 expresses, then Dan would be a victorious tribe over others that might seem more powerful.

D. Gad (19).

Even though Gad will be raided by marauding bands, he will fight valiantly. That border raids would be the lot of Gad is emphasized by the word plays in the verse—four of the six words play on the name: *gād* *g^edûd y^egûdennû w^ehû' yāgûd 'āqēb* (the plays using the verbs *gûd* and *gādad*). The name Gad probably means "fortune," as was determined in the naming narrative (30:11). But *g^edûd,* translated "marauding bands," is related to the root *gādad* ("to cut off"). The verb "overcome" or "attack" comes from the root *gûd.* The sounds of the words thus work together to stress the point of the oracle that eventually Gad would overcome these marauding bands.

E. Asher (20).

The oracle predicts that Asher would be fertile and productive, so much so that he would provide delicacies to royalty. The word *š^emēnâ,* "fertile" or "fat" (related to *šemen,* "fat" or "oil"), is probably an adjective modifying the word "bread," even though there is disagreement in gender. When the word is used to describe the ground, the idea of quality and quantity of harvest is present (Isa. 30:23)—"Asher's food is abundant."

The second clause of the oracle describes what Asher would do with his abundant produce—deliver it to the court. The choice of the term "delicacies" (*ma'ădannîm* < *'ēden*) signifies that the produce was delightful or pleasurable. It is probably not ordinary food but delicacies that kings would afford.

F. Naphtali (21).

Naphtali would be a free mountain people, as the play on the name may suggest (see Skinner, *Commentary on Genesis,* p. 387; and J. Lewy, "The Old West Semitic Sun-god Ḥammu," *HUCA* 18 [1944]: 452). But the specific point of this oracle is that Naphtali would be a messenger with a message of victory.

The imagery of Naphtali as a hind let loose conveys swiftness and agility, especially in battle (Ps. 18:33; 2 Sam. 22:34). The verb "let loose" (*š^elūḥá* < *šālaḥ*) is frequently used in military contexts where a message is being sent (e.g., see 1 Kings 14:6 and Gen. 32:19).

The second clause reveals what the message is—"words of beauty" (*'imrê-šāper*). The word translated "beauty" (*šāper*) could perhaps be translated as "message" (*šipru,* in the Amarna letters). In this case it means simply that he gives the words of the message. If "beauty" is retained as the reading, then it suggests good news.

G. Benjamin (27).

Although Joseph is treated before Benjamin in the order of the chapter, I shall comment on Benjamin within the section of short aphorisms. Benjamin, according to the oracle, would be so successful that he would be able to share with others of his substance.

Like Judah, Benjamin is compared to an animal, specifically, a wolf.

It is no less voracious an animal than the lion but usually kills far more than it can eat. That is the picture given here, for Benjamin would divide the spoil (y^ehallēq šālāl). Here again, success is predicted for a son of Jacob.

VI. God gives ultimate blessing and victory to those who patiently endure persecution and opposition (22–26).

The fourth major section concerns Joseph. Jacob treated this son more lavishly than all the others, for here lay the coveted blessing (as the Chronicler noted, in 1 Chron. 5:1–2). Jacob took up the promise of fruitfulness from the name of Ephraim and lavished prosperity and blessing on Joseph's tribes.

A. Joseph as a prosperous tribe is attacked by his enemies (22–23).

The description of Joseph begins with a phrase traditionally translated as "fruitful bough" (bēn pōrāt). The word "bough" was chosen over "son" because Joseph is pictured here as a vine extending over the wall, an image of prosperity. A greater problem concerns the meaning of pōrāt, translated "fruitful." The form seems to be an active participle, feminine singular, from the root pārâ, "to be fruitful." The literal rendering of the phrase would thus be "son of fruitfulness." The theme of fruitfulness has appeared before in the line from Rachel: God at first withheld fruit from her womb (30:2) but later made her fruitful (v. 22). Then Joseph himself was made fruitful with the birth of Ephraim (41:52).

The picture is made complete with the explanation that he is by a well and extending over a wall. Joseph, then, would be healthy and fruitful.

But Joseph's prosperity spurs attacks from his enemies (v. 23). His enemies showed bitterness toward him, shot their arrows at him, and hated him. Arrows are used literally or figuratively (for malicious words) in the Bible. Although there is not enough information to determine which is meant here, it is clear that people tried to destroy Joseph's prosperity. This pressure began, it may be recalled, in Joseph's life with his brothers; the oracle extends that envy into the future as a prediction.

B. Joseph was successfully defended by the God of his father (24–25a).

Joseph would be able to resist such attacks because the God of his father would save him (w^eya'z^erekkā) and bless him (wîbār^ekekkā). Joseph would be firm in his position through supernatural assistance.

The first description of God is in the expression "from the hands of the Mighty One of Jacob [mîdê 'ăbîr ya'ăqōb]." The image of the hands of the Lord is frequent in passages of judgment and deliverance (e.g., Exod. 9:3; Deut. 2:15; Judg. 2:16). Here it is strengthened by the term "Mighty One" ('ăbîr). This title speaks of how powerful God is (see Ps. 132:2; Isa. 49:26). Joseph himself acknowledged that his power came from God (Gen. 40:8; 41:16; 45:5–8).

The next line further develops the concept of God in this oracle: "From thence is the Shepherd [rō'eh], the Stone ['eben] of Israel." Since there is no clear antecedent for miššām, "from there," many would follow some of the versions and read the prepositional phrase miššēm, "from the name of," thereby forming a closer parallel with "from God" in verse 25a.

The God who defends Joseph is a Shepherd, one who is able to lead and defend his people (48:15 and 35:3). He is also the Stone of Israel, that is, one who is stable and unchanging (see Isa. 8:14, where "stone" and "rock" are parallel). He is the "God of your father" ('ēl 'ăbîkā), a description that reminds the reader of the ancestral calling and promised blessings (31:5; 32:9–10; 46:3). Finally, he is described as "Almighty" (šadday). These last two titles seem to fit the last two verbs: the God of the father would save him, and the Almighty would bless him. Without the help and blessing of God, Joseph could not have made it as far as he had, and his descendants would not make it further.

C. The blessing gave Joseph a superior position over his brothers (25b–26).

Five times in these last verses the word "blessings" (birkōt) is used to describe the lavish treatment of Joseph. To bless someone, as we have seen throughout Genesis, means to give success to someone, and especially success in fertility (1:22, 28, and the patriarchal stories). Jacob declared that God would bestow his power on Joseph so that the latter could continue to be successful and fruitful. Here the oracle delineates blessing in agricultural pursuits, blessing of livestock, and blessing of descendants. A comparison of this blessing at the end of Genesis with the blessing of God for humankind at the beginning of creation reveals that the prized blessing handed down by the patriarchs retained much of God's original desire for his firstborn of creation. Here Joseph received that bounty of the firstborn, which, as we have seen, would be divided among his sons, Ephraim and Manasseh. This blessing would exceed anything given to any of the progenitors, according to this oracle. (Many commentators, however, prefer the reading "mountains" to "progenitors," making the line parallel with the next and signifying that the blessing extended to the everlasting hills.) By saying that the blessing extends to the hills, it selects the places of choice agricultural lands for the blessing terminology, for they were a symbol of fertility (Isa. 5:1; Deut. 33:15; Ps. 72). In short, the blessing on Joseph would be so great that it would exceed anything that anyone could imagine from a very fertile land (Pehlke, "Exegetical and Theological Study," p. 236).

Just as Joseph had overcome hatred and opposition to become successful in Egypt by the power of God, so too would his tribe continue to have the greatest of blessings. Jacob discerned the faithful perseverance of his favorite son and the blessing of God richly on him, and so in his final blessing he confirmed that work of God on Joseph.

The section concludes with an editorial note about these being the twelve tribes of Israel and about Jacob's blessing each one of them. They shared in the richest blessings in accordance with their faithfulness and their characteristics.

All the sons of Jacob were blessed to carry the Abrahamic covenant forward, for they all became founders of tribes that went up out of Egypt as the seed of Abraham. In this sense the oracle can be called a blessing, even though it appears that some were passed over and some elevated to leadership and double blessing. Joseph and Judah came to the fore, as indeed they had in the story of Joseph. Joseph received a double portion so that Ephraim and Manasseh would have equal shares with the other sons; and out of the promises given to Abraham, kingship was reserved for Judah. The various promises made to Abraham were here channeled to the tribes, all sharing in some way in accord with their lives and traits. The words of the patriarch were general but clearly anticipated favor and responsibility in the tribes of Israel.

Besides the general ideas of comfort through prophecy, hope for the future, or the plan of God in blessing through the seed of Abraham, there is a clear idea here about rewards. On the basis of the lives of these men, God through Jacob endowed rewarding positions in the future land for their descendants. Their families would all be there in the Promised Land, but in different capacities. *The actions of believers determine their future portion in the sure blessing of God.* As is often the case, the activities and nature of the parents will affect the destinies of the descendants. It was true for Adam and Eve, and it was true for the sons of Jacob.

Bibliography

Allegro, J. M. "Further Messianic References in Qumran Literature." *JBL* 75 (1956): 174–87.

——— . "A Possible Mesopotamian Background to the Joseph Blessing of Gen. 49." *ZAW* 64 (1952): 249–51.

Armerding, Carl. "The Last Words of Jacob: Genesis 49." *BibSac* 112 (1955): 320–28.

Battenfield, James R. "Hebrew Stylistic Development in Archaic Poetry: A Text-Critical and Exegetical Study of the Blessing of Jacob." Th.D. diss., Grace Seminary, 1976.

Bennetch, John H. "The Prophecy of Jacob." *BibSac* 95 (1938): 417–35.

Blenkinsopp, J. "The Oracle of Judah and the Messianic Entry." *JBL* 80 (1961): 55–64.

Buchanan, G. W. "Eschatology and the End of Days." *JNES* 20 (1961): 188–93.

Carmichael, Calum M. "Some Sayings in Genesis 49." *JBL* 88 (1969): 435–44.

Cassuto, U. "Biblical and Canaanite Literature." In *Biblical and Oriental Studies*, vol. 2, p. 39. Jerusalem: Magnes, 1973.

Coppens, J. "La bénédiction de Jacob." *VTS* 6 (1957): 97–115.

Dahood, M. "Is 'Eben Yisrael' a Divine Title?" *Bib* 40 (1959): 1002–7.

Gevirtz, Stanley. "The Issachar Oracle in the Testament of Jacob." *ErIs* 12 (1975): 104–12.

———. "The Reprimand of Reuben." *JNES* 30 (1971): 87–98.

Good, E. M. "The 'Blessing' on Judah." *JBL* 82 (1963): 427–32.

Gordon, R. P. "Targum Onkelos to Genesis 49:4 and a Common Semitic Idiom." *JQR* 66 (1976): 224–26.

Greenfield, J. C. "Ugaritic Lexicographical Notes." *JCS* 21 (1967): 89.

Held, Moshe. "Philological Notes on the Mari Covenant Rituals." *BASOR* 200 (1970): 35.

Lindblom, J. "The Political Background of the Shiloh Oracle." *VTS* 1 (1953): 78–87.

Mayes, A. D. H. "Israel in the Pre-Monarchy Period." *VT* 23 (1973): 151–70.

Mendolsohn, I. "On the Preferential Status of the Eldest Son." *BASOR* 156 (1959): 38–40.

Moran, W. L. "Gen. 49, 10 and Its Use in Ezek. 21, 32." *Bib* 39 (1958): 405–25.

Pehlke, Helmuth. "An Exegetical and Theological Study of Genesis 49:1–28." Th.D. diss., Dallas Theological Seminary, 1985.

Peters, J. P. "Jacob's Blessing." *JBL* 6 (1886): 99–116.

Reider, Joseph. "Etymological Studies in Biblical Hebrew." *VT* 4 (1954): 276.

Smyth, K. "The Prophecy Concerning Judah." *CBQ* 7 (1945): 290–305.

Sonne, Isaiah. "Genesis 49:25–26." *JBL* 65 (1946): 303–6.

Speiser, E. A. "I Knew Not the Day of My Death." *JBL* 74 (1955): 252–56.

Vawter, Bruce. "The Canaanite Background of Genesis 49." *CBQ* 17 (1955): 1–18.

Yadin, Yigael. "Some Notes on the Commentaries on Genesis 49 and Isaiah from Qumran Cave 4." *IEJ* 7 (1957): 66–68.

68

Deaths and Unfulfilled Promises
(Gen. 49:29–50:26)

This last section of the book reports the deaths of Jacob and Joseph—each to be buried in the ancestral home and not in Egypt. Their deaths and the manner of the burials represent the belief that Egypt was not their home. The future of God's people lay elsewhere, and they knew it. This passage confirms the point of Abraham's purchase of the cave of Machpelah and all that was said at that point in the study about hope beyond the grave.

The passage can be divided between the two patriarchs, Jacob and Joseph. Genesis 49:29–50:14 records the final events of the life and death of Jacob: his farewell speech (49:29–32), the report of his death (49:33), the dirge (50:1–3), and the account of the burial procession with lamentation (50:4–14). Genesis 50:15–26 brings to a close the story of Joseph. It includes the brothers' speech (v. 15), their message to Joseph (vv. 16–17), their audience with Joseph (vv. 17–18), and Joseph's speech of reconciliation (vv. 19–21). Then follows Joseph's death report and the promise of the exodus (vv. 22–26).

Theological Ideas

Out of this unit come two prominent theological ideas. First, and perhaps the more striking, is the theology of Joseph that God's sovereign plan used the evil intents of human beings. God was able to turn human wickedness to serve his divine purpose. Consequently, if it was "the will of God" throughout, Joseph had no right to retaliate or need to forgive—God does both.

Second, death is a major theme in the passage—specifically, how believers die when the promises are yet unfulfilled. Believers fully expect them to be fulfilled, and so will anticipate them for the ones who live on, as well as for themselves in the world to come. This confidence explains the patriarchs' desire to be carried to the land of Canaan for burial and the announcement that God would surely visit them and deliver them from Egypt.

Structure and Synthesis

Structure

Jacob's commission for burial in Canaan was given to Joseph in 47:29–31 and to all the brothers in 49:29–32. These two instruction passages frame the account that begins with the announcement of Jacob's death in 47:29 and ends with the death itself in 49:33. The report of Joseph's grief in 50:1 is the response to the death of Jacob, and the burial in Canaan (vv. 12–14) is the goal of the account of the journey (vv. 4–11).

The repetition of the motif of Joseph's reconciliation with his brothers serves to strengthen the point after the death of the father. The little unit (vv. 15–21) is a self-contained scene. There is apprehension, sending a messenger, and face-to-face dialogue. The crucial words that form the ground for the reconciliation are in the middle of Joseph's answer (vv. 19–20). The reiteration of this motif seems to round off the narrative by recalling the theme of reconciliation from 45:3–8.

Two final sections (vv. 22–26) have been added to bring the story to a close and to provide a transition to the Book of Exodus. They summarize Joseph's life and Joseph's last words.

Summary Message

In compliance with the instruction of Jacob, Joseph gained permission from Pharaoh to bury his father in the Land of Promise; and in response to his brothers' fears, Joseph assured them of his favor in spite of their past actions, promising, before he died, that God's promises would be fulfilled.

Exegetical Outline

I. Joseph, in compliance with his father's instructions, gained permission from Pharaoh to bury the patriarch in the land of Canaan (49:29–50:14).
   A. After giving explicit instructions concerning the place of his burial, Jacob died (49:29–33).
      1. Realizing that he was about to die, Jacob gave specific instructions concerning his burial place (29–32).
      2. Jacob died (33).
   B. Joseph directed the physicians to embalm Jacob in preparation for his burial (50:1–3).
      1. Joseph mourned over the death of his father (1).
      2. Joseph directed the physicians to begin the embalming process (2).
      3. During the embalming period Jacob was mourned by the Egyptians (3).
   C. In order to carry out Jacob's wishes, Joseph obtained permission from Pharaoh to leave for Canaan (50:4–6).
      1. Joseph asked permission to bury his father in Canaan (4–5).
      2. Pharaoh granted Joseph permission to take his father's body back to Canaan (6).
   D. Joseph led the burial procession of his father to the land of Canaan (50:7–11).
      1. Along with Joseph went the dignitaries of Egypt to the burial (7).
      2. Leaving only the children and cattle behind, all the Israelite households attended the burial (8–9).
      3. The intense mourning of the burial party aroused the attention of the Canaanites (10–11).
   E. The sons of Jacob thus did as he had instructed them (50:12–14).
II. Joseph, in response to his brothers' fears of retaliation for their past sins, assured them of his kindness to them and of God's purposes (50:15–21).
   A. The brothers, fearing that Joseph would now punish them, begged him to forgive them and attributed such a wish to Jacob (15–18).
   B. Joseph, explaining that, although they had meant harm, God meant it for good, promised his kind favor to them (19–21).

III. Joseph, after a full and prosperous life, died in faith that the promises would be fulfilled (50:22–26).

Development of the Exposition

I. The death and burial of a believer provides one of the greatest opportunities to demonstrate the abiding faith in the future promises (49:29–50:14).

A. The death (49:29–33).

The death of Jacob begins to draw the book to a close. Once more the patriarchal grave became important, as Jacob instructed Joseph to bury him there with the fathers. Jacob died, after 147 years of struggle and sorrow had come to an end. Infirmities were many; sins, not a few. But throughout, Jacob retained that unquenchable desire for the blessing of God. There was deep piety that habitually relied on God, in spite of everything else. He had learned in his life the true source of blessings, and he fought with God and man to be privileged to hand that blessing on to his sons.

B. The burial (50:1–14).

The burial of Jacob was in accord with the faith. Joseph had the body embalmed for burial and then asked permission to go up and bury him. The period of embalming was seldom less than a month, and normally took forty days. Here the Egyptians mourned him for seventy days, just two days short of the time of the mourning for Pharaoh.

The procession to Canaan was led by Joseph (vv. 7–14). Along the way the mourning of the Egyptians gave rise to the name Abel Mizraim. The word play on this name serves to retain the event in the memory of Israel. The place 'ābēl miṣrayim probably once meant "the meadow of Egypt." But the very mention of that name would now recall 'ēbel miṣrayim, the "mourning of Egypt."

The family of Jacob, with its attendant company of Gentiles, rehearsed, as it were, the future homecoming of the nation in fulfillment of the promises to Israel. Once more the children of Israel would leave Egypt, taking with them the bones of the patriarch (see Exod. 13:19). Here, however, the pilgrimage to the Land of Promise was only temporary; the grave was only a claim to the land. Moses would lead the next pilgrimage to Canaan.

II. Fears and anxieties after the passing of a believer provide one of the greatest opportunities for demonstrating faith in the sovereignty of God (50:15–21).

A tension arose among the brothers. Fearing that, now that Jacob had died, Joseph would deal harshly with them, the brothers sent to Joseph, pleading with him for forgiveness. Their great fear led them to attempt to deceive Joseph into thinking that Jacob had left this request. The impact of the request reduced Joseph to tears.

Joseph's statement is one of the classic theological statements of the book: "But as for you, you thought evil [rā'â] against me, but God meant it for good [ṭōbâ]" (v. 20). The sovereign plan of God, designed to save many people alive, in some way incorporated the evil of the brothers and used it as the means of bringing about the good. On the basis of his confidence in the ways of the Lord, Joseph was able to comfort his brothers and relieve their fears.

Relationships among God's people may sometimes be tense, especially when, through death, leadership changes hands. But believers can use this to demonstrate God's sovereign design, even through human failures. They may do so through forgiveness and kindness.

III. The prospect of dying without receiving the promises provides one of the greatest opportunities for demonstrating faith in the future deliverance (50:22–26).

Joseph died in Egypt after a long and fruitful life in faithful service to God. Like his father before him, he requested that his bones be taken out of the land of Egypt at the great deliverance. This deliverance, he reassured them, would take place when God intervened to fulfill the promises of the fathers. His expression "God will surely visit you" (pāqōd yipqōd 'ĕlōhîm) guarantees that the fulfillment of the promises lay in the future (as Exod. 3:16–17 affirms). The verb pāqad, "visit," signifies divine intervention for the sake of blessing or cursing—both, in the case of the exodus, in which Israel was delivered at the expense of the Egyptians. The word usually carries the connotation that destinies would be changed by the visitation from on high. (See appendix 4.)

It is interesting to note that the Book of Genesis falls silent on this note of the expectancy of the visitation, just as the Old Testament itself does, until Zacharias identifies the birth of Jesus as the long-awaited visitation (Luke 1:68). The New Testament also ends with the expectation of the visitation from heaven for the ultimate redemption and final fulfillment of God's promised blessing—"Come, Lord Jesus" (Rev. 22:20).

Believers are convinced that their future in God's program lies elsewhere and that this current world is but part of a pilgrimage to that land. They know that God will surely visit and deliver his people, in spite of death and discouragement. *Those who trust the Lord to bring about his promised blessings in his own inscrutable ways will dem-*

onstrate their faith through the adverse circumstances of life. If believers wholeheartedly trust in the sovereignty of God, death will lose its power over them, and persecution and antagonism will fade into his sovereign plan, providing a spirit of confidence and kindness.

The book thus ends with the promise yet unfulfilled but with the expectancy of the visitation from on high. The company of the faithful thus waits in expectation for that day when the promised seed will be victorious over the curse and establish in reality the long-awaited blessing promised by God.

Bibliography

Andre, Gunnel. *Determining the Destiny: PQD in the Old Testament.* Lund: CWK Gleerup, 1980.

Grossfeld, Bernard. "The Translation of Biblical Hebrew פקד in the Targum, Peshitta, Vulgate, and Septuagint." *ZAW* 96 (1984): 83–101.

The Interpretation of Genesis 1:1–3

The Major Views

Original Creation

One view takes Genesis 1:1 to be the first part of the first day of creation. Leupold, Keil, and, to a certain extent, Cassuto follow this view. Such a view takes verse 1 as an independent, narrative sentence recording the first part of the work of God in creation on the first day (Leupold, *Exposition of Genesis*, vol. 1, p. 42). Verse 2 records three disjunctive, parallel clauses that describe the condition of the earth immediately after the creation of the universe (Keil, *Biblischer Commentar*, vol. 1, p. 49). Leupold calls them the deficiencies of the creation (i.e., those things that in the purpose of God were consecutively to be supplied). Verse 3, then, is an independent narrative sentence showing the manner in which God worked—by his Word (Leupold, *Exposition of Genesis*, vol. 1, p. 51).

In this view, the verb "create," *bārā'*, is taken here to mean creation out of nothing. The clauses in Genesis 1:2 are taken in a neutral sense, implying only raw materials from which God formed the earth as we now know it.

The Gap Theory

George H. Pember (*Earth's Earliest Ages and Their Connection with Modern Spiritualism and Theosophy* [New York: Revell, n.d.]), Hengstenburg, and the

718

Scofield Reference Bible (1st ed.) defend a different view. For them, verse 1 is an independent, narrative sentence describing the original, perfect creation. Between verses 1 and 2, the fall of Satan occurred, in which the earth underwent cataclysmic change as a result of divine judgment. Verse 2 is an independent, narrative sentence describing the condition of the universe after the fall of Satan. Verse 3 is an independent, narrative sentence describing the first step in the process of reconstruction and reformation of the judged earth.

This view also takes the verb "create" as representing creation out of nothing. The disjunctive clauses in verse 2 are interpreted as descriptions of chaos and are connected with Jeremiah 4:23–26, Isaiah 24:1, and Isaiah 45:18. The verb *hāyâ* is given the sense of "become" (not "was"), describing the transition to the chaotic state.

A Relative Beginning

There are several variations of the view that takes the first few verses of Genesis as a relative beginning. First, there is the view of Rashi, Ibn Ezra, and the *New English Bible*. Genesis 1:1 is a dependent, temporal clause. Verse 2 is the first main clause, the apodosis, describing the condition of the earth "when God began to create." This interpretation takes *bᵉrē'šît* as a noun in construct. The clause after *bᵉrē'šît* would then be a noun clause in the genitive case. "Created," *bārā'*, is not absolute creation, because it presupposes the existence of the earth of verse 2. *Wᵉhā'āreṣ*, "now the earth," would then introduce the main clause of the protasis-apodosis relationship. There are several weaknesses with this view, as the exegesis will show: the first word is probably not a construct noun; and the clauses in verse 2 are circumstantial *dependent* clauses.

Second, there is the view of E. A. Speiser in *Genesis* (Anchor Bible), which is reflected in the translation of the Torah by the Jewish Publication Society (1962). Genesis 1:1 is the prologue to the creation account in the form of a temporal clause. Verse 2 is parenthetical and consists of three clauses that are circumstantial to verse 1. The first day of creation begins with Genesis 1:3, which is an independent, narrative sentence, the apodosis of the temporal clause begun in verse 1. "When God began to create the heaven and the earth (the earth being unformed and void . . .), God said. . . ." This interpretation also takes the first word of the text as a noun in construct with a verbal form. The verb *bārā'* refers to a reforming or reshaping. The circumstantial clauses describe the state of things when God began to reshape them.

Third, there is the view of Merril F. Unger (*Unger's Bible Handbook: Unger's Bible Commentary*). Genesis 1:1 is an independent narrative sentence describing not an absolute beginning but a relative beginning. Verse 2 consists of three clauses that are circumstantial to verse 1, all describing the situation at the time of the principal action of verse 1 and giving the reason for that action. The first day actually begins in verse 3. Verses 1 and 2 thus give background information to Genesis 1:3. "In the beginning God fashioned the heavens and the earth, for the earth was waste and void . . ., and God said. . . ." This interpretation understands the first prepositional phrase as a temporal phrase with the noun in the absolute state. Unger places the "gap" during which Satan fell *before* Genesis 1:1. "In the beginning" is a relative beginning in which the cosmos was reshaped for the latecomer—man. Brought into existence before sin entered the universe (Ezek. 28; Isa. 14), the original earth was designed to be the habitation of God's first sinless angelic creatures (Job 38; Isa. 45). The pristine, sinless earth was evidently the place where sin began in God's hitherto sinless universe in connection with the revolt of Satan. *Bārā'*, then, refers not to creation out of nothing in this chapter but to a reshaping or refashioning.

Fourth, there is the view of E. J. Young (*Studies in Genesis One*). Young takes Genesis 1:1 as a summary topic statement that answers the question, "Who made all these things?" Verse 2 consists of three clauses that are circumstantial to the main clause of verse 3, stating the condition of the earth when created and until God began to form it into its present shape. Genesis 1:3 is the main clause describing the first act of God in forming the present universe. Young takes *bᵉrē'šît* as a prepositional phrase in the absolute state. To him it defines the absolute beginning. The verb *bārā'* refers to the total process of Genesis 1 and the six days of creation. This verb, he says, refers to creation out of nothing. The clauses in verse 2 are also taken by Young to be neutral. In fact, for him the threefold statement of circumstances seems to imply order—they merely describe the earth as uninhabitable.

Fifth, there is the view of Gerhard von Rad, G. Bush, B. Waltke, and others. Genesis 1:1 is a summary statement of everything that is unfolded step by step in the following verses (von Rad, *Genesis*, p. 47). Verse 2 consists of three clauses that are circumstantial to verse 3 and describe the condition of the earth when God spoke. Genesis 1:3 is an independent, narrative sentence describing the first action in the process of bringing the earth into its present order. In this view *bᵉrē'šît* is a temporal prepositional phrase with the noun in the absolute state. The term would refer not to the absolute beginning but to the beginning of the heaven and the earth as we know them. The verb *bārā'* does not refer to creation out of nothing but indicates a reforming or refashioning. The verb summarizes the activity of God over the six days of creation, a work of refashioning a world that had come under judgment. The three circumstantial clauses of Genesis 1:2 are far from neutral in their description. They describe a world that has passed under divine judgment and that is in a chaotic state; they are not simply raw material. The *wāw*, "and," prefixed to the first word of verse 2 must be taken as a disjunctive introducing the clauses and cannot chronologically follow verse 1. If this chaos is a result of the fall of Satan, that fall did not occur between verses 1 and 2 but before the creation of Genesis 1.

In this fifth view, there was an original creation that cannot be dated (see John 1:3 and Heb. 11:3). The fall of Satan and some of the angels took place before Genesis 1 (see Ezek. 28; Isa. 45; Jer. 4:23–26); the result of their fall was judgment and chaos. Genesis 1 records the re-creation or restoration of the cosmos (God's first act of salvation).

Evaluation of the Text

In this section I list the basic elements in the verses and give what I believe an exegetical analysis of the evidence shows.

Bᵉrēʾšît, "in the beginning"

The form of this word is either absolute or construct. Out of fifty-one occurrences, only a few are in the absolute state (e.g., Lev. 2:12; Isa. 46:10; Neh. 12:44). If it were taken as a construct here, however, the verb of 1:1 would stand in a dependent genitive clause (as happens in Hos. 1:2 and Num. 3:1). Cassuto (*Commentary on Genesis*, vol. 1, p. 19) argues that, if bᵉrēʾšît were taken as construct, then verse 2 would begin with wattᵉhî or hāyᵉtâ. Moreover, it should be noted that the Masoretes (note the disjunctive accent with the word) as well as the ancient versions understood the form as an absolute.

According to the lexicons the word can mean (1) the first phase or step in a course of events (e.g., the beginning of strife, wisdom, or knowledge, in various passages), (2) the first product or issue, (3) the first fruits or (4) the chief or choicest parts. In this passage the word would refer to the first phase of the universe as we know it.

Bārāʾ, "created"

For a study of this word, see Appendix 2. The study will show that God is always the subject and that the result is always something perfect, new, fresh, or whole. It describes the work of shaping, reshaping, or bringing to perfection. It may be defined as "to fashion anew"—a divine activity.

ʾĕlōhîm, "God"

This noun is the specialized use of the plural form for God. It has been variously explained as (1) honorific title (plural of respect); (2) plural of intensity, a focus on the characteristics of the stem (GKC §124d–e); (3) plural of majesty, summing up the several characteristics belonging to the idea, besides possessing the secondary sense of an intensification of the original idea (GKC §124g–i); or (4) potential plural, indicating the wealth of the potentials of the divine being (Leupold, *Exposition of Genesis*, vol. 1, p. 43).

Haššāmayim wᵉhāʾāreṣ, "the heavens and the earth"

This expression is probably a merism for the whole universe and all that is in it. Keil says it denotes the universe, for which there is no single word in the Hebrew language (*Biblischer Kommentar*, vol. 1, p. 47).

Wᵉhāʾāreṣ, "now the earth"

Verse 2 begins with the standard formation of a disjunctive wāw on a non-verb followed by the verb hāyᵉtâ, the perfect tense. The wāw introduces clauses here that are circumstantial to the main verb of the narrative, wayyōʾmer of verse 3. While most circumstantial clauses are placed after the clause they modify, Davidson says that at times the concomitant event or clause is placed first with the effect of greater vividness (A. B. Davidson, *Hebrew Syntax* [Edinburgh: T. & T. Clark, 1902], §141, p. 188)

The construction at the beginning of verse 2 rules out a sequence between verses 1 and 2, making a translation of "became" for the verb improbable. "Now the earth was waste and void" is the way these words would be translated. The clause states the circumstances prior to verse 3, not the results of verse 1. If God "created" the universe, and if the descriptions in verse 2 tell the condition of what he created, there are problems for the meanings of the words involved.

Tōhû wābōhû, *"waste and void"*

The traditional meaning of these two words has been "waste and void." The first word describes a trackless waste, physical emptiness, chaos, or ruin (Isa. 24:10; 34:11; 45:18). In a metaphorical sense it is used for what is base and futile (see 1 Sam. 12:21; Isa. 29:21). It basically describes that which lacks form.

The second word in the couplet occurs only two other times, both times with tōhû, to mean "empty." In both passages the word describes divine judgment (Jer. 4:23 and Isa. 34:11). The joining of the two in the prophetic literature builds an interpretation that is similar to Genesis 1. The fact is that God says things are good only when these conditions of verse 2 begin to be rectified. That "waste and void" is not good can also be seen in Isaiah 45:18—he created not a waste but something to be inhabited! God did not create tōhû.

Ḥōšek, *"darkness"*

This term is not used in the Bible for what is good. It is frequently used, however, in conjunction with divine judgment, apart from its normal description of darkness, night, and evil (metaphorically). In judgment it comes in the plagues on Egypt (Exod. 10:21–23), on the wicked (1 Sam. 2:9), on the enemies of the psalmist (Ps. 35:6), as a symbol of death (Job 3:4–5), and for the day of the Lord (Joel 2:2). Darkness and deep gloom are carried throughout the New Testament as well with this significant meaning. Darkness is not a positive good for human beings but a part of the chaotic state; it is the first thing that God corrects, and when he corrects it by the creation of light, he pronounces that creation of light "good." Darkness will be finally eliminated in the eschaton.

Teôm, *"the deep"*

This word has been often connected with the name of the defeated goddess Ti'amat, from whose carcass the god Marduk created the world. Many have seen it as a mythical borrowing from the pagans. Alexander Heidel (*Babylonian Genesis*, 2nd ed. [Chicago: University of Chicago Press, 1951], pp. 98–101), however, observes that the goddess's name is related to the Akkadian *tamtu*, "salty sea," and the male counterpart is *apsu*, which as a noun means "fresh water." The two words are thus personified (deified) natural forces. The Akkadian *tamtu* is cognate to the Ugaritic *thm*, "ocean, deep."

The term teôm in the Book of Genesis would serve a great polemic value against the pagan world. The "deep" is the ocean. In the ancient world it was looked upon as the symbol of chaos. It was an enemy to be conquered, a force to be reckoned with. It was the symbol of the abyss and the netherworld. It was not something conducive to life but a part of death. In Genesis, however, it is part of the chaotic state that Israel's God controls.

In view of the syntax of the first three verses and the meanings of all the words chosen, the view of Gerhard von Rad seems to carry the most exegetical support. That is, verse 1 is the summary statement of the contents of chapter 1 of Genesis (actually 1:3–2:3). Verse 2 provides circumstantial clauses that describe the state of the earth when God spoke—it was waste and void, enveloped in darkness, covered with the deep, but the Spirit of God was hovering over the face of the waters. The first day of creation would actually begin with verse 3, although verse 2 provides the circumstances. The chapter records the bringing of creation as we know it out of chaos. For the initial creation, or original creation, one has to look elsewhere in the Bible.

This view in no wise teaches evolution or allows for it. It states that the original work was thrown into darkness and chaos and that, in six days by special divine acts, God created the universe we know. It simply recognizes that "beginnings" with God are not necessarily absolute beginnings. The text is concerned not with the original creative activity of God but with the bringing of the universe we know into its present shape.

APPENDIX **2**

Bārāʾ, "to Create"

The verb *bārāʾ* is important in the discussion about creation. The common assumption that the word means "creation out of nothing" must be examined in conjunction with the determination of the precise meanings in biblical usage.

Etymology

Definition

The dictionaries offer "shape, create, fashion" as the basic meanings for *bārāʾ*. The English word "create" is most frequently used to translate *bārāʾ*; it can be used for creating from nothing or making out of existing materials.

Hebrew Cognates

The only related word is the feminine noun *bᵉrîʾâ*, "a creation, thing created." Its only use is in Numbers 16:30, where it describes the Lord's bringing about "something totally new"—the earth's swallowing the rebels.

Cognate Languages

Akkadian. BDB lists the Assyrian *barû* with the meaning "to make, create," as a cognate of *bārāʾ*. Instead of giving this meaning for *barû*, however, the *Chicago Assyrian Dictionary* defines *barû* as (1)"to look upon, to watch over," and (2)"to be hungry."

724

BDB also suggests *bārā'* be compared with Assyrian *banû*, which means (1)"to build, construct, form," (2)"to engender, produce," (3)"to create," and (4)"to devise a plan." The correspondence of *banû* with *bārā'* would involve an interchange between the *n* and the *r* (cf. Hebrew *bēn* and Aramaic *bār*, both meaning "son"). The connection finds additional support in that *banû* is the verb in the Babylonian creation story, *Enuma Elish*: "[Ea] created [ibna] mankind out of [Kingu's] blood" (tablet 6, line 33). Akkadian *banû*, however, is probably cognate to Hebrew *bānâ*, which is also used in the creation section of Genesis: "And the LORD fashioned [*wayyiben*] the rib into a woman" (2:22).

Arabic. The cognate word *barā'a* is probably a loan-word, "create." Old South Arabic has a root *br'*, "to build"; one dialect has the meaning "bring forth, give birth to."

Aramaic. Both Aramaic and Syriac have the verb *brā'*, "to create." The word is not used in the Aramaic portions of the Old Testament, but in later Aramaic and Hebrew the rabbinical usage carries forward the biblical meanings of "create."

From this survey it seems safe to say that the Hebrew verb *bārā'*, "create," is not well attested in the cognate languages. Only by joining apparent homonyms can any substantial cognate material be collected. For example, Bernhardt suggests that the Hebrew root *br'* had an original meaning of "separate, divide" (*TDOT*, vol. 2, p. 245). But this idea incorporates the definitions of homonyms with the meanings of "cut, sculpt, sharpen" along with "create, shape, fashion." There is not enough evidence to support such a theory.

Usage

Bārā' is used in the *qal* some thirty-eight times and in the *niphal* ten times, all of which are in contexts consistent with the idea of "create." We may divide the examples into three, more specific categories of meaning.

The Formation of the Universe and Its Contents

The most common usage of *bārā'* applies to God's making the universe and everything in it.

The universe. *Bārā'* summarizes the work of God in producing what human beings never produce or think to produce. The first verse of the Bible summarizes such a work: "In the beginning God created [*bārā'*] the heavens and the earth." The context of Genesis 1 and of passages such as Psalm 33:9 explains that the means of this creating was God's powerful Word.

Other passages fit this first point as well. Genesis 2:3 summarizes the creation of the heaven and the earth and all the contents with *bārā'*. Isaiah also uses *bārā'* to say that the Lord created the heavens (42:5), the stars (40:26) and the ends of the earth (v. 28). The psalmist also affirms that God created the north and the south (89:12), probably a merism for the whole world.

Cosmic forces. *Bārā'* is also used to describe God's producing the forces of nature. Amos describes the Lord as the one who formed (< *yāṣar*) the mountains and created (< *bārā'*) the wind (4:13). "Darkness" is also a result of God's creative power: "I form [< *yāṣar*] the light and create [< *bārā'*] darkness, I make [< *'āśâ*] peace and create [< bārā'] evil" (Isa. 45:7). Darkness (*ḥōšek*) in this text is paralleled to evil (*ra'*) by virtue of the repetition of *bārā'*. These words are used differently in Isaiah; they may stress the evil forces of darkness, of painful calamity, or of distressing situations, in contrast to light and peace.

Living creatures. Bārā' is used in Genesis to describe the creation of humankind. Three times the verb is used in Genesis 1:27. It is also used this way in Genesis 5:1–2; 6:7; Deuteronomy 4:32; and Isaiah 45:12. The Scripture thereby stresses that humankind is exclusively the product of God's creative act. Since the account in Genesis 2:7 specifies that the man was formed (< *yāṣar*) from the dust of the ground, it may be concluded that *bārā'* here describes a formation using pre-existing material. *Bārā'*, then, can describe the transforming of dust into a body.

One verse that needs further discussion is Psalm 89:47—"Remember how short my time is; why have you made [*bārā'tā*] all mankind [*kol-benê-'ādām*] in vain?" The idea is that, since God created man in the beginning, he is also the creator of the human race.

Bārā' is also used in Genesis 1:21 for the making of the great sea creatures. The verb may have been chosen purposefully here: since the great sea creatures were feared and venerated among the nations, the writer perhaps wished to stress that they were also a part of God's creation.

The Establishment of the Nation Israel

A second category for the use of *bārā'* applies to the creation of Israel. Isaiah records the declaration of the Lord: "I am the LORD, your Holy One, the Creator [*bôrē'*] of Israel, your King" (43:15). The same chapter also uses Jacob as the object of *bārā':* "But now, thus says the LORD who created you [*bōrā'ăkā*], O Jacob, and he who formed you, O Israel" (43:1). The same idea appears to be the point of Malachi 2:10; the prophet says, "Have we not all one father? Has not one God created us [*berā'ānû*]?" He bases his message on the national unity they share as the people of God.

Bārā' describes not only the forming of the nation but also the inclusion of believers within it. Referring to the regathering of his sons, God mentions "every one that is called by my name, for I have created him [*berā'tîw*] for my glory" (Isa. 43:7). Perhaps Qohelet's use of the word carries something of this idea as well: "Remember now your Creator [*bôre'eykā*] in the days of your youth" (Eccles. 12:1).

Transformation for the Renewal of Things

The third category includes those passages that describe God's work of making things new. The prophets in particular use *bārā'* to describe future transformations or restorations. Isaiah records, "I create [*bôrē'*] new heavens and a new earth" (65:17). In the same context of anticipated new beginnings he adds, "But be glad and rejoice forever in that which I create [*bôrē'*], for I am about to create [*bôrē'*] Jerusalem as a rejoicing, and her people as a joy" (v. 18).

Nature also will be renovated (41:18–20). In fact, the entire coming restoration is called a creation of the Lord's (45:8).

Bārā' also conveys the idea of renewal. Psalm 51:10 says, "Create [*b^erā'*] in me a clean heart, O God, and renew [*ḥaddēš*] within me a steadfast spirit." The two verbs together show that the request is for the *renewal* of the spiritual attitudes. A similar use is found in Isaiah 57:19, which says, "I create [*bôrē'*] the fruit of the lips." The point here is that, when the Lord heals someone, he inspires praise once again.

The emphasis in using *bārā'* for such transformations may be on their being totally new. Jeremiah 31:22 explicitly uses it this way: "For the LORD has created [*bārā'*] a new thing [*ḥādāšâ*] on the earth." In Numbers 16:30, the "new thing" is expressed by the noun derived from the verb: "but if the LORD make a new thing [*w^e'im-b^erî'â yibrā'*]."

In all these samples the action of *bārā'* is that of transforming something into a new condition. With the exception of the Numbers passage, that transformation is always to something far better.

Synonyms

The major synonyms of *bārā'* are *yāṣar* and *'āśâ*. *Yāṣar* means "to form, fashion (something purposefully)." It is the activity of an artist, as may be illustrated from its participial form, which means "potter." Whereas the significance of *bārā'* is that something new and perfect is produced, *yāṣar* suggests that what is formed is by design. The other synonym, *'āśâ*, simply means "to do, make" and is too broad to be helpful here. The verb *bānâ*, "to build," also may be used synonymously with creation words. It may describe the physical construction of a building but may also be used for creation (as with the formation of Eve, in Gen. 2:22) or procreation (e.g., building the house of Israel, in (Ruth 4:11).

Translations

In the Greek translations of the Old Testament books several words are used to translate *bārā'*, the most common being *ktizō* (which also translates *yāṣar* and *qānâ*, among others). In classical use the term meant "to people a place" or "to make habitable." In the New Testament it is used for the creation by God (Col. 1:16; Eph. 3:9) as well as the transforming of believers (Eph. 2:10; 4:24).

The second major word used in the Greek is *poieō*, "to do, make." This word is far too general to give any help in this study. It most naturally translates *'āśâ*. It translates *bārā'*, however, in Genesis 1:1, 21, 27; 5:1–2; 6:7; Isaiah 42:5; 43:1; 45:7, 18; 65:18. Aquila, however, preferred the precision of *ktizō* in the creation accounts.

Several other Greek words are used for *bārā'*, especially in the prophets, but they do not help us in this study.

Significance

The word *bārā'* is used exclusively for the activity of God in which he *fashions something anew*. The word can be used for creating something out of nothing, but that idea must come from the context and not from the inherent meaning of this word.

Bārā' has the nuances *shaping, forming, or transforming*. Its emphasis lies in the fact that what is produced is new and fresh and good. While many English words could be used in the translations, "create" serves very well because it has been elevated by association with the Creator. This usage is fitting, since *bārā'* is never found with a human subject.

APPENDIX **3**

The Faith of Abraham at Worship

In this appendix I wish to determine as specifically as possible the biblical picture of Abraham's faith—that is, what the text says or implies that he believed and how that belief manifested itself in worship. The source of the information is basically the scriptural traditions, but we cannot ignore the extrabiblical context as well.

The Evidence

Extrabiblical Evidence

We know from Joshua 24:2 that the ancestors lived beyond the great river Euphrates and worshiped other gods. We also know that Ur and Haran were centers of activity for Abram's family (Gen. 12:4; 15:7). From archaeological data we know the beliefs of people in these ancient centers of civilization, which Abraham was probably familiar with.

A survey of ancient religious texts (esp. *Atraḫasis*) provides us with the data. The family perhaps knew about creation, a great flood, longevity of famous ancestors, and even the confusion of languages. Abram's family would have believed that there were supernatural beings that controlled destiny, that humankind was to serve god(s) in this life, that sacrifice, prayer, proclamation, and hymns were acceptable forms of worship, and that there was life after death. Whether Abraham was ever a polytheist at heart is too difficult to say

729

(Joshua seems to distinguish him from the ancestors). It is clear, though, that with the call of the Lord he became a true monotheist.

The Biblical Evidence

The specific points about Abraham's Yahwistic faith and worship come from the Scripture itself. Within the biblical material, however, we must follow certain cautions. First, priority must be given to statements that the text reports Abraham as saying. Second, great importance must be given to reports of what God said to Abraham. Here, however, we may ask how this information was communicated to Abraham, or how it was known to the writer. Third, a distinction must be made between the historical report and the editorial interpretation. In places, the wording of the text may reflect the theological interpretation of Moses or of another inspired editor.

Of lesser importance, but still useful, are other events in Abraham's world. Here we have to assume that, since they are in the Bible, they must have become part of the family's tradition early on and that Abraham knew about these interchanges between God and the pagan individuals.

It is also important to remember that Abraham grew in his knowledge of the truth. This factor may have importance in trying to determine what theological ideas led to the various religious practices; however, since the precise chronology of the stories and the exact timing of the growth of knowledge cannot be determined, the matter is not of great importance here. On the whole, the faith of Abraham at the beginning would have had less content than at the time of the sacrifice of Isaac.

Abraham's Belief

For the sake of convenience the data will be arranged systematically rather than chronologically. This format provides the opportunity of capturing the general picture of Abraham's beliefs, even though parts of it developed gradually.

The Nature of God

First, God is alive—in contrast to the pagan deities. God spoke to Abraham and his relatives (12:1–3, 4; 13:14; 16:8–9; 21:12; etc.); he appeared to people (12:7; 15:1 [in a vision]; 18:1; 20:3 [in a dream to Abimelech]); he saw people in their needs (16:13); and he heard their cries (v. 11; 21:17).

Second, God is the sovereign Lord. Abraham knew that the Lord was the true Creator of the universe (14:22); that he raised up nations and made kings (17:6); that he could give the land to whomever he wished (13:15); that he brought plagues on people (12:17); that he judged nations for their sin (13:13; 15:14, 16; chaps. 18–19); and that he protected his covenant by preventing sin (20:6). God also protected his people like a shield (15:1) by delivering the enemies into their hands (14:20) and by providing for them in the wilderness (16:7; 21:19). God could provide life (17:16), and he could destroy it (18:23). All these activities demonstrated the power of the Lord as well, so aptly summarized in the Lord's question, "Is anything too marvelous for the LORD?" (18:14).

Then, God is the righteous Judge. Abraham believed that the Lord was the Judge of the whole earth (18:25) and the God of heaven (24:7). He learned that the Lord was able to discern the heart, for he was omniscient (18:13, 15); he knew that God was just in his decisions (15:16; 18:25) and would spare the wicked for the sake of the righteous (v. 26). He also knew that the punishment of sin was death (20:3, 7).

Fourth, God is gracious. The predominant theme through these chapters is that God graciously elected Abram to be his worshiper and made specific promises to him (12:1–3). These promises were for blessings for Abraham and his descendants (12:1–3; 15:4–5; 22:17). The promise of blessings also came through a priest (14:19), and their fulfillment was observed by pagans (21:22).

The essence of the relationship between God and Abraham is expressed in Genesis 15:6. In response to the Word of God that called Abram out of polytheism and promised him physical and spiritual blessings, Abram "believed the LORD." For this act of faith (leaving Ur and embarking on a walk with God), God gave him righteousness. Since this verse is the writer's explanation of Abram's relationship with God, it would be difficult to determine how much Abraham understood about imputed righteousness. He simply put his life and destiny in the Lord by leaving Ur. Consequently, Moses says, he was credited with righteousness.

The form of the grace of God was his covenant. Genesis 15:7–21 shows that the Lord graciously made a covenant with Abram and his descendants. He prescribed the ritual for its formation (15:9) and established its reliability by fulfilling (in part) its promises (17:7), proving himself to be their God (v. 8). He prophesied the future history of his covenant people because he established destiny (15:13) in accordance with his plan to bless the world (12:3).

At the heart of the covenant promise was fertility—it came from the Lord and not pagan gods. The promise of God to multiply Abraham's seed was repeated often to the patriarch (13:16; 15:5; 17:2). God would also multiply the seed of Hagar (16:10). Conversely, God could prevent childbirth (15:3) and close the womb (20:17–18).

God's gracious dealings were also revealed in his providential intervention in the lives of his people. Notable is the coming of the Lord to eat Abraham's meal (18:8) in order to reveal his plans. This manifestation was with angels. Later Abraham told his servant that the Lord would send his angel to lead him on the journey (24:7, 21, 27; see also 12:7).

Finally, God is faithful. Abraham ultimately knew that God was faithful in keeping his promises (12:7; 21:1–7). His faithfulness was also seen in the provision of the animal anticipated by Abraham (22:8) and in the preservation of Lot in accord with his Word to Abraham (19:29).

The Nature of Human Beings

First, people are frail and sinful. Abraham had no false concepts about human nature, as did the pagans. He knew that he was but dust and ashes (18:27) and that, in the face of death, he could only prepare for the future descendants (chaps. 23–24). He recognized that humans could be divided into the righteous and the wicked (18:23), the latter being the future recipients of God's wrath (chap. 19). People who feared the Lord would obey him (20:11), but such fear had to be tested at times (22:1).

Second, people have covenant responsibilities. The righteous, that is, those who live in covenant relationship with the Lord, had to live in conformity to his will. The righteous were instructed to be perfect (see 17:1). Abraham specifically was instructed to make the sacrifice for establishing the covenant (15:9) and to keep the sign of the covenant (17:9). At times God commanded the unexpected (22:1). At other times he called on them to learn of his good promises (13:14–18).

Finally, people have hope for the future. Abraham was told of God's plan for his death and for the bondage and deliverance of his descendants in Egypt (15:13–16) so that he might rest in confidence in the Lord. But Abraham also knew that the promises were not exhausted in his life and so bought the burial cave in Canaan (chap. 23) because he knew that the promises would be fulfilled there. In short, there was hope beyond the grave.

It should be clear from this survey that Abraham probably had a good understanding of the nature and work of the Lord in relation to sinful humankind. In this connection, two New Testament passages need explanation.

In John 8:56, Jesus said, "Abraham rejoiced to see my day, and he saw [it] and was glad." The verse does not specify very much, but "my day" seems to refer to the manifestation of the promised Christ. One may suppose that, in offering up Isaac (Gen. 22), Abraham may have been given a greater vision of the meaning of the promise. His faith could be called a vision of the day of the Lord, meaning that he understood the Lord's plan to provide substitution for the sacrifice of the human. Genesis 22 does provide the motto of worship: "In the mount of the LORD it will be seen" (v. 14). This interpretation would be taking the words of Jesus in their general sense. It would be hard to prove from these words that Abraham saw the crucifixion act of the incarnate Lord. Jesus' main point was that he was before Abraham—he was the Lord—and that Abraham believed in him. The midrash *Genesis Rabba* says that Abraham saw the whole history of his descendants in the vision in Genesis 15 and "rejoiced with the joy of the Law." Perhaps Jesus was using some such early Jewish tradition in pressing his claim to the Pharisees.

Hebrews 11:19 interprets why Abraham offered up Isaac—he reasoned that God was able to raise him up from the dead, "whence he also received him in a figure." Abraham's faith was strong enough to obey, in spite of conflicting words from God. He knew that the promise of God could not fail, and so he relinquished Isaac. It is clear that the ancient world knew that there was life after death, but there is no clear statement about resurrection from the dead. The closest hint of such a belief in Genesis is the motivation for the purchase of the cave (chap. 23). Abraham believed in the creative power of God that transcended death or the barren womb; that power could maintain Isaac as the promised seed, even if he was sacrificed. The writer of the Book of Hebrews identifies this confidence as an early belief in resurrection. Either the writer of Hebrews is providing additional information regarding what Abraham actually knew, or he is interpreting for his audience the kind of faith Abraham had (i.e., Abraham may not have fully understood resurrection, but he knew that God could overcome death to make Isaac the seed). The former view weakens the nature of the test; the later view fits some of the patterns of interpretation of Old Testament passages in the Book of Hebrews.

Abraham's Worship

Abraham's knowledge of God inspired in him the fear of the Lord (22:12) and faith in the Lord (15:6). These responses, of course, are at the heart of worship. The following survey includes private and public acts of worship as they relate to belief.

Sacrifice

The first thing that Abram did upon arriving in the land was to build an altar (12:7), a custom that he followed frequently (v. 8; 13:18; etc.). There is no mention of sacrifice per se, but one may assume some offering was made on the altars. Genesis 22 supports this assumption, for Isaac naturally wondered where the animal was.

That sacrifice was a gift to God, a substitution for the devotee and an act of homage and surrender, would have been clear to the patriarch. But the sacrifice of Isaac was another matter. Abraham had faith and hope, and that hope came to reality with Isaac. A sacrifice would be a fitting way to express gratitude for the birth of a son. But what could he offer that was more than a mere token? God's instruction for him to offer the boy was strange and painful, but to offer the child would be the greatest act of sacrifice possible. In a sense, and true to the nature of sacrifice, Abraham was offering up himself at that altar. When the real victim was surrendered, then a ram was all that was needed for the symbolic expression of surrender. By this time Abraham had learned that to sacrifice to the Lord was at the heart of worship and that to please God in worship required that he surrender his will in compliance with God's instruction.

Proclamation

At the altars that he built, Abraham "made proclamation of the LORD by name" (12:8; see also 4:26; etc.). Genesis 21:33 records that Abraham planted a grove and there called out in the name of the Lord again. The ideas bound up in the "name of the Lord" would certainly include the above survey of the nature of God. Abraham's witness to his new faith had much content.

Prayer

Prayer was also an important part of the response of Abraham and his household to the Lord. The greatest example of his prayer is the bold, yet humble, intercession for Sodom (chap. 18). But Abraham also prayed for Abimelech so that the people of Gerar would not be destroyed (20:7, 17). Prayer also played an important part in his servant's mission (24:12). It is clear that the patriarch inspired submission to the will of God. Perhaps the mention of Abraham's being a prophet (20:7) is connected with his praying.

Praise and Worship

Abraham's gratitude was expressed in humble adoration as he would fall on his face (17:3), bow to the ground (18:2), or rejoice (21:1–7). His praise also took the form of commemorative naming, that is, keeping the event in the memory of the righteous (16:14–15; 22:14). His servant also worshiped in gratitude (24:26), praising God for leading him to the fulfillment of his prayer (vv. 27, 48, 52).

Tithes

According to Genesis 14:20, Abraham paid tithes of all he had to Melchizedek, priest of the Most High God. The act was a natural gesture of his submission, a recognition that God had granted him his wealth.

Oaths

Another expression of his devotion to the Lord was in the religious practices of making oaths. He solemnized his oath by appealing to the Lord in Genesis 14:22. He again made an oath in Genesis 21:23 and had his servant do likewise in 24:3, 9. These oaths expressed his reverence for the Lord.

Circumcision

Since circumcision was the sign of the covenant, to comply with this rite was to keep covenant (17:10, 24–27; 21:4). This observance became a regular ritual of the believing community.

Ethical Conduct

Proper acts of worship will result in proper ethical conduct (i.e., knowledge of God leads to worship of God and in turn to obedience to God). Genesis 26:4–5 records that Abraham obeyed everything that the Lord commanded him to do. This statement harmonizes with the point of the revelation in 18:19, namely, that Abraham was to be righteous and to teach righteousness. He was to live in integrity (17:1; see also 20:5), protect the covenant (15:11), and ensure that the blessing was passed on (23:4, 17–20; 25:1–11).

The Relation of Faith and Worship

The following brief list displays the immediate motivation for Abraham's (and his family's) acts of worship:

built an altar (12:7–8)	after the Lord's confirming appearance
built an altar (13:18)	after the Lord's comforting promises
paid tithes (14:20)	after the priestly blessing following the victory
took an oath (14:22)	after the temptation from the king of Sodom
prepared the sacrifice and protected the covenant (Chap. 15)	after (or in) the vision of the Lord in a dream

gave a commemorative name (16:14–15)	after Hagar was saved by the Lord
bowed to the ground (17:3)	after the Lord appeared to him
was circumcised (17:10, 24)	in compliance with the divine command
interceded (Chap. 18)	after hearing of judgment
interceded (20:7, 17)	after the request of Abimelech in face of doom
rejoiced (21:1–7)	after the fulfillment of a promise
swore by the Lord (21:23–24)	after pagans agreed to peace
sacrificed (Chap. 22)	in obedience to the test and in fear of the Lord
swore (24:3, 9)	to begin the solemn mission
prayed (24:12)	for leading in the mission
praised and worshiped (24:26–27)	after the answer to the prayer

It seems clear enough that worship in the life and family of Abraham was a spontaneous response to divine intervention, whether a solemn command, a visitation, or a marvelous provision. The acts of worship not only reflect the beliefs of the worshiper; they express the attitudes of submission, dependence, and gratitude as well.

Pāqad, "to Visit"

The verb *pāqad* has a wide range of meanings that call for special attention. The common translation "to visit" is somewhat misleading if it is understood in the modern sense, and so a contextual study of the passages is in order.

Etymology

Definition

The dictionaries list the basic meanings of *pāqad* as "to attend to, visit, muster, appoint, entrust."

Hebrew Cognates

Hebrew has several words that are derived from the verb. One noun, *pᵉquddâ*, means "visitation" but more specifically "punishment" in Hosea 9:7 and "prison" in Jeremiah 52:11. It also has the meaning "store" or "storage" in Isaiah 15:7, "overseeing" in 1 Chronicles 26:30, and "mustering" fighters in 2 Chronicles 17:14. This range of meanings parallels the range for the verb.

The word for "overseer" or "commissioner" is *pāqîd* (Gen. 41:34; Judg. 9:29).

The idea of "appointing" is also attested with related words. *Piqqûd* is a "precept," that is, something appointed to be obeyed (Ps. 19:8). The noun *mipqād* is "appointment" in 2 Chronicles 31:13, and an "appointed place" in

Ezekiel 43:21. It also is translated "muster" in 2 Samuel 24:9. *Piqqādôn* is a "deposit" or "store" in Genesis 41:36.

Cognate Languages

The root *pāqad* is well attested in the cognate languages. The dictionaries record that it occurs in Akkadian with essentially the same meanings as Hebrew. In the Ugaritic texts *pqd* has the meaning "to give orders." In Phoenician it means "to attend to, provide." The Syriac cognate means "to visit." Arabic has the meanings "to lose, miss, give attention to." And Ethiopic has the word with the meanings "to visit, muster, desire, need." All these meanings in the cognate languages parallel the usage of the Hebrew word.

Usage

To Attend To

Pāqad occurs in several contexts where the idea seems to have something to do with "attending to" something or someone.

To pay attention to, to observe. In a few passages the idea of the verb is that of close examination or observation, with the intent to do something to benefit or punish. For example, the psalmist says, "What is man that you are mindful [< *zākar*] of him, or the son of man that you visit [< *pāqad*] him?" (8:4). Or, "I remember [*pāqadtî*] that which Amalek did to Israel, how he laid wait" (1 Sam. 15:2). In spite of the various ways that the English versions have rendered this verb, the idea in these contexts is clearly that of observing something with the intent to act.

To see to something. Some passages use the word in the sense of the intended action, not just the examination. The idea of "seeing to" something conveys this sense. An example is found in Zechariah 11:16, which says, "I will raise up a shepherd in the land who shall not attend to [*yipqōd*] those who are cut off."

To seek. Also connected to the idea of looking for or taking note of something is the category of seeking, that is, looking for a remedy or for something missing. For example, Isaiah says, "LORD, in trouble have they sought you [*pᵉqādûkā*]; they poured out a prayer when your chastening was upon them" (26:16). Similarly we read: "If your father at all miss me [*pāqōd yipqᵉdēnî*] . . ." (1 Sam. 20:6). The first sample uses the word for seeking that finds expression in prayer. The second uses it in the sense of seeking in vain.

All the samples in this first category, then, have the idea of paying attention to, looking after, looking for, or remembering with the intent of doing something.

To Visit

This second category includes usages that describe some kind of intervention (usually by God) for blessing or punishment. The translation "visit" may be somewhat archaic in view of modern English usage, but it still is retained in several of the English translations. Moreover, *Webster's Dictionary, The American College Dictionary, The Oxford English Dictionary,* and *The Amer-*

ican Heritage Dictionary all include as part of the usage of "visit" the concepts found in these passages, that is, to come to comfort or aid, to assail, to plague, or to afflict with suffering. The use of this English word for the category description is thus acceptable, even though each passage must be explained as to its precise sense.

Intervention for good. A number of passages use the word to describe blessing. One type of blessing is childbirth—the speaker attributes the birth of a long-expected child as a work of God. Genesis 21:1 reports that the Lord "visited" Sarah and that she gave birth to Isaac. First Samuel 2:21 reports the same with regard to Hannah.

Another blessing that comes through divine visitation is growth in the fields. Ruth 1:6 says, "She had heard that the LORD had visited [*pāqad*] his people by giving them bread" (Ruth 1:6). And the psalmist says, "You visit [*pāqadtā*] the earth and water it" (65:9). Probably the point of the Ruth passage is that of the psalm, namely, that the Lord ended the famine—it rained, crops grew, and the people made bread.

A third blessing that this word introduces is deliverance from oppression. Two passages clearly show it to be the means of escape from bondage: "God will surely visit you [*pāqōd yipqōd*] and will bring you out of this place" (Gen. 50:24–25). And, "After seventy years have been accomplished at Babylon, I will visit ['*epqōd*] you and perform my good word to you in causing you to return to this place" (Jer. 29:10).

The idea of deliverance can also be personal when God visits his servant. The psalmist says, "O visit me [*poqdēnî*] with your salvation" (106:4); and Jeremiah says, "O LORD, you knew; remember me and visit me [*ûpoqdēnî*] and revenge me of my persecutors" (15:15). When *pāqad* is used to describe the Lord's intervention for good, some deliverance or benefit will be granted. It is interesting to note that the concept of "remembering" appears in some of these passages, as it did in those under the first category of "attending to" something.

Intervention for punishment. A second group of passages uses the word to describe some kind of intervention as punishment. Punishment for sin is clearly expressed in Exodus: "I, the LORD your God, am a jealous God, visiting [*pōqēd*] the iniquity of the fathers on the children" (20:5). The passage is saying that the children often pay for the sins their ancestors committed. Another passage that expresses punishment concerns the sin of the golden calf: "when I visit [*poqdî*] I will visit [*ûpāqadtî*] their sin on them" (Exod. 32:34). The verb seems to have two slightly different senses here: when the Lord intervenes in their life (a neutral connotation), it will be for punishment for sin (negative connotation).

In some contexts the emphasis is more on the judgment that is the punishment. For example, Hosea says, "Now will he remember their iniquities and visit [*we̓yipqōd*] their sins, and they shall return to Egypt" (8:13). Amos says, "When I visit the transgression of Israel upon him, I will visit [*ûpāqadtî*] the altars of Bethel also" (and the horns of the altar will be cut off and fall to the ground) (3:14). Isaiah says, "In that day the LORD with his awesome and great, strong sword will punish [*yipqōd ʿal*] Leviathan" (27:1). And again Isaiah says that the Lord will water and keep a vineyard "lest any harm [*pen yipqōd*] it" (v. 3). In all these samples the verb describes punishment inflicted in some way by intervention.

Intervention for testing. The word also describes suffering at the hand of God as a form of testing, not punishment. Job asks, "What is man . . . that you should visit him [*wattipqᵉdennû*] every morning and test him [*tibḥānennû*] every moment?" (7:17–18).

To Number

This category may be a development of the first idea of observing or examining with some preparation in mind—usually for war. Numbers records, "You shall number [*tipqᵉdû*] them (males, twenty years old and able to fight) by their armies" (1:3). David said to Joab, "Go through all the tribes . . . and number [*ûpiqdû*] the people . . . that I may know the number of them" (2 Sam. 24:2).

To Appoint

This fourth category is closely related to that of "seeing to" something, but these passages emphasize the appointing of someone. For example, Genesis says, "And the captain of the guard charged [*wayyipqōd*] Joseph with them, and he served them" (40:4). The law prescribed: "They shall make [*ûpāqᵉdû*] captains of the armies to lead the people" (Deut. 20:9). And finally, Cyrus says of the Lord, "And he has charged me [*pāqad ʿālay*] to build a house in Jerusalem" (2 Chron. 36:23).

Summarizing the usage in the *qal* (and *niphal*) stem, we may say that the basic ideas are "to attend to" something, examine or observe it, see to it, look for it; "to intervene," used of God's visiting with benefits or punishment or sufferings; "to number" by examining or observing for the purpose of warfare; or "to appoint" or entrust someone with the responsibilities of overseeing or attending to someone.

To Muster

A couple of passages use the verb in the *piel-hithpael* system with the idea of mustering armies. This sense is clearly related to the *qal* meaning of numbering armies for the purpose of fighting but appears to be more intensive, that is, rousing the troops to fight. Isaiah, for example, says, "The LORD of hosts musters [*mᵉpaqqēd*] the host of the battle" (13:4).

To Entrust

The last category of meaning to be surveyed concerns the use in the *hiphil-hophal* system. The basic concept here is that of entrusting something or someone into another's care. The following illustrations show the range of this category. Genesis records that Potiphar made Joseph overseer (*wayyapqîdēhû*) over his house (39:4). The law instructed: "You shall appoint [*hapqēd*] the Levites over the tabernacle of the testimony" (Num. 1:50). The prophet-historian reported that Rehoboam made shields "and committed them" (w^e-$hipq\hat{i}d$) to the chief of the guard (1 Kings 14:27). And finally, Isaiah says, "At Michmash he would lay up [$yapq\hat{i}d$] his implements" (10:28).

It should be clear from this brief survey of the usage of $p\bar{a}qad$ that there are common motifs that run through the uses—ideas of attending to something or seeing to something—which leads to the idea of intervention to bless or punish, the enlisting of people for military intervention, or the appointing or entrusting of such responsibilities to individuals. It should be clear that no one English word can be used for each of the categories.

Gunnel Andre, in his book *Determining the Destiny: PQD in the Old Testament*, proposes that the basic idea behind the word is "to determine the destiny." This understanding fits very well many of the passages, especially where the Lord is said to "visit" people in blessing or judgment.

In the Book of Genesis two key passages use the word with the idea of great blessing. The birth of Isaac is explained as a visitation from the Lord, a divine intervention in the lives of Abraham and Sarah to provide the promised seed and alter the destiny of the family forever. And then at the end of the book, Joseph announced that God would surely visit them and deliver them from Egypt. This visitation also was a divine intervention to fulfill the promises made to the fathers.

Bibliography

Commentaries on Genesis

Aberbach, Moses, and Bernard Grossfeld. *Targum Onkelos to Genesis: A Critical Analysis Together with an English Translation of the Text (Based on A. Sperber's Edition).* New York: Ktav, 1982.

Brueggemann, Walter. *Genesis. Interpretation: A Bible Commentary for Teaching and Preaching.* Atlanta: John Knox, 1982.

Bush, George. *Notes, Critical and Practical on the Book of Genesis.* 2 vols. New York: Ivison, Phinney, 1857. Reprint. Minneapolis: James Family Christian Publishers, 1979.

Calvin, John. *Commentaries on the First Book of Moses, Called Genesis.* 2 vols. Translated by John King from the Latin [1554] and Compared with the French Edition [1563]. Edinburgh: For the Calvin Translation Society, 1847. Reprint. Edinburgh: Banner of Truth, 1965.

Candlish, Robert S. *Studies in Genesis.* Edinburgh: A. & C. Black, 1868. Reprint. Grand Rapids: Kregel, 1979.

Cassuto, Umberto. *A Commentary on the Book of Genesis.* 2 vols. Vol. 1, *From Adam to Noah, Genesis I–VI:8;* vol. 2, *From Noah to Abraham, Genesis VI:9–XI:32:* With an Appendix: A Fragment of Part III. Translated by Israel Abrahams. Jerusalem: Magnes, 1961–64.

Coats, George W. *Genesis, with an Introduction to Narrative Literature.* Forms of Old Testament Literature, edited by Rolf Knierim and Gene M. Tucker, vol. 1. Grand Rapids: Eerdmans, 1983.

Colson, F. H., and G. H. Whitaker, eds. and trans. *Philo, with an English Translation.* 10 vols. Loeb Classical Library. Cambridge: Harvard University Press; London: W. Heinemann, 1929–35. (Vols. 1–6 deal with subjects in Genesis.)

Davis, John J. *Paradise to Prison: Studies in Genesis.* Grand Rapids: Baker, 1975.

Delitzsch, Franz. *A New Commentary on Genesis.* 6th ed. 2 vols. Translated by Sophia Taylor. Edinburgh: T. & T. Clark, 1888–89.

Dillmann, A. *Genesis, Critically and Exegetically Expounded.* Translated by William B. Stevenson. Edinburgh: T. & T. Clark, 1897.

Dods, Marcus. *The Book of Genesis.* Expositor's Bible. London: Hodder & Stoughton, 1893.

Driver, S. R. *The Book of Genesis, with Introduction and Notes.* 15th ed. Edited, with an Appendix by G. R. Driver. Westminster Commentaries. London: Methuen, 1948.

Grossfeld, Bernard. "A Commentary on the Text of a New Palestinian Targum (Codex Neofiti I) on Genesis 1–25." Ph.D. diss., Johns Hopkins University, 1968.

Gunkel, Hermann. *Genesis übersetzt und erklärt.* 5th ed. Göttinger Handkommentar zum Alten Testament, vol. 1, no. 1. Göttingen: Vandenhoeck & Ruprecht, 1922.

Jacob, Benno. *Das erste Buch der Tora: Genesis übersetzt und erklärt.* Berlin: Schocken, 1934.

——— . *The First Book of the Bible: Genesis, Interpreted by B. Jacob.* His commentary abridged, edited, and translated by E. J. Jacob and W. Jacob. New York: Ktav, 1974.

Keil, Carl Friedrich. *Biblical Commentary on the Old Testament. Vol. 1, The Pentateuch.* Translated by James Martin. Edinburgh: T. & T. Clark, 1866.

Kidner, Derek. *Genesis: An Introduction and Commentary.* Tyndale Old Testament Commentaries. London: Tyndale; Downers Grove, Ill.: Inter-Varsity, 1967.

Leupold, Herbert Carl. *Exposition of Genesis.* 2 vols. Grand Rapids: Baker, 1942.

Luther, Martin. *Lectures on Genesis.* 8 vols. Edited by Jaroslav Pelikan and Helmut Lehman. Translated by George V. Schick and Paul D. Pahl from *In primum librum Mose enarrationes.* St. Louis: Concordia, 1958–70.

——— . *Luther's Commentary on Genesis: A New Translation.* 2 vols. Translated by J. Theodore Mueller from *In primum librum Mose enarrationes.* Grand Rapids: Zondervan, 1958.

Michaeli, Frank. *Le Livre de la Genèse.* 2 vols. Collection "La Bible Ouverte." Neuchâtel: Delachaux & Niestle, 1957–60.

Rad, Gerhard von. *Genesis: A Commentary.* Rev. ed. Translated by John H. Marks from *Das erste Buch Mose übersetzt und erklärt.* Old Testament Library. London: SCM; Philadelphia: Westminster, 1973. (Rev. according to the 9th German ed., 1972.)

——————. *Old Testament Theology.* 2 vols. Translated by D. M. G. Stalker. New York: Harper & Row, 1962.

Richardson, Alan. *Genesis I–XI.* Torch Bible Commentaries. London: SCM, 1953.

Ryle, Herbert E. *The Book of Genesis.* Cambridge Bible for Schools and Colleges. Cambridge: Cambridge University Press, 1914.

Sarna, Nahum M. *Understanding Genesis: The Heritage of Biblical Israel.* New York: McGraw-Hill, 1966.

Scharbert, Josef. *Genesis 1–11 erklärt.* Die Neue Echter Bibel, pt. 5, no. 1. Würzburg: Echter, 1983.

Skinner, John. *A Critical and Exegetical Commentary on Genesis.* 2d ed. International Critical Commentary. Edinburgh: T. & T. Clark, 1910.

Speiser, E. A. *Genesis: Introduction, Translation, and Notes.* Anchor Bible. Edited by W. R. Albright and D. N. Freedman. Garden City, N.Y.: Doubleday, 1964.

Spurrell, George James. *Notes on the Hebrew Text of the Book of Genesis.* 2d ed. London: Froude, 1896.

Stigers, Harold G. *A Commentary on Genesis.* Grand Rapids: Zondervan, 1976.

Vawter, Bruce. *On Genesis: A New Reading.* Garden City, N.Y.: Doubleday, 1977.

Westermann, Claus. *Genesis.* 3 vols. Biblischer Kommentar Altes Testament, vol. 1, nos. 1–3. Neukirchen-Vluyn: Neukirchener, 1974–82. (Translated by John J. Scullion as *Genesis: A Commentary.* 3 vols. London: SPCK; Minneapolis: Augsburg, 1984–86.)

Monographs on Genesis

Blenkinsopp, Joseph. *From Adam to Abraham.* Glen Rock, N.J.: Paulist, 1965.

Cassuto, Umberto. *La questione della Genesi.* Firenze: F. le Monnier, 1934.

Childs, Brevard S. *Myth and Reality in the Old Testament.* Naperville, Ill.: Allenson, 1960.

Davis, J. D. *Genesis and Semitic Tradition.* Grand Rapids: Baker, 1980.

Fishbane, Michael, *Text and Texture.* New York: Schocken, 1979.

Fokkelmann, Jan P. *Narrative Art in Genesis: Specimens of Stylistic and Structural Analysis.* Studia Semitica Neerlandica, 17. Assen: Van Gorcum, 1975.

Gage, Warren Austin. *The Gospel of Genesis: Studies in Protology and Eschatology.* Winona Lake, Ind.: Carpenter, 1984.

Gemser, B. et al. *Studies on the Book of Genesis.* OTS 12 (1958).

Green, W. H. *The Unity of the Book of Genesis.* 1895. Reprint. Grand Rapids: Baker, 1979.

Gunkel, Hermann. *The Legends of Genesis.* Translated by W. H. Carruth from the Introduction to the 1st ed. of *Genesis übersetzt und erklärt.* Chicago: Open Court, 1901: Reprint. New York: Schocken, 1964, with an introduction by W. F. Albright.

Külling, S. R. *Zur Datierung der "Genesis-P-Stücke."* Kampen: Verlag J. H. Kok, N.V., 1964.

Ryle, Herbert E. *The Early Narratives of Genesis.* 2d ed. London: Macmillan, 1900.

Sant, C. "The Literary Structure of the Book of Genesis." Diss., Malta, 1953.

Thompson, D. "The Genesis Messenger Stories and Their Theological Significance: Two Methods." Diss., Tübingen, 1971–72.

Vos, Howard F. *Genesis and Archaeology.* Chicago: Moody, 1963. Rev. ed. Grand Rapids: Zondervan, 1985.

Westermann, Claus. *Genesis 1–11.* Erträge der Forschung, 7. Darmstadt: Wissenschaftliche Buchgemeinschaft, 1972.

———. *Genesis 12–50.* Erträge der Forschung, 48. Darmstadt: Wissenschaftliche Buchgemeinschaft, 1975.

Wiseman, P. J. *Ancient Records and the Structure of Genesis: A Case for Literary Unity.* Edited by D. J. Wiseman. Nashville: Nelson, 1985. (Rev. ed. of *New Discoveries in Babylonia About Genesis* [1936].)